	Thomas Aquinas *1225–1274*	*Summa Theologica*★ (*c. 1265–1274*)
1337	Hundred Years War begins.	
1348–1350	The Black Plague ravages Europe.	
c. 1440	Johannes Gutenberg, a German printer, invents movable type.	
1492	Columbus discovers America.	
	Desiderius Erasmus *1466–1536*	*On the Freedom of the Will* (*1524*)
	Niccolò Machiavelli *1469–1527*	*The Prince*★ (*1513*)
	Martin Luther *1483–1546*	*On the Bondage of the Will*★ (*1525*)
1517	The Protestant Reformation begins in Germany.	
1519–1522	Magellan circumnavigates the globe.	
	John Calvin *1509–1564*	*Institutes of the Christian Religion* (*1536*)
1543	Publication of Copernicus's *Revolution of Heavenly Bodies*.	
1558–1603	Reign of Queen Elizabeth I of England.	
	Francis Bacon *1561–1626*	*Novum Organum* (*1620*)
1618	Thirty Years War begins.	
1638	Galileo's *Discourse on Two New Sciences* published.	
1643	Civil War begins in England.	
	Thomas Hobbes *1588–1679*	*Leviathan*★ (*1651*)
	René Descartes *1596–1650*	*Meditations on First Philosophy*★ (*1641*)
	Blaise Pascal *1623–1662*	*Pensées*★ (*1670*)
	Baruch Spinoza *1632–1677*	*On the Improvement of the Understanding*★ (*1677*)
1687	Newton's *Principia* published.	
1688	The "Glorious Revolution" deposes James II of England.	
	John Locke *1632–1704*	*An Essay Concerning Human Understanding*★ (*1690*) Two Treatises of Government★ (*1690*)
	Gottfried Wilhem von Leibniz *1646–1716* **George Berkeley** *1685–1753*	*...es of*
	Jonathan Edwards *1703–1758*	

The Questions of Philosophy

OTHER BOOKS BY JOHN K. ROTH AND FREDERICK SONTAG

John K. Roth and Frederick Sontag

The American Religious Experience: The Roots, Trends and Future of American Theology, 1972

God and America's Future, 1977

The Defense of God, eds., 1985

John K. Roth

Freedom and the Moral Life: The Ethics of William James, 1969

Problems of the Philosophy of Religion, 1971

American Dreams: Meditations on Life in the United States, 1976

A Consuming Fire: Encounters with Elie Wiesel and the Holocaust, 1979

The American Dream (with Robert H. Fossum), 1981

Approaches to Auschwitz: The Holocaust and Its Legacy (with Richard L. Rubenstein), 1987

Frederick Sontag

Divine Perfection: Possible Ideas of God, 1962

The Existentialist Prolegomena: To a Future Metaphysics, 1969

The Future of Theology: A Philosophical Basis for Contemporary Protestant Theology, 1969

The Crisis of Faith: A Protestant Witness in Rome, 1969

The God of Evil: An Argument from the Existence of the Devil, 1970

God, Why Did You Do That? 1970

The Problems of Metaphysics, 1970

How Philosophy Shapes Theology: Problems in the Philosophy of Religion, 1971

Love Beyond Pain: Mysticism within Christianity, 1977

Sun Myung Moon and the Unification Church, 1977

What Can God Do? 1979

A Kierkegaard Handbook, 1979

The Elements of Philosophy, 1984

The Questions of Philosophy

JOHN K. ROTH
Claremont McKenna College

FREDERICK SONTAG
Pomona College

WADSWORTH PUBLISHING COMPANY

Belmont, California
A Division of Wadsworth, Inc.

Philosophy Editor: Kenneth King
Editorial Associate: Debbie Fox
Production Editor: Deborah McDaniel
Managing Designer: Donna Davis
Print Buyer: Barbara Britton
Designer: Lisa Mirski
Copy Editor: Brenda Griffing
Cover: Lisa Mirski

Printed in the United States of America   49

1 2 3 4 5 6 7 8 9 10—92 91 90 89 88

Library of Congress Cataloging-in-Publication Data
Roth, John K.
    The questions of philosophy.

    Bibliography: p.
    Includes index.
    1. Philosophy—Introductions. I. Sontag, Frederick.
II. Title.
BD21.R647   1988   100   87-6261
ISBN   0-534-08064-2

Acknowledgments

The photos on the following pages appear with permission of the Bettmann Archives: Pp. 2, 3, 13, 17, 29, 34, 40, 55, 70, 81, 87, 92, 99, 109, 116, 122, 129, 137, 151, 176, 180, 183, 189, 200, 213, 219, 230, 250, 261, 268, 285, 292, 300, 305, 315, 322, 331, 342, 348, 364, 376, 384, 393, 405, 415, 421, 428, 435, 448, 458, 468, 476, 490, 506

The photo on p. 157 appears by permission of Wide World Photos.

The photo on p. 163 appears by permission of the Master and Fellows of Trinity College, Cambridge.

The photos on pp. 255 and 503 appear with permission from the Granger Collection.

Excerpt on p. 27 from "Letters to a Young Poet" is from *Selected Works*, Volume I, by Rainer Maria Rilke, translated by M.D. Herter. Reprinted by permission of W.W. Norton & Company, Inc., the Hogarth Press, and the estate of Rainer Maria Rilke.

For our grandchildren, present and future

BUT RACHEL WAS BEAUTIFUL
AND WELL FAVORED.
Genesis 29:17

Contents

Readings within Chapters

Preface

*I*n 1981 John Roth received an invitation to lecture at Doshisha University in Kyoto, Japan. The offer included responsibility to teach an introduction to Western philosophy for Japanese undergraduates. His host, Professor Kenji Yoshida, explained that he would need a manuscript so he could translate Roth's English into Japanese. Thus the idea for this book was born.

Frederick Sontag, Roth's former philosophy teacher, long-time friend, and colleague, was one of the first to know about the Doshisha opportunity. As we talked about it, we decided to put our experience to work. In combination, this includes more than fifty years of experience devoted to introducing students to philosophy, plus joint authorship of three books and numerous articles. We converted Professor Yoshida's request into *The Questions of Philosophy.*

What were the most important insights about Western philosophy to present to beginning Japanese students? That question initially governed our planning, but we finally concluded that newcomers to this field of study—whatever their nationality, tradition, or age—are in much the same position. Of all the subjects first encountered by college and university students, philosophy is the least likely to be familiar. They probably have studied literature, history, social and natural sciences, and mathematics. Many have had

some exposure to religion, too. But before they arrive on campus, relatively few students have had any significant introduction to the questions of philosophy.

Although Japanese and American students are sometimes required to study philosophy, large numbers still do so by choice. Yet even those who elect introductory courses are not usually motivated by prior knowledge of the history of philosophy. Especially in the United States, they lack such background almost completely. Likewise, they are virtually unaware of the technical issues that professionals in the field spend their lives arguing about. Instead, students at home or abroad usually start to study philosophy because they assume that an introductory course will help them understand themselves and life's meanings. A successful introduction to philosophy should capitalize on these impulses. Our book does so in three major ways.

We Emphasize Questions

Most new students come to philosophy with questions, not doctrines, in mind. Typically these questions are about "life's problems." As our table of contents indicates, we link these concerns to the philosophical tradition by following Immanuel Kant's suggestion that the basic questions of philosophy are three: What can I know? What should I do? What may I hope?

Everything in life hinges on whether any person can rightly claim to possess knowledge. Furthermore, hardly an hour passes without our asking whether we ought to do some things and not others. These issues keep people thinking about the future. Questions about the meaning and destiny of our lives—individually and collectively—are never far from our attention.

Philosophy revolves around questions. Thus, in each chapter we introduce a major issue, illustrate its connection with everyday life, and show how that issue has been a focal point of the historical figures we link to it. In addition to providing background about each thinker, our approach indicates how the same question provokes different responses and how debate involving those responses leads to still other perspectives. As we do this historical analysis, however, our main intent is not to make the reader a budding expert in intellectual history. Rather, the goal is to let historical reflection encourage students to think critically for themselves about the perennial and current questions of life.

We Stress Philosophy's Variety

At a time when educators are concerned to introduce students to the classics of Western thought, this book offers an extensive range of coverage. While emphasizing many of philosophy's most crucial questions—no single book could deal with them all—it also stresses the variety of approaches and responses philosophers have made to them. We highlight major figures, including Plato and Aristotle, Descartes and Hume, plus American philosophers such as William James and John Rawls. But lesser-known thinkers—even some who do not fit the conventional stereotype of "philosopher"—have also made important contributions to philosophical inquiry, and they receive attention, too. Pascal and Royce are examples of the former kind; the novelist Ayn Rand and the recent winner of the Nobel Peace Prize, Elie Wiesel, illustrate the latter.

The variety of philosophers represented in this book tells us that philosophy does not yield final answers on which everyone agrees. On the contrary, philosophers approach and answer the questions of philosophy in diverse ways, which suggests that no one philosopher is completely correct. That possibility confronts our readers with a challenge: they eventually will be responsible for figuring out their own personal responses. As the Study Questions at the end of each chapter suggest—they are not the standard "review questions" but prods for further reflection—we try to show that the traditional questions of philosophy are still very much alive. We also urge our readers to explore the various ways in which philosophers work. As that process unfolds, we want them to recognize each philosopher as a friend who has important convictions to share. We want them to understand, however, that they are still left to decide which of these insights are the most important for them. At its best, philosophy is an adventure of ideas. By wrestling with life's puzzles concerning knowledge, action, and hope, we receive valuable insights that cannot be acquired in any other way.

We Offer Diverse Options for Teaching and Learning

This book lends itself to a semester-long course in which the class can devote a week to each of its thirteen chapters. Other possibilities exist as well, because every chapter contains a balance of primary source material and our interpretive explanations, incorporating substantial quotations from the philosophers under consideration. If students read nothing except our text, they will still get a firsthand impression of a writer's style and outlook. Fitting our book's other emphases, however, we set a framework that enables students to encounter the primary source readings as well, and we encourage them to think critically along with the author of each selection to form their own outlook. The primary source readings and our explanations are at once integrated and separable. Thus, the book can be used to maximize or minimize the attention placed on any one of the questions or philosophers.

A Word of Thanks

Our work was not completed during John Roth's stay in Japan. We discovered anew how difficult it is to write about the questions of philosophy in succinct ways that are accessible to beginners. It took six more years for us to complete in California a project whose beginnings spanned the Pacific.

We hope this book will be a reliable guide for readers who seek their own answers to the questions of philosophy. If it succeeds, much credit belongs to the many people who offered us advice and support along the way. Not only Kenji Yoshida but also Professor Yoshimori Hiraishi of Doshisha University deserve thanks. Closer to home, we benefited immensely from the editorial review done by Alex Holzman. If this book reads at all easily, credit goes to his constant effort to help us say clearly what we mean. The word processing center at Claremont McKenna College—with special thanks to Pat Padilla—did a heroic job of turning out the many drafts and revisions. Our Wadsworth editor, Kenneth King, worked with us from start to finish to realize the multifaceted text we envisaged. We are greatly indebted to him and also to Debbie McDaniel, who cared so well for the manuscript during the final production process.

Two Pomona College students deserve a special word of thanks. Heather Martin carried a burden of detail, and Colin Brayton prepared the glossaries single-handedly. If the reader finds these helpful in understanding philosophical terms, it will be due almost entirely to Colin's understanding of how to make complex terms intelligible.

In addition to those already mentioned, we received excellent counsel from the numerous philosophers who reviewed our work at various stages, among whom are the following: H. Michael Awalt, Belmont College; Margaret Knapke, University of Dayton; Ann Mahoney, Mesa Community College; Louis Pojman, University of Mississippi; C. Merrill Proudfoot, Park College; Janine Randal, Angelo State University; Nani L. Ranken, Indiana University at Kokomo; Alan S. Rosenbaum, Cleveland State University; George J. Stack, SUNY at Brockport; and Manuel Velasquez, University of Santa Clara. We thank them, too, each and all.

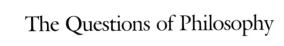

The Questions of Philosophy

INTRODUCTION

All the interests of my reason, speculative as well as practical, combine in the three following questions:
1. *What can I know?*
2. *What ought I to do?*
3. *What may I hope?*

IMMANUEL KANT
Critique of Pure Reason

CHAPTER ONE

What Is Philosophy?

*E*veryone asks questions, but "What is philosophy?" is not usually one of them. Yet that question is important. Human civilization has been changed because Greek thinkers began to ask that question 2500 years ago. Much later, Karl Marx asked whether philosophy should change the world as well as understand it, and revolution followed. We assume an answer to this question when we try to learn what we can know, seek to decide what we ought to do, or take stock of our destiny. Although there are various ways of dealing with those issues, they are all questions of **philosophy.*** One may wonder about the best ways to cope with them, but the best way to approach these questions is to begin by asking: What is philosophy?

To introduce you to the various answers given to the question "What is philosophy?", we offer you the answers several philosophers have given. Plato is "the father of philosophy" and a master of the art of dialogue; Auguste Comte wants to revolutionize and modernize the traditional approach; Josiah Royce joins philosophy with religion. Taken together, all of them can help you decide: "What is philosophy?"

*Boldfaced terms, including those in the primary source readings, are defined in the Glossary at the end of the chapter.

Socrates, Plato, and the Method of Dialogue

Philosophers do not always agree when you ask them what philosophy is, and their answers have given birth to more than one

SOCRATES c. 470–399 B.C.

philosophical view. Often such inquiry begins by turning all the way back to Socrates (c. 470–399 B.C.). He lived in Athens, and the state convicted him of "corrupting the youth." Socrates questioned traditional beliefs. In the eyes of the country's leaders, this amounted to "corruption." For this offense he was sentenced to die by drinking hemlock, a deadly poison. He gave his reply to these charges in the dialogue we have selected for you to read. We know little directly about what Socrates thought, because he wrote nothing down. It was his student Plato (427–347 B.C.) who immortalized him by writing a series of brilliant **dialogues** featuring Socrates as the main speaker. Athens at the time of Socrates was an important cradle for the birth of philosophy and the democratic spirit. All roads in philosophy seem to lead back to Athens and the time of Plato/ Socrates, and Plato's dialogues present Socrates' views for us.

Are the Questions More Important Than the Answers to the Questions?

As Plato portrayed him, Socrates was a master at asking questions and stimulating critical reflection. We call this approach to philosophy the **"Socratic method,"** or sometimes "the method of dialogue." Although he thought he could point out what was wrong in the way the participants in a dialogue phrased their ideas, Socrates did not claim to possess knowledge or **wisdom.** The most he would say was that he was aware of his own ignorance, whereas other people failed to recognize theirs. Some in ancient Greece (as well as today) claimed to be "wise men," but for Socrates the philosophical spirit is always born out of the realization that we lack true wisdom. Those who pursue philosophy in Socratic fashion do not claim to have knowledge that is final and complete. In its Greek origins, "philosophy" simply

PLATO   427–347 B.C.

means "the love of wisdom." To be moved by the feeling of love, Plato had Socrates explain, tells you that you do not fully possess what you desire. Otherwise, desire would not arise. You know only enough to be aware of what you would like to have and to realize that you do not yet possess it. Still, that realization is sufficient to provide hope. If you know that you do not possess wisdom, you at least know that much. Philosophers are not "lost individuals"; they occupy a middle ground between ignorance and wisdom. To know that you do not know is, in a sense, to know more than do those who are blind to their deficiencies.

In his famous seventh Epistle, Plato tells us that it is not possible to capture truth in written form, to be offered to others as ultimate statements.

> If I thought it possible to deal adequately with the subject in a treatise or a lecture for the general public, what finer achievement would there have been in my life than to write a work of a great benefit to mankind and to bring the nature of things to light for all men.[1]

Understanding philosophy does not come about in that way. Truth cannot be put in a fixed form and handed over to someone else.

> Acquaintance with it must come rather after a long period of instruction in the subject itself and of close companionship, when suddenly, like a blaze kindled by a leaping spark, it is generated in the soul and at once becomes self-sustaining. (341 c–d, P. 94.)[†]

Plato felt that if you want to become a philosopher, you must engage in dialogue. That is, you must learn to profit from discussion. Seeking knowledge is a communal enterprise. We need to be corrected by our discussions with others, if we do not want to go astray. Without the give and take of mutual exchange, we might settle for a prepackaged "truth" someone offers us. Philosophy should be a life of joint inquiry and struggle, a theme Plato repeats in many of his dialogues.

Plato's Ideal of the Philosopher-King and His Vision of Philosophy

Plato's best-known work is *The Republic.* In this dialogue he offers us his theories about education and the human soul. But what is particularly important, he gives us his description of the ideal state. In all Plato's dialogues, the question of what philosophy is and does is always under discussion, no matter what the official topic. When he

---

†Throughout this text, page numbers in parentheses refer to the source cited in the previous numbered note.

describes the ideal republic, Plato defines the role philosophy should play, what it should be and do. Plato felt that political states fail and turn corrupt because their leaders are neither wise nor seekers after wisdom. But he was also harsh in his judgment of philosophers. Although they seek wisdom, they do nothing to put into practice the knowledge they gain. As leaders they are too often so inept and unimpressive that no one will listen to them. Considering this situation, Plato made this proposal to remedy both faults:

> Until philosophers are kings, or the kings and princes of this world have the spirit and power of philosophy, and political greatness and wisdom meet in one, and those commoner natures who pursue either to the exclusion of the other are compelled to stand aside, critics will never rest from their evils—no, nor the human race, as I believe—and then only will this our State have a possibility of life and behold the light of day.[2]

To be a philosopher for Plato means that you have a passion to seek wisdom; you want to know the truth. Not everyone, however, shares such a feeling or does much about it. Indeed, Plato believed that "philosophy, then, the love of wisdom, is impossible for the multitude" (V, 494, 1:754). Accordingly, the majority are bound either to disapprove or to be indifferent to those who pursue wisdom as being impractical. His famous "allegory of the cave" in Book VII of *The Republic* illustrates that seeking wisdom can be a lonely pursuit. We know this because constant questioning can bring any project to a halt. Being agreeable is a more congenial social attitude.

In this allegory Plato pictures men who spend their lives in a cavern as prisoners. They are chained down so that all they can do is watch the shadows cast on the wall by a fire. They cannot even turn their heads to discover that the fire is the cause of the shadows. But one man eventually is freed and turns to discover the source of the shadows, which before he had thought were the only real objects in the world. Later he is brought up out of the cave and into the light. Having lived in the darkness for so long, the man who climbs out of the cave finds the light painful at first. When he adjusts, he is able to look toward the sun itself, the source of the light. He is entranced by its beauty. He would gladly stay above ground, lost in contemplation of the bright new world he has discovered. However, he returns to the cave and tells the prisoners that their world is unreal; but they ignore him or berate him for his trouble. They do not appreciate being told that they have been deceived. They prefer the shadows they know to a reported bright world they have not seen.

In our own society, many of us live in a kind of cave. We might use the example of people who still smoke and enjoy it and refuse to give it up. The medical/scientific evidence is overwhelming that smoking can cause cancer. In spite of this, we refuse to stop smoking, and we ignore those who chide us. Or, there are those who won't wear seat belts in cars when statistics prove that seat belts prevent serious injury. Human beings do not always appreciate being told what is good for them. Vices have a strong hold on us, often against all reason. Plato, of course, is speaking of even greater forms of blindness, when we do not admit the reality of any form of life except the one before us.

Is Love the Real Source and Driving Force in Philosophy?

In his claim that philosophers do not possess wisdom, Plato suggested that the love of wisdom is a middle state lying between ignorance and the full possession of wisdom. The philosophers in our world are those who spend their lives living "in between." But why, if they can never possess wisdom fully, do they keep trying to find it? The answer is the same as the explanation of why they started out on the search in the first place. Some men and women feel a stirring to know, to learn, and to be rid of ignorance. But if you are gripped by such a desire you must have already discerned, however dimly, something of what you want to know. Feeling the stirring of love within tells you that you have glimpsed what you need to cure your ignorance. Nevertheless, the feeling of desire will persist as long as the object is not fully in your possession. In this way, love draws you on. It inspires you to search and to ask questions. Due to the desire love induces, you struggle to rise from your ignorance.

Plato believes that love is always the love of beauty and not of deformity. Thus, when the philosopher feels the stirring of love, he knows he has had an apprehension of something that must be beautiful, something that lies behind the drab world he sees.

> For God mingles not with man; but through Love all the intercourse and converse of God with man, whether awake or asleep, is carried on.[3]

> He [Love] is by nature neither mortal nor immortal, but alive and flourishing at one moment when he is in plenty, and dead at another moment, and again alive by reason of his . . . nature. . . . Therefore Love is also a philosopher or lover of wisdom, and being a lover of wisdom is in a mean between the wise and the ignorant. (203–4, 1:329.)

Yet, we mortals are not content to be happy only for a moment, to love only for a time, or to achieve knowledge but for an instant. Love is entrancing and it causes us to pursue particular objects of beauty. As a consequence, we are led up the ladder in search of Beauty itself. Plato describes Beauty itself as something

> . . . absolute, separate, simple and everlasting, which without diminution and without increase or any change is imparted to the evergrowing and perishing beauties of all

other things. He who . . . ascending under the influence of true love begins to perceive that Beauty is not far from the end. (211, 1:335.)

The destiny of the lover is to remain in between, at one time excited, at another exhausted. Yet love leads us from individual beautiful things on to understand what Beauty is itself, Beauty not in one instance but Beauty in general. In this sense love is the philosophers' helper, because it keeps us searching and will not let us stop short of knowing the truth.

Where Will the Love of Wisdom Take Us?

Of course, not everyone pictures the life of philosophy as Plato did. Still, he is a good teacher for the novice in philosophy, because he makes the search for wisdom that love induces seem appealing, even if eventually we go on to think of philosophy in other ways. In his dialogue *Phaedrus*, Plato takes up the question of what love's effects are, what love does to us. What are its virtues and its risks? By way of explanation, Plato tells his readers a poetic myth or **allegory.** Where the important issues are concerned, he often considered **myth** and **symbol** to be a more accurate vehicle of discourse than a direct description could ever be. In the Gospels, Jesus constantly used parables, rather than direct statement, to convey his truth. In our society, movies serve the director's purpose in the same way. Woody Allen's *The Purple Rose of Cairo,* for example, is an allegory. Although it is fiction, it tells us something true about illusions and dreams versus our real life and its drabness. Movies can tell us things straightforward statement cannot.

Plato's myth about love describes the **soul** as something that once had wings and traversed the whole universe. What we must understand about ourselves, in our present state of ignorance, is why the soul's wings fell from it and are lost.

The wing is the corporeal element which is most akin to the divine, and which by nature tends to soar aloft and carry that which gravitates downwards into the upper region, which is the habitation of the gods. The divine is beauty, wisdom, goodness, and the like; and by these the wing of the soul is nourished, and grows apace; but when fed upon evil and foulness and the opposite of good, wastes and falls away.[4]

Under the influence of love we "grow wings," we are borne aloft; we expand and develop new experiences. But as we exist now, we seldom have the feeling of being borne aloft. Through the love of wisdom, we attempt to rise and to see life from a perspective higher than our ordinary one.

Plato also depicts the soul in the image of a charioteer who drives two steeds. The charioteer represents our reason. One horse, the white one, represents our courageous side. It is easy to track and guide. But the other, the black one, representing our appetites, is difficult and unruly. The charioteer, our rational side, tries to keep the two horses working together. As long as he can do this, the soul soars through the heavens and discerns Beauty itself and the true nature of reality. But unfortunately, such harmony does not last. Eventually the black horse starts to pull the soul back to earth as the charioteer loses control. Then, the soul plunges to earth. Thereafter, according to Plato's story in the *Phaedrus,* we spend our lives down on earth trying to regain the vision we had while we were borne aloft in perfect harmony. Love is our guide in this attempt to recapture our lost vision.

Yet love is not always sheer bliss. Desire can drive us to madness, which makes philosophy a dangerous pursuit. Those who love Beauty may be touched by madness. Because of this, some may at times become irrationally possessed. However, Plato thought it worth our while to take that risk of following love's guidance, since only love has the power to move us to any great height or to cause us to put forth any unusual effort. And Plato thought we must make an extraordinary effort if we are to learn much. We cannot be sure where following the love of wisdom will take us. Our only choice, if we do not accept the risk of following love, is to remain chained in a cave watching the flickering shadows on a wall. Never to learn that the shadows in front of us are not reality—that is the real danger we should fear, not the possible excess that being driven by love may produce. We must learn not to fear being led on a never-ending quest. In the first of the two excerpts that follow, you will read Plato's famous "allegory of the cave," a passage from *The Republic* in which Socrates helps his young friend Glaucon understand what the struggle for knowledge involves. Apparently inquiries of this kind got Socrates into serious trouble, as Plato indicated in the *Apology*, the source of the second reading. This dialogue is Plato's version of Socrates' speech to the court that convicted him of atheism and corrupting of the youth of Athens. Socrates received a death sentence. Do you think his version of philosophy is something worth dying for? Socrates speaks first.

And now, I said, let me show in a figure how far our nature is enlightened or unenlightened:—Behold! human beings living in an underground den, which has a mouth open towards the light and reaching all along the den; here they have been from their childhood, and have their legs and necks chained so that they cannot move, and can only see before them, being prevented by the chains from turning round their heads. Above and behind them a fire is blazing at a distance, and between the fire and the prisoners there is a raised way; and you will see, if you look, a low wall built along the way, like the screen which marionette players have in front of them, over which they show the puppets.

I see.

And do you see, I said, men passing along the wall carrying all sorts of vessels, and statues and figures of animals made of wood and stone and various materials, which appear over the wall? Some of them are talking, others silent.

You have shown me a strange image, and they are strange prisoners.

Like ourselves, I replied; and they see only their own shadows, or the shadows of one another, which the fire throws on the opposite wall of the cave?

True, he said; how could they see anything but the shadows if they were never allowed to move their heads?

And of the objects which are being carried in like manner they would only see the shadows?

Yes, he said.

And if they were able to converse with one another, would they not suppose that they were naming what was actually before them?

Very true.

And suppose further that the prison had an echo which came from the other side, would they not be sure to fancy when one of the passers-by spoke that the voice which they heard came from the passing shadow?

No question, he replied.

To them, I said, the truth would be literally nothing but the shadows of the images.

That is certain.

And now look again, and see what will naturally follow if the prisoners are released and disabused of their error. At first, when any of them is liberated and compelled suddenly to stand up and turn his neck round and walk and look towards the light, he will suffer sharp pains; the glare will distress him, and he will be unable to see the realities of which in his former state he had seen the shadows; and then conceive someone saying to him, that what he saw before was an illusion, but that now, when he is approaching nearer to being and his eye is turned towards more real existence, he has a clearer vision—what will be his reply? And you may further imagine that his instructor is pointing to the objects as they pass and requiring him to name them—will he not be perplexed? Will he not fancy that the shadows which he formerly saw are truer than the objects which are now shown to him?

Far truer.

And if he is compelled to look straight at the light, will he not have a pain in his eyes which will make him turn away to take refuge in the objects of vision which he can see, and which he will conceive to be in reality clearer than the things which are now being shown to him?

True, he said.

And suppose once more, that he is reluctantly dragged up a steep and rugged ascent, and held fast until he is forced into the presence of the sun himself, is he not likely to be pained and irritated? When he approaches the light his eyes will be dazzled, and he will not be able to see anything at all of what are now called realities.

Not all in a moment, he said.

He will require to grow accustomed to the sight of the upper world. And first he will see the shadows best, next the reflections of men and other objects in the water, and then the objects themselves; then he will gaze upon the light of the moon and the stars and the spangled heaven; and he will see the sky and the stars by night better than the sun or the light of the sun by day?

Certainly.

Last of all he will be able to see the sun, and not mere reflections of him in the water, but he will see him in his own proper place, and not in another; and he will contemplate him as he is.

Certainly.

He will then proceed to argue that this is he who gives the season and the years, and is the guardian of all that is in the visible world, and in a certain way the cause of all things which he and his fellows have been accustomed to behold?

Clearly, he said, he would first see the sun and then reason about him.

And when he remembered his old habitation, and the wisdom of the den and his fellow-prisoners, do you not suppose that he would felicitate himself on the change, and pity them?

Certainly, he would.

And if they were in the habit of conferring honors among themselves on those who were quickest to observe the passing shadows and to remark which of them went before, and which followed after, and which were together; and who were therefore best able to draw conclusions as to the future, do you think that he would care for such honors and glories, or envy the possessors of them? Would he not say with Homer,

Better to be the poor servant of a poor master,

and to endure anything, rather than think as they do and live after their manner?

Yes, he said, I think that he would rather suffer anything than entertain these false notions and live in this miserable manner.

Imagine once more, I said, such an one coming suddenly out of the sun to be replaced in his old situation; would he not be certain to have his eyes full of darkness?

To be sure, he said.

And if there were a contest, and he had to compete in measuring the shadows with the prisoners who had never moved out of the den, while his sight was still weak, and before his eyes had become steady (and the time which would be needed to acquire this new habit of sight might be very considerable), would he not be ridiculous? Men would say of him that up he went and down he came without his eyes; and that it was better not even to think of ascending; and if anyone tried to loose another and lead him up to the light, let them only catch the offender, and they would put him to death.

No question, he said.

This entire allegory, I said, you may now append, dear Glaucon, to the previous argument; the prison-house is the world of sight, the light of the fire is the sun, and you will not misapprehend me if you interpret the journey upwards to be the ascent of the soul into the intellectual world according to my poor belief, which, at your desire, I have expressed—whether rightly or wrongly God knows. But, whether true or false, my opinion is that in the world of knowledge the idea of good appears last of all, and is seen only with an effort; and, when seen, is also inferred to be the universal author of all things beautiful and right, parent of light and of the lord of light in this visible world, and the immediate source of reason and truth in the intellectual; and that this is the power upon which he who would act rationally either in public or private life must have his eye fixed.

I agree, he said, as far as I am able to understand you.

Moreover, I said, you must not wonder that those who attain to this beatific vision are unwilling to descend to human affairs; for their souls are ever hastening into the upper world where they desire to dwell; which desire of theirs is very natural, if our allegory may be trusted.

Yes, very natural.

And is there anything surprising in one who passes from divine contemplations to the evil state of man, misbehaving himself in a ridiculous manner; if, while his eyes are blinking and before he has become accustomed to the surrounding darkness, he is compelled to fight in courts of law, or in other places, about the images or the shadows of images of justice, and is endeavoring to meet the conceptions of those who have never yet seen absolute justice?

Anything but surprising, he replied.

Anyone who has common sense will remember that the bewilderments of the eyes are of two kinds, and arise from two causes, either from coming out of the light or from going into the light, which is true of the mind's eye, quite as much as of the bodily eye; and he who remembers this when he sees anyone whose vision is perplexed and weak, will not be too ready to laugh; he will first ask whether that soul of man has come out of the brighter life, and is unable to see because unaccustomed to the dark, or having turned from darkness to the day is dazzled by excess of light. And he will count the one happy in his condition and state of being, and he will pity the other; or, if he

have a mind to laugh at the soul which comes from below into the light, there will be more reason in this than in the laugh which greets him who returns from above out of the light into the den.

That, he said, is a very just distinction.

But then, if I am right, certain professors of education must be wrong when they say that they can put a knowledge into the soul which was not there before, like sight into blind eyes.

They undoubtedly say this, he replied.

Whereas, our argument shows that the power and capacity of learning exists in the soul already; and that just as the eye was unable to turn from darkness to light without the whole body, so too the instrument of knowledge can only by the movement of the whole soul be turned from the world of becoming into that of being, and learn by degrees to endure the sight of being, and of the brightest and best of being, or in other words, of the good.[5]

There are many reasons why I am not grieved, O men of Athens, at the vote of condemnation. I expected it, and am only surprised that the votes are so nearly equal; for I had thought that the majority against me would have been far larger; but now, had thirty votes gone over to the other side, I should have been acquitted. And I may say, I think, that I have escaped Meletus. I may say more; for without the assistance of Anytus and Lycon, anyone may see that he would not have had a fifth part of the votes, as the law requires, in which case he would have incurred a fine of a thousand drachmae.

And so he proposes death as the penalty. And what shall I propose on my part, O men of Athens? Clearly that which is my due. And what is my due? What return shall be made to the man who has never had the wit to be idle during his whole life; but has been careless of what the many care for—wealth, and family interests, and military offices, and speaking in the assembly, and magistracies, and plots, and parties. Reflecting that I was really too honest a man to be a politician and live, I did not go where I could do no good to you or to myself; but where I could do the greatest good privately to every one of you, thither I went, and sought to persuade every man among you that he must look to himself, and seek virtue and wisdom before he looks to his private interests, and look to the state before he looks to the interests of the state; and that this should be the order which he observes in all his actions. What shall be done to such an one? Doubtless some good thing, O men of Athens, if he has his reward; and the good should be of a kind suitable to him. What would be a reward suitable to a poor man who is your benefactor, and who desires leisure that he may instruct you? . . .

Perhaps you think that I am braving you in what I am saying now, as in what I said before about the tears and prayers. But this is not so. I speak rather because I am convinced that I never intentionally wronged anyone, although I cannot convince you— the time has been too short; if there were a law at Athens, as there is in other cities, that a capital cause should not be decided in one day, then I believe that I should have convinced you. But I cannot in a moment refute great slanders; and, as I am convinced that I never wronged another, I will assuredly not wrong myself. I will not say of myself that I deserve any evil, or propose any penalty. Why should I? Because I am afraid of the penalty of death which Meletus proposes? When I do not know whether death is a good or an evil, why should I propose a penalty which would certainly be an evil? Shall I say imprisonment? And why should I live in prison, and be the slave of the magistrates of the year—of the Eleven? Or shall the penalty be a fine, and imprisonment until the fine is paid? There is the same objection. I should have to lie in prison, for money I have none, and cannot pay. And if I say exile (and this may possibly be the penalty which you will affix), I must indeed be blinded by the love of life, if I am so irrational as to expect that when you, who are my own citizens, cannot endure my discourses and words, and have found them so grievous and odious that you will have no more of them, others are likely to endure me. No indeed, men of Athens, that is not very likely. And what a life should I lead, at my age, wandering from city to city, ever changing my place of exile, and always being driven out! For I am quite sure that wherever I go, there, as here, the young men will flock to me; and if I drive them away, their elders will drive me out at their request; and if I let them come, their fathers and friends will drive me out for their sakes.

Someone will say: Yes, Socrates, but cannot you hold your tongue, and then you may go into a foreign city, and no one will interfere with you? Now I have great difficulty in making you understand my answer to this. For if I tell you that to do as you say would be a disobedience to the God, and therefore that I cannot hold my tongue, you will not believe that I am serious; and if I say again that daily to discourse about virtue, and of those other things about which you hear me examining myself and others, is the greatest good of man, and that the unexamined life is not worth living, you are still less likely to believe me. Yet I say what is true, although a thing of which it is hard for me to persuade you. Also, I have never been accustomed to think that I deserve to suffer any harm. Had I money I might have estimated the offense at what I was able to pay, and not have been much the worse. But I have none, and therefore I must ask you to proportion the fine to my means. Well, perhaps I could afford a mina, and therefore I propose that penalty: Plato, Crito, Critobulus, and Apollodorus, my friends here, bid me say thirty minae, and they will be the sureties. Let thirty minae be the penalty; for which sum they will be ample security to you.

Not much time will be gained, O Athenians, in return for the evil name which you will get from the detractors of the city, who will say that you killed Socrates, a wise man; for they will call me wise, even although I am not wise, when they want to reproach you.

If you had waited a little while, your desire would have been fulfilled in the course of nature. For I am far advanced in years, as you may perceive, and not far from death. I am speaking now not to all of you, but only to those who have condemned me to death. And I have another thing to say to them: You think that I was convicted because I had no words of the sort which would have procured my acquittal—I mean, if I had thought fit to leave nothing undone or unsaid. Not so; the deficiency which led to my conviction was not of words—certainly not. But I had not the boldness or impudence or inclination to address you as you would have liked me to do, weeping and wailing and lamenting, and saying and doing many things which you have been accustomed to hear from others, and which, as I maintain, are unworthy of me. I thought at the time that I ought not to do anything common or mean when in danger: nor do I now repent of the style of my defense; I would rather die having spoken after my manner, than speak in your manner and live. For neither in war nor yet at law ought I or any man to use every way of escaping death. Often in battle there can be no doubt that if a man will throw away his arms, and fall on his knees before his pursuers, he may escape death; and in other dangers there are other ways of escaping death, if a man is willing to say and do anything. The difficulty, my friends, is not to avoid death, but to avoid unrighteousness; for that runs faster than death. I am old and move slowly, and the slower runner has overtaken me, and my accusers are keen and quick, and the faster runner, who is unrighteousness, has overtaken them. And now I depart hence condemned by you to suffer the penalty of death—they too go their ways condemned by the truth to suffer the penalty of villainy and wrong; and I must abide by my award—let them abide by theirs. I suppose that these things may be regarded as fated—and I think that they are well.

And now, O men who have condemned me, I would fain prophesy to you; for I am about to die, and in the hour of death men are gifted with prophetic power. And I prophesy to you who are my murderers, that immediately after my departure punishment far heavier than you have inflicted on me will surely await you. Me you have killed because you wanted to escape the accuser, and not to give an account of your lives. But that will not be as you suppose: far otherwise. For I say that there will be more accusers of you than there are now; accusers whom hitherto I have restrained: and as they are younger they will be more inconsiderate with you, and you will be more offended at them. If you think that by killing men you can prevent someone from censuring your evil lives, you are mistaken; that is not a way of escape which is either possible or honorable; the easiest and the noblest way is not to be disabling others, but to be improving yourselves. This is the prophecy which I utter before my departure to the judges who have condemned me.

Friends, who would have acquitted me, I would like also to talk with you about the thing which has come to pass, while the magistrates are busy, and before I go to the place at which I must die. Stay then a little, for we may as well talk with one another while there is time. You are my friends, and I should like to show you the meaning of this event which has happened to me. O my judges—for you I may truly call judges—I should like to tell you of a wonderful circumstance. Hitherto the divine faculty of which the internal oracle is the source has constantly been in the habit of opposing me even about trifles, if I was going to make a slip or error in any matter; and now as you see there has come upon me that which may be thought, and is generally believed to be, the last and worst evil. But the oracle made no sign of opposition, either when I was leaving my house in the morning, or when I was on my way to the court, or while I was speaking, at anything which I was going to say; and yet I have often been stopped in the middle of a speech, but now in nothing I either said or did touching the matter in hand has the oracle opposed me. What do I take to be the explanation of this silence? I will tell you. It is an intimation that what has happened to me is a good, and that those of us who think that death is an evil are in error. For the customary sign would surely have opposed me had I been going to evil and not to good.

Let us reflect in another way, and we shall see that there is great reason to hope that death is a good; for one of two things—either death is a state of nothingness and utter unconsciousness, or, as men say, there is a change and migration of the soul from this world to another. Now if you suppose that there is no consciousness, but a sleep like the sleep of him who is undisturbed even by dreams, death will be an unspeakable gain. For if a person were to select the night in which his sleep was undisturbed even by dreams, and were to compare with this the other days and nights of his life, and then were to tell us how many days and nights he had passed in the course of his life better and more pleasantly than this one, I think that any man, I will not say a private man, but even the great king will not find many such days or nights, when compared with the others. Now if death be of such a nature, I say that to die is gain; for eternity is then only a single night. But if death is the journey to another place, and there, as men say, all the dead abide, what good, O my friends and judges, can be greater than this? If indeed when the pilgrim arrives in the world below, he is delivered from the professors of justice in this world, and finds the true judges who are said to give judgment there, Minos and Rhadamanthus and Aeacus and Triptolemus, and other sons of God who were righteous in their own life, that pilgrimage will be worth making. What would not a man give if he might converse with Orpheus and Musaeus and Hesiod and Homer? Nay, if this be true, let me die again and again. I myself, too, shall have a wonderful interest in there meeting and conversing with Palamedes, and Ajax the son of Telamon, and any other ancient hero who has suf-

fered death through an unjust judgment; and there will be no small pleasure, as I think, in comparing my own sufferings with theirs. Above all, I shall then be able to continue my search into true and false knowledge; as in this world, so also in the next; and I shall find out who is wise, and who pretends to be wise, and is not. What would not a man give, O judges, to be able to examine the leader of the great Trojan expedition; or Odysseus or Sisyphus, or numberless others, men and women too! What infinite delight would there be in conversing with them and asking them questions! In another world they do not put a man to death for asking questions: assuredly not. For besides being happier than we are, they will be immortal, if what is said is true.

Wherefore, O judges, be of good cheer about death, and know of a certainty, that no evil can happen to a good man, either in life or after death. He and his are not neglected by the gods; nor has my own approaching end happened by mere chance. But I see clearly that the time had arrived when it was better for me to die and be released from trouble; wherefore the oracle gave no sign. For which reason, also, I am not angry with my condemners, or with my accusers; they have done me no harm, although they did not mean to do me any good; and for this I may gently blame them.

Still I have a favor to ask of them. When my sons are grown up, I would ask you, O my friends, to punish them; and I would have you trouble them, as I have troubled you, if they seem to care about riches, or anything, more than about virtue; or if they pretend to be something when they are really nothing—then reprove them, as I have reproved you, for not caring about that for which they ought to care, and thinking that they are something when they are really nothing. And if you do this, both I and my sons will have received justice at your hands.

The hour of departure has arrived, and we go our ways—I to die, and you to live. Which is better God only knows.[6]

AUGUSTE COMTE   1798–1857

Auguste Comte and Philosophy as a New Science

Perhaps the only **absolute** fact in philosophy is that philosophers do not agree about what philosophy is. Although some philosophers still turn back to Plato, his world of love and myth does not appeal to everyone. Some later thinkers want to be rid of philosophy's past. They want to bypass the poetic myths Plato accepted and revise philosophy radically along the model of a modern science. Those who propound this revolution are all too aware that previous philosophers, such as Plato, asked questions without any intention of stating definitive conclusions. But modern science has altered our lives and achieved unexpected heights. Beginning in the seventeenth century, many intellectuals felt science might offer final answers. But has this

proved to be true? If it has, these innovators asked, shouldn't we change our conception of philosophy and make it into something radically new? Plato was acceptable as a philosopher in his day, but has modern science put an end to his approach?

These sentiments are at the roots of the "positive philosophy" developed by Auguste Comte (1798–1857). He and Plato are centuries apart, not only in time but also in the way they looked at the world. Born in France as the son of ardent Catholics, Comte received a solid scientific education. Then, for seven years he worked as the personal secretary to the French social philosopher Saint-Simon, who wanted to reorganize society based on scientific principles. Under Saint-Simon's influence, Comte became convinced that the power of scientific thinking could produce a beneficial reorganization of human society. Comte lived in a time when people believed in progress and trusted that science would produce this. Differences of opinion developed, however, and Comte's friendship with Saint-Simon deteriorated. Indeed, Comte was unable to obtain a permanent university teaching position due to Saint-Simon's opposition. He had to support himself by tutoring in mathematics, supplemented by contributions from his followers. Lectures given to a private audience in 1829 became the basis for his *Course of Positive Philosophy,* a six-volume work written between 1830 and 1842. Plagued by poor health throughout his life, Comte died in isolation but not without having made major contributions, which included laying the foundation for a new "science" of sociology.

Can Philosophy Be Brought into the Modern World?

Comte's philosophy begins by surveying the growth of human knowledge over the centuries. Comte looked on philosophy as progressive and as continually developing, as opposed to being always the same in its approach. In trying to understand what philosophy is, each of us must decide whether it does develop along evolutionary lines or whether ancient theories, such as Plato's, are still true today. Comte thought there were three stages in the history of philosophy: first the **theological** or religious period, then the **metaphysical** or speculative one, and finally the scientific or the **empirical.** If he was right, this means that only the latest form of scientific or empirical knowledge can be valid today. Comte wanted philosophy to stop searching for the origins of the **universe** and to content itself with establishing the laws of relations among empirical phenomena or the data our senses produce. He assumed that this could be done. But can all of human experience be formulated into rules that apply to everyone? That **assumption** has been questioned. Some philosophers have said yes; others, no.

Comte wanted everyone to agree about philosophy, what it is, and what it concluded. He thought we could do so if only we would use the same **scientific method.** We know that Plato doubted that all humanity would ever agree completely, partly because truth could not be stated finally. Comte, however, was confident that we could now do much better and so eliminate philosophical discord at last. If he was correct, the outcome will affect our whole conception of philosophy. But why did Comte think that such definite results were possible in his day when they were not before? The answer, he believed, was that a sound understanding of the empirical procedures of science could provide what previously was missing. Human intelligence has "come of age."

> All competent thinkers agree with [Francis] Bacon that there can be no real knowledge except that which rests upon observed facts. This fundamental maxim is evidently indis-

putable if it is applied, as it ought to be, to the mature state of our intelligence.[7]

Do Human Reason and Science Mature in the Same Way?

In making his proposal to revise philosophy and in naming it the "**positive** philosophy," Comte assumed that something crucial had happened in the history of humankind. For some time, said Comte, philosophers had struggled unsuccessfully with complex questions about the world and human existence. But, he thought, suddenly he and his contemporaries had become capable of moving to a new stage of victory. After dealing with religious and metaphysical speculation for centuries, they could begin to discover the true pattern of human development. Once this discovery had been completed, people could move on to outline invariable natural laws.

> . . . (T)he human mind, by simply confining itself to researches of an entirely possible order, can find therein inexhaustible food for its highest form of activity without attacking inaccessible problems. (P. 10.)

Comte thought earlier philosophers had reached too far. If we ask only the question of how to promote human happiness, and do not ask questions about universal justice, science can aid us in solving our immediate problems.

We live, thought Comte, in the time of a fundamental revolution that will allow us to answer questions definitely in a way Socrates could never have hoped. He had to settle for asking questions. Now we can answer them. Such a prospect makes the future of philosophy quite exciting. The scientific revolution began with mathematics and physics, but social phenomena can also now be described in a rigorous scientific form. Comte was convinced that the obstacles facing philosophy could now be overcome.

All our fundamental conceptions having thus been rendered homogeneous, philosophy will be constituted finally in the positive state. Its character will henceforth be unchangeable. (P. 13.)

Philosophy, Comte thought, had strayed into considering **abstract** areas (e.g., God). Now the fundamental questions of human life can be resolved into one philosophical view, not many, as had been the case.

If this is possible, what happens to all previous philosophy? As we study Plato, will we think that the philosophy he developed in his time in Athens is still relevant and can teach us something? If we accept Comte's theory of progress and evolution, all previous theories will be rendered insignificant except for their historical interest. As we try to determine what philosophy is, we realize that it does not remain the same throughout time. But must we treat it as an enterprise that is strictly modern and contemporary? Comte's answer was yes. He was impatient for his group of properly trained scientists to get on with their crucial task in philosophy's newly enlightened age, since scientific method has given us the procedure to pursue philosophy.

Is Philosophy a Means to Organize Society?

Plato wanted philosophy not just to speculate but to be joined to effective action. Comte was even more optimistic about his philosophy and its ability to solve social ills.

We may look upon the positive philosophy as constituting the only solid basis of the social reorganization that must terminate the crisis in which the most civilized nations have found themselves for so long. (P. 28.)

Philosophy can have this decisive effect, Comte thought, because our political and moral crisis is due only to the intellectual anarchy we inherited from the past. Positive philosophy, he believed, can organize our thought into a scientific system and thus cure society's moral crisis.

If we are to reach this goal, we must attain a large measure of agreement among philosophers. Thus, one of the most important questions about philosophy is whether philosophers will always disagree, or whether in a scientific age it is possible finally to achieve **unanimity** of thought. Comte thought his "positive philosophy" was destined to prevail against all alternatives. The question we need to ask is whether philosophy is organized in such a way that one view can ever dominate. Or is divergence of opinion a constant philosophical fact with which we must learn to live? If the latter is our situation, unanimity will never appear.

Socrates made popular the dialogue form of philosophy. He wanted us to engage in shared inquiry, an exchange of questions and answers. Comte's aim was the unity of all philosophy, something Plato never achieved. Comte hoped to reach this unity through the use of a common, agreed, scientifically derived method, one very different from Socrates' method of questions and discussion. To accomplish this, certain conditions had to be fulfilled. Comte thought the groundwork for this unity had now been laid and that philosophy could be something different from what it had been in the past.

Is Philosophy Historical or Scientific in Its Approach?

You can tell what someone thinks philosophy is all about by how he or she approaches it—whether it is presented as a contemporary science, for example, or by considering a series of historical authors. If we study Plato and the Socratic method, we do so because we think it relevant and applicable today. If it is, philosophy cannot be an exact science. The physical sciences are not historical in their basic approach, so a fundamental choice must be made. If Comte was right, only the offerings of modern science are relevant for philosophy. If he was not, a contemporary theory may have no advantage over what is ancient.

Comte wanted philosophy to lead us to what he called social physics (sociology). He included in this mathematics, astronomy, physics, chemistry, physiology, and biology. Each has unique aspects, but he thought unity could be found among them. Philosophy's first job would be to discern that common basis and then to build on what has been learned. By organizing our knowledge in this way, philosophy could reorganize society on a scientific footing. Plato's emphasis, on the other hand, was on the art of inquiry and on learning to rephrase the questions we ask.

Plato's method of telling myths and using poetic symbols would be far too imprecise for Comte. Mathematical precision takes precedence over discussion.

> I shall show that the possibility of applying mathematical analysis to the study of different phenomena, and so obtaining for such study the highest possible degree of precision and coordination, is in exact proportion to the rank that these phenomena occupy in my encyclopedic scale. . . . It is, therefore, mathematical science that must constitute the true starting point of all rational scientific education, whether general or special. (Pp. 60, 67.)

Once it has based itself on scientific laws, and its method of **verification,** philosophy must build an encyclopedia that contains all knowledge. The eighteenth-century Encyclopedists had started this task; now science can complete it and transform philosophy into an exact science. Aiming at nothing less than the revolution of our intellectual system, this goal is ambitious, as Comte fully realized. But if our human situation has not changed fundamentally since ancient times, those who expect philosophy to produce this precision and finality may be disillusioned if

they find themselves asking the same questions Socrates did, moving no further than a continual dialogue.

Mathematics and the method of quantifiable data combine to offer philosophy a new basis, Comte thought. We have studied forms of life in the biological laboratory and known much more about them today. Why not do the same for human nature and human ambition? Comte unfortunately did not go far toward realizing this new unifying scheme himself. But his was the great vision. It was his genius to see that the methods of modern science could be applied to human problems, even though he could not apply them far enough to validate the vision with which his positive philosophy began. The selection that follows, like all those in this section, is from *Introduction to Positive Philosophy*, a twentieth-century edition/translation of Comte's six-volume work (1830–42) alluded to earlier.

In order to explain properly the true nature and peculiar character of the positive philosophy, it is indispensable that we should first take a brief survey of the progressive growth of the human mind viewed as a whole; for no idea can be properly understood apart from its history.

In thus studying the total development of human intelligence in its different spheres of activity, from its first and simplest beginning up to our own time, I believe that I have discovered a great fundamental law, to which the mind is subjected by an invariable necessity. The truth of this law can, I think, be demonstrated both by reasoned proofs furnished by a knowledge of our mental organization, and by historical verification due to an attentive study of the past. This law consists in the fact that each of our principal conceptions, each branch of our knowledge, passes in succession through three different theoretical states: the theological or fictitious state, the metaphysical or abstract state, and the scientific or positive state. In other words, the human mind—by its very nature—makes use successively in each of its researches of three methods of philosophizing, whose characters are essentially different and even radically opposed to each other. We have first the theological method, then the metaphysical method, and finally the positive method. Hence, there are three kinds of philosophy or general systems of conceptions on the aggregate of phenomena which are mutually exclusive of each other. The first is the necessary starting point of human intelligence; the third represents its fixed and definitive state; the second is destined to serve only as a transitional method.

In the theological state, the human mind directs its researches mainly toward the inner nature of beings, and toward the first and final causes of all the phenomena that it observes—in a word, toward absolute knowledge. It therefore represents these phenomena as being produced by the direct and continuous action of more or less numerous supernatural agents, whose arbitrary intervention explains all the apparent anomalies of the universe.

In the metaphysical state, which is in reality only a simple general modification of the first state, the supernatural agents are replaced by abstract forces, real entities or personified abstractions, inherent in the different beings of the world. These entities are looked upon as capable of giving rise by themselves to all the phenomena observed, each phenomenon being explained by assigning it to its corresponding entity.

Finally, in the positive state, the human mind, recognizing the impossibility of obtaining absolute truth, gives up the search after the origin and hidden causes of the universe and a knowledge of the final causes of phenomena. It endeavors now only to discover, by a well-combined use of reasoning and observation, the actual laws of phenomena—that is to say, their invariable relations of succession and likeness. The explanation of facts, thus reduced to its real terms, consists henceforth only in the connection established between different particular phenomena and some general facts, the number of which the progress of science tends more and more to diminish. (Pp. 1–2.)

Josiah Royce and the Religious Aspect of Philosophy

Philosophy experiences periods of being "born again." Its Western forms first appeared in ancient Greece. Later, philosophy flourished in Europe and traveled across the Atlantic to the New World. At first philosophy was not easily separated from the political and religious concerns the immigrants brought with them to America. But as the United States began to mature in the nine-

JOSIAH ROYCE 1855–1916

teenth century, American philosophy became more self-conscious. We find that new outlook in the work of Josiah Royce (1855–1916) who was born in the Gold Rush town of Grass Valley, California.

After spending his early years teaching in San Francisco and the University of California at Berkeley, Royce moved east to continue his career at Harvard. William James, whom we will meet, became his friendly philosophical rival. At the turn of the century, the two dominated philosophy in the United States and shared international acclaim. Royce summed up his prolific career by saying that "my deepest motives and problems have centered about the Idea of the Community."[8] He spent his life refining an elaborate theory that emphasized both the interrelatedness of all things, events, and persons, and his conviction that God—or the **Absolute,** as Royce liked to say—is the origin and destiny of all that exists. Thus, the way of philosophy leads Royce to the question: Is philosophy different from religion? He created his own novel response, and this fascination involved him with all the philosophers of the past. If Plato was content to raise questions, Royce wanted to come closer to offering answers. If Comte thought science could set philosophy on a new path, Royce felt religion could combine with ancient philosophical questions to give us guidance for living.

Is Philosophy Different from Religion?

Socrates spoke about the gods, and Plato meditated on love. Both wondered why the world exhibits the order it does, and they urged people to follow what they discovered to be good. Even Comte, who had little use for God, found that a religion based on the love and service of humanity had a role to play in his philosophy. Of course, 'religion' for him meant a devotion to science as the

creation of human nature. Some philosophers reject religion completely, even in Comte's sense. But if you think about the similarities between philosophy and religion, it is not easy to separate the two, because they share so many links. **Religion** offers a guide to life; philosophy offers ethical advice. Still, philosophy and religion are not the same. How are they best compared and contrasted?

Many of Royce's basic ideas can be found in *The Religious Aspect of Philosophy* (1885). One of the first questions raised in that book is: What is religion? Three elements stand out in his reply.

> A religion must teach some moral code, must in some way inspire a strong feeling of devotion to that code, and in so doing must show something in the nature of things that answers to the code or that serves to reinforce the feeling. A religion is therefore practical, emotional, and theoretical; it teaches us to do, to feel, and to believe, and it teaches . . . belief as a means to its teaching of the action and of the feeling.[9]

In defining religion, Royce wanted a general statement that could apply universally. He did not advocate a particular religious faith, nor was he suggesting that any one religious community possessed the truth. Royce's topic—what is religion?—is a philosophical question. Although religion is the subject, his method in thinking about religion was not necessarily religious. His goal was to discover the nature of religion and how it relates to everything that is. His conclusion was that wherever we find religion it involves: (1) a moral code, (2) elements such as ritual, myth, and sacred texts that inspire enthusiasm and dedication toward the moral code, and (3) a theoretical factor, namely, a view about the nature of reality as a whole.

"Religion," said Royce, "invites the scrutiny of philosophy, and philosophy may not neglect the problems of religion" (p. 4). Philosophy has two functions as it examines religion. On the one hand philosophy has an **analytical** function. It examines religion's assumptions about morality and reality. It checks to see what justifies such assertions and whether those warrants are sound. On the other hand, Royce believes that philosophy is more than just critical. It seeks answers to questions such as: What should I do? For what can I hope? At this point, philosophy and religion should stand on common ground, in spite of the failure of some philosophers to see this.

Two Types of Philosophy

Royce denied that philosophy can replace religion. While religion is concerned with practical activity, philosophy stresses theoretic understanding. Optimistically, Royce played down the power of philosophy to discredit religion. He urged instead that the relationship between the two be complementary. Religion needs philosophy, he believed, because the philosopher engages in the critical and analytical tasks required to ground religion firmly. Our practical decisions need theory to be sure our decisions are properly investigated. One discovers that religion is an important expression of humanity's hope as well as a matter of practical activity. Philosophy can thus receive insights and suggestions from religion that uncover answers to life's fundamental questions.

Royce distinguished between philosophy as *purely theoretic* and philosophy as *religious*. Purely theoretic philosophy must take the truth as it is, however dreadful that truth may be. Theoretic philosophy must have passion for the truth alone. It must discover and state the truth with serenity, without either approbation or condemnation. In a word, it must be objective. Royce continues to draw the distinction as follows:

But religious philosophy has other objects in addition to these. Religious philosophy is indeed neither the foe nor the mistress of theoretic philosophy. Religious philosophy dares not be in opposition to the truths that theory may have established. But over and above these truths it seeks something else. It seeks to know their value. It comes to the world with other interests, in addition to the purely theoretical ones. It wants to know what in the world is worthy of worship as the good. It seeks not merely the truth, but the inspiring truth. It defines for itself goodness, moral worth, and then it asks, *What in this world is worth anything?* Its demands in this regard are boundless. It will be content only with the best it can find. Having formulated for itself its ideal of worth, it asks at the outset: *Is there then, anywhere in the universe, any real thing of Infinite Worth?* If this cannot be found, then and then only will religious philosophy be content with less. Then it will still ask: *What in this world is worth most?* It cannot make realities, but it is determined to judge them. It cannot be content with blind faith, and demands the actual truth as much as theoretical philosophy demands it; but religious philosophy treats this truth only as the material for its ideal judgments. It seeks the ideal among the realities. (Pp. 8, 9.)

Religion is just as necessary as philosophy, since philosophy without religion could become idle speculation. Royce also felt that religion keeps us focused on ideal realities and not merely mundane ones. We know that the real world offers us mundane realities; we take a job and we raise a family. In contrast, religion lifts our attention to another world, where we strive to achieve ideals as well as to know facts. Similarly, passing your philosophy course will require a certain amount of mundane work. But in addition, studying philosophy might lift your sights, encouraging you to strive for new ideals in your life. Insofar as it does this, philosophy is "religious."

Should Philosophy Abandon Hope?

Royce spent his life working out a vision of religious philosophy. As you read through his work you repeatedly find the theme that philosophy should have a critical and a constructive side. Philosophy develops our critical faculties, but it should also deal with our doubts. Even where those elements are present together, however, they do not solve our dilemma but rather intensify the effort to know what philosophy is.

As a teacher of beginning students, Royce found that their difficulty with philosophy was not due to technical and abstract philosophical language but to "the confusing variety of the doctrines of the philosophers."[10] After all, students study thinkers who have labored for years to develop their views, but they do so in the hope that true insight will emerge. Instead, the result turns out to be a snarl of **premises,** methods, and conclusions that often disagree. Even where there is general agreement, no two philosophers ever see eye to eye or speak exactly alike. Dante's warning to those at the gates of hell, "Abandon all hope, ye who enter here," is apt counsel for the student who wanders into the labyrinth of philosophy. Royce, however, drew anything but a pessimistic conclusion about this situation. His search for a sound religious philosophy produced an alternative.

> What I want to suggest here is that the truth about this world is certainly so manifold, so paradoxical, so capable of equally truthful and yet seemingly opposed descriptions, as to forbid us to declare a philosopher wrong in his doctrine merely because we find it easy to make plausible a doctrine that at first sight appears to conflict with his own. . . . What if all the aspects should contain truth? What if our failure thus far to find and to state the absolute philosophy were due to the fact, not that all the philosophies thus far have been essentially false, but that the truth is

> so wealthy as to need not only these, but yet other and future expressions to exhaust its treasury. (P. 13.)

In other words, we may have to abandon the hope of finding a single truth such as the one sought by Comte. But still we should rejoice in the abundance of the possible roads to truth.

Do Things Hang Together?

The view stated above attracted Royce because, for him, philosophy was a critical reflection on how we act in our world. Living is what we do, said Royce, and living involves passion, faith, doubt, and courage. "Critical inquiry into what all these things mean and imply," Royce asserted, "is philosophy" (p. 1). The point he wanted to underscore is that there is variety in philosophy because there are so many varied individuals in the world. Our experiences and critical reflections are bound to differ. However, Royce was struck with another fact: we all have experiences and a capacity to reflect that give us a great deal in common. The multiplicity in life still constitutes a unity in the sense that thought continually searches for this unity. Even though we are different and our experiences conflict, we know that the world is not a sheer plurality. Somehow all things fit together in one grasp.

With that insight, Royce hoped that he could find what he calls an absolute philosophy. Such a philosophy would have to emphasize the diversity life contains. The reach of thought might always exceed our grasp, but Royce was undaunted. He died believing he had seen what the basic form of reality must be.

> This theory is that the whole universe, including the physical world also, is essentially one live thing, a mind, one great Spirit, infinitely wealthier in his experiences than we are, but for that reason to be compre-

hended by us only in terms of our own wealthiest experience. . . . But the point is that *if* the universe is a live thing, a spiritual reality, we, in progression towards a comprehension of its nature, must needs first comprehend our own life. And in doing this we shall pass through all sorts of conflicting moods, theories, doctrines; and these doctrines, in the midst of their conflict and variety, will express, in fragmentary ways, aspects of the final doctrine, so that . . . the truth will be the whole. (P. 17.)

Royce was convinced that reality is rational, purposeful, and knowable. He also believed that the destructive aspects of conflict ultimately could be overcome. Justice, truth, and beauty would prevail. Not every philosophical outlook views the world that way, but Royce, by noting the diversity in life while maintaining nevertheless its essential unity, represents a middle ground between Plato and Comte. He sees one truth—though not the same one as Comte—but he also sees the Platonic need for a perpetual quest and constant dialogue.

There is little question that Royce's view was religious, in the sense of lifting our vision away from the mundane, although there is disagreement about his broader vision. He gave us a view of philosophy that represents an effort to learn how and why all things are related as they are. This perspective is an example of the **"coherence theory of truth,"** which holds that the only real test for truth lies in considering all things together in their widest possible scope. It differs from the **"correspondence theory"** offered by some philosophers, which tells us to test individual claims by seeing how they correspond to a limited set of facts. Royce offers us a clear alternative to such a restriction. In the accompanying selection from *The Religious Aspect of Philosophy* (1885), Royce invites each of us to recognize how natural it is to philosophize and how important it is to go for the broad scope and "the big picture."

Philosophy, in the proper sense of the term, is not a presumptuous effort to explain the mysteries of the world by means of any superhuman insight or extraordinary cunning, but has its origin and value in an attempt to give a reasonable account of our own personal attitude towards the more serious business of life. You philosophize when you reflect critically upon what you are actually doing in your world. What you are doing is of course, in the first place, living. And life involves passions, faiths, doubts, and courage. The critical inquiry into what all these things mean and imply is philosophy. We have our faith in life; we want reflectively to estimate this faith. We feel ourselves in a world of law and of significance. Yet why we feel this homelike sense of the reality and the worth of our world is a matter for criticism. Such a criticism of life, made elaborate and thorough-going, is a philosophy.

If this assumption of mine be well-founded, it follows that healthy philosophizing, or thorough-going self-criticism, is a very human and natural business, in which you are all occasionally, if not frequently engaged, and for which you will therefore from the start have a certain sympathy. Whether we will it or no, we all of us do philosophize. The difference between the temperament which loves technical philosophy and the temperament which can make nothing of so-called metaphysics is rather one of degree than of kind. The moral order, the evils of life, the authority of conscience, the intentions of God, how often have I not heard them discussed, and with a wise and critical skepticism, too, by men who seldom looked into books. The professional student of philosophy does, as his constant business, precisely what all other people do at moments. In the life of nonmetaphysical people, reflection on destiny and the deepest truths of life occupies much the same place as music occupies in the lives of appreciative, but much distracted amateurs. The constant student of philosophy is merely the professional musician of reflective thought.

He daily plays his scales in the form of what the scoffers call "chopping logic." He takes, in short, a delight in the technical subtleties of his art which makes his enthusiasm often incomprehensible to less devoted analysts of life. But his love for speculation is merely their own natural taste somewhat specialized. He is a sort of miser, secretly hoarding up the treasures of reflection which other people wear as the occasional ornaments of intercourse, or use as a part of the heavier coinage of conversation. If, as nonprofessional philosophers, you confine your reflections to moments, the result is perhaps a serious talk with a friend, or nothing more noteworthy than an occasional hour of meditation, a dreamy glance of wonder, as it were, at this whole great and deep universe before you, with its countless worlds and its wayward hearts. Such chance heart searchings, such momentary communings with the universal, such ungrown germs of reflection, would under other circumstances develop into systems of philosophy. If you let them pass from your attention you soon forget them, and may then even fancy that you have small fondness for metaphysics. But, none the less, all intelligent people, even including the haters of metaphysics, are despite themselves occasionally metaphysicians. (Pp. 1–3.)

Summary

On the first leg of our journey through the realms of philosophy, we discovered that philosophy is both one thing and many things. Plato, Comte, and Royce agreed that philosophy is a search for truth and for knowledge of a fundamental kind. They believed that human reason, rightly used, can distinguish appearance from reality and falsehood from truth. It is beneficial to inquire critically, even when the effort is arduous or frustrating. Few of the major figures in Western philosophy would quarrel with these conclusions.

However, the thinkers presented in this first chapter are at odds over basic questions. Plato sought simply to sensitize us to fundamental issues by the spirit of dialogue and to leave us with the questions and an unending dialogue. Comte was restless with such inconclusiveness in view of what he felt were the achievements of modern science that could be transferred to philosophy. Royce wanted to wed philosophy to a religious quest, which he thought represented the spirit of philosophy.

These differences will increase in the pages that follow. Some of the disagreements revolve around these questions: (1) What methods should philosophy employ? (2) To what extent can ignorance be dispelled? (3) In what sense can there be progress in philosophy, and does philosophy require every student to begin anew and at the same place? (4) Can philosophy continue without certainty, or can it attain completeness and finality? (5) How is philosophy related to and also different from science and religion?

These issues bring us back to our original point of departure: What is philosophy, and what are its questions? Philosophy keeps us young by constantly forcing us to start at the beginning to ask the old questions over again. Yet as students, you may ask: What good will it do me to ask these "old questions" over again? One answer has just been given—asking questions keeps us young. Furthermore, all philosophers are convinced that these questions are not idle; sooner or later, they are questions life will force you to ask. At the moment you will have other interests, too, and may prefer baseball or rock concerts. But maturity and responsibility, we are convinced, will sooner or later raise these questions for you. Why not start to live the life of continued dialogue, with yourself, with your friends, and with all the philosophers past and present. The premise of the **dialectic** technique is that mutual inquiry is the only road to self-discovery and truth.

GLOSSARY

absolute free of all qualifications; independent; nonrelative; unchanging; eternal. Royce used the term (capitalized) to refer to God or to Reality as an unconditioned, all-inclusive totality.

abstract a quality of the type of thinking that works with concepts that are entirely general, excluding the consideration of the particular instances to which those general concepts might be applied; for instance, in *The Republic*, Plato develops a concept of justice that is abstract in the sense that it is intended to refer to 'justice' in and of itself, a method of inquiry he believes must take precedence over questions of whether certain particular actions actually possess the quality of being just.

allegory a type of story used for teaching, in which the relations between the people, things, and events in the story stand symbolically for an altogether separate, often abstract, state of affairs. See **symbol.**

analytical referring to the method of inquiry that divides things or ideas into their simplest parts and studies the relations that hold among these parts.

apology as it is used by Plato for the title of the dialogue relating Socrates' final speech to his accusers, and contrary to ordinary usage, "apology" has the sense, not of an excuse or a tacit admission of wrongdoing, but of a defense and justification of one's actions.

assumption a principle that is accepted uncritically, taken for granted, without the support of proof or argument. Often an assumption is employed as the major premise of an argument. See **premise.**

cause a hidden or underlying entity, process, or principle that is taken to determine or explain the nature of the phenomena that are present to the senses. See **phenomenon.**

coherence theory of truth the theory that truth is not a property of individual, isolated judgments or statements, but that the truth must involve a judgment's being consistent with a large body of other judgments, forming a part of an interconnected, rational system.

correspondence theory of truth the theory that regards individual statements as true if they simply agree with the facts to which they refer, and as false if they simply do not.

dialectic the use of questions and answers as a method of philosophical inquiry, weighing the strengths and weakness of differing or opposing viewpoints with the aim of reaching a new, more complete, and more balanced understanding of the issue at hand.

dialogue a discussion between two persons, developed by the exchange of questions and answers, assertion and objections, first used as a literary framework for philosophical writings by Plato. In philosophy, a dialogue will often be **dialectical.**

empirical pertaining to knowledge obtained from and justified by an appeal to experience, in particular to sense experience.

ideal a concept or principle that embodies a vision of some kind of perfection or excellence and serves to direct human conduct and awareness toward goals of higher than ordinary significance; sometimes used in a negative sense to indicate that a conduct or principle is a product of pure imagination, embodying a degree of perfection that is not really attainable, given the limitations of our faculties of knowledge and the objective reality as we are actually able to know it.

metaphysical concerned with the study of that which is most basic and fundamental in reality. Comte's account of the development of philosophy designates the metaphysical as an intermediary stage between theological thought and positive science, in which the supernatural deities of theology are replaced by abstract entities.

myth a traditional story, usually of unknown origin but claiming a basis in history, that is employed to explain, illustrate, or justify some practice or belief.

optimism an outlook that anticipates the best outcome in any given situation and believes that good triumphs over evil.

pessimism an outlook that stresses the inevitability of misfortune.

phenomenon from a Greek term meaning "what is shown," an object or event in the world, considered in terms of the way it is experienced by or appears to some sentient observer, as opposed to what it might possibly be like in itself or what underlying reality might be causally responsible for the way reality appears to us.

philosophy a term derived from the Greek *philein* ("to love") and *sophia* ("wisdom"). In general, philosophy is the love of wisdom in the sense of advancing human understanding about what is fundamentally true and good.

positive Comte's term for a method of philosophical inquiry that, taking its inspiration from scientific method, would abandon metaphysical speculation in favor of an attempt to catalogue exhaustively the laws governing the observable order of the world, impelling philosophy progressively and systematically toward a conclusive set of answers to all questions that can meaningfully be asked.

premise in a philosophical argument, a primary assumption on which subsequent claims of the argument rely and from which these claims may be logically derived. See **assumption.**

religion the beliefs, practices, and institutions that express human experience and ideas of that which is taken to be holy, divine, sacred, or ultimate in power and value.

scientific method refers to procedures used to advance human knowledge by collecting data through observation and experiment and by formulating, testing, and confirming provisional suggestions *(hypotheses)* by appealing to such data.

"Socratic method" the form of **dialogue** and **dialectic** technique employed by Socrates to clarify ideas, by means of a persistent questioning aimed at a successive sharpening of definitions.

soul the term used by Socrates and Plato to refer to the animating part of a human being, consisting of appetites, will, and intellect.

symbol an object that is taken to stand for or suggest something other than itself, especially an object used to represent an abstract quality.

theological pertaining to the study of the nature of the divine, the sacred, and the ultimate, often for the purpose of creating or supporting **religious doctrines** (see **religion**). For Comte, theological thought represented a first tentative step toward positive science but was destined for extinction because it made claims that could not be verified, hence was incapable of providing the consensus among rational people that is the test of true knowledge. For Royce, on the other hand, theological thought functions as a means of guaranteeing the **coherence** of religious doctrines as a necessary condition for the existence of cohesion in human communities.

unanimity accord or agreement, in philosophy a goal of inquiry, that enables people to agree clearly and rationally on what is to be considered fundamentally good, true, just, etc.

universe in philosophy, this term often refers to everything that exists.

verification showing some statement to be true by appealing to empirical evidence in its favor, or to formal rules of reasoning that guarantee the validity of its derivation from other statements that can themselves be checked against the empirical evidence.

wisdom knowledge and understanding that show us how to live rightly and well; see **philosophy.**

STUDY QUESTIONS

1. Do you agree with Plato that dialogue, engaging different points of view, is helpful in facing life's problems, even though it involves uncertainty and tentativeness?

2. Would you be content simply to explore the questions of life, even if you knew answers were not forthcoming? Or, do you think answers to some of life's problems can be found?

3. Do you agree with Comte that the achievements of modern science have, or should have, changed the goals and methods of philosophy drastically?

4. Can you give an example of the way in which you think the findings of modern science have definitely answered one of the questions of philosophy raised in this chapter?

5. As you understand the meaning of 'religion,' do you agree with Royce on the intimate relation between religion and philosophy? Can you give an example?

6. Do you see any problems if philosophy were to become tied to "religious philosophy"? Would this help or hinder its ability to reach all people with its questions?

NOTES

[1] Plato, Epistle VII (341d), in *Thirteen Epistles of Plato*, trans. L. A. Post (Oxford: Clarendon, 1925), p. 94.

[2] Plato, *The Republic* (V, 473), in *The Dialogues of Plato*, trans. B. Jowett (New York: Random House, 1920), 1:737.

[3] Plato, *Symposium* (203), in *The Dialogues of Plato*, 1:328.

[4] Plato, *Phaedrus* (246), in *The Dialogues of Plato*, 1:251.

[5] Plato, *The Republic* (VII, 514–18), in *The Dialogues of Plato*, 1:773–77.

[6] Plato, *Apology* (36–42), in *The Dialogues of Plato*, 1:418–23.

[7] Auguste Comte, *Introduction to Positive Philosophy*, trans. Paul Descours and Frederick Ferré (Indianapolis: Bobbs-Merrill, 1970), p. 4. Copyright © 1970 by Macmillan Publishing Company. Reprinted by permission of the publisher.

[8] Josiah Royce, "Words of Professor Royce at the Walton Hotel at Philadelphia, December 29, 1915," in *The Hope of the Great Society* (New York: Macmillan, 1916), p. 126.

[9] Josiah Royce, *The Religious Aspect of Philosophy* (New York: Harper Torchbooks, 1958), pp. 3–4.

[10] Josiah Royce, *The Spirit of Modern Philosophy* (New York: W. W. Norton, 1967), p. 3.

I

WHAT CAN I KNOW?

. . . *Be patient toward all that is unsolved in your heart and try to love the* questions themselves *like locked rooms and like books that are written in a very foreign tongue. Do not now seek the answers, which cannot be given you because you would not be able to live them. And the point is, to live everything.* Live *the questions now. Perhaps you will then gradually, without noticing it, live along some distant day into the answer.*

RAINER MARIA RILKE
Letters to a Young Poet

CHAPTER TWO

Can I Know the External World?

"*D*o you really know him or her?" "What do you know about politics or physics?" "How do you know a philosophy paper is due next week?" Without thinking twice, we sometimes answer quickly, but we do not respond quite so easily when questions involve "knowledge" and "knowing." We realize that mistakes happen. There is also a difference between opinion and warranted belief; our perceptions of truth and falsity differentiate our judgments. "I'm not sure," or "I can't say." The questions people ask us often produce those responses and make us wonder what it means to know.

Epistemology is what philosophers call the study of questions about knowledge and knowing. One of its principles is that knowledge claims are sound if and only if they involve true and justified beliefs. Major disputes in philosophy turn on the meaning of those terms, but in general philosophers hold that knowledge means **justified true belief.** We can have beliefs and still lack knowledge if our beliefs are false. Unfortunately, we can also have true beliefs and still lack knowledge, at least in the deepest sense, because we fail to understand how or why a **belief** is true. **Justification** involves finding such an understanding, but philosophers are usually hard to satisfy when justification is the issue. "Can I know the external world?"

is a question that proves the point. For example, consider the sky and sea, persons and places, projects and things that occupy our attention. Surely we think they exist and that they are essentially as we experience them to be. But is that the case? How could such beliefs be justified?

We inhabit a world. Apparently it differs from us and we from it. At least experience commonly distinguishes between the knower and the known, between the objects we encounter and the "I" who interacts with them. Physical objects and other persons, we sometimes say, are external to us. Apparently they are also independent of each other, even if they are somehow related. Furthermore, we typically assume that we experience the world directly—as it is in itself—and also accurately, after taking into account the possibilities of illusion, misperception, and faulty judgment. If we ask how this happens, however, the difficulty of clarifying and justifying our beliefs looms large. For when common sense thinks twice, things may not turn out as they seemed at first.

The issues sketched here especially concerned three British philosophers: Locke, Berkeley, and Hume. These philosophers of **empiricism** regarded sense **experience** as the sole originating source of knowledge. Their approach criticized adherents of **rational-**

ism, such as Descartes, Spinoza, and Leibniz, whom we shall meet later in other chapters. According to the empiricists, the rationalists overemphasized the ideal of mathematical certainty and put too much trust in reason's ability to obtain knowledge without careful sense experience.

If the rationalists were overconfident about the power of unaided reason, the British empiricists faced problems, too. In ways their own analyses did not anticipate, sense experience proved a less than completely reliable source for knowledge of the external world. **Skepticism,** the position that our knowledge claims always remain subject to doubt, held on more emphatically than these thinkers hoped. Immanuel Kant, the fourth philosopher discussed in this chapter, tried to rescue knowledge from skepticism's devastation, but his success was restricted as well. As we study each of these philosophers in more detail, we will learn one of philosophy's lessons, namely, that the external world may not be what it seems.

J O H N   L O C K E   1632–1704

John Locke and the Nature of Experience

"Since it is the *understanding* that sets man above the rest of sensible beings, and gives him all the advantage and dominion which he has over them, it is certainly a subject, even for its nobleness, worth our labor to inquire into."[1] Thus, John Locke (1632–1704) introduced *An Essay Concerning Human Understanding* (1690). Published the same year as *Two Treatises of Civil Government,* which strongly influenced modern political theories of democracy, including Thomas Jefferson's writing of the Declaration of Independence, Locke's *Essay* sparked inquiries that have intrigued philosophers ever after.

Oxford-trained, Locke studied medicine and became the personal physician and close adviser to the Earl of Shaftesbury, a leading London statesman. In an England wracked by political turmoil, Shaftesbury stood trial for treason in 1681. Although Shaftesbury was acquitted, suspicion also fell on Locke. In 1683 he fled to Holland, where he wrote extensively. Remaining active politically, Locke made friends with Prince William and Princess Mary of Orange. When they were called to the British throne after James II was overthrown in the "Glorious Revolution" of 1688, Locke returned with them. Well situated to advance his favorite ideas, which included religious toleration and freedom of the press, he also published a number of works he had written in exile, among them the *Essay* and his *Two Treatises.*

Laying a Foundation

The purpose of Locke's *Essay* was "to inquire into the original, certainty, and extent of *human knowledge,* together with the grounds and degrees of *belief, opinion,* and *assent*" (p. 244). This project, Locke reported, had origins in the winter of 1670–71 when he and some friends discussed questions about morality and religion. One argument led to another, without reaching a resolution; question followed question with too little agreement. Locke eventually decided the priorities were misplaced; knowledge about morality and religion necessitated a sound epistemological foundation. As he later put the point,

> If we can find out how far the understanding can extend its view, how far it has faculties to attain certainty, and in what cases it can only judge and guess, we may learn to content ourselves with what is attainable by us in this state. (P. 245.)

Note that Locke believed in some cases the most we can do is "judge and guess." People often fail to recognize the limits of human understanding. Instead they presume to know more than they do. Contrary to the rationalists' expectations, Locke held that we are unlikely to find much certainty. But that outcome, he added, should not cripple us with doubt. "Our business here is not to know all things," he said, "but those which concern our conduct" (p. 246). Used properly, human reason is equal to that task.

The Importance of Ideas

Locke apologized for using the word **"idea"** so much, but he explained he would let the term "stand for whatsoever is the *object* of the understanding when a man thinks" (p. 247). Everyone admits we have ideas, and thus Locke announced that our first job is to determine how they arise. This is the proper strategy, he thought, because without ideas knowledge is impossible. The knowledge ideas can contain, moreover, is a function of how they are produced, organized, and related.

In good empirical fashion, Locke appealed "to everyone's own observation and experience" in showing how ideas exist (p. 248). This appeal, unfortunately, yielded neither the clarity nor the agreement he sought. For Locke's starting point—ideas—introduced hard problems straightaway, and his solutions did not satisfy the critics. One of the problems involved Locke's assertion that ideas are the objects of human understanding. If this principle is true, how can our knowledge be of the external world? Are we not trapped inside our own minds?

It was not Locke's intention to suggest that we lack knowledge of a world different from our minds. On the contrary, he never seriously doubted that material objects exist, and he confidently held that we know them through ideas. His concern therefore was to grasp how ideas occurred and thereby to outline the boundaries of human knowledge. But Locke's definition of ideas and his assumptions about the distinctions between them and their objects raised questions that his theory did not—and perhaps could not—answer. That outcome, however, did not make Locke a philosophical failure.

The questions of philosophy rarely have simple right or wrong answers. Philosophers may think they have settled a problem, but, like everyone else, they are not immune from thinking they know more than they do. Instead of settling issues, philosophers usually explore them further. In this process they may show—at times inadvertently and against their expressed intentions—how a particular perspective does not work as well as they thought it would. The result is to reveal new avenues of thought. One way or another, all the thinkers in this book fit this pattern. If we view philosophy as inquiry that aims at insight—not at fixed answers—then Locke's unresolved issues are no less important than the positive conclusions he defended.

The Attack on Innate Ideas

According to Locke, all ideas come from experience and, in particular, from "sensation or reflection" (p. 248). Locke's development of this thesis rejected a favorite belief of many rationalistic philosophers, namely, that we possess *innate ideas.* He interpreted this doctrine to mean that we share principles that are neither learned nor derived from experience; they are part of the mind at birth. Locke contended that there was no solid evidence to support this teaching. If the supposed evidence in its favor was universal human agreement on certain propositions, Locke questioned the universality. The existence of idiots, savages, and children, he pointed out, was enough to falsify the claim that there are any judgments—logical, moral, political, religious, or otherwise—about which human beings universally agree. Even if there were universal agreement, moreover, it would be insufficient to show that ideas are innate. When we trace how the so-called innate ideas appear, they invariably follow after particular sensory experiences and do not precede them.

Locke did not deny that there were self-evident truths. They would be deniable only at the cost of self-contradiction, but he held that self-evidence does not entail the existence of innate ideas. Even proofs about God's existence, argued Locke, do not depend on them. For unlike some later empiricists he believed that arguments based on experience could warrant a belief in God. Add to these objections Locke's conviction that the doctrine of innate ideas encouraged authoritarianism and laziness of mind, and it is not difficult to see why he claimed that all ideas come exclusively from experience.

Back to Experience

The thoroughness of Locke's rejection of innate ideas can be seen in his famous invitation to return to experience as the origin of ideas: "Let us then suppose the mind to be . . . white paper, void of all characters, without any ideas; how comes it to be furnished? . . . Whence has it all the materials of reason and knowledge?" (p. 248). Locke answers, first, that sensation is the "great source of most of the ideas we have" (p. 249). Through the senses we get "several distinct perceptions of things"—for example, "yellow, white, heat, cold, soft, hard, bitter, sweet" (p. 248). Reflection, the second source, provides "the understanding with another set of ideas which could not be had from things without." It encompasses "perception, thinking, doubting, believing, reasoning, knowing, willing, and all the different actings of our own minds" (p. 249). Including the capacity for memory and contemplation, reflection produces ideas by observing the mind's internal activity as well as by concentrating on sensory content that the mind has already received.

Locke's first image of the mind as a **tabula rasa,** a blank slate, turns out to be much more complicated than it looks. Even "white paper" has a structure before anything can be entered on it. In addition, Locke's full theory entails the mind's being active as well as a more-or-less passive recipient of sense data. His contention about the nonexistence of innate ideas—at least as he understood them—may be valid, but the issue is whether the mind brings features of its own to our experience. Locke did reckon with it, but only enough to convince his successors that a more thorough analysis was needed.

Meanwhile, besides differentiating **sensation** and **reflection,** Locke's epistemology included another crucial distinction: all our experience consists of *simple* or *complex* ideas. A color seen, a sound heard, warmth felt, an odor smelled—all are simple ideas of sense. Such simple ideas are the first building blocks of knowledge. They cannot be analyzed into simpler components. Nor can the mind invent or destroy them by itself, a conviction of Locke's that underscores again his commitment to the existence of real objects in an external world as the causes of the mind's content. Where simple ideas are concerned, the mind is mostly passive. Once we possess simple ideas, however, the mind actively unites, relates, and abstracts from them in a vast number of ways. Thus arise the complex ideas that are also necessary to account for our experience.

Primary and Secondary Qualities

Locke's theory of knowledge depends on a dualistic distinction between the knower and the known, between physical objects in the world and sensations and ideas in the mind. If Locke correctly described the origin and structure of our ideas, it still remains to ask whether those ideas convey the **world** to us accurately. Remember that Locke did not think of human experience as the measure or source of reality, but he did believe that the mind has no immediate objects except its own ideas. With their references to atoms, forces, and mathematical relations, moreover, the sciences increasingly suggested that there might be a considerable difference between the world as commonly experienced and the world as it exists objectively. Locke's position, then, was that our ideas *represent* reality. His theory about how they do so involved him in one more crucial distinction: the difference between primary and secondary **qualities**.

Primary qualities—for example, size, shape, motion, and mass—are utterly inseparable from the physical objects represented by ideas, and Locke therefore judged those qualities to exist independently of the

human mind. They have objective existence, and the test for their presence is that no material object ever is or can be experienced without them. Other qualities, contended Locke, have subjective existence; that is, they depend on a perceiver for their existence. Such **secondary qualities** include sense data such as warmth, color, smell, taste, and sound. They do not exist in things themselves, according to Locke, although objects contain the power to cause us to experience them. By Locke's reckoning, it follows that no object is, for example, red in itself. But some objects do possess properties that make us experience red when our ideas represent their characteristics properly.

Do We Know the External World as It Really Is?

One further point about Locke's theory of qualities deserves notice because of the complications it created for him. Neither primary nor secondary qualities float about freely. Instead, thought Locke, they subsist in something. If we ask what has shape or color, for instance, we might refer to something solid and extended. But those primary qualities are not things in themselves, either. In Locke's view, they are properties of something, and this something he called **substance.**

If there is an underlying substance that upholds the physical qualities of sensible things, there must also be something that does the same where intellectual activities such as thinking, willing, denying, and doubting are concerned. Matter, said Locke, is the first kind of substance; the second he designated as mind. But Locke also recognized that his claims about substance were not without problems. Chief among them is the fact that what a substance is in itself escapes us, because our experience is only of its qualities. Thus, the most essential aspects of existence itself apparently elude our comprehension. Locke was never more serious than when he stressed that there are limits to what human persons can know.

In spite of the difficulties that made it necessary for Locke to answer "no" as well as "yes" to our question "Can I know the external world?", he insisted that the response was still "mostly yes." But Locke's epistemological theory made his successors less confident. Unresolved problems developed, ironically, from the very point Locke regarded as the most obvious, namely, that there is real knowledge but also a fundamental dualism between the knower and the known. As most of us do, Locke believed ideas can accurately represent a reality external to the observer. But if our experience is so thoroughly a matter of ideas, how do we know that the ideas represent—or are caused by—substances or anything at all, let alone that they do so accurately? Locke contended that our ideas could fit those patterns, but Berkeley, Hume, and Kant were unpersuaded that his belief—however true it might be—was justified.

While arguing that we can have knowledge of the external world, even Locke had suggested that things in themselves are not exactly as they seem to us. But the next three philosophers we meet concluded that Locke had not pushed far enough. They modified his answer to the question "Can I know the external world?" It would have to read: "Yes and no, but mostly no." See if you can anticipate further why and how that trend emerged as you consider a final excerpt from Locke's *Essay Concerning Human Understanding* (1690).

---

15. *Ideas of primary qualities are resemblances; of secondary, not.* From whence I think it is easy to draw this observation, that the ideas of primary qualities of bodies are resemblances of them, and their patterns do really exist in the bodies themselves; but the ideas produced in us by these secondary qualities have no resemblance of them at all. There is nothing like our ideas existing in the bodies themselves. They are, in the bodies we denominate from them, only a power to produce those sensations in us; and what is sweet, blue, or warm in idea, is but the certain bulk, figure, and motion of the insensible parts in the bodies themselves, which we call so.

16. Flame is denominated *hot* and *light;* snow, *white* and *cold;* and manna, *white* and *sweet,* from the ideas they produce in us, which qualities are commonly thought to be the same in those bodies that those ideas are in us, the one the perfect resemblance of the other, as they are in a mirror, and it would by most men be judged very extravagant, if one should say otherwise. And yet he that will consider that the same fire that at one distance produces in us the sensation of warmth, does at a nearer approach produce in us the far different sensation of pain, ought to bethink himself what reason he has to say, that his idea of warmth which was produced in him by the fire, is actually in the fire, and his idea of pain which the same fire produced in him the same way is not in the fire. Why is whiteness and coldness in snow and pain not, when it produces the one and the other idea in us, and can do neither but by the bulk, figure, number, and motion of its solid parts?

17. The particular bulk, number, figure, and motion of the parts of fire or snow are really in them, whether anyone's senses perceive them or no; and therefore they may be called *real* qualities, because they really exist in those bodies. But light, heat, whiteness, or coldness, are no more really in them than sickness or pain is in manna. Take away the sensation of them; let not the eyes see light or colors, nor the ears hear sounds; let the palate not taste, nor the nose smell; and all colors, tastes, odors and sounds, as they are such particular ideas, vanish and cease, and are reduced to their causes, i.e., bulk, figure, and motion of parts. (P. 267.)

GEORGE BERKELEY 1685–1753

George Berkeley and Subjectivism

George Berkeley (1685–1753) is often referred to as Bishop Berkeley, because he was in fact a bishop of the Church of England. Born in Ireland, he attended Trinity College, Dublin, and taught there. He became interested in the American colonies and spent three years in Newport, Rhode Island, making plans for the college he hoped to found. While there he influenced the early American philosopher Jonathan Edwards, the Puritan divine, whom we will meet in Chapter Six. After he returned to Ireland, he became bishop of

Cloyne, a position he held for eighteen years. Berkeley was not in the ordinary sense a professional philosopher, although as a young man he wrote important works on that subject, including his *Essay Towards a New Theory of Vision* (1709), *A Treatise Concerning the Principles of Human Knowledge* (1710), and *Three Dialogues Between Hylas and Philonous* (1713). Among his main concerns was the belief that philosophy was so involved in abtruse questions involving dubious assumptions that, if he could help us see the folly in our ways, the problems might disappear, leaving time for more important matters.

Berkeley studied Locke, and from him he learned the distinction between primary and secondary qualities. The primary qualities, such as extension, are in the object, while the secondary qualities, such as color, vary with the individual perception. This mysterious world of extension lying behind our perceptions, but on which they depend, was what Berkeley thought caused us problems. Its philosophical perplexities took up time that we could better spend on other matters.

Abstract Ideas

Wanting to be "less disturbed with doubts and difficulties than other men," Berkeley felt there was no flaw in our faculties but only in the use we made of them.[2] False principles of human knowledge have permitted the intrusion of doubt and uncertainty, all of which might have been avoided. A lot of the avoidance of error depends on seeing the function of language correctly and recognizing when it is abused. Berkeley focused particularly on the belief that there are abstract ideas. Locke had given us an account of how our ideas are formed and used, and he suggested that we come to general ideas by abstracting from a series of particular ideas.

However, one consequence of Locke's notion is that either we have ideas that correspond to nothing in the real world we perceive, or else there are underlying substances never perceived as such. Berkeley responded to this dilemma by stating the belief that every idea we can conceive refers to some particular size and shape, so that in reality we never really conceive of a completely abstract idea—for example, a man of no particular size or shape. Yet we do use words which we take to refer to abstract general ideas. How is that possible, if in fact it turns out that we really cannot conceive of any idea that is not in some way particular?

Following Locke, Berkeley asked whether in fact "a word becomes general by being made the sign, not of an abstract general idea, but of several particular ideas." His conclusion regarding this matter is "that I do not deny absolutely that there are general ideas, but only that there are any *abstract* general ideas." What happens is that "an idea which considered in itself is particular, becomes general by being made to represent or stand for all other particular ideas of the same sort" (p. 515). What this argument leads us to conclude is that abstract ideas do not really exist but come into existence only because language allows us to use words so that what in itself is particular becomes general by being made a sign for a group of particular things. Were it not for language, we would never come to think of general abstract ideas, since our perceptions give us only particulars. Abstract and general ideas are not what we first come to know but are formed later, and become the source of confusion if we do not see that they represent nothing objective but arise only from words and language.

To Be Is to Be Perceived

Berkeley shared Locke's belief that the objects of human knowledge are all ideas. More than Locke, however, Berkeley wondered how we could ever get "outside ideas" to compare them with the material objects Locke assumed to exist as the cause of ideas. Berkeley felt that Locke's views led to skepticism, since we could never know directly the objects that were supposedly the source of our ideas. In an attempt to avoid skepticism, Berkeley proposed an **idealism** or **subjectivism,** that is, a scheme in which all objects composing our world are collections of ideas, nothing else. He felt this was not against common sense but actually in accord with it, since we think the things before us are directly known, and ideas are what fit such descriptions.

Esse est percipi—"to be is to be perceived" (p. 524). This is Berkeley's most famous philosophical phrase, and that principle is the essence of his **"subjective idealism."** The latter phrase does not mean that there is no real world or that we can make of the world anything we wish. God's existence guarantees that things do not pass in and out of existence as we individually cease to perceive them. It is just that there is no unthinking material substance behind ideas, lying there unperceived but still somehow the source of our perceptions. Since an idea can be like nothing but an idea, the cause of ideas must be "an incorporeal active substance or spirit" (p. 531). God provides the world's existence with its continuity, coherence, and presence in our minds.

That the things we see with our eyes and touch with our hands do exist, really exist, Berkeley has no doubt. It is just that they are nothing different from ideas. As for God's keeping them in existence when we are not perceiving what we call material objects, a limerick that once appeared in a student newspaper sums up Berkeley's position:

There once was a man who said God
Must think it exceedingly odd
That this juniper tree
Should continue to be
When there's no one about on the Quad!

To which the printed reply came:

> Dear Sir:
> Your astonishment's odd
> Since I'm always about on the Quad
> That's why the juniper tree
> Should continue to be
> Since perceived by
>> Yours faithfully,
>> God

What Counts as Common Sense?

Real fire, contends Berkeley, is not different from the idea of fire. He thought his theory accounted for what we accept as **common sense,** but most people have felt something odd about this proposition. For example, Dr. Samuel Johnson, the eighteenth-century British lexicographer and author—responded to Berkeley's theory by kicking a stone and exclaiming, "Thus I refute him." Dr. Johnson's kick, of course, did not banish Berkeley's idealism, but it does suggest that common sense resists identifying objects with ideas. Yet the question of how we can know those objects remains. Berkeley thought he had solved that problem by his theory of ideas, which includes the proposition that "God is known as certainly and immediately as any other mind or spirit whatsoever distinct from ourselves" (p. 574). That belief will not strike everyone as being "common sense," either.

Berkeley's answer to our question "Can I know the external world?" is that there is no world other than and "external to" the world of ideas we all experience. This idealism is a subjectivism, but only in the sense that we need not refer to objects other than and unlike ideas to support or to cause the ideas we experience. Berkeley saw his theory as eliminating unnecessary suppositions that do not help to explain our knowledge but in fact cause us trouble. A world unperceived by us, as an unseen source of the ideas we do experience, is unnecessary. Dr. Johnson was

right in the sense that the stone we kick is solid and can bring on pain, but Berkeley argues that we need no notion of "material substance" to account for what we really experience. As we began by noting, our ideas are all of particular things, but the universal and abstract ideas we think we need and think we actually deal with really exist only in our language and are in fact the result of our use of words.

Berkeley wrote largely in response to Locke, whose theories he took seriously but wanted to simplify. Later commentators often think Berkeley proposed an unreal world as a substitute rather than the "hard, solid" world we experience. But this was not at all Berkeley's intention. He argued that his world of ideas is perfectly real and has all the qualities we always experience. Keep that point in mind as you read more of Berkeley's thought. Hume, as we shall see, does move toward the skepticism Berkeley hoped to avoid, but perhaps for reasons other than the ones Berkeley saw inherent in Locke's theory of a material substance behind our ideas. Again responding to the problem of skepticism, Kant will not postulate an external world we can know by means of or outside of our ideas. His solution will be a more complicated, and perhaps more ingenious, "subjectivism." See if you can tell why the following passages from Berkeley's *Treatise Concerning the Principles of Human Knowledge* (1710) moved Hume and Kant to think otherwise.

---

9. And as the mind frames to itself abstract ideas of qualities or modes, so does it, by the same precision or mental separation, attain abstract ideas of the more compounded beings which include several coexistent qualities. For example, the mind having observed that Peter, James, and John resemble each other in certain common agreements of shape and other qualities, leaves out of the complex or compounded

idea it has of Peter, James, and any other particular man, that which is peculiar to each, retaining only what is common to all, and so makes an abstract idea wherein all the particulars equally partake; abstracting entirely from and cutting off all those circumstances and differences which might determine it to any particular existence. And after this manner it is said we come by the abstract idea of man, or, if you please, humanity, or human nature; wherein it is true there is included color, because there is no man but has some color, but then it can be neither white, nor black, nor any particular color, because there is no one particular color wherein all men partake. So likewise there is included stature, but then it is neither tall stature, nor low stature, nor yet middle stature, but something abstracted from all these. And so of the rest. Moreover, there being a great variety of other creatures that partake in some parts, but not all, of the complex idea of man, the mind, leaving out those parts which are peculiar to men, and retaining those only which are common to all the living creatures, frames the idea of *animal*, which abstracts not only from all particular men, but also all birds, beasts, fishes, and insects. The constituent parts of the abstract idea of animal are body, life, sense, and spontaneous motion. By *body* is meant body without any particular shape or figure, there being no one shape or figure common to all animals, without covering, either of hair, or feathers, or scales, etc., nor yet naked: hair, feathers, scales, and nakedness being the distinguishing properties of particular animals, and for that reason left out of the *abstract idea*. Upon the same account the spontaneous motion must be neither walking, nor flying, nor creeping; it is nevertheless a motion, but what that motion is it is not easy to conceive. (Pp. 512–13.)

12. By observing how ideas become general we may the better judge how words are made so. And here it is to be noted that I do not deny absolutely there are general ideas, but only that there are any *abstract* general ideas; for in the passages we have quoted

wherein there is mention of general ideas, it is always supposed that they are formed by abstraction, after the manner set forth [above]. Now, if we will annex a meaning to our words, and speak only of what we can conceive, I believe we shall acknowledge that an idea which considered in itself is particular, becomes general by being made to represent or stand for all other particular ideas of the same sort. To make this plain by an example, suppose a geometrician is demonstrating the method of cutting a line in two equal parts. He draws, for instance, a black line of an inch in length: this, which in itself is a particular line, is nevertheless with regard to its signification general, since, as it is there used, it represents all particular lines whatsoever; so that what is demonstrated of it is demonstrated of all lines, or, in other words, of a line in general. And, as that particular line becomes general by being made a sign, so the *name* "line," which taken absolutely is particular, by being a sign is made general. And as the former owes its generality not to its being the sign of an abstract or general line, but of all particular right lines that may possibly exist, so the latter must be thought to derive its generality from the same cause, namely, the various particular lines which it indifferently denotes. (P. 515.)

It is evident to anyone who takes a survey of the objects of human knowledge, that they are either ideas (1) actually imprinted on the senses, or else such as are (2) perceived by attending to the passions and operations of the mind, or lastly (3) ideas formed by help of memory and imagination, either compounding, dividing, or barely representing those originally perceived in the aforesaid ways. By sight I have the ideas of lights and colors, with their several degrees and variations. By touch I perceive hard and soft, heat and cold, motion and resistance, and of all these more and less either as to quantity or degree. Smelling furnishes me with odors, the palate with tastes, and hearing conveys sounds to the mind in all their variety of tone and composition. And as several of these are observed to accompany each other, they come to be marked by one name, and so to be reputed as one thing. Thus, for example, a certain color, taste, smell, figure, and consistence, having been observed to go together, are accounted one distinct thing, signified by the name "apple." Other collections of ideas constitute a stone, a tree, a book, and the like sensible things; which, as they are pleasing or disagreeable, excite the passions of love, hatred, joy, grief, and so forth.

2. But besides all that endless variety of ideas or objects of knowledge, there is likewise something which knows or perceives them, and exercises divers operations, as willing, imagining, remembering, about them. This perceiving, active being is what I call *mind, spirit, soul,* or *myself.* By which words I do not denote any one of my ideas, but a thing entirely distinct from them wherein they exist, or, which is the same thing, whereby they are perceived; for the existence of an idea consists in being perceived.

3. That neither our thoughts, nor passions, nor ideas formed by the imagination, exist without the mind, is what everybody will allow. And it seems no less evident that the various sensations or ideas imprinted on the sense, however blended or combined together (that is, whatever objects they compose), cannot exist otherwise than in a mind perceiving them. I think an intuitive knowledge may be obtained of this by anyone that shall attend to what is meant by the term "exist" when applied to sensible things. The table I write on I say exists—that is, I see and feel it; and if I were out of my study I should say it existed—meaning thereby that if I was in my study I might perceive it, or that some other spirit actually does perceive it. There was an odor, that is, it was smelt; there was a sound, that is, it was heard; a color or figure, and it was perceived by sight or touch. This is all that I can understand by these and the like expressions. For as to what is said of the absolute existence of unthinking things without any relation to their being perceived, that seems perfectly unintelligi-

ble. Their *esse* is *percipi*, nor is it possible they should have any existence out of the minds of thinking things which perceive them.

4. It is indeed an opinion strangely prevailing amongst men, that houses, mountains, rivers, and in a word all sensible objects, have an existence, natural or real, distinct from their being perceived by the understanding. But with how great an assurance and acquiescence soever this principle may be entertained in the world, yet whoever shall find in his heart to call it in question may, if I mistake not, perceive it to involve a manifest contradiction. For what are the forementioned objects but the things we perceive by sense? and what do we perceive *besides our own ideas or sensations?* and is it not plainly repugnant that any one of these, or any combination of them, should exist unperceived?

5. If we thoroughly examine this tenet it will perhaps be found at bottom to depend on the doctrine of *abstract ideas.* For can there be a nicer strain of abstraction than to distinguish the existence of sensible objects from their being perceived, so as to conceive them existing unperceived? Light and colors, heat and cold, extension and figures—in a word the things we see and feel—what are they but so many sensations, notions, ideas, or impressions on the sense? And is it possible to separate, even in thought, any of these from perception? For my part, I might as easily divide a thing from itself. I may, indeed, divide in my thoughts, or conceive apart from each other, those things which perhaps I never perceived by sense so divided. Thus I imagine the trunk of a human body without the limbs, or conceive the smell of a rose without thinking on the rose itself. So far, I will not deny, I can abstract, if that may properly be called abstraction which extends only to the conceiving separately such objects as it is possible may really exist or be actually perceived asunder. But my conceiving or imagining power does not extend beyond the possibility of real existence or perception. Hence, as it is impossible for me to see or feel anything without an actual sensation of that thing, so it is impossible for me to

conceive in my thoughts any sensible thing or object distinct from the sensation or perception of it.

6. Some truths there are so near and obvious to the mind that a man need only open his eyes to see them. Such I take this important one to be, to wit, that all the choir of heaven and furniture of the earth, in a word all those bodies which compose the mighty frame of the world, have not any subsistence without a mind, that their *being* is to be perceived or known; that consequently so long as they are not actually perceived by me, or do not exist in my mind or that of any other created spirit, they must either have no existence at all, or else subsist in the mind of some Eternal Spirit; it being perfectly unintelligible, and involving all the absurdity of abstraction, to attribute to any single part of them an existence independent of a spirit. To be convinced of which, the reader need only reflect and try to separate in his own thoughts the *being* of a sensible thing from its *being perceived*. (Pp. 523–25.)

16. But let us examine a little the received opinion. It is said extension is a mode or accident of matter, and that matter is the *substratum* that supports it. Now I desire that you would explain to me what is meant by matter's *supporting* extension. Say you, I have no idea of matter and therefore cannot explain it. I answer, though you have no positive, yet, if you have any meaning at all, you must at least have a relative idea of matter; though you know not what it is, yet you must be supposed to know what relation it bears to accidents, and what is meant by its supporting them. It is evident "support" cannot here be taken in its usual or literal sense—as when we say that pillars support a building; in what sense therefore must it be taken?

17. If we inquire into what the most accurate philosophers declare themselves to mean by *material substance*, we shall find them acknowledge they have no other meaning annexed to those sounds but the idea of *Being in general*, together with the relative notion of its supporting accidents. The general idea of Being appeareth to me the most abstract and incomprehensible of all other; and as for its supporting accidents, this, as we have just now observed, cannot be understood in the common sense of those words; it must therefore be taken in some other sense, but what that is they do not explain. So that when I consider the two parts or branches which make the signification of the words *material substance*, I am convinced there is no distinct meaning annexed to them. But why should we trouble ourselves any farther, in discussing this material *substratum* or support of figure and motion, and other sensible qualities? Does it not suppose they have an existence without the mind? And is not this a direct repugnancy, and altogether inconceivable? (P. 528.)

20. In short, if there were external bodies, it is impossible we should ever come to know it; and if there were not, we might have the very same reasons to think there were that we have now. Suppose (what no one can deny possible) an intelligence without the help of external bodies, to be affected with the same train of sensations or ideas that you are, imprinted in the same order and with like vividness in his mind. I ask whether that intelligence hath not all the reason to believe the existence of corporeal substances, represented by his ideas, and exciting them in his mind, that you can possibly have for believing the same thing? Of this there can be no question; which one consideration were enough to make any reasonable person suspect the strength of whatever arguments he may think himself to have for the existence of bodies without the mind. (P. 529.)

33. The ideas imprinted on the senses by the Author of nature are called *real things;* and those excited in the imagination, being less regular, vivid, and constant, are more properly termed *ideas*, or *images* of *things*, which they copy and represent. But then our sensations, be they never so vivid and distinct, are nevertheless ideas, that is, they exist in the mind, or are perceived by it, as

truly as the ideas of its own framing. The ideas of sense are allowed to have more reality in them, that is, to be more strong, orderly, and coherent than the creatures of the mind; but this is no argument that they exist without the mind. They are also less dependent on the spirit, or thinking substance which perceives them, in that they are excited by the will of another and more powerful spirit; yet still they are *ideas,* and certainly no idea, whether faint or strong, can exist otherwise than in a mind perceiving it. (P. 533.)

DAVID HUME 1711–1776

David Hume and the Appeal of Skepticism

John Locke's position is sometimes called *representational realism* because he thought that true ideas *correspond* to the real objects of a world external to our minds. Bishop Berkeley, however, was unconvinced that Locke had bridged the gap between subject and object so that our claims to know could be justified. He rejected a correspondence between ideas and material things, for the only thing that really corresponds to an idea is another idea, he said. Berkeley's *idealism* therefore excluded Locke's material things; instead, only "mental substance" exists. Our sensations, for example, are not *of* tables and chairs. Rather tables and chairs are bundles of sensations. Ours is not a world of things but of ideas alone.

Locke moved away from a direct **realism** that equates the qualities of sense experience with the properties of things in themselves. Berkeley went further still by questioning whether, apart from ideas created by God, there is an external world different in kind at all. He nevertheless held that we could know that reality is in fact the way our ideas present it. His world differed substantially from ordinary interpretations, but that outcome did not make it impossible for us to justify common sense's belief that we know reality in itself.

Although Locke and Berkeley are important in epistemology, neither rivals the thinker for whom they paved the way. David Hume (1711–1776) knew their work, and he was attracted to their empirical approach. But he went on to radicalize empiricism so that we are left to wonder whether we can have any knowledge beyond what is actually disclosed in sense experience. More devastating, Hume makes us face the possibility that even the disclosures of sense experience produce results far more problematic than we think. All the theories discussed in this book have been influential, but few show more lasting power than Hume's skepticism.

His brief autobiography states that Hume was born in Edinburgh, Scotland, studied law, then worked in business. At the age of 23, however, Hume took a small allowance from his family and went to France to study philosophy and to write. He had high hopes for *A Treatise of Human Nature* and was disappointed when its publication in 1739 aroused little interest. Hume returned to Britain, but his reputation as an atheist and a skeptic blocked his appointment to a professorship at the University of Edinburgh. So he continued to write while serving on various diplomatic missions to France and other countries. His *History of England* (1759, 1762) was one of the first important accounts of that country. Among his most important philosophical writings are the posthumously published *Dialogues Concerning Natural Religion*, which will be discussed in Chapter Eleven, and *An Enquiry Concerning Human Understanding* (first published in 1748), which provides the most precise statement of Hume's outlook.

Three Types of Skepticism

In *An Enquiry Concerning Human Understanding*, Hume distinguished between **antecedent** and **consequent skepticism,** which are versions of the doctrine that more or less denies the validity of our claims to have knowledge.

This analysis led Hume both to accept and to reject some aspects of these positions. Hume found his example of antecedent skepticism in the rationalistic philosophy of René Descartes, which we will examine in more detail in Chapter Three. Seeking to find a point of certainty from which he could deduce other equally certain truths, Descartes proposed the use of "methodological doubt." By questioning the validity of all beliefs, Descartes hoped to discover at least one basic feature of our existence that could stand unchallenged and hence qualify as the point of certainty he needed. Descartes thought he had discovered his point of certainty in our own existence, which is undeniably involved in the very experience of doubting. Although you can be mistaken about the existence of the world or even of parts of your body, doubt about your fundamental existence cannot be sustained. No matter how much you doubt, you must exist for your doubt to occur. Since doubting is a form of thinking, Descartes expressed his famous insight in the following form: *Cogito, ergo sum* (I think, therefore I am).

Hume concluded that this programmatic doubt sounded more promising than it actually was. If doubt is as radical as Descartes demands, Hume argued, eventually the doubter would have to question the reliability of even the rational faculties he used to draw conclusions about his own existence. On Descartes's own principles, these faculties must be regarded as suspect. Had Descartes truly doubted the trustworthiness of his reason, he never would have escaped doubt, since nothing is to escape the test of doubt. We must have proof of reason's veracity before we can accept the Cartesian claim to know our existence with certainty. But since this claim for knowledge rests on assumptions about the trustworthiness of our faculties, we can no longer regard it as absolutely certain. The program of Descartes, Hume asserted, is an impossibility. If we call everything into question, we cannot later legitimately claim to have knowledge. If we have left anything untouched as an assumption in order to claim that we can have knowledge, as Hume thought Descartes had done, we must give up the possibility of certainty.

Some elaboration on the last point will enable us to see Hume's position more clearly. According to Hume, "All the objects of human reason or inquiry may naturally be divided into two kinds, to wit, *relations of ideas* and *matters of fact.*"[3] Relations of ideas (for example, that 3 times 5 is equal to half of 30) can be known to be true **a priori.** That is, such truths are demonstrable without empirical observation, and they are absolutely certain because their denial is contradictory. But, according to Hume, they tell us nothing about matters of fact and existence. On the other hand, knowledge of matters of fact and existence is neither obtainable a priori nor is it demonstrable and absolutely certain. Hume based this view on the principle that "Whatever *is* may *not be.* No negation of a fact can involve a contradiction. The nonexistence of any being, without exception, is as clear and distinct an idea as its existence" (p. 688). Knowledge of matters of fact, then, can come only through empirical experience and can never be without potential error.

Although Hume rejected Descartes's antecedent skepticism, his emphasis on human fallibility led him to a less radical version that he believed would be helpful in avoiding error. If before accepting claims as true we have some skepticism about their validity, we will be more likely to test them empirically. This approach will not give us absolute certainty where matters of fact are concerned, but it will help us establish sound beliefs. Experience, for example, leads us to believe that the sun will rise each morning. No good comes, Hume believes, from subjecting that proposition to extreme doubt. But if we examine the basis of our firm beliefs about the sun, we find that they rest on a series of limited experiences, nothing more. We have no absolute reasons to believe our future experience is guaranteed to be the same. We should continue to hold our beliefs about the sun's behavior but be aware of the limited basis these convictions have in our actual experience.

Unlike antecedent skepticism, Hume's second type—consequent skepticism—is not a methodological tool. Rather, it is the result of particular philosophical inquiries. Moving on from the discovery that sense experience can be illusory and rational inference erroneous, the conclusion is drawn that genuine knowledge is an impossibility. This skepticism, admitted Hume, is more difficult to refute than the antecedent skepticism of Descartes. Nevertheless, Hume argued against it in two ways. First, if pushed to an extreme, such skepticism results in no good. Its effect is utterly debilitating. It would so undermine human confidence that all action would be curtailed. Second, our natural inclinations and beliefs are so strong that they simply will not be destroyed, even by a confrontation with consequent skepticism. This skepticism, in short, is unwarranted due to **practical** consideration. Our natural desire is to live and act, which makes practical concerns take precedence over the radical objections our reasoning abilities bring up about our sense experience or even reason itself.

On the other hand, our encounter with consequent skepticism has a healthy effect. It impresses on us that practical conviction is not the same as rational demonstration, and this leads to a sharper awareness of the precariousness of all existence. As with antecedent skepticism, then, Hume acknowledged that we can learn from consequent skepticism even if we cannot adopt it entirely. We need to be careful about the assumptions and beliefs we hold as we start an investigation. And as we draw conclusions, we also need to be aware of the limits of our senses and our reason. All things considered, Hume argued, a third type of **skepticism—mitigated** as he called it—is the best stance to take. It places an emphasis on the need to be ever alert about error.

One further point needs to be underscored about the skepticism Hume recommends. He thinks our claims about matters of fact are always fallible. Our knowledge of matters of fact is grounded in experience, and the possibility of error lurks there continually. Nevertheless, by staying within the realm of our empirical experiences, by seeking evidence there and by testing our judgments, we may be able to avoid serious mistakes. But if we go beyond our capabilities to support or refute judgments with empirical evidence, our thinking is sure to have a misleading effect. It will lead us to think that we both have a capacity to know, and actually do know, matters of fact that are really beyond us. The results of such thinking can only be confusion and error. Life already has enough uncertainty and difficulty without introducing claims for knowledge that are unwarranted because they lack a sound empirical grounding. But these considerations raise a new question: What conditions must hold before Hume thinks we are justified in claiming to have knowledge of matters of fact?

Impressions and Ideas

Hume's philosophy leaves us with the conclusion that we are forced to take some things as granted or given. Given that base, his theory of experience, which echoes but does not duplicate Locke's, contends that all the contents of our conscious experience can be broken down into two categories: **impressions** and **ideas.** Hume uses "impressions" to refer to "all our more lively perceptions, when we hear, or see, or feel, or love, or hate, or desire, or will" (p. 593). In Hume's vocabulary, they differ from ideas not so much in content but rather in the forcefulness and vivacity with which they strike us. According to Hume, no ideas are innate. All are ultimately derived from impressions; they are either images based on memory of impressions or thoughts about impressions, the latter often involving our faculty of imagination. This allows the production of ideas that may have no direct correlate in the sphere of impressions.

Hume further elaborated the relation between impressions and ideas by stating that both can be either *simple* or *complex*. A complex impression is composed of simple impressions. Moreover, every simple idea originates in a simple impression to which it corresponds directly. A complex idea, on the other hand, need not come directly from a complex impression to which it corresponds. Instead, complex ideas can be derived

from a variety of simple or complex impressions, or they can be made from other ideas. To illustrate Hume's perspective, we may feel love, and we may derive from this impression the idea that we should spend more time with the object of our affection. The feeling of love is simple, direct, and lively; the idea of a long-term relationship is more complex and may be less direct and lively. We can, of course, form a complex impression too by adding together all our feelings of love on a variety of occasions, and out of this form complex ideas about our future life. But above all else, Hume's thesis remains that all human experience and thought have their origin in sensory impressions. There are two further implications of importance to note about this crucial point in Hume's theory.

Echoing Berkeley, the first involves our understanding of the meaning of words and **propositions.** Although all our thinking originates with impressions, thought can carry us far away from the original starting points. In fact, Hume suggests, we can move so far that the terms we use and the assertions we make may lack clarity or significance. The test for clarity and significance is simply to see from what impressions the terms and propositions in question are derived. By showing the connections between (1) words and propositions and (2) impressions, or by discovering an essential lack or confusion of connection, we can indicate the presence or absence of clarity and significance in the terms and propositions we are examining.

Second, if sense impressions are the given factors in experience, the structure of our experience is such that we can never have full clarity and absolute certainty about their origin. Although we can think about these fundamental sense impressions, we never get the objective distance from them we would need to examine their ultimate grounding. Any claims to such a perspective or to explaining these origins definitively will be unwarranted speculations. With this argument, Hume carries empiricism to a conclusion more radical than either Locke or Berkeley reached. For example, Hume thinks it is simply beside the point and also misleading to argue whether there are two kinds of substance or only one. Knowledge of such matters is not ours to have. All we can actually know are the appearances presented to us in our perceptions. Such appearances are sometimes referred to as phenomena, and for that reason Hume's position has been called **phenomenalism.**

More can be said with respect to ideas. Not only can we obtain a valid theory concerning their origin, which Hume claimed he had produced, but it is also possible to describe how ideas get organized in our experience. For instance, analysis of experience indicates that we have two faculties, memory and imagination, that play a vital part in our mental processes. Memory allows us to retain impressions with exactness, although with less vividness than in the original instance. Imagination allows us to order and arrange ideas in various ways. According to Hume, however, the possibilities available on this score are regulated by three general principles of association. Our ideas tend naturally to follow or to be associated with one another when their contents (1) involve a resemblance, (2) are contiguous in time or space, or (3) are related in terms of cause and effect. Hume believed that all the complex ideas that originate in our minds involve at least one of these three principles. He did not, however, offer proof that his list of principles was exhaustive, nor did he claim to have an account of their origin. Like simple sense impressions, they are given factors in experience.

Causes and Effects

At no point was Hume's philosophy more devastating to claims about knowledge of an external world—or knowledge of anything, for that matter—than in his analysis of **causality.** This especially interested him because "all reasonings concerning matter of fact seem to be founded on the relation of *cause* and *effect*. By means of that relation alone we can go beyond the evidence of our memory and senses" (p. 599). In addition to being one of the natural ways in which ideas are initially associated in the mind, the relation of cause and effect emerges as a basic reasoning principle in our conscious efforts to explore and understand the world. It is by thinking of cause-and-effect relations that we seek and assert connections between our immediate experience and the past and future. Obviously, the cause-and-effect relationship is crucial, and therefore it behooves us to be as clear as possible about the nature of the relation and the grounds we possess for using it as we do.

What is involved when we employ the relation of cause and effect? Does our use of it have a demonstrable rational foundation? Hume suggests that when we think of cause-and-effect relations between two or more things, we usually mean that one is immediately or approximately contiguous with the other, and that the one we are designating as the cause is to some degree temporally prior to the other. These conditions alone, however, do not establish a cause-and-effect relationship. Since it is conceivable that X can be contiguous with and temporally prior to Y without being the cause of Y, something more is required. Hume thinks that we add the idea that there is a **necessary connection** between X and Y in the situation where X is said to be the cause of Y. Without the addition of the idea that every event or thing must have some cause that necessarily produces it, the ordinary understanding of cause-and-effect relations would not exist.

Hume's analysis places great importance on the idea of a necessary connection. When he probed the foundation on which it rests, two approaches seemed available: (1) one could argue that the use of the concept is valid on a priori grounds; or (2) one could argue that the use is sufficiently grounded by an appeal to our experience. Hume attacked the first option by arguing that it is neither intuitively certain nor demonstrable a priori that everything that begins to exist must have a cause. This proposition is a crucial factor in our idea of a necessary connection, and if we cannot show that every thing or event must have a cause, the concept of necessary connection is on shaky ground indeed. Hume made short work of the claim that the proposition in question is intuitively certain. It is not intuitively certain because it is possible to think of some thing's coming into existence without being caused and yet not fall into contradiction. Nothing in the idea of "coming into existence," claimed Hume, necessarily entails the idea of "being caused to exist."

A similar fate awaited the attempt to demonstrate a priori that everything that begins to exist must have a cause. For example, it was argued that a denial of this principle leads to absurdity. If something started to exist without a cause, it would (1) have to cause itself or (2) be caused by nothing. Both alternatives are impossible. The first is impossible because it entails the absurdity of a thing's having to exist prior to itself in order to cause itself. The second is impossible because it is clear that nothing cannot be the cause of anything. Since the results of denying the principle are absurd, the principle itself must be affirmed, in which case the idea of necessary connection gained support.

These rationalistic arguments, Hume retorted, are not as neat as they look. In fact, they have a common, fatal flaw: they assume the validity of the very principle in question. It is absurd to say that something can come into being without having a cause outside itself only if one is already committed to the principle that everything that comes into being must have such a cause. Hume thought this shortcoming proved that our use of the concept of necessary connection cannot be adequately grounded a priori by appeals to intuition or rational demonstration.

What about the possibility of grounding our use of the concept of necessary connection by an appeal to experience? First, Hume reminds us, the experience of any particular object or event does not force us to think in terms of a cause of the object or event. In itself, no experience of an object or event necessarily implies the existence of any other object or event. If we look at sensory experiences, however, we can begin to see how the idea of a necessary connection emerges. In experience we frequently find that in addition to being contiguous and in temporal succession, things are *constantly conjoined*. For instance, on countless occasions we have seen one object (e.g., a billiard ball) hit a second with the result that the second moves. Now, Hume suggested, when we find two objects related in this way over a period of time, we attribute a causal power to the first, and we conclude that there is a necessary connection between the two.

Is such an attribution rationally grounded? Does it give us knowledge of the world in the ways we commonly suppose? Hume thinks not. Although we may directly experience the constant conjunction of things, Hume denies that there are any impressions that clearly correspond to the idea of causal power, which is crucial to the idea of necessary connection. Constant conjunction differs from necessary connection. Moreover, no matter how frequently the constant conjunction of things may have been observed, it does not follow that the relationship will continue to hold. To think this will be so is to smuggle in a principle asserting the *uniformity of nature*. But such a principle cannot be demonstrated as eternally binding, since change is always conceivable. In addition, it cannot even be argued that the continuation of the uniformity of nature is a strong probability, because arguments concerning probability already assume some version of the principle of the uniformity of nature. And unless we assume some uniformity in nature, it makes no sense to say that anything is probable. Hume is certain that we do believe that nature is uniform, and that idea figures into our use of the concept of necessary connection, but this does not mean that either factor in our experience is based on reasoning immune to skepticism.

Challenging Locke in particular, Hume also dismissed the possibility that the idea of necessary connection could be directly grounded in internal feelings or states (for example, willing to move my arm and then seeing or feeling it move). We have a feeling of **volition.** Here, too, all that we really observe or feel, according to Hume's empiricism, is a constant conjunction of events. The repetition of the conjunction, no matter how extensive, is not the same thing as necessary connection. Hume's conclusion, then, is that the presence of the concept of necessary connection in human experience indicates a basic but ultimately puzzling fact about the human mind. From the constant conjunction of things in our experience, the idea of necessary connection emerges as a powerful habit of thought. Why it exists is not fully clear. What is clear is that the idea is not completely rational, and thus knowledge claims based on it are beliefs that lack the firm justification we commonly attribute to them.

Hume's World of Uncertainty

Hume leaves us in a world of epistemological uncertainty. Although he acknowledged that practical belief and habit will win out, he argued that we cannot know whether there is a real world that directly corresponds to our experiences in any way. His analysis of causality suggests that the world we find ourselves inhabiting is largely a construction of our own minds, an outcome that goes well beyond the conclusions of Locke and Berkeley.

Where matters of fact are concerned, Hume urges us to replace the concepts of certainty and rational demonstration with those of fallibility and practical belief. We will continue to think in terms of causality and necessary connection, but Hume's investigations turn up nothing to suggest that these ideas have more than a subjective origin. Not only do things or events fail to entail specific causes, but it is even possible to conceive of things or events as coming to be without having been caused at all. Locke and Berkeley would never have thought of such a thing, but virtually anything can happen in Hume's world—except knowledge of an external world. And yet the story does not end there, for if Locke and Berkeley prepared the way for Hume, he did the same for Kant, who would take even more seriously than Hume the suggestion that a relationship such as cause and effect is something the mind contributes to experience. In that regard, Kant said that Hume awakened him from "dogmatic slumbers." If you want to save knowing more than Hume did, but recognize that you will have to go beyond him to do so, see if you can find a path to take by reflecting on the following passage from Hume's mid-eighteenth-century work, *An Enquiry Concerning Human Understanding.*

OF THE IDEA OF NECESSARY CONNECTION

Part I The great advantage of the mathematical sciences above the moral consists in this, that the ideas of the former, being sensible, are always clear and determinate, the smallest distinction between them is immediately perceptible, and the same terms are still expressive of the same ideas, without ambiguity or variation. An oval is never mistaken for a circle, nor a hyperbola for an ellipse. The isosceles and scalenum are distinguished by boundaries more exact than vice and virtue, right and wrong. If any term be defined in geometry, the mind readily, of itself, substitutes, on all occasions, the definition for the term defined: or even when no definition is employed, the object itself may be presented to the senses, and by that means be steadily and clearly apprehended. But the finer sentiments of the mind, the operations of the understanding, the various agitations of the passions, though really in themselves distinct, easily escape us, when surveyed by reflection; nor is it in our power to recall the original object, as often as we have occasion to contemplate it. Ambiguity, by this means, is gradually introduced into our reasonings: similar objects are readily taken to be the same: and the conclusion becomes at last very wide of the premises.

One may safely, however, affirm, that, if we consider these sciences in a proper light, their advantages and disadvantages nearly compensate each other, and reduce both of them to a state of equality. If the mind, with greater facility, retains the ideas of geometry clear and determinate, it must carry on a much longer and more intricate chain of reasoning, and compare ideas much wider of each other, in order to reach the abstruser truths of that science. And if moral ideas are apt, without extreme care, to fall into obscurity and confusion, the inferences are always much shorter in these disquisitions, and the intermediate steps, which lead to the conclusion, much fewer than in the sciences which treat of quantity and number. In reality, there is scarcely a proposition in Euclid so simple, as not to consist of more parts, than are to be found in any moral reasoning which runs not into chimera and conceit. Where we trace the principles of the human mind through a few steps, we may be very well satisfied with our progress; considering how soon nature throws a bar to all our inquiries concerning causes, and reduces us to an acknowledgment of our ignorance. The chief obstacle, therefore, to our improvement in the moral or metaphysical sciences is the obscurity of the ideas, and ambiguity of the terms. The principal difficulty in the

mathematics is the length of inferences and compass of thought, requisite to the forming of any conclusion. And, perhaps, our progress in natural philosophy is chiefly retarded by the want of proper experiments and phenomena, which are often discovered by chance, and cannot always be found, when requisite, even by the most diligent and prudent inquiry. As moral philosophy seems hitherto to have received less improvement than either geometry or physics, we may conclude, that, if there be any difference in this respect among these sciences, the difficulties, which obstruct the progress of the former, require superior care and capacity to be surmounted.

There are no ideas, which occur in metaphysics more obscure and uncertain, than those of *power, force, energy,* or *necessary connection,* of which it is every moment necessary for us to treat in all our disquisitions. We shall, therefore, endeavor, in this section, to fix, if possible, the precise meaning of these terms, and thereby remove some part of that obscurity, which is so much complained of in this species of philosophy.

It seems a proposition, which will not admit of much dispute, that all our ideas are nothing but copies of our impressions, or, in other words, that it is impossible for us to *think* of anything, which we have not antecedently *felt,* either by our external or internal senses. I have endeavored [in an earlier section of the *Enquiry*] to explain and prove this proposition, and have expressed my hopes, that, by a proper application of it, men may reach a greater clearness and precision in philosophical reasonings, than what they have hitherto been able to attain. Complex ideas may, perhaps, be well known by definition, which is nothing but an enumeration of those parts or simple ideas, that compose them. But when we have pushed up definitions to the most simple ideas, and find still some ambiguity and obscurity; what resource are we then possessed of? By what invention can we throw light upon these ideas, and render them altogether precise and determinate to our intellectual view! Produce the impressions or original sentiments, from which the ideas are copied. These impressions are all strong and sensible. They admit not of ambiguity. They are not only placed in a full light themselves, but may throw light on their correspondent ideas, which lie in obscurity. And by this means, we may, perhaps, attain a new microscope or species of optics, by which, in the moral sciences, the most minute, and most simple ideas may be so enlarged as to fall readily under our apprehension, and be equally known with the grossest and most sensible ideas, that can be the object of our inquiry.

To be fully acquainted, therefore, with the idea of power or necessary connection, let us examine its impression; and in order to find the impression with greater certainty, let us search for it in all the sources, from which it may possibly be derived.

When we look about us towards external objects, and consider the operation of causes, we are never able, in a single instance, to discover any power or necessary connection; any quality, which binds the effect to the cause, and renders the one an infallible consequence of the other. We only find, that the one does actually, in fact, follow the other. The impulse of one billiard ball is attended with motion in the second. This is the whole that appears to the *outward* senses. The mind feels no sentiment or *inward* impression from this succession of objects: consequently there is not, in any single, particular instance of cause and effect, anything which can suggest the idea of power or necessary connection.

From the first appearance of an object, we never can conjecture what effect will result from it. But were the power or energy of any cause discoverable by the mind, we could foresee the effect, even without experience; and might, at first, pronounce with certainty concerning it, by mere dint of thought and reasoning.

In reality, there is no part of matter, that does ever, by its sensible qualities, discover any power or energy, or give us ground to imagine, that it could produce anything, or be followed by any other object, which we could denominate its effect. Solidity, extension, motion; these qualities are all complete in themselves, and never point out any other event which may result from them. The scenes of the universe are continually shifting, and one object follows another in an uninterrupted succession; but the power of force, which actuates the whole machine, is entirely concealed from us, and never discovers itself in any of the sensible qualities of body. We know, that, in fact, heat is a constant attendant of flame; but what is the connection between them, we have no room so much as to conjecture or imagine. It is impossible, therefore, that the idea of power can be derived from the contemplation of bodies, in single instances of their operation; because no bodies ever discover any power, which can be the original of this idea.*

Since, therefore, external objects as they appear to the senses, give us no idea of power or necessary connection, by their operation in particular instances, let us see, whether this idea be derived from reflection on the operations of our own minds, and be copied from any internal impression. It may be said that we are every moment conscious of internal power; while we feel, that, by the simple command of our will, we can move the organs of our body, or direct the faculties of our mind. An act of volition produces motion in our limbs, or raises a new idea in our imagination. This influence of the will we know by consciousness. Hence we acquire the idea of power or energy, and are certain, that we ourselves and all other intelligent beings are possessed of power. This idea, then, is an idea of reflection, since it arises from reflecting on the operations of our own mind, and on the command which is exercised by will, both over the organs of the body and faculties of the soul.

*Mr. Locke, in his chapter on power, says, that, finding from experience, that there are several new productions in matter, and concluding that there must somewhere be a power capable of producing them, we arrive at last by this reasoning at the idea of power. But no reasoning can ever give us a new original, simple idea; as this philosopher himself confesses. This, therefore, can never be the origin of that idea.

We shall proceed to examine this pretension; and first with regard to the influence of volition over the organs of the body. This influence, we may observe, is a fact, which, like all other natural events, can be known only by experience, and can never be foreseen from any apparent energy or power in the cause, which connects it with the effect, and renders the one an infallible consequence of the other. The motion of our body follows upon the command of our will. Of this we are every moment conscious. But the means, by which this is effected; the energy, by which the will performs so extraordinary an operation; of this we are so far from being immediately conscious, that it must for ever escape our most diligent inquiry.

For *first*, Is there any principle in all nature more mysterious than the union of soul with body; by which a supposed spiritual substance acquires such an influence over a material one, that the most refined thought is able to actuate the grossest matter? Were we empowered, by a secret wish, to remove mountains, or control the planets in their orbit; this extensive authority would not be more extraordinary, nor more beyond our comprehension. But if by consciousness we perceived any power or energy in the will, we must know this power; we must know its connection with the effect; we must know the secret union of soul and body, and the nature of both these substances; by which the one is able to operate, in so many instances, upon the other.

Secondly, We are not able to move all the organs of the body with a like authority; though we cannot assign any reason besides experience, for so remarkable a difference between one and the other. Why has the will an influence over the tongue and fingers, not over the heart and liver? This question would never embarrass us, were we conscious of a power in the former case, not in the latter. We should then perceive, independent of experience, why the authority of will over the organs of the body is circumscribed within such particular limits. Being in that case fully acquainted with the power

or force, by which it operates, we should also know, why its influence reaches precisely to such boundaries, and no farther.

A man, suddenly struck with palsy in the leg or arm, or who had newly lost those members, frequently endeavors, at first to move them, and employ them in their usual offices. Here he is as much conscious of power to command such limbs, as a man in perfect health is conscious of power to actuate any member which remains in its natural state and condition. But consciousness never deceives. Consequently, neither in the one case nor in the other, are we ever conscious of any power. We learn the influence of our will from experience alone. And experience only teaches us, how one event constantly follows another; without instructing us in the secret connection, which binds them together, and renders them inseparable.

Thirdly, We learn from anatomy that the immediate object of power in voluntary motion, is not the member itself which is moved, but certain muscles, and nerves, and animal spirits, and, perhaps, something still more minute and more unknown, through which the motion is successfully propagated, ere it reach the member itself whose motion is the immediate object of volition. Can there be a more certain proof that the power, by which this whole operation is performed, so far from being directly and fully known by an inward sentiment or consciousness, is, to the last degree, mysterious and unintelligible? Here the mind wills a certain event: immediately another event, unknown to ourselves, and totally different from the one intended, is produced: this event produces another, equally unknown: till at last, through a long succession, the desired event is produced. But if the original power were felt, it must be known: were it known, its effect also must be known; since all power is relative to its effect. And vice versa, if the effect be not known, the power cannot be known nor felt. How indeed can we be conscious of a power to move our limbs, when we have no such power; but only that to move certain animal spirits, which, though they produce at last the motion of our limbs, yet operate in such a manner as is wholly beyond our comprehension?

We may . . . conclude . . . that our idea of power is not copied from any sentiment or consciousness of power within ourselves, when we give rise to animal motion, or apply our limbs, to their proper use and office. That their motion follows the command of the will is a matter of common experience, like other natural events: but the power or energy by which this is effected, like that in other natural events, is unknown and inconceivable.[†]

Shall we then assert, that we are conscious of a power or energy in our own minds, when, by an act or command of our will, we raise up a new idea, fix the mind to the contemplation of it, turn it on all sides, and at last dismiss it for some other idea, when we think that we have surveyed it with sufficient accuracy? I believe the same arguments will prove, that even this command of the will gives us no real idea of force or energy.

First, It must be allowed, that, when we know a power, we know that very circumstance in the cause, by which it is enabled to produce the effect: for these are supposed to be synonymous. We must, therefore, know

---

[†]It may be pretended that the resistance which we meet with in bodies, obliging us frequently to exert our force, and call up all our power, this gives us the idea of force and power. It is this *nisus,* or strong endeavor, of which we are conscious, that is the original impression from which this idea is copied. But, *first,* We attribute power to a vast number of objects, where we never can suppose this resistance or exertion of force to take place; to the Supreme Being, who never meets with any resistance; to the mind in its command over its ideas and limbs, in common thinking and motion, where the effect follows immediately upon the will, without any exertion or summoning up of force; to inanimate matter, which is not capable of this sentiment. *Secondly,* This sentiment of an endeavor to overcome resistance has no known connection with any event: what follows it, we know by experience; but could not know it *a priori.* It must, however, be confessed, that the animal *nisus,* which we experience, though it can afford no accurate precise idea of power, enters very much into that vulgar, inaccurate idea, which is formed of it.

both the cause and effect, and the relation between them. But do we pretend to be acquainted with the nature of the human soul and the nature of an idea, or the aptitude of the one to produce the other? This is a real creation; a production of something out of nothing: which implies a power so great that it may seem, at first sight, beyond the reach of any being, less than infinite. At least it must be owned, that such a power is not felt, nor known, nor even conceivable by the mind. We only feel the event, namely, the existence of an idea, consequent to a command of the will: but the manner, in which this operation is performed, the power by which it is produced, is entirely beyond our comprehension.

Secondly, The command of the mind over itself is limited, as well as its command over the body; and these limits are not known by reason, or any acquaintance with the nature of cause and effect, but only by experience and observation, as in all other natural events and in the operation of external objects. Our authority over our sentiments and passions is much weaker than that over our ideas; and even the latter authority is circumscribed within very narrow boundaries. Will anyone pretend to assign the ultimate reason of these boundaries, or show why the power is deficient in one case, not in another?

Thirdly, This self-command is very different at different times. A man in health possesses more of it than one languishing with sickness. We are more master of our thoughts in the morning than in the evening; fasting, than after a full meal. Can we give any reason for these variations, except experience? Where then is the power, of which we pretend to be conscious? Is there not here, either in a spiritual or material substance, or both, some secret mechanism or structure of parts, upon which the effect depends, and which, being entirely unknown to us, renders the power or energy of the will equally unknown and incomprehensible?

Volition is surely an act of the mind, with which we are sufficiently acquainted. Reflect upon it. Consider it on all sides. Do you find anything in it like this creative power, by which it raises from nothing a new idea, and with a kind of fiat, imitates the omnipotence of its Maker, if I may be allowed so to speak, who called forth into existence all the various scenes of nature? So far from being conscious of this energy in the will, it requires as certain experience as that of which we are possessed, to convince us that such extraordinary effects do ever result from a simple act of volition.

The generality of mankind never find any difficulty in accounting for the more common and familiar operations of nature—such as the descent of heavy bodies, the growth of plants, the generation of animals, or the nourishment of bodies by food; but suppose that, in all these cases, they perceive the very force or energy of the cause, by which it is connected with its effect, and is forever infallible in its operation. They acquire, by long habit, such a turn of mind, that, upon the appearance of the cause, they immediately expect with assurance its usual attendant, and hardly conceive it possible that any other event could result from it. It is only on the discovery of extraordinary phenomena, such as earthquakes, pestilence, and prodigies of any kind, that they find themselves at a loss to assign a proper cause, and to explain the manner in which the effect is produced by it. It is usual for men, in such difficulties, to have recourse to some invisible intelligent principle as the immediate cause of that event which surprises them, and which, they think, cannot be accounted for from the common powers of nature. But philosophers, who carry their scrutiny a little farther, immediately perceive that, even in the most familiar events, the energy of the cause is as unintelligible as in the most unusual, and that we only learn by experience the frequent *conjunction* of objects, without being ever able to comprehend anything like *connection* between them. Here, then, many philosophers think themselves obliged by reason to have recourse, on all occasions, to the same principle, which the vulgar never appeal to but in cases that appear miraculous and supernatural. They acknowledge mind and intelligence to be,

not only the ultimate and original cause of all things, but the immediate and sole cause of every event which appears in nature. They pretend that those objects which are commonly denominated *causes*, are in reality nothing but *occasions;* and that the true and direct principle of every effect is not any power or force in nature, but a volition of the Supreme Being, who wills that such particular objects should forever be conjoined with each other. Instead of saying that one billiard ball moves another by a force which it has derived from the author of nature, it is the Deity himself, they say, who, by a particular volition, moves the second ball, being determined to this operation by the impulse of the first ball, in consequence of those general laws which he has laid down to himself in the government of the universe. But philosophers advancing still in their inquiries discover that, as we are totally ignorant of the power on which depends the mutual operation of bodies, we are no less ignorant of that power on which depends the operation of mind on body, or of body on mind; nor are we able, either from our senses or consciousness, to assign the ultimate principle in one case more than in the other. The same ignorance, therefore, reduces them to the same conclusion. They assert that the Deity is the immediate cause of the union between soul and body; and that they are not the organs of sense, which, being agitated by external objects, produce sensations in the mind; but that it is a particular volition of our omnipotent Maker, which excites such a sensation, in consequence of such a motion in the organ. In like manner, it is not any energy in the will that produces local motion in our members; it is God himself, who is pleased to second our will, in itself impotent, and to command that motion which we erroneously attribute to our own power and efficacy. Nor do philosophers stop at this conclusion. They sometimes extend the same inference to the mind itself, in its internal operations. Our mental vision or conception of ideas is nothing but a revelation made to us by our Maker. When we voluntarily turn our thoughts to any object, and raise up its image in the fancy, it is not the will which creates that idea; it is the universal Creator, who discovers it to the mind, and renders it present to us.

Thus, according to these philosophers, everything is full of God. Not content with the principle, that nothing exists but by his will, that nothing possesses any power but by his concession; they rob nature, and all created beings, of every power, in order to render their dependence on the Deity still more sensible and immediate. They consider not that, by this theory, they diminish, instead of magnifying, the grandeur of those attributes, which they affect so much to celebrate. It argues surely more power in the Deity to delegate a certain degree of power to inferior creatures, than to produce everything by his own immediate volition. It argues more wisdom to contrive at first the fabric of the world with such perfect foresight that, of itself, and by its proper operation, it may serve all the purposes of providence, than if the great Creator were obliged every moment to adjust its parts, and animate by his breath all the wheels of that stupendous machine.

But if we would have a more philosophical confutation of this theory, perhaps the two following reflections may suffice.

First, It seems to me that this theory of the universal energy and operation of the Supreme Being is too bold ever to carry conviction with it to a man, sufficiently apprised of the weakness of human reason, and the narrow limits to which it is confined in all its operations. Though the chain of arguments which conduct to it were ever so logical, there must arise a strong suspicion, if not an absolute assurance, that it has carried us quite beyond the reach of our faculties, when it leads to conclusions so extraordinary, and so remote from common life and experience. We are got into fairy land, long ere we have reached the last steps of our theory; and *there* we have no reason to trust our common methods of argument, or to think that our usual analogies and probabilities have any authority. Our line is too short to fathom such immense abysses. And

however we may flatter ourselves that we are guided, in every step which we take, by a kind of verisimilitude and experience, we may be assured that this fancied experience has no authority when we thus apply it to subjects that lie entirely out of the sphere of experience. But on this we shall have occasion to touch afterwards.

Secondly, I cannot perceive any force in the arguments on which this theory is founded. We are ignorant, it is true, of the manner in which bodies operate on each other: their force or energy is entirely incomprehensible: but are we not equally ignorant of the manner or force by which a mind, even the supreme mind, operates either on itself or on body? Whence, I beseech you, do we acquire any idea of it? We have no sentiment or consciousness of this power in ourselves. We have no idea of the Supreme Being but what we learn from reflection on our own faculties. Were our ignorance, therefore, a good reason for rejecting anything, we should be led into that principle of denying all energy in the Supreme Being as much as in the grossest matter. We surely comprehend as little the operations of one as of the other. Is it more difficult to conceive that motion may arise from impulse than that it may arise from volition? All we know is our profound ignorance in both cases.

Part II But to hasten to a conclusion of this argument, which is already drawn out to too great a length: we have sought in vain for an idea of power or necessary connection in all the sources from which we could suppose it to be derived. It appears that, in single instances of the operation of bodies, we never can, by our utmost scrutiny, discover anything but one event following another, without being able to comprehend any force or power by which the cause operates, or any connection between it and its supposed effect. The same difficulty occurs in contemplating the operations of mind on body— where we observe the motion of the latter to follow upon the volition of the former, but are not able to observe or conceive the tie which binds together the motion and volition, or the energy by which the mind produces this effect. The authority of the will over its own faculties and ideas is not a whit more comprehensible: so that, upon the whole, there appears not, throughout all nature; any one instance of connection which is conceivable by us. All events seem entirely loose and separate. One event follows another; but we never can observe any tie between them. They seem *conjoined*, but never *connected*. And as we can have no idea of anything which never appeared to our outward sense or inward sentiment, the necessary conclusion *seems* to be that we have no idea of connection or power at all, and that these words are absolutely without any meaning, when employed either in philosophical reasonings or common life.

But there still remains one method of avoiding this conclusion, and one source which we have not yet examined. When any natural object or event is presented, it is impossible for us, by any sagacity or penetration, to discover, or even conjecture, without experience, what event will result from it, or to carry our foresight beyond that object which is immediately present to the memory and senses. Even after one instance or experiment where we have observed a particular event to follow upon another, we are not entitled to form a general rule, or foretell what will happen in like cases; it being justly esteemed an unpardonable temerity to judge of the whole course of nature from one single experiment, however accurate or certain. But when one particular species of event has always, in all instances, been conjoined with another, we make no longer any scruple of foretelling one upon the appearance of the other, and of employing that reasoning which can alone assure us of any matter of fact or existence. We then call the one object, *cause*; the other, *effect*. We suppose that there is some connection between them; some power in the one, by which it infallibly produces the other, and operates with the greatest certainty and strongest necessity.

It appears, then, that this idea of a necessary connection among events arises from a number of similar instances which occur of the constant conjunction of these events; nor can that idea ever be suggested by any one of these instances, surveyed in all possible lights and positions. But there is nothing in a number of instances, different from every single instance, which is supposed to be exactly similar; except only, that after a repetition of similar instances, the mind is carried by habit, upon the appearance of one event, to expect its usual attendant, and to believe that it will exist. This connection, therefore, which we *feel* in the mind, this customary transition of the imagination from one object to its usual attendant, is the sentiment or impression from which we form the idea of power or necessary connection. Nothing farther is in the case. Contemplate the subject on all sides; you will never find any other origin of that idea. This is the sole difference between one instance, from which we can never receive the idea of connection, and a number of similar instances, by which it is suggested. The first time a man saw the communication of motion by impulse, as by the shock of two billiard balls, he could not pronounce that the one event was *connected;* but only that it was *conjoined* with the other. After he has observed several instances of this nature, he then pronounces them to be *connected*. What alteration has happened to give rise to this new idea of *connection*? Nothing but that he now *feels* these events to be *connected* in his imagination, and can readily foretell the existence of one from the appearance of the other. When we say, therefore, that one object is connected with another, we mean only that they have acquired a connection in our thought, and give rise to this inference, by which they become proofs of each other's existence: a conclusion which is somewhat extraordinary, but which seems founded on sufficient evidence. Nor will its evidence be weakened by any general diffidence of the understanding, or skeptical suspicion concerning every conclusion which is new and extraordinary. No conclusions can be more agreeable to skepticism than such as make discoveries concerning the weakness and narrow limits of human reason and capacity.

And what stronger instance can be produced of the surprising ignorance and weakness of the understanding than the present? For surely, if there be any relation among objects which it imports to us to know perfectly, it is that of cause and effect. On this are founded all our reasonings concerning matter of fact or existence. By means of it alone we attain any assurance concerning objects which are removed from the present testimony of our memory and senses. The only immediate utility of all sciences, is to teach us, how to control and regulate future events by their causes. Our thoughts and inquiries are, therefore, every moment, employed about this relation: yet so imperfect are the ideas which we form concerning it, that it is impossible to give any just definition of cause, except what is drawn from something extraneous and foreign to it. Similar objects are always conjoined with similar. Of this we have experience. Suitably to this experience, therefore, we may define a cause to be *an object, followed by another, and where all the objects similar to the first are followed by objects similar to the second.* Or in other words *where, if the first object had not been, the second never had existed.* The appearance of a cause always conveys the mind, by a customary transition, to the idea of the effect. Of this also we have experience. We may, therefore, suitably to this experience, form another definition of cause, and call it, *an object followed by another, and whose appearance always conveys the thought to that other.* But though both these definitions be drawn from circumstances foreign to the cause, we cannot remedy this inconvenience, or attain any more perfect definition, which may point out that circumstances in the cause, which gives it a connection with its effect. We have no idea of this connection, nor even any distinct notion what it is we desire to know, when we endeavor at a conception of it. We say, for instance, that the vibration of this string is the cause of this particular sound. But what do we mean by that affirmation? We either mean *that this vibration is followed by this sound, and that all similar vibrations have been followed by similar sounds: Or, that this vibration is followed by this sound, and that upon the appearance of one the mind anticipates the senses, and forms immediately an idea of the other.* We may consider the relation of cause and effect in either of these two lights; but beyond these, we have no idea of it.

To recapitulate, therefore, the reasonings of this section: every idea is copied from some preceding impression or sentiment; and where we cannot find any impression, we may be certain that there is no idea. In all single instances of the operation of bodies or minds, there is nothing that produces any impression, nor consequently can suggest any idea of power or necessary connection. But when many uniform instances appear, and the same object is always followed by the same event, we then begin to entertain the notion of cause and connection. We then feel a new sentiment or impression, to wit, a customary connection in the thought or imagination between one object and its usual attendant; and this sentiment is the original of that idea which we seek for. For as this idea arises from a number of similar instances, and not from any single instance, it must arise from that circumstance, in which the number of instances differ from every individual instance. But this customary connection or transition of the imagination is the only circumstance in which they differ. In every other particular they are alike. The first instance which we saw of motion communicated by the shock of two billiard balls (to return to this obvious illustration) is exactly similar to any instance that may, at present, occur to us; except only, that we could not, at first, *infer* one event from the other; which we are enabled to do at present, after so long a course of uniform experience. I know not whether the reader will readily apprehend this reasoning. I am afraid that, should I multiply words about it, or throw it into a greater variety of lights, it would only become more obscure and intricate. In all abstract reasonings there is one point of view which, if we can happily hit, we shall go farther towards illustrating the subject than by all the eloquence in the world. This point of view we should endeavor to reach, and reserve the flowers of rhetoric for subjects which are more adapted to them. (Pp. 620–33.)

Immanuel Kant and His Copernican Revolution

The writings of Immanuel Kant (1724–1804) have had worldwide influence. Yet of all the philosophers discussed in this book, his biography is probably the least exciting. Kant is sometimes called the "provincial philosopher" because he seldom left his Prussian hometown, Königsberg, which is now in East

IMMANUEL KANT 1724–1804

Germany. The residents, it is said, could set their watches by Kant's appearance on the streets, so regular was his habitual walk every day after lunch. Not much involved in public affairs, he came from a simple religious background. Although his philosophy became extremely sophisticated, there is a sense in which he never left his spiritual roots. Kant went to the University of Königsberg and then he spent most of his life there teaching and writing. His main works are *Critique of Pure Reason* (first edition, 1781; second edition, 1787), *Prolegomena to Any Future Metaphysics* (1783), *Foundations of the Metaphysics of Morals* (1785), *Critique of Practical Reason* (1788), *Critique of Judgment* (1790), and *Religion within the Limits of Reason Alone* (1793).

The impressive rise of modern science played an important part in Kant's philosophy. To understand why this is so, recall Kant's statement that Hume woke him from a dogmatic slumber. Hume's theory about impressions and ideas led Hume to conclude that we lacked any certain knowledge about causes and effects. In fact, certainty of any kind was hardly available. Kant recognized, however, a body of knowledge in physics and mathematics it was important to account for. Not only did this knowledge involve cause and effect, it also seemed to offer certainty. But, if Hume was correct, how could these things be? Given the existence of what Kant took to be an undeniable body of scientific learning, he felt that philosophers must meet Hume's challenge and show how it is possible to have genuine scientific knowledge.

On one crucial point Kant agreed with Hume. Our unexamined experience is uncertain and offers an inadequate basis for science. Thus, the certainties that science has uncovered must find their basis outside our vacillating, uncriticized experience. That line of thought made Kant realize that what we bring to experience could be of decisive importance.

What We Bring to Experience

Agreeing with the empiricists, Kant said that all human knowledge begins with experience. But he added an important qualification: "It does not follow that it all arises out of experience."[4] Kant thought space and time provided two key examples. No object is imaginable without spatiality being implied. Moreover, all our perceptions, whether of objects external to us or of our own feelings and thoughts, follow each other temporally. Space and time, concluded Kant, are not things that are merely discovered empirically. They are the very forms into which all perceptual experiences are cast. They do not determine the precise content of perceptual experience. This content depends largely on the things we encounter. Contrary to Berkeley, this analysis led Kant to distinguish between a **"noumenal"** and a **"phenomenal"** reality. The latter is reality as it appears to us, while the former is reality as it exists apart from the order we introduce.

The order we introduce in experience is not restricted to **forms of intuition,** as Kant sometimes called space and time. Knowledge has roots in perceptual experiences, but it also entails the application of human understanding or reason to the sensory content. As Kant liked to put the point, "Without sensibility no object would be given to us, without understanding no object would be thought. Thoughts without content are empty, intuitions without concepts are blind" (p. 93). Knowledge entails the organization of sense experience so that judgments can be made. Kant argued that this organization means bringing sensory content into relation with an active intellectual power. By examining the characteristic logical forms that are present in the judgments we make, Kant concluded that the reality of these logical forms requires the existence of twelve basic *categories of the understanding.* Through these **categories,** sensory content is organized, and judgments are made possible.

One of these categories involves causes and effects, which Kant linked with judgments that have the logical form "If . . . then. . . . " The significance of these **hypothetical** judgments depends on the reality of causal relationships between things. Moreover, many of the basic concepts of our language (for example, to make, to create, to produce, and the like) imply the relationship of cause and effect. Thus, Kant argued that the relationship is also fundamental in our organization of experience and in our knowledge. It is not a relationship that is merely discovered through experiences, but it stands as a foundational organizing principle that makes our experience and knowledge possible.

The order we contribute to experience, according to Kant, provides the stability and certainty of scientific knowledge. We can experience things only in particular formal ways, and science is possible because of that fact. Kant called this finding his **"Copernican revolution."** Instead of taking the position that human experience and knowledge must conform to the objects we encounter, Kant revolutionized the theory of knowledge by arguing that we ought to regard objects in experience as conforming to our capacities for perception and judgment.

The basis for our real knowledge, then, does not come from experience exclusively but is in part necessarily prescribed to experience by us. Having failed to make this discovery, Hume's philosophy could hardly avoid a skeptical outcome, for it analyzed only our ideas in experience and not what is presupposed for their very existence. But Hume's failure was only partial in Kant's eyes, for in his awakened state Kant saw that he had not been able to save scientific knowledge cheaply. In short, if human knowledge always involves a constructive contribution from the mind, then the world that appears in our experience cannot automatically be equated with the world in itself. That world may be structured, but we cannot know it as such. Human understanding dictates to our experience and so informs it, but our rational capacities are not sufficiently powerful to give us demonstrable conclusions about things in themselves.

The Future of Metaphysics

The fullest exposition of Kant's "Copernican revolution" occurred in his *Critique of Pure Reason*. A worthwhile summary, however, exists in the *Prolegomena to Any Future Metaphysics*. Kant took "metaphysics" to be a dogmatic branch of philosophy that made pronouncements about all of existence and God. Hume, believed Kant, was right: such rigidity in theory is misleading, even impossible. Thus, before any new interpretation of reality could be written, Kant argued, philosophers must reconsider the foundations for metaphysics. Kant's revision turned out to be so thorough that he ended this brief work by deciding that metaphysics, insofar as it discusses God and "noumena," is not possible even though reason is constantly tempted to think it can answer all the questions it asks. But in the process of putting metaphysics "on hold," Kant did claim to discover the basis for the certainty he sought. Since it was the ground for our experience only, this foundation, however, did not enable us to know things in themselves as Kant thought metaphysics wanted to do.

Kant distrusted ungrounded speculation. He also feared skepticism, for he felt it was out of tune with what the science of his day had accomplished. His strategy in finding a middle way between the extremes of skepticism and dogmatism involved a technical vocabulary. His fundamental position, however, is less complicated than it looks. Essen-

tially Kant believed that the human mind orders experience by means of forms and categories that exist prior to experience. These are not the innate ideas Locke attacked, but they do exist as conditions that must be present to account for the experience we actually have. The world-as-experienced and the world-independent-of-experience may or may not be the same, however—we just cannot know for sure. Kant's gain is that we can have certainty within experience. The cost is that we must recognize that our knowledge is severely limited. By seeing that the world-as-experienced revolves around us, we uncover a certainty Hume overlooked. But we do so at the price of ignorance about things in themselves. Metaphysics has a limited future at best.

Synthetic A Priori Judgments

The basic issue between Hume and Kant can be outlined in another way as well. Kant believed that there are **synthetic a priori** judgments and tried to show how they are possible, while Hume thought that there are no judgments of this kind. Hume argued that all our meaningful judgments are concerned either with relations of ideas or with matters of fact. Judgments concerned with the former are true a priori—they hold universally and necessarily—and their truth does not depend on empirical testing. However, these judgments are true a priori only because the **predicate** is already contained at least implicitly in the subject of the judgment (as, for example, in the claim that all triangles have three angles). To use Kant's term, such judgments are **analytic.** According to Hume, these judgments do not, strictly speaking, give us new information, and they tell us nothing about matters of fact. They are, however, necessarily true because of the meaning of their terms. On the other hand, meaningful judgments about matters of fact (such as,

"Many roses are red") are understood by Hume to be neither necessary and universal nor true by virtue of the meaning of their terms. To use Kant's term, such judgments are **synthetic a posteriori.** Here the subject does not contain the predicate, and the truth status of the judgment depends on empirical testing.

Hume would say that all judgments are either analytic a priori or synthetic a posteriori, but Kant argued that some judgments fall into neither of these groups. Some judgments are *synthetic a priori,* and these are of special interest to science and philosophy because they convey new information—the judgment's predicate is not already contained in its subject. Yet their truth is necessary, universal, and not dependent on empirical testing. Although the existence of these judgments in metaphysics is uncertain, Kant claimed we find numerous instances of them in the mathematical and physical sciences. For Kant, then, the question was not whether we have any certain knowledge, but rather, since we do have it, "How is it possible for human reason to produce such knowledge entirely a priori?"[5] The answer to that question, Kant believed, lay in the structuring power that the mind brings to experience.

How Is Knowledge Possible?

According to Kant, we know some important things that do not depend on experience. But how can this be, since it would seem contradictory to say that we can know anything about experience a priori? It is not contradictory to say so, Kant held, if we are not claiming to know the particulars of experience but only its formal properties. That is, we do not have certainty that my wife will attend tonight's party, but we do know prior to the event that her appearance or nonappearance will involve our perceiving her in time. Likewise, we may not know the color of my wife's new dress or how she will look in it, but we do know before she arrives that she will appear to us in space. Empirical experience does not tell us these things about time and space; they are discovered as the very conditions for individual experience. We do not learn them *from* experience but prescribe them *to* experience.

Your mind does not possess particular content prior to experience, but it does have the form of all empirical knowledge prior to any particular sensation. Form, then, is independent of content and also more certain and universal than individual experiences. But this means that "we can know objects only as they appear to us (to our senses), not as they are in themselves" (p. 30). We have obtained certainty, but its source lies in us, not in the objects as we experience them. The forms of space and time actually make the appearance of objects possible.

Experience, said Kant, "can never teach us the nature of things in themselves" (p. 40). But nevertheless we can learn the universal laws of nature, since "nature" is what comes to us through experience, and we have discovered something universal and necessary about experience itself. To avoid confusion and error, we must stay within these boundaries and not ask questions about things in themselves that we cannot answer. We cannot avoid using concepts such as quantity, quality, and relation. These are among the organizing categories of experience. Kant thought Hume looked in the wrong place when he tried to derive causality from experiences. It is an organizing principle in our perception and is in our mind as a form of our understanding prior to any particular experiences. Without such a principle, experience would be chaotic. But that is precisely what experience is not. It is always ordered, and if Kant could not explain why that was the case, he did believe that he had shown how. See if you agree with him as you study some additional passages from the

Prolegomena, which has challenged students for more than two centuries.

1. OF THE SOURCES OF METAPHYSICS

If it becomes desirable to organize any knowledge as science, it will be necessary first to determine accurately those peculiar features which no other science has in common with it, constituting its peculiarity; otherwise the boundaries of all sciences become confused, and none of them can be treated thoroughly according to its nature.

The peculiar characteristic of a science may consist of a simple difference of object, or of the sources of knowledge, or of the kind of knowledge, or perhaps of all three conjointly. On these, therefore, depends the idea of a possible science and its territory.

First, as concerns the sources of metaphysical knowledge, its very concept implies that they cannot be empirical. Its principles (including not only its maxims but its basic notions) must never be derived from experience. It must not be physical but metaphysical knowledge, namely, knowledge lying beyond experience. It can therefore have for its basis neither external experience, which is the source of physics proper, nor internal, which is the basis of empirical psychology. It is therefore *a priori* knowledge, coming from pure understanding and pure reason.

But so far metaphysics would not be distinguishable from pure mathematics; it must therefore be called *pure philosophical* knowledge. . . .

2. CONCERNING THE KIND OF KNOWLEDGE WHICH CAN ALONE BE CALLED META-PHYSICAL

a. On the Distinction between Analytical and Synthetical Judgments in General. The peculiarity of its sources demands that metaphysical knowledge must consist of nothing but *a priori* judgments. But whatever be their origin or their logical form, there is a distinction in judgments, as to their content, according to which they are either merely *explicative,* adding nothing to the content of knowledge, or *expansive,* increasing the given knowledge. The former may be called *analytical,* the latter *synthetical,* judgments.

Analytical judgments express nothing in the predicate but what has been already actually thought in the concept of the subject, though not so distinctly or with the same (full) consciousness. When I say: "All bodies are extended," I have not amplified in the least my concept of body, but have only analyzed it, as extension was really thought to belong to that concept before the judgment was made, though it was not expressed. This judgment is therefore analytical. On the contrary, this judgment, "All bodies have weight," contains in its predicate something not actually thought in the universal concept of body; it amplifies my knowledge by adding something to my concept, and must therefore be called synthetical.

b. The Common Principle of All Analytical Judgments Is the Law of Contradiction. All analytical judgments depend wholly on the **law of contradiction,** and are in their nature a priori cognitions, whether the concepts that supply them with matter be empirical or not. For the predicate of an affirmative analytical judgment is already contained in the concept of the subject, of which it cannot be denied without contradiction. In the same way its opposite is necessarily denied of the subject in an analytical, but negative, judgment, by the same law of contradiction. Such is the nature of the judgments: "All bodies are extended," and "No bodies are unextended (that is, simple)."

For this very reason all analytical judgments are a priori even when the concepts are empirical, as, for example, "Gold is a yellow metal"; for to know this I require no experience beyond my concept of gold as a yellow metal. It is, in fact, the very concept, and I need only analyze it without looking beyond it.

c. Synthetical Judgments Require a Different Principle from the Law of Contradiction. There are synthetical a posteriori judgments of empirical origin; but there are also others which are certain a priori, and which spring from pure understanding and reason. Yet they both agree in this, that they cannot possibly spring from the principle of analysis, namely, the law of contradiction, alone. They require a quite different principle from which they may be deduced, subject, of course, always to the law of contradiction, which must never be violated, even though everything cannot be deduced from it. I shall first classify synthetical judgments.

1. *Judgments of Experience* are always synthetical. For it would be absurd to base an analytical judgment on experience, as our concept suffices for the purpose without requiring any testimony from experience. That body is extended is a judgment established a priori, and not an empirical judgment. For before appealing to experience, we already have all the conditions of the judgment in the concept, from which we have but to elicit the predicate according to the law of contradiction, and thereby to become conscious of the necessity of the judgment, which experience could not in the least teach us.

2. *Mathematical Judgments* are all synthetical. This fact seems hitherto to have altogether escaped the observation of those who have analyzed human reason: it even seems directly opposed to all their conjectures, though it is incontestably certain and most important in its consequences. For as it was found that the conclusions of mathematicians all proceed according to the law of contradiction (as is demanded by all **apodictic** certainty), men persuaded themselves that the fundamental principles were known from the same law. This was a great mistake, for a synthetical proposition can indeed be established by the law of contradiction, but only by presupposing another synthetical proposition from which it follows, but never by that law alone.

First of all, we must observe that all strictly mathematical judgments are a priori, and not empirical, because they carry with them necessity, which cannot be obtained from experience. But if this be not conceded to me, very good; I shall confine my assertion to *pure mathematics*, the very notion of which implies that it contains pure a priori and not empirical knowledge.

It must at first be thought that the proposition $7 + 5 = 12$ is a mere analytical judgment, following from the concept of the sum of seven and five, according to the law of contradiction. But on closer examination it appears that the concept of the sum of $7 + 5$ contains merely their union in a single number, without its being at all thought what the particular number is that unites them. The concept of twelve is by no means thought by merely thinking of the combination of seven and five; and, analyze this possible sum as we may, we shall not discover twelve in the concept. We must go beyond these concepts, by calling to our aid some **intuition** which corresponds to one of the concepts—that is, either our five fingers or five points (as Segner has it in his *Arithmetic*)—and we must add successively the units of the five given in the intuition to the concept of seven. Hence our concept is really amplified by the proposition $7 + 5 = 12$, and we add to the first concept a second concept not thought in it. Arithmetical judgments are therefore synthetical, and the more plainly according as we take larger numbers; for in such cases it is clear that, however closely we analyze our concepts without calling intuition to our aid, we can never find the sum by such mere dissection.

Just as little is any principle of geometry analytical. That a straight line is the shortest path between two points is a synthetical proposition. For my concept of straight contains nothing of quantity, but only a quality. The concept "shortest" is therefore altogether additional and cannot be obtained by any analysis of the concept "straight line." Here, too, intuition must come to aid us. It alone makes the synthesis possible. What usually makes us believe that the predicate of such apodictic judgments is already contained in our concept, and that the judgment is therefore analytical, is the duplicity of the expression. We must think a certain predicate as attached to a given concept, and necessity indeed belongs to the concepts. But the question is not what we must join in thought *to* the given concept, but what we actually think together with and in it, though obscurely; and so it appears that the predicate belongs to this concept necessarily indeed, yet not directly but indirectly by means of an intuition which must be present. . . .

3. *Metaphysical Judgments,* properly so called, are all synthetical. We must distinguish judgments pertaining to metaphysics from metaphysical judgments properly so called. Many of the former are analytical, but they only afford the means for metaphysical judgments, which are the whole end of the science and which are always synthetical. For if there be concepts pertaining to metaphysics (as, for example, that of substance), the judgments springing from simple analysis of them also pertain to metaphysics, as, for example, substance is that which only exists as subject, etc.; and by means of several such analytical judgments we seek to approach the definition of the concepts. But as the analysis of a pure concept of the understanding (the kind of concept pertaining to metaphysics) does not proceed in any different manner from the dissection of any other, even empirical, concepts, not belonging to metaphysics (such as, air is an elastic fluid, the elasticity of which is not destroyed by any known degree of cold), it follows that the concept indeed, but not the analytical judgment, is properly metaphysical. This science has something peculiar in the production of its a priori cognitions, which must therefore be distinguished from the features it has in common with other rational knowledge. Thus the judgment that all the substance in things is permanent is a synthetical and properly metaphysical judgment.

If the a priori concepts which constitute the materials and tools of metaphysics have first been collected according to fixed principles, then their analysis will be of great value; it might be taught as a particular part (as a *philosophia definitiva*), containing nothing but analytical judgments pertaining to metaphysics, and could be treated separately from the synthetical which constitute metaphysics proper. For indeed these analyses are not of much value except in metaphysics, that is, as regards the synthetical judgments which are to be generated by these previously analyzed concepts.

The conclusion drawn in this section then is that metaphysics is properly concerned with synthetical propositions a priori, and these alone constitute its end, for which it indeed requires various dissections of its concepts, namely, analytical judgments, but wherein the procedure is not different from that in every other kind of knowledge, in which we merely seek to render our concepts distinct by analysis. But the generation of a priori knowledge by intuition as well as by concepts, in fine, of synthetical propositions a priori, especially in philosophical knowledge, constitutes the essential subject of metaphysics. (Pp. 13–19, boldface added to identify glossary terms.)

HOW IS PURE MATHEMATICS POSSIBLE?

6. Here is a great and established branch of knowledge, encompassing even now a wonderfully large domain and promising an unlimited extension in the future, yet carrying with it thoroughly apodictic certainty, that is, absolute necessity, and therefore resting upon no empirical grounds. Consequently it is a pure product of reason; and, moreover, it is thoroughly synthetical. (Hence the question arises:) "How then is it possible for human reason to produce such knowledge entirely a priori?"

Does not this faculty (which produces mathematics), as it neither is nor can be based upon experience, presuppose some ground of knowledge a priori, which lies deeply hidden but which might reveal itself by these its effects if their first beginnings were but diligently ferreted out? . . .

10. . . . Now, the intuitions which pure mathematics lays at the foundation of all its cognitions and judgments which appear at once apodictic and necessary are space and time. For mathematics must first present all its concepts in intuition, and pure mathematics in pure intuition; that is, it must construct them. If it proceeded in any other way, it would be impossible to take a single step; for mathematics proceeds, not analytically by dissection of concepts, but synthetically, and if pure intuition be wanting there is nothing in which the matter for synthetical judgments a priori can be given. Geometry is based upon the pure intuition of space. Arithmetic achieves its concept of number by the successive addition of units in time, and pure mechanics cannot attain its concepts of motion without employing the representation of time. Both representations, however, are only intuitions; for if we omit from the empirical intuitions of bodies and their alterations (motion) everything empirical, that is, belonging to sensation, space and time still remain, which are therefore pure intuitions that lie a priori at the basis of the empirical. Hence they can never be omitted; but at the same time, by their being pure intuitions a priori, they prove that they are mere forms of our sensibility, which must precede all empirical intuition, that is, perception of actual objects, and comformably to which objects can be known a priori, but only as they appear to us.

11. The problem of the present section is therefore solved. Pure mathematics, as synthetical cognition a priori, is possible only by referring to no other objects than those of the senses. At the basis of their empirical intuition lies a pure intuition (of space and of time) which is a priori, because the latter intuition is nothing but the mere form of sensibility, which precedes the actual appearance of the objects, since in fact it makes them possible. Yet this faculty of intuiting a priori affects not the matter of the phenomenon (that is, the sensation in it, for this constitutes that which is empirical), but its form, namely, space and time. Should

any man venture to doubt that these are determinations adhering not to things in themselves, but to their relation to our sensibility, I should be glad to know how he can find it possible to know a priori how their intuition will be characterized before we have any acquaintance with them and before they are presented to us. Such, however, is the case with space and time. But this is quite comprehensible as soon as both count for nothing more than formal conditions of our sensibility, while the objects count merely as phenomena: for then the form of the phenomenon, that is, pure intuition, can by all means be represented as proceeding from ourselves, that is, a priori. (Pp. 28, 30–31.)

HOW IS PURE SCIENCE OF NATURE POSSIBLE?

29. In order to test Hume's problematical concept, . . . the concept of cause, we are first given a priori, by means of logic, the form of a conditional judgment in general; that is, we have one cognition given as antecedent and another as consequent. But it is possible that in perception we may meet with a rule of relation which runs thus: that a certain appearance is constantly followed by another (though not conversely); and this is a case for me to use the hypothetical judgment and, for instance, to say if the sun shines long enough upon a body it grows warm. Here there is indeed as yet no necessity of connection or concept of cause. But I proceed and say that, if this proposition, which is merely a subjective connection of perceptions, is to be a proposition of experience, it must be seen as necessary and universally valid. Such a proposition would be that the sun is by its light the cause of heat. The empirical rule is now considered as a law, and as valid, not merely of appearances but valid of them for the purposes of a possible experience which requires universal and therefore necessarily valid rules. I therefore easily comprehend the concept of cause, as a concept necessarily belonging to the mere

form of experience, and its possibility as a synthetical union of perceptions in consciousness in general; but I do not at all comprehend the possibility of a thing in general as a cause, because the concept of cause denotes a condition not at all belonging to things, but to experience. For experience can be nothing but objectively valid knowledge of appearances and of their succession, only so far as the earlier can be conjoined with the later according to the rule of hypothetical judgments.

30. Hence if even the pure concepts of the understanding are thought to go beyond objects of experience to things in themselves *(noumena)*, they have no meaning whatever. They serve, as it were, only to decipher appearances, that we may be able to read them as experience. The principles which arise from their reference to the sensible world only serve our understanding for empirical use. Beyond this they are arbitrary combinations without objective reality, and we can neither know their possibility a priori nor verify—or even render intelligible by any example—their reference to objects; because examples can only be borrowed from some possible experience, and consequently the objects of these concepts can be found nowhere but in a possible experience.

This complete (though to its originator unexpected) solution of Hume's problem rescues for the pure concepts of the understanding their a priori origin and for the universal laws of nature their validity as laws of the understanding, yet in such a way as to limit their use to experience, because their possibility depends solely on the reference of the understanding to experience, but with a completely reversed mode of connection which never occurred to Hume—they do not derive from experience, but experience derives from them.

This is, therefore, the result of all our foregoing inquiries: "All synthetical principles a priori are nothing more than principles of possible experience" and can never be referred to things in themselves, but to appearances as objects of experience. And hence pure mathematics as well as a pure science of nature can never be referred to anything more than mere appearances, and can only represent either that which makes experience in general possible, or else that which, as it is derived from these principles, must always be capable of being represented in some possible experience. (Pp. 59–60.)

Summary

We asked the question "Can I know the external world?" and we have now reviewed four responses to that issue. More than many philosophers who respond to major questions, Locke, Berkeley, Hume, and Kant lived relatively close to each other in time. They were concerned about the same problems; they were aware of the views of those before them and commented on them. All wanted us to stay close to actual sense experience, but they differed as to what they thought we could legitimately claim as verified knowledge on that basis. Each offers an answer that lets us know about an "external world," but, interestingly enough, each also differs on how you know it and with what degree of justification.

As you reflect on the problems involved, notice how important "ideas" are for all four men. Yet, notice that there is little agreement as to just what "ideas" are, how they arise, or what confidence we can place in them. Each offers a different proposal. Notice also how important the notion of "experience" is to each man. They want to base their philosophical theories on "experience" and to stay close to it. But, unfortunately, they cannot agree on what "experience" means or exactly how it arises. Study your own "ideas" and your own notion of "experience" and see how your views compare to these four theories.

GLOSSARY

analytic refers to the type of proposition whose truth can be determined without comparing the proposition to any particular phenomena it is supposed to describe, by comparing its logical structure and the meanings of its terms to the rules governing the "relations of ideas." See **propositions, relations of ideas.**

apodictic from the Greek *apodeitikos* meaning "demonstrable," referring to the expression of necessary truths.

a posteriori term for the type of **proposition** that can be verified only "after the fact"; a proposition about the *contingent*, that is, the unpredictable, that which is necessarily dependent on experience.

a priori term for the type of proposition that can be verified independently of, and *prior* to, experience, which cannot be disconfirmed by any particular experience because its content is "relations of ideas" rather than "matters of fact."

belief an attitude of confidence about the truth of a proposition, whether this confidence is justified or not; a disposition to confirm some particular opinion as knowledge of the truth.

categories the table of twelve fundamental concepts Kant believed must be grafted onto the data of raw experience, or 'intuition,' to render these data intelligible for the purposes of a human understanding of the world.

causality the concept of a specific type of relation between two events, a relation of **necessary connection.** Hume thought this concept resulted from bringing together the observed condition of the proximity of the two events in space and time with a subjective idea of necessary connection imposed by the mind in the act of understanding. Kant echoed this account of the origin of causality when he explained it as the application of the logical **category** having the form "if . . . then . . . " to the **intuition** of the two phenomena occurring together.

"common sense" that which is taken to be most natural or reasonable to believe; as used by the empiricists, the term conveys a sense of the potential simplicity and transparency to knowledge of the world as we experience it, underlying their efforts to build theories about the nature of knowledge and reality without relying on speculations about the existence of entities outside the real world of simple experience to explain the possibility and specific conditions of knowledge and truth.

"Copernican revolution" the phrase used by Kant to characterize the importance of his doctrines for clarifying philosophical thinking, in analogy to the discovery by Copernicus that the planets revolve around the sun, not the earth, as previous astronomers had believed.

empiricism the school of epistemology whose position is that all **ideas,** including abstract ideas such as those used in mathematics, are in some way constructed out of and reducible to the simplest kinds of sensory experience. Sometimes also referred to as *sensationalism.* See **sensation.** The counterpart to **rationalism.**

epistemology the division of philosophy that is concerned with theories about the origin, structure, and possible scope of human knowledge; often, this goes hand in hand with an attempt to formulate and clarify the procedures by which reliable knowledge can be attained and by which claims to knowledge can be evaluated.

expansive Kant's term for judgments or propositions that enlarge the scope of knowledge by containing in the *predicate* information that goes beyond merely *defining* the subject. Kant thought the property of expansiveness defined **synthetic** propositions.

experience the product of the contact between the data originating in the **world** and the faculties of sense, memory, and conceptual understanding possessed by sentient beings; often described as a relationship between a mind that appropriates these data and "the given," the objective features of the world that serve as grist to its mill. The central issue between **rationalism** and **empiricism** hinges on the extent to which "experience" conceived in this philosophical way can be sufficient by itself to account for the existence of general and abstract forms of knowledge. See **common sense.**

explicative Kant's term for propositions that add nothing to the sum of knowledge; that is, the **analytic** propositions in which certain basic terms are defined, or as he put it, in which the predicate is contained in, or defines the meaning of, the subject of the proposition.

"forms of intuition" the concepts that govern the fundamental structure of experience of the world; "space" and "time" are two such concepts in Kant's theory, supplied by the mind in intuition but giving us little or no reason to believe in their objective existence outside the mind.

hypothetical refers to the type of proposition that can be confirmed only by experience, a confirmed hypothesis expressed in an *expansive* judgment.

idea most often conceived philosophically as a representation in the mind of some kinds of objects not in or of the mind, either wholly external or peripheral to it.

idealism a family of metaphysical views often, but not always, associated with **rationalism** in epistemology; any doctrine that holds that reality is essentially composed of thought and is perfectly rational in its structure, or that ideas are the kinds of objects we are capable of knowing with the most certainty, as Berkeley believed.

impressions Hume's term for what Locke called "simple ideas," though Hume suggests a basic distinction in kind between the impressions of perception and the more abstract ideas used to compare and categorize impressions and to manage the relations among other ideas. Hume also distinguishes between "simple" and "complex" types of *both* impressions and ideas.

intuition(s) Kant's term for the impression(s) or act(s) of perception, which he attempted to

analyze into their necessary, or **a priori,** components and their contingent, empirical, or **a posteriori** components. He believed intuitions necessarily involved the application of a priori forms of intuition to the "unsynthesized manifold of apperception" if the idea of a stable, comprehensible world was to be confirmed as a real possibility.

justification a metaphysical procedure by which a proposition claiming the status of knowledge is defended against skepticism by showing how it follows from observable facts or from other propositions that themselves follow from observable facts, or by showing that it is analytic.

"justified true belief" a formula that is widely accepted as a general philosophical definition of knowledge. A claim to knowledge is successful if (1) it is believed by someone; (2) that person can produce concrete evidence to validate his belief; and (3) this justification supports a claim that actually corresponds with the facts. So, a person who correctly believes a thing to be true without being able to justify his belief cannot be said to know that thing, since he still will not have sufficient reason to believe himself to be correct. Whether a person can believe without knowing himself to be justified (as with the case of religious belief), and what criteria define an adequate justification, are central topics of **epistemology.**

law of contradiction Kant's criterion for distinguishing synthetic from analytic propositions: analytic propositions are those whose contradictions would necessarily imply an absurdity, whereas the contradiction of a synthetic proposition may be clearly true if the original proposition is not in accord with the experience referred to.

necessary connection the idea Hume believed we infer rather arbitrarily, without sound reasons based on experience itself, from the experience of two events that are "constantly conjoined" in space and time.

noumenal beyond the scope of perception and knowledge; the "in-itself" or "essential" (see **substance**); referring to the world as it would appear without the ordering imposed on it by the mind in the act of perception.

phenomenal available to intuition or the senses; apparent; perceptible; tangible; referring to the world as experienced, prior to any attempt to analyze experience in terms of what is dependent on and independent of the mind of the person to whom the experience belongs.

phenomenalism Hume's doctrine that the only class of objects with which we are actually in contact for the sake of knowledge are things we are able to sense and whose conception must be limited to the specific ways in which it is possible for us to sense them—that is, *phenomena.*

practical (see **common sense**) what Hume distinguished from the **theoretical** as being what is convenient to believe about the world from the point of view of the real problems and familiar features of life as it is ordinarily, prephilosophically lived and experienced. It is the sense of the practical, Hume believed, that ought to lead to our adopting a *mitigated* form of skepticism, an awareness of our own potential fallibility that does not undermine our confidence in our ability to make sound judgments on a regular basis. Radical skepticism contradicts the way in which we actually live and originates from purely theoretical considerations special to philosophy.

predicate the component of a proposition that modifies and qualifies the proposition's subject; for instance, in the proposition "roses are red, fragrant, and expensive," the predicate is the set of adjectives modifying "roses."

primary qualities in Locke, the general qualities of the object, as for instance extension and continuity through time, that necessarily inhere in any object whatsoever as a condition of the object's being recognizable *as* an object.

propositions potential beliefs or claims to knowledge about the world, expressed in words and capable of being tested against both the observable facts and some standard of meaningfulness. Often said to be composed of a subject and a **predicate,** which defines or explains the meaning of the subject. See **analytic, synthetic.**

quality a particular and observable attribute of an object that, in combination with other qualities, composes our conception of the object. Locke distinguished between **primary** and **secondary** qualities but found it necessary to speak of **substance** to account for the quality of unity or self-identity we believe objects to possess.

rationalism the school of epistemology that maintains that certainty of knowledge can be attained but only insofar as reality admits of being understood in accordance with purely rational principles, like those of mathematics and physics. A radical form of this view is that the basic structure of the world may be to a large extent only a projection of rational ideas that belong to the predetermined structure of the mind.

realism a family of metaphysical views often associated with empiricism in epistemology; the doctrine that the ideas of the mind represent reality as it is, like an image on a photographic plate.

reflection introspection, self-observation; in Locke's scheme, the form of experience from which "complex" ideas are derived and in which primary qualities are grasped, as the result of a person's being simultaneously aware of the immediate content of his senses and the disposition of his own mind to interpret that content in a way consistent with past experience. See **quality, substance.**

secondary qualities in Locke, the qualities of objects (color, shape, apparent size, etc.) that can vary from observation to observation, depending on the conditions under which the object is observed, the perspective of the observer, and the context in which the object is viewed.

sensation simple perception of external objects; for Locke, the simpler of the two basic forms of experience from which ideas can be derived from the mind, especially the ideas he called "simple," which are taken to refer to the sensible qualities of material objects they are used to represent.

skepticism a philosophical attitude characterized by the attempt to cast a shadow of doubt over claims to knowledge, particularly claims that most people would regard as being **common sense,** not subject to doubt. Hume distinguished between **antecedent, consequent,** and **mitigated** skepticism and believed that extreme forms of skepticism originated from an unreasonable demand for absolute certainty that always will be overruled by both the inevitable fallibility of human knowledge and the force of habitual, unskeptical ways of conceiving things.

subjective idealism Berkeley's doctrine that the proper objects of knowledge are the ideas or impressions that enter the mind through perception; he denied that there are real objects existing independently of their being perceived by some mind.

subjectivism the type of doctrine that holds that what determines our sense of reality is to a greater extent the subjective concepts we impose on our experience.

substance the unchanging unity underlying the apparent qualities, both primary and secondary, of things in the world, posited by Locke. Locke believed there were two main categories of substance, material and mental; Berkeley believed that only mental substance is real.

synthetic refers to the type of proposition that can be verified only by comparing it to the empirical phenomena it is supposed to describe.

synthetic a posteriori knowledge accumulated after experience and thus requiring no special explanation of its possibility.

synthetic a priori in Kant's classification of the types of knowledge, the kind of knowledge expressed by a proposition that has the paradoxical quality of being *both* dependent on experience in order for us to have a concept of it (synthetic) *and* necessarily capable of being known prior to experience, in fact forming a precondition of experience. Chief among this class of propositions Kant included the laws of natural science, especially of the physics of his day.

tabula rasa literally, "blank slate"; used by Locke to refer to the quality of the unexperienced mind, in which he believed there exist no "innate ideas."

theoretical an attitude toward reality that is a counterpart to the **practical** standpoint, with which philosophical thinking is identified because philosophy introduces new, very abstract concepts into thought, which produce conclusions and consequences that seem meaningless, trivial, or counterintuitive from the point of view of **common sense.**

volition the cause of purposeful human action; the ability to will or intend some state of affairs; the capacity of a human being to initiate events causally connected with his or her own body and according to the individual's own purposes. Hume believed that our conception of **causality** was in part due to our regarding events in the world as being analogous to the necessary connection between our willful acts and their consequences.

world the subject matter of **experience,** the totality of things that can possibly engage the attention and interest of sentient beings. Whether the "external world" includes elements that lie beyond the potential scope of human intelligence, and if it does, to what degree, are fundamental issues of contention between rationalists and empiricists.

STUDY QUESTIONS

1. What are the strengths and weaknesses of Locke's suggestion that the human mind is originally like a blank slate?

2. Trace how Locke thinks your mind works to expand its ideas. Does he seem to have described correctly the source of ideas?

3. Can you accept Locke's distinction between primary and secondary qualities? To what extent is the distinction helpful?

4. After you reflect on Locke's theory of knowledge, are you more or less convinced that you have knowledge of an external world?

5. Do you understand why Berkeley objected to Locke's notion of primary qualities, and can you see why Berkeley thought the idea led to further problems?

6. When Berkeley argues that "to be is to be perceived" or that we know only ideas, do you think he can account for all experience as you know it?

7. Do you find Hume more, or less, "empirical" than Locke or Berkeley? In general, do you think these three empiricists give an accurate and adequate account of human experience and understanding?

8. Can you see why Hume felt driven to some form of skepticism, and can you distinguish his "mitigated" skepticism from more radical kinds? Does or should Hume's skepticism change any of the ways you think or act?

9. Using Hume's theories, can you adequately account for your belief in cause-and-effect relations? What are the most important implications of Hume's analysis of causality?

10. Why do you think Kant was unsatisfied with Hume's philosophy? Do you see anything in your experience that cannot be accounted for if you accept Hume's theory, and, if so, does Kant provide the needed rationalization?

11. As Kant explains how certainty enters our knowledge, do you find his explanation of its origin satisfactory?

12. In your view, does Kant satisfactorily answer the question "Can I know the external world?" Why, or why not?

NOTES

[1]John Locke, *An Essay Concerning Human Understanding*, in *The English Philosophers from Bacon to Mill*, ed. Edwin A. Burtt (New York: Modern Library, 1939), p. 244.

[2]George Berkeley, *A Treatise Concerning the Principles of Human Knowledge*, in *The English Philosophers from Bacon to Mill*, p. 510.

[3]David Hume, "An Enquiry Concerning Human Understanding," in *The English Philosophers from Bacon to Mill*, p. 598.

[4]Immanuel Kant, *Critique of Pure Reason*, trans. Norman Kemp Smith (London: Macmillan, 1963), p. 41.

[5]Immanuel Kant, *Prolegomena to Any Future Metaphysics*, trans. Lewis White Beck (Indianapolis: Bobbs-Merrill, 1979), p. 30. Copyright 1950 by Macmillan Publishing Company, renewed 1978 by Lewis White Beck. Reprinted by permission of the publisher.

CHAPTER THREE

Can I Know My "Self"?

A sk yourself: "Who am I?" At first the answer may seem obvious. One might say, "I am a student." Countless other details could be added. You are a man or a woman. You have a name. You have specific parents, brothers, and sisters. You were born at a definite time and place; you belong to a particular nationality; and you have your own history and future. In short, you are unique. Without too much difficulty, you can provide a description of your identity that makes you different from other persons in the world.

"Who am I?" Answers are easy to find; yet they do not settle the question once and for all. Even after we mention numerous facts, we may still wonder who we are, because our existence points toward the question of how new selves are created. It seems as if everything about us could have been different. Even if we hold that everything is inevitable, that every event must be just as it is, we may still wonder why this must be so. We know much about who we are, but even our "answers" leave us wondering: What do we know after all? Who am I? Can I know my "self"? These are the perennial questions of philosophy.

As we explore these questions with you, we will offer a variety of approaches taken by widely different philosophers. If the questions are puzzling, it should be obvious that no single answer can tell us all we need

to know. René Descartes, the celebrated French rationalist, offers a straightforward attempt to answer the question in clear terms. David Hume, the British empiricist, likes clear ideas as well as Descartes, but he will differ about the degree of certainty we can reach on this subject. In fact, as you will see, the "self" is a very elusive reality for Hume. Hume's compatriot, Adam Smith, is usually thought of in connection with economic theory. However, his theories rest on a very definite view of who we are as human beings, and they reflect ideas widely held today. Sigmund Freud, the father of modern psychoanalysis, has much to tell us about our hidden self. But perhaps our most unusual thinker is Martin Buber, the Jewish theologian, whose views are associated with mysticism. As Buber adds his novel perspective, we hope the contrast of the five views will prove enlightening for you.

René Descartes and the Search for Knowledge in His Own Existence

In 1641 René Descartes completed one of the most important books in Western philosophy, *Meditations on First Philosophy*. This French thinker lived in a time of abundant

RENÉ DESCARTES   1596–1650

of the certainty and the evidence of its arguments. As you read the views of other philosophers, you will find many who support Descartes in this quest, while some will argue that we should settle for less than certainty. Descartes's goal was to make philosophy approximate mathematical certainty. He looked for "the true method of arriving at the knowledge of everything my mind was capable of attaining,"[1] and to this end, he formulated four rules.

> The first was never to accept anything as true that I did not know evidently to be so. . . . The second, to divide each of the difficulties I was examining into as many parts as possible. . . . The third . . . commencing with the simplest and easiest to know objects, to rise gradually as by degrees to the knowledge of the most composite things. And last, everywhere to make enumerations so complete and reviews so general that I would be sure of having omitted nothing. (P. 10.)

genius. Shakespeare was writing *The Merchant of Venice* in 1596, the year Descartes was born. When the philosopher died in 1650, Isaac Newton was 7 years old. Meanwhile, European explorations in North and South America had opened up the New World, and the work of Galileo, Kepler, and Copernicus was disrupting long-held assumptions about the universe. Within Christianity itself, the great schisms of the Protestant Reformation had split the Catholic Church, yielding denominations outside the authority of Rome. Descartes, therefore, believed it was time to reconsider the basic questions of philosophy. He was unwilling to trust old foundations that were crumbling; he wanted a new philosophical beginning.

Descartes's interests were wide. He contributed to biology and physiology. He was also a distinguished mathematician. In his *Discourse on Method* (1637), he reported that he took great pleasure in mathematics because

Deception and Doubt

As Descartes applied his first rule in the *Meditations,* four years later, he emphasized how easy it is to take things for granted. No person's judgments are totally free of error. Making mistakes is a common experience. What intrigued Descartes, however, was the possibility that we might be more deeply in error than our ordinary awareness suggests. Descartes wondered: Is it possible to know with certainty that one is not perpetually deceived? We think we are awake, but might we not simply be dreaming of being awake? We think we are encountering physical objects, but might not all these be illusions? Apparently we can distinguish between true and false judgments, but perhaps even what we take as demonstrably true is part of a deceptive scheme so subtle that it escapes detection. We think we know our selves with certainty, but do we really?

Descartes was "forced to admit that there is nothing, among the things I once believed to be true, which it is not permissible to doubt" (p. 59). If knowledge is equated with certainty, the only way to determine whether knowledge is possible is to turn the threat of **doubt** into a tool which philosophy can employ systematically. In short, philosophy ought to use doubt rigorously to see if it can locate a point where doubt itself reveals what is indubitable. If such a position could be reached, that foundation could be used to ground the knowledge philosophy seeks.

To facilitate his rigorous application of doubt, Descartes supposed that there exists "not a supremely good God, the source of truth, but rather an evil genius, as clever and deceitful as he is powerful, who has directed his entire effort to misleading me" (p. 60). This hypothetical demon seemed to demolish Descartes's world, his experience, and even his convictions about his own identity. Given the criterion that nothing liable to doubt ought to be accepted as certainly true, Descartes saw that neither his sense experiences nor his memories could be accepted at face value. In reality the world might be very different from what it appeared to be. In fact, Descartes himself might not be Descartes at all. No genuine knowledge is possible unless there is a way to show conclusively that, at least in one instance, there is no gap between appearance and reality, between what we think to be true and what is true.

The Existing "I"

Radical doubt makes it conceivable that "there is nothing at all in the world: no heaven, no earth, no minds, no bodies" (p. 61). Could it also be the case, Descartes wondered, that even one's own existence was an illusion, the most cunning deception of all? That question was the pivot on which Descartes's philosophy turned. But finally his discovery was that his own existence withstood all the power

of radical doubt. Even in order to be deceived, I must exist. That claim, Descartes concluded, is indubitable. Not even the evil genius, reasoned Descartes, could undermine that certainty.

> Deceive me as he will, he can never bring it about that I am nothing so long as I shall think that I am something. Thus it must be granted that, after weighing everything carefully and sufficiently, one must come to the considered judgment that the statement "I am, I exist" is necessarily true every time it is uttered by me or conceived in my mind. (P. 61.)

Descartes knew that this claim about his own existence was only the barest of beginnings. After being certain that he existed, the next crucial step was to ask "Now who is this 'I' whom I know?" (p. 63). Since Descartes would not admit anything he could not prove to be necessarily true, his self-knowledge was severely limited. If he knew that he existed, he might still be deceived, for example, about what his senses told him or even about whether he had a real body. Only what was **"clear and distinct,"** to use Cartesian terms, would necessarily be true. That the philosopher existed as "a thing that thinks," which is to say as "a thing that doubts, understands, affirms, denies, wills, refuses, and which also imagines and senses" (p. 63), this was his first clear and distinct idea. At this point, Descartes concluded, he had retrieved his own existence and his mental life from the clutches of doubt. Consciousness seemed secure, but what of physical bodies and objects? We can be sure our thinking world is indubitably real, but what of realities external to our mind?

God and the World

Descartes never denied that physical objects exist. Nor did he believe that human experience is trapped inside its own consciousness, never to achieve contact with an outside world. Such things were as subject to doubt as his commonsense convictions turned out to be. Descartes's problem was to secure knowledge against all doubt. Having satisfied himself that his mental existence was indubitable, he pressed on to see if he could get the world back with proof of its certainty too. The route to that destination, however, turned out to be indirect.

Although Descartes believed that his own existence could be guaranteed against doubt because his very doubt presupposed his own existence, the world's existence needed additional insurance. The existence of God would seem to provide this, so Descartes focused on securing knowledge in that area. Since our idea of God is the idea of a perfect being, it is clear and distinct, Descartes reasoned. Since the idea of perfection involves necessary existence, one cannot think of God except as existing. Descartes argued that his idea of a perfect being entailed the existence of God as its source, because Descartes could locate nothing within himself with power sufficient to produce such an idea. In addition, God's perfection excludes the possibility that God is a deceiver. Fortunately, Descartes concluded, "everything that I clearly and distinctly perceive is necessarily true," because God "certainly has not given me a faculty such that, when I use it properly, I could ever make a mistake" (pp. 88, 79).

The existence of God does not mean that the world always has been the way it appears to be. We need to use reason to obtain clarity and distinctness, but Descartes thought it possible to be sure of at least what is seen as clear and distinct. We have a strong inclination to believe that our experience is caused by actually existing corporeal objects. In fact, that inclination is so strong that it would be impossible to vindicate God from the charge of deceit if our experience did not include such objects. For the same reason, we can trust that the external world actually is the way it appears, if we critically analyze our experience using the criteria of clarity and distinctness. In addition, if we can make indubitable knowledge claims within these boundaries, how much more are we able to make them with respect to our own bodies and the existence of other persons? These realities are intimately conjoined with us. Again, Descartes emphasized that particular judgments can be mistaken; they must be tested for their clarity and distinctness. But at the end of his *Meditations*, Descartes was convinced that he had won back knowledge of his own existence, of God, and of a world of physical objects, other persons, and his own bodily reality.

How Certain Could Descartes Be?

Descartes's philosophy points out a fundamental paradox, namely, that our critical reflection entails the existence of what makes such reflection possible. Existence does not begin with questions. There must be something to ask about and some person to do the questioning. These must be in existence first. Descartes thought that his personal identity as a "thinking thing" was indubitable because it was a necessary condition for deception and doubt to take place. **Certainty,** he argued, depends on clarity and distinctness. A factor of undeniability is present in these properties.

You may be clear that you are in pain, for your suffering is unmistakable. But distinctness characterizes experience only to the extent that the exact quality of the pain and its difference from other feelings are definitely focused. Using this criterion, many things seemed certain to Descartes about our question "Who am I?" Descartes thought that knowledge of his own existence, his own "self," was indubitable. He claimed that his self could be defined at first as "a thinking thing." Although ultimately he concluded that his body was real and that his sensory experiences could be trusted once critically evaluated, he was convinced that neither his body nor his environment was essential to his personal existence. This dualism of mind and body, this separation of mental from physical reality, led Descartes to defend the soul's immortality, but the question remains whether his own criteria for true knowledge entitled him to claim certainty for this conviction.

Many philosophers have disagreed with Descartes because his criteria of clarity and distinctness, when closely examined, turn out to be vague and imprecise. Consider, for example, one of the rules of inquiry Descartes listed in his *Discourse on Method*. Constant review is always important in inquiry, he tells us. But why should we have to keep up such review, if clarity and distinctness are sufficient to confer certainty? Presumably we might monitor individual situations just to be sure that our experience has been properly evaluated and our judgments well made. Doing so, moreover, might solidify our conviction that the required procedures have been properly followed and that our certainty is real. Descartes's insistence on review, however, is more troublesome than those explanations suggest. Urging review in itself implies that one might be mistaken. Indeed, even one's previous reviews might be in error. You might be confident that certainty is present, the conditions of clarity and distinctness having been fulfilled, but the counsel to review casts a shadow of doubt, even if for practical purposes one concludes that such review has continued long enough.

Descartes's findings about his own identity are not necessarily in error, but perhaps he cannot claim quite as much certitude for them as he wanted. Practically speaking, it rarely occurs to us to doubt our own existence. If that reality is not certain, probably nothing is. But problems arise when we ask what our existence involves. Descartes's answer to the question "Who am I?" is, after all, an interpretation of experience. Admittedly that experience is *his* experience, but who or what is *he*? A feeling and thinking person. Each of us knows at least that much if we know anything. And we distinguish experience quite naturally in terms of "I" and "you," "mine" and "yours." One of the dilemmas of our existence is that we find it practically impossible to deny that we are persons, and yet we seem not to know exactly what "being a person" means in general or even for our particular identity.

More important, as you study the following excerpt from the *Meditations on First Philosophy* (1641), consider whether Descartes simply assumed some aspects of our experience to be certain when, if we examine them carefully, they may not prove to be. Descartes may take for granted our knowledge of what it means to be a self. We may not understand the self as well as he thinks, however, and the grounds of our information may not be as certain as we think. Shortly, David Hume will also raise these questions for us. He assents to much of what Descartes says. He also grounds knowledge on experience, but he is not so sure that we have examined "experience" closely enough to see how reliable it can be as a basis for knowledge of the self.

MEDITATION ONE: CONCERNING THOSE THINGS THAT CAN BE CALLED INTO DOUBT

Several years have now passed since I first realized how many were the false opinions that in my youth I took to be true, and thus how doubtful were all the things that I subsequently built upon these opinions. From the time I became aware of this, I realized that for once I had to raze everything in my life, down to the very bottom, so as to begin again from the first foundations, if I wanted to establish anything firm and lasting in the sciences. But the task seemed so enormous that I waited for a point in my life that was so ripe that no more suitable a time for laying hold of these disciplines would come to pass. For this reason, I have delayed so long that I would be at fault were I to waste on deliberation the time that is left for action. Therefore, now that I have freed my mind from all cares, and I have secured for myself some leisurely and carefree time, I withdraw in solitude. I will, in short, apply myself earnestly and openly to the general destruction of my former opinions.

Yet to this end it will not be necessary that I show that all my opinions are false, which perhaps I could never accomplish anyway. But because reason now persuades me that I should withhold my assent no less carefully from things which are not plainly certain and indubitable than I would to what is patently false, it will be sufficient justification for rejecting them all, if I find a reason for doubting even the least of them. Nor therefore need one survey each opinion one after the other, a task of endless proportion. Rather—because undermining the foundations will cause whatever has been built upon them to fall down of its own accord—I will at once attack those principles which supported everything that I once believed.

Whatever I had admitted until now as most true I took in either from the senses or through the senses; however, I noticed that they sometimes deceived me. And it is a mark of prudence never to trust wholly in those things which have once deceived us.

But perhaps, although the senses sometimes deceive us when it is a question of very small and distant things, still there are many other matters which one certainly cannot doubt, although they are derived from the very same senses: that I am sitting here before the fireplace wearing my dressing gown, that I feel this sheet of paper in my hands, and so on. But how could one deny that these hands and that my whole body exist? Unless perhaps I should compare myself to insane people whose brains are so impaired by a stubborn vapor from a black bile that they continually insist that they are

kings when they are in utter poverty, or that they are wearing purple robes when they are naked, or that they have a head made of clay, or that they are gourds, or that they are made of glass. But they are all demented, and I would appear no less demented if I were to take their conduct as a model for myself.

All of this would be well and good, were I not a man who is accustomed to sleeping at night, and to undergoing in my sleep the very same things—or now and then even less likely ones—as do these insane people when they are awake. How often has my evening slumber persuaded me of such customary things as these: that I am here, clothed in my dressing gown, seated at the fireplace, when in fact I am lying undressed between the blankets! But right now I certainly am gazing upon this piece of paper with eyes wide awake. This head which I am moving is not heavy with sleep. I extend this hand consciously and deliberately and I feel it. These things would not be so distinct for one who is asleep. But this all seems as if I do not recall having been deceived by similar thoughts on other occasions in my dreams. As I consider these cases more intently, I see so plainly that there are no definite signs to distinguish being awake from being asleep that I am quite astonished, and this astonishment almost convinces me that I am sleeping.

Let us say, then, for the sake of argument, that we are sleeping and that such particulars as these are not true: that we open our eyes, move our heads, extend our hands. Perhaps we do not even have these hands, or any such body at all. Nevertheless, it really must be admitted that things seen in sleep are, as it were, like painted images, which could have been produced only in the likeness of true things. Therefore at least these general things (eyes, head, hands, the whole body) are not imaginary things, but are true and exist. For indeed when painters wish to represent sirens and satyrs by means of bizarre and unusual forms, they surely cannot ascribe utterly new natures to these creatures. Rather, they simply intermingle the members of various animals. And even if they concoct something so utterly novel that its likes have never been seen before (being utterly fictitious and false), certainly at the very minimum the colors from which the painters compose the thing ought to be true. And for the same reason, although even these general things (eyes, head, hands, and the like) can be imaginary, still one must necessarily admit that at least other things that are even more simple and universal are true, from which, as from true colors, all these things—be they true or false—which in our thought are images of things, are constructed.

To this class seems to belong corporeal nature in general, together with its extension; likewise the shape of extended things, their quantity or size, their number; as well as the place where they exist, the time of their duration, and other such things.

Hence perhaps we do not conclude improperly that physics, astronomy, medicine, and all the other disciplines that are dependent upon the consideration of composite things are all doubtful. But arithmetic, geometry, and other such disciplines—which treat of nothing but the simplest and most general things and which are indifferent as to whether these composite things do or do not exist—contain something certain and indubitable. For whether I be awake or asleep, two plus three makes five, and a square does not have more than four sides; nor does it seem possible that such obvious truths can fall under the suspicion of falsity.

All the same, a certain opinion of long standing has been fixed in my mind, namely that there exists a God who is able to do anything and by whom I, such as I am, have been created. How do I know that he did not bring it about that there be no earth at all, no heavens, no extended thing, no figure, no size, no place, and yet all these things should seem to me to exist precisely as they appear to do now? Moreover—as I judge that others sometimes make mistakes in matters that they believe they know most

perfectly—how do I know that I am not deceived every time I add two and three or count the sides of a square or perform an even simpler operation, if such can be imagined? But perhaps God has not willed that I be thus deceived, for it is said that he is supremely good. Nonetheless, if it were repugnant to his goodness that he should have created me such that I be deceived all the time, it would seem, from this same consideration, to be foreign to him to permit me to be deceived occasionally. But we cannot make this last assertion.

Perhaps there are some who would rather deny such a powerful God, than believe that all other matters are uncertain. Let us not put these people off just yet; rather, let us grant that everything said here about God is fictitious. Now they suppose that I came to be what I am either by fate or by chance or by a continuous series of events or by some other way. But because being deceived and being mistaken seem to be imperfections, the less powerful they take the author of my being to be, the more probable it will be that I would be so imperfect as to be deceived perpetually. I have nothing to say in response to these arguments. At length I am forced to admit that there is nothing, among the things I once believed to be true, which it is not permissible to doubt—not for reasons of frivolity or a lack of forethought, but because of valid and considered arguments. Thus I must carefully withhold assent no less from these things than from the patently false, if I wish to find anything certain.

But it is not enough simply to have made a note of this; I must take care to keep it before my mind. For long-standing opinions keep coming back again and again, almost against my will; they seize upon my credulity, as if it were bound over to them by long use and the claims of intimacy. Nor will I get out of the habit of assenting to them and believing in them, so long as I take them to be exactly what they are, namely, in some respects doubtful as by now is obvious, but nevertheless highly probable, so that it is much more consonant with reason to believe them than to deny them. Hence, it seems to me, I would do well to turn my will in the opposite direction, to deceive myself and pretend for a considerable period that they are wholly false and imaginary, until finally, as if with equal weight of prejudice* on both sides, no bad habit should turn my judgment from the correct perception of things. For indeed I know that no danger or error will follow and that it is impossible for me to indulge in too much distrust, since I now am concentrating only on knowledge, not on action.

Thus I will suppose not a supremely good God, the source of truth, but rather an evil genius, as clever and deceitful as he is powerful, who has directed his entire effort to misleading me. I will regard the heavens, the air, the earth, colors, shapes, sounds, and all external things as nothing but the deceptive games of my dreams, with which he lays snares for my credulity. I will regard myself as having no hands, no eyes, no flesh, no blood, no senses, but as nevertheless falsely believing that I possess all these things. I will remain resolutely fixed in this meditation, and, even if it be out of my power to know anything true, certainly it is within my power to take care resolutely to withhold my assent to what is false, lest this deceiver, powerful and clever as he is, have an effect on me. But this undertaking is arduous, and laziness brings me back to my customary way of living. I am not unlike a prisoner who might enjoy an imaginary freedom in his sleep. When he later begins to suspect that he is sleeping, he fears being awakened and conspires slowly with these pleasant illusions. In just this way, I spontaneously fall back into my old beliefs, and dread being awakened, lest the toilsome wakefulness which follows upon a peaceful rest have to be spent thenceforward not in the light but among the inextricable shadows of the difficulties now brought forward.

*A "prejudice" is a prejudgment, that is, an adjudication of an issue without having first reviewed the appropriate evidence.

MEDITATION TWO: CONCERNING THE NATURE OF THE HUMAN MIND: THAT THE MIND IS MORE KNOWN THAN THE BODY

Yesterday's meditation filled my mind with so many doubts that I can no longer forget about them—nor yet do I see how they are to be resolved. But, as if I had suddenly fallen into a deep whirlpool, I am so disturbed that I can neither touch my foot to the bottom, nor swim up to the top. Nevertheless I will work my way up, and I will follow the same path I took yesterday, putting aside everything which admits of the least doubt, as if I had discovered it to be absolutely false. I will go forward until I know something certain—or, if nothing else, until I at least know for certain that nothing is certain. Archimedes sought only a firm and immovable point in order to move the entire earth from one place to another. Surely great things are to be hoped for if I am lucky enough to find at least one thing that is certain and indubitable.

Therefore I will suppose that all I see is false. I will believe that none of those things that my deceitful memory brings before my eyes ever existed. I thus have no senses: body, shape, extension, movement, and place are all figments of my imagination. What then will count as true? Perhaps only this one thing: that nothing is certain.

But on what grounds do I know that there is nothing over and above all those which I have just reviewed, concerning which there is not even the least cause for doubt? Is there not a God (or whatever name I might call him) who instills these thoughts in me? But why should I think that, since perhaps I myself could be the author of these things? Therefore am I not at least something? But I have already denied that I have any senses and any body. Still, I hesitate; for what follows from that? Am I so tied to the body and to the senses that I cannot exist without them? But I have persuaded myself that there is nothing at all in the world: no heaven, no earth, no minds, no bodies. Is it not then true that I do not exist? But certainly I should exist, if I were to persuade myself of something. But there is a deceiver (I know not who he is) powerful and sly in the highest degree, who is always purposely deceiving me. Then there is no doubt that I exist, if he deceives me. And deceive me as he will, he can never bring it about that I am nothing so long as I shall think that I am something. Thus it must be granted that, after weighing everything carefully and sufficiently, one must come to the considered judgment that the statement "I am, I exist" is necessarily true every time it is uttered by me or conceived in my mind.

But I do not yet understand well enough who I am—I, who now necessarily exist. And from this point on, I must take care lest I imprudently substitute something else in place of myself; and thus be mistaken even in that knowledge which I claim to be the most certain and evident of all. To this end, I shall meditate once more on what I once believed myself to be before having embarked upon these deliberations. For this reason, then, I will set aside whatever can be refuted even to a slight degree by the arguments brought forward, so that at length there shall remain precisely nothing but what is certain and unshaken.

What therefore did I formerly think I was? A man, of course. But what is a man? Might I not say a rational animal? No, because then one would have to inquire what an "animal" is and what "rational" means. And then from only one question we slide into many more difficult ones. Nor do I now have enough free time that I want to waste it on subtleties of this sort. But rather here I pay attention to what spontaneously and at nature's lead came into my thought beforehand whenever I pondered what I was. Namely, it occurred to me first that I have a face, hands, arms, and this entire mechanism of bodily members, the very same as are discerned in a corpse—which I referred to by the name "body." It also occurred to me that I eat, walk, feel, and think; these actions I used to assign to the soul as their cause. But what this soul

was I either did not think about or I imagined it was something terribly insubstantial—after the fashion of a wind, fire, or ether—which has been poured into my coarser parts. I truly was not in doubt regarding the body; rather I believed that I distinctly knew its nature, which, were I perhaps tempted to describe it such as I mentally conceived it, I would explain it thus: by "body," I understand all that is suitable for being bounded by some shape, for being enclosed in some place, and thus for filling up space, so that it excludes every other body from that space; for being perceived by touch, sight, hearing, taste, or smell; for being moved in several ways, not surely by itself, but by whatever else that touches it. For I judged that the power of self-motion, and likewise of sensing or of thinking, in no way pertains to the nature of the body. Nonetheless, I used to marvel especially that such faculties were found in certain bodies.

But now what am I, when I suppose that some deceiver—omnipotent and, if I may be allowed to say it, malicious—takes all the pains he can in order to deceive me? Can I not affirm that I possess at least a small measure of all those traits which I already have said pertain to the nature of the body? I pay attention, I think, I deliberate—but nothing happens. I am wearied of repeating this in vain. But which of these am I to ascribe to the soul? How about eating or walking? These are surely nothing but illusions, because I do not have a body. How about sensing? Again, this also does not happen without a body, and I judge that I really did not sense those many things I seemed to have sensed in my dreams. How about thinking? Here I discover that thought is an attribute that really does belong to me. This alone cannot be detached from me. I am; I exist; this is certain. But for how long? For as long as I think. Because perhaps it could also come to pass that if I should cease from all thinking I would then utterly cease to exist. I now admit nothing that is not necessarily true. I am therefore precisely only a thing that thinks; that is, a mind, or soul, or intellect, or reason—words the meaning of which I was ignorant before. Now, I am a true thing, and truly existing; but what kind of thing? I have said it already: a thing that thinks.

What then? I will set my imagination going to see if I am not something more. I am not that connection of members which is called the human body. Neither am I some subtle air infused into these members, not a wind, not a fire, not a vapor, not a breath—nothing that I imagine to myself, for I have supposed all these to be nothing. The assertion stands: the fact still remains that I am something. But perhaps it is the case that nevertheless, these very things which I take to be nothing (because I am ignorant of them) in reality do not differ from that self which I know. This I do not know. I shall not quarrel about it right now; I can make a judgment only regarding things which are known to me. I know that I exist; I ask now who is this "I" whom I know. Most certainly the knowledge of this matter, thus precisely understood, does not depend upon things that I do not yet know to exist. Therefore, it is not dependent upon any of those things that I feign in my imagination. But this word "feign" warns me of my error. For I would be feigning if I should "imagine" that I am something, because imagining is merely the contemplation of the shape or image of a corporeal thing. But I know now with certainty that I am, and at the same time it could happen that all these images—and, generally, everything that pertains to the nature of the body—are nothing but dreams. When these things are taken into account, I would speak no less foolishly were I to say: "I will imagine so that I might recognize more distinctly who I am," than were I to say: "Now I surely am awake, and I see something true, but because I do not yet see it with sufficient evidence, I will take the trouble of going to sleep so that my dreams might show this to me more truly and more evidently." Thus I know that none of what I can comprehend by means of the imagination pertains to this understanding that I have of myself. Moreover, I know that I must be most diligent about withdrawing my mind from these

things so that it can perceive its nature as distinctly as possible.

But what then am I? A thing that thinks. What is that? A thing that doubts, understands, affirms, denies, wills, refuses, and which also imagines and senses.

It is truly no small matter if all of these things pertain to me. But why should they not pertain to me? Is it not I who now doubt almost everything, I who nevertheless understand something, I who affirm that this one thing is true, I who deny other things, I who desire to know more things, I who wish not to be deceived, I who imagine many things against my will, I who take note of many things as if coming from the senses? Is there anything in all of this which is not just as true as it is that I am, even if I am always dreaming or even if the one who created me tries as hard as possible to delude me? Are any of these attributes distinct from my thought? What can be said to be separate from myself? For it is so obvious that it is I who doubt, I who understand, I who will, that there is nothing through which it could be more evidently explicated. But indeed I am also the same one who imagines; for, although perhaps as I supposed before, no imagined thing would be wholly true, the very power of imagining does really exist, and constitutes a part of my thought. Finally, I am the same one who senses or who takes note of bodily things as if through the senses. For example, I now see a light, I hear a noise, I feel heat. These are false, since I am asleep. But I certainly seem to see, hear, and feel. This cannot be false: properly speaking, this is what is called "sensing" in me. But this is, to speak precisely, nothing other than thinking.

From these considerations I begin to know a little better who I am. But it still seems that I cannot hold back from believing that bodily things—whose images are formed by thought, and which the senses themselves examine—are much more distinctly known than this unknown aspect of myself which does not come under the imagination. And yet it would be quite strange if the very things which I consider to be doubtful, unknown, and foreign to me are comprehended by me more distinctly than what is true, what is known—than, in fine, myself. But I see what is happening: my mind loves to wander and does not allow itself to be restricted to the confines of truth. Let it be that way then: let us allow it the freest rein in every respect, so that, when we pull in the reins at the right time a little later, the mind may suffer itself to be ruled more easily.

Let us consider those things which are commonly believed to be the most distinctly comprehended of all: namely the bodies which we touch and see. But not bodies in general, for these generic perceptions are often somewhat more confused; rather let us consider one body in particular. Let us take, for instance, this piece of wax. It has very recently been taken from the honeycombs; it has not as yet lost all the flavor of its honey. It retains some of the smell of the flowers from which it was collected. Its color, shape, and size are obvious. It is hard and cold. It can easily be touched, and if you rap on it with a knuckle it makes a sound. In short, everything is present in it that appears to be needed in order that a body can be known as distinctly as possible. But notice that while I am speaking, it is brought close to the fire; the remaining traces of the honey flavor are purged; the odor vanishes; the color is changed; the original shape disappears. Its magnitude increases, it becomes liquid and hot, and can hardly be touched; and now, when you knock on it, it does not emit any sound. Up to this point, does the same wax remain? One must confess that it does: no one denies it; no one thinks otherwise. What was there then in the wax that was so distinctly comprehended? Certainly none of the things that I reached by means of the senses. For whatever came under taste or smell or sight or touch or hearing by now has changed, yet the wax remains.

Perhaps the wax was what I now think it is: namely that it really never was the sweetness of the honey or the fragrance of the flowers, not this whiteness, not a figure, not

a sound, but a body which a little earlier manifested itself to me in these ways, and now does so in other ways. But just what precisely is this thing which I imagine thus? Let us direct our attention to this and see what remains after we have removed everything which does not belong to the wax: only that it is something extended, flexible, and subject to change. What is this flexible and mutable thing? Is it not the fact that I imagine that this wax can change from a round to a square shape, or from the latter to a rectangular shape? Not at all: for I comprehend that the wax is capable of innumerable changes, yet I cannot survey these innumerable changes by imagining them. Therefore this comprehension is not accomplished by the faculty of imagination. What is this extended thing? Is this thing's extension also unknown? For it becomes larger in wax that is beginning to liquefy, greater in boiling wax, and greater still as the heat is increased. And I would not judge rightly what the wax is if I did not believe that this wax can take on even more varieties of extension than I could ever have grasped by the imagination. It remains then for me to concede that I in no way imagine what this wax is, but perceive it by the mind only. I am speaking about this piece of wax in particular, for it is clearer in the case of wax in general. But what is this wax which is perceived only by the mind? It is the same that I see, touch, and imagine; in short it is the same as I took it to be from the very beginning. But we must take note of the fact that the perception of the wax is neither by sight, nor touch, nor imagination, nor was it ever so (although it seemed so before), but rather an inspection on the part of the mind alone. This inspection can be imperfect and confused, as it was before, or clear and distinct, as it is now, according to whether I pay greater or less attention to those things of which the wax consists.

But meanwhile I marvel at how prone my mind is to errors; for although I am considering these things within myself silently and without words, nevertheless I latch onto words themselves and I am very nearly deceived by the ways in which people speak. For we say that we see the wax itself, if it is present, and not that we judge it to be present from its color or shape. Whence I might conclude at once: the wax is therefore known by eyesight, and not by an inspection on the part of the mind alone, unless I perhaps now might have looked out the window at the men crossing the street whom I say I am no less wont to see than the wax. But what do I see over and above the hats and clothing? Could not robots be concealed under these things? But I judge them to be men; thus what I believed I had seen with my eyes, I actually comprehend with nothing but the faculty of judgment which is in my mind.

But a person who seeks to know more than the common crowd should be ashamed of himself if he has come upon doubts as a result of an encounter with the forms of speech devised by the common crowd. Let us then go forward, paying attention to the following question: did I perceive more perfectly and evidently what the wax was when I first saw it and believed I had known it by the external sense—or at least by the common sense, as they say, that is, the imaginative power—than I know it now, after having examined more diligently both what the wax is and how it is known. Surely it is absurd to doubt this matter. For what was there in the first perception that was distinct? What was there that any animal could not have seemed capable of possessing? But when I distinguish the wax from its external forms, as if having taken off its clothes, as it were, I look at the naked wax, even though at this point there can be an error in my judgment; nevertheless I could not perceive it without a human mind.

But what am I to say about this mind, or about myself? For as yet I admit nothing else to be in me over and above my mind. What, I say, am I who seem to perceive this wax so distinctly? Do I not know myself not only much more truly and with more certainty, but also much more distinctly and evidently? For if I judge that the wax exists from the fact that I see it, certainly it follows much

more evidently that I myself exist, from the fact that I see the wax. For it could happen that what I see is not truly wax. It could happen that I have no eyes with which to see anything. But it could not happen that, while I see or think I see (I do not now distinguish these two), I who think am not something. Likewise, if I judge that the wax exists from the fact that I touch it, the same thing will again follow: I exist. If from the fact that I imagine, or from whatever other cause, the same thing readily follows. But what I noted regarding the wax applies to all the other things that are external to me. Furthermore, if the perception of the wax seemed more distinct after it became known to me not only from sight or touch, but from many causes, how much more distinctly I must be known to myself; for there are no considerations that can aid in the perception of the wax or any other body without these considerations demonstrating even better the nature of my mind. But there are still so many other things in my mind from which one can draw a more distinct knowledge of the mind, so that those things which emanate from a body seem hardly worth enumerating.

But lo and behold, I have arrived on my own at the place I wanted. Since I know that bodies are not, properly speaking, perceived by the senses or by the faculty of imagination, but only by the intellect, and since, moreover, I know that they are not perceived by being touched or seen, but only insofar as they are expressly understood, nothing can be more easily and more evidently perceived by me than my mind. But because an established habit of belief cannot be put aside so quickly, it is appropriate to stop here, so that by the length of my meditation this new knowledge may be more deeply impressed on my memory. (Pp. 57–67.)

David Hume and the Idea of Self

Philosophy thrives on doubt, because doubt exposes our questionable convictions. But

Like Descartes, Hume asked, "Can I know my 'self'?" But Hume's empirical approach produced an analysis and a conclusion very different from those of Descartes. Language, noted Hume, permits us to speak of one's "self." When we speak that way, we apparently refer to something definite and real. Indeed, with Descartes in mind, Hume's *A Treatise of Human Nature* (1739) observed that "there are some philosophers who imagine we are every moment intimately conscious of what we call our self; that we feel its existence and its continuance in existence and are certain beyond the evidence of demonstration both of its perfect identity and simplicity."[2] He understood how these convictions arose, but he found such certainties less than firmly grounded.

The Origins of the Idea of Self

In Chapter Two, we saw that Hume accepted the principle that all ideas ultimately derive from sense impressions. From what impression, Hume went on to ask, could the idea of self originate? He could not see before him any sense impression corresponding to a "self." Unfortunately, Hume found, "This question is impossible to answer without a manifest contradiction and absurdity; and yet it is a question which must necessarily be answered if we would have the idea of self pass for clear and intelligible" (p. 251). The problem, Hume argued, is that we cannot trace the idea of self back to any impression that would entail the clear sense of **identity** we think the idea of self conveys. Far from supporting the claim that we endure as essentially the same persons through time, Hume's analysis of experience suggested something different:

> For my part, when I enter most intimately into what I call *myself*, I always stumble on some particular perception or other, of heat or cold, light or shade, love or hatred, pain or pleasure. I never can catch *myself* at any

DAVID HUME 1711–1776

philosophy often tries to get beyond doubt, too. Descartes's method of employing doubt until one locates an indubitable foundation provides a historic example. This attempt fascinated David Hume (1711–1776), the British philosopher we met in Chapter Two, but Descartes's work left him unconvinced. Although Descartes appealed to "experience" in the *Meditations*, Hume thought Descartes relied too much on abstract rational principles and too little on careful empirical observation. As you will become aware, many philosophers claim to be true to experience. But even among empiricists, who hold that sense perception is the sole source of human knowledge, 'experience' is interpreted differently.

time without a perception, and never can observe any thing but the perception. When my perceptions are removed for any time, as by sound sleep, so long am I insensible of *myself*, and may truly be said not to exist. And were all my perceptions removed by death, and could I neither think, nor feel, nor see, nor love, nor hate after the dissolution of my body, I should be entirely annihilated, nor do I conceive what is farther requisite to make me a perfect nonentity. If anyone upon serious and unprejudiced reflection, thinks he had a different notion of *himself*, I must confess that I can reason no longer with him. (P. 252.)

What am I as a self? Hume's answer is: " . . . nothing but a bundle or collection of different perceptions" (p. 252). That answer, however, raises another important question. What leads us to suppose that a particular bundle of perceptions belongs to a person, to me or to you? Hume's explanation indicates that we have two faculties, memory and imagination, each of which plays a part in our mental processes. **Memory** allows us to retain impressions with exactness, although these are now less vivid than the original instance. **Imagination** allows us to formulate, order, and arrange ideas in a variety of ways. The possibilities available to us, as you can recall from Chapter Two, are regulated by three general principles of **association.** Our ideas tend naturally to follow or to be associated with one another when (1) they involve a resemblance, (2) when they are contiguous in time or space, or (3) when they are related in terms of cause and effect. We see women in various countries in various dress, but still they resemble one another so we associate them. We make associations. We see baseball players and baseball diamonds contiguous in time and space so we also associate these. But the relation of ideas by cause and effect may be the most crucial association of all. Hume understands cause and effect to be the constant conjunction of phenomena. We

see steam coming from a factory whistle and hear a sound following, and we assume the steam is the cause of the sound. We have always had the two experiences (sight of steam, hearing sound) together in a temporal sequence.

Hume was disposed to believe that all the complex ideas that originate in our minds involve at least one of these three principles. Where personal identity is concerned, resemblance and the constant conjunction among our experiences are the crucial factors. Memory and imagination link experiences that are similar and closely conjoined. We link together a series of experiences we have had and build these into the notion of a person. We call this our **self,** although we have no direct experience of such a thing but only a series of separate experiences we link together. Therein lies the basis for our sense of personal identity, insubstantial though it may be.

Did Hume's Account Satisfy Him?

If Hume applied his theory of experience consistently to the problem of personal identity, and if he was justified in concluding that philosophers such as Descartes had claimed greater degrees of self-knowledge than they deserved, nonetheless Hume did not rest content with his own position on these matters. In an "Appendix" to his *Treatise of Human Nature,* he expressed some reservations about his discussion of human identity. These are particularly noteworthy because Hume's later work remains largely silent on this topic. In the "Appendix" Hume admitted that his reflections on selfhood had taken him into a labyrinth, although he still felt confident that his analysis of the uncertainty of experience was correct. Ideas are ultimately derived from impressions, but impressions alone are not sufficient to produce the idea of self. Such an idea is the creation of memory and imagination. It is our product, something we manufacture rather than perceive, although it is real enough to us. However, Hume went on to say,

> . . . having thus loosened all our particular perceptions, when I proceed to explain the principle of connection, which binds them together, and makes us attribute to them a real simplicity and identity, I am sensible that my account is very defective, and that nothing but the seeming evidence of the precedent reasonings could have induced me to receive it. (P. 635.)

What perplexed Hume was his explanation of how one particular group of experiences comes to be identified as "mine" and another as "yours." He felt he had not accounted for either the particularity of that division or the strong sense that we have that one of them belongs to me, another to you. In addition, Hume knew that he constantly used personal pronouns, not to mention terms such as mind, imagination, and memory, as though these pointed to more than bundles of perceptions. Indeed, Hume never escaped the implication that there is something behind his impressions, something that feels, thinks, loves, and hates. But we do not actually see this "I" or experience this "self" in sensory impressions. This does not mean that the "I" or "self" does not exist, only that we have no right to think we know the self directly.

Yet, is it true that we lack all experience of ourselves, as Hume asserted? Was Hume as "empirical" in his outlook as he thought? Do we actually begin every time with only a "simple" sense impression? From the outset of our existence, our experience seems complex. Hume's own account of personal identity left him uneasy. As you think about Hume further, consider whether the dissatisfaction expressed in the following selection from the *Treatise of Human Nature* (1739) was perhaps due to the philosopher's sensing that the

question "Can I know my 'self'?" leaves us hidden to ourselves.

There are some philosophers who imagine we are every moment intimately conscious of what we call our *self;* that we feel its existence and its continuance in existence; and are certain, beyond the evidence of a demonstration, both of its perfect identity and simplicity. The strongest sensation, the most violent passion, say they, instead of distracting us from this view, only fix it the more intensely, and make us consider their influence on *self* either by their pain or pleasure. To attempt a further proof of this were to weaken its evidence; since no proof can be derived from any fact of which we are so intimately conscious; nor is there anything of which we can be certain if we doubt of this.

Unluckily all these positive assertions are contrary to that very experience which is pleaded for them; nor have we any idea of *self,* after the manner it is here explained. For, from what impression could this idea be derived? This question it is impossible to answer without a manifest contradiction and absurdity; and yet it is a question which must necessarily be answered, if we would have the idea of self pass for clear and intelligible. It must be some one impression that gives rise to every real idea. But self or person is not any one impression, but that to which our several impressions and ideas are supposed to have a reference. If any impression gives rise to the idea of self, that impression must continue invariably the same, through the whole course of our lives, since self is supposed to exist after that manner. But there is no impression constant and invariable. Pain and pleasure, grief and joy, passions, and sensations succeed each other, and never all exist at the same time. It cannot therefore be from any of these impressions, or from any other, that the idea of self is derived; and consequently there is no such idea.

But further, what must become of all our particular perceptions upon this hypothesis? All these are different, and distinguishable, and separable from each other, and may be separately considered, and may exist separately, and have no need of anything to support their existence. After what manner therefore do they belong to self, and how are they connected with it? For my part, when I enter most intimately into what I call *myself*, I always stumble on some particular perception or other, of heat or cold, light or shade, love or hatred, pain or pleasure. I never can catch *myself* at any time without a perception, and never can observe anything but the perception. When my perceptions are removed for any time, as by sound sleep, so long am I insensible of *myself*, and may truly be said not to exist. And were all my perceptions removed by death, and could I neither think, nor feel, nor see, nor love, nor hate, after the dissolution of my body, I should be entirely annihilated, nor do I conceive what is further requisite to make me a perfect nonentity. If anyone, upon serious and unprejudiced reflection, thinks he has a different notion of *himself*, I must confess I can reason no longer with him. All I can allow him is, that he may be in the right as well as I, and that we are essentially different in this particular. He may, perhaps, perceive something simple and continued, which he calls *himself*, though I am certain there is no such principle in me.

But setting aside some metaphysicians of this kind, I may venture to affirm of the rest of mankind, that they are nothing but a bundle or collection of different perceptions, which succeed each other with an inconceivable rapidity, and are in a perpetual flux and movement. Our eyes cannot turn in their sockets without varying our perceptions. Our thought is still more variable than our sight; and all our other senses and faculties contribute to this change; nor is there any single power of the soul, which remains unalterably the same, perhaps for one moment. The mind is a kind of theater, where several perceptions successively make their appearance; pass, repass, glide away, and mingle in an infinite variety of postures and situations. There is properly no *simplicity* in it at one time, nor *identity* in different, whatever

natural propension we may have to imagine that simplicity and identity. The comparison of the theater must not mislead us. They are the successive perceptions only, that constitute the mind; nor have we the most distant notion of the place where these scenes are represented, or of the materials of which it is composed.

What then gives us so great a propension to ascribe an identity to these successive perceptions, and to suppose ourselves possessed of an invariable and uninterrupted existence through the whole course of our lives? In order to answer this question we must distinguish betwixt personal identity, as it regards our thought or imagination, and as it regards our passions or the concern we take in ourselves. The first is our present subject; and to explain it perfectly we must take the matter pretty deep, and account for that identity, which we attribute to plants and animals, there being a great analogy betwixt it and the identity of a self or person.

We have a distinct idea of an object that remains invariable and uninterrupted through a supposed variation of time; and this idea we call that of *identity* or *sameness*. We have also a distinct idea of several different objects existing in succession, and connected together by a close relation; and this to an accurate view affords as perfect a notion of *diversity* as if there was no manner of relation among the objects. But though these two ideas of identity, and a succession of related objects, be in themselves perfectly distinct, and even contrary, yet it is certain that, in our common way of thinking, they are generally confounded with each other. That action of the imagination, by which we consider the uninterrupted and invariable object, and that by which we reflect on the succession of related objects, are almost the same to the feeling, nor is there much more effort of thought required in the latter case than in the former. The relation facilitates the transition of the mind from one object to another, and renders its passage as smooth as if it contemplated one continued object. This resemblance is the cause of the confusion and mistake, and makes us substitute the notion of identity, instead of that of related objects. However at one instant we may consider the related succession as variable or interrupted, we are sure the next to ascribe to it a perfect identity, and regard it as invariable and uninterrupted. Our propensity to this mistake is so great from the resemblance above mentioned, that we fall into it before we are aware; and though we incessantly correct ourselves by reflection, and return to a more accurate method of thinking, yet we cannot long sustain our philosophy, or take off this bias from the imagination. Our last resource is to yield to it, and boldly assert that these different related objects are in effect the same, however interrupted and variable. In order to justify to ourselves this absurdity, we often feign some new and unintelligible principle that connects the objects together, and prevents their interruption or variation. Thus we feign the continued existence of the perceptions of our senses, to remove the interruption, and run into the notion of a *soul*, and *self*, and *substance*, to disguise the variation. But, we may further observe, that where we do not give rise to such a fiction, our propension to confound identity with relation is so great that we are apt to imagine something unknown and mysterious, connecting the parts, beside their relation; and this I take to be the case with regard to the identity we ascribe to plants and vegetables. And even when this does not take place, we still feel a propensity to confound these ideas, though we are not able fully to satisfy ourselves in that particular, nor find anything invariable and uninterrupted to justify our notion of identity. . . .

As memory alone acquaints us with the continuance and extent of this succession of perceptions, it is to be considered, upon that account chiefly, as the source of personal identity. Had we no memory, we never should have any notion of causation, nor consequently of that chain of causes and effects, which constitute our self or person. But having once acquired this notion of causation from the memory, we can extend the same chain of causes, and consequently the identity of our persons beyond our

memory, and can comprehend times, and circumstances, and actions, which we have entirely forgot, but suppose in general to have existed. For how few of our past actions are there, of which we have any memory? Who can tell me, for instance, what were his thoughts and actions on the first of January 1715, the eleventh of March 1719, and the third of August 1733? Or will he affirm, because he has entirely forgot the incidents of these days, that the present self is not the same person with the self of that time, and by that means overturn all the most established notions of personal identity? In this view, therefore, memory does not so much *produce* as *discover* personal identity, by showing us the relation of cause and effect among our different perceptions. It will be incumbent on those who affirm that memory produces entirely our personal identity, to give a reason why we can thus extend our identity beyond our memory.

The whole of this doctrine leads us to a conclusion, which is of great importance in the present affair, viz. that all the nice and subtle questions concerning personal identity can never possibly be decided, and are to be regarded rather as grammatical than as philosophical difficulties. Identity depends on the relations of ideas; and these relations produce identity, by means of that easy transition they occasion. But as the relations, and the easiness of the transition may diminish by insensible degrees, we have no just standard by which we can decide any dispute concerning the time when they acquire or lose a title to the name of identity. All the disputes concerning the identity of connected objects are merely verbal, except so far as the relation of parts gives rise to some fiction or imaginary principle of union, as we have already observed.

What I have said concerning the first origin and uncertainty of our notion of identity, as applied to the human mind, may be extended with little or no variation to that of *simplicity*. An object, whose different coexistent parts are bound together by a close relation, operates upon the imagination after much the same manner as one perfectly simple and indivisible, and requires not a much greater stretch of thought in order to its conception. From this similarity of operation we attribute a simplicity to it, and feign a principle of union as the support of this simplicity, and the center of all the different parts and qualities of the object. . . .

Upon a more strict review of the section concerning *personal identity*, I find myself involved in such a labyrinth that, I must confess, I neither know how to correct my former opinions, nor how to render them consistent. If this be not a good *general* reason for skepticism, it is at least a sufficient one (if I were not already abundantly supplied) for me to entertain a diffidence and modesty in all my decisions. I shall propose the arguments on both sides, beginning with those that induced me to deny the strict and proper identity and simplicity of a self or thinking being. . . .

When I turn my reflection on *myself*, I never can perceive this *self* without some one or more perceptions; nor can I ever perceive anything but the perceptions. It is the composition of these, therefore, which forms the self.

We can conceive a thinking being to have either many or few perceptions. Suppose the mind to be reduced even below the life of an oyster. Suppose it to have only one perception, as of thirst or hunger. Consider it in that situation. Do you conceive anything but merely that perception? Have you any notion of *self* or *substance*? If not, the addition of other perceptions can never give you that notion.

The annihilation which some people suppose to follow upon death, and which entirely destroys this self, is nothing but an extinction of all particular perceptions; love and hatred, pain and pleasure, thought and sensation. These, therefore, must be the same with self, since the one cannot survive the other.

Is *self* the same with *substance*? If it be, how can that question have place, concerning the substance of self, under a change of substance? If they be distinct, what is the difference betwixt them? For my part, I have a notion of neither, when conceived distinct from particular perceptions.

Philosophers begin to be reconciled to the principle, *that we have no idea of external substance, distinct from the ideas of particular qualities.* This must pave the way for a like principle with regard to the mind, *that we have no notion of it, distinct from the particular perception.* . . .

In short, there are two principles which I cannot render consistent, nor is it in my power to renounce either of them, viz. *that all our distinct perceptions are distinct existences,* and *that the mind never perceives any real connection among distinct existences.* Did our perceptions either inhere in something simple and individual, or did the mind perceive some real connection among them, there would be no difficulty in the case. For my part, I must plead the privilege of a skeptic, and confess that this difficulty is too hard for my understanding. I pretend not, however, to pronounce it absolutely insuperable. Others, perhaps, or myself, upon more mature reflections, may discover some hypothesis that will reconcile those contradictions. (Pp. 251–263, 635–636.)

Adam Smith and Self-Interest

One of David Hume's close friends was Adam Smith (1723–1790), a philosopher best known as the father of capitalist economic theory. Smith was not introspective like Descartes, nor was he greatly perplexed about the problem of human identity that haunted Hume. In his major work, *An Inquiry into the Nature and Causes of the Wealth of Nations* (1776), Smith took up the theme that "a man must always live by his work." He explored our question "Who am I?" by examining human behavior in socioeconomic situations. Smith was less concerned about the individual who thinks about himself or herself in isolation and more

A D A M   S M I T H   1723–1790

about "a certain propensity in human nature . . . to truck, barter, and exchange one thing for another."[3] Who am I? In Smith's view, the answer to that question depends on the work I do, the economic system in which my life unfolds, and the fact that "every man is rich or poor according to the degree in which he can afford to enjoy the necessaries, conveniences, and amusements of human life" (1:47).

The Natural Order of Things

In *The Theory of Moral Sentiments* (1759), which preceded *The Wealth of Nations*, Smith argued that human nature is endowed by God, the "Author of Nature," with a natural inclination to love. It seemed clear to Smith that although human conduct involves a high degree of self-love or **self-interest,** it also may be motivated by a **sympathy** for others. This sympathy can neither be reduced to self-interest nor explained completely in terms of its usefulness. In short, concern for others is as fundamental a feature of human existence as a concern for oneself. But these two inclinations do not always harmonize; people usually care more about their own immediate concerns than about the interests of others. Hence, besides counting on the natural inclination of sympathy and the power of moral philosophy to balance the scales, we need legal sanctions and governmental institutions to regulate human conduct.

Smith recognized that societies change and may in any event take many forms. As he observed basic patterns of societal development, he decided that the structure of a society changes as its mode of subsistence does. Smith believed that the impetus for change stemmed from the human striving to improve material conditions. Hence, human history included four states of development. Beginning with social life oriented around hunting, human societies evolved into pasturing communities, then into agricultural groups, and finally into economic systems based on industrial manufacturing and monetary exchange. The latest stage brought into existence laborers who worked for a wage and owners of large stocks of capital. These social roles and their corresponding institutions were new elements in human history, and to a significant extent, they were not the consequences of conscious human planning. Their appearance was welcome nonetheless, because it signaled progress. As Adam Smith saw things, history moved forward under the **"invisible hand"** of the forces of supply and demand in the market. Human life would be enhanced if our conduct conformed to "the natural order of things" as ordained by God and as revealed through the right use of reason.

The Division of Labor

Repeatedly Smith referred to what struck him as "natural." Nothing is more so, he argued, than the type of labor found in an industrial, modernized economy.

> The greatest improvement in the productive powers of labor, and the greater part of the skill, dexterity, and judgment with which it is anywhere directed, or applied, seem to have been the effects of the division of labor. (1:13.)

This **division of labor** is possible just to the extent that opportunities for economic exchange exist. It enables one person to devote energy in a specialized direction with the confidence that such effort will provide for subsistence and will perhaps even yield prosperity. Indeed, if markets are large and open, the division of labor can be extended to take full advantage of humanity's diverse talent. Such effort, promised Smith, will enlarge the wealth of nations.

In the work of sustaining a human community, if at first we divide up our labor—you grow food, he builds houses, and I make tools—we can simply trade the fruits of our individual labors. However, as society grows and more and more people are involved, we need other less cumbersome methods for exchange. Then money develops as a substitute for the actual exchange of goods. As labor becomes specialized, admitted Smith, the produce of an individual's own labor can supply but a very small part of the worker's wants. Far from being unfortunate, however, Smith looked on this consequence as a great step forward. Because as it is divided and specialized, labor creates a surplus production, which can be traded. This activity is facilitated still further when money replaces barter as a means of exchange. Mutual benefit results because self-interest in the market produces competition, which regulates supply to fit demand and tends thereby to make favorable prices for consumers. At least these things will happen, Smith claimed, if the market is allowed to function freely in its natural ways. **Laissez-faire** was Smith's plea: let a market economy operate without artificial props or restraints. Then the benignly lawful regularities of nature, which encompass economic life, will advance human progress. Adam Smith knew what it means to be a self in such a system.

Human Beings Need Each Other

No person can live without help from others. As the division of labor increases, Smith went on to say, our dependence on one another increases. But how can we expect to obtain all the help we need? Although Smith believed that human beings have a natural inclination to be sympathetic, he also had observed that it was unreasonable to expect assistance from the **benevolence** of others. We are far more likely to obtain what we need or want if we can appeal to the self-love in others and make this work for us. As Smith aptly put the point, "It is not from the benevolence of the butcher, the brewer, or the baker, that we expect our dinner, but from their regard to their own interest" (1:26–27). In brief, no one can reasonably expect something for nothing, at least not very often. Butcher, brewer, and baker produce their goods because they hope to obtain what they need or want by providing things others must have to live, or may crave if subsistence does not require them. Likewise, one can count on obtaining life's necessities and advantages only if one has something of value to offer in return.

Our ability to obtain the necessities and advantages of life depends on the wealth we possess. Smith thought that wealth could be measured in accordance with the amount of labor that a person could command or afford to purchase. "Labor," he wrote, "is the real measure of the exchangeable value of all commodities" (1:47). He noted, however, that this labor theory of self-value has problems. Not only is it complicated to compare different quantities and qualities of labor, but the workings of the market make such considerations secondary to the quantity of another good or the amount of money one can obtain in exchange for the goods one has produced. Further complications intrude when we realize that for Smith labor itself becomes a **commodity**. Most people have no products to sell directly; they work in an industrial system of mass production. The resulting products are owned by those who have put up the capital to buy raw materials and the equipment needed to manufacture the goods. Labor is simply an additional item the owners must purchase. For most persons, who they are will be determined by the price they can fetch for the labor they have to sell.

Equal work deserves equal pay, but as Smith explains, there are many kinds of labor, some deserving better pay than others. The proper variations, he thought, are determined by the agreeableness or disagreeableness of the labor, the ease and cost of learning the skills involved, the constancy of employment one can expect, the degree of trust committed to a worker, and the amount of risk involved in pursuing a particular trade. Ease and the cost of learning the skills involved in a job were the most important of these factors for Smith:

> When any expensive machine is erected, the extraordinary work to be performed by it before it is worn out, it must be expected, will replace the capital laid out upon it, with at least the ordinary profits. A man educated at the expense of much labor and time to any of those employments which require extraordinary dexterity and skill may be compared to one of those expensive machines. (1:118.)

Smith argued that a man so trained should be paid more to compensate for the time and expense required to learn the skill. Indeed, hardly anyone could be lured into learning such a trade unless the effort were to be well repaid. But more intriguing for us as we consider the question, "Can I know my 'self'?" is comparison of a human life to that of a machine. If Smith is correct in saying that we need each other because we have to work to live, his economic interpretation of self-interest also implies that, in working to live, we run the risk of distorting our image of who we are. On the one hand, Smith has argued for human **value** by saying that capital is just as necessary to purchase a worker's training as to purchase the plant itself. But on the other hand, there is an unmistakable implication that human beings are like commodities we buy and treat as investments. The comparison of human value to the worth of machines may have negative implications when we ask "Who am I?" or "What does it mean to be a 'self'?"

Beyond Economics?

Descartes claimed certainty about his own identity only when he had stripped himself of his social relationships and defined his identity as a thinking thing. Adam Smith countered that approach with an economic theory that began with human beings in social relationships and then described human existence in terms of labor and self-interest. Smith's perspective emphasizes simple facts about social organization that are practically undeniable; it has a power that Descartes's theory cannot touch. Descartes, however, did suggest that our personal identity cannot easily be equated with social roles and economic functions. While Smith does not make that equation either, his theory contains the seeds for such an outlook.

Hence, if David Hume's skepticism is aptly applied to Descartes, it may also be in order where the results of Smith's economic philosophy are concerned. That is, Smith takes as obvious the use of economic roles as a basis for defining human nature, just as Descartes took the existence of the self for granted. Just as Hume proved that our direct impressions of the self were less securely based than Descartes thought, so we may apply a little skepticism to the now common assumption that economic roles obviously define the man or the woman.

The wealth of nations (and by extension, of individual selves) would grow, Smith thought, if economic practices were rationalized. Production could be rendered more efficient through specialization. Progress would be assisted by expanded trade in enlarged markets, industrialized production, and increased mobility. If only the natural course of events were allowed to unfold freely, self-interest—tempered by infusions of human sympathy—would work in conjunction with the guidance of an "invisible hand" to assure progress.

Smith's *Theory of Moral Sentiments* took sympathy to be at the core of human nature, but *The Wealth of Nations* makes one wonder about that claim. The latter describes a world of buying and selling, profit and loss, supply and demand. There human sympathy for others is even less evident than the invisible hand of the marketplace. Cost-effectiveness, getting the most for the least, will tend to govern calculations in a domain in which wealth means power, whereupon productivity may take precedence over people. Adam Smith was correct: a person must have food to eat, and food is earned by sweat from somebody's brow. Each of us as a self is known in part by what the individual produces and by what he or she does in the marketplace. But the marketplace, even Smith's free and naturally ordered one, can obscure us from each other if it only partly reveals who we are. Figuratively if not literally, we buy and sell not only products but each other. If we trade our selves as commodities, it is not difficult to lose sight of our humanity. To the

extent that we fail to keep our other human traits in view, we cannot fully appreciate who we are. We are indeed beings who "truck, barter, and exchange," but that only partially answers the question "Who am I?" As you consider more of Smith's outlook in the following excerpt from *An Inquiry into the Nature and Causes of the Wealth of Nations*, ask whether self-understanding needs to move beyond economics.

This division of labor, from which so many advantages are derived, is not originally the effect of any human wisdom, which foresees and intends that general opulence to which it gives occasion. It is the necessary, though very slow and gradual, consequence of a certain propensity in human nature which has in view no such extensive utility; the propensity to truck, barter, and exchange one thing for another.

Whether this propensity be one of those original principles in human nature, of which no further account can be given; or whether, as seems more probable, it be the necessary consequence of the faculties of reason and speech, it belongs not to our present subject to inquire. It is common to all men, and to be found in no other race of animals, which seem to know neither this nor any other species of contracts. . . . In civilized society [man] stands at all times in need of the cooperation and assistance of great multitudes, while his whole life is scarce sufficient to gain the friendship of a few persons. In almost every other race of animals each individual, when it is grown up to maturity, is entirely independent, and in its natural state has occasion for the assistance of no other living creature. But man has almost constant occasion for the help of his brethren, and it is in vain for him to expect it from their benevolence only. He will be more likely to prevail if he can interest their self-love in his favor, and show them that it is for their own advantage to do for him what he requires of them. Whoever offers to another a bargain of any kind, proposes to do this. Give me that which I want, and you shall have this which you want, is the meaning of every such offer; and it is in this manner that we obtain from one another the far greater part of those good offices which we stand in need of. It is not from the benevolence of the butcher, the brewer, or the baker, that we expect our dinner, but from their regard to their own interest. We address ourselves, not to their humanity but to their self-love, and never talk to them of our own necessities but of their advantages. Nobody but a beggar chooses to depend chiefly upon the benevolence of his fellow-citizens. Even a beggar does not depend upon it entirely. . . . (1:25–27.)

Every individual is continually exerting himself to find out the most advantageous employment for whatever capital he can command. It is his own advantage, indeed, and not that of the society, which he has in view. But the study of his own advantage naturally, or rather necessarily leads him to prefer that employment which is most advantageous to the society. . . .

Every individual who employs his capital in the support of domestic industry, necessarily endeavors so to direct that industry that its produce may be of the greatest possible value.

The produce of industry is what it adds to the subject or materials upon which it is employed. In proportion as the value of this produce is great or small, so will likewise be the profits of the employer. But it is only for the sake of profit that any man employs a capital in the support of industry; and he will always, therefore, endeavor to employ it in the support of that industry of which the produce is likely to be of the greatest value, or to exchange for the greatest quantity either of money or of other goods.

But the annual revenue of every society is always precisely equal to the exchangeable value of the whole annual produce of its industry, or rather is precisely the same thing with that exchangeable value. As every individual, therefore, endeavors as much as he can both to employ his capital in the support of domestic industry, and so to direct that industry that its produce may be of the greatest value; every individual necessarily labors to render the annual revenue of the society as great as he can. He generally, indeed, neither intends to promote the public interest, nor knows how much he is promoting it. By preferring the support of domestic to that of foreign industry, he intends only his own security; and by directing that industry in such a manner as its produce may be of the greatest value, he intends only his own gain, and he is in this, as in many other cases, led by an invisible hand to promote an end which was no part of his intention. Nor is it always the worse for the society that it was no part of it. By pursuing his own interest he frequently promotes that of the society more effectually than when he really intends to promote it. I have never known much good done by those who affected to trade for the public good. It is an affectation, indeed, not very common among merchants, and very few words need be employed in dissuading them from it. (1:454–56.)

Sigmund Freud and the Unconscious

Thus far we have discussed three very different views about our knowledge of the self, what the self is like, and how certain we can be about it. Descartes raised radical doubts but found certainty in the self. Hume questioned the basis for Descartes's certainty but agreed that we must make practical decisions about the self and ought not to let doubt overwhelm us. Adam Smith brought social and economic considerations to the fore as he explored human nature. A fourth thinker, the Austrian Sigmund Freud (1856–1939), championed the idea of the hidden nature of the self. The idea that a part of our thinking process is unconscious was neither new nor Freud's invention. It is just that he gave

SIGMUND FREUD   1856–1939

have not turned out as Freud hoped is another matter.

Freud belongs in any investigation of the question "Can I know my 'self'?" because he made it impossible to investigate our thought process without considering the unconscious. Philosophers, particularly those who consider themselves to be "rationalists," have on the whole preferred to deal only with the conscious mind as they explore self-knowledge. Should it turn out that a significant part—Freud would say the most important part—of thought is determined by the unconscious, the philosopher's job would become more difficult. In fact, any hope to establish a base of certainty about our conscious thought process would be doomed. Yet when we ask "Who am I?", we must consider what portion of our self might lie beyond our immediate observation.

Freud's Once-in-a-Lifetime Discovery

When Freud started his career in medicine, he was interested in seemingly unsolvable cases of mental illness. At first he approached this task through the specialty of neurology, but he found research into the physiology of the brain to be a dead end. He achieved a certain success with hypnosis, but then decided that its "cures" were too temporary. It was Freud's analysis of dreams that set him on the path to important formulations and to fame. Freud became fascinated by his patients' reported dreams, which were inexplicable by any standard applications of thought or memory. (Philosophers, of course, have not usually dealt much with dreams.) Freud practiced in the matrix of a very conservative society, the Vienna of the nineteenth and early twentieth century, and the theories he developed about the sexual basis for most mental problems were difficult for his Victorian contemporaries to accept. Briefly, however, Freud decided that dreams contained coded messages on matters either

it new prominence and a scientific foundation in medical psychiatry. In fact, as the founder of modern **psychoanalysis,** Freud revolutionized the treatment of the mentally ill by his investigation into the **unconscious.** A medical doctor, Freud was not a professionally trained philosopher. On the contrary, he was quite suspicious of philosophy, for he wanted to found a new science and feared that philosophy was too theoretical and subject to continuous disagreement. Freud hoped that physicians all over the world would accept his hypothesis of the importance of the unconscious and establish it as scientific by means of a compilation of case studies of mental illness. That things

taboo in society or too painful for the person to handle. What, he asked himself, censors these messages and translates them into dream symbolism?

Freud's theory about the process of dream construction implied that much of importance in our thought goes on out of our consciousness. Our conscious thought process offers us only a partial story; mechanisms other than cogitation determine what we are aware of on a conscious level. The unconscious part of thought often controls, but how are we to know what this unconscious is? Prescientific man acknowledged that dreams contained important interpretive material, Freud pointed out; but the age of scientific analysis had considered dream interpretation to be superstition. Now, Freud asserted, dreams should once again be at the center of our search for understanding. "One day," he tells us, "I discovered to my great astonishment that the view of dreams which came nearest to the truth was not the medical but the popular one, half-involved though it still was in superstition."[4]

If we can understand how dreams are formed, we may learn what lies in the unconscious. What set Freud apart from the conscious rationalist was his belief that you cannot achieve understanding of dreams by a direct frontal attack. Instead, he developed his method of **"free association,"** in which the patient reports whatever comes to mind in connection with a dream. Gradually, relationships appear that were not visible in the original dream. Freud postulated that the dream itself was only the conscious end-product of a much more complicated process going on behind the scenes. "I was led," he reports, "to regard the dream as a sort of *substitute* for the thought process, full of meaning and emotion" (p. 26). Much is compressed or condensed into the small scope of the dream, and it is this latent content of the dream that we need to uncover. Behind it Freud located a "significant experience,"

one now blocked from conscious memory. When in the dream process of "displacement" we insert substitutes for facets of remembered experience, we expose ourselves to material that is too painful for us to think about consciously. For example, if I dream of encountering a strange figure on the ski slopes, I may, with the assistance of a psychoanalyst, come to realize that the dream has changed the setting and participants of a simple yet painful childhood experience that was connected, not to skiing, but to a harsh confrontation with my father.

Freud has suggested that dreams are formed by the same process that governs a great deal of thought. If so, what we need to gain is not knowledge of more conscious thought but an understanding of what is going on *behind* the scenes. In sleep, our censor (the superego) relaxes its grip, but only in an indirect or disguised way. Dreams distort in order to disguise what otherwise would be too disagreeable to contemplate. We fulfill our wishes in dreams in ways we could not do while waking. But if we are to understand what dreams are telling us about the self, we must find a way to decode them.

How Do We Gain Knowledge of Unseen Forces?

Freud asks himself: What operates in this indirect fashion to construct dreams? To describe what seems to operate behind conscious activity, Freud postulated his theory of the unconscious. In a series of lectures given at the University of Vienna from 1915 to 1917, Freud tried to explain to skeptical medical students all that he had discovered about the operation of the unconscious and the determinative part it plays in our conscious thought and action. He formulated his ideas about a method of treatment called "psychoanalysis" in which the patient talks and the analyst looks for clues, symbols of what is hidden in the patient's unconscious.

This analytic technique is termed *free association*. Freud wanted medical doctors to see psychoanalysis not as a mysterious philosophy, but as " . . . a method of medical treatment for those suffering from nervous disorders."[5] This sounds far removed from philosophy, but many philosophers have thought of philosophy as a way to deal with human problems, too. However, medical training makes doctors accustomed to use their physical senses. Thus, much about medical practice makes the doctor suspicious of psychoanalysis, which deals not only with symptoms that cannot be directly seen, touched, smelled, or heard but also with intangibles like unconscious thought. Psychoanalysis does not use any physical treatment. "In psychoanalysis," Freud reports, "nothing happens but an exchange of words between the patient and the physician" (p. 21).

In primitive societies words were often thought to possess special powers. Words retain this ancient magical power for Freud, and "the dialogue which constitutes the analysis will admit of no audience; the process cannot be demonstrated" (p. 22). Those who count on empirical confirmation will be frustrated. Furthermore, psychoanalysis is an individual treatment, involving only patient and doctor. It is learned through the study of one's own personality.

> . . . Two tenets of psychoanalysis . . . offend the whole world and excite its resentment; the one conflicts with the intellectual, the other with moral and aesthetic prejudices. . . . The first of these displeasing propositions . . . is this: that mental processes are essentially unconscious. . . . [The second] . . . consists in the assertion that impulses, which can only be described as sexual . . . play a particularly large part, never before sufficiently appreciated, in the causation of nervous and mental disorders. (Pp. 25–27.)

Since the time Freud first wrote, we have come to accept his notions as almost commonplace. But they remain revolutionary insofar as they tell us how we can learn about our hidden self. We tend to look for big items in our thought, for instance; but Freud looked to little slips in speech to find evidence about the hidden nature of thought. "So let us not undervalue small signs," he says (p. 31). This makes the pursuit of knowledge about the self a genuinely tricky business. If the errors we make in speech turn out to tell us more than some of our conscious assertions, and to be more important, we know that the important part of our thought, contrary to what we might like to believe, goes on behind the scenes. The errors we make demonstrate that conscious thought is a compromise, forced on us because we cannot say directly all that we would like to. Our internal censor will not permit it. But some fragments of forbidden thoughts slip by and may reveal secrets of the mind that allow the analyst to uncover for us "what we really think."

Interpretation, Freud tells us, means discovering a hidden meaning. But he intends to use this technique to turn an esoteric art into a modern science. How can the analyst uncover the knowledge the patient has hidden beneath the surface of his mind and does not even know he possesses? The analyst must carefully reconstruct what lies in the unconscious by piecing together small bits of evidence supplied unwittingly by slips of the tongue and by dreams. Then a scheme must be devised to decode dreams that reveal the message the unconscious mind is trying to slip by its censor. The psychoanalyst must look for every little sign and symbol and question the patient until some slim connection is discovered that assists them in recovering the hidden story from the unconscious. Freud did not want this approach to rest on a speculative system of ideas; he wanted a new scientific method to take dream interpretation out of the hands of mystics and establish it as modern science.

How New Knowledge Will Release Us from Old Problems

"The day will come," Freud boldly asserted, "when every little piece of knowledge will be converted into power, and into therapeutic power" (p. 267). He started with strange, hidden facts about the workings of the mind, and yet he hoped to build an indisputable method of understanding the self fully. Part of his technique rested on the assumption that everything has meaning, that no small fact is without significance. There are no accidents, ultimately, so it is our task to find out what these supposed bits and pieces "really mean." The mind works in strange ways, but all this can be sorted out and deciphered. However, everything is connected to the detailed biography of the individual, so that gaining knowledge is a slow, laborious task in which nothing can be taken for granted. The behind-the-scenes activity of the unconscious remains our basic postulate. "The fact that it is possible to find meaning in neurotic symptoms by means of analytic interpretation is an irrefutable proof of the existence . . . of unconscious mental processes" (p. 290).

The problem with philosophers who deal only with the way the conscious mind works, Freud tells us, is that "their psychology of consciousness is incapable of solving the problems of dreams and hypnosis."[6] Thus, if we want to know how the mind works we learn more from its unconscious and hidden activity than from its waking, simple, rational operation. We need to refer to the unseen mechanism of the mind when we encounter odd facts that are not easily explainable. We have discovered a coherent organizing principle for mental processes, which Freud calls the **ego**. But the ego is a hindrance to our understanding in the sense that it resists our intrusions to seek for thoughts, repressed from consciousness, which still disturb us. Consciousness is only the surface of our mental apparatus and should not be taken as ultimate. In Freud's terms, the **id** is also one of the self's important parts; it represents all those drives and desires that are hidden from our view.

Freud's id represents our passions, so that in his view our rational, conscious thought is much influenced if not determined by passion. And there is yet another part to the mind, which Freud labels the **superego**. This creates our ideal images, often instilled by early childhood training. Thinking simply cannot be straightforward. Emotion (id) and ideals (superego) play a certain role. We must look beyond reason to discover the origins of thought and what shapes it. If so, psychology becomes the basis for philosophical understanding, although in an earlier era it was part of philosophy.

The Anatomy of Knowing

For Freud, the id "contains everything that is inherited . . . above all . . . the instincts. . . . One portion of the id has undergone a special development . . . which henceforth acts as an intermediary between the id and the external world. This region of our mental life had been given the name of *ego*. . . . The ego pursues pleasure and seeks to avoid unpleasure. . . . The long period of childhood . . . forms within [the] ego a special agency in which [the] parental influence is prolonged. It has received the name of *superego*."[7]

The id seeks satisfaction of its desires, but the function of the superego is to limit them. Thus, the dynamics of thought develop as a struggle between these two forces, the ego and the id. In this struggle, some desires are repressed, and this sets up the source of our trouble. The id is simple raw desire; the ego is the constructed image of the self, but the superego is that controlling censor, the ethical and inhibiting director, that lets the id know what it can and cannot express directly.

"We assume," says Freud, "that in mental life some kind of energy is at work" (p. 44). We cannot know how the mind works until we chart the course of this energy. Unfortunately, however, the laws of the unconscious are not the same as the laws of the conscious mind. "The governing laws of logic have no sway in the unconscious; it might be called the Kingdom of the Illogical" (p. 53). Logic, then, is confined to the surface of the mind and misses the region where our conscious thoughts are made. Our selves are only partly logical and rational. Freud tells us that "the data of conscious self-perception . . . have proved themselves in every respect inadequate to fathom the profusion and complexity of the processes of the mind" (pp. 104–5).

Understanding Thinking as the Solution to a Mystery

Freud has described how we think in a manner as complex as it is fascinating. To him, understanding how the self operates is like solving a riddle. As a medical doctor, Freud was sure he had left philosophy and religion behind by discovering that unseen determinant of thought which can now be brought to light once and for all. But despite all the accomplishments of modern psychiatry, this has not quite proved to be the case. However, that is not our primary concern in studying Freud. Our question concerns the unconscious and its determining role in how we understand ourselves. Regardless of whether these forces work as Freud outlined them, if these unseen forces exist in any form and if they operate in ways different from conscious thought, we must somehow make

the unknown become known before we learn much of importance about the self.

Freud offers us one theory: the development of and the ongoing clash between the id, the ego, and the superego. Freud pieced together this information by solving (he thought) the puzzle of how dreams are formed and what their symbolic messages mean to say. He became convinced he knew how we think and why. The problem is whether the unconscious operations become clearly revealed only if we accept Freud's theory to start with. He was certain we would soon all come to endorse one theory (his) and thus put speculation and uncertainty behind us. But if different explanations are possible, the hidden processes in thought may remain as mysterious as they always have been. If what we need to know about how we think is not easily visible for us to see and agree upon, our theories about the unseen parts of the mind remain by definition at least partly speculative and thus subject to disagreement. Freud's *General Introduction* and *New Introductory Lectures*, selections from which follow, were intended for the layperson, but his explorations raise questions as well as answers.

I do not know what knowledge any of you may already have of psychoanalysis, either from reading or from hearsay. But having regard to the title of my lectures—Introductory Lectures on Psychoanalysis—I am bound to proceed as though you knew nothing of the subject and needed instruction, even in its first elements.

One thing, at least, I may presuppose that you know—namely, that psychoanalysis is a method of medical treatment for those suffering from nervous disorders; and I can give you at once an illustration of the way in which psychoanalytic procedure differs from, and often even reverses, what is customary in other branches of medicine. Usually, when we introduce a patient to a new form of treatment we minimize its difficulties and give him confident assurances of its success. This is, in my opinion, perfectly justifiable, for we thereby increase the probability of success. But when we undertake to treat a neurotic psychoanalytically we proceed otherwise. We explain to him the difficulties of the method, its long duration, the trials and sacrifices which will be required of him; and, as to the result, we tell him that we can make no definite promises, that success depends upon his endeavors, upon his understanding, his adaptability, and his perseverance. We have, of course, good reasons, into which you will perhaps gain some insight later on, for adopting this apparently perverse attitude. . . .

First of all, there is the problem of the teaching and exposition of the subject. In your medical studies you have been accustomed to use your eyes. You see the anatomical specimen, the precipitate of the chemical reaction, the contraction of the muscle as the result of the stimulation of its nerves. Later you come into contact with the patients; you learn the symptoms of disease by the evidence of your senses; the results of pathological processes can be demonstrated to you, and in many cases even the exciting cause of them in an isolated form. On the surgical side you are witnesses of the measures by which the patient is helped, and are permitted to attempt them yourselves. Even in psychiatry, demonstration of patients, of their altered expression, speech, and behavior, yields a series of observations which leave a deep impression on your minds. Thus a teacher of medicine acts for the most part as an exponent and guide, leading you as it were through a museum, while you gain in this way a direct relationship to what is displayed to you and believe yourselves to have been convinced by your own experience of the existence of the new facts.

But in psychoanalysis, unfortunately, all this is different. In psychoanalytic treatment nothing happens but an exchange of words between the patient and the physician. The patient talks, tells of his past experiences and present impressions, complains, and expresses his wishes and his emotions. The physician listens, attempts to direct the patient's thought-processes, reminds him, forces his attention in certain directions, gives him explanations, and observes the reactions of understanding or denial thus evoked. The patient's unenlightened relatives—people of a kind to be impressed only by something visible and tangible, preferably by the sort of 'action' that may be seen at a cinema—never omit to express their doubts of how "mere talk can possibly cure anybody." Their reasoning is of course as illogical as it is inconsistent. For they are the same people who are always convinced that the sufferings of neurotics are purely "in their own imagination." Words and magic were in the beginning one and the same thing, and even today words retain much of their magical power. By words one of us can give to another the greatest happiness or bring about utter despair; by words the teacher imparts his knowledge to the student; by words the orator sweeps his audience with him and determines its judgments and decisions. Words call forth emotions and are universally the means by which we influence our fellow-creatures. Therefore let us not despise the use of words in psychotherapy and let us be content if we may overhear the words which pass between the analyst and the patient.

But even that is impossible. The dialogue which constitutes the analysis will admit of no audience; the process cannot be demonstrated. One could, of course, exhibit a neurasthenic or hysterical patient to students at a psychiatric lecture. He would relate his case and his symptoms, but nothing more. He will make the communications necessary to the analysis only under the conditions of a special affective relationship to the physician; in the presence of a single person to whom he was indifferent he would become mute. For these communications relate to all his most private thoughts and feelings, all that which as a socially independent person he must hide from others, all that which, being foreign to his own conception of himself, he tries to conceal even from himself.

It is impossible, therefore, for you to be actually present during a psychoanalytic treatment; you can only be told about it, and can learn psychoanalysis, in the strictest sense of the word, only by hearsay. This tuition at second hand, so to say, puts you in a very unusual and difficult position as regards forming your own judgment on the subject, which will therefore largely depend on the reliance you can place on your informant.[8]

With regard to the two alternatives—that the ego and the superego may themselves be unconscious, or that they may merely give rise to unconscious effects—we have for good reasons decided in favor of the former. Certainly, large portions of the ego and superego can remain unconscious, are, in fact, normally unconscious. That means to say that the individual knows nothing of their contents and that it requires an expenditure of effort to make him conscious of them. It is true, then, that ego and conscious, repressed and unconscious do not coincide. We are forced fundamentally to revise our attitude towards the problem of conscious and unconscious. At first we might be inclined to think very much less of the importance of consciousness as a criterion, since it has proved so untrustworthy. But if we did so, we should be wrong. It is the same with life: it is not worth much, but it is all that we have. Without the light shed by the quality of consciousness we should be lost in the darkness of depth-psychology. Nevertheless we must try to orientate ourselves anew.

What is meant by "conscious," we need not discuss; it is beyond all doubt. The oldest and best meaning of the word "unconscious" is the descriptive one; we call "unconscious" any mental process the existence of which we are obliged to assume—because, for instance, we infer it in some way from its effects—but of which we are not directly aware. We have the same relation to that mental process as we have to a

mental process in another person, except that it belongs to ourselves. If we want to be more accurate, we should modify the statement by saying that we call a process "unconscious" when we have to assume that it was active *at a certain time*, although *at that time* we knew nothing about it. This restriction reminds us that most conscious processes are conscious only for a short period; quite soon they become *latent*, though they can easily become conscious again. We could also say that they had become unconscious, if we were certain that they were still something mental when they were in the latent condition. So far we should have learnt nothing, and not even have earned the right to introduce the notion of the unconscious into psychology. But now we come across a new fact which we can already observe in the case of errors. We find that, in order to explain a slip of the tongue, for instance, we are obliged to assume that an intention to say some particular thing had formed itself in the mind of the person who made the slip. We can infer it with certainty from the occurrence of the speech-disturbance, but it was not able to obtain expression; it was, that is to say, unconscious. If we subsequently bring the intention to the speaker's notice, he may recognize it as a familiar one, in which case it was only temporarily unconscious, or he may repudiate it as foreign to him, in which case it was permanently unconscious. Such an observation as this justifies us in also regarding what we have called "latent" as something "unconscious." The consideration of these dynamic relations puts us in a position to distinguish two kinds of unconscious: one which is transformed into conscious material easily and under conditions which frequently arise, and another in the case of which such a transformation is difficult, can only come about with a considerable expenditure of energy, or may never occur at all. In order to avoid any ambiguity as to whether we are referring to the one or the other unconscious, whether we are using the word in the descriptive or dynamic sense, we make use of a legitimate and simple expedient. We call the unconscious which is only latent, and so can easily become conscious, the "preconscious," and keep the name "unconscious" for the other. We have now three terms, "conscious," "preconscious," and "unconscious," to serve our purposes in describing mental phenomena. Once again, from a purely descriptive point of view, the "preconscious" is also unconscious, but we do not give it that name, except when we are speaking loosely, or when we have to defend in general the existence of unconscious processes in mental life.[9]

MARTIN BUBER 1878–1965

Martin Buber and Transcending the Self

Many thinkers have contributed to the recent rise of the general public's interest in Jewish thought, but few are better known than Martin Buber (1878–1965). For many years he taught in German universities, but after Hitler came to power, he emigrated to Palestine, and continued his scholarly career at the Hebrew University. The work that did the most to bring Buber to popular attention was *I and Thou* (1923). Written in a poetic style and drawing on insights from Jewish mysticism, the book is quite different from the analytical approach that has characterized much philosophy in the twentieth century. As we seek answers for the questions that perplex us, we ought to be careful not to cut off any approach that might prove helpful. Whether we come to agree with Buber or not, exploring his suggestions casts traditional philosophy into relief against an exceptional background as we continue to investigate "Can I know my 'self'?"

You Are Not Alone

Descartes focused intently on the individual self in answering the question "Who am I?" By analyzing his own thoughts, he assumed

he could come to a certain knowledge of the essential self. But Buber was convinced that a purely rational, analytic approach could not provide satisfactory knowledge of the self and that no individual could be understood alone. He wanted us to focus on our attitude toward other human beings, although for Buber the primary person we face is God. Buber treats God as a self not unlike ourselves. He wants to show us that to do so tells us something significant about human nature, rather than to treat persons as mere commodities as Adam Smith did. Buber argued that any personal relationship is subjective, even where God is concerned. When we confront another subject, we become different from the self that deals with animals or inanimate objects. Although much modern philosophy had consciously tried to separate itself from religion, Buber thought that because in confronting God we learn more than we do from human creatures, the divine dimension was crucial. This is true because God may only be addressed, not expressed.

Buber is convinced that such a mystical relationship can tell us more about who we are than any rational discourse could. For one thing, confronting God is a present task each of us must engage in, not a matter of historical knowledge, which we can dismiss. It must be dealt with now. Since it requires a meeting of persons, we cannot deal with it objectively, as we would if it were objects that confronted us. This view poses a challenge to philosophy. Is there, we are forced to ask, something either inappropriate or distorting in a rational or impersonal approach to our question? Must philosophy go "beyond rationalism" (as well as economics) in order to reveal our identity? Perhaps certain essential features in human nature never come to light until we explore all sides of our nature. In Buber's case the core of human nature comes to light in the religious dimension.

Dialogue: The Context for Self-Understanding

Martin Buber has a simple explanation of why Descartes's attempt to understand the self may not succeed for the rest of us: the French philosopher tried to do it alone. Buber argues that the true self is never found alone. "I" is not the primary word, only "the combination **I–Thou**."[10] Not "I–It," though we relate to objects too, but "I–Thou is the crucial relationship." "For the I of the primary word I–Thou is a different I than that of the primary word I–It" (p. 3). Buber challenges us to consider how the self will appear different in different **contexts.** It is entirely possible that a Descartes might come to find out something about the self by individual meditation, but a suspicion will haunt any certainty he claimed. The self has other contexts, and it might appear quite different in another light. Can we claim to know the answer to the question "Who am I?" until we have explored every possible relationship the self might come into?

Buber suggests that this task includes God, which involves us in added difficulties, and that the self is never understood until it looks beyond itself, or at least until it overcomes individual isolation. Dialogue, whether with God or another human, forces us to go outside ourselves, and we become vulnerable. Painful and uncertain as this can be, the self is not seen in full if we miss this experience. And Buber is convinced that we cannot avoid God in our experience of any other person. "In each Thou we address the eternal Thou" (p. 60).

You Cannot Be a Self Alone

"Through the Thou a man becomes I," Buber argues (p. 28). If this is so, it's no wonder those who analyze the individual as he or she exists alone continually run into problems. The self simply cannot exist alone; it becomes; and this happens only in the relationship of dialogue. We face a fundamental issue: Is the self something that always exists, something that can be located and its essence stated? If Buber is right, the self never is; it only becomes. It does not exist as essentially the same thing from its beginning. Often we treat persons as if they were objects in order to be able to organize them. The drill sergeant shouts orders to his company. He cannot consider individuals when he is trying to teach military drills. But in pursuing this practical necessity, we misunderstand what a self is if we do not accept the risk of introducing chaos by treating the objects we try to organize as individual persons. Thus when the individual soldier faints because he is ill, the sergeant must give up shouting orders and treat the person in a different manner. "Without It man cannot live. But he who lives with It alone is not a man," Buber concluded (p. 34).

Our temptation, of course, is to deal only with "the world of It," that is, only with persons as commodities, because it is easier to do so, as Adam Smith argued. To take each person individually and to relate to him or her as such, is time-consuming and demanding. But those who treat the world as only objective, which we tend to do in the name of rationalism, miss that element of the self in which its freedom is expressed. Descartes wanted "knowledge," and Buber admits that only by treating all persons as if they were "things" amenable to objective study can absolute knowledge be attained. Thus, those who accept a personal, subjective approach give up all hope of achieving final knowledge. But they also may discover a wider area of the self and recognize its potential freedom. Each individual must decide to be free by treating others as individuals and dealing with every one on an individual basis. Freedom is not simply given to us. Dialogue forces us to recognize our need for decision, as monologue never does, and this reveals the possibility of human freedom when we venture out of the world of objects into the realm of persons.

Selves Reveal God and Vice Versa

Descartes, you remember, included God in his argument for certain knowledge by appealing to his idea of God for protection against the possibility of total deception. But God is an objective idea for Descartes, one that appears the same in everyone's mind. Descartes's God is encountered as a rational idea and not as a person, but Buber suggests that elaborate objective arguments for God's existence are not only unnecessary but unsuccessful. God is encountered only in other persons, he argues, not as a rational necessity. We experience God only in meeting other people, not in considering ideas. Thus, God is involved in every human encounter, and to encounter God can expand

our understanding of other persons and ourselves. Although a mystical relationship may develop, our individual I never becomes one with God. There is no final union of man with God for Buber, because dialogue is possible only as long as both I and Thou remain separate individuals. Our experience of God is more like confrontation rather than merging.

On this point Buber differs from some traditional mystics and is "more philosophical." That is, he does not seek a loss of self or even union with God. Rather, he wants greater understanding of the self via the divine encounter, with both self and God remaining individual. But everything cannot become clear, as Descartes hoped, in this way of encountering God. "We have come near to God, but not nearer to unveiling being or solving its riddle" (p. 111). If all came out as Descartes wanted, self-understanding should provide a standard of clarity and distinctness whereby all judgments could be evaluated. But if Buber is right, our necessary involvement with others in dialogue, and particularly with God, while it increases our self-understanding, ends more with a riddle than with final clarity. But do riddles, if we accept them, reveal something about the human self we need to know, even if the process of dealing with God and others as individuals is painful and the resulting knowledge less certain than philosophers often want?

The Self Is Known in Its Struggles

Although *I and Thou* is probably Buber's most widely known book, his total written work is immense. As is obvious, the Jewish religious tradition, and in particular its mystical heritage, are the setting within which Buber thinks self-understanding can come. Those of a more modern persuasion might dismiss him as not being "philosophical," but to do so assumes a single, perhaps too narrow, definition of philosophy. Certainly Buber considered himself a philosopher, at least in part.

Descartes left human values out of account, and he wanted to do so because he thought it would interfere with the clarity and certainty he sought. It is typical that Buber treats the problem of good and evil as so important that he feels "the struggle must begin within one's soul—all else will follow upon this."[11] The good and evil we face in searching for knowledge of the self, he thinks, lead us to "an adequate awareness of the opposites inherent in all being in the world" (p. 74). The struggle with good and evil introduces complexities and makes it more difficult to understand "Who I am." But if this awareness of opposites is inherent in everything, the self cannot escape complexity, and our self-understanding remains partial unless we accept that conflict. Hard as it is to deal with, one learns something important about the self in observing the struggle between good and evil.

For Buber, evil can be perceived only by watching ourselves. "A man only knows factually what 'evil' is insofar as he knows about himself" (p. 88). If we want to know who we are, we ought not to shirk from the encounter with evil that is in us, although you remember that the primary awareness of the self comes from our encounter with others. But as this indicates, Buber argues that our aim is to transcend the self: "Only through mastering unmitigated evil does existence attain to transfiguration" (p. 103). Descartes liked the use of systematic doubt as a means to self-knowledge, but Buber thinks using doubt offers difficulties: "He does not choose, he doubts. Doubt is unchoice, indecision. Out of it evil arises" (p. 104). He is not convinced that we all seek the clear self-knowledge Descartes thought we did. Life is "the uncanny game of hide-and-seek in the obscurity of the soul, in which it, the single human soul, evades itself, avoids itself, hides

from itself" (p. 111). Therefore, Buber is less optimistic than Descartes about our ability to locate answers through self-study and, ultimately, to achieve full self-knowledge. Read his own words, from *I and Thou*.

To man the world is twofold, in accordance with his twofold attitude.

The attitude of man is twofold, in accordance with the twofold nature of the primary words which he speaks.

The primary words are not isolated words, but combined words.

The one primary word is the combination *I–Thou*.

The other primary word is the combination *I–It*; wherein, without a change in the primary word, one of the words *He* and *She* can replace *It*.

Hence the *I* of man is also twofold.

For the *I* of the primary word *I–Thou* is a different *I* from that of the primary word *I–It*. . . .

There is no *I* taken in itself, but only the *I* of the primary word *I–Thou* and the *I* of the primary word *I–It*.

When a man says *I* he refers to one or other of these. The *I* to which he refers is present when he says *I*. Further, when he says *Thou* or *It*, the *I* of one of the two primary words is present.

The existence of *I* and the speaking of *I* are one and the same thing.

When a primary word is spoken the speaker enters the word and takes his stand in it.

The spheres in which the world of relation arises are three.

First, our life with nature. There the relation sways in gloom, beneath the level of speech. Creatures live and move over against us, but cannot come to us, and when we address them as *Thou*, our words cling to the threshold of speech.

Second, our life with men. There the relation is open and in the form of speech. We can give and accept the *Thou*.

Third, our life with spiritual beings. There the relation is clouded, yet it discloses itself; it does not use speech, yet begets it. We perceive no *Thou*, but none the less we feel we are addressed and we answer—forming, thinking, acting. We speak the primary word with our being, though we cannot utter *Thou* with our lips.

But with what right do we draw what lies outside speech into relation with the world of the primary word?

In every sphere in its own way, through each process of becoming that is present to us we look out toward the fringe of the eternal *Thou;* in each we are aware of a breath from the eternal *Thou;* in each *Thou* we address the eternal *Thou*.[12]

Summary

Answering the question "Can I know the 'self'?" is more difficult if, as Buber claims, there is no single, consistent self that is always there. We must keep looking for "the real self," or the self that appears when the natural self is understood in new contexts. He tells us: "The real self appears only when it enters into relation with the Other."[13] In trying to discover who and what the self is, we could hardly have greater contrasts than those offered by Descartes, Hume, Adam Smith, Freud, and Buber. The rationalist Descartes believes that certain knowledge is possible and that achieving it is only a matter of finding the right method and applying it introspectively. Hume is the skeptic who does not deny all knowledge of the self but does think that certainty is impossible and that the knowledge we achieve is much more insecurely based than most of us suppose. Nevertheless, Hume agrees that getting on with the practical business of life in some sense presupposes the existence of the self. Adam Smith suggests that personal identi-

ties depend on economics. Freud, who holds that much about the self is hidden, is optimistic that we can uncover these aspects and gain full rational knowledge of the self. Buber doubts that science is enough. He urges a more mystical quest if we are to know ourselves. We must encounter others, search for God, wrestle with evil, and transcend the conventional distinctions between subject and object if we are to know who we are. The contrasts between these five views on self-knowledge leave us with more questions than answers, but thereby the questions are enlarged. We should realize how much is involved in attempting to answer the question "Can I know my 'self'?" If we really come to understand the questions we ask, we have, after all, come a long way from ignorance even if we are still far from the end of our search.

"Can I know my 'self'?" may at first seem like an abstract question, but life makes us encounter it. Each child, for example, must define himself or herself against parents and other family members to become a distinct individual. To do so is at least implicitly to answer the question "Who am I?" Moreover, in defining a role for ourselves, choosing a profession, becoming something, we must answer the question "Who am I?" for ourselves. If we don't, others will answer it for us by automatically classifying us according to what they see.

Furthermore, as should be evident by now, none of the philosophical questions this book raises exists in isolation. To deal with "Can I know the self?" involves us in other questions. In Part II, for example, we will consider questions about ethics and human conduct. How we respond to these will depend on what we decide individual selves are like. In addition to coming to grips with each question we raise, you will find philosophy more interesting if at the same time you work on the interrelationship between all the questions.

GLOSSARY

association in Hume's psychological theory, the grouping of impressions or ideas by the imagination on the basis of some perceived affinity or resemblance; the idea of the substantial self is held by Hume to be the product of just such an imaginative association of some general features of actual experience with the features of the self.

benevolence (see **sympathy**) a term descriptive of a feature of human nature conceived as capable of acting out of a motive other than pure **self-interest;** "good will."

certainty the state of a mind that is confident in its belief and free of **doubt;** or, as Descartes held, a property of a claim to knowledge that, like propositions of mathematics such as "1 + 1 = 2," cannot be doubted.

"clear and distinct" Descartes's criteria describing the properties of knowledge of the necessarily true, the *indubitable;* if a thing or idea could always be intuited clearly and could always be decisively differentiated from other things, it must be real or true. The self, or *cogito,* as Descartes called it, is in the Cartesian view the primary example of a clear and distinct idea.

commodity an item considered in terms of its relation to the satisfaction of human needs and desires, and consequently to its value as an object of economic exchange. The labor power of human beings, Smith implies, becomes a commodity as societies become progressively industrialized.

context the environment or setting of an event or thing; 'universe of discourse,' milieu; the whole situation of which particular things form a part and from which particular things derive their specific meanings. These specific meanings may vary from context to context, though the thing remains unchanged in itself.

division of labor a technique of organizing manufacturing and other forms of productive work, in which production is divided up into many simple subtasks, creating a working environment in which each article is produced by a long series of workers specializing in the repetitive performance of one simple subroutine, rather than by single craftsmen, each responsible for a whole article.

doubt the state of a mind that is highly cognizant of the potential for error, deception, misconception, and misperception in the sphere of ordinary judgments. Descartes's *methodological* doubt served him as a means for boiling away everything in the mind that can be suspected of a susceptibility to doubt, leaving as a residue that which cannot be doubted, the existence of the "I" which thinks, even though by thinking it becomes the *subject* of error, misconception, etc.

ego in Freud's theory, the conscious component of the self, or the *constructed image* of the self with which a person identifies himself or herself. Freud thought of the ego as interposed between the id and superego and the world, attempting to coordinate the demands of the subjective drives and prohibitions with the practical problems of living in the world.

free association a technique of **psychoanalysis** in which the patient reports verbally and spontaneously his associations with words produced by the analyst, thereby revealing patterns of thought that reflect the structure and dynamics of his unconscious mind.

id in psychoanalytic theory, the aspect of the self that is constituted by the basic animal instincts and drives of the organism.

identity the defining quality of objects that, as Hume says, "remain invariable and uninterrupted through a supposed variation in time." Self-identity of the personality, Hume thought, was a tenuous though practically necessary idea supported mainly by the faculties of **memory** and **imagination.**

imagination the faculty of mind in Hume's theory that is responsible for our awareness of the possibilities of association of ideas, impressions, and memories, which provides an important basis for our conception of the unity and continuity of our self; the faculty that links together particular ideas and remembered impressions to create the idea of unities continuously existing through time.

interpretation a method of psychoanalysis that begins with the assumption that some forms of behavior and experience are not to be taken at face value, but as expressing some "hidden meaning." These provide important clues to latent, unconscious processes, hidden from the direct observation of the scientist or the casual observer, and sometimes at odds with conscious, rational mental life. Dreams are the most important source of material for psychoanalytic interpretation; the dream-images are interpreted as symbolizing, sometimes in very oblique ways, fundamental psychic conflicts.

invisible hand in the economic theory of Adam Smith, a "natural" process of social, cultural, and economic growth and progress governed and determined solely by the law of supply and demand in an unregulated marketplace. This law motivates innovations in technology and the division of labor; such innovations in the workplace affect in their turn the structure of relations between people in society, which affects the sense of self of individuals. Individuals define themselves chiefly in terms of their place in a clearly defined social order structured by the market of labor and the value it assigns to various occupations.

"I–Thou" Buber's idea of a fundamental *context*, which deeply affects the meaning of the concept of the self; the concept of the self has very different meanings in the context of our relations with other persons and in the context of our relations with inanimate objects and commodities, Buber believed.

laissez-faire the doctrine that economic systems will function most efficiently if not interfered with by any outside agency, being left free to follow the "natural law" of supply and demand and its beneficial consequences for society in channeling self-interest into socially productive activity. From the French phrase meaning roughly "leave it be" or "hands off."

memory the faculty of mind in Hume's model of the self that provides material to support our belief that our self is a singular entity existing continuously through time.

psychiatry the branch of medical science that deals with mental and neurological disorders, in which **psychoanalysis** is one widely practiced method of diagnosis and treatment.

psychoanalysis a method of diagnosis and treatment of mental illness founded by Sigmund Freud and based on the assumption that many symptoms of psychic disorder can be explained only by reference to a realm of unconscious mental processes, where experiences and wishes unacceptable to the conscious self continue to affect the person who has attempted to suppress them, even if he is not consciously aware of them.

self the object of the idea of personal identity; the concept that organizes experiences by conceiving them as belonging to a specific and self-contained consciousness. For Hume, the self is a fiction or abstraction in that it cannot be discerned directly in the field of sensory experience, but must be inferred from certain tenuous assumptions of continuity and unity in the field of experience itself. For Freud, the conscious self or ego is also fictional, a constructed image a person creates of himself, which is often at odds with and undermined by deeper unconscious processes. For Smith and Buber, the mean of the concept of self depends on context: Smith sees the self-image determined by the relation of the person to the kind of labor that sustains his life and the structure of social relations this entails; to Buber, social relations—relations to other persons—define for the self a context radically different from that consisting of the relation between a person and the commodities he uses.

self-interest Smith's conception of the fundamental motivation governing human behavior; in his view, the self is defined by the activity of acquiring commodities necessary for sustaining its own material well-being by means of the creation of value through labor equivalent to the value of the commodities it requires.

superego the "censor" of the unconscious mind, where **taboos** and other constraining principles and forces originate and reside. In Freud's theory of the economy of the unconscious, the superego provides a check and balance to the insistent demands of the id for gratification of its unqualified desires.

sympathy in Smith's moral philosophy, a generous, charitable, understanding attitude toward other persons that clashes with the attitude of **self-interest,** which Smith believes must define social relations according to the "natural law" of policity economy.

taboo a deeply felt aversion to or prohibition against particular forms of behavior, such as incest or murder, stemming from a fear of the sanctions imposed on such behavior as determined by a given cultural context.

unconscious the realm of psychological activity Freud thought was separate from and sometimes at odds with the beliefs of the conscious personality-construct, or ego.

value the property of being desirable or necessary for human existence; the relative importance of a thing in relation to human needs and desires.

STUDY QUESTIONS

1. Should I be concerned with the questions "Can I know my 'self'?" and "Who am I?" If so, what gives rise to these questions. If not, why not?

2. Does Descartes's search for certainty seem important to you where the self is concerned?

3. Do you understand Descartes's use of doubt, and does it seem to you possible to overcome doubt?

4. What role does Descartes assign to God in self-understanding, and do you think an idea of God can function in this way?

5. State how you see Hume's form of doubt as differing from Descartes's.

6. What does "skepticism" mean for Hume, and how does it affect our search for self-knowledge?

7. Do you understand the basis for Adam Smith's view of human nature, and do you agree or disagree with him?

8. If you think Freud is not, strictly speaking, a philosopher, what is "philosophical" about his theory of the self?

9. According to Freud, what role does emotion play in helping or hindering our search for knowledge of the self?

10. If Buber has been called a "mystic," do you see why and how this relates to his view of the self?

11. Do you think we can understand ourselves alone, or does understanding require interaction with others?

12. Like Descartes, Buber sees God as important in the process of self-understanding. How do these philosophers differ, then?

NOTES

[1]René Descartes, *Discourse on Method* and *Meditations on First Philosophy,* trans. Donald A. Cress. Reprinted by permission of Hackett Publishing Co., Inc., Indianapolis, Indiana.

[2]David Hume, *A Treatise of Human Nature,* ed. L. A. Selby-Bigge (Oxford: Clarendon, 1946), p. 251.

[3]Adam Smith, *An Inquiry into the Nature and Causes of the Wealth of Nations,* ed. R. H. Campbell and A. S. Skinner, 2 vols. (Indianapolis: Liberty Press, 1981), 1:25.

[4]See Sigmund Freud, *On Dreams,* trans. James Strachey (New York: Norton, 1951), p. 15.

[5]See Sigmund Freud, *A General Introduction to Psychoanalysis*, trans. Joan Riviere (New York: Pocket Books, 1975), p. 19.

[6]Sigmund Freud, *The Ego and the Id*, trans. James Strachey (New York: Norton, 1962), p. 3.

[7]Sigmund Freud, *An Outline of Psychoanalysis*, trans. James Strachey (New York: Norton, 1949), pp. 14–16.

[8]Freud, *General Introduction*, pp. 19–22.

[9]Sigmund Freud, *New Introductory Lectures on Psychoanalysis*, trans. W. J. H. Sprott (London: The Hogarth Press, Ltd., 1949), pp. 94–96. From *The Standard Edition of the Complete Psychological Works of Sigmund Freud*. Translated and edited by James Strachey. Reprinted by permission of Sigmund Freud Copyrights Ltd., The Institute of Psycho-Analysis, The Hogarth Press, and W.W. Norton & Company, Inc.

[10]Martin Buber, *I and Thou*, trans. Walter Kaufmann (New York: Charles Scribner's, 1958), p. 3. Reprinted with the permission of Charles Scribner's Sons and T & T Clark, Scotland; Copyright © 1970 Charles Scribner's Sons, Introduction copyright © 1970 Walter Kaufmann.

[11]Martin Buber, *Good and Evil* (New York: Charles Scribner's, 1952), p. 64.

[12]Buber, *I and Thou*, pp. 3–4, 6.

[13]Martin Buber, *Eclipse of God*, trans. Maurice S. Friedman et al. (New York: Harper & Row, 1952), p. 97.

CHAPTER FOUR

How Can I Acquire Knowledge?

When do we possess knowledge? Of what does it consist? How is it different from mere opinion? Epistemology, you recall, is the technical name given to the part of philosophy concerned with such issues, but these are everyday concerns as well. Consider, for example, the question: "How do you know?" We employ it constantly with countless variations. How do you know it is going to rain? How do you know Abraham Lincoln was President of the United States? How do you know the Soviet Union produces more military weapons than the United States? How do you know it is right to do this, wrong to do that? Coming up with good answers for such questions is no trivial matter.

Among the answers offered, we find some more satisfactory because they fulfill the conditions required of valid claims for knowledge. What those conditions are or should be, however, is itself one of the major issues in philosophy. To outline those conditions entails critical reflection about the question "How can I acquire knowledge?" Thinking and knowing are closely related. They are not identical, of course, because one can think false thoughts, reason incorrectly, and make erroneous judgments. Until we decide how we *ought* to think, we can never be clear about the degree to which knowledge is ours.

To help you explore these questions and make certain distinctions, we will use a vari-

ety of philosophers as illustrations. Aristotle is one of the great classical thinkers of Greece, and every philosopher would agree that he helped to divide philosophy into its various fields of interest and to outline the questions of epistemology. Francis Bacon is known as one of the founding thinkers of the modern period, and his views have been widely influential in producing methods for testing our knowledge claims. Baruch Spinoza created a whole system, which he titled *Ethics*, but it was based on his theory about the nature of God. That theory, in turn, provided the context in which he discussed how we should go about acquiring knowledge. Charles S. Peirce, an American pragmatist, wanted to change our view about how we think we think. Miguel de Unamuno, a Spanish existentialist, was even more radical in his attempt to make us look at knowing in new ways. Each of these philosophers has a different view about how we think and how we attain knowledge. The variety in their approaches should cast a new light on the question "How can I acquire knowledge?"

Aristotle and the Desire to Know

Aristotle (384–322 B.C.) said that "all men by nature desire to know."[1] He did not draw that conclusion by observing every human

ARISTOTLE 384–322 B.C.

being in the world, but neither did he fabricate it out of thin air. Observable data entered into his claim. He had an ability to reflect on such data and to formulate a judgment that extended beyond the actual cases he could enumerate. But Aristotle's statement about our desire to know also involves a basic assumption that all human beings share a common nature. In short, it rests on a definition of what it means to be human.

Aristotle's proposition that all men by nature desire to know depends on two assumptions: first, that human experience can disclose reality; and, second, that our powers of reason are trustworthy guides to interpret experience and reveal the truth about reality to us. Common sense might regard such convictions as obvious, but Aristotle held them partly because of Plato's influence.

Headed for a medical career at the age of 17, Aristotle was sent to study in Athens. Although biology remained an interest, his work at Plato's academy led him also into the questions of philosophy. Aristotle became Plato's most distinguished student, though his philosophical differences with Plato caused him to found his own school, the Lyceum. Aristotle eventually tutored Philip of Macedon's son Alexander, a young man who would one day rule the Mediterranean world. After Alexander's death his empire declined and Aristotle fled, reportedly to spare Athens from "sinning twice against philosophy" (that is, putting him to death, as the precedent of Socrates suggested). Aristotle did live on, and so great is his reputation that he has sometimes been called, simply "the Philosopher."

Aristotle's Departure from Plato

Plato spawned but could not satisfy Aristotle's philosophical concerns. In fact, Aristotle's approach to philosophy diverged from Plato's in important ways. Where Plato stressed the dialogue form, for example, Aristotle abandoned it in favor of a straightforward declarative style. Plato used poetic myths because he felt his speculations could never be put into words that expressed his thoughts literally. Aristotle on the other hand strove for clarity through precise literal definitions and distinctions. Both, however, stressed analysis based on observations about the physical world and the use of logic to categorize the various types of judgments and arguments, and they agreed that "All persons by nature desire to know."

If we put the question "How can I acquire knowledge?" to Plato and Aristotle, they would give very different answers. If we all thought completely alike, it would be difficult to account for such differences. On the other hand, our differences are only partial. Otherwise we could not account for the fact that human disagreement is less than total and that we can at least understand our differences. But what about the ways in which we ought to think? If we are going to be reasonable, must we all think alike about the fundamental issues? Or, are basic differences in thinking inevitable, perhaps even desirable? Aristotle's study of such issues led him to a logic philosophers still use for systematic inquiry. Plato, on the other hand, left us with the dialogue method, which is content to ask questions, clarify them, and leave the answer to each of us who asks the question.

The Vocabulary of Philosophy

Aristotle's major achievements include cataloguing and defining the vocabulary of philosophy. The key terms in our vocabulary, Aristotle said, are the fundamental **categories** that structure our life and are those that human reason must employ in order to comprehend what is real. For example, we encounter existing individuals, things such as men and horses, or "substances" as Aristotle termed them. These all exhibit **quantity** and **quality.** As we look out a window we may see two cats, one white and the other black, but we understand what we see by using the categories of quantity and quality.

When our minds function properly, Aristotle tells us, our judgments about the things we encounter correspond to those actual things. Such agreement is possible because the categories of judgment (that is, the way we place things in groups by their common features) fit the categories reflected in the nature of existing things themselves. Philosophy's task is to discern what qualities are common to the objects we group together and the ways in which they can be regarded as one or many, discrete or continuous. This requires studying the **relations** among things, including the way we affect each other and produce change. Although the sciences also

study features of reality, in Aristotle's view philosophy is unique because it ultimately becomes

> . . . a science which investigates being as being and the attributes which belong to this in virtue of its own nature. Now this is not the same as any of the so-called special sciences; for none of these others treats universally of being as being. They cut off a part of being and investigate the attribute of this part; this is what the mathematical sciences for instance do. (1003a, P. 731.)

Since Aristotle's time, "metaphysics" has been the name given to philosophy when it studies "being as being." The goal of metaphysics is to discern the **first principles** that structure all existence or all **being.** In addition to exploring how all reality involves substance, quantity, quality, relation, and **change,** it seeks to know how existence is characterized by the categories of time and place, possibility and actuality, necessity and contingency, universality and particularity. The aim of this effort is to arrive at genuine knowledge. But it can be achieved if and only if the vocabulary of philosophy reflects the nature of the real world itself. Aristotle thought this kind of vocabulary could be developed and he offered his categories (quantity, quality, substance, etc.) as the basis for it. In opposition to Plato, Aristotle was quite sure words could be refined sufficiently to capture reality for us.

Judgments and Inferences

If we did not have adequate categories for reality, we might experience the world in a crude sense, but we could not reason about it or put it into words. However, thinking involves much more than using categories, indispensable as they are. Judgments and **inferences** are essential, too. Through them we reason about what we claim to know. Judgments, which philosophers sometimes call propositions, assert or deny that something is the case. Our ability to communicate depends on them. Aristotle tried to describe when the judgments we make are trustworthy and when they are not. In particular he wanted to identify when one was reasoning legitimately by inferring one proposition from another. All of us make hundreds of inferences a day, deriving one judgment from another. Aristotle wanted to determine when such inferences are valid and when they are made in ways that lead us astray. In short, he wanted to differentiate between inferences drawn from sound reasoning and those made through faulty reasoning or even through no reasoning at all.

We are least likely to be led astray, Aristotle believed, when we have "unqualified scientific knowledge of a thing." Such knowledge would be ours when we

> . . . know the cause on which the fact depends, as the cause of that fact and of no other, and, further, that the fact could not be other than it is. . . . Consequently the proper object of unqualified scientific knowledge is something which cannot be other than it is.[2]

"The sun rises in the east and sets in the west," for example, is something that cannot be other than it is. It is true for all, and upon examination is found to be necessary and so it is "unqualified scientific knowledge." Aristotle's description of "unqualified scientific knowledge" set a standard he wanted us to approximate in every field of inquiry.

Leaving aside the gross blunders people make when they misperceive or reason hastily, Aristotle noted that "all instruction given or received by way of argument proceeds from preexistent knowledge" (71a, p. 110). In reasoning or **"argument,"** as Aristotle used that term, the goal is to prove that something is the case. This can be done inductively by investigating several particular things and then forming a general judgment about those

things. "All Japanese have black hair," we learn by this kind of investigation. Or we can prove something deductively by using other knowledge we already have and exploring to discover what further knowledge can be drawn from it. "All men are mortal," for example, we know to be true because we already know that mortality is one of the characteristics of human beings, and all men are human. Or we may use a combination of the two methods. Aristotle explored the errors of logic people make in getting from particular things or given premises to conclusions. But his crucial point was that all argument has to begin somewhere. The truth of the conclusions the argument tries to prove can be only as certain as the truth of the propositions with which it begins and on which it rests.

Where Does Knowledge Begin?

Knowledge produced through argumentation, Aristotle contended, depends on "preexistent knowledge." Such knowledge is of two kinds: it is either an accurate understanding of some fact, or it is an adequate comprehension of the meaning of the terms a given proposition contains. That is, we either explore human life more completely and observe human action, or we look further into the meaning of the terms 'men' and 'mortal.' But where do these starting points themselves originate? How are we to know whether they actually possess the ingredients we need to draw on to gain new knowledge? Taking up the latter question, Aristotle tried to identify what he called **necessary premises,** that is, the assumptions you find you must make and cannot avoid. Ultimately, a necessary premise is one that does not need to be proved and is the basis for other proofs. Aristotle called "the basic truths of every genus those elements in it the existence of which cannot be proved" (76a, p. 124). These basic truths, argued Aristotle, are propositions "which we must necessarily believe" (76b, p. 125). They are so compelling as to be undeniable.

The source for these necessary premises lies both in experience itself and in the nature of our ability to think, which Aristotle regarded as able to duplicate the structure of existence. Two examples illustrate what Aristotle meant. "It is impossible," wrote Aristotle, "to affirm and deny simultaneously the same predicate of the same subject." You cannot, for example, say that this chalk is white and at the same time say that this piece of chalk is not white. He supplemented that principle of noncontradiction with what we now call the principle of excluded middle; that is, "every predicate can be either truly affirmed or truly denied of every subject" (77a, p. 126). Aristotle spoke of these principles as laws. He believed that they govern all reality, not only human thought. Such principles involve propositions that we must necessarily believe and they are the basis for all argument. If we deny that they are true, in denying them we will either use those principles implicitly or speak nonsense. We cannot escape the binding force of these laws of logic, Aristotle contended, because quite literally they reflect the way things are. Were things not that way, there would be no universe for us, let alone any human minds to seek knowledge of it.

The Mark of an Educated Man

The number of propositions "which we must necessarily believe" might be few, since most claims we make do not have the binding effect of the principles just outlined. But Aristotle persisted in his conviction that genuine knowledge is "scientific knowledge," which entails comprehending the facts and the causes of why they could not be other than they are. As Aristotle recognized, however, these standards of rigor are not uniformly applicable to all areas of human experience.

Nor does it follow that we lack all knowledge when we do not have it in its purest forms. Hence, when Aristotle began his inquiries into ethics and politics—noting that "every art and every inquiry, and similarly every action and pursuit, is thought to aim at some good; and for this reason the good has rightly been declared to be that at which all things aim"—he added that it is difficult to determine what the chief good might be.[3] Deeming politics the inquiry that explores the chief good for humankind, he argued that this investigation would be

. . . adequate if it has as much clearness as the subject-matter admits of, for precision is not to be sought for alike in all discussions, any more than in all the products of the crafts. Now fine and just actions, which political science investigates, admit of much variety and fluctuation of opinions, so that they may be thought to exist only by convention, and not by nature. And goods also give rise to a similar fluctuation because they bring harm to many people; for before now men have been undone by reason of their wealth, and others by reason of their courage. We must be content, then, in speaking of such subjects and with such premises to indicate the truth roughly and in outline, and in speaking about things which are only and for the most part true and with premises of the same kind to reach conclusions that are no better. . . . It is the mark of an educated man to look for precision in each class of things just so far as the nature of the subject admits; it is evidently equally foolish to accept probable reasoning from a mathematician and to demand from a rhetorician scientific proofs. (1094b, P. 936.)

In other words, the kind of knowledge we can have depends on the kind of subject matter we are investigating. Some subjects lead to precise knowledge, others do not.

Aristotle urged people to tailor their method of inquiry to the subject matter involved. We can do so, he believed, and still obtain knowledge in each case, because existence itself is rational; it is adapted to our ways of thinking if we use our resources well. Nowhere is this underlying theme more apparent than in Aristotle's enumeration of the four types of cause one must comprehend to possess "unqualified scientific knowledge." The physical objects and the people we meet, for example, are a composite of **matter** and **form.** The 'matter' of the pot is the clay the potter uses; its form is the shape he or she gives it. The object could not be what it is without both matter and form. Hence Aristotle spoke of material and formal causes. In addition, most things are brought into existence; they are acted on by other things, and they may also have the power to change themselves and to influence others. This factor Aristotle called efficient causality. Most importantly he also believed that nature does nothing without purpose, which is to say that things do not happen without good reasons. Aristotle was persuaded that every existing thing has a nature that impels it to be what it ought to be. Impediments from outside or flaws from within can frustrate fulfillment of this final cause, as Aristotle called it. But if by nature we desire to know, that desire should be trusted and pursued. Knowledge can be obtained, and with it wisdom, virtue, happiness, and a sound ordering for the state and its citizens. Taken together, those elements identify our final cause, that is, the purpose for which human life exists.

When it comes to stating how we acquire knowledge, and how we "know when we know," nothing is more important to Aristotle than discovering **causes.** We know a thing when we know its causes, **formal, material, efficient,** and **final.** For him knowledge is a knowledge of causes, and when we know the causes of any object or situation, we have obtained knowledge. To seek knowledge is to seek causes. Others—for example, David Hume—will question our ability to be sure of causal relationships, but

it fits Aristotle's confidence to believe that the mind can know the world directly and categorize it correctly. Thus, he felt we could determine the causes and thus find reliable knowledge.

Did Aristotle Assume Too Much?

Aristotle's optimistic reflections on how we do and ought to think may give us reason to pause. His definition of genuine knowledge assumes the possibility of the very thing that is in question. When Aristotle held that "the proper object of unqualified scientific knowledge is something which cannot be other than it is," he took for granted that the way our mind functions accurately corresponds to what reality is in itself.

Aristotle gave us a philosophical vocabulary of great power. He analyzed the many ways, both sound and unsound, in which we make judgments and inferences, and he recognized that different subject matters require modifications in our methods of inquiry and that some resulted in a less certain kind of knowledge. He stressed that the validity of our claims to know depends on the validity of our starting points, and he looked for firm beginnings. But Aristotle's largest assumption is that human reason, when it functions properly, gives us an accurate account of the way things are in themselves. Is this one of those propositions we must necessarily believe? More than one philosopher has denied that Aristotle was entitled to take this fundamental starting point for granted. If he was wrong, then knowledge is not what Aristotle said it was. Aristotle may have the power of common sense on his side, but philosophy must put common sense to the test. That does not mean that the beliefs of common sense will be scuttled; it does mean that they may not emerge unscathed.

How can we acquire knowledge? In different ways for different subjects, Aristotle would say, but we may do so with the confidence that a proper use of reason will take us as close as we can get to the unqualified scientific knowledge that is the model all thinking should emulate. As the following passage from Book II of Aristotle's *Metaphysics* indicates, knowledge depends on understanding causes. Follow his train of thought and see if you agree.

---

1. The investigation of the truth is in one way hard, in another easy. An indication of this is found in the fact that no one is able to attain the truth adequately, while, on the other hand, we do not collectively fail, but everyone says something true about the nature of things, and while individually we contribute little or nothing to the truth, by the union of all a considerable amount is amassed. Therefore, since the truth seems to be like the proverbial door, which no one can fail to hit, in this respect it must be easy, but the fact that we can have a whole truth and not the particular part we aim at shows the difficulty of it.

Perhaps, too, as difficulties are of two kinds, the cause of the present difficulty is not in the facts but in us. For as the eyes of bats are to the blaze of day, so is the reason in our soul to the things which are by nature most evident of all.

It is just that we should be grateful, not only to those with whose views we may agree, but also to those who have expressed more superficial views; for these also contributed something, by developing before us the powers of thought. It is true that if there had been no Timotheus we should have been without much of our lyric poetry; but if there had been no Phrynis there would have been no Timotheus. The same holds good of those who have expressed views about the truth; for from some thinkers we have inherited certain opinions, while the others have been responsible for the appearance of the former.

It is right also that philosophy should be called knowledge of the truth. For the end of theoretical knowledge is truth, while that of practical knowledge is action (for even if they consider how things are, practical men do not study the eternal, but what is relative and in the present). Now we do not know a truth without its cause; and a thing has a quality in a higher degree than other things if in virtue of it the similar quality belongs to the other things as well (e.g., fire is the hottest of things; for it is the cause of the heat of all other things); so that that which causes derivative truths to be true is most true. Hence the principles of eternal things must be always most true (for they are not merely sometimes true, nor is there any cause of their being, but they themselves are the cause of the being of other things), so that as each thing is in respect of being, so is it in respect of truth.

2. But evidently there *is* a first principle, and the causes of things are neither an infinite series nor infinitely various in kind. For (1) neither can one thing proceed from another, as from matter, *ad infinitum* (e.g., flesh from earth, earth from air, air from fire, and so on without stopping), nor can the sources of movement form an endless series (man for instance being acted on by air, air by the sun, the sun by Strife,* and so on without limit). Similarly the final causes cannot go on *ad infinitum*—walking being for the sake of health, this for the sake of happiness, happiness for the sake of something else, and so one thing always for the sake of another. And the case of the essence is similar. For in the case of intermediates, which have a last term and a term prior to them, the prior must be the cause of the later terms. For if we had to say which of the three is the cause, we should say the first; surely not the last, for the final term is the cause of none; nor even the intermediate, for it is the cause only of one. (It makes no difference whether there is one intermediate or more, nor whether they are infinite or finite in number.) But of series which are infinite in this way, and of the infinite in

---

*The illustration is taken from the cosmology of Empedocles.

general, all the parts down to that now present are alike intermediates; so that if there is no first there is no cause at all.

Nor can there be an infinite process downwards, with a beginning in the upward direction, so that water should proceed from fire, earth from water, and so always some other kind should be produced. For one thing comes *from* another in two ways—not in the sense in which "from" means "after" (as we say "from the Isthmian games come the Olympian"), but either (i) as the man comes from the boy, by the boy's changing, or (ii) as air comes from water. By "as the man comes from the boy" we mean "as that which has come to be from that which is coming to be, or as that which is finished from that which is being achieved" (for as becoming is between being and not being, so that which is becoming is always between that which is and that which is not; for the learner is a man of science in the making, and this is what is meant when we say that *from* a learner a man of science is being made); on the other hand, coming from another thing as water comes from air implies the destruction of the other thing. This is why changes of the former kind are not reversible, and the boy does not come from the man (for it is not that which comes to be something that comes to be as a result of coming to be, but that which exists after the coming to be; for it is thus that the day, too, comes from the morning—in the sense that it comes after the morning; which is the reason why the morning cannot come from the day); but changes of the other kind are reversible. But in both cases it is impossible that the number of terms should be infinite. For terms of the former kind, being intermediates, must have an end, and terms of the latter kind change back into *one another;* for the destruction of either is the generation of the other.

At the same time it is impossible that the first cause, being eternal, should be destroyed; for since the process of becoming is not infinite in the upward direction, that which is the first thing by whose destruction something came to be must be noneternal.

Further, the *final cause* is an end, and that sort of end which is not for the sake of something else, but for whose sake everything else is; so that if there is to be a last term of this sort, the process will not be infinite; but if there is no such term, there will be no final cause, but those who maintain the infinite series eliminate the Good without knowing it (yet no one would try to do anything if he were not going to come to a limit); nor would there be reason in the world; the reasonable man, at least, always acts for a purpose, and this is a limit; for the end is a limit.

But the *essence*, also, cannot be reduced to another definition which is fuller in expression.[†] For the original definition is always more of a definition, and not the later one; and in a series in which the first term has not the required character, the next has not it either.—Further, those who speak thus destroy science; for it is not possible to have this till one comes to the unanalyzable terms. And knowledge becomes impossible; for how can one apprehend things that are infinite in this way?[‡] For this is not like the case of the line, to whose divisibility there is no stop, but which we cannot think if we do not make a stop (for which reason one who is tracing the infinitely divisible line cannot be counting the possibilities of section), but the whole line also must be apprehended by something in us that does not move from part to part.—Again, nothing infinite can exist; and if it could, at least the notion of infinity is not infinite.

But (2) if the *kinds* of causes had been infinite in number, then also knowledge would have been impossible; for we think we know, only when we have ascertained the causes, but that which is infinite by addition cannot be gone through in a finite time.

3. The effect which lectures produce on a hearer depends on his habits; for we demand the language we are accustomed to,

---

[†]That is, one can reduce the definition of man as "rational animal" to "rational sensitive living substance," but one cannot carry on this process *ad infinitum.*

[‡]That is, *actually* infinite.

and that which is different from this seems not in keeping but somewhat unintelligible and foreign because of its unwontedness. For it is the customary that is intelligible. The force of habit is shown by the laws, in which the legendary and childish elements prevail over our knowledge about them, owing to habit. Thus some people do not listen to a speaker unless he speaks mathematically, others unless he gives instances, while others expect him to cite a poet as witness. And some want to have everything done accurately, while others are annoyed by accuracy, either because they cannot follow the connection of thought or because they regard it as pettifoggery. For accuracy has something of this character, so that as in trade so in argument some people think it mean. Hence one must be already trained to know how to take each sort of argument, since it is absurd to seek at the same time knowledge and the way of attaining knowledge; and it is not easy to get even one of the two.

The minute accuracy of mathematics is not to be demanded in all cases, but only in the case of things which have no matter. Hence its method is not that of natural science; for presumably the whole of nature has matter. Hence we must inquire first what nature is: for thus we shall also see what natural science treats of [and whether it belongs to one science or to more to investigate the causes and the principles of things].[4]

FRANCIS BACON   1561–1626

Francis Bacon and the Inductive Method

Aristotle continues to influence the quest for knowledge, but not every philosopher finds his impact entirely beneficial. In the seventeenth century, for example, Francis Bacon (1561–1626) thought the Aristotelian tradition needed substantial correction. For much of the Middle Ages (c. 500–1400), the Western world had largely forgotten or lost the learning of ancient Greece and Rome. The

Renaissance, which began in the fourteenth century, renewed interest in important texts recently recovered from antiquity. Aristotle's influence grew—so much that Bacon felt it dangerous.

Avoiding Bondage to the Past

Bacon feared that bondage to the past might result from his contemporaries' enthusiasm for antiquity. Instead of looking back, philosophers and scientists should wake up to the age in which they lived. According to Bacon, doing so required breaking the bad habits that prevent people from acquiring knowledge. Specifically, under the influence of Aristotelian ways, learning was hampered by too exclusive a reliance on **deduction.** Its strategy involved the **syllogism,** a form of reasoning in which a major premise (for example, "All mammals are warm-blooded") and a minor premise ("Cats are mammals") yielded a necessary conclusion ("Cats are warm-blooded"). Moving from the general to the particular, the syllogism promised certainty, but Bacon took this deductive approach to be inadequate. With too much haste, generalizations were made and conclusions drawn. Instead of stressing the importance of detailed observation and experimentation—the keys to acquiring scientific knowledge—the emphasis fell on logical consistency. In short, making sure that conclusions followed from premises in necessary Aristotelian order did not yield knowledge for Bacon, let alone advance our insight.

Aristotle's collected logical treatises were known as the *Organon.* Convinced that there must be a corrective to the shortcomings of the Aristotelian approach, Bacon proposed a "New Organon." Along with *The Advancement of Learning* (1605), however, his *Novum Organum* (1620) was the only finished part of a planned six-volume study. Called *Instauratio Magna (Great Renewal),* its aim was to appraise the methods and accomplishments of experimental science.

Before we explore Bacon's program for acquiring knowledge, note that he was more a man of practical affairs, although his career had its ups and downs, than a retiring, meditative sort. Born into an influential family, Bacon entered Trinity College, Cambridge, when he was 12. Four years later he assisted the English ambassador to France. Although his father's death left him impoverished, Bacon won a seat in Parliament by the age of 23. His status waxed and waned during the reign of Elizabeth I, but Bacon's fortunes improved with the succession of James I. Eventually knighted, he also became lord chancellor. At the height of his power, however, Bacon was convicted of taking bribes.

He lost his place at court and died deeply in debt.

Bacon's political concerns sparked his interests in science and philosophy. He tried unsuccessfully to enlist the king's support for new scientific enterprises, for Bacon believed that science was much more than an academic matter. With scientific knowledge, humankind could increase its mastery of nature, enhance political power, and improve the quality of life. Bacon had no laboratory; nor did he make scientific discoveries of lasting importance. Even his writings about science remained incomplete. Yet no one rivaled him as a herald of the coming scientific age. By refining the method for acquiring scientific knowledge, Bacon emphasized practicality in philosophy.

Knowledge Is Power

Unimpressed by philosophy's contributions—they seemed more a hindrance to progress than a help—Bacon found inspiration in the geographical discoveries of Marco Polo and Columbus, the technological advances represented by gunpowder and printing, and the explorations of scientists such as Copernicus. These practical efforts succeeded where those of speculative philosophers failed because the former entailed the careful gathering of data, their critical interpretation, the carrying out of experiments, and the discernment of nature's secrets by planned and organized observation targeted on nature's regularities. Science and technology promised a new world. The right kind of philosophy, contended Bacon, could hasten its discovery.

Bacon detailed this outlook in his "Aphorisms Concerning the Interpretation of Nature and the Kingdom of Man," the best-known portions of the *Novum Organum.* Central to his view is the proposition that

> Human knowledge and human power meet in one; for where the cause is not known the

effect cannot be produced. Nature to be commanded must be obeyed; and that which in contemplation is as the cause is in operation as the rule.[5]

According to Bacon, knowledge is power. Its **utility** makes knowledge valuable. Lacking knowledge, life is confusion; nothing of significance can be accomplished. But when knowledge exists, we can make plans and fulfill goals. We can imagine, invent, and achieve the discoveries that make progress.

Bacon agreed with Aristotle that to acquire knowledge means to understand the causes of events. Such understanding requires reasoning, but neither can come from the mind alone. But when Bacon stressed that nature must be obeyed before its processes will serve our desires, he went further than Aristotle in stressing that we must become more patient, disciplined observers:

> Man, being the servant and interpreter of nature, can do and understand so much and so much only as he has observed in fact or in thought of the course of nature: beyond this he neither knows anything nor can do anything. (P. 28.)

Speculation must give way to painstaking empirical study. The payment for that effort, Bacon said, is well worth the trouble. The resulting knowledge yields power.

Debunking the Idols

"Go to facts themselves for everything"— that was Bacon's way to acquire knowledge.[6] Scientific breakthroughs show us what can be done by implementing that procedure, but Bacon still had two concerns. First, the proper method of inquiry had to be used systematically. Second, instances of the systematic use of an appropriate method of inquiry were more the exception than the rule. Too many of "the sciences we now possess," held Bacon, "are merely systems for the nice ordering and setting forth of things already invented;

not methods of invention or directions for new works."[7] Outmoded forms of inquiry hold progress back. Bacon had the Aristotelian tradition in mind when he added, "The logic now in use serves rather to fix and give stability to the errors which have their foundation in commonly received notions, than to help the search after truth. So it does more harm than good" (p. 29). Nothing less than "a reconstruction of the sciences" was needed.[8] Philosophy could have a leading role by articulating the requirements for a new method of inquiry.

To launch his reconstruction project, Bacon thought philosophy must debunk "four classes of idols which beset men's minds. To these four distinctions I have assigned names—called the first class *Idols of the Tribe*; the second, *Idols of the Cave*; the third, *Idols of the Marketplace*; the fourth, *Idols of the Theater.*"[9] Collectively, these idols are counterproductive habits of thought that deserve to be swept away. The "idols of the tribe" lurk in tendencies common to human nature. We tend to think, for example, that sense perception gives us direct and truthful access to reality. Anticipating the insights of Locke, Berkeley, Hume, and Kant—the philosophers we met in Chapter Two—Bacon stressed that this assumption must be criticized because we too easily overlook the fact that our "seeing" does not necessarily show us things as they really are. Human sense experience, essential though it is, does not constitute the measure of all things. We must learn to see objectively, a task that requires us to be alert for occasions when emotion, feeling, and inference are self-deceptive.

If the "idols of the tribe" deceive humankind, each individual must reckon with his or her peculiar prejudices, which Bacon called "idols of the cave." Here Bacon recalls Plato's allegory in which people imprisoned in a cave mistake appearance (shadows) for reality. Each of us has uncriticized blind spots and pet theories. Bacon recommends that we treat with special suspicion any outlook that gives us special satisfaction. We all tend to believe what we like to believe, but that path does not lead to knowledge.

A third target, the "idols of the marketplace," emerges from the words we use in everyday business. Their meanings are often vague and ambiguous, but they solidify our impressions and beliefs nonetheless. Social and political opinion can be powerful, but such power contains no assurance of truth. Unless we guard against "the ill and unfit choice of words," their impact can "force and overrule the understanding and throw all into confusion" (p. 35).

Philosophy itself bears particular responsibility for the "idols of the theater." Many of its speculations claim to be true accounts of reality, but in fact they are closer to stage plays depicting unreal worlds of human creation. Specifically, Bacon faults three types of false philosophy. Exemplified by Aristotle, the first trusts nonempirical inference too much; its result is **sophistry.** Although more experimental, a second draws sweeping conclusions from too little data; its result is pseudoscience. The third mixes philosophy and religion indiscriminately; its result is **superstition.**

The Inductive Method

Exposing the idols that enslave the mind, Bacon understood, is only half the battle. Bad habits die hard. To prevent their resurgence and to ensure that we remain on the path that leads to genuine insight, an experimental approach is needed. Properly employed, it produces truly scientific knowledge, which consists of understanding the cause of an event and how the cause and its effect reflect general laws of nature. To achieve these ends, Bacon explained, entails more than drawing generalizations from particulars—"induction by simple enumeration," as this process is sometimes known. For example, if one

wanted to explore what causes heat, a subject that greatly interested Bacon, it would not be sufficient to list cases in which heat is present, identify conditions they share, and then generalize that those conditions cause heat. Nature does not reveal its structure so easily. A more sophisticated method of induction is needed, one that employs the **"process of Exclusion"** (p. 113).

To identify the cause of heat or any other phenomenon, Bacon recommended a four-part process of **induction.** The first task is to identify all the known cases in which the property occurs. Second, one must note the cases in which the property is absent, paying special attention to those that are closely related in appearance to the former cases. For instance, the sun, moon, and stars are all heavenly bodies, but the sun is hot and the moon is not. Grasping what makes the difference is crucial for the acquisition of knowledge about the cause of heat. Third, we must identify instances in which the property in question is more or less present. Finally, the process of exclusion comes into play. The various lists are compared and analyzed to identify the conditions that are always present when the property exists, always absent when the property is missing, and present in amounts corresponding to the amounts of the property's presence. The result of this analysis can be considered to identify the cause of the phenomenon.

Precision and Imprecision

Bacon was an enemy of vagueness and imprecision and also of philosophies that claimed greater clarity and precision than they possessed. He hoped to develop an inductive approach to knowledge that would "establish progressive stages of certainty."[10] He thought he had gone far in that direction, but his approach was not without problems. It is doubtful, for example, that empirical observation typically should or even can proceed along the lines of Bacon's cumbersome lists. Although Bacon criticized induction by enumeration, his own approach relied on it unrealistically. To his credit, Bacon may even have been aware of this, because he understood that however promising his process of exclusion, it might prove insufficient to produce the knowledge he sought. For even after exclusion had done its work, we could be left with complex conditions, thus leaving the identification of causes imprecise and problematic. At that point, Bacon admitted, one might have to make an educated guess—follow a hunch—and then test to see if the resulting explanation held in the particular cases.

Bacon detested hasty generalizations and syllogistic demonstrations based on them. In resisting the abuses of those procedures, however, he underplayed what his own inductive method led him to sense, namely, that it is difficult to do meaningful observation unless and until we possess a **hypothesis**—a tentative, working explanation—to guide our inquiry. To be able to form a good working hypothesis, which is akin to knowing how to ask the right questions, is as essential for the acquisition of knowledge as the careful observation of facts. Later philosophers such as Charles S. Peirce—we will meet him soon—refined the analysis of induction that Bacon encouraged, exploring how we observe, form a tentative explanation, and test its validity by seeing whether the expectations created by the working hypothesis pan out.

Although he did not take the inductive method as far as it needed to go, Bacon made an important beginning, and nowhere more brilliantly than in his discussion of the idols of the mind. For whenever we observe, hypothesize, test, and revise our thinking—including the use of the inductive method itself—Bacon warned us not to rest content with what we would like to believe. Ask yourself whether the acquisition of knowl-edge requires even more than Bacon's *Great Instauration* as you reflect on the following excerpt from that work.

Having thus coasted past the ancient arts, the next point is to equip the intellect for passing beyond. To the second part therefore belongs the doctrine concerning the better and more perfect use of human reason in the inquisition of things, and the true helps of the understanding; that thereby (as far as the condition of mortality and humanity allows) the intellect may be raised and exalted, and made capable of overcoming the difficulties and obscurities of nature. The art which I introduce with this view (which I call Interpretation of Nature) is a kind of logic; though the difference between it and the ordinary logic is great, indeed immense. For the ordinary logic professes to contrive and prepare helps and guards for the understanding, as mine does; and in this one point they agree. But mine differs from it in three points especially: viz., in the end aimed at, in the order of demonstration, and in the starting point of the inquiry.

For the end which this science of mine proposes is the invention not of arguments but of arts; not of things in accordance with principles, but of principles themselves; not of probable reasons, but of designations and directions for works. And as the intention is different, so accordingly is the effect: the effect of the one being to overcome an opponent in argument, for the other to command nature in action.

In accordance with this end is also the nature and order of the demonstrations. For in the ordinary logic almost all the work is spent about the syllogism. Of induction the logicians seem hardly to have taken any serious thought, but they pass it by with a slight notice, and hasten on to the formulae of disputation. I on the contrary, reject demonstration by syllogism, as acting too confusedly, and letting nature slip out of its hands. For although no one can doubt that things which agree in a middle term agree with one another (which is a proposition of mathematical certainty), yet it leaves an opening for deception; which is this. The syllogism consists of propositions; propositions of words; and words are the tokens and signs of notions. Now if the very notions of the mind (which are as the soul of words and the basis of the whole structure) be improperly and overhastily abstracted from facts, vague, not sufficiently definite, faulty in short in many ways, the whole edifice tumbles. I therefore reject the syllogism; and that not only as regards principles (for to principles the logicians themselves do not apply it) but also as regards middle propositions; which, though obtainable no doubt by the syllogism, are, when so obtained, barren of works, remote from practice, and altogether unavailable for the active department of the sciences. Although therefore I leave to the syllogism and these famous and boasted modes of demonstration their jurisdiction over popular arts and such as are matter of opinion (in which department I leave all as it is), yet in dealing with the nature of things I use induction throughout, and that in the minor propositions as well as the major. For I consider induction to be that form of demonstration which upholds the sense, and closes with nature, and comes to the very brink of operation, if it does not actually deal with it.

Hence it follows that the order of demonstration is likewise inverted. For hitherto the proceeding has been to fly at once from the sense and particulars, up to the most general propositions, as certain fixed poles for the argument to turn upon, and from these to derive the rest by middle terms: a short way, no doubt, but precipitate; and one which will never lead to nature, though it offers an easy and ready way to disputation. Now my plan is to proceed regularly and gradually from one axiom to another, so that the most general are not reached till the last; but then when you do come to them you find them to be not empty notions, but well defined, and such as nature would really recognize as her first principles, and such as lie at the heart and marrow of things.

But the greatest change I introduce is in the form itself of induction and the judgment made thereby. For the induction of which the logicians speak, which proceeds by simple enumeration, is a puerile thing; concludes at hazard; is always liable to be upset by contradictory instance; takes into account only what is known and ordinary; and leads to no result.

Now what the sciences stand in need of is a form of induction which shall analyze experience and take it to pieces, and by a due process of exclusion and rejection lead to an inevitable conclusion. And if that ordinary mode of judgment practiced by the logicians was so laborious, and found exercise for such great wits, how much more labor must we be prepared to bestow upon this other, which is extracted not merely out of the depths of the mind, but out of the very bowels of nature.[11]

Baruch Spinoza and the Improvement of the Understanding

If we are going to acquire knowledge, we must use language properly. Otherwise it becomes impossible to communicate and thus share what we have learned. No philosopher believed more strongly that we can obtain knowledge, and specifically that words can demonstrate the truth, than Baruch Spinoza (1632–1677), a Sephardic Jew who was born in the Netherlands because his family had fled Spain to avoid religious persecution. At the time, Holland was among the most tolerant European states, but even there it was Spinoza's fate to be harassed by those who did not share his views. Early on he became intrigued by Descartes's philosophy and the development of modern science and mathematics. Because he held unorthodox views and sought to express them in public, he was banned from the synagogue and so

BARUCH SPINOZA 1632–1677

Spinoza's reputation among a European elite. One supporter offered him a professorship in a German university, but Spinoza declined, feeling that a private life would give him greater intellectual freedom.

Spinoza's most influential treatise, *Ethics*, was published posthumously in 1677. It reflected his conviction that philosophers could use words to demonstrate the truth if they employed them with mathematical precision. *Ethics* applies the procedures of geometrical **proof** to the nature of God and the world. Throughout his writings, one finds a concern for defining truth and for identifying the proper methods for stating it. Not surprisingly, one of his works that appeared posthumously is *On the Improvement of the Understanding*. Although unfinished, it reveals his confidence that we can acquire trustworthy knowledge. Spinoza viewed the world as possessing an intelligible structure according to which every event is in principle comprehensible as a necessary part of the whole.

The Quest for the True Good

Before Spinoza could be optimistic that we can acquire knowledge if we learn to use words properly, he had to be converted to the life of philosophy. Thus, he starts *On the Improvement of the Understanding* by reporting how experience "taught me that the events of everyday life are empty and futile."[12] Philosophy, he was convinced, could change this. He therefore resolved to inquire whether there is some true good that, if found, he could enjoy forever in continuous and supreme happiness. This quest led him to reject the pursuit of fame and wealth, which seemed to unsettle rather than to improve the mind. "The more we possess of fame and wealth," he observed, "the greater is our desire to increase them." Pursuing these "ordinary objects of desire," Spinoza sur-

left his Amsterdam home. Living quietly in the Netherlands, he supported his yearning to write by working as a lens grinder. Finally settling in The Hague, he died there before reaching his 45th birthday.

Goethe, the famous German poet, called Spinoza a "God-intoxicated man." But ironically Spinoza stirred controversy in his own day because his thought—a version of pantheism, which holds that all things are aspects of God—flouted religious tradition. Branded an atheist, Spinoza could publish few of his writings, and even those added fuel to the fire. The philosopher was not without friends, however, and they circulated his manuscripts privately, enhancing

mised, "would keep me from discovering a better way of life" (p. 4).

Spinoza decided that words encompass the truth only if we give up uncertain goods in favor of the one good whose nature is certain. If love of perishable things creates disturbance and prevents realization of our proper goal, "love of an eternal and infinite thing nourishes the mind with pure happiness and is free from sorrow" (p. 5). This can be beneficial no matter what your role in life. We must learn to distinguish "good" and "bad," or else we are blocked from the truth. Yet, writes Spinoza, "nothing considered by itself can be called either perfect or imperfect" (p. 4). We need to discover what makes us label some things "good" and some "bad."

The Ways of Knowing

The first step we need to make is to become clear about the ways of knowing. Spinoza believed there are essentially four (pp. 7–8):

1. Knowledge through hearsay or some arbitrary sign (e.g., date of birth).

2. Knowledge resulting from uncritical experience, that is, from experience which has not been subjected to full reasoning, so that we accept the evidence of random events without testing one experience by others. For instance, a medical cure may "work" even if we don't know why.

3. Knowledge by inferring the essence of one thing from another, but not adequately, either (a) by inferring the cause from the effect or (b) by inferring the necessary presence of a particular property from a universal conception. For example, we may try to determine the size of the sun from the fact that objects get smaller as we get farther from them.

4. Finally, knowledge by comprehending a thing through its essence alone or through its proximate cause. For example, we can

see that 2 is related to 4 as 3 is related to 6; that is immediately apparent.

Of these ways of knowing, only the fourth kind is "without risk of error" (p. 10). Its importance is obvious, because as long as error is possible, we cannot be sure that words do reflect the truth. Spinoza thought he could justify that confidence.

The issue hinges on finding the right method for attaining true knowledge. Here Spinoza joined Descartes in defending a commonly held principle in modern thought: epistemological uncertainty is due to our failure to follow the proper method of inquiry. Yet, with so much previous failure, why should Spinoza think that we could succeed now in finding this foolproof path and thus speak the truth once and for all? Like Comte in the nineteenth century, Spinoza rested his trust on science and mathematics. The methods that produce progress in those areas of inquiry also give philosophy hope for improved understanding.

A proper method of inquiry should tell us when we find true ideas and how to distinguish them. Since we need to be certain, this method must exhibit **finality**. Persuaded that such finality is obtainable, Spinoza asserted that "to be certain of truth, we require no other sign than that of having a true idea" (p. 12). Hence, we do not have to know that we know. Such a regression could lead to infinity and thus eliminate certainty. As an example, we can go back to Descartes's belief that our knowledge of our own existence is beyond doubt. We simply need to consider our thought process to see that it is impossible to doubt our own existence as thinking beings. Since our existence is indubitable, it can form a basis for certainty. True ideas are those that give insight about the essence of things. When that principle is applied to the nature of knowledge itself, we see that knowledge is achieved when proper methods of inquiry are followed. "Method in this sense," Spinoza explains, "is nothing but knowledge reflecting on itself. Of knowledge, there will be no methodology unless knowledge exists first" (p. 13).

According to Spinoza, method and knowledge both exist. The power to find true ideas, moreover, resides within us. But this capacity is not of our own making. Like the objects we know, and indeed like knowledge itself, human reason is an aspect of God. That is, Spinoza believed that our finite minds are a part of the infinite intellect of God and that we achieve knowledge when we come to see our minds as part of a larger whole. Hence improvement of our understanding and awareness of God go together. Religion and philosophy complement one another, as Josiah Royce also argued. For Spinoza, human understanding moves toward fulfillment as it "reflects on the knowledge it has of the most perfect being" (p. 14). Spinoza was convinced that our understanding of one thing as true depended on our grasp of the whole of the world and God, now phrased in mathematically precise forms. If we improve our powers of understanding, the method for finding truth is available. Since truth "reveals itself as such we need no other tools than truth and good reasoning" (p. 15). Superstitions have no place in truth. Proper reasoning will not admit them, nor will it permit us to mistake true ideas for those that are confused, merely hypothetical, or ultimately false.

because "doubt is never due to the object that is doubted" (p. 28). Put another way, Spinoza thinks that a false idea can never be clear and distinct, for such ideas do not correspond to reality. If we use reason to divide complex things, and if we then examine each simple part separately, confusion will vanish. Reality itself is essentially clear and distinct, Spinoza reckoned, and thus reason can and should operate that way as well. When properly formed, our words reveal truth.

Multiple confusions, Spinoza argued, prevent us from using words to tell the truth. But Spinoza believed we can think our way beyond all confusion. Sound thinking enables us to use words with greater care. To do so is crucial, because Spinoza points out that words "belong to the realm of the senses" (p. 32). We use words to communicate ideas, but "words are invented freely and in conformity with the public's level of intelligence. They therefore signify things as they exist for the senses and the imagination, but not for the intellect" (p. 32). Spinoza gave "ordinary language" anything but a privileged position. It is far more likely to contain confusion than clarity and distinctness. According to Spinoza, "We affirm and deny many things because the nature of words allows it, but not the nature of things. We will easily confuse falsity with truth if we do not realize this" (p. 33). A mind that is improved by his guidelines, Spinoza implies, will know how language ought to be used.

Conceiving Things Clearly and Distinctly

Spinoza had great confidence in the powers of reason. Rationalists agree in asserting that fiction and falsehood need not plague us "as long as we conceive things clearly and distinctly" (p. 22). He was convinced not only of the necessity of clear and distinct ideas but also of the possibility of our forming them,

Philosophy and Self-Help

If truth is distinguished from falsity by intrinsic factors and not by external ones, we can locate truth by an internal examination. The basis for this optimism is Spinoza's claim that truth manifests itself through clear ideas. Without that fortunate possibility, we would be left to an endless examination of external objects, resulting in endless words but not truth. Our search for truth would become never-ending. Spinoza acknowledged that our powers of understanding are not infinite, but, given the presence of truth in simple ideas, our power to state the truth is sufficient if we adopt the right procedures. Philosophical self-help is the key to success. Nothing keeps us from truth except ourselves. Avoiding error is a matter of following the rules that yield improvement of the understanding. Now that those rules are known in the age of modern science and mathematics, Spinoza advises us, there is no longer any reason for words to fail to convey the truth. Simply stated, these rules are:

1. Make sure that each individual idea is clearly defined.

2. Make sure that the relationships between ideas are clearly understood.

3. Make sure that our movements of thought occur step by step, in the proper order.

When all these things are done, truth will be ours, according to Spinoza, because ideas properly conceived reveal what is real. Now read more of what Spinoza said in *Improvement of the Understanding,* and see if you trust reason as much as he did.

I will state only briefly here what I mean by the true good and also what the supreme good is. To understand this properly it must be realized that good and bad are relative terms, so that the same thing can be called good and bad, or perfect and imperfect, in different respects. Nothing considered by itself can be called either perfect or imperfect, particularly if we are aware that all things that come into being do so in accordance with the same eternal order and the fixed laws of nature. Human weakness does not readily comprehend this order. But man conceives of the possibility of a much more powerful human nature than his. As he sees nothing in the way of acquiring such a nature, he is encouraged to seek the means which

can lead him to such a perfection. He calls everything that can serve as means to such perfection a true good. The supreme good is to enjoy, together with other men if possible, such a nature. We shall show in its place what this nature is, that it is the knowledge of the union of the mind with the whole of nature.

The end to which I aspire is to attain such a nature and to seek that many men acquire it with me. My pursuit of happiness is not complete without the endeavor to have many others achieve the same power of reasoning as myself, so that their reason and desire be fully cooperative with my own. For this purpose we must acquire sufficient knowledge of the nature of things and we must establish the sort of society which will enable the greatest possible number of people to achieve the goal in peace and without undue difficulty. This will require the study of moral philosophy as well as the theory of education. Medicine will have to be included, as health is of no small significance as a means to our end. Mechanical science is not to be despised, for through art we can make many laborious things easy and thus gain much time and comfort in life. Above all a way must be found to improve the intellect and purify it as much as possible right at the start, so that it will not be encumbered with errors and will understand things properly. It is clear that I wish to direct all sciences to one end and purpose: the achievement of the highest human perfection. Whatever in the sciences does not further this will have to be rejected as useless. All of our actions as well as our thoughts must be directed to this end.

Having laid down these rules, I will now proceed to my foremost task, the correction of the intellect, the rendering it capable of the reasoning that is necessary for our goal. The natural method of doing this requires that I begin by reviewing all ways of reasoning which I have until now employed for affirming or denying anything with assurance, so that I may select the best of these ways and begin to know my own powers and the nature which I desire to render perfect. Unless I am mistaken, they all can be reduced to four:

1. Knowledge through hearsay or some arbitrary sign.
2. Knowledge resulting from uncritical experience, that is, from experience which has not been subjected to full reasoning, so that we accept the evidence of random events without testing one experience by others.
3. Knowledge by inferring the essence of one thing from another, but not adequately, either (a) by inferring the cause from the effect or (b) by inferring the necessary presence of a particular property from a universal conception.
4. Finally, knowledge by comprehending a thing through its essence alone or through its proximate cause.

Examples will make all this clearer. From hearsay alone I know the day of my birth, who brought me into life, and like things about which I have never been in doubt. From mere experience I know that I shall die. I believe this because I have found that other men died, even though they did not all live the same length of time or die from the same disease. I also know from mere experience that oil has the property of feeding a fire and water of extinguishing it, that the dog is a barking animal and that man is a rational animal—in short, practically everything that is required for the conduct of life. An example of inferential knowledge is my deducing that the soul is united to the body from the fact that I experience the feelings of my own body but not those of other bodies, whereby I take the union of body and soul to be the cause of the feelings I experience. But this inference does not enable me to know fully what the nature of this feeling and this union is. Likewise, from my knowledge of visual perception and particularly its property of making one and the same thing appear larger or smaller depending on my distance from it, I infer that the

sun is larger than it appears, and many other things. Finally, a thing is known through its essence alone, for instance when, in knowing a thing, I know the very nature of this knowledge, or when, by knowing the essence of the soul, I know that it is united to the body. By this kind of knowledge I know that two and three are five and that two lines which are parallel to a third are parallel to each other, etc. The things, however, which until now I have been able to know in this way have been very few.

To proceed now toward selecting the best of these ways of knowing, I should begin by briefly enumerating the steps that must be taken to attain our end. We must achieve exact knowledge of our nature which we desire to perfect, and as much of the nature of things as is necessary to enable us (1) to establish correctly the differences, similarities, and oppositions of things, (2) to determine exactly the extent to which things can or cannot be acted on, [and] (3) to compare the nature and powers of things with those of man. In this way the highest perfection to which man can attain will easily become apparent.

Having stated this, let us see to which kind of knowledge we should give preference. As to the first kind, it is obvious that hearsay knowledge, quite apart from its uncertainty, does not, as our illustrations have made clear, give us the essence of things. Because the existence of an individual thing is not known unless its essence is known, as will be shown later, such certainty as hearsay may give us is not scientific in character. Simple hearsay, without rational examination, is an ineffectual way of gaining knowledge. Neither does the second kind of knowledge furnish us the ideas we seek to discover. It is very uncertain and indefinite knowledge and yields only the accidental properties of natural objects which are never clearly known unless their essences are first known. Hence this kind of knowledge must be rejected too. The third kind of knowledge furnishes us true ideas of things, and it enables us to make inferences without the risk of error. But it is not by itself the means of achieving the perfection we aim at. Only the fourth kind of knowledge grasps adequately the essence of things without the risk of error. It is, therefore, the most useful knowledge. I shall endeavor to explain how we may acquire this knowledge and thus be able to understand things previously not understood.

A true idea (for we have true ideas) is something different from its object. A circle is one thing, the idea of a circle another. The idea of a circle does not have a periphery and a center, just as the idea of a body is not that body itself. An idea, being different from its object, constitutes a knowable entity of its own. Considered as an actual essence of its own, an idea can become the object of another idea-essence which again, regarded in itself, is a real and knowable entity, and so to infinity.

Peter, for example, is something real. The true idea of Peter is an intellectual essence representing Peter, that is, an entity real in itself and entirely different from Peter himself. As the idea of Peter is a real entity having its own particular essence, it will in turn be something intelligible and the object of another idea which will contain ideationally all that the idea of Peter contains actually. This idea of the idea of Peter also has its own essence which can become the object of another idea and so to infinity. Everyone can confirm this when he is aware at the same time of knowing Peter and knowing that he knows, or knowing that he knows he knows, etc. It follows that in order to know the essence of Peter, I need not know the idea of Peter, and much less the idea of the idea of Peter. To know a thing I need not know that I know and still less that I know I know, just as it is not necessary to know the nature of the circle in order to know the nature of the triangle. (But, in contrast, to know that I know, I must necessarily first know.)

It is clear, therefore, that certainty consists in nothing but the idea itself, that is, in the way in which we experience an actual essence. To be certain of truth, we require

no other sign than that of having a true idea. For, as I have shown, to possess knowledge it is not necessary that I know I know. It also follows that nobody can know what is the highest certainty unless he has adequate ideas of things; for certainty consists in adequate ideas. As truth needs no external sign, but it suffices to know the ideational essences of things (or, what is the same, their adequate ideas) to dispel all doubt, it follows that true method does not consist in looking for the signs of the truth of our ideas after we have acquired them, but in the methodical search for the truth, the adequate ideas, or the ideational essences of things (all these terms are synonymous).

In another sense method means the theory of systematic thinking and reasoning. That is, method in this sense does not consist in the systematic thinking that leads to the knowledge of the causes of things and much less in that knowledge itself. It consists in the knowledge whereby we know what true knowledge is, differentiating it from other forms of knowledge, and inquiring into its nature to enable us to know our powers of thought and to discipline our mind so that it will make true knowledge the standard of its operations. This knowledge enables us to formulate definite rules and to keep the mind from wasting itself on useless operations. Method in this sense is nothing but knowledge reflecting upon itself, the ideas of ideas. Because knowledge must exist before there can be knowledge of knowledge, there will be no methodology unless knowledge exists first. Good method, therefore, consists in showing how the mind is to be guided to conform to the standard of already existing true knowledge. Further, since the relation which exists between two ideas is the same as the relation which exists between the actual essences of which they are the ideas, it follows that the knowledge which reflects on the idea of the most perfect being will be superior to the knowledge which reflects on any other idea. The perfect method, therefore, will show how the mind is to be guided so as to measure up to the standard set by the idea of the most perfect being. (Pp. 6–13.)

THE DEFINITION OF TRUTH

Because it belongs to the very nature of thought to form true ideas, as was shown in the first part of our discussion of method, we must turn now to the question of what is meant by the powers and strength of the intellect. The chief function of method is to enable us to know, as best we can, the nature and power of the intellect. We must then (in accordance with what was said in the second part of our discussion) deduce the nature and power of the intellect from the definition itself of truth or intellect. The difficulty is that we do not as yet possess rules for the discovery of true definitions and that to establish such rules we would first need to know the nature or definition of truth or intellect and its power. It follows either that the definition of the intellect or of truth must be self-evident or that knowledge is impossible. Now we do not possess a fully self-evident definition of the intellect. But because the properties of the intellect can, as everything else, be known clearly and distinctly only if its nature is first known, the definition of the intellect will make itself manifest in the clear and distinct knowledge we have of its properties. Let me, therefore, enumerate and analyze the properties of the intellect and thus begin with the intellectual tools which are native with us. The properties of truth or intellect which I find preeminent and know clearly are the following:

1. True knowledge is certain knowledge. This means that we know that the thing exists in reality as it is represented in our ideas.

2. Some ideas are formed simply, some are derived from other ideas. The idea of quantity is formed simply, without reference to other ideas. But the idea of motion requires the idea of quantity.

3. Ideas that are formed simply express what is unlimited. Ideas formed by reference to other ideas are of what is finite. Even quantity becomes finite when it is viewed as due to a cause, as when body is viewed as arising from the motion of the plane, the plane as arising from the motion of the line, the line from the motion of the point. These ideas do not serve to give us knowledge of what quantity is but merely to place it in a finite context. This is clear when we conceive line, plane, and body as arising by certain motions, although the idea of motion presupposes that of quantity. But we could not conceive of the infinitely extended motion required for the formation of the line unless we had the idea of infinite quantity.

4. Positive ideas are formed before negative ones.

5. The intellect views things, not from the perspective of time, but from the perspective of eternity and infinity and hence has no regard to the number and duration of things. Our senses, however, perceive things as being of determinate number, duration, and quantity.

6. Clear and distinct ideas follow from the necessity of our nature alone and hence are subject to our control. The opposite is the case with confused ideas. They are often formed against our will.

7. Ideas which are formed by reference to other ideas can be formed in many ways. For example, we can define an ellipse as the figure created by a pencil which is moved along a string that is attached to two centers, or as an infinite number of points that have a definite and invariant relation to a given straight line, or as the section of a cone cut in an oblique plane such that the angle of inclination is greater than the angle of the vertex of the cone; and we can add an infinite number of other definitions.

8. The more an idea expresses the perfection of its object, the more perfect is the idea itself. We admire an architect's plan of a splendid temple more than that of a little chapel.

I will not here discuss other aspects of mental activity, such as love, happiness, etc., for they do not pertain to our present purposes and cannot be understood unless we have knowledge of the intellect which is prior to everything else.

False and fictitious ideas (as I have abundantly shown) do not give us any positive knowledge. It is due to our ignorance that they are held to be knowledge. False and fictitious ideas as such cannot, therefore, teach us anything about the essential nature of thought. Such knowledge must be derived from the study of the positive properties just enumerated which will yield us the common nature from which these properties necessarily follow and on which they depend completely for their existence. (Pp. 38–40.)

Charles S. Peirce and the Doctrine of Fallibilism

Two thousand years after Aristotle searched for unqualified scientific knowledge, a group of American intellectuals, some of them local teachers of philosophy, organized a philosophical discussion group in Cambridge, Massachusetts. They debated issues provoked by Charles Darwin's evolutionary biology and Auguste Comte's positivistic claim that science and science alone could ensure reliable knowledge and progress. One member of this "Metaphysical Club" was Charles Sanders Peirce (1839–1914). This brilliant if eccentric man was a philosopher's philosopher who could not communicate easily with a popular audience. Peirce toiled in poverty and obscurity, but he left behind series of writings that make him one of the fathers of American pragmatism.

Peirce regarded Aristotle as "the prince of philosophers."[13] Like Aristotle, Peirce wanted

CHARLES SANDERS PEIRCE 1839–1914

to clarify how we do and ought to think. But despite this admiration, Peirce ultimately broke with Aristotle on the notion of certainty. In a theory he sometimes called the doctrine of **fallibilism,** Peirce concluded that human knowledge, scientific or not, is never unqualified. Error, thought Peirce, is a permanent possibility. In meetings of the Metaphysical Club, he explored the evidence for and the implications of that claim. One result was an essay entitled "The Fixation of Belief," which Peirce published in 1877.

The Irritation of Doubt

Although Aristotle was content to settle for such rigor as a given subject matter allowed, philosophers were more impressed by his claim that the purest form of knowing has no possibility of error. For centuries much of Western philosophy was obsessed by a quest for certainty. Peirce's scientific and mathematical inclinations made him desire precision, too, but he felt that philosophy's quest for certainty led into a blind alley. The way out, Peirce believed, was to reevaluate how scientific knowledge advances and how scientific method works. Peirce's approach involved a description of the fundamental context for inquiry and, reminiscent of Bacon's idols, an appraisal of four ways to form beliefs.

Peirce launched his investigation by marking the differences between doubt and belief. He found doubt to be

> . . . an uneasy and dissatisfied state from which we struggle to free ourselves and pass into the state of belief; while the latter is a calm and satisfactory state which we do not wish to avoid, or to change to a belief in anything else. On the contrary, we cling tenaciously, not merely to believing, but to believing just what we do believe. Thus, both doubt and belief have positive effects upon us, though very different ones. Belief does not make us act at once, but puts us into such a condition that we shall behave in a certain way, when the occasion arises. Doubt has not the least effect of this sort, but stimulates us to action until it is destroyed.[14]

To believe something is to be prepared to act in some specifiable way and to expect some specifiable set of experiences. Students believe that if they go to the college dining hall between certain hours in the morning, breakfast will be provided, and so they develop the habit of going there, expecting coffee and so on for their satisfaction. Moreover, beliefs are reinforced as long as we get the expected results. When there is a break-down in that pattern however (we find the dining hall closed one holiday), we have to stop and reconsider. As Peirce put it: "The irritation of doubt causes a struggle to attain a state of belief. I shall term this struggle *inquiry*" (p. 99). **Inquiry** begins when beliefs break down. The opposite of belief, then, is not disbelief, which actually is a form of belief, but doubt. Doubt is the state of uneasiness in which we lack either a firm course of action or a clear set of expectations. It requires us to find our way anew. "Hence," concluded Peirce, "the sole object of inquiry is the settlement of opinion" (p. 100).

Belief and Truth

Before analyzing how to remove the irritation of doubt, Peirce spelled out some ramifications of his account of how we think. Some philosophers, Peirce admitted, would question whether the only goal of inquiry is to settle opinion. They would argue instead that inquiry's objective is to arrive not merely at an opinion but at a *true* opinion. In this instance, however, Peirce was concerned more with the way people actually do think than with the way in which they ought to think, and his observations led him to conclude that inquiry ceases when a firm belief, whether true or false, is obtained. Inquiry begins again, of course, if experience forces us to call the new belief into question. Even so, Peirce went on to say, "the most that can be contended is that we seek for a belief that we shall *think* to be true. But we think each one of our beliefs to be true, and, indeed, it is mere tautology to say so" (p. 100).

Peirce did not want to blur the distinction between (1) thinking that a belief is true and (2) its actually being true. The line between the two is crucial, but it is also fine, because truth is disclosed in the arena of experience. Truth, wrote Peirce, is "that character of a proposition which consists in this, that belief in the proposition would, with sufficient experience and reflection, lead us to such conduct as would tend to satisfy the desires we should then have. To say that truth means more than this is to say that it has no meaning at all" (p. 100). Our expectations and experiences do not make truth, at any rate not by themselves. Nonetheless truth is a function of experience. It cannot be conceived without at least implicit reference to the experiences that a given belief creates for us and the satisfaction of the expectations we have. Truth has an absolute, objective status in Peirce's philosophy. It is found only to the extent that beliefs are critically focused to produce the expectations that experience actually fulfills. Believing that something is the case is definitely not enough to make it so. At the same time, Peirce's interpretation makes plain that, practically speaking, the term "truth" has meaning only in relation to our beliefs about experience.

Furthermore, Peirce suggested that ultimate and final knowledge will elude any individual or group. Such knowledge would exist only if experience involved an exhaustive grasp of its past and present and if it lacked a future in which new events could happen. Thus, when Peirce claimed that a finally true opinion would be one that a complete human investigation would be bound ultimately to agree upon, he described an ideal that human experience might advance toward but could never fully attain. This conclusion, however, did not plunge Peirce into skepticism and despair. On the contrary, he had clarified those points about experience and truth to sweep away what he called "some vague and erroneous conceptions of proof" (p. 100).

Philosophy's Big Mistake

Philosophy's big mistake, claimed Peirce, was its insistence on trying to find what is both unnecessary and impossible to obtain,

namely, "ultimately and absolutely indubitable propositions" (p. 101). Because the meaning of a proposition involves a web of related expectations about experience, Peirce doubted that any proposition could genuinely be one that is ultimately and absolutely indubitable. This, however, is not as tragic as many philosophers feared. Inquiry can advance, Peirce contended, if we accept that it can be free from actual but not theoretical doubt. Indeed, Peirce said, that procedure is the one we follow whenever we inquire; we never occupy a position from which we can examine all assumptions at once.

One fact is inescapable: to inquire at all we have to start somewhere, and that means we have to make some assumptions. If we are careful about our methods of inquiry, said Peirce, we can lay claim to a form of knowledge and even to demonstration, though we must recognize that our claims to know and to demonstrate are fallible and subject to revision. We cannot regard them as absolute, but it is useless to lament the limits within which human investigation must operate.

Three Inadequate Ways to Fix Belief

Without regret, Peirce set aside the quest for certainty. Instead, his fundamental questions became: What are the available ways for setting opinion? Which one is best? Peirce discussed four options. Three of them—the methods of tenacity, authority, and a priori appeals to reason—have a long history and have exerted great influence. Unfortunately, they are also deficient. The method of tenacity fixes belief by individual choice and by subjective liking. Often arbitrary, this approach ignores the public dimension of knowledge. Specifically, it overlooks the fact that "we shall necessarily influence each other's opinions; so that the problem becomes how to fix belief, not in the individual merely, but in the community" (p. 103). Nor does this method leave us any option for dealing with error, except by yet another tenacious affirmation of belief. The method of authority is more communally oriented. Yet it, too, ultimately falls back on the dictates of a single group or person and involves all the dangers of subjectivism that haunt the method of tenacity.

Although it does emphasize critical reflection, what Peirce calls the "a priori method" turns out to be little better than the first two. In calling this method a priori, Peirce meant that we use it to form judgments on the basis of what seems "agreeable to reason." The problem, according to Peirce, is that what is "agreeable" depends too much on the individual's introspection and not enough on external observation carried on by a community of investigators. Peirce's special target was the Cartesian position that certainty and genuine knowledge arise when ideas emerge as "clear and distinct" after being submitted to radical doubt and rigorous criticism. This approach does involve a more extensive use of reason than the method of tenacity, and it requires individuals to free themselves from dogma. But it harbors a dangerous subjectivism. That an idea or claim appears clear and distinct, even after extensive rational criticism, is no absolute guarantee of its certain truth. Appeals to "clarity and distinctness," claimed Peirce, still leave us with the possibility of error. If we use this approach to belief, error comes as a nasty surprise and can be dealt with only by refixing belief through another a priori appeal to reason. However, no a priori appeal to reason is sufficient to prevent experience from destroying our dearest certainties.

The Self-Corrective Method of Science

Certainty is scarce in Peirce's world. Infallible revelations have been imparted to no groups or individuals. The possibility of error is permanent and pervasive. Even a person's introspective judgments are not immune from doubt. Peirce's fallibilism is strong because he believed that having knowledge entails making claims and judgments about experience. Where claims and judgments are made, interpretation takes place. According to Peirce, interpretations of experience are always fallible. We are warranted in holding any given interpretation only as long as critically sifted evidence, empirically obtained and publicly grounded, bears it out. Yet even fulfilling those conditions does not absolutely guarantee knowledge and truth.

For Peirce, scientific method incorporates an accurate understanding of our human predicament in inquiry and provides the only adequate way to fix belief. Scientific method recognizes that human claims are fallible and insists, therefore, on regarding our claims as hypothetical and in need of verification by a community of investigators. In short, this method is self-corrective in ways the other methods are not. Faced with error, the other methods Peirce considered respond only through fresh acts of tenacious affirmation or by appeals to authority, "clarity and distinctness," or self-evidence. Scientific method escapes the embarrassing and often disastrous consequences of pronouncing a claim to be certain only to have it contradicted later.

Since it places a premium on the permanent possibility of error, scientific method does not allow absolute assertions. It tests claims and actively hunts for mistakes. As experience unfolds, judgments and facts, expectations and consequences are closely and critically examined. Where they harmonize confidence in our possession of truth increases, but it is never completely unshakable. If they clash, experience must be reappraised. Creative inquiry then occurs, and new hypotheses are formed and tested with the hope that they will be more adequate. Peirce's scientific men and women give up trust in their capacity to discern the truth and accept the fact that existence is risk-filled. They agree to live with fallible probabilities, not deceptive certainties.

Making Our Ideas Clear

In 1878, a year after "The Fixation of Belief" appeared, Peirce published another article, "How to Make Our Ideas Clear." He built on a thesis in the earlier essay, namely, that a scientific approach can be used in many areas of life, including philosophy. Peirce argued that improvements in scientific method were possible. In particular, Peirce claimed, scientific method could be improved by a defined procedure to clarify the meanings of ideas.

In scientific work, let alone life in general, clarity seldom reigns supreme. But it is crucial to know what ideas mean, because clarity is a fundamental condition for devising and carrying out tests to determine the truth or falsity of propositions and theories. A procedure that could systematically perform this operation would also help us to clarify situations in which people use the same terms but actually say different things. It would also be crucial in recognizing occasions of different words being used with disagreement although the intended meaning is really the same, or at least close enough to make the disputes mainly verbal.

Broadly speaking, Peirce's pragmatism, or pragmaticism as he became fond of calling it, can be equated with fallibilism. More precisely, it is a theory of meaning whose fundamental principle says that "our idea of anything *is* our idea of its sensible effects."[15] Peirce illustrated what he meant by inviting us to think about what is intended when we affirm that an object, say a diamond, is "hard." Clarity about the meaning of "hard," he stated, entails our thinking about the behavior of the thing in experience. Hence, if something is "hard," it cannot be easily scratched. Expanding his notion that meaning involves actions and reactions that are matters of experience, Peirce summarized his outlook as follows:

> . . . consider what effects, which might conceivably have practical bearings, we conceive the object of our conception to have. Then, our conception of these effects is the whole of our conception of the object. (P. 124.)

This perspective is not as simple as it may appear, but the gist of Peirce's plan is straightforward enough. He wanted ideas and theories to have an empirical grounding, that is, a referent we can point to in actual experience. If they fail to specify some possible difference of practice, they either lack meaning altogether or they are not functioning with the meanings we thought they conveyed. Everything is brought down to a concrete level. When these pragmatic principles operate, we have to lay our cards on the table. We can try to understand what people mean by getting them to specify what kinds of thought and action they are referring to in using their terms. And we will get clear about these meanings just to the degree that the procedure is carried out.

Peirce had high hopes for his pragmatic theory of meaning. Although it did not attract much notice at first and later was interpreted in ways that displeased him, Peirce thought that a pragmatic rebellion against vagueness and confusion could foster a new cooperation in the search for truth that would benefit all humankind. He saw that the clarification of meaning, seemingly a simple task, might be enormously complex. It could lead from concept to concept, from experience to experience, without a foreseeable end. He even acknowledged that "our perversity and that of others may indefinitely postpone the settlement of opinion; it might even conceivably cause an arbitrary proposition to be universally accepted as long as the human race should last" (p. 133). But his more characteristic position was that "it is unphilosophical to suppose that, with regard to any given question (if it has a clear meaning), investigation would not bring forth a solution of it, if it were carried far enough" (p. 134). Moreover, banking on the increased influence that science might have, Peirce saw scientific investigation as a great humanizing force. It "strongly influences those who pursue it to subordinate all motives of ambition, fame, greed, self-seeking of every description."[16] Peirce's enthusiasm may have been excessive, but the intent was to increase communal understanding and knowledge.

How Clear Can We Be?

Peirce was attracted to the method of scientific inquiry for three major reasons. It employed a procedure that was public and open to anyone to use. It also had a self-corrective quality, and it involved individuals working cooperatively to approach a common and universal goal. Just as Aristotle did much to establish the basic vocabulary of philosophy, Peirce's pragmatism helped to lessen philosophy's obsession about certainty, and move it to approach experience with an empirical and a fallibilistic orientation. Peirce's ambitions for science were less grandiose than those of Aristotle, Bacon, or Spinoza. But like them he did hope that greater agreement might prevail in human experience than had been the case before. He believed in principle that for every clearly formulated problem there could be a rational solution. Reappraising our methods of inquiry could direct us toward that goal, even in a world in which error is a permanent possibility.

As a twentieth century full of violence and conflict bears painful witness, Peirce's hope has gone largely unfulfilled. Why? Human perversity, as Peirce proclaimed, deserves much of the blame. People allow fixed beliefs to govern their conduct, and the tenacity with which people cling to such notions, even when vast amounts of evidence stand in opposition, is notorious. The theory of the inherent superiority of one race over another, for example, has little evidence to support it. Yet tension based on racism continues to plague society. Part of the problem is that Peirce's outlook is not easily implemented so as to effect a change in human attitudes. The problem is further complicated, however, because it is not even clear that implementing Peirce's method would produce all the results he anticipated. Ironically, the puzzling question "How clear can we be?" intrudes again just when Peirce thought he had solved the problem of how to make our ideas clear.

Perhaps "clarity" is a relative matter. As Aristotle reminded us, the precision possible in science often is not available in politics or in individual experience. Sometimes this difficulty is due to human perversity. Sometimes it is a function of diversity. Peirce assumed that every human mind can work in the same way, but each may work differently from others. Although not absolutely different, to be sure, variations in experience keep us thinking in divergent ways, in practice, even if we agree on basic methodological principles. Philosophers, including Peirce, often lament the disagreements that result from different human experiences. Considering the particularity and diversity of individual experiences, perhaps it is more surprising that people agree as much as they do.

Even when we do know what we want to say and succeed in saying what we mean, exact meaning remains hard to fix. Meaning is felt, intuited, as much as it is verbally specified. It is not clear that the meaning we experience can always be captured in words that transmit specifiable expectations. Even when we do specify meaning verbally, emotion is often generated, too. Our words have meanings, but they communicate imprecisely. They often resist our efforts at clarification. Not even the public access provided by the methods of science and the pragmatic approach to clarity can completely remove emotion. Peirce's own experience in employing scientific method should have made it clear to him that an individual's personal experience involves elements that elude the best-trained community of investigators. Otherwise, why wouldn't everyone adopt Peirce's theory? The most that his pragmatic methods may be able to accomplish is to point out that our experiences of ambiguity and confusion are real and irreducible.

How do we think? Peirce's basic answer is: Not as clearly as we should. But that answer leads to another question: How clearly can we think? And what are the risks involved in thinking as clearly as we can? Read some of Peirce's 1877 essay, "The Fixation of Belief," and ask whether thinking can give us perfectly clear answers to those questions.

I V

The irritation of doubt causes a struggle to attain a state of belief.* I shall term this struggle *inquiry*, though it must be admitted that this is sometimes not a very apt designation.

The irritation of doubt is the only immediate motive for the struggle to attain belief. It is certainly best for us that our beliefs should be such as may truly guide our actions so as to satisfy our desires; and this reflection will make us reject any belief which does

not seem to have been so formed as to insure this result. But it will only do so by creating a doubt in the place of that belief. With the doubt, therefore, the struggle begins, and with the cessation of doubt it ends. Hence, the sole object of inquiry is the settlement of opinion. We may fancy that this is not enough for us, and that we seek not merely an opinion, but a true opinion. But put this fancy to the test, and it proves groundless; for as soon as a firm belief is reached we are entirely satisfied, whether the belief be false or true. And it is clear that nothing out of the sphere of our knowledge can be our object, for nothing which does not affect the mind can be a motive for a mental effort. The most that can be maintained is that we seek for a belief that we shall *think* to be true. But we think each one of our beliefs to be true, and, indeed, it is mere tautology to say so.†

That the settlement of opinion is the sole end of inquiry is a very important proposition. It sweeps away, at once, various vague and erroneous conceptions of proof. A few of these may be noticed here.

1. Some philosophers have imagined that to start an inquiry it was only necessary to utter or question or set it down on paper, and have even recommended us to begin our studies with questioning everything! But the mere putting of a proposition into the interrogative form does not stimulate the mind to any struggle after belief. There must be a real and living doubt, and without all this, discussion is idle.

2. It is a very common idea that a demonstration must rest on some ultimate and absolutely indubitable propositions. These, according to one school, are first principles of a general nature; according

---

*Doubt, however, is not usually hesitancy about what is to be done then and there. It is anticipated hesitancy about what I shall do hereafter, or a feigned hesitancy about a fictitious state of things. It is the power of making believe we hesitate, together with the pregnant fact that the decision upon the make-believe dilemma goes toward forming a bona fide habit that will be operative in a real emergency. It is these two things in conjunction that constitute us intellectual beings. [Added in 1893.]

†For truth is neither more nor less than that character of a proposition which consists in this, that belief in the proposition would, with sufficient experience and reflection, lead us to such conduct as would tend to satisfy the desires we should then have. To say that truth means more than this is to say that it has no meaning at all. [1903.]

to another, are first sensations. But, in point of fact, an inquiry, to have that completely satisfactory result called demonstration, has only to start with propositions perfectly free from all actual doubt. If the premises are not in fact doubted at all, they cannot be more satisfactory than they are.[‡]

3. Some people seem to love to argue a point after all the world is fully convinced of it. But no further advance can be made. When doubt ceases, mental action on the subject comes to an end; and, if it did go on, it would be without a purpose, except that of self-criticism.

V

If the settlement of opinion is the sole object of inquiry, and if belief is of the nature of a habit, why should we not attain the desired end by taking any answer to a question, which we may fancy, and constantly reiterating it to ourselves, dwelling on all which may conduce to that belief, and learning to turn with contempt and hatred from anything which might disturb it? This simple and direct method is really pursued by many men. I remember once being entreated not to read a certain newspaper lest it might change my opinion upon free trade. "Lest I might be entrapped by its fallacies and misstatements" was the form of expression. "You are not," my friend said, "a special student of political economy. You might, therefore, easily be deceived by fallacious arguments upon the subject. You might, then, if you read this paper, be led to believe in protection. But you admit that free trade is the true doctrine; and you do not wish to believe what is not true." I have often known this system to be deliberately adopted. Still oftener, the instinctive dislike of an undecided state of mind, exaggerated into a vague dread of doubt, makes men cling spasmodically to the views they already take. The man feels that if he only holds to his belief without

wavering, it will be entirely satisfactory. Nor can it be denied that a steady and immovable faith yields great peace of mind. It may, indeed, give rise to inconveniences, as if a man should resolutely continue to believe that fire would not burn him, or that he would be eternally damned if he received his *ingesta* otherwise than through a stomach pump. But then the man who adopts this method will not allow that its inconveniences are greater than its advantages. He will say, "I hold steadfastly to the truth and the truth is always wholesome." And in many cases it may very well be that the pleasure he derives from his calm faith overbalances any inconveniences resulting from its deceptive character. Thus, if it be true that death is annihilation, then the man who believes that he will certainly go straight to heaven when he dies, provided he have fulfilled certain simple observances in this life, has a cheap pleasure which will not be followed by the least disappointment. A similar consideration seems to have weight with many persons in religious topics, for we frequently hear it said, "Oh, I could not believe so-and-so, because I should be wretched if I did." When an ostrich buries its head in the sand as danger approaches, it very likely takes the happiest course. It hides the danger, and then calmly says there is no danger; and, if it feels perfectly sure there is none, why should it raise its head to see? A man may go through life, systematically keeping out of view all that might cause a change in his opinions, and if he only succeeds—basing his method, as he does, on two fundamental psychological laws—I do not see what can be said against his doing so. It would be an egotistical impertinence to object that his procedure is irrational, for that only amounts to saying that his method of settling belief is not ours. He does not propose to himself to be rational, and indeed, will often talk with scorn of man's weak and illusive reason. So let him think as he pleases.

But this method of fixing belief, which may be called the method of tenacity, will be unable to hold its ground in practice. The social impulse is against it. The man who

[‡]Doubts about them may spring up later; but we can find no propositions which are not subject to this contingency. [1903.]

adopts it will find that other men think differently from him, and it will be apt to occur to him in some saner moment that their opinions are quite as good as his own, and this will shake his confidence in his belief. This conception, that another man's thought or sentiment may be equivalent to one's own, is a distinctly new step, and a highly important one. It arises from an impulse too strong in man to be suppressed, without danger of destroying the human species. Unless we make ourselves hermits, we shall necessarily influence each other's opinions; so that the problem becomes how to fix belief, not in the individual merely, but in the community.[17]

Miguel de Unamuno and the Tragic Sense of Life

In 1913, the year before Charles Peirce's death, Spanish philosopher Miguel de Unamuno (1864–1936) published a book entitled *The Tragic Sense of Life*. Unamuno, a Roman Catholic, agreed with Aristotle: human beings naturally desire knowledge. But he held that this desire will ultimately be frustrated. It was Unamuno's impression that "reason is essentially skeptical."[18] He thought that reason's questions cast doubt on our beliefs and that this skeptical quality of reason combined with other elements in our existence to give life a tragic sense. Yet those circumstances need not leave people in despair. The tragic sense of life, Unamuno affirmed, contains resources that can check hopelessness. "The skepticism of the reason encounters the despair of the heart and this encounter leads to the discovery of a basis—a terrible basis—for consolation to build on" (p. 105).

The Man of Flesh and Bone

Unamuno, a novelist as well as a philosopher, spent most of his career at the Univer-

MIGUEL DE UNAMUNO 1864–1936

sity of Salamanca, where he was professor of Greek. He was also politically active. Coming from the Basque region of Spain, an area with a long history of dissent from the Spanish establishment, Unamuno took an independent line that often put him at odds with the ruling powers. Forced into exile for much of the 1920s, he was able to return to Spain in the 1930s, but he drew little satisfaction from the policies of either side during the Spanish Civil War. During the last year of his life he was under house arrest. Unamuno followed Socrates in affirming that the philosopher should be a gadfly calling into question what is taken for granted, probing fundamental assumptions, and above all unmasking human pretentiousness and insisting on honesty. These factors led Unamuno to emphasize: "The man we have to do with is the man of flesh and bone—I, you, reader of mine, the other man yonder, all of us who walk solidly on the earth" (p. 1).

Unamuno thought philosophy was neglecting something vital as it searched for knowledge. Too much stress was being placed on the universal, not enough on the particular. But man in general does not philosophize; individual persons do. Moreover, they do so not merely to obtain absolute truth or objective knowledge. Instead, said Unamuno, the philosopher "philosophizes in order to live" (p. 29). What Unamuno meant is that, as we think, our basic yearnings assert themselves. Abstractly stated, the need is to form "a complete and unitary conception of the world and of life," but that need derives from flesh and bone (p. 2). We are beings who are born, suffer, and die, and our philosophy is therefore more like poetry than science. It has autobiographical elements that are too often overlooked. "Our philosophy," contended Unamuno, "springs from our feeling towards life itself. And life, like everything affective, has roots in subconsciousness, perhaps in unconsciousness" (p. 3). Freud, as we have seen, developed this theme into a modern psychology, but it is interesting to see it argued by Unamuno, the humanist existentialist philosopher, as well as by the founder of psychoanalysis.

Aristotle recognized that exactitude escapes us when a given subject matter is too complex. Peirce stressed fallibility because our judgments could not be guaranteed against the possibility of error. Neither of them, however, emphasized that there is an irreducible subjective element that filters into all the ways we think. They made allowance for whim and bias, of course. But it was Unamuno who suggested that feeling and the personal aspects of experience unavoidably color our thinking, even in ways that remain veiled. Unamuno believed that a philosopher usually "philosophizes either in order to resign himself to life, or to seek some

finality in it, or to distract himself and forget his griefs, or for pastime and amusement" (p. 29).

Why and Wherefore

Unamuno denied that we seek knowledge simply for the sake of knowledge, truth only for the sake of truth. On the contrary, he asserted, "the 'why' interests us only in view of the 'wherefore' " (p. 32). Inquiry, Unamuno concurred with Peirce, aims at the settlement of opinion, but Unamuno stressed even more how practical that settlement really is. It aims at understanding what our destiny shall be. More accurately, the settlement of opinion seeks to obtain an interpretation of the "wherefore" that makes as much sense of life as honesty permits. To know the "wherefore" is to be able to state the aims of our life and why we pursue the goals we choose. Life struck Unamuno as fundamentally tragic. As he explored the "wherefore," he found that neither the facts of life nor our thoughts and emotions about them mesh together in a way that provides tranquility. Instead they produce feelings of conflict and struggle reflecting an irreducible tension between the head and the heart caused by the simple fact that human beings die.

Philosophers reflect at length about experience, but they differ both in the particular experiences each emphasizes and in the ways they think about experience in general. Aristotle and Peirce said relatively little about death. Unamuno thinks that a consideration of death is crucial in any appraisal of how we think. His strongest claim about death is that "I do not want to die—no; I neither want to die nor do I want to want to die; I want to live for ever and ever and ever" (p. 45). Unamuno intentionally wrote in the first-person singular. His report about death is his feeling. He offered no proof that it inevitably must be shared by every man and woman, but he surmised that the feeling he expressed was universal.

Granted, some people take their own lives or give them up voluntarily. Unamuno could see that in some instances life becomes unbearable and death is welcomed. In the former cases, the longing for death comes only when life-affirming forces are drained away beyond the point of being replenished. As for cases of the latter type, a love for life is still visible, since voluntary death actually affirms life. You make the decision to die for a cause or reason, rather than deserting life because you cannot stand it any longer. The most critical point for Unamuno, though, is that the thirst for life is not assuaged. Death has many whys but no obvious wherefore. We die for many reasons, but we never know the outcome or final purpose. We can determine why we act, but we cannot know life's ultimate meaning or aim. Therein lies the tragic sense of life and Unamuno's "answer" to how we acquire knowledge.

The Skepticism of Reason

Where death is concerned, the skepticism of reason becomes overwhelming, because there is overriding evidence against our hope that death is not absolute and final. An analysis based solely on **reason** tells us that death leaves behind a corpse, nothing more or less. To think otherwise is to defy empirical facts irrationally. Testimony against the ultimate annihilation of the individual person can be heard, but we are unlikely to be persuaded by reason alone. Unamuno agreed that the meaning of death is precisely what our reason tells us, namely, the ultimate disappearance of the individual. And the lingering influence of the individual is a sort of impersonal immortality that little interested Unamuno. What he longed for, and what his reason denied him, was an assurance that the grave was not the end of one's life.

In Unamuno's estimate, neither skeptical reason nor death is final, however. Paradoxically, what Unamuno implied is that thinking goes further than reason itself. Unamuno's philosophy, for example, is certainly an instance of thinking, but he refuses to limit his thinking to the use of reason alone. Unamuno argued that neither the head nor the heart ever operates in isolation. Hence, if skepticism threatens our hope for immortality, a passion for life is not therefore rendered helpless by our thinking. Reason and **faith**—the latter was Unamuno's designation for his passionate hope for immortality—are enemies. But "in the depths of the abyss, the despair of the heart and of the will and the skepticism of reason meet face to face and embrace like brothers" (p. 106). Within that embrace, the tragic sense of life, though not eliminated, can be dealt with effectively.

No less than the head, the heart knows that death awaits us all. Its yearning for life beyond death is prompted by our feeling of the inevitability of death. The heart's despair is only intensified by reason, for the latter offers no consolation, no support for our yearning. It adds fuel to the fires of despair. The sheer hopelessness of this situation, however, makes a reversal possible. If skepticism and despair cannot be removed, they eventually turn upon themselves. This opens the door a crack. Things do not necessarily have to be the way reason, or even the heart's despair, makes them appear to be. No leap to a certainty beyond uncertainty is honest in this situation, Unamuno admitted. Nevertheless, a faith that affirms something different from despair, in spite of and even because of skepticism and uncertainty, remains an option.

Two Kinds of Thinking

"Reason and faith are two enemies," said Unamuno, "neither of which can maintain itself without the other" (p. 111). If reason were not sustained by trust that life has purpose, skepticism would leave us without consolation or incentive. Life cannot continue to reason just for its own sake, but life can encourage reason to carry on if it outlines a purpose. On the other hand, faith is unthinkable without reason and in particular without reason's skepticism. For example, wrote Unamuno, "the most robust faith . . . is based on uncertainty" (p. 187). Where there is no uncertainty, there can be no faith. For Unamuno, faith is belief in spite of compelling evidence to the contrary; it is trust in spite of good "reasons" to think that trust might be misplaced. The outcome of this relationship, however, is not a harmonious reconciliation between reason and faith. This fact remains: "Life cheats reason and reason cheats life" (p. 116). Life cannot supply the certainty reason demands, but reason cannot carry on without meaning.

The rational, stated Unamuno, tends to be against life. Existence is in process; reason puts it into fixed compartments. Life moves; reason locks it into unchanging forms. Understanding demands a fixed focus, but reason cheats life nonetheless. Life, however, returns reason's favor. It cheats reason when life defies, even contradicts, reason's dictates. We "think out" a solution to some problems in life—marriage, for example. But then a shift in our personal relationships, in the emotions of the personalities involved, makes it hard to accept rational analysis. We would have had no reason to think unless life made the problem meaningful for us, and yet often life moves so fast that by the time it has been carefully worked out, reason's analysis is no longer useful.

Unamuno believed that "life is contradiction" (p. 14), although he never said that existence itself is contradictory. He believed, rather, that existence could be irrational. To say this may not be understandable within the categories of reason alone. For Una-

muno, our individual lives are riddled by contradictions; existence pulls us in fundamentally opposite directions. To the question "Is death ultimate?", for example, one part of us says "yes," another "no." Such contradiction is a fact of life; it comes from our life experience, and it is not solely logical and theoretical. Many would like reason to prevail in life, and sometimes it does. But in the matter of life and death, life may cheat reason. As humans we may insist on denying death's victory. The struggle between two kinds of thinking—the thinking of reason and our faith in life—continues. Unamuno wanted it that way. "For my part," he insisted, "I do not wish to make peace between my heart and my head, between my faith and my reason—I wish rather that there should be war between them" (p. 119).

Never-Ending Longing

The refusal to make peace between his heart and his head characterized Unamuno's outlook. As he put it,

> . . . my soul at least . . . longs ever to approach and never to arrive, it longs for never-ending longing, for an eternal hope which is eternally renewed but never wholly fulfilled. And together with all this, it longs for an eternal lack of something and an eternal suffering. (P. 256.)

The human thirst for life is an urge to go on living life as we know it, removing only waste, boredom, and death. Suffering, however, has a place. Suffering heightens our awareness of existence. Human life is stretched out into a future that entails both the joy of hope and the anguish of waiting. Love is "the most tragic thing in the world" because we can never confirm it to be right by using reason; yet it drives human energies" (p. 132). This happens both through the suffering we experience directly and through our recognition that others suffer. We are drawn to do what we can to relieve their agony.

Unamuno understood that his never-ending longing was a function of his finite and contingent existence. As much as we may want a total explanation of why we exist, such cannot be seen along our limited horizons. We sense that there is nothing necessary, certainly nothing permanent, about our earthly life, and no human being, claimed Unamuno, can be content with the prospect of eventual annihilation. But does Unamuno's longing make any difference, or is it only a flickering of consciousness bracketed by the twin mysteries of birth and death? He could not be sure. He believed, however, that the longing stood no chance of fulfillment without the existence of God. "We need God," asserted Unamuno, "not in order to understand the *way*, but in order to feel and sustain the ultimate *wherefore*, to give a meaning to the Universe" (p. 152). If his never-ending longing was to have a chance for fulfillment, something more was needed than a principle that explained how the world came to be. Wrote Unamuno:

> The only way to give finality to the world is to give it consciousness. For where there is no consciousness there is no finality, finality presupposing a purpose. (P. 52.)

A God with personal qualities, then, is required to sustain the ultimate "wherefore." Once more, however, the tragic sense of life intrudes. If we want to redeem ourselves and our world from eternal nonexistence, we need a God who cares for and sustains finite creatures. But final knowledge that such a God exists is not to be found. To the contrary, human reason offers plenty of contrary evidence, and this leaves Unamuno's never-ending longing in never-ending frustration. But once more Unamuno rose to the occasion and turned despair itself into a foundation for a different kind of belief. To believe in God is not to know conclusively

that God exists but rather to long for God's existence, he said. Uncertainty is a precondition for faith; it makes hope possible. The crucial link between hope and faith, Unamuno went on to say, is that "we believe what we hope for" (p. 52).

Unamuno's parting wish for the readers of *The Tragic Sense of Life*, from which the following reading is excerpted, was "May God deny you peace, but give you glory" (p. 330). We think in order to live, but the attempt to acquire knowledge should not be a tranquil effort. It has to involve "uncertainty, doubt, perpetual wrestling with the mystery of our final destiny, mental despair, and the lack of any solid and stable dogmatic foundation" (p. 256). In contending with this knowledge, Unamuno believed, the glory he wished for his readers might be theirs. Do you share that understanding?

The man we have to do with is the man of flesh and bone—I, you, reader of mine, the other man yonder, all of us who walk solidly on the earth.

And this concrete man, this man of flesh and bone, is at once the subject and the supreme object of all philosophy, whether certain self-styled philosophers like it or not.

In most of the histories of philosophy that I know, philosophic systems are presented to us as if growing out of one another spontaneously, and their authors, the philosophers, appear only as mere pretexts. The inner biography of the philosophers, of the men who philosophized, occupies a secondary place. And yet it is precisely this inner biography that explains for us most things.

It behooves us to say, before all, that philosophy lies closer to poetry than to science. All philosophic systems which have been constructed as a supreme concord of the final results of the individual sciences have in every age possessed much less consistency and life than those which expressed the integral spiritual yearning of their authors.

And, though they concern us so greatly, and are, indeed, indispensable for our life and thought, the sciences are in a certain sense more foreign to us than philosophy. They fulfill a more objective end—that is to say, an end more external to ourselves. They are fundamentally a matter of economics. A new scientific discovery, of the kind called theoretical, is, like a mechanical discovery—that of the steam engine, the telephone, the phonograph, or the airplane—a thing which is useful for something else. Thus the telephone may be useful to us in enabling us to communicate at a distance with the woman we love. But she, wherefore is she useful to us? A man takes an electric tram to go to hear an opera, and asks himself, Which, in this case, is the more useful, the tram or the opera?

Philosophy answers to our need of forming a complete and unitary conception of the world and of life, and as a result of this conception, a feeling which gives birth to an inward attitude and even to outward action. But the fact is that this feeling, instead of being a consequence of this conception, is the cause of it. Our philosophy—that is, our mode of understanding or not understanding the world and life—springs from our feeling towards life itself. And life, like everything affective, has roots in subconsciousness, perhaps in unconsciousness.

It is not usually our ideas that make us optimists or pessimists, but it is our optimism or our pessimism, of physiological or perhaps pathological origin, as much the one as the other, that makes our ideas.

Man is said to be a reasoning animal. I do not know why he has not been defined as an affective or feeling animal. Perhaps that which differentiates him from other animals is feeling rather than reason. More often I have seen a cat reason than laugh or weep. Perhaps it weeps or laughs inwardly—but then perhaps, also inwardly, the crab resolves equations of the second degree.

And thus, in a philosopher, what must needs most concern us is the man. (Pp. 50–51.)

Summary

When we compare Aristotle, Bacon, Spinoza, Peirce, and Unamuno, we see that each answers the question "How can I acquire knowledge?" in a distinctive manner. Aristotle is the technician; he builds a precisely defined vocabulary to attack the problem. Bacon places his hopes in a method of induction. Spinoza stresses the necessity of obtaining clear and distinct ideas, which he believes will correspond with reality. Peirce, the pragmatist, is suspicious of any claim that we possess certainty but hopes that the fallible methods of science will be sufficiently self-corrective to keep error at bay. Unamuno sets the whole question about knowing into the context of our search for meaning as we try to deal with the tragic sense of life.

Knowing is a puzzling process, but philosophers have often hoped that it would all be made plain one day. Perhaps this can be done by using one philosophical theory or another as the basis for your explanation, but unfortunately for the human desire to solve its problems once and for all, no philosophy seems to stand as exclusively or finally correct. Philosophy can give answers, but these answers in turn raise new questions. We should remember that truth may be so rich as to be partly found in many theories but too rich to be fully contained by any one of them.

No single chapter can explain how we know. That is at least a life-long project. But in presenting these diverse thinkers, we hope the diversity in each approach will itself produce insights. If, as Aristotle said, individually we fail but collectively we may succeed, then by contrasting theories we might come to understand better how we acquire knowledge. Thus, to summarize this chapter, review the central theory of each thinker and see if you can reconcile them or, if not, choose among them. Considering the alternatives, ask yourself: Which is the closest to the way I think knowledge can be acquired?

GLOSSARY

argument unlike the ordinary connotation of a dispute between two or more persons, a sustained monologue, or *discourse*, composed of systematic reasoning and aimed at an exhaustive exposition and analysis of the subject matter.

being an existing thing; also, the property all existing things possess in common, regardless of their **category;** what is referred to by the various senses of the word "is."

categories types, kinds, or classes of things, grouped together according to similarity and distinguished by lack of similarity; in Aristotle, the ten most fundamental kinds of expression out of which propositions can be constructed, corresponding to the ten most fundamental kinds of **beings.**

cause, efficient the agency, power, or dynamic process that brings about the transformation of the matter composing a thing. Aristotle's favorite example is the production of a work of art or craft: the sculptor is the efficient cause of the sculpture he produces.

cause, final the purpose for which a thing is made, the function it is designed to serve.

cause, formal the **form** that is realized by a being, the *model* or prototype of a thing or class of things; that which the object is made to represent or resemble.

cause, material the matter of which a thing is composed; for instance, the clay is the material cause of the urn into which it is formed by the craftsman.

causes in Aristotle, the various kinds of beings out of which other beings come to be; Aristotle's notions of the four "causes" are less like the modern concept of "cause" as employed by Hume or Kant than like what we might call an "explanation." See above.

change the process in and by which things are altered or transformed, the principles of which Aristotle thought to explain fully by applying the notion of the four **causes.**

deduction a form of the method of reasoning called **inference,** in which necessary conclusions are reached by applying analytic defini-tions and laws of logical derivation to some original premise to derive its logical consequences. See **syllogism.**

faith an unconditional belief in something that cannot be or has not been proved, justified, or verified, such as belief in a religious or political doctrine or in a metaphysical theory.

fallibilism C. S. Peirce's doctrine that the starting point of philosophical inquiry should be the realization that certainty is a practical impossibility.

finality for Spinoza, the absolute certainty that must characterize true knowledge, which he believed could be found in principles that are indubitable, like the knowledge of our own existence and the principles of mathematics.

first principles the fundamental laws governing the relation between Being and the various kinds of beings, laws the branch of philosophy called *metaphysics* seeks to discover and to formulate in precise concepts.

form the shape or contours of a thing, abstracted from the matter on which the shape is imposed in a particular realization of the form.

hypothesis the tentative, working assumptions, subject to revision in light of further evidence that invalidates them, which form the core of scientific method as Bacon conceived it.

induction the form of reasoning that begins with a substantial body of propositions about observable phenomena and concludes with either a generalization or a prediction, instead of with a necessary truth as in the case of arguments of **deduction.**

inference the process of deriving propositions or beliefs on the basis of other propositions, rather than from direct experience; the branch of philosophy called *logic* is concerned with formulating the standards of validity (see **valid**) for this process.

inquiry in C. S. Peirce's definition, the pursuit of knowledge motivated by the innate propensity of human beings to be made uneasy by the psychological state of doubt and so to prefer and actively pursue a state of belief.

matter the substance of which an entity is composed, abstracted from the particular **form** imposed upon it in a particular object.

necessary premise (see **first principle**) an undeniable proposition on which Aristotle thought a compelling argument should, ideally, be based.

"process of Exclusion" Bacon's phrase for the inductive method, which should form the basis for the discovery of causes in science. In it, observed phenomena are extensively catalogued according to the precise conditions under which they occur, then analyzed to pick out the particular combinations of conditions and observable properties that form a systematic pattern.

proof a piece of reasoning that demonstrates the validity of another piece of reasoning by showing how it derives its conclusions according to rules of inference whose validity is already established.

quality one of Aristotle's categories, containing all the expressions referring to the perceptible properties of things.

quantity another Aristotelian category, containing the expressions referring to the different numbers of things there can be.

reason the faculty of rationality in human beings, which Unamuno stressed must coexist with a capacity for **faith** in light of reason's inability to provide as much certainty as rationalist philosophers have demanded of it.

relation the Aristotelian category expressing the various ways in which things can be conceptually connected to one another, including spatial relations like "is on top of" as well as more abstract relations like "is similar to."

sophistry fallacious, pseudological argumentation designed to mislead or persuade under false pretenses of validity.

superstition a variety of belief based on irrational speculation about the supernatural rather than the real, scientifically discoverable causes of things; one of the afflictions of thought that Bacon thought could be overcome by a universal adoption of scientific procedures.

syllogism the type of deductive inference forming the core of Aristotelian logic, composed of a major premise stating a categorical fact ("All men are mortal") and a minor premise stating a particular matter of fact ("Socrates is a man"), and concluding with the inference derived from combining the two premises ("Socrates must be mortal").

utility practicality, usefulness; the quality of scientific knowledge that Bacon thought established its primacy over other less precise methods of attempting to understand the natural world.

STUDY QUESTIONS

1. What does Aristotle think is most important in the knowing process?

2. In what way would you understand Aristotle's theory to be "scientific"?

3. To what extent is Bacon correct that we believe what we want to believe? Does his method of induction provide an adequate remedy for that tendency?

4. If you were to describe what is involved in sound observation and explanation, would your account differ from Bacon's?

5. Could reliance on Bacon's method of induction itself become an "idol of the mind"?

6. Few philosophers could be further apart in their approaches than Bacon and Spi-

noza. Can you formulate what you think Spinoza wants to accomplish by his method and how his approach would differ fundamentally from Bacon's?

7. Can our understanding be improved by internal inspection, as Spinoza hoped? Why or why not?

8. Does Peirce's theory seem to you to be "modern"? If so, in what way?

9. Do Aristotle and Peirce differ on what they would call scientific? Explain this.

10. If Unamuno is called an existentialist, do you see what this might mean for his theory of knowledge?

11. If Unamuno is right, are there things our reason cannot accomplish?

12. Can you state the ways in which the views of Aristotle, Bacon, Spinoza, Peirce, and Unamuno might be similar and the ways in which you think they are radically different?

NOTES

[1] Aristotle, *Metaphysics* (980a), trans. W. D. Ross, in *The Basic Works of Aristotle*, ed. Richard McKeon (New York: Random House, 1941), p. 689. Reprinted by permission of Oxford University Press.

[2] Aristotle, *Posterior Analytics* (71b), trans. G.R.G. Mure, in *The Basic Works of Aristotle*, p. 111.

[3] Aristotle, *Nicomachean Ethics* (1094a), trans. W. D. Ross, in *The Basic Works of Aristotle*, p. 935.

[4] Aristotle, *Metaphysics* (993b–995a), pp. 712–15.

[5] Francis Bacon, *Novum Organum* ("Aphorisms Concerning the Interpretation of Nature and the Kingdom of Man"), in *The English Philosophers from Bacon to Mill*, ed. Edwin A. Burtt (New York: Modern Library, 1939), p. 28.

[6] Francis Bacon, Preface to *The Great Instauration*, in *The English Philosophers from Bacon to Mill*, p. 19.

[7] Bacon, *Novum Organum* ("Aphorisms"), in *The English Philosophers from Bacon to Mill*, p. 29.

[8] Bacon, Preface to *The Great Instauration*, p. 19.

[9] Bacon, *Novum Organum* ("Aphorisms"), p. 34.

[10] Francis Bacon, Preface to *Novum Organum*, p. 25.

[11] Bacon, Preface to *The Great Instauration*, pp. 15–16.

[12] Baruch Spinoza, *On the Improvement of the Understanding*, trans. Joseph Katz (New York: Liberal Arts Press, 1958), p. 3. Copyright 1958 by Macmillan Publishing Company. Reprinted by permission of the publisher.

[13] Charles S. Peirce, "The Doctrine of Necessity," in *Charles S. Peirce: Selected Writings*, ed. Philip P. Wiener (New York: Dover, 1958), p. 162. Reprinted by permission of Dover Publications, Inc.

[14] Charles S. Peirce, "The Fixation of Belief," in *Charles S. Peirce: Selected Writings*, p. 99.

[15] Charles S. Peirce, "How to Make Our Ideas Clear," in *Charles S. Peirce: Selected Writings*, p. 124.

[16] From Peirce's review of *Clark University, 1889–1899: Decennial Celebration*, dated April 20, 1900, in *Charles S. Peirce: Selected Writings*, p. 334.

[17] Peirce, "The Fixation of Belief," pp. 52–55.

[18] Miguel de Unamuno, *The Tragic Sense of Life in Men and in Peoples*, trans. J. E. Crawford Flitch (London: Macmillan, 1921), p. 90.

CHAPTER FIVE

What Does "Truth" Mean?

*A*n old adage tells us: a picture is worth a thousand words. Although that adage points out the deficiencies in language, words often are adequate to convey what we mean, in spite of their shortcomings. The importance of words in our search for truth is undeniable, as anyone knows who has tried to help a sick animal. The ability to use words makes us human, but to what extent do words hinder us or reveal the truth? We need to ask that question. Otherwise, we cannot know how words can disclose truth to us. As we explore that issue, we will again meet Plato and his theory about the nature of ideas. William James offers the practical advice of an American pragmatist, and A. J. Ayer will bring us closer to our own times with a view on how to clear up obscurities. In the present day, Ludwig Wittgenstein, the fourth philosopher discussed in this chapter, is the one most often associated with the effort to reform philosophy so that our words can reveal truth. The approach and the methods we use are all important. We need to think through our notion of philosophy before we speak. We cannot automatically assume that the words we utter will convey truth to others as we hope they will.

Like the air we breathe, we often take **language** for granted. Nevertheless, it functions in an amazing variety of ways. Family ties and friendships, politics and poetry, science and technology, business and pleasure—all these and more depend on our use of words. Not the least of all, words reflect and to some extent determine our ability to ask questions and receive answers. Words fascinate philosophers for these reasons. At first glance, it seems that we can speak or write truthfully about virtually anything and everything. Yet philosophers wonder not only whether words actually reflect the truth in specific cases but also whether in other cases words can reveal the truth at all.

First and foremost, we must be sure we know what we mean by **"truth."** The distinction between truth and falsity is vital to our search. If we cannot define truth, plans may be misguided, choices imprudent, and lives put at risk. Unfortunately, overcoming our inability to state the truth can be just as difficult as the possession of truth is important. Lying and self-deception thrive in unclarity. But even when truth is grasped, claims about it may be precarious. Consider the experience of making an "honest mistake." You believed sincerely that you had acted according to what was true, but later you found you were wrong. Often we do not control truth—at least not completely. That realization prompts philosophers to inquire about the nature of language and its relation to truth. Such philosophical questions improve our understanding by revealing where our use of language is limited. We learn how to clarify the meaning of basic concepts and to ask again, "What does 'truth' mean?"

Plato and the Nature of Ideas

As we ask about the meaning of truth, few philosophers offer a better starting point than Plato. As we saw in Chapter One, he is the first major and still well-known philosopher in the Western tradition. More important, few things occupied Plato more than trying to understand what truth means and how we can be sure we have found it. For him, this question was tied to the theory of "ideas" he formulated. "Ideas" show us what truth means for Plato and how he thought we can find it. Plato was sensitive to the variety of meanings our important terms such as "justice" have and how little we agree about these meanings. When brought to light, such differences reveal how fundamental our disagreements are, but this discovery also starts us on our search to find the truth. Remember that Plato wrote in dialogue form. The method of dialogue itself, that is, asking and discussing questions, is central in his search for truth.

The Socratic Quest

Plato's dialogues often feature his teacher, Socrates. That they often end on an inconclusive note suggests something important about Plato's view of truth. As we noted in Chapter One, a famous letter by Plato indicates his doubt that truth can be written down in a direct, literal discourse. Without mutual inquiry, truth does not appear, but even with such efforts, its appearance is not easy to discern, let alone state once and for all in simple words.

Plato's picture of the "Socratic quest" suggests that philosophers are largely searchers rather than question answerers. As we start

out, we stand somewhere between complete ignorance and full knowledge. To search, we must have begun with some idea of what we are seeking. We start, then, with some innate knowledge, but, Plato insisted, it must be developed. The question-and-answer procedure of dialogue helps us to do this. At times, truth may be grasped in a flash after a time of searching, but Plato added that we do not control this outcome. For example, as we commonly use them, terms such as "justice" and "virtue" have many meanings. To learn their essential meanings requires clarification. No guarantee exists that we will make this discovery, but in the course of dialogue we may be led to an apprehension of the truth.

Such apprehension, however, is not easily communicated; it cannot simply be handed over to others. Plato's point is that the search *is* the discovery. Not just the conclusion but the path we use to reach it are crucial dimensions of the truth. Each person must go through the search for himself or herself. And this is not only the case during our early education. The philosophical life is basically a permanent quest. Yet, odd as it seems, this insight does not mean that truth does not exist. According to Plato, it is there—fixed, final, and permanent. To explain how life is an eternal quest and yet that truth exists absolute and eternal, we must turn to Plato's theory of ideas.

Recalling the Truth

The *Meno* is a dialogue in which Plato asks questions of an unschooled slave boy. Upon being questioned, Meno is able to "recall" the correct answers to hard geometrical problems he has never seen before. Plato postulates that we all know the truth but not always consciously. Under questioning, we may recall it. Plato's theory of "**recollection**," as it is often called, illustrates his basic belief that truth exists and that it can be apprehended by our minds and used to guide us. To show how this apprehension occurs, Plato suggested that there are separately existing **Forms** of all things. These Ideas, as he sometimes designated them, are eternal and unchanging. They exist beyond our conventional perceptions of space and time. Indeed, Plato speculates that our own souls may have existed prior to our earthly lives. In that state, we knew the truth much better than we do now. Having been thrown into a material world at birth, we have forgotten what we knew before our minds became distracted, but still we may recall some truth if we try.

Our words "man," "chair," and "justice," and the objects in the world that we call by those names, Plato contended, are each individual representations of universal Forms. Studying individual objects, or considering topics such as virtue or justice, can lead our minds to grasp the Forms that each of these things embodies. Plato did not deny that there are many kinds of men, many kinds of chairs, and many views of justice, but he did hold that all individual things participate in Forms that make them knowable. Grasping the Forms of things, according to Plato, is essentially what "truth" involves.

The Discovery of Universals

In another dialogue, *Theatetus,* Plato wrote that "the mind, by a power of her own, contemplates the universals in all things."[1] We can grasp concepts such as "man," "chair," and "justice" because our minds mesh with what is real when we use these concepts properly. Thus, "knowledge does not consist in impressions of sense, but in reasoning about them" (186, 2:189). Sense experience may be the occasion for such reflection, but it is through thought that we grasp the Ideas that lie behind the visible, changing world of everyday life.

In Plato's most widely known dialogue, *The Republic,* the participants cannot agree on the meaning of "justice," since it has diverse meanings in ordinary experience. So the participants discuss justice, allowing Plato to make the point that just as knowledge and opinion are different, so there are two worlds. Belief involves us with appearances that are less than fully real. But knowledge must apprehend what is fully real, the world of Forms: "Now, that which imparts truth to the known and the power of knowing to the knower is what I would have you term the idea of good, and this you will deem to be the cause of science, and of truth in so far as the latter becomes the subject of knowledge."[2] We may think we know things simply through empirical observation, but Plato thought that what gives us knowledge and truth—not just opinion—is a grasp of the Forms behind the particular objects. Truth involves **universal** concepts, and without them, there can be no comprehension of **particulars.**

The Journey of the Dialectic

Plato defined "dialectic" as the journey we take to seek the truth, the apprehension of his universal Forms or Ideas. The method of dialogue starts us out; questions lead us; but essentially we are drawn on toward truth by the grasp of universal Forms, such as goodness, which lie behind the world of individual objects and our experience of them. This journey could not take place, Plato believed, unless the world of Forms did exist. Truth is eternal and immutable, and it is the ever-changing nature of our earthly existence that prompts us to seek it. Because we experience many kinds of goodness, we are led to ask what is the "Goodness itself" in which all the particular instances of goodness share.

As the best illustration of what Plato means by Ideas and how we can find them, recall the allegory of the cave we read in Chapter One. There Plato likened the quest for truth to a quest for light and, more than that, a quest for the light behind the flickering shadows in our world. We see the shadows in front of us and some of us accept these as ultimately real. But the philosophers, the inquirers, search instead for the source of the light that illuminates them and will not settle for less. The Platonic symbol for truth has always been light, which means the final grasp of the Ideas, the universal Forms, which exist independently of our changing world, but which alone explain it. When we grasp the form Goodness or Justice, we have discovered the universal quality in which all particular instances of goodness or justice share. Such knowledge of Forms is truth, because they do not change as our beliefs do. The passage that follows comes from *The Republic,* just after Plato's story about the cave. Socrates sums up what dialectic involves. In doing so, he tells us more about truth by distinguishing between knowledge and opinion.

And so, Glaucon, I said, we have at last arrived at the hymn of dialectic. This is that strain which is of the intellect only, but which the faculty of sight will nevertheless be found to imitate: for sight, as you may remember, was imagined by us after a while to behold the real animals and stars, and last of all the sun himself. And so with dialectic; when a person starts on the discovery of the absolute by the light of reason only, and without any assistance of sense, and perseveres until by pure intelligence he arrives at the perception of the absolute good, he at last finds himself at the end of the intellectual world, as in the case of sight at the end of the visible.

Exactly, he said.

Then this is the progress which you call dialectic?

True.

But the release of the prisoners from chains, and their translation from the shadows to the images and to the light, and the ascent from the underground den to the sun, while in his presence they are vainly trying to look on animals and plants and the light of the sun, but are able to perceive even with their weak eyes the images in the water [which are divine], and are the shadows of true existence (not shadows of images cast by a light of fire, which compared with the sun is only an image)—this power of elevating the highest principle in the soul to the contemplation of that which is best in existence, with which we may compare the raising of that faculty which is the very light of the body to the sight of that which is brightest in the material and visible world— this power is given, as I was saying, by all that study and pursuit of the arts which has been described.

I agree in what you are saying, he replied, which may be hard to believe, yet, from another point of view, is harder still to deny. This however is not a theme to be treated of in passing only, but will have to be discussed again and again. And so, whether our conclusion be true or false, let us assume all this, and proceed at once from the prelude or preamble to the chief strain, and describe that in like manner. Say, then, what is the nature and what are the divisions of dialectic, and what are the paths which lead thither; for these paths will also lead to our final rest.

Dear Glaucon, I said, you will not be able to follow me here, though I would do my best, and you should behold not an image only but the absolute truth, according to my notion. Whether what I told you would or would not have been a reality I cannot venture to say; but you would have seen something like reality; of that I am confident.

Doubtless, he replied.

But I must also remind you, that the power of dialectic alone can reveal this, and only to one who is a disciple of the previous sciences.

Of that assertion you may be as confident as of the last.

And assuredly no one will argue that there is any other method of comprehending by any regular process all true existence or of ascertaining what each thing is in its own nature: for the arts in general are concerned with the desires or opinions of men, or are cultivated with a view to production and construction, or for the preservation of such productions and constructions; and as to the mathematical sciences which, as we were saying, have some apprehension of being true—geometry and the like—they only dream about being, but never can they behold the waking reality so long as they leave the hypotheses which they use unexamined, and are unable to give an account of them. For when a man knows not his own first principle, and when the conclusion and intermediate steps are also constructed out of he knows not what, how can he imagine that such a fabric of convention can ever become science?

Impossible, he said.

Then dialectic, and dialectic alone, goes directly to the first principle and is the only science which does away with hypotheses in order to make her ground secure; the eye of the soul, which is literally buried in an outlandish slough, is by her gentle aid lifted upwards; and she uses as handmaids and helpers in the work of conversion, the sciences which we have been discussing. Custom terms them sciences, but they ought to have some other name, implying greater clearness than opinion and less clearness than science: and this, in our previous sketch, was called understanding. But why should we dispute about names when we have realities of such importance to consider?

Why indeed, he said, when any name will do which expresses the thought of the mind with clearness?

At any rate, we are satisfied, as before, to have four divisions; two for intellect and two for opinion, and to call the first division science, the second understanding, the third belief, and the fourth perception of shadows, opinion being concerned with becoming, and intellect with being; and so to make a proportion:

As being is to becoming, so is pure intellect to opinion.

And as intellect is to opinion, so is science to belief, and understanding to the perception of shadows.

But let us defer the further correlation and subdivision of the subjects of opinion and of intellect, for it will be a long enquiry, many times longer than this has been.

As far as I understand, he said, I agree.

And do you also agree, I said, in describing the dialectician as one who attains a conception of the essence of each thing? And he who does not possess and is therefore unable to impart this conception, in whatever degree he fails, may in that degree also be said to fail in intelligence? Will you admit so much?

Yes, he said; how can I deny it?

And you would say the same of the conception of the good? Until the person is able to abstract and define rationally the idea of good, and unless he can run the gauntlet of all objections, and is ready to disprove them, not by appeals to opinion, but to absolute truth, never faltering at any step of the argument—unless he can do all this, you would say that he knows neither the idea of good nor any other good; he apprehends only a shadow, if anything at all, which is given by opinion and not by science; dreaming and slumbering in this life, before he is well awake here, he arrives at the world below, and has his final quietus.

In all that I should most certainly agree with you.

And surely you would not have the children of your ideal State, whom you are nurturing and educating—if the ideal ever becomes a reality—you would not allow the future rulers to be like posts, having no reason in them, and yet to be set in authority over the highest matters?

Certainly not.

Then you will make a law that they shall have such an education as will enable them to attain the greatest skill in asking and answering questions?

Yes, he said, you and I together will make it.

Dialectic, then, as you will agree, is the coping-stone of the sciences, and is set over them; no other science can be placed higher—the nature of knowledge can no further go? I agree, he said. (532–34; 1:791–94.)

William James and the Meaning of Truth

All philosophers are indebted to Plato and his dialectical method of inquiry. But fewer feel obliged to express gratitude for the discoveries Plato made in his dialogues; to his successors some of his conclusions seem profoundly misleading. For example, William James (1842–1910) was not convinced that Plato performed a service by teaching of "concepts as forming an entirely separate world and [treating] this as the only object fit for the study of immortal minds."[3] One of the misleading features of Plato's theory of Ideas, James believed, was that it led to an understanding of truth that did not square with experience. James's philosophy is a version of the **pragmatism** introduced by Charles S. Peirce and later elaborated by John Dewey, whom we will meet later. He offered us an interpretation of truth vastly different from Plato's.

WILLIAM JAMES 1842–1910

What Is Pragmatism?

The career of William James, which began with the study of medicine, was an intellectual and spiritual odyssey that went from physiology to philosophy, with pioneering contributions to psychology in between. Elder brother of the distinguished novelist Henry James, William was a Harvard professor and the best-known American philosopher of his day. A gifted writer and an eloquent speaker, he was much in demand at home and abroad. An invitation to lecture at the Lowell Insti-

tute in Boston during the winter of 1906–7 led to a famous book called *Pragmatism* (1907). James subtitled it: *A New Name for Some Old Ways of Thinking.* His pragmatism, however, was more than that, and the issues it raised provoked a storm of controversy.

Pragmatism, James reports, consists of two parts. It is a method for the determination of meaning, and it is a theory about the nature of truth. Taking up the problem of meaning, James urged that "the whole function of philosophy ought to be to find out what difference it will make to you and me, at definite instants of our life, if this **world-formula** or that world-formula be the true one."[4] The way to such discoveries, he argued, required special attention to words: "You must bring out of each word its practical cash-value, set it at work within the stream of your experience" (p. 53). To avoid merely verbal disputes and to settle those that are genuine, we need a way of obtaining agreement concerning the meaning of our concepts and theories. James believed that the proper way to do this is to analyze a theory for its practical consequences in our future experience. A meaningful theory will lead to some specifiable expectations concerning our activities in the world. If we give a full account of those expectations, this will elucidate the meaning in question.

James counted Socrates, but not necessarily Plato, among the fathers of pragmatism. Both emphasized the practical aspects and agreed with positivism "in its disdain for verbal solutions, useless questions, and metaphysical abstractions" (pp. 53–54). But in its pragmatic guise, James contended, "the empiricist attitude" takes on "a more radical . . . form than it has ever yet assumed" (p. 51). Applied persistently, a pragmatic approach to meaning will tell us whether there are substantial differences between conflicting views. If none can be specified, the dispute between them is merely verbal and the debate should end. On the other hand, if there are substantial differences in the views, an outline of the concrete differences should influence our future beliefs and our efforts to obtain the evidence required to settle disagreement. Suppose one person tells us that socialism is the best economic political system, while another advocates capitalism. We should be able to examine two societies—for instance, Sweden and the United States—and find empirical evidence to tell us that one works better than the other.

James's approach was broadly empirical; that is, he sought for concrete data all could see. No concept or theory is barred from consideration. The search is for experiential data to help us differentiate between claims, but unlike the British philosopher A. J. Ayer, whom we meet next, James never suggested that certain restrictions were demanded by logic. Specifically, it did not occur to James to label moral, religious, or metaphysical claims as "meaningless," as being beyond the realms of truth and falsity altogether. Disputes about these claims, he thought, might well be useless, but the validity of that judgment would depend more on the disputants' lack of clarity than on the meaninglessness of words and propositions themselves.

For James the aim was always to determine the possible concrete expectations that our use of language contains. He did not, as we will find Ayer doing, set up a criterion for meaning—claiming it to be empirical when all the while it was another "fixed principle" of rationalism—then pronouncing as "meaningless" every candidate that did not meet the criterion. James was optimistic about the degree to which clarity can be obtained and about the amount of agreement it will yield. He was open to a range of meaning for "truth."

Two More Basic Points

We want to know the meaning of our beliefs, but even more we want to know whether they are true. James believed this problem arose because we had not carried out a pragmatic analysis of the meaning of "truth." James provided it. His intent was to remove ambiguities in the concept of truth, but he really did more to reveal how uncertain we are when we wonder if or how words can reveal the truth. According to James, a commonsense understanding of truth involves two basic points. First, truth is a property of some ideas or beliefs. Importantly, this view implies that truth and falsity do not exist if there are no ideas. There can still be states of affairs without consciousness, but these would constitute bare existence without truth or falsity. Truth is not just a function of existence but of awareness and judgment. Second, true ideas "agree" with reality. But, James tells us, problems lurk in that formula. It is ambiguous because there are different views about what is meant by our ideas' agreeing with reality. He believes, however, that the issue can be clarified if we remember that ideas and beliefs are essentially guides for organizing and structuring our world. They give us expectations about future experience. It is natural, therefore, to say that the truth or falsity of an idea, or its agreement or disagreement with reality, depends on obtaining or failing to obtain corroboration of the expectations that follow from the idea in question. James sums up as follows:

> *True ideas are those that we can assimilate, validate, corroborate, and verify. False ideas are those that we cannot.* That is the practical difference it makes to us to have true ideas; that, therefore, is the meaning of truth, for it is all that truth is known-as. (P. 201.)

When James states that "truth" means validation, corroboration, and **verification** because that is "all that truth is known-as," he means this: we can say that a belief is true or false only when we test it experientially and find that the expectations it gives us about future events are either fulfilled or unfulfilled. Experiences of corroboration or disconfirmation constitute the meaning of truth.

James and His Critics

James's analysis undercut the traditional view that truth is eternal, unchanging, complete. According to this tradition, we might discover truth but should not think that we create it. James took a different position. Impressed that human experience and the world we inhabit are continually changing, he stressed that verification is temporal and

ongoing. As long as experience continues, corroboration is incomplete. Our truth claims remain fallible. Thus, when we speak of the truth of an idea, we should remember that it is true only "insofar as" it has been verified, or that it is true "just to the extent that" it has been confirmed.

An interesting example is heliocentricity. When Aristotle said the sun went around the earth, observations seemed to verify it, and in that sense his theory was *true*. Only after more accurate observation created anomalies (more than a thousand years later) did Copernicus suggest that the earth revolved around the sun. And when experience showed that model to work better than Aristotle's, it became true and Aristotle's, which had been true, became false. If corroboration and verification are temporal processes, truth itself is temporal. Truth is a property of ideas, and if we inhabit a world in which both facts and ideas are changing, truth itself changes. "The truth of an idea," wrote James, "is not a stagnant property inherent in it. Truth *happens* to an idea. It *becomes* true, is *made* true by events" (p. 201). Our words can reveal truth, but, according to James, they can never do so with completeness and finality as long as there is a future to unfold.

James's views clash with the claim that truth is absolute, eternal, and forever unchanging. He argues that thinking in absolutes takes us beyond actual experience, which does not demonstrate that the truth is complete, fixed, and unchanging, although experience does show that some ideas, like the Copernican model, have been validated for a very long time. At best, James contends, the notion of absolute truth serves as a helpful limiting concept. It refers to what would be the case if all possible inquiry and experience were completed. But as a limiting concept, absolute truth remains unattainable; it reminds us instead of our finitude and fallibility. James even rejected the idea that God has a complete awareness that constitutes absolute truth. He found no compelling evidence in its favor but also regarded divine omniscience as constituting a morally abhorrent determinism.

Already aroused, James's critics were further irritated by his choice of words. For instance, he equated "true" ideas with those that are "useful" or **"expedient."** He suggested that the "true" idea is the one that "works." Such language, it seemed to his critics, did not itself reflect the truth. Granted, if an idea were true, it would be useful or expedient, but to equate expedient and useful ideas with true ones went too far. Terms such as "expedient" and "useful," James's critics insisted, are dangerously subjective and ambiguous. Linking them with truth would reduce truth to opinion, such that even false beliefs might be "true" if they somehow "worked" for individuals.

Additional problems plagued James's theory of truth. His language, the critics claimed, radically relativized ethics and religion. To say that the truth of ethical or religious claims is inextricably related to their usefulness, expediency, or workability leads to a subjectivism that allows people to justify any action or belief that is useful for them. James, by endorsing the possibility that a proposition could be "true for me" even if in fact it was mistaken, might encourage people to flout sound logical standards.

Retreating from Subjectivism

James spent much time answering his critics. Consider the following passage from *Pragmatism:*

> *"The true,"* to put it very briefly, *is only the expedient in the way of our thinking, just as "the right" is only the expedient in the way of our behaving.* Expedient in almost any fashion; and expedient in the long run and on the whole of course; for what meets expediently all the experience in sight won't necessarily

meet all farther experiences equally satisfactorily. Experience, as we know, has ways of *boiling over,* and making us correct our present formulas. (P. 222.)

When James says that the truth of a belief or theory depends on its expediency over "the long run" and "on the whole," he stresses the importance of repeated testing of our ideas plus the need for consistency and coherence among all of our beliefs and theories. These qualifications are communal. They invalidate a narrowly subjective interpretation of "expediency" and "usefulness."

Pragmatism, James continued, does not admit of a belief that can be both expedient or useful and totally false at the same time. The very definition of a belief's expediency and truth is that it gives us expectations that do get fulfilled. If a claim does so, it is true to that extent; but a claim that gives us expectations that experience never fulfills will not be true in any respect. James insisted that a proposition may point to many different practical consequences. He regarded a proposition as true only insofar as we can verify the expectations it creates. At the crux of the matter, moreover, is the need to obtain public as well as personal evidence for our beliefs so that we have consistency and coherence in our thoughts and actions.

Do James's Own Words Reveal the Truth?

William James thought his theory of truth was essentially correct. His critics disagreed. Consider one reason for the difference: the truth or falsity of a theory of truth depends on the nature of reality itself. But complete and final knowledge about the nature of reality is precisely what we lack. Hence, we are probably destined to remain with a multiplicity of views about truth. We have to assess the evidence to identify those that are the more adequate. The evidence we will obtain, however, is not likely to be overwhelming enough to produce universal agreement, even if we follow James's own pragmatic procedures for making our ideas clear. One of James's strengths is that he understood these considerations. His theory of truth reflects them. He believed, though he knew that he could not prove it conclusively, that we confront an open future in a world of freedom. He did not see how we could make sense of life on any other terms. It followed, James thought, that the nature of truth itself should agree with those conditions. Therefore, he contended, truth must be "in the making."

In stating his theory of truth, James no doubt used words that left him open to charges of unwarranted subjectivism. Nor is it clear that he put all those indictments to rest. But he did challenge a tradition about truth that was not as clear as it appeared to be. While showing that possession of truth depends on an ongoing, critical sifting of experience, which depends on checking to see whether the expectations created by propositions and theories are fulfilled, he helps us to understand what "truth" means. Test that claim as you read these passages from *Pragmatism* (1907).

Some years ago, being with a camping party in the mountains, I returned from a solitary ramble to find everyone engaged in a ferocious metaphysical dispute. The *corpus* of the dispute was a squirrel—a live squirrel supposed to be clinging to one side of a tree trunk; while over against the tree's opposite side a human being was imagined to stand. This human witness tries to get sight of the squirrel by moving rapidly round the tree, but no matter how fast he goes, the squirrel moves as fast in the opposite direction, and always keeps the tree between himself and the man, so that never a glimpse of him is caught. The resultant metaphysical problem now is this: *Does the man go round the squirrel or not?* He goes round the tree, sure enough, and the squirrel is on the tree; but does he go round the squirrel? In the unlimited leisure of the wilderness, discussion had been worn threadbare. Everyone had taken sides, and was obstinate; and the numbers on both sides were even. Each side, when I appeared, therefore appealed to me to make it a majority. Mindful of the scholastic adage that whenever you meet a contradiction you must make a distinction, I immediately sought and found one, as follows: "Which party is right," I said, "depends on what you *practically mean* by 'going round' the squirrel. If you mean passing from the north of him to the east, then to the south, then to the west, and then to the north of him again, obviously the man does go round him, for he occupies these successive positions. But if on the contrary you mean being first in front of him, then on the right of him, then behind him, then on his left, and finally in front again, it is quite as obvious that the man fails to go round him, for by the compensating movements the squirrel makes, he keeps his belly turned towards the man all the time, and his back turned away. Make the distinction, and there is no occasion for any farther dispute. You are both right and both wrong according as you conceive the verb 'to go round' in one practical fashion or the other."

Although one or two of the hotter disputants called my speech a shuffling evasion, saying they wanted no quibbling or scholastic hair-splitting, but meant just plain honest English "round," the majority seemed to think that the distinction had assuaged the dispute.

I tell this trivial anecdote because it is a peculiarly simple example of what I wish now to speak of as *the pragmatic method*. The pragmatic method is primarily a method of settling metaphysical disputes that otherwise might be interminable. Is the world one or many? Fated or free? Material or spiritual? Here are notions either of which may or may not hold good of the world; and disputes over such notions are unending. The pragmatic method in such cases is to try to interpret each notion by tracing its respective practical consequences. What difference would it practically make to anyone if this notion rather than that notion were true? If no practical difference whatever can be traced, then the alternatives mean practically the same thing, and all dispute is idle. Whenever a dispute is serious, we ought to be able to show some practical difference that must follow from one side or the other's being right. (Pp. 43–46.)

Truth, as any dictionary will tell you, is a property of certain of our ideas. It means their "agreement," as falsity means their disagreement, with "reality." Pragmatists and intellectualists both accept this definition as a matter of course. They begin to quarrel only after the question is raised as to what may precisely be meant by the term "agreement," and what by the term "reality," when reality is taken as something for our ideas to agree with. (P. 193.)

Pragmatism . . . asks its usual question. "Grant an idea or belief to be true," it says, "what concrete difference will its being true make in any one's actual life? How will the truth be realized? What experiences will be different from those which would obtain if the belief were false? What, in short, is the truth's cash value in experiential terms?"

The moment pragmatism asks this question, it sees the answer: *True ideas are those that we can assimilate, validate, corroborate, and verify. False ideas are those that we cannot.* That is the practical difference it makes to us to have true ideas; that, therefore, is the meaning of truth, for it is all that truth is known-as.

This thesis is what I have to defend. The truth of an idea is not a stagnant property inherent in it. Truth *happens* to an idea. It *becomes* true, is *made* true by events. Its verity *is* in fact an event, a process: the process namely of its verifying itself, its veri-*fication*. Its validity is the process of its valid-*ation*. (Pp. 200–201.)

A. J. Ayer and the Restrictions of Positivism

In asking "What does 'truth' mean?" Plato and William James ended up far apart. But their answers to that question by no means exhausted the options. Another viewpoint that proved influential came from the British philosopher A. J. Ayer (b. 1910). If James thought Plato went too far in thinking that we could apprehend an unchanging truth, Ayer questioned more severely than James whether words could tell the truth at all. After graduating from Oxford in 1932, Ayer spent time at the University of Vienna, where he was influenced by a philosophical group known as the "Vienna Circle." Its membership included scientists, mathematicians, and philosophers of science. Believing that much traditional philosophy consisted of assertions that could not possibly be verified experientially, they wanted to find a much more rigorously scientific base for human thought, and they used the tools of mathematical logic for this purpose. They called their movement **Logical Positivism.** Already sympathetic to similar strands of thought in the work of Bertrand Russell and Ludwig Wittgenstein, Ayer found the positivists' position persuasive. As he developed it in his own ways, Ayer linked the positivist program to the demand for empirical **verification** of every assertion. Ayer believed that words could reveal truth to us only if language were guarded by rigorous boundaries.

Verification as the Foundation of Truth

First published in 1936, *Language, Truth and Logic* remains Ayer's most famous book. It promulgated a verification principle whose application, according to Ayer, would bring clarity to philosophers and truth to us all. This principle, Ayer explained in a new introduction written for the 1946 edition,

A . J . A Y E R b. 1910

when we can point to some sense experience that is relevant to the truth of our words. We say: "AIDS is a fatal disease" and point to actual deaths attributed beyond a doubt to acquired immune deficiency syndrome. Metaphysics, which Ayer regarded as claiming knowledge of reality that transcends the worlds of science and common sense, is ruled out by these criteria. "Philosophy," said Ayer, "is not a source of speculative truth," and since "many traditional disputes of philosophers are, for the most part, as unwarranted as they are unfruitful," restrictions on metaphysics should be welcomed (pp. 26, 33). Words can report the truth, but to do so they must be linked precisely to empirical data or else be judged merely analytic.

Solving Puzzles

Ayer thinks the philosopher's task is more "to 'solve puzzles' than to discover truths" (p. 26). He warns philosophers to avoid speaking of a reality that transcends the limits of sense experience, for no statement referring to such reality "can possibly have any literal significance" (p. 34). Those who do so, far from using words to tell the truth, create nonsense. The philosopher solves puzzles by exposing that nonsense. We should use the following litmus test: "A sentence is factually significant to a given person, if, and only if, he knows how to verify the proposition which it purports to express—that is, if he knows what observations would lead him to accept the proposition as being true, or reject it as being false" (p. 35).

A sentence failing that test may still have emotional significance, which is one of Ayer's ways of acknowledging the difference between a mere jumble of words and the vast array of grammatically correct formulations we can make with words. Still, many of those formulations cannot be cognitively meaningful. They may express human feel-

promised to provide "a criterion by which it can be determined whether or not a sentence is literally meaningful. A simple way to formulate it would be to say that a sentence had literal meaning if and only if the proposition it expressed was either analytic or empirically verifiable."[5]

If a statement is true by virtue of the definitions we give to words, argued Ayer, then it is analytic. "Man is a rational animal" is analytically true, because we define "man" as such. Although the second concept is less easily pinned down, to speak of a statement as "empirically verifiable" essentially entails "some possible sense-experience [that] should be relevant to the determination of its truth or falsehood" (p. 31). We can tell what is true

ing—"God exists" would be a crucial example for Ayer—but beyond that they convey no information. Such words do not convey truth. Philosophers who think words can reflect the truth in any simple way come under ceaseless attack from Ayer's criteria. And while some philosophers with positivistic sympathies are willing to bestow a dubious honor by calling the metaphysician "a kind of misplaced poet" (p. 44), Ayer contends that this description merely robs the poet to pay the philosopher. In most cases, the poet's words do not defy sound criteria for cognitive meaning. When the poet does use language to achieve an artistic effect that goes beyond those boundaries, he or she usually knows it. On the other hand, states Ayer, philosophers no more intend to write poetry than they intend to write nonsense. Their plight is that they often do not know what they are doing.

Ayer would say that much of philosophy is "literally senseless" (p. 45). This outcome indicates how differently philosophers regard the implications of mathematics and science where telling the truth is the issue. Descartes would not reject Ayer's claim that "there is no field of experience which cannot, in principle, be brought under some form of scientific law" (p. 48). Nor would he quarrel when Ayer asserts that "all general problems are at least theoretically capable of being solved" (p. 50). But Descartes's understanding of science, mathematics, and logic nevertheless leads him to see the problems differently. He thought the mind could discern truth on its own, whereas Ayer insists that the test of success must be an empirical perspective that "enables us to predict future experience, and so to control our environment" (p. 50). This position is close to that of James's American pragmatism. That is, practical effects are the only real test for truth. The difference, however, is that Ayer's use of this principle is much more restrictive than James would have thought sensible.

Philosophers Analyze and Clarify

What holds philosophy back, Ayer contended, is its attempt to answer unanswerable questions by speaking of things that transcend common sense. According to Ayer, his verification principle can put a stop to such nonsense and thereby keep philosophy true to its proper calling. That calling is "wholly independent of metaphysics" and "essentially analytic" (pp. 55–56). Philosophy, in brief, "is a department of logic" (p. 57). When philosophy is regarded that way,

> The question "What is truth?" is reducible to the question "What is the analysis of the sentence '*p* is true'?" (P. 89.)

What if *p* stands for the sentence "Stealing is wrong" or "God loves you"? Such uses of words purport to tell the truth, but Ayer thinks them deceptive. To clarify his position, he reminds us that propositions are of two kinds: analytic and synthetic. "A proposition is analytic when its validity depends solely on the definition of the symbols it contains and synthetic when its validity is determined by the facts of experience" (p. 78). Analytic propositions show how words relate, but they do not give us information about matters of fact. Synthetic propositions, on the other hand, can give information about matters of fact because they are verifiable. The proposition "AIDS is found in certain groups in our population" can be checked by demographic study. Analytic propositions—tautologies, as they are sometimes called—can be absolutely true, but they convey no factual information. Synthetic propositions, on the other hand, carry factual information, but they are not absolute: "Empirical propositions are one and all hypotheses, which may be confirmed or discredited in actual sense-experience" (pp. 94–95).

Ayer's appraisal is that sentences such as "Stealing is wrong" and "God loves you" are not **tautological** so they are not analytic. Nor are they empirical; no relevant factual tests are possible to show their truth or falsity. The function of words in ethics is to express and "to arouse feeling, and so to stimulate action," but not to convey factual truth (p. 108). For similar reasons, "all utterances about the nature of God are nonsensical" (p. 115). Religious words of any kind, whether articulated by believers, atheists, or agnostics, cannot reveal the truth in any way. As for the appeal to religious experience that some persons might make to undercut Ayer's views, he replies:

> The fact that people have religious experiences is interesting from the psychological point of view, but it does not in any way imply that there is such a thing as religious knowledge, any more than our having moral experience implies that there is such a thing as moral knowledge. The theist, like the moralist, may believe that his experiences are cognitive experiences, but, unless he can formulate his "knowledge" in propositions that are empirically verifiable, we may be sure that he is deceiving himself. (Pp. 119–20.)

Why Are We Deceived?

Finding the right compartments for our various pursuits is important to A. J. Ayer. Instead of making logic a department of philosophy, as philosophers traditionally have done, he makes philosophy a department of logic. In addition, his verification principle leads him to categorize ethics and religion as "nothing more than a department of psychology and sociology" (p. 112). But in what category does Ayer's very own philosophy—especially its restrictive criteria—belong? His doctrines are not mere tautologies. But are they empirically verifiable, either? If not, where do they fit? Ayer can place them within logic, but that does not lay to rest every question about how Ayer can justify the exclusive status he wants his

philosophy to possess with respect to other theories.

In a word, is there one and only one criterion for truth? Is Ayer's empirical verifiability the test to which all persons should assent? Ayer thinks philosophers have been sloppy in stating what truth means. To remedy those defects, he proposes a strict standard for truth. Ayer rightly calls into question many things we may have taken for granted, including the truth of ethical and religious propositions. He does so, moreover, in an electrifying fashion. According to Ayer, for example, when Jesus said "Blessed are the pure in heart, for they shall see God" (Matt. 5:8), he could not possibly have made a cognitively meaningful statement because that sentence does not meet Ayer's strict philosophical standards. Yet millions of persons have staked hope on at least the possible truth of those and other words that Jesus preached in the Sermon on the Mount. Countless examples of a similar kind can be found from other religious traditions, too.

Ayer helps us to rethink what expressing truth means, but we need to assess the authority of his theory as well. Ayer's criteria may say more about himself and his desire for absolute clarity than about the way we find truth in the words spoken to us in the world. Can truth actually appear in imprecise words? Why should only what is clear and empirically verifiable be true? That would be convenient if true. But we do pursue truth in obscure forms and some find truth revealed in words that seem far from empirical observation. Our task remains: to account for how the truth we seem to find can tell us what "truth" really means. Check the extent to which the following passage from the 1946 edition of *Language, Truth and Logic* advances your understanding in that regard.

The traditional disputes of philosophers are, for the most part, as unwarranted as they are unfruitful. The surest way to end them is to establish beyond question what should be the purpose and method of a philosophical inquiry. And this is by no means so difficult a task as the history of philosophy would lead one to suppose. For if there are any questions which science leaves it to philosophy to answer, a straightforward process of elimination must lead to their discovery.

We may begin by criticizing the metaphysical thesis that philosophy affords us knowledge of a reality transcending the world of science and common sense. Later on, when we come to define metaphysics and account for its existence, we shall find that it is possible to be a metaphysician without believing in a transcendent reality; for we shall see that many metaphysical utterances are due to the commission of logical errors, rather than to a conscious desire on the part of their authors to go beyond the limits of experience. But it is convenient for us to take the case of those who believe that it is possible to have knowledge of a transcendent reality as a starting point for our discussion. The arguments which we use to refute them will subsequently be found to apply to the whole of metaphysics.

One way of attacking a metaphysician who claimed to have knowledge of a reality which transcended the phenomenal world would be to inquire from what premises his propositions were deduced. Must he not begin, as other men do, with the evidence of his senses? And if so, what valid process of reasoning can possibly lead him to the conception of a transcendent reality? Surely from empirical premises nothing whatsoever concerning the properties, or even the existence, of anything superempirical can legitimately be inferred. But this objection would be met by a denial on the part of the metaphysician that his assertions were ultimately based on the evidence of his senses. He would say that he was endowed with a faculty of intellectual intuition which enabled him to know facts that could not be known through sense-experience. And even if it could be shown that he was relying on empirical premises, and that his venture into

a nonempirical world was therefore logically unjustified, it would not follow that the assertions which he made concerning this nonempirical world could not be true. For the fact that a conclusion does not follow from its putative premise is not sufficient to show that it is false. Consequently one cannot overthrow a system of transcendent metaphysics merely by criticizing the way in which it comes into being. What is required is rather a criticism of the nature of the actual statements which comprise it. And this is the line of argument which we shall, in fact, pursue. For we shall maintain that no statement which refers to a "reality" transcending the limits of all possible sense-experience can possibly have any literal significance; from which it must follow that the labors of those who have striven to describe such a reality have all been devoted to the production of nonsense. (Pp. 33–34.)

The criterion which we use to test the genuineness of apparent statements of fact is the criterion of verifiability. We say that a sentence is factually significant to any given person, if, and only if, he knows how to verify the proposition which it purports to express—that is, if he knows what observations would lead him, under certain conditions, to accept the proposition as being true, or reject it as being false. If, on the other hand, the putative proposition is of such a character that the assumption of its truth, or falsehood, is consistent with any assumption whatsoever concerning the nature of his future experience, then, as far as he is concerned, it is, if not a tautology, a mere pseudoproposition. The sentence expressing it may be emotionally significant to him; but it is not literally significant. And with regard to questions the procedure is the same. We inquire in every case what observations would lead us to answer the question, one way or the other; and, if none can be discovered, we must conclude that the sentence under consideration does not, as far as we are concerned, express a genuine question, however strongly its grammatical appearance may suggest that it does.

As the adoption of this procedure is an essential factor in the argument of this book, it needs to be examined in detail.

In the first place, it is necessary to draw a distinction between practical verifiability, and verifiability in principle. Plainly we all understand, in many cases believe, propositions which we have not in fact taken steps to verify. Many of these are propositions which we could verify if we took enough trouble. But there remain a number of significant propositions, concerning matters of fact, which we could not verify even if we chose; simply because we lack the practical means of placing ourselves in the situation where the relevant observations could be made. A simple and familiar example of such a proposition is the proposition that there are mountains on the farther side of the moon. No rocket has yet been invented which would enable me to go and look at the farther side of the moon, so that I am unable to decide the matter by actual observation. But I do know what observations would decide it for me, if, as is theoretically conceivable, I were once in a position to make them. And therefore I say that the proposition is verifiable in principle, if not in practice, and is accordingly significant. On the other hand, such a metaphysical pseudo-proposition as "the Absolute enters into, but is itself incapable of, evolution and progress," is not even in principle verifiable. For one cannot conceive of an observation which would enable one to determine whether the Absolute did, or did not, enter into evolution and progress. Of course it is possible that the author of such a remark is using English words in a way in which they are not commonly used by English-speaking people, and that he does, in fact, intend to assert something which could be empirically verified. But until he makes us understand how the proposition that he wishes to express would be verified, he fails to communicate anything to us. And if he admits, as I think the author of the remark in question would have admitted, that his words

were not intended to express either a tautology or a proposition which was capable, at least in principle, of being verified, then it follows that he has made an utterance which has no literal significance even for himself.

A further distinction which we must make is the distinction between the "strong" and the "weak" sense of the term "verifiable." A proposition is said to be verifiable, in the strong sense of the term, if, and only if, its truth could be conclusively established in experience. But it is verifiable, in the weak sense, if it is possible for experience to render it probable. In which sense are we using the term when we say that a putative proposition is genuine only if it is verifiable?

It seems to me that if we adopt conclusive verifiability as our criterion of significance, as some positivists have proposed, our argument will prove too much. Consider, for example, the case of general propositions of law—such propositions, namely, as "arsenic is poisonous"; "all men are mortal"; "a body tends to expand when it is heated." It is of the very nature of these propositions that their truth cannot be established with certainty by any finite series of observations. But if it is recognized that such general propositions of law are designed to cover an infinite number of cases, then it must be admitted that they cannot, even in principle, be verified conclusively. And then, if we adopt conclusive verifiability as our criterion of significance, we are logically obliged to treat these general propositions of law in the same fashion as we treat the statements of the metaphysician.

In face of this difficulty, some positivists have adopted the heroic course of saying that these general propositions are indeed pieces of nonsense, albeit an essentially important type of nonsense. But here the introduction of the term "important" is simply an attempt to hedge. It serves only to mark the authors' recognition that their view is somewhat too paradoxical, without in any way removing the paradox. Besides, the difficulty is not confined to the case of general propositions of law, though it is there revealed most plainly. It is hardly less obvious in the case of propositions about the remote past. For it must surely be admitted that, however strong the evidence in favor of historical statements may be, their truth can never become more than highly probable. And to maintain that they also constituted an important, or unimportant, type of nonsense would be unplausible, to say the very least. Indeed, it will be our contention that no proposition, other than a tautology, can possibly be anything more than a probable hypothesis. And if this is correct, the principle that a sentence can be factually significant only if it expresses what is conclusively verifiable is self-stultifying as a criterion of significance. For it leads to the conclusion that it is impossible to make a significant statement of fact at all.

Nor can we accept the suggestion that a sentence should be allowed to be factually significant if, and only if, it expresses something which is definitely confutable by experience. Those who adopt this course assume that, although no finite series of observations is ever sufficient to establish the truth of a hypothesis beyond all possibility of doubt, there are crucial cases in which a single observation, or series of observations, can definitely confute it. But, as we shall show later on, this assumption is false. A hypothesis cannot be conclusively confuted any more than it can be conclusively verified. For when we take the occurrence of certain observations as proof that a given hypothesis is false, we presuppose the existence of certain conditions. And though, in any given case, it may be extremely improbable that this assumption is false, it is not logically impossible. We shall see that there need be no self-contradiction in holding that some of the relevant circumstances are other than we have taken them to be, and consequently that the hypothesis has not really broken down. And if it is not the case that any hypothesis can be definitely confuted, we cannot hold that the genuineness of a proposition depends on the possibility of its definite confutation.

Accordingly, we fall back on the weaker sense of verification. We say that the question that must be asked about any putative statement of fact is not, Would any observations make its truth or falsehood logically certain? but simply, Would any observations be relevant to the determination of its truth or falsehood? And it is only if a negative answer is given to this second question that we conclude that the statement under consideration is nonsensical. (Pp. 35–38.)

Ludwig Wittgenstein and the Boundaries of Language

Finding their own routes to what Spinoza called "the improvement of the understanding," James and Ayer developed two of the twentieth century's more important philosophical movements: pragmatism and logical positivism. Similarly motivated, Vienna-born Ludwig Wittgenstein (1889–1951) forged a third, **linguistic analysis,** introduced in his most important book, *Philosophical Investigations* (1953). Wittgenstein's engineering studies took him to England in 1908. There his interests shifted to mathematics and logic, and by 1912 he was at Cambridge as one of Bertrand Russell's students. During World War I, he served in the Austrian army and also wrote a strangely titled book: *Tractatus Logico-Philosophicus*. Appearing in 1921, it was one of the few works Wittgenstein published himself.

Much of this man's thoughts come to us from his notebooks and from his students at Cambridge after World War II. Wittgenstein would refer to his work as "philosophical remarks," which he likened to "sketches of landscapes . . . made in the course of . . . long and involved journeyings."[6] Nearly all those philosophical travels explored questions about truth.

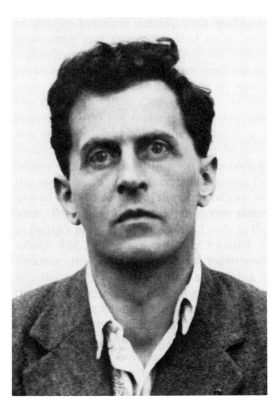

LUDWIG WITTGENSTEIN 1889–1951

Wittgenstein's First Aim in Philosophy

Sometimes philosophers decide that even their own words do not reveal truth, and so they head off in a different direction. Wittgenstein's career illustrates this point; there are clear "earlier" and "later" phases in his philosophy. In particular, Wittgenstein changed his mind about the *Tractatus*. The preface to that book proclaimed that "the *truth* of the thoughts that are here set forth seems to me unassailable and definitive. I therefore believe myself to have found, on all essential points, the final solution of the problems."[7] Such confidence rivaled that of any rationalist, but in Wittgenstein's case it did not last. The problems Wittgenstein thought he had

solved can be summed up in two questions: How can combinations of words represent facts? and How can sentences reveal that something is the case? The answer, he argued, is that propositions are logical pictures of possible facts. In a picture of an object or a scene, a correspondence exists between the picture's elements and those of the object or scene portrayed. According to the "early Wittgenstein," words and facts, including their complex configurations, work like that, too.

From the outset, Wittgenstein knew that he was not empirically describing the way we observe language working. But he did think that he had uncovered a structure that language and the world possess when words reveal truth. The theory nevertheless left him unsatisfied. What bothered him was the possibility that his account of language was more an invention foisted on the facts than an unassailable conclusion of logic. This doubt prompted new investigations, and with them came the rejection of three assumptions. Contrary to what he had first thought, Wittgenstein contended, it will not do to think that language is essentially employed for one purpose, namely, to state facts. Nor is it correct to hold that sentences get their meaning in one fundamental way, namely, by "picturing" facts. Finally, we ought not to take for granted the notion that all verbal expression depends on a single logical structure.

Ordinary Language

Leaving his early followers puzzled, Wittgenstein reformulated his philosophical quest. "What is your aim in philosophy?" he would ask himself in *Philosophical Investigations*. "To show the fly," he replied, "the way out of the fly-bottle."[8] The image of a trapped fly futilely buzzing itself into exhaustion struck Wittgenstein as aptly depicting what philosophers, including himself, had been up to for years. Just as the fly needed someone to shoo it out, philosophy needed relief from the puzzles that kept it bottled up.

Wittgenstein's reconsideration of the *Tractatus* left him still convinced that the issue of whether words can reveal truth lies at the heart of philosophy's problems. In no way did he give up his persuasion that philosophers must be vigilant about language. Wittgenstein continued to hold that "what can be said at all can be said clearly, and what we cannot talk about we must pass over in silence."[9] But now he also emphasized that "philosophical problems arise when language *goes on holiday*."[10] Too often, Wittgenstein contended, philosophers use language sensibly at the beginning of their inquiries only to ask questions or propound claims that are odd. Failing to notice the oddity, they draw conclusions whose bizarre qualities are not reduced by the sincerity with which philosophers advance them. Plato tells us there are universal ideas existing outside space and time, and we think we agree without realizing the consequences of such a statement.

The "later" Wittgenstein tries less to solve the questions of philosophy than to dissolve them. "The philosopher's treatment of a question," he says, "is like the treatment of an illness" (p. 91). The objective is to make the disease go away. Or, we might say, philosophy's business is to put philosophy out of business, for at its best "philosophy only states what everyone admits" (p. 156). But what does everyone admit? The resolution for that question, according to Wittgenstein, can be found by paying close attention to the workings of **ordinary language**. Those workings are multiple and varied, but the fly's way out of the fly-bottle depends on careful analysis. The uses of words are as diverse as the functions of a carpenter's tools, just as sawing and hammering are two very different, if related, activities. We carry on equally diverse "language-games," as Wittgenstein dubs them.

Language-Games

Wittgenstein was not being frivolous when he spoke of "**language-games.**" In fact, he chose the term with care. Games are many things. They display "**family resemblances,**" to use another of his terms, but they also have diffuse aims and require multiple skills. Although concepts and rules have a role in games, they too vary. Rules, for example, are explicit at some times, indefinite at others, and on some occasions stipulated as play occurs. Something that makes sense in one game, moreover, will not in another. A batter hitting a baseball does not score a touchdown worth six points even if he rounds all the bases, reaches home plate, and so on. So when we use words, it is important to understand what game is being played, especially when we employ language to tell the truth.

At one point, Wittgenstein asks his readers to "review the multiplicity of language-games in the following examples, and in others:

Giving orders, and obeying them

Describing the appearance of an object, or giving its measurements

Constructing an object from a description (a drawing)

Reporting an event

Speculating about an event

Forming and testing a hypothesis

Presenting the result of an experiment in tables and diagrams

Making up a story; and reading it

Play acting

Singing catches

Guessing riddles

Making a joke; telling it

Solving a problem in practical arithmetic

Translating from one language into another

Asking, thanking, cursing, greeting, praying" (pp. 11–12).

By calling attention to this variety, Wittgenstein suggests that the activity of using language is "a form of life" (p. 11). Each language-game both assumes and creates a **context**. Consider next some of the intriguing inferences Wittgenstein drew from those observations.

Is Truth Ever Context-Free?

Asking whether words can reveal truth is a question that should make us wonder what language-game is being played. Certainly, as Wittgenstein would point out, some words do not reveal the truth because they are not used with that intention. But when we do use words to state what is true, we need to be careful to understand how that process differs from case to case. Wittgenstein illustrates that claim in the following statements:

> All testing, all confirmation and disconfirmation of a hypothesis take place already within a system. . . . The *truth* of certain empirical propositions belongs to our **frame of reference.** . . . Whether a proposition can turn out false after all depends on what I make count as determinants for that proposition.[11]

Family resemblances exist among the different language-games in which truth is sought. But it is one thing to confirm that Joan Benoit won a gold medal in the marathon at the 1984 Olympic Games and quite another to confirm the truth of a mathematical theorem. For corroboration to occur in either of these cases, however, much has to be taken for granted. "My *life*," affirms Wittgenstein, "consists in my being content to accept many things" (p. 44).

We could say that Wittgenstein calls attention to the glasses on one's nose. Their impact on vision should not be overlooked. Figuratively, Wittgenstein suspected that all sight is colored by spectacles of one kind or another, which means that we never attain an absolute, **context-free** perspective. We can be confident about whether words state the truth in specific situations in which particular language-games are played, but if the goal is to find words that state "truth" absolutely, our quest is useless. Philosophers create problems first by forgetting the everyday use of language and then by sending it off "on holiday" to play impossible language-games instead. We say "God is all-good" and forget how much evil we find in front of us.

Hope beyond Theory

According to Wittgenstein's philosophical theory, words cannot do all we expect of them. When their limits are reached, it behooves us to be silent. We cannot present God accurately in words, for example, and we should not try. Such wisdom, he understood, is hard to accept and even more difficult to practice. A profoundly human tendency makes us want to transcend the finite, transitory nature of our earthly lives. Hence, we "run against the boundaries of language." Wittgenstein thought that "this running against the walls of our cage is perfectly, absolutely hopeless," but, as he said in a 1929 lecture at Cambridge University, the attempt remained one that "I cannot help respecting deeply, and I would not for my life ridicule it."[12]

In that lecture, with his mind moving away from the *Tractatus* and toward the *Philosophical Investigations*, Wittgenstein proposed that "if a man could write a book on Ethics which really was a book on Ethics, this book would, with an explosion, destroy all the other books in the world" (p. 449). His point was this: our world is full of value judgments, but we cannot know what is *really* good and evil—absolutely, not contextually—because every value judgment we can possibly make is situated contextually. The desired book on ethics would destroy all other books and it would destroy our world, because such a book is not compatible with its existence.

It did not follow for Wittgenstein, however, that ethics was worthless. Nor were aesthetic judgments or religious practices. They were not "meaningless" as Ayer thought they were. Life cannot be human without valuing and hoping. It is just that the forms people give to these dimensions of life will vary, and none in this world can be certified as absolute, despite claims to the contrary. William James also thought our judgments could only be relative and contextual. Experience, Wittgenstein pointed out, suggests as much when we recognize that "certain events would put me into a position in which I could not go on with the old language-game any further. In which I was torn away from the *sureness* of the game."[13] Wittgenstein was torn away from the unassailability of his *Tractatus*. But read on and consider whether his later views about language are subject to revision as well.

Think of the tools in a toolbox: there is a hammer, pliers, a saw, a screwdriver, a rule, a glue pot, glue, nails, and screws. The functions of words are as diverse as the functions of these objects. (And in both cases there are similarities.)

Of course, what confuses us is the uniform appearance of words when we hear them spoken or meet them in script and print. For their *application* is not presented to us so clearly. Especially not, when we are doing philosophy!

It is like looking into the cabin of a locomotive. We see handles all looking more or less alike. (Naturally, since they are all supposed to be handled.) But one is the handle of a crank which can be moved continuously (it regulates the opening of a valve); another is the handle of a switch, which has only two effective positions, it is either off or on; a third is the handle of a brake lever—the harder one pulls on it, the harder it brakes; a fourth, the handle of a pump—it has an effect only so long as it is moved to and fro.

When we say: "Every word in language signifies something" we have so far said *nothing whatever*, unless we have explained *exactly what* distinction we wish to make. . . .

Imagine someone's saying: "*All* tools serve to modify something. Thus the hammer modifies the position of the nail, the saw the shape of the board, and so on."—And what is modified by the rule, the glue pot, the nails?—"Our knowledge of a thing's length, the temperature of the glue, and the solidity of the box."—Would anything be gained by this assimilation of expressions?

The word "to signify" is perhaps used in the most straightforward way when the object signified is marked with the sign. Suppose that the tools A uses in building bear certain marks. When A shows his assistant such a mark, he brings the tool that has that mark on it.

It is in this and more or less similar ways that a name means and is given to a thing.— It will often prove useful in philosophy to say to ourselves: naming something is like attaching a label to a thing.

What about the color samples that A shows to B: are they part of the *language*? Well, it is as you please. They do not belong among the words; yet when I say to someone: "Pronounce the word 'the'," you will count the second "the" as part of the sentence. Yet it has a role just like that of a color sample [in the apple-buying language]; that is, it is a sample of what the other is meant to say.

It is most natural, and causes least confusion, to reckon the samples among the instruments of the language. . . .

It will be possible to say: In [most languages] we have different *kinds of word*. . . . But how we group words into kinds will depend on the aim of the classification—and on our own inclination.

Think of the different points of view from which one can classify tools or chessmen.

Do not be troubled by the fact that [some] languages . . . consist only of orders. If you want to say that this shows them to be incomplete, ask yourself whether our language is complete:—whether it was so before the symbolism of chemistry and the notation of the infinitesimal calculus were incorporated in it; for these are, so to speak, suburbs of our language. (And how many houses or streets does it take before a town begins to be a town?) Our language can be seen as an ancient city: a maze of little streets and squares, of old and new houses, and of houses with additions from various periods; and this surrounded by a multitude of new boroughs with straight regular streets and uniform houses.

It is easy to image a language consisting only of orders and reports in battle.—Or a language consisting only of questions and expressions for answering yes and no. And innumerable others.—And to imagine a language means to imagine a form of life.
. . .

But how many kinds of sentence are there? Say assertion, question, and command?—There are *countless* kinds: countless different kinds of use of what we call "symbols," "words," "sentences." And this multiplicity is not something fixed, given once for all; but new types of language, new language-games, as we may say, come into existence, and others become obsolete and get forgotten. . . .

Here the term "language-game" is meant to bring into prominence the fact that the *speaking* of language is part of any activity, or of a form of life. . . .

Someone might object against me: "You take the easy way out! You talk about all sorts of language-games, but have nowhere said what the essence of a language-game, and hence of language, is: what is common to all these activities, and what makes them into language or parts of language. . . . "

And this is true.—Instead of producing something common to all that we call language, I am saying that these phenomena have no one thing in common which makes us use the same word for all—but that they are *related* to one another in many different ways. And it is because of this relationship, or these relationships, that we call them all "language." I will try to explain this.

Consider for example the proceedings that

we call "games." I mean board games, card games, ballgames, Olympic games, and so on. What is common to them all?—Don't say: "There *must* be something common, or they would not be called 'games'"—but *look and see* whether there is anything common to all.—For if you look at them you will not see something that is common to *all*, but similarities, relationships, and a whole series of them at that. To repeat: don't think, but look!—Look for example at board games, with their multifarious relationships. Now pass to card games; here you find many correspondences with the first group, but many common features drop out, and others appear. When we pass next to ballgames, much that is common is retained, but much is lost.—Are they all "amusing"? Compare chess with noughts and crosses. Or is there always winning and losing, or competition between players? Think of patience. . . . Look at the parts played by skill and luck; and at the difference between skill in chess and skill in tennis. . . . And we can go through the many, many other groups of games in the same way; can see how similarities crop up and disappear.

And the result of this examination is: we see a complicated network of similarities overlapping and criss-crossing: sometimes overall similarities, sometimes similarities of detail.

I can think of no better expression to characterize these similarities than "family resemblances"; for the various resemblances between members of a family: build, features, color of eyes, gait, temperament, etc., etc., overlap and criss-cross in the same way.—And I shall say: "games" form a family. . . .

One might say that the concept "game" is a concept with blurred edges.—"But is a blurred concept a concept at all?"—Is an indistinct photograph a picture of a person at all? Is it even always an advantage to replace an indistinct picture by a sharp one? Isn't the indistinct one often exactly what we need? . . .

When philosophers use a word—"knowledge," "being," "object," "I," "proposition," "name"—and try to grasp the *essence* of the thing, one must always ask oneself: is the word ever actually used in this way in the language-game which is its original home? . . .

For philosophical problems arise when language *goes on holiday.* . . .

What we do is to bring words back from their metaphysical to their everyday use. . . .

What is your aim in philosophy?—To show the fly the way out of the fly-bottle.[14]

Summary

In this chapter our guiding question has been, "What does 'truth' mean?" Plato felt that Forms, eternal and immutable, hold the truth about all things, whether we grasp them or not. James's idea was different: he urged us to test our beliefs in practice. If they work, we know they convey truth just because they are effective in practical life. A. J. Ayer's approach was more restrictive. We must check our theories against clear empirical data. Our propositions cannot claim to be meaningful, let alone true, unless that procedure is rigorously followed. Wittgenstein asked us to think about the problem in yet another way. Language has multiple uses and also various

limitations. The key to understanding "truth" is to see how the word actually functions in the language-games of life. When we do this well, we will see when words can convey truth and when they cannot.

Before you study philosophy, you may naturally think that it will not be too difficult to think clearly and to express the truth you find. If philosophy appears to complicate the situation, the reason may be that the issues surrounding truth are really more complex than we think at first. Whoever is closest to the truth among these four philosophers, our problem is still to keep examining what "truth" means and how we use that word. Then we must decide what, if anything, we can do to force words, to state truth for us.

With this chapter's consideration of what truth means, we conclude Part I: "What can I know?" Thus far, we have tried to suggest something of what philosophy means, and we hope that you now have a feeling and even, in Rilke's words, a love for its questions. We have spoken about the "external" world and the self. We have asked how knowledge can be acquired. All these issues—and more—remain alive as we move on to Part II, which has for its central question, "What should I do?"

GLOSSARY

analytic philosophy Ayer's conception of philosophy as concerned mainly with distinguishing between meaningful and meaningless sentences, where the criterion of meaning is the verifiability (see **verification**) of a given sentence, the possibility of specifying a procedure for checking it against empirical facts; all meaningful propositions, in Ayer's view, can be analyzed into propositions that can be so verified, and their logical consequences.

context See **frame of reference.**

context-free the property attributed to knowledge of the **universal;** independent of any particular situation or instance.

expedient relevant to or helpful for some particular purpose. James did not think that the question of truth could be separated from the question of the relative *expediency* of the various ways of conceptualizing a given state of affairs.

family resemblance Wittgenstein's term for a principle of unity of a class or category of things that is less precise and definite than the common essence suggested by the concept of the **universal** or the Platonic **Form;** such general concepts, like the concept of a "game," have many marginal cases—"blurred edges," as Wittgenstein puts it—where it is not clear that they apply.

Forms Plato's term for his conception of **universals,** the eternal, transcendent Ideas in which particular entities participate and which must be grasped if we are to have knowledge of the truth.

frame of reference the particular context in which language is used, including the unique perspective, or practical interests and priorities, of the communicants, and the conventional rules of communication that are taken to apply to that particular type of situation or activity.

language a system of concrete symbols that function as a medium for the communication of information, ideas, and feelings.

"language-games" Wittgenstein's term for the variety of different kinds of activity that can be performed using language; Wittgenstein stressed that this diversity precludes any philosophical theory about the nature of language that conceives of language as a unified phenomenon; the various "language-games" are at least as dissimilar among themselves as they are similar, a situation that corresponds to the variety of purposes and situations to which language can pertain. The unity of this variety is not one constituted by a common *essence*, he thought, but by what he called **"family resemblance."**

linguistic analysis the philosophical method founded by Wittgenstein on the assumption that the definition of truth depends to a large extent on the actual nature of language, the medium through which truth is grasped.

Logical Positivism the influential school of philosophy founded in Austria in the 1930s by the group of philosophers known as the Vienna Circle. These philosophers believed that all metaphysical problems were pseudo-problems resulting from an idealization of certain features of the grammar of natural languages (much as Berkeley believed that the notion of "abstract ideas" was a product of language's power over our thought; see Chapter Two). This situation leads to senseless disputes over issues that are really only the product of semantic confusion. Philosophy's task, in their view, is to provide a criterion of meaningfulness for the evaluation of sentences in order to dispel, much as Bacon wished to do, thinking that was misleading, superstitious, and unclear. For these philosophers the problem of truth was reducible to the problem of the **verification** of meaningful propositions through scientific procedures of evaluating evidence.

"ordinary language" the central concept of **linguistic analysis;** a notion of language based on the variety of ways in which language is actually used, rather than on some idealization of it based on logic or scientific method, which is used to describe the relationship of language to the world.

particulars individual, independently existing entities, conceived apart from their similarity and dissimilarity to other entities.

pragmatism the philosophical movement founded by the Americans Peirce, James, and Dewey around the turn of the century, based on the assumption that the pursuit of truth is a practical, ongoing, and unfinalizable process, limited by the finite capacities of human reason and guided and determined by the concrete practical interests of human beings. In the pragmatic view, philosophy should begin with the realization that absolute truth is merely an ideal limit, like the concept of infinity in calculus, and not a practical possibility. Like the Logical Positivists, the pragmatists considered it an important part of philosophy's task to distinguish between genuine disagreements and disputes based on confusions over the meaning of philosophical terms.

"recollection" Plato's doctrine that knowledge of truth depends on our ability to "recall" the realm of transcendent Ideas with which our souls were acquainted before we commenced our earthly existence.

tautological a synonym for the characteristic of what Kant called *analytic* propositions in which the predicate defines the meaning of, hence is identical with, the subject; according to Ayer, the only kind of proposition that can have a higher status than that of a "probable hypothesis"; redundant, circular, trivial.

truth agreement between concepts and reality, between the world as represented through language and the world as it actually is.

universals Forms, essences, absolute generalities; concepts denoting those properties characteristic of, or forming the common essence of, particular entities of various kinds.

verification corroboration, confirmation; the correlation of sentences with empirical evidence that lends credibility to their claim to represent truth. Ayer distinguishes between "strong" and "weak" notions of verification; "strong" verification carries a demand for virtual certainty in confirming a statement, while "weak" verification requires only that the *probability* of its being true be established. Ayer thinks the latter is the only practical procedure.

"world-formula" James's term for a self-contained, coherent view of reality; James's pragmatism supports the existence of a variety of such views, some of which can genuinely conflict with others without being entirely true or entirely false.

STUDY QUESTIONS

1. Can you understand what Plato means by Forms or Ideas, and can you find these appearing in your own experience?

2. Do you find your own struggle to obtain truth anything like Plato's allegory of the cave? Why?

3. Does James's pragmatism seem to you peculiarly "American" in its approach to truth?

4. What strengths and/or weaknesses do you see in the pragmatic theory of truth that James developed?

5. Do the restrictions of Ayer's criteria seem to be "the right way to go" to find truth?

6. What do you think Ayer is trying to achieve? Is his goal one that we ought to accept?

7. Can you explain what Wittgenstein was trying to accomplish when he emphasized "language-games"?

8. Have you ever experienced language to be an obstacle, either in a discussion or in consideration of a personal issue? If so, could Wittgenstein's philosophy be of help?

NOTES

[1] Plato, *Theatetus* (185), in *The Dialogues of Plato*, trans. B. Jowett (New York: Random House, 1920), 2:188.

[2] Plato, *The Republic* (508), in *The Dialogues of Plato*, 1:770.

[3] William James, *Some Problems of Philosophy: A Beginning of an Introduction to Philosophy* (New York: Longmans, Green, 1911), p. 76.

[4] William James, *Pragmatism: A New Name for Some Old Ways of Thinking* (New York: Longmans, Green, 1907), p. 50.

[5]A. J. Ayer, *Language, Truth and Logic*, 2nd ed. (New York: Dover, n.d.), p. 5. Reprinted by permission of the publisher.

[6]Ludwig Wittgenstein, *Philosophical Investigations*, trans. G.E.M. Anscombe. Reprinted by permission of Basil Blackwell.

[7]Ludwig Wittgenstein, *Tractatus Logico-Philosophicus*, trans. D. F. Pears and B. F. McGuinness (New York: Humanities, 1963), p. 5.

[8]Wittgenstein, *Investigations*, p. 103.

[9]Wittgenstein, *Tractatus*, 3.

[10]Wittgenstein, *Investigations*, p. 19. Wittgenstein's italics.

[11]Ludwig Wittgenstein, *On Certainty*, ed. G.E.M. Anscombe and G. H. von Wright and trans. Denis Paul and G.E.M. Anscombe (New York: Harper Torchbooks, 1972), pp. 16, 9, 2.

[12]Ludwig Wittgenstein, "A Lecture on Ethics," in *Ethics: Selections from Classical and Contemporary Writers*, ed. Oliver A. Johnson, 4th ed. (New York: Holt, Rinehart & Winston, 1978), p. 453. The lecture is reprinted from *The Philosophical Review* 74, no. 1 (1965).

[13]Wittgenstein, *On Certainty*, p. 82.

[14]Wittgenstein, *Investigations*, pp. 6–7, 11, 19, 31–32, 34, 48.

WHAT SHOULD I DO?

Philosophy . . . "bakes no bread," as has been said, but it can inspire our souls with courage. . . . Philosophy's results concern us all most vitally. . . .

WILLIAM JAMES
Pragmatism

CHAPTER SIX

Am I Free to Act?

*I*n response to our first major question, "What can I know?", philosophers urge us to analyze how we think and how we decide what to believe. They also recommend how we *should* think, and they propose beliefs we *ought* to hold. Everyday experience contains a similar mixture. We deal constantly with factual matters, but we also make value judgments, issue prescriptive statements, and formulate normative appraisals. In short, we try to figure out what we ought to do, what is good and right. We distinguish these factors from what we consider wrong and what is simply the way events turn out. How *should* they have come out, we ask.

Many factors enter into such evaluations: our cultural background, religious training, the influences of parents, teachers, and friends, to mention but a few. Philosophers take all those features into account, but in exploring the variations on the question "What should I do?", they want to learn whether our attitudes about right and wrong are simply the reflections of culture or whether they rest on critically appraised foundations. They wonder, for example, whether all men and women have rights and duties in common. Philosophers seek to discover what a good life involves and to see if the qualities that make life good are valid regardless of time and place. They also ask whether human history evidences progress

in achieving what is good. Philosophy, in turn, asks us to decide how we can educate people so that they are more likely to achieve worthwhile goals.

As we explore the question "What should I do?", we will divide our explorations among five related questions. We first ask "Am I free to act?" (Chapter Six) because the answer to that question has much to do with determining what we *can* do. If our actions are totally determined, the question of what we *ought* to do may be very different from what it first appears. Next we ask "Do rules govern my actions?" (Chapter Seven). This question is important because if there are such rules, they are the basis we need to help us decide what we ought to do. The question "How do I make right decisions?" (Chapter Eight) is closely related, since in fact our actions depend on deciding when a decision is "right" and what makes it so. "Do I have rights in society?" (Chapter Nine) obviously bears on our question of what we ought to do, since we need to put every action into a social context, not simply an individual one. Last, we will discuss "Can I make society better?" (Chapter Ten), for what we ought to do depends, at least in part, on what influence we feel our actions can have.

As we approach our first question, "Am I free to act?", we will meet six authors who have quite different answers. First, we consider together the views of two Protestant reformers, Martin Luther and John Calvin, plus the thought of the Renaissance humanist, Erasmus, and Jonathan Edwards, who is often regarded as America's first original philosopher–theologian. With Arthur Schopenhauer we have an example of a nineteenth-century German philosopher who worried a great deal about how human free will could fit into the scientific scheme of nature. We have met William James in Chapter Five, but this American pragmatist appears again because of his important contributions to the debate between advocates of determinism and freedom. Finally, Jean-Paul Sartre propounds the views of twentieth-century **existentialism**, which stresses individual freedom perhaps more than any other philosophy.

One critical issue underlies the questions in this section. It arises when we think about the words "ought" and "should." To ask whether you ought or ought not do something implies that you have a choice. To expect someone to do something when there is no possibility that he or she can accomplish the action would be absurd, even cruel. Moral judgments and ethical requirements both assume that various forms of human conduct are possible. They depend on the assumption that human lives are not strictly determined in advance but are at least partly free. Nevertheless, the question of whether humans have free will is one of the fundamental issues of philosophy. Even when philosophers affirm freedom, they do not always agree about its nature and its boundaries. Philosophy wrestles with those problems and so do we all. For instance, why are you reading these words? Must you do it? You are free to set this book aside right now, aren't you?

No matter what your response to the questions above, a basic issue remains. Are you freely choosing to read these words? Could you be doing something different at this very moment? Or is your present activity inevitable, unavoidable, and determined such that it could not be otherwise? Now consider the news broadcast you heard last night. Did those disasters and crimes have to happen? Could the individuals and nations involved have acted differently? Your answers are important. Our lives seem to follow a particular path into an unknown future because we make decisions freely. On the other hand, we know that human dealings do not occur in a vacuum. They are strands in an intricate web, a conceptual framework of cause-and-effect relationships that tells us much about why life as a whole has one design and not another. Although we feel free, we may yet discover powerful forces and instincts that drive us from within as well as from outside. Is your present activity the inevitable effect of preceding causes, even if you do not grasp what all the causes may be or how they combine to produce what is happening? Such reflections lead us back to the question "Am I free to act?"

Luther, Erasmus, Calvin, and Edwards on Free Will

It is not usual to turn to the German Protestant reformer who opposed the pope and the Roman hierarchy for philosophical insight about decision making. As a theologian and churchman, Martin Luther (1483–1546) was rather negative in his attitude toward philosophy. Luther, however, did carry on a debate with Desiderius Erasmus (1466–1536), the famous Dutch humanist, over the issue of **free will.** You must admit that this question is fundamental where decision making is concerned. If in fact we are not free to act, it is useless to talk about practical decision making, for all our decisions must already have been determined. Luther raises this question in the context of God's determination of all events, but the basic issue is the

MARTIN LUTHER 1483–1546

DESIDERIUS ERASMUS 1466–1536

same with or without God. Luther, it is clear, did not believe in the freedom of the human will, and we will see why. Erasmus did, and Luther challenged him to a debate, or at least Luther responded to Erasmus as if they were engaged in a debate on free will.

Is Human Freedom Possible?

Are we free to make decisions of our own, or is agonizing over some decision a futile enterprise because the outcome has been determined in advance? The humanist Erasmus wanted us to have free will, but in the debate with Luther, who based his arguments on Scripture, Erasmus was primarily concerned to show that Scripture does not require a servitude of the will. Nevertheless, Erasmus admitted that "there is hardly a more

tangled labyrinth than that of 'free choice'."[1] As you can see, this question is important to other philosophers and theologians too. Erasmus wrote his essay on free will in a reflective mood, but he had Luther in mind. "Many different views about free choice have been handed down from the ancients about what I have, as yet, no fixed conviction, except that I think there to be a certain power of free choice" (p. 37). As you will see, for reasons of his own Luther is much more fixed in his opinion; but as far as free choice is concerned, what is important is that it not flatly be ruled out. It is enough for Erasmus that there are very varying opinions so that at least free will might be an option for us. Erasmus puts the argument on Luther's ground by saying that the question is "whether God foreknows anything contingently" (p. 37). The issue: Is an event or action in doubt until we decide, in which case no action takes place necessarily? Erasmus seems willing to admit that God foreknows our future decisions, but he focuses on whether God could know them contingently, that is, knowing that an alternative has not yet been chosen. This would break the deadlock of absolute fixity and give us some leverage in making our choices. God would foreknow only their contingency, not their absolute determination. Erasmus opposes his view to Luther's. He paraphrases Luther's position as follows: "Whatever is done by us is done not by free choice but by sheer necessity" (p. 41). It is easy to see that, if Luther is right, our situation in decision making is quite other than we might hope.

To placate Luther, Erasmus says that Scripture's authority is not in dispute. "Our battle," he contends, "is about the meaning of Scripture" (p. 43). The debate primarily takes the form of arguing over whether Scripture itself absolutely requires the believer to accept **determinism.** If it does not, then free will is an open question, and we might be able actively to make decisions for ourselves without having their outcome determined in advance. In any case, Erasmus asserts, "there is a whole choir of saints who support free choice" (pp. 44–45). Furthermore, Erasmus goes on to say that there are "many places in the Holy Scriptures which seem to set forth free choice" (p. 47). If he is correct, at least the evidence is not all on one side, and we are allowed to argue the question. Erasmus then goes on to tell what he means by "free choice," and every philosopher knows that clear definition is a necessary first important step: "By free choice in this place we mean a power of the human will by which a man can apply himself to things which lead to eternal salvation, or turn away from them" (p. 47). Luther's primary aim, on the other hand, is to prevent anyone from saying that we can in any way accomplish our own salvation. Because Luther

wants to reserve this power totally for God, he stands against free will on theological grounds.

What Blocks Our Freedom, Hence Our Decisions?

At the base of the issue is the question of whether our reason has been obscured by **sin.** Taking the religious notion of "original sin" as described in Genesis, Luther had argued that Adam's sin rendered our reason incapable of free decision. Erasmus does not argue against the fact of sin in human nature. Rather, he says that reason "is obscured by sin but not altogether extinguished" (p. 48). If that is true, then although we may not be fully in command of our faculties, we might have enough power left to influence our decisions. Whether one believes in the religious notion of original sin or not, the issue is basic. We all know that at times we have trouble choosing or arriving at even a simple decision. Erasmus' question is whether we are free in those moments when we are cool, rational, and self-controlled. It would do us no good to be free in some abstract sense if we lacked the power to follow through on a decision. Where free choice is concerned, any limitation on our power is as important as the contention that the choice has been made for us.

Erasmus appealed to the notion of **divine grace.** Even if we have damaged our powers by sin, God's grace could restore us so that "the will is made free to that extent" (p. 49). Again, Erasmus has not raised only a religious issue, since many things might inhibit our being decisive (for example, drug use, stress). But if we can be restored, a temporary inability need not block our power to be decisive, once such blocks have been removed. Erasmus also argued that if the will has not been free to begin with, it makes no sense to say that we sin. If we are in possession of the freedom to sin, it remains possible that, once the burden of sin has been removed, we could become free to act on our own again: "For although free choice is damaged by sin, it is nevertheless not extinguished by it" (p. 51). Erasmus went on to argue that God sets choices before us, which must indicate that God grants us a free will to choose. "God shows what is good, what is evil, shows the different rewards of death and life, leaves man freedom to choose" (p. 54). Why should Scripture urge us to strive after better things unless we are free to choose? Why issue us the Ten Commandments if we are not free to keep them?

Where there is unrelieved perpetual necessity there can be no good or bad, Erasmus argued. A tendency both toward virtue and toward sin may be implanted in us, but "it is this flexible will which is called free choice" (p. 77). In battling Luther, Erasmus tried to show: (1) that Scripture is not absolutely clear in denying free will and thus leaves the door open; (2) that sin, although a fact, does not prove absolutely that no power of choice is left or that our ability to decide, once damaged, could not be restored; and (3) that all exhortations to do good and shun the wrong are pointless unless we have some power to choose among alternatives. As we said, despite its theological setting, the issues Erasmus raised can be extended to any discussion of free will. Most important, as we try to teach ourselves to make practical decisions efficiently and wisely, we must know that our effort is not in vain. Just what powers of freedom do we have? It is no use trying to make practical decisions if in fact our human powers are blocked.

Martin Luther and the Bondage of the Will

When Luther replied after reading Erasmus' essay, he did not so much argue with Erasmus as ridicule his position. "You say nothing on the important subject," contends Luther, "that has not been said before. . . . Your book struck me as so cheap and paltry that I felt profoundly sorry for you."[2] Luther thought that every Christian should embrace his position that determinism is the plain truth and that Scripture is not obscure on the matter of free will. Only our ignorance interferes with our seeing the truth: "Let miserable men, therefore, stop imputing with blasphemous perversity the darkness and obscurity of their own heart to the whole clear Scriptures of God" (p. 111). Luther put the issue plainly: "For you cannot possibly know what free choice is unless you know what the human will can do, and what God does, and whether he foreknows necessarily" (p. 118). Luther moved on to resolve the issue as follows: "Here, then, is something fundamentally necessary and salutary for a Christian, to know that God foreknows nothing contingently but that he foresees and proposes and does all things by his immutable, eternal, and infallible will. Here is the thunderbolt by which free will is completely prostrated and shattered" (p. 118). If then it is determined now (either by God's knowledge or by the laws of science) what I will do tomorrow, it is false that I am free to do otherwise.

Luther, then, did not respond directly to Erasmus' points; he simply asserted that Christian doctrine (which for him is one fixed thing) requires the denial of free will. Luther did say that if we label any act we do as "contingent," it is indefinite only from our point of view, not from God's, since divinity has a knowledge of all future contingent events. "Every thing that comes into being does so necessarily, if the action of God is necessary," Luther tells us, although he admits that every action is not necessary in the same way that God's existence is necessary (p. 120). Luther's argument is ultimately based on the question of whether we can be certain of God's offer of salvation. "For if you doubt or disdain to know that God foreknows all things, not contingently, but necessarily and immutably, how can you believe his promises and place a sure trust and reliance on them?" (p. 120). Thus, we see that it was Luther's desire to be absolutely certain about God's power to offer salvation that made him bind all human actions so that there could be nothing contingent in God's sight.

Do Other Considerations Determine How We Make Decisions?

Luther's position also depended on his conviction that "the Word of God and the traditions of men are irreconcilably opposed to one another" (p. 131). In this case, Erasmus' argument for our belief in freedom of the will, or our need for freedom in our practical life, is cut short. Luther feels that it may be true that we need free will, but that tells us nothing about how God operates. Luther's aim was clearly to humble men and women before God; he was afraid that allowing any degree of free will would lead to human arrogance. To humble a person, he thought, we must be certain that our own salvation is utterly beyond our power and depends entirely on God alone. "But when a man has no doubt that every thing depends on the will of God, then he completely despairs of himself and chooses nothing for himself, but waits for God to work; then he has come close to grace, and can be saved" (p. 131). Thus, Luther did not really deal with the question of free will and our practical decisions. He could not allow it and still hold the view of utter dependence on God, which he thought necessary for salvation. Whether or not we share Luther's theological views, this is a good illustration of how many arguments about free will are decided by ulterior considerations. We must deal with these and respond to them, before we can move on to decide about our practical choices.

"Free choice is plainly a divine term, and can be properly applied to none but the Divine

Majesty alone," Luther concluded (p. 141). Such a position, however, raises more questions than it answers, because it involves: (1) Luther's being absolutely sure about God's nature, and (2) Luther's apparent certainty that what God possesses no human being can have. Despite his Protestantism, Luther takes absolute determinism to be a matter of church doctrine, and "it is impossible for the church to err, even in the smallest article" (p. 154). That statement sounds strange coming from one who opposed papal authority on so many issues. Again we see Luther's connection of human freedom with his determination that the Christian faith requires full determination. Luther argued that God must give those who are elected a clear and certain law that leaves no ground for uncertainty. Speaking of the Law and the Prophets, he said "What sort of witness is it if it is obscure?" (p. 161). He does not think God would give us obscure or ambiguous Scriptures, but that position also assumes that Luther was correct in his analysis of how God operates.

If Scripture is "crystal clear," as Luther vehemently maintained, there certainly have been and are many intelligent people who are needlessly puzzled. Luther did say that Scripture is clear in itself; we just do not understand it. This is possible but certainly difficult to explain as long as uncertainty over our decisions remains. Luther further stated that our belief in free will is the work of Satan, which is a hard argument to deal with. "It is Satan's work to prevent men from recognizing their plight and to keep them presuming that they can do everything they are told" (p. 193). Of course, one could argue that we would understand our plight better if we saw every action of ours as a result of our own free **choice**. Luther wanted to bring people to despair so that they would accept God's grace, and he thought holding out for the absolute determinism of our actions was the means to do this. He admitted that God might have a secret will unknown to us, but he put that possibility aside and insisted we stay only with Scripture, which is fixed and clear. Luther did say that it would be unjust of God to demand free choice if such were not possible, but he overlooked the fact that the argument can be turned the other way around. That is, if God demands choices of us (and in our everyday life we surely face many decision points), he must have granted us at least some freedom to respond.

Luther's arguments are instructive, however, because they show us that the question of free will is connected to a whole nest of issues. Luther had a fixed view of God's nature, the clarity of Scripture, and the necessity to bind human will in order to make persons receptive to the Christian gospel. For Luther, free will represented human arrogance, which he found abhorrent. Even outside this theological/religious context, whenever we question our freedom to make the practical decisions that confront us daily, a whole nest of problems becomes involved, which cannot be decided in isolation. This will be seen if we consider any practical decision before us. Shall we go to a movie tonight? Shall I divorce my husband or wife? No issue is simple, nor does any question stand in isolation. To decide wisely one way or another, we must both understand the background and appreciate the complexity of an issue. If free will is a fragile reed, before making any decision we must ask what circumstances would allow us to be free to decide, if we could create them?

John Calvin and the Demand for Determinism

Though we human beings often demand freedom, might there also be times when necessity seems acceptable? Necessity may give a certain comfort to the natural scientist, since it seems to guarantee that human

JOHN CALVIN 1509–1564

beings will not be able to interfere with the orderliness of nature, which science attempts to translate into fixed laws. A feeling of being determined may also relieve us of some **responsibility** for our actions. As we shall see, some people consider human **freedom** to be an immense burden.

John Calvin (1509–1564) had another reason to deny human freedom. He believed that God controlled the universe; hence any human interference in the form of independent decisions would jeopardize God's absolute control. More important, Calvin believed that God had promised to do certain things for mankind. Therefore, God limited human freedom to allow himself to do his work. So you see, we do not simply sit down and say, "Which do we like best, freedom or determinism?" Instead, the issue is closely bound up with other beliefs we hold important.

A lawyer by training, Calvin worked in Geneva and became widely known as the founder of a religious movement, now called Calvinism. Following Luther, he is perhaps the most important figure in the Protestant Reformation. His major work is the *Institutes of the Christian Religion* (1536), but he sets forth the doctrine that concerns us here in a simpler work, *Concerning the Eternal Predestination of God*. First of all, it is important to note that Calvin is bent on giving God a free hand. He speaks of "the free **election** of God, by which He adopts for Himself whom He will out of the lost and damned generation of man."[3] Also, it is impossible for all beings to be completely free. The freedom of some might lead to the determination of others. So zealous is Calvin in guarding the concept of God's freedom that he is willing to compromise human freedom. We must realize that, historically, not everyone has prized individual freedom as highly as we who live in the late twentieth century. During the Reformation, the debate often centered on the question of "who is saved," and all other issues seemed subordinate. For Calvin, God must be free to elect whomever he wills for salvation, and that is Calvin's primary value. Calvin does not want people to imagine that whether they are elected by God is a matter that lies within their free choice.

Calvin speaks of "the inscrutable judgment of God" (p. 58). This idea should make us pause to consider whether it is possible for us to penetrate to the final origins of human behavior if God is involved in our actions. Of course, in Calvin's view human actions ultimately find their explanation in God. In the modern scientific world, it may be that many reject God because they want to study human nature on its own and would like to explain our behavior without reference to any transcendental being such as God. Calvin, of course, found the answers to all

questions in his understanding of God. However, even if today we exclude God to simplify matters, there still is a question as to whether human behavior is fully open to our inspection. It has been our modern assumption that we either can explain human behavior fully or will soon be able to. This assumption has led some philosophers to a doctrine of determinism not unlike Calvin's, although for entirely different reasons. Calvin believed that God was free to call "whom He condescends to call" and to make religious whom God will (p. 63). On the other hand, modern men and women who are enamored of scientific explanation are sometimes afraid that human freedom will interfere with the scientific explanation of human nature by introducing too much uncertainty.

Has Human Nature Lost Its Capacity for Freedom?

Calvin's position is complicated by his belief in the traditional Christian doctrine of the fall of humankind. That is, human beings were free and were created to lead a perfect existence, but they damaged or lost this capacity through error and sin. Calvin speaks of "man's depravity," which came about by the original abuse of freedom so that it led to the decreased capacity of all who came afterwards.[4] Man "by sinning forfeited the privileges conferred on him at his creation," Calvin reports (1:28). It is not simply a matter of whether being human by itself offers us free will, but whether our ancestors destroyed such a capacity by their sinful actions. Furthermore, we need to know if the fall was predestined to occur.

Since for Calvin God's essence "is incomprehensible, utterly transcending all human thought," our ability to understand humanity's original freedom and how it was lost forever is made more difficult by God's involvement in that crucial event (1:51). Furthermore, human understanding needs help from outside itself (i.e., from God) if it is to restore itself. For Calvin, human reason cannot stand on its own. Thus, we must at least ask whether human reason is adequate to decide the question of freedom. The tendency in modern times notwithstanding, we should not simply assume that ability.

In addition to believing that we have been deprived of liberty, Calvin is sure that we talk about our liberty simply as an excuse. "For, some under the pretext of this liberty, cast off all obedience to God and precipitate themselves into the most unbridled licentiousness" (2:131). In the modern world we tend to think that freedom is an unquestionable good, but Calvin is convinced that people often use the notion that we are free as an excuse for bad behavior. Such liberty as Calvin allows to be good is that which turns us from external things to our internal spiritual nature: "Christian liberty is, in all its branches a spiritual thing, all the virtue of which consists in appeasing terrified consciences before God" (2:135). Modern thinkers have argued that human reason gives us the capacity to decide freely, if only we learn to reason properly. But for Calvin, human reason has been corrupted and broken and so cannot be depended on. Others (for example, Sigmund Freud) have thought that our actions are controlled by our unconscious mind. Calvin thinks we reason consciously but that corruption has weakened human reason so as to render it ineffective. Thus, Calvin teaches us not to assume that freedom is always good or that reason is always dependable.

Calvin makes us see that we are mistaken if we simply assume that human freedom is desirable and possible. We make assumptions about the unquestioned power of reason that may be overly optimistic. Furthermore, there may be reasons that point to determinism as a preferable hypothesis. Certainly it makes explaining the world a much simpler matter. Also, 'freedom' can

mean many things. But basically we usually think we are "free" if it lies within our power to decide and thus to determine our own actions at least partially by the power of our own will. The final truth could lie, however, between the two extremes of being absolutely free and being completely determined. It is easier if we can assert that the same things are possible for all persons. But in point of fact some may have damaged their capacity for freedom—for example, by their decision to use hard drugs, if not through actions that damage others, as Calvin proposes. Or, some situations may allow us the exercise of freedom and others not. In this case, freedom would depend on our ability to seize the right moment. We may well be determined in some matters and open to freedom in others. After all, even Calvin, who prefers **predestination** in human action for God's sake, sees some possibility that we might still retain a "spiritual freedom."

Freedom of the Will Revised

Jonathan Edwards (1703–1758) disclaimed dependence on Calvin. Yet the Puritan tradition, from which this important philosophical theologian came, was clearly influenced by the Geneva thinker. Born in colonial Connecticut, Edwards attended Yale College. Locke and Berkeley were among the philosophers who influenced him most. But Edwards felt that God had called him to be a minister. For almost twenty years he led a church in Northampton, Massachusetts, but eventually he clashed with the membership and accepted an Indian mission post at Stockbridge, Massachusetts. All the while, he wrote prolifically, and while in Stockbridge he authored *Freedom of the Will* (1754). Like many of his works, this one explored God's absolute sovereignty and human dependence on God. But it also defended an intriguing notion of freedom. In 1757 Edwards

JONATHAN EDWARDS   1703–1758

became president of what is now Princeton University and died at Princeton the following year.

Edwards's discussion of freedom begins with a definition of the **will**, which he regarded as "that by which the mind chooses anything."[5] If the soul is to act voluntarily, it must act electively. Locke had suggested that "will" means a power or ability to prefer or choose. One question, Edwards pointed out, involves the relationship between volition and preference. In every volition, he concluded, there is a preference. "A man never, in any instance," claimed Edwards, "wills anything contrary to his desires, or desires anything contrary to his will" (p. 139). Thus, the motive that "is the strongest . . . determines the will" (p. 141). The decisive influence comes from what we perceive as "good." Therefore, Edwards contended, "the will always is as the greatest good is" (p. 142). It does not follow, of course, that our wills always get their way. Even our judgments about what is good are often mistaken. Still, the will's activity is determined by the greatest apparent good. As you can see, in spite of the theological context of the question, Edwards has a more philosophical approach than Luther or Calvin. His stress here is not on God or explicitly religious concerns. Rather, he wants to pin down what "free will" means. We follow what is agreeable, Edwards thought, and "the will always follows the last dictate of the understanding" (p. 148).

When Edwards says that the will is always determined by the strongest motive, he leaves the will free in one sense, but the question of what "freedom" means remains. He tries to clarify the situation by reflecting on "necessity." Edwards held, for example, that "anything . . . is *necessary* when we cannot help it, let us do what we will" (p. 150). But this does not hold in our action, he argued, for we are governed precisely by what we will, and what we will is governed in turn by our strongest motive. Yet the range of freedom still remains at issue, as we can see when Edwards adds that what he wants to show is that "Necessity is not inconsistent with Liberty" (p. 152). The point is that Edwards allows us freedom in the sense that our motives prevail—we are self-determining, according to Edwards—but the catch is that our motives and their impact are themselves the necessary effects of causes.

"Nothing," claimed Edwards, "ever comes to pass without a cause" (p. 181). An act of the will is the effect of a cause. The same is true of the motives that govern the will. Our liberty resides in our "power of willing as we please" (p. 192). But what "we please" is not as free as we think, because Edwards sees every event as the result of previous causes that determined it. Edwards wants to retain some meaning for "free will" but not so much that our acts are without causes that determine them necessarily. His "freedom" means only that we are not constrained by necessity to act contrary to our strongest motives. As for the motives themselves, they are links in a deterministic chain of causes and effects nonetheless.

Philosophy Shapes Edwards's Views

It is clear that Luther's protest against Erasmus stemmed from the religious doctrine Luther wished to protect. Although not so adamant, Calvin equally shaped his notions on free will from his theological motives. There is nothing wrong with this, as long as one is clear about what the determining factor is. Jonathan Edwards certainly has his theological concerns, and yet he finds Locke and a philosophical style of analyzing the question of free will the most useful. This gives us one example of the helpfulness of philosophical study. In dealing with a tangled religious issue, Edwards turned to Locke to help him distinguish several issues surrounding the question.

We are probably all prone to take an issue like "freedom of the will" and assert the position we think suits us best without too much consideration of alternatives. Luther is quite clear about what causes him to take the view he does, as is Calvin. However, both Erasmus and Edwards try to step back a pace and examine the complex questions involved, trying to determine what must be distinguished before a meaningful decision can be reached. Of course, those who share Luther's or Calvin's convictions may agree with them about free will, but the wider issue is what we can do to convince others who do not begin by sharing our basic assumptions. Phi-

losophers tend more to look at background assumptions than to defend any particular view. Watch for these possibilities as you examine more of the thought of Luther, Calvin, and Edwards.

FROM *ON THE BONDAGE OF THE WILL*
By Martin Luther

Here, then, is something fundamentally necessary and salutary for a Christian, to know that God foreknows nothing contingently, but that he foresees and purposes and does all things by his immutable, eternal, and infallible will. Here is a thunderbolt by which free choice is completely prostrated and shattered, so that those who want free choice asserted must either deny or explain away this thunderbolt, or get rid of it by some other means. However, before I establish this point by my own argument and the authority of Scripture, I will first deal with it in your words.

Was it not you, my dear Erasmus, who asserted a little earlier that God is by nature just, by nature most merciful? If this is true, does it not follow that he is immutably just and merciful—that as his nature never changes, so neither does his justice or mercy? But what is said of his justice and mercy must also be said of his knowledge, wisdom, goodness, will, and other divine attributes. If, then, the assertion of these things concerning God is, as you state, religious, pious, and salutary, what has come over you that you now contradict yourself by asserting that it is irreverent, inquisitive, and vain to say that God foreknows necessarily? You declare that the will of God is to be understood immutable, yet you forbid us to know that his foreknowledge is immutable. Do you, then, believe that he foreknows without willing or wills without knowing? If his foreknowledge is an attribute of his will, then his will is eternal and unchanging, because that is its nature; if his will is an attribute of his foreknowledge, then his foreknowledge is eternal and unchanging, because that is its nature.

From this it follows irrefutably that everything we do, everything that happens, even if it seems to us to happen mutably and contingently, happens in fact nonetheless necessarily and immutably, if you have regard to the will of God. For the will of God is effectual and cannot be hindered, since it is the power of the divine nature itself; moreover it is wise, so that it cannot be deceived. Now, if his will is not hindered, there is nothing to prevent the work itself from being done, in the place, time, manner, and measure that he himself both foresees and wills. If the will of God were such that, when the work was completed, the work remained but the will ceased—like the will of men, which ceases to will when the house they want is built, just as it also comes to an end in death— then it could be truly said that things happen contingently and mutably. But here the opposite happens; the work comes to an end and the will remains, so remote is it from possibility that the work itself, during its production and completed existence, should exist or persist contingently. To happen contingently, however—in order that we may not misuse terms—means in Latin, not that the work itself is contingent, but that it is done by a contingent and mutable will, such as there is not in God. Moreover, a work can only be called contingent when *from our point of view* it is done contingently and, as it were, by chance and without our expecting it, because our will or hand seizes on it as something presented to us by chance, when we have thought or willed nothing about it previously.[6]

DEFINITION OF PROVIDENCE

By John Calvin

By His providence, God rules not only the whole fabric of the world and its several parts, but also the hearts and even the actions of men. A mass of literature confronts anyone who will write on this subject. But since I have already so dealt with the subject as to give considerable satisfaction to sound and fair readers, I shall summarize it now with as much brevity as is possible. It cannot be hoped that what I say will match in splendor the greatness and excellence of the subject. I shall refer in a few words to what was expounded at greater length in my *Institutes*; and, if authority is needed, I shall attach scriptural proof. Thus I shall dispose of the sinister and malignant observations of Pighius and others like him, which evilly distort what is well said, lest pious minds should be hindered or disturbed.

We mean by providence not an idle observation by God in heaven of what goes on in earth, but His rule of the world which He made; for He is not the creator of a moment, but the perpetual governor. Thus the providence we ascribe to God belongs not only to His eyes but to His hands. So He is said to rule the world in His providence, not only because He watches the order of nature imposed by Himself, but because He has and exercises a particular care of each one of His creatures. For it is indeed true, that, as the creation of the world was beautifully ordained by the admirable wisdom of God, so it is unable to persist in being unless it be sustained by His virtue. That the sun should daily rise for us, that in its swift course it has degrees so fitly tempered, that the separate orbits of the stars are wonderfully undisturbed, that the seasons continually recur; that the earth yields its annual produce for the nourishment of men, that the elements and particles do not cease to discharge their office, that finally the fertility of nature never fails as though it were fatigued—this is to be ascribed solely to His directing hand who once made all things. Psalm 104 is nothing but a eulogy of this universal providence. So too Paul declares, when he says that in Him we live and move and have our being (Acts 17:28). Since this is the essential property of the one God, so faith must consider the secret vitality it communicates, by which it comes about that creatures exist, though they will also soon perish.

PROVIDENCE REFERS TO PAST AS WELL AS FUTURE

Two other distinctions add some light. The first is that the providence of God is to be referred to past as well as future time; the other, that, sometimes with and sometimes without and sometimes contrary to all means, the highest power is to be ascribed to Him who ordains and creates all things. To consider the reference to past time: if anything follows according to one's wish or desire, let mortal man not sacrifice to his own net, as Habakkuk says (1:16), not exalt his prudence or virtue or good fortune; let him not make the offering to men or creatures which is properly God's own. But let him be persuaded that God is the prime author of his blessing, however it come about. But in adversity, let him rest in this consolation: As God pleased, so it has come about; by revolting against God, I profit nothing and only involve myself in the guilt of impious contumacy. Then let the memory of his past life come before him, so that, from the punishments inflicted upon him, he may learn his sins. As for future time, the providence of God is to be thought of in this way by pious minds. There is always an intention in His promises and threats. If there should be any discrepancy, there will remain no building up in the fear of God and no progress in faith. But the man who observes the omnipotence of God in the mirror of His word will not only rise above the innumerable perils of the world on the wings of faith, but also be less subdued and humiliated by daily aggravations. When I said that the providence of God is to be considered along with the means employed, I meant that if anyone give help to those who labor in the last extremity, the deliverance is not human, but divine by the hand of man. The sun rises daily, but it is God that gives light to the earthly globe. The earth produces fruit, but it is God that supplies bread and by bread imparts vigor to us in our need. In a word, when inferior causes, like veils, withdraw God from our sight, as they usually do, we must penetrate higher by the eye of faith, so

as to discern God's hand working in these instruments. Christ teaches by an example how to look away from the means and give place to the providence of God, when He repelled the assault of Satan with the shield: Man does not live by bread alone, but by every word that proceeds from the mouth of God (Matt. 4:4). For, as He knew the power of God needed no external support, He concludes that it is supplied without bread as well as being mercifully supplied by bread. Hence, we are to guard against being so attached to inferior means, as to think that the hand of God alone by itself cannot supply us abundantly with all help. Apart from mere means, the providence of God attains its deserved praise from us, when we are persuaded that it is superior to all obstacles and we conquer all assembled terrors by faith alone. For this is a real wrestling school in which God tests our faith, for every day obstacles arise to impede His counsel up and down through all creation. What then is to be done? If only faith will ascend to the level of divine power, it will without great trouble overcome all agents that seem to oppose it.[7]

CONCERNING THE NATURE OF THE WILL

By Jonathan Edwards

It may possibly be thought that there is no great need of going about to define or describe the "will"; this word being generally as well understood as any other words we can use to explain it: and so perhaps it would be, had not philosophers, metaphysicians, and polemic divines brought the matter into obscurity by the things they have said of it. But since it is so, I think it may be of some use, and will tend to the greater clearness in the following discourse, to say a few things concerning it.

And therefore I observe, that the will (without any metaphysical refining) is plainly, that by which the mind chooses anything. The faculty of the will is that faculty or power or principle of mind by which it is capable of choosing: an act of the will is the same as an act of choosing or choice.

If any think 'tis a more perfect definition of the will to say that it is that by which the soul either chooses or refuses, I am content with it: though I think that 'tis enough to say, it's that by which the soul chooses: for in every act of will whatsoever, the mind chooses one thing rather than another; it chooses something rather than the contrary, or rather than the want or nonexistence of that thing. So in every act of refusal, the mind chooses the absence of the thing refused; the positive and the negative are set before the mind for its choice, and it chooses the negative; and the mind's making its choice in that case is properly the act of the will: the will's determining between the two is a voluntary determining; but that is the same thing as making a choice. So that whatever names we call the act of the will by—choosing, refusing, approving, disapproving, liking, disliking, embracing, rejecting, determining, directing, commanding, forbidding, inclining, or being averse, a being pleased or displeased with—all may be reduced to this of choosing. For the soul to act voluntarily, is evermore to act electively.

Mr. Locke says, "The will signifies nothing but a power or ability to prefer or choose." And in the foregoing page says, "The word 'preferring' seems best to express the act of volition"; but adds, that "it does it not precisely; for [says he] though a man would prefer flying to walking, yet who can say he ever wills it?" But the instance he mentions don't [sic] prove that there is anything else in "willing" but merely "preferring": for it should be considered what is the next and immediate object of the will, with respect to a man's walking or any other external action—which is not his being removed from one place to another, on the earth, or through the air: these are remoter objects of preference—but such or such an immediate exertion of himself. The thing nextly chosen or preferred when a man wills to walk is not his being removed to such a place where he would be, but such an exertion and motion of his legs and feet, etc. in order to [do] it. And his willing such an alteration in his body in the present moment is nothing else but

his choosing or preferring such an alteration in his body at such a moment, or his liking it better than the forbearance of it. And God has so made and established the human nature, the soul being united to a body in proper state, that the soul preferring or choosing such an immediate exertion or alteration of the body, such an alteration instantaneously follows. There is nothing else in the actings of my mind, that I am conscious of while I walk, but only my preferring or choosing, through successive moments, that there should be such alterations of my external sensations and motions, together with a concurring habitual expectation that it will be so, having ever found by experience that on such an immediate preference, such sensations and motions do actually instantaneously, and constantly arise. But it is not so in the case of flying: though a man may be said remotely to choose or prefer flying, yet he don't choose or prefer, incline to or desire, under circumstances in view, any immediate exertion of the members of his body in order to [do] it, because he has no expectation that he should obtain the desired end by any such exertion; and he don't prefer or incline to any bodily exertion or effort under this apprehended circumstance, of its being wholly in vain. So that if we carefully distinguish the proper objects of the several acts of the will, it will not appear by this, and suchlike instances, that there is any difference between "volition" and "preference"; or that a man's choosing, liking best, or being best pleased with a thing are not the same with his willing that thing, as they seem to be according to those general and more natural notions of men, according to which language is formed. Thus an act of the will is commonly expressed by its pleasing a man to do thus or thus; and a man's doing as he wills, and doing as he pleases, are the same thing in common speech.

Mr. Locke says, "The will is perfectly distinguished from desire; which in the very same action may have a quite contrary tendency from that which our wills set us upon. A man [says he] whom I cannot deny, may oblige me to use persuasions to another, which, at the same time I am speaking, I may wish may not prevail on him. In this case 'tis plain the will and desire run counter." I don't suppose that "will" and "desire" are words of precisely the same signification: "will" seems to be a word of a more general signification, extending to things present and absent. "Desire" respects something absent. I may prefer my present situation and posture, suppose sitting still, or having my eyes open, and so may will it. But yet I can't think they are so entirely distinct, that they can ever be properly said to run counter. A man never, in any instance, wills anything contrary to his desires, or desires anything contrary to his will. The forementioned instance, which Mr. Locke produces, don't prove that he ever does. He may, on some consideration or other, will to utter speeches which have a tendency to persuade another, and still may desire that they may not persuade him: but yet his will and desire don't run counter at all: the thing which he wills, the very same he desires; and he don't will a thing, and desire the contrary in any particular. In this instance, it is not carefully observed, what is the thing willed, and what is the thing desired: if it were, it would be found that will and desire don't clash in the least. The thing willed on some consideration is to utter such words; and certainly, the same consideration so influences him that he don't desire the contrary; all things considered, he chooses to utter such words, and don't desire not to utter 'em. And so as to the thing which Mr. Locke speaks of as desired, viz. that the words, though they tend to persuade, should not be effectual to that end, his will is not contrary to this; he don't will that they should be effectual, but rather wills that they should not, as he desires. In order to prove that the will and desire may run counter, it should be shown that they may be contrary one to the other in the same thing, or with respect to the very same object of will or desire: but here the objects are two; and in each, taken by themselves, the will and desire agree. And 'tis no wonder that they should not agree in different things, however little distinguished they are in their nature. The will may not agree with the will, nor desire agree with desire, in different things. As in this very instance which Mr. Locke mentions, a person may, on some consideration, desire to use persuasions, and at the same time may desire they may not prevail; but yet nobody will say that desire runs counter to desire; or that this proves that desire is perfectly a distinct thing from desire. The like might be observed of the other instance Mr. Locke produces, of a man's desiring to be eased of pain and so forth.

But not to dwell any longer on this, whether desire and will, and whether preference and volition be precisely the same things or no; yet, I trust it will be allowed by all, that in every act of will there is an act of choice; that in every volition there is a preference, or a prevailing inclination of the soul, whereby the soul, at that instant, is out of a state of perfect indifference, with respect to the direct object of the volition. So that in every act, or going forth of the will, there is some preponderation of the mind or inclination, one way rather than another; and the soul had rather have or do one thing than another, or than not to have or do that thing; and that there, where there is absolutely no preferring or choosing, but a perfect continuing equilibrium, there is no volition.

CONCERNING THE DETERMINATION OF THE WILL

By "determining the will," if the phrase be used with any meaning, must be intended, causing that the act of the will or choice should be thus, and not otherwise: and the will is said to be determined, when, in consequence of some action, or influence, its choice is directed to, and fixed upon a particular object. As when we speak of the determination of motion, we mean causing the motion of the body to be such a way, or in such a direction, rather than another.

To talk of the determination of the will

supposes an effect, which must have a cause. If the will be determined, there is a determiner. This must be supposed to be intended even by them that say the will determines itself. If it be so, the will is both determiner and determined; it is a cause that acts and produces effects upon itself, and is the object of its own influence and action.

With respect to that grand inquiry, what determines the will, it would be very tedious and unnecessary at present to enumerate and examine all the various opinions which have been advanced concerning this matter; nor is it needful that I should enter into a particular disquisition of all points debated in disputes on that question, whether the will always follows the last dictate of the understanding. It is sufficient to my present purpose to say, it is that motive, which, as it stands in the view of the mind, is the strongest, that determines the will. —But it may be necessary that I should a little explain my meaning in this.

By "motive," I mean the whole of that which moves, excites, or invites the mind to volition, whether that be one thing singly, or many things conjunctly. Many particular things may concur and unite their strength to induce the mind; and when it is so, all together are as it were one complex motive. And when I speak of the "strongest motive," I have respect to the strength of the whole that operates to induce to a particular act of volition, whether that be the strength of one thing alone, or of many together.[8]

ARTHUR SCHOPENHAUER 1788–1860

Arthur Schopenhauer and the Paradoxes of Freedom

As indicated in the preceding section, not everyone is passionately interested in allowing human freedom. Some people have reasons to oppose or fear it. Another thinker who found freedom worrisome was Arthur Schopenhauer (1788–1860). Born into a family of wealthy German merchants, he stud-

ied medicine for a time but ended up pursuing philosophy instead. He taught at the University of Berlin, but had difficulty attracting an audience for his lectures because he insisted on giving them at the same hours as his colleague Hegel, who was then the leading philosopher in all Europe. Arrogant and brooding, Schopenhauer slept with a loaded pistol at hand and took extensive precautions against disease. It is not surprising that his name is associated with pessimism. He did not trust reason as had been fashionable among eighteenth-century European philosophers. The notion of inevitable progress held little attraction for him. Yet Schopenhauer felt it important to spell out his philosophy. His most important work is entitled *The World as Will and Idea* (1818). There and in other writings, too, his interest in freedom and its paradoxes is apparent. We sometimes think that to talk about freedom is to be an optimist about human nature. But not all who are interested in freedom are optimists. It is possible to be absorbed in the notions of will and freedom just because you are pessimistic about their ultimate use, which tended to be the case with this gloomy German philosopher.

Is Freedom Merely a Negative Concept?

In his brief *Essay on the Freedom of the Will* (1841), Schopenhauer wrote: "This concept [freedom] turns out to be negative: It signifies merely the absence of any hindrance and restraint."[9] We think of animate beings as being able to originate movements from their own will. "Animals and men are called free when their actions are not hindered by any physical or material obstacles" (p. 4). Thus, "whenever an animate being acts only from its will, it is, in the physical sense, free" (p. 4). We tend to think of freedom positively as being a great good. Schopenhauer questions this.

In addition, we also have thoughts about our intellectual and moral freedom. Motives, more than physical objects, are involved in this case. "Consequently, to ask whether the will itself is free, is to ask whether the will is in accordance with itself" (p. 6). By way of contrast, he says, "something is necessary which follows from a given sufficient ground. . . . But since the mark of freedom is absence of necessity, that which is free would have to be independent of any and would therefore have to be defined as absolutely accidental. . . . A free will then would be the will which is not determined by grounds" (ibid.). Schopenhauer approaches freedom "metaphysically"; that is, he seeks to learn what principles lie beneath it and therefore determine or support it.

Must We Will Self-Consciously?

When a person wills, Schopenhauer tells us, "His will is always directed to an object and can be thought of only in relation to an object" (p. 14). He continues:

> What does it mean to will something? It means the following: The volition, which initially is itself only an object of the self-consciousness, comes into being as a result of something which belongs to the consciousness of other things and hence is an object of the cognitive faculty. (P. 14.)

Thus, Schopenhauer is telling us that we don't act or will in a vacuum. We sometimes think our decisions spring internally from our will. But objects we perceive outside our selves are always involved. We try to decide whether we should marry a certain person, but the nature of that person and the way we perceive him or her has a great deal, perhaps everything, to do with determining how we will act. A motive intends to change the object in some way and so reacts to it. But the question is whether, given the existence of this object for cognition, the volition must take place. Schopenhauer asks: "Does the entrance of a motive into the consciousness necessarily bring absolute volition, or does the will retain complete freedom either to will or not to will" (p. 14)? We often wish a number of things, but the problem is we can will only one of them. But given the fact that we do choose,

> The question is whether in that choice . . . his own willing of one thing and not the other could possibly have been somehow different from what it actually was. (P. 20.)

To ask whether people could will differently is to ask whether they could be other than themselves. "And that [one] does not know" (p. 20). The question of human freedom cannot be answered without deciding what human nature is like, and our nature in particular.

Does Freedom Interfere with the Laws of Causality?

The problem is that all the changes that take place in the external world are subject to the laws of causality, Schopenhauer is convinced. "Therefore, whenever and wherever they occur, they always occur necessarily and inevitably" (p. 29). How can human freedom be reconciled with this assumed uniformity in nature? Animals have motives that move them, but these are always perceptual and actual. That is, they see and feel things in their world and simply respond to them. Thus, they have little choice. But by virtue of our capacity for nonperceptual ideas by means of which we think and reflect, Schopenhauer argues, human beings have "an infinitely larger field of vision which includes the absent, the past, and the future" (p. 35). Our ideas go beyond immediate perception and so expand our options for freedom.

Persons are relatively free by being free of immediate compulsion. But the problem is that our thought becomes a motive. And if all motives are causes, all motivation carries with it necessity. As we investigate this problem, we are hampered by the fact that concepts and thoughts are independent of the present surroundings and are therefore hidden from the spectator. "It is erroneous to think that our self-consciousness contains the certainty of a free will" (pp. 42–43). "If freedom of the will were so posed, every human action would be an inexplicable miracle—an effect without a cause" (p. 47). Schopenhauer lifts some restrictions on the scope of human freedom, but this cannot go beyond the bounds of causal relationships. We are still subject to laws.

Freedom Can Never Be a Simple Matter

According to Schopenhauer, "For any man, in any situation, two contrary actions are equally possible. . . . The inborn character of man determines in essentials even the goals toward which he inalterably strives" (p. 58). In Schopenhauer's view, freedom of the will turns out in the end to be determined by nature. Ironically, having set out to stress freedom of the will, he concludes that freedom of the will would mean an existence without an essence. That is, we have a nature and cannot act independently from it. Schopenhauer asks his crucial question:

> To a given man under given circumstances, are two actions possible or only one? The answer of all who think deeply: "Only one." (P. 69.)

In spite of his quest for freedom, Schopenhauer concludes: "Everything that happens, from the largest to the smallest, happens necessarily. . . . The voluntary, just as such, is necessary, just by virtue of the motive without which volition is no more possible than without a subject who wills" (p. 62). Schopenhauer admits that this result annuls all freedom of human action and subjects it to the strictest necessity. Actions are determined by our human nature and character, Schopenhauer answers. We are born as a certain kind of being and this is unchangeable. Each person proves to be the product of two factors: his character along with a motive. Our motives move us and give us a sense of spontaneous freedom, but all must fit within our given nature.

Can "Freedom" Actually Turn Out to Mean "Necessity"?

Schopenhauer concludes by tying the two concepts of **character** and **motive** together: "Man does at all times what he wills, and yet he does this necessarily" (p. 98). This outcome means that each of us already is what he or she wills. Objectively we know that behavior is subject to the laws of causality. "Subjectively, however, everyone feels that he always does only what he wills" (p. 99).

Schopenhauer claims that this account does not eliminate freedom, but only moves it to a higher realm. Freedom becomes 'transcendental,' he says, but he does not tell us how this in any way releases our actions from necessity.

Human freedom is connected to the will, and motives take over in human nature to determine the will. Thus, for Schopenhauer, the causal chain is longer and more indirect for human beings than for animals, but the ultimate necessity that governs us is no less strict. Where freedom is concerned we have to ask: Free to do what? And Schopenhauer's answer is: to express our nature. Freedom means the freedom not to be determined by outside physical forces but to be able to express our internal nature, even if that is equally determined. But now we need to ask ourselves: Is this an acceptable meaning of human freedom? Of course, as we proceed to consider this, we must recognize that Schopenhauer's assumption of a causality throughout nature that determines the will is just that, an assumption. Should it not be true, much changes. Perhaps he thought that natural science in his day required the assumption of necessary causes in nature, but as you read the next passage, from *Essay on Freedom of the Will*, consider whether science in the twentieth century is still that inflexible.

Thus that assumption on which the necessity of the operations of *all* causes rests is the inner being of every thing—be it merely a general natural force which manifests itself in it, or be it life force, or be it will. In every case the particular being, of whatever type, will react according to its special nature, whenever causes act upon it. This law, to which all things in the world are subject without exception, was expressed by the scholastics in the formula *operari sequitur esse.* According to it, the chemist tests substances by means of reagents, and a man tries out another man by means of tests which he applies to him. In all cases the external causes will necessarily call forth that which is hidden in a being; for this being cannot react otherwise than according to its nature.

Here one must be reminded that every existence presupposes an essence, that is, every thing-in-being must be *something*, must have a definite nature. It cannot exist and yet be nothing, it cannot be something like the *ens metaphysicum*, that is, a thing which simply *is* and no more than *is*, without any definitions and properties, and consequently, without a definite way of acting which flows from them. As little as an essence yields a reality without an existence (as Kant expounded in the familiar example of the 100 talers), just as little can an existence do this without an essence. For every thing-in-being must have a nature which is essential and peculiar to it, in virtue of which it is what it is, which this being always maintains, and whose manifestations are called forth of necessity by causes; while on the other hand this nature itself is by no means the effect of those causes, nor can it be modified by them. But all this is just as true of man and his will as of all other beings in nature. He too has an essence in addition to existence, that is, fundamental properties which make up his character and require only an outside inducement in order to reveal themselves. Consequently, to expect that a man should act one time in one way, another time quite differently, in response to the same cause, would be no different than to expect that the same tree which bore cherries this summer should bear pears in the next. Freedom of the will, when carefully analyzed, means an existence without an essence, which means that something *is* and at the same time *is nothing*, which in turn means *is not*, and consequently is a self-contradiction.

The question of the freedom of the will is really a touchstone by which one can distinguish the deeply thinking minds from the superficial ones, or it is a milestone at which their ways part, all the former maintaining the necessary occurrence of an action when the character and the motive are given, and the latter, together with the great masses, clinging to the freedom of the will. There is also a type of a middle-of-the-roader who, feeling embarrassed, tacks back and forth, shifts the target for himself and others, hides behind words and phrases, or turns and twists the question so long that one no longer knows what it amounted to. This was what Leibniz did, who was much more of a mathematician and a learned man than a philosopher. But in order to make such vacillating talkers face the question, one must put it to them in the following way and insist that they answer it.

1. To a given man under given circumstances, are two actions possible, or only one?—The answer of all who think deeply: only one.

2. Let us consider that a man's character remains unchanged and also that the circumstances whose influence he had to experience were necessarily determined throughout and down to the least detail by external causes, which always take place with strict necessity and whose chain, entirely consisting of likewise necessary links, continues into infinity. Could the completed life course of such a man turn out in any respect, even the smallest, in any happening, any scene, differently from the way it did?—No! is the consistent and correct answer.

The conclusion from both propositions is: everything that happens, from the largest to the smallest, happens necessarily. *Quidquid fit necessario fit.*

Anyone who is frightened by these propositions has still to learn some things and unlearn others. But then he will realize that they are the most abundant source of comfort and tranquility. Our acts are indeed not a first beginning; therefore nothing really new comes through them into being. But this is true: *through that which we do we only find out what we are.* (Pp. 59–60.)

William James and the Dilemma of Determinism

In Chapter Five, where the guiding question was "What does 'truth' mean?", we met William James (1842–1910), the American pragmatist who believed that true ideas are those we can verify experientially. James thought the answer to the question "Am I free to act?" must be either yes or no. As he put the point in a well-known essay "The Dilemma of Determinism" (1884), "the truth *must* lie with one side or the other and its lying with one side makes the other false."[10] But which side was true? Although James defended a theory of freedom against determinism, he knew it would not be easy to verify human freedom of action.

For James, one reason for the difficulty of showing that we are free to act was the confusion philosophers had brought to the definition of freedom. In fact, James was not sure that the word was meaningful any longer. He summed up the **dilemma** as follows:

> Old-fashioned determinism was what we may call *hard* determinism. It did not shrink from such words as **fatality,** bondage of the will, necessitation, and the like. Nowadays, we have a *soft* determinism which abhors harsh words, and, repudiating fatality, necessity, and even predetermination, says that its real name is freedom; for freedom is only necessity understood, and bondage to the highest is identical with freedom. (P. 149.)

Edwards and Schopenhauer were two philosophers James had in mind when he mentioned "soft determinism." To ensure that his view of freedom would not be confused with Schopenhauer's, James employed the word **chance** to emphasize that he defended the opposite of determinism—"hard" or "soft." "Chance" was not an ideal choice of terms because it suggests randomness or capriciousness, and James never claimed that human action lacks order and purpose. But he willingly accepted the liabilities of "chance" to make unmistakable his view that freedom and determinism are radically different. Here is how James made the contrast:

> What does determinism profess? It professes that those parts of the universe already laid down absolutely appoint and decree what the other parts shall be. The future has no ambiguous possibilities hidden in its womb: the part we call the present is compatible with only one totality. . . . Indeterminism, on the contrary, says that the parts have a certain amount of loose play on one another, so that the laying down of one of them does not necessarily determine what the others shall be. It admits that possibilities may be in excess of actualities, and that things not yet revealed to our knowledge may really in themselves be ambiguous. (P. 150.)

The Vise of Determinism

Sharp differentiation between freedom and determinism, James understood, was far from enough to show that we are free to act. On the contrary, there is strong evidence to support determinism. James knew this because, in addition to being a distinguished philosopher, he was one of the founders of modern psychology. His scientific understanding convinced him that natural disasters and human affairs do not unfold in a vacuum. They are strands of an intricate web of cause-and-effect relationships.

Are we free agents or puppets on a string? Our lives move into an unknown future, and they seem to follow a particular path because we make decisions freely. But if we live forward, we understand backward. We know the present largely by means of the past. The feeling of freedom counts for less than we think because in retrospect we discover powerful forces and instincts that drive us from within as well as from the outside.

Apparently such an analysis requires us to say that what we are doing now is the effect of preceding causes, even if we do not grasp what all the causes may be or exactly how they combine to produce what happens. Carried to its logical conclusion, James thought, this line of reasoning meant that nothing can be other than it is. Real possibilities vanish. The commonsense conviction that present choices produce genuinely new results because they are free—not beyond the influence of environment and previous events, but not totally controlled by them either—turns into a self-deception.

Sense and Nonsense

The vise of determinism threatened to squeeze freedom out of existence. James detested the *feeling* of that squeeze. As an avenue to truth, feeling cannot be trusted completely; it needs to be interpreted and tested by critical reflection. But James believed that gut-level feeling should be taken seriously as well. Looking for a match between the two, James held to the following intuition: when feeling and thinking do not jibe, the first step is not to scrap feeling but to see whether our thinking about it should be revised. That principle focused his attack on determinism and led to his support for the view that we are free to act.

James knew philosophers who thought that determinism was required to make sense of existence. Their contention was that unless one can develop cause-and-effect accounts in which the past always explains the present completely, knowledge and especially science fall by the way. James found such assumptions neither necessary nor convincing. Far from making existence intelligible, determinism made it nonsensical. To make his case, James chose as an example a brutal killing in Brockton, Massachusetts, discussed in the accompanying reading.

Savage murder, James argued, rightly creates feeling of abhorrence and regret. The meaning of such feelings is that an actual happening, in this case the killing, ought not to have happened. The meaning of that **"ought,"** in turn, is that the killing was avoidable. If determinism is valid, such feelings of abhorrence and regret cannot be other than they are, but neither is it possible in any meaningful sense to say that the murder could not have been. It was an unavoidable next link in a chain already forged. If determinism makes sense, James could find little of it in a scenario including an event that ought not to have happened and yet could not possibly have been otherwise. As far as sense is concerned, that discrepancy gave James enough evidence to assert that determinism offers people a promissory note that can never be cashed.

Note James's strategy. He gave no proof for indeterminism; nor did he claim that determinism was conclusively wrong. The latter might be true, but the issue is whether it is incumbent on us, or even desirable, to believe that it is. James thought not, because determinism needlessly makes common sense nonsensical. As for the lingering charge that any nondeterministic approach renders scientific knowledge impossible, James claimed that such an indictment was sound only if science actually required a deterministic base. Another alternative exists, and its validity is greater.

Scientific knowledge, James believed, is best understood as the result of tested hypotheses. Such knowledge is obtained by seeing and judging what happens. The seeing and judging are always fallible. They can result in inferences about causes and effects, laws of nature, and fundamental principles, but these interpretations can be made without assuming determinism. Thus, science can never prove that determinism is real. In fact, James asserted, a view of reality much more in tune with what scientists actually do, not

to mention what people feel in response to tragic death, is one that finds existence in process, moving into an open future. Freedom, not hard or soft determinism, is the hypothesis that best fits the sense of human experience.

The Faith-Ladder

Life, believed James, confronts us with "mutually exclusive alternatives of which only one can be true at once; so that we must choose, and in choosing murder one possibility. The wrench is absolute: "Either–or!"[11] If determinism cannot be rigorously demonstrated, the same is also true for freedom. Thus, according to James, these views are best understood as mutually exclusive postulates that are full of moral significance about the nature of the world. James contended that when a person is faced by such postulates and conclusive proof is not forthcoming, he or she has the right—even the responsibility—to choose in favor of the view that best makes sense of his or her existence. A person continues to live even when objective evidence is incomplete. In such cases the sensible thing to do is consider the available facts and choose the course of belief and action that best fits the attempt to carve out a meaningful life for oneself.

One of James's most important philosophical contributions calls attention to the relationship between a positive belief in the reality of freedom and the act of choosing itself. This relationship is illustrated well by an entry in the diary James kept as a young man. He describes the outcome of his wrestling with determinism as follows:

> I think that yesterday was a crisis in my life. I finished the first part of Renouvier's second *Essais* and see no reason why his definition of free will—"the sustaining of a thought *because I choose to* when I might have other thoughts"—need be the definition of an illusion. At any rate, I will assume for the

present—until next year—that it is no illusion. My first act of free will shall be to believe in free will.[12]

James thought that human freedom centered in our conscious capacity to *pay attention*. As he attended to the logic of belief in freedom, he concluded it was completely fitting that such belief should involve an individual's definite choice. Since conclusive evidence is not available for deciding the freedom–determinism issue on objective grounds, the possibility that either position might be true remains open. But if freedom is a reality, it is appropriate that a choice is required in regard to our belief in it. Freedom implies a freely chosen attitude toward itself. If we are free, there is no necessity to regulate our belief in freedom. "Am I free to act?" The answer may be either yes or no. A conscious choice does not prove freedom's reality, but it is required if we are to view ourselves as free in the face of possible arguments to the contrary. By making such choices, we move ourselves in the direction of freedom.

On August 26, 1910, James died after hiking in the mountains of New Hampshire. He left incomplete an introductory textbook for his Harvard philosophy students. James planned to dedicate the book to Charles Renouvier, the French writer who forty years earlier had started him toward a philosophy of freedom. Published posthumously, *Some Problems of Philosophy* concludes by outlining a reasoning process called the "**faith-ladder**." It moves this way:

1. There is nothing absurd in a certain view of the world being true, nothing self-contradictory.

2. It *might* have been true under certain conditions.

3. It *may* be true, even now.

4. It is *fit* to be true.

5. It *ought* to be true.

6. It *must* be true.

7. It *shall* be true, at any rate for *me*.[13]

The "faith-ladder," parts of which are illustrated in what has gone before, summarizes James's way of arguing for freedom and against determinism. Although James thought that life made good sense only if we are free to act, he saw that it would not make good sense to expect the reality of freedom to be demonstrable or real freedom to be consistent with one's being determined to believe that freedom is real. Freedom, including belief in freedom, rightly involves risk and choice. "Freedom's first deed," wrote James, "should be to affirm itself. We ought never to hope for any other method of getting at the truth if indeterminism be a fact."[14] While you read more of his "Dilemma of Determinism," can you decide freely whether his account makes better sense than those of Edwards, Schopenhauer, and other determinists?

I wish first of all to show you just what the notion that this is a deterministic world implies. The implications I call your attention to are all bound up with the fact that it is a world in which we constantly have to make what I shall, with your permission, call judgments of regret. Hardly an hour passes in which we do not wish that something might be otherwise; and happy indeed are those of us whose hearts have never echoed the wish of Omar Khayam—

> That we might clasp, ere closed, the book of fate,
> And make the writer on a fairer leaf
> Inscribe our names, or quite obliterate.
>
> Ah! Love, could you and I with fate conspire
> To mend this sorry scheme of things entire,
> Would we not shatter it to bits, and then
> Remould it nearer to the heart's desire?

Now, it is undeniable that most of these regrets are foolish, and quite on a par in point of philosophic value which the criticisms on the universe of that friend of our infancy, the hero of the fable "The Atheist and the Acorn":

Fool! had that bough a pumpkin bore,
Thy whimsies would have worked no more, etc.

Even from the point of view of our own ends, we should probably make a botch of remodeling the universe. How much more then from the point of view of ends we cannot see! Wise men therefore regret as little as they can. But still some regrets are pretty obstinate and hard to stifle—regrets for acts of wanton cruelty or treachery, for example, whether performed by others or by ourselves. Hardly anyone can remain *entirely* optimistic after reading the confession of the murderer at Brockton the other day: how, to get rid of the wife whose continued existence bored him, he inveigled her into a desert spot, shot her four times, and then, as she lay on the ground and said to him, "You didn't do it on purpose, did you, dear?" replied, "No, I didn't do it on purpose," as he raised a rock and smashed her skull. Such an occurrence, with the mild sentence and self-satisfaction of the prisoner, is a field for a crop of regrets, which one need not take up in detail. We feel that, although a perfect mechanical fit to the rest of the universe, it is a bad moral fit, and that something else would really have been better in its place.

But for the deterministic philosophy the murder, the sentence, and the prisoner's optimism were all necessary from eternity; and nothing else for a moment had a ghost of a chance of being put into their place. To admit such a chance, the determinists tell us, would be to make a suicide of reason; so we must steel our hearts against the thought. And here our plot thickens, for we see the first of those difficult implications of determinism and monism which it is my purpose to make you feel. If this Brockton murder was called for by the rest of the universe, if

it had to come at its preappointed hour, and if nothing else would have been consistent with the sense of the whole, what are we to think of the universe? Are we stubbornly to stick to our judgment of regret, and say, though it *couldn't* be, yet it *would* have been a better universe with something different from this Brockton murder in it? That, of course, seems the natural and spontaneous thing for us to do; and yet it is nothing short of deliberately espousing a kind of pessimism. The judgment of regret calls the murder bad. Calling a thing bad means, if it mean anything at all, that the thing ought not to be, that something else ought to be in its stead. Determinism, in denying that anything else can be in its stead, virtually defines the universe as a place in which what ought to be is impossible—in other words, as an organism whose constitution is afflicted with an incurable taint, an irremediable flaw. The pessimism of a Schopenhauer says no more than this—that the murder is a symptom; and that it is a vicious symptom because it belongs to a vicious whole, which can express its nature no otherwise than by bringing forth just such a symptom as that at this particular spot. Regret for the murder must transform itself, if we are determinists and wise, into a larger regret. It is absurd to regret the murder alone. Other things being what they are, *it* could not be different. What we should regret is that whole frame of things of which the murder is one member. I see no escape whatever from this pessimistic conclusion if, being determinists, our judgment of regret is to be allowed to stand at all.

The only deterministic escape from pessimism is everywhere to abandon the judgment of regret. That this can be done, history shows to be not impossible. The devil, *quo ad existentiam,* may be good. That is, although he be a *principle* of evil, yet the universe, with such a principle in it, may practically be a better universe than it could have been without. On every hand, in a small way, we find that a certain amount of evil is a condition by which a higher form of good is brought. There is nothing to prevent anybody from generalizing this view, and trusting that if we could but see things in the largest of all ways, even such matters as this Brockton murder would appear to be paid for by the uses that follow in their train. An optimism *quand même*, a systematic and infatuated optimism like that ridiculed by Voltaire in his *Candide,* is one of the possible ideal ways in which a man may train himself to look on life. Bereft of dogmatic hardness and lit up with the expression of a tender and pathetic hope, such an optimism has been the grace of some of the most religious characters that ever lived.

Throb thine with Nature's throbbing breast,
And all is clear from east to west.

Even cruelty and treachery may be among the absolutely blessed fruits of time, and to quarrel with any of their details may be blasphemy. The only real blasphemy, in short, may be that pessimistic temper of the soul which lets it give way to such things as regrets, remorse, and grief.

Thus, our deterministic pessimism may become a deterministic optimism at the price of extinguishing our judgment of regret.

But does not this immediately bring us into a curious logical predicament? Our determinism leads us to call our judgments of regret wrong, because they are pessimistic in implying that what is impossible yet ought to be. But how then about the judgments of regret themselves? If they are wrong, other judgments, judgments of approval presumably, ought to be in their place. But as they are necessitated, nothing else *can* be in their place; and the universe is just what it was before—namely, a place in which what ought to be appears impossible. . . .

But this brings us right back, after such a long detour, to the question of indeterminism and to the conclusion of all I came here to say tonight. For the only consistent way of representing a pluralism and a world whose parts may affect one another through their conduct being either good or bad is the indeterministic way. What interest, zest, or

excitement can there be in achieving the right way, unless we are enabled to feel that the wrong way is also a possible and a natural way—nay, more, a menacing and an imminent way? And what sense can there be in condemning ourselves for taking the wrong way, unless we need have done nothing of the sort, unless the right way was open to us as well? I cannot understand the willingness to act, no matter how we feel, without the belief that acts are really good and bad. I cannot understand the belief that an act is bad, without regret at its happening. I cannot understand regret without the admission of real, genuine possibilities in the world. Only *then* is it other than a mockery to feel, after we have failed to do our best, that an irreparable opportunity is gone from the universe, the loss of which it must forever after mourn.

If you insist that this is all superstition, that possibility is in the eye of science and reason impossibility, and that if I act badly 'tis that the universe was foredoomed to suffer this defect, you fall right back into the dilemma, the labyrinth, of pessimism and subjectivism, from out of whose toils we have just wound our way.

Now, we are of course free to fall back, if we please. For my own part, though, whatever difficulties may beset the philosophy of objective right and wrong, and the indeterminism it seems to imply, determinism, with its alternative of pessimism or romanticism, contains difficulties that are greater still. But . . . I [have] expressly repudiated . . . the pretension to offer any arguments which could be coercive in a so-called scientific fashion in this matter. And I consequently find myself . . . obliged to state my conclusions in an altogether personal way. This personal method of appeal seems to be among the very conditions of the problem; and the most anyone can do is to confess as candidly as he can the grounds for the faith that is in him, and leave his example to work on others as it may.

Let me, then, without circumlocution say just this. The world is enigmatical enough in all conscience, whatever theory we may take up toward it. The indeterminism I defend, the free-will theory of popular sense based on the judgment of regret, represents that world as vulnerable, and liable to be injured by certain of its parts if they act wrong. And it represents their acting wrong as a matter of possibility or accident, neither inevitable nor yet to be infallibly warded off. In all this, it is a theory devoid either of transparency or of stability. It gives us a pluralistic, restless universe, in which no single point of view can ever take in the whole scene; and to a mind possessed of the love of unity at any cost, it will, no doubt, remain forever inacceptable. A friend with such a mind once told me that the thought of my universe made him sick, like the sight of the horrible motion of a mass of maggots in their carrion bed.

But while I freely admit that the pluralism and the restlessness are repugnant and irrational in a certain way, I find that every alternative to them is irrational in a deeper way. The indeterminism with its maggots, if you please to speak so about it, offends only the native absolutism of my intellect—an absolutism which, after all, perhaps, deserves to be snubbed and kept in check. But the determinism with its necessary carrion, to continue the figure of speech, and with no possible maggots to eat the latter up, violates my sense of moral reality through and through. When, for example, I imagine such carrion as the Brockton murder, I cannot conceive it as an act by which the universe, as a whole, logically and necessarily expresses its nature without shrinking from complicity with such a whole. And I deliberately refuse to keep on terms of loyalty with the universe by saying blankly that the murder, since it does flow from the nature of the whole, is not carrion. There are *some* instinctive reactions which I, for one, will not tamper with. The only remaining alternative, the attitude of gnostical romanticism, wrenches my personal instincts in quite as violent a way. It falsifies the simple objectivity of their deliverance. It makes the gooseflesh the murder excites in me a sufficient reason for the perpetration of the crime. It

transforms life from a tragic reality into an insincere melodramatic exhibition, as foul or as tawdry as anyone's diseased curiosity pleases to carry it out. And with its consecration of the *roman naturaliste* state of mind, and its enthronement of the baser crew of Parisian *littérateurs* among the eternally indispensable organs by which the infinite spirit of things attains to that subjective illumination which is the task of life, it leaves me in presence of a sort of subjective carrion considerably more noisome than the objective carrion I called it in to take away.

No! better a thousand times, than such systematic corruption of our moral sanity, the plainest pessimism, so that it be straightforward; but better far then that the world of chance. Make as great an uproar about chance as you please, I know that chance means pluralism and nothing more. If some of the members of the pluralism are bad, the philosophy of pluralism, whatever broad views it may deny me, permits me, at least, to turn to the other members with a clean breast of affection and an unsophisticated moral sense. And if I still wish to think of the world as a totality, it lets me feel that a world with a *chance* in it of being altogether good, even if the chance never come to pass, is better than a world with no such chance at all. That "chance" whose very notion I am exhorted and conjured to banish from my view of the future as the suicide of reason concerning it, that "chance" is—what? Just this—the chance that in moral respects the future may be other and better than the past has been. This is the only chance we have any motive for supposing to exist. Shame, rather, on its repudiation and its denial! For its presence is the vital air which lets the world live, the salt which keeps it sweet.[15]

Jean-Paul Sartre and the Burden of Freedom

If Schopenhauer was a pessimist, one might wonder what to call a philosopher who wrote a novel entitled *Nausea*. Jean-Paul Sartre

JEAN-PAUL SARTRE 1905–1980

(1905–1980), the author of this important book, was born in Paris. His university training, which included time in Germany, focused on literature and philosophy. Sartre was teaching in Paris when World War II began. Sent to the front, he was captured by the Germans and imprisoned for nine months. When he was returned to France in 1941, he served in the Resistance movement. He remained politically active after the war, espousing Marxist causes much of the time. Offered the Nobel Prize in literature in 1964, Sartre refused to accept the honor.

Existentialism is the label most frequently associated with Sartre's name. As Sartre developed that philosophy, which he took to be optimistic even though its critics did not, existentialism accented freedom, the difficulties it brings to human existence, and the chances we have to overcome them. These themes dominated *Nausea*, which was published in 1938. Its main character, a historian named Roquentin, is writing a biography, but finds it increasingly difficult to carry out his project because he cannot be sure whether he is describing or creating the subject of his work. How much of the biography is a factual, objective account, and how much of it is really Roquentin's own construction? The answer is unclear, but Roquentin becomes convinced that his interpretations color everything he writes. Hence, he gives up the biography. At the novel's end, he considers trying his hand at fiction.

Fiction and Philosophy

Roquentin's shifting project reveals much more than a mere change of plans. As Sartre traces Roquentin's efforts to write a biography, he is recording our human struggle to cope with all existence. *Nausea* emerges as part of that struggle. This includes the physical feeling but, as Sartre used the idea, it is nothing so tame as acid indigestion or motion sickness. The **nausea** Sartre described is a condition that combines disorientation, queasiness, and even revulsion brought on by an awareness of the uncertainty that characterizes our situation in life. This is due to the extensive freedom human beings possess.

Roquentin discovered that his own interpretation influenced and formed everything he experienced. Why that should be the case, indeed why anything should exist at all, he could not fathom. He found that the world is everywhere particularized. The tree you see, for instance, exists with its specific leaves and bark, colors and textures. Reasons for that can be given, but none of them fully accounts for that particular thing. **Existence** is so definitely real and yet so unnecessary and inexplicable—especially his own—that it made Roquentin nauseous. As Roquentin came to realize, nausea resulted largely from his sense of freedom, since our existence condemns us to be free. Without having been consulted in advance, we are thrown into life to make of it what we can. We do and we must shape it by our own choosing. Far from exulting in this freedom, Roquentin found it a heavy burden. Even if freedom allowed for creativity, he came to realize, the nausea caused by his struggle to cope with existence would never be far away. Even if controlled, repressed, or forgotten for a time, it would well up again and require him to define once more his relation to the choices before him.

If *Nausea* is Sartre's best known fiction, *Being and Nothingness* (1943), which elaborates many of the themes in Roquentin's experience, remains the most important nonfiction expression of Sartre's existential philosophy. The book reflects an outlook tempered by Sartre's resistance to the Nazis during World War II. At one point in *Being and Nothingness* Sartre states that "man is a useless passion."[16] That remark might seem to counsel despair. But while Sartre did want his pronouncement to describe the human predicament, he also wanted it to challenge men and women to make an honest, humanistic response to it. Both the description and the challenge depend on human freedom. In fact, no Western philosopher has gone further than Sartre in giving an emphatically affirmative answer to the question "Am I free to act?"

Two Types of Being

As Sartre explored human existence, he became intrigued by what he called **prereflective** experience. Such experience, he explained, is the kind we have prior to think-

ing about what we are doing or before we look back at what we have done. For example, if you ski down a slope, you are aware, but you probably are not thinking about skiing or about yourself because *you are doing* the skiing. Sartre noted that the prereflective experience, which comes before our thinking about experience, always has the quality of being *of* something. In short, it has content. That content, he affirmed, transcends and often resists our analysis; consider how difficult it is to describe everything about skiing or even to describe the exact techniques we use to ski. Sartre's general term for this "something" that we always encounter is "being-in-itself."

Of **being-in-itself,** Sartre concluded, we can say only that it exists and that it is different from "being-for-itself." His reason for this claim reflects Roquentin's dilemma in attempting to write an objective biography. Consciousness, or **being-for-itself** (our awareness of what we meant to become) as Sartre called it, permits individual opinions to appear. As Sartre described the role played by consciousness, he spoke of it as "negating" being-in-itself. In this way being is broken apart into *this* and *not this, that* and *not that.* Take away this power of consciousness to accomplish **negation** and we are powerless to describe being-in-itself. Hence apart from saying simply that being-in-itself is real, Sartre argued, we cannot describe it directly. We can portray being as it is experienced, but what it is in itself remains hidden. Our consciousness, however, does alter being-in-itself, and we can observe the results of its discriminating activity.

Existence and Essence

Sartre proclaimed that "existence precedes essence," and this formula is basic for understanding his view of human existence and our freedom (p. 568). He characterized consciousness not so much in positive terms but by emphasizing its negating power in relation to being-in-itself. Sartre interpreted human consciousness as a form of being that is always seeking to transcend itself but never fully finishes its task. It seemed to Sartre that we humans move to leave behind what we have been and to become what we are not. We are always headed somewhere; we are never fixed, complete, and static. Short of death, there is a perpetual process of negation and a continuous movement into a future of possibility and uncertainty.

What one will become is indefinite until consciousness determines it. We are what we become more than we become what we are. In that sense, our existence precedes the formation of our essence. For example, you think you have the potential talent to become an architect. But you are not already an architect in your nature. Rather, you must act, take steps to become an architect, study, work, and then as a result of your activity you may form that essence: "architect." But you did not exist in that role in any way except in imagination prior to your actions. What you do defines what you become, not some inner essence in your nature working its way out.

Sartre identified the negating power of consciousness with human freedom. The fact that we can move beyond what we are toward that which we are not, he argued, signifies freedom. Whenever we act freely, there is a sense in which we leave something behind. We negate what we have been in order to try to become what we are not. Hence, not only does existence precede essence but, Sartre claimed, "freedom is existence" (p. 567). According to Sartre, a person's life is characterized by freedom, by choosing what one will be and how one will see the world one inhabits. The determination of what one is results from our individual choices and not from a series of determined causes outside of or even within oneself.

Reaching toward God

Being-in-itself and being-for-itself are the two fundamental modes of being according to Sartre. Although being-for-itself is dependent on being-in-itself, since consciousness is always of something, he does not think it possible to say why consciousness exists. No necessity enters in; being simply is. It cannot be thought away, but nonetheless, contended Sartre, being and therefore being-for-itself are contingent. Consciousness did not have to be, and the fact that it exists shows its contingency all the more because our passions to achieve our desires for being-for-itself are ultimately unfulfillable. What Sartre had in mind is encapsulated in his claim that "to be man means to reach toward being God" (p. 566).

You are what you are, or what you have become by your actions. But you reach forward into the future for more than that: what you want to become. Yet this depends on circumstances and your decisions. Sartre was an atheist, but he used the idea of God to drive home his points. Thus, Sartre points out that God is static in his existence; you are not, but you would like to be certain about your future. For instance, you know how to act; you have studied acting. But you want to become a prominent actress and adopt name roles. Nothing is certain about your future, however. Not even your native talent can guarantee it. God can be certain of his future. You cannot be, no matter how much you wish for it. Too much depends on too many decisions yet to be made.

Let us consider two questions about Sartre's theory that should make his position clearer. First, did Sartre prove or only assume that reality of human freedom? The best answer is: neither. What impressed him was that whenever we describe or interpret experience, we always encounter the possibility that things could be other than we find them.

To any question of the form "Is it true that such-and-such is the case?" the answer could always be "No." That outcome, Sartre thought, leaves us needing to choose what we will believe and do. Whether we realize this or not, Sartre argued, our choices are inescapable and are being made constantly. Moreover, to think of those choices as other than free seemed to him false, for the affirmation of any form of determinism is itself a choice that did not have to be made.

Nor should that choice be made, Sartre believed, just because the experience of feeling free accompanies choice. Insofar as we seek to understand why people act as they do, free choice explains more than an appeal to deterministic principles and psychological laws. The former does so with a finality that the other account cannot muster. A free choice, Sartre contended, grounds itself in a way that no principle or law ever can. In trying to discover deterministic principles, we are always driven further back, from one principle to another before it. Once accepted, free choice needs nothing beyond that decisive act to explain itself, Sartre believes.

Even if we decide that Sartre's analysis is correct, can we accuse him of going too far in outlining the degree of freedom that men and women possess? Far from having lives permeated by freedom, it has been argued that most persons feel hemmed in on every side. Many cannot find enough food to eat, let alone strive toward being God. Sartre was aware of such difficulties; his account emphasizes that human existence is always lived in particular concrete and individual situations. These situations reveal how finite we are and how full of suffering existence can be. Yet Sartre contended that the structure of human freedom remains such that any person in any situation will always seek to be something.

Ultimately, in our seeking we try to achieve a complete self-identity in which we com-prehend ourselves totally and are no longer constantly at a distance from ourselves. To accomplish this task, Sartre argued, would be to become God, but no person can succeed in this undertaking. In fact, he claimed that the idea of God is contradictory. Consciousness, he concluded, excludes self-identity; self-identity also excludes consciousness. Consciousness always has the quality of being stretched out ahead of itself. It always moves beyond itself. If you became completely self-identical and unchanging, you would not be conscious any more.

When we think of our future, for example, our thought naturally reaches beyond what we presently are. To be simply identified with what we are would exclude our future. Again, you want to be an architect; you want to be that consciousness, but you are not that now. You reach ahead to think of the architect you would become. But even when you become an architect in fact, your thought will reach beyond that to future plans, to new buildings you want to design. Where our drive to become self-identical is concerned, we are forever doomed to frustration. Human freedom makes our existence "a useless passion."

Responsibility and Bad Faith

As Sartre characterized it, freedom ironically hems us in. This is because our lives are always situated in definite times and places. Freedom goes hand in hand with consciousness, and our future projects leave us forever short of fulfillment. At the same time, this freedom makes us responsible for ourselves. Sometimes, Sartre said, we choose our own world and even our own birth. Such statements may seem excessive, but Sartre's point was that so long as we choose to live, we have in effect chosen to be born. Additionally, insofar as the world has significance, such significance is a result of consciousness. Our consciousness of being alive is what allows us to choose the goals and purposes we confront as we meet other persons or project our own future, our "for-itself."

We are responsible, Sartre asserted, for making what we can of the world. Because such responsibility is awesome, our freedom can be dreadful, and we may try to flee from it. Sartre called that flight **bad faith.** Unlike lying, a situation in which I know the truth and try to hide it from others, "in bad faith it is from myself that I am hiding the truth" (p. 49). Whenever we deny ourselves by ignoring or repressing the fact that our free decisions are crucial ingredients in determining the situations we are in, bad faith intrudes. In its place Sartre wanted to put honesty and responsibility. Even though he called human existence a useless passion because it is so radically free, that same freedom makes it possible for us to do the best we can with the life we have.

On this point, you might want to compare Sartre and Unamuno. Both urge us to make responsible choices, and both see human nature as placed in a world less than what we might desire. Yet we can act; that is our salvation, both men agree. It was Sartre's view that doing the best we can, first and foremost, requires an honest appraisal of the degree to which we are responsible for ourselves. We have to choose what shall be good and what evil; such norms are not fixed in advance. Wherever norms do exist, someone has chosen them to be authoritative. That does not mean that values are arbitrary or irrational, but it does mean that we have to decide what we ought to do.

Sartre's Final Point

The power of Sartre's theory stems from his emphasis on consciousness. By identifying consciousness with a power that differen-

tiates being by negation and by then linking consciousness and freedom, Sartre could say that we ourselves make the world what it is. Granted, we do not construct it from nothing. Something appears; it resists us so that we are rarely able to have our own way. What appears, however, is always a function of being-for-itself's interacting with being-in-itself. That interaction constitutes the world. Consciousness cannot make the world by itself, but without consciousness no world exists. Hence at no point can one escape the impact of consciousness and its free choice-making.

Some critics find Sartre's stress on the importance of human reponse to be extreme and his distinction between being-in-itself and being-for-itself an oversimplification. But Sartre still has one final point in his favor—he shares it with James—where the issue of freedom is concerned: to reject freedom or to accept determinism would entail a decision. A negative answer to the question "Are we free?" undercuts itself. Since from the very meaning of freedom there are options among which we must choose, the indeterminate state of our existence leads us to the conclusion that freedom is real, even though we may not be able to prove that proposition with finality. The degree of freedom we possess remains uncertain. It varies from time to time and from place to place, and it depends on our evaluations of rights and duties, our sense of the limits of our freedom, and our ability to decide. Reflecting on these matters may lead us to question Sartre's appraisal that human existence is a useless passion, but however the debate turns out, the question of human freedom has a central place in our thought, as the following selection from Sartre's essay "Existentialism Is a Humanism" helps to show.

Atheistic existentialism, of which I am a representative, declares with greater consistency that if God does not exist there is at least one being whose existence comes before its essence, a being which exists before it can be defined by any conception of it. That being is man or, as Heidegger has it, the human reality. What do we mean by saying that existence precedes essence? We mean that man first of all exists, encounters himself, surges up in the world—and defines himself afterward. If man as the existentialist sees him is not definable, it is because to begin with he is nothing. He will not be anything until later, and then he will be what he makes of himself. Thus, there is no human nature, because there is no God to have a conception of it. Man simply is. Not that he is simply what he conceives himself to be, but he is what he wills, and as he conceives himself after already existing—as he wills to be after that leap towards existence. Man is nothing else but that which he makes of himself. That is the first principle of existentialism. And this is what people call its "subjectivity," using the word as a reproach against us. But what do we mean to say by this, but that man is of a greater dignity than a stone or a table? For we mean to say that man primarily exists—that man is, before all else, something which propels itself toward a future and is aware that it is doing so. Man is, indeed, a project which possesses a subjective life, instead of being a kind of moss, or a fungus or a cauliflower. Before that projection of the self nothing exists; not even in the heaven of intelligence: man will only attain existence when he is what he purposes to be. Not, however, what he may wish to be. For what we usually understand by wishing or willing is a conscious decision taken—much more often than not—after we have made ourselves what we are. I may wish to join a party, to write a book, or to marry—but in such a case what is usually called my will is probably a manifestation of a prior and more spontaneous decision. If, however, it is true that existence is prior to essence, man is responsible for what he is. Thus, the first effect of existentialism is that it puts every man in possession of himself

as he is, and places the entire responsibility for his existence squarely upon his own shoulders. And, when we say that man is responsible for himself, we do not mean that he is responsible only for his own individuality, but that he is responsible for all men. The word "subjectivism" is to be understood in two senses, and our adversaries play upon only one of them. Subjectivism means, on the one hand, the freedom of the individual subject and, on the other, that man cannot pass beyond human subjectivity. It is the latter which is the deeper meaning of existentialism. When we say that man chooses himself, we do mean that every one of us must choose himself; but by that we also mean that in choosing for himself he chooses for all men. For in effect, of all the actions a man may take in order to create himself as he wills to be, there is not one which is not creative, at the same time, of an image of man such as he believes he ought to be. To choose between this or that is at the same time to affirm the value of that which is chosen; for we are unable ever to choose the worse. What we choose is always the better; and nothing can be better for us unless it is better for all. If, moreover, existence precedes essence and we will to exist at the same time as we fashion our image, that image is valid for all and for the entire epoch in which we find ourselves. Our responsibility is thus much greater than we had supposed, for it concerns mankind as a whole. If I am a worker, for instance, I may choose to join a Christian rather than a Communist trade union. And if, by that membership, I choose to signify that resignation is, after all, the attitude that best becomes a man, that man's kingdom is not upon this earth, I do not commit myself alone to that view. Resignation is my will for everyone, and my action is, in consequence, a commitment on behalf of all mankind. Or if, to take a more personal case, I decide to marry and to have children, even though this decision proceeds simply from my situation, from my passion or my desire, I am thereby committing not only myself, but humanity as a whole, to the practice of monogamy. I am thus responsible for myself and for all men, and I am creating a certain image of man as I would have him to be. In fashioning myself I fashion man. . . .

As for "despair," the meaning of this expression is extremely simple. It merely means that we limit ourselves to a reliance upon that which is within our wills, or within the sum of the probabilities which render our action feasible. Whenever one wills anything, there are always these elements of probability. If I am counting upon a visit from a friend, who may be coming by train or by tram, I presuppose that the train will arrive at the appointed time, or that the tram will not be derailed. I remain in the realm of possibilities; but one does not rely upon any possibilities beyond those that are strictly concerned in one's action. Beyond the point at which the possibilities under consideration cease to affect my action, I ought to disinterest myself. For there is no God and no prevenient design, which can adapt the world and all its possibilities to my will. When Descartes said, "Conquer yourself rather than the world," what he meant was, at bottom, the same—that we should act without hope. . . .

Furthermore, although it is impossible to find in each and every man a universal essence that can be called human nature, there is nevertheless a human universality of *condition*. It is not by chance that the thinkers of today are so much more ready to speak of the condition than of the nature of man. By his condition they understand, with more or less clarity, all the *limitations* which a priori define man's fundamental situation in the universe. His historical situations are variable: man may be born a slave in a pagan society, or may be a feudal baron, or a proletarian. But what never vary are the necessities of being in the world, of having to labor, and to die there. These limitations are neither subjective nor objective, nor rather there is both a subjective and an objective aspect of them. Objective, because we meet with them everywhere and they are everywhere recognizable: and subjective because they are *lived* and are nothing if man does not live them—if, that is to say, he does not freely determine himself and his existence in relation to them. And, diverse though man's purposes may be, at least none of them is wholly foreign to me, since every human purpose presents itself as an attempt either to surpass these limitations, or to widen them, or else to deny or to accommodate oneself to them. Consequently every purpose, however individual it may be, is of universal value. Every purpose, even that of a Chinese, an Indian, or a Negro, can be understood by a European. To say it can be understood means that the European of 1945 may be striving out of a certain situation toward the same limitations in the same way, and that he may reconceive in himself the purpose of the Chinese, of the Indian, or the African. In every purpose there is universality, in this sense that every purpose is comprehensible to every man. Not that this or that purpose defines man forever, but that it may be entertained again and again. There is always some way of understanding an idiot, a child, a primitive man, or a foreigner if one has sufficient information. In this sense we may say that there is a human universality, but it is not something given; it is being perpetually made. I make this universality in choosing myself; I also make it by understanding the purpose of any other man, of whatever epoch. This absoluteness of the act of choice does not alter the relativity of each epoch.

What is at the very heart and center of existentialism is the absolute character of the free commitment, by which every man realizes himself in realizing a type of humanity—a commitment always understandable, to no matter whom in no matter what epoch—and its bearing upon the relativity of the cultural pattern which may result from such absolute commitment. One must observe equally the relativity of Cartesianism and the absolute character of the Cartesian commitment. In this sense you may say, if you like, that every one of us makes the absolute by breathing, by eating, by sleeping, or by behaving in any fashion whatsoever. There is no difference between free being—being as self-committal, as existence choosing its essence—and absolute being. And there is no difference whatever between being as an absolute, temporarily localized—that is, localized in history—and universally intelligible being.[17]

Summary

No resolution of this chapter's question "Am I free to act?" can be absolutely final just because human freedom is as elusive as it is important. But our discussion does show how the sides line up on some of the most important aspects. Luther, Calvin, Edwards, and Schopenhauer are determinists of one kind or another. A religious context affects the discussions by Luther, Calvin, and, to a lesser extent, Edwards. Schopenhauer employs a more scientific approach. But whatever the starting point, these thinkers seem convinced that all events are the effects of prior causes that necessitate them.

Erasmus, James, and Sartre dissent from determinism. They find it contrary to human experience. In that regard they support our ordinary beliefs that decisions can be made freely. But on the other hand, they are not sure that we can prove the existence of freedom. There is evidence for determinism, they recognize, but, in addition, the logic of freedom itself requires that a decision be made as to whether freedom is real. Particularly if that decision is affirmative, however, we may be led to wonder how human conduct should be governed and what part moral rules might play in that process. Those are the subjects for our next chapter.

GLOSSARY

bad faith Sartre's term for the various ways in which people attempt to evade responsibility for their lives by denying the reality of their own freedom.

being-for-itself Sartre's term for the mode of existence that is defined by its ability to become aware of itself as existing, to form a self-concept, and to conceive of a variety of possible futures for itself on the basis of that self-concept.

being-in-itself Sartre's term for the mode of being, characteristic of inanimate objects and animals, that has no consciousness of itself as such, that cannot become an object of its own cognition, and therefore cannot become the subject of deliberate choices about its own actions. See **prereflective**.

chance the element of uncertainty and unpredictability in human life, stemming from the limited capacity of human knowledge, which supports the idea that freedom of choice is at least a possibility for human beings.

character See **motive;** for Schopenhauer, the overall pattern of *motives* that determines the course a human life will take and the unique form a human personality will assume, given external conditions favorable to development.

choice an act of self-determination, a free and conscious decision between real alternatives that are clearly recognized and whose significance for ourselves is clearly understood.

contingency as opposed to *determined*, that which can be otherwise, what happens by accident, or that which is the result of deliberation and free decision.

determinism the doctrine that the dominance over the world of the laws of cause and effect is so complete that the determination of the future lies completely outside the power of human beings. Luther coupled the inability to make free choices with the biblical notion of original sin (see **sin**) and, along with Calvin, associated the idea of a deterministic universe with the omnipotence of God. James, on the other hand, distinguished between "hard" determinism such as Luther's and "soft" determinism, a view that, like Schopenhauer's, tries to interpret the concepts of determinism and freedom so as to reconcile them with each other.

dilemma from the Latin for "two-horned"; a choice or decision for which there exists no satisfactory reason for accepting one side over another.

divine grace Erasmus' term for the process by which the power to act decisively that is lost by human beings through original **sin** can be redeemed if God wills it.

election Calvin's notion of the origin of salvation; salvation could never be the fruit of human endeavor, but only the product of God's grace. See **fatality; predestination.**

existence in Sartre's philosophy, the brute fact of things as they are, which always stands in opposition to how we imagine things *could* be and resists the realization of the *essence*, or ideal state of things—that is, the potential we see in ourselves. See **being-in-itself.**

existentialist movement the philosophical movement that, following the writings of Kierkegaard, Sartre, and others, flourished in Europe during the period from the end of World War II until the late 1960s. Existentialism emphasizes the radical extent of human freedom and attempts to deal seriously with its consequences for people's day-to-day existence.

"faith-ladder" James's model of the process of reasoning by which a rational belief in the freedom of the will can be arrived at.

fatality a force of predestination or predetermination that is believed to govern the course of human lives.

freedom conceived positively, the ability to function as an ultimate cause, to originate actions in absolute independence from other causal factors; conceived negatively, the absence of objective obstacles to the course of action dictated by our will and our desires, which themselves may still be subject to causal laws governing their operation. Calvin believed that only God could determine whether our souls would be saved or damned, and therefore what appears to be our liberty to choose between piety and a life of vice merely reflects God's preordained design for our lives. James, however, thought that since neither the positive idea of freedom nor the idea of universal determinism was obviously absurd, it must be possible in principle to choose freely between them; our sense of what the world could and ought to be like, he said, is left open to be determined by the specific spiritual needs of human lives as they are actually lived, rather than by the abstract requirements of metaphysical or theological theories.

free will the idea of human volition as an independent origin of events, on a par with those operating in the world of nature; in other words, the idea that human actions can make a significant difference in determining the order of things. The theological debate over the validity of this concept focuses on the degree to which human volition is subject to God's deliberate designs for the destiny of humanity. A more philosophical approach to the issue is the question of whether the will is subject to laws of the same kinds that govern other natural phenomena. Schopenhauer tried to resolve this question by defining freedom of the will as the absence of external obstacles to the will's achieving its fullest expression according to the laws internal to the will that govern its development.

motives reasons for acting, the basic interests and needs that actions are aimed at fulfilling; Schopenhauer used the term to refer to those universal and constitutive features of human nature that fundamentally determine the range and types of disposition toward the world that our will can assume.

nausea Sartre's metaphor for the characteristically human response to the radical uncertainty and indeterminacy that defines the life of a person who recognizes himself as *being-for-itself;* the character Roquentin in Sartre's novel experiences this "nausea" in response to the gulf between the dizzying sense of possibility entailed by his awareness of his own existence and the inexplicable definiteness of the objects that compose his world and the **prereflective** lives of other people.

negation the capacity of *being-for-itself* that Sartre believes constitutes its essential difference from *being-in-itself,* the capacity to recognize that things could be other than the way they are at the present moment, and the capacity to move consciously toward actualizing one's own potential in an infinite variety of ways.

normative evaluative, judgmental; a type of statement that attributes moral or aesthetic qualities like superiority or inferiority, rightness or impropriety, to a thing, action, or state of affairs. See **responsibility.**

"ought" a word commonly used to carry the persuasive force of a **prescriptive** statement, implying that the speaker has strong reasons for deciding an issue in a given way, reasons the hearer must also accept.

paradox a concept or argument that seems highly ambiguous or self-contradictory. For Schopenhauer, the coexistence of the concepts of freedom and necessity in our usual way of thinking seems to pose a paradox.

predestination Calvin's doctrine that the fact of God's absolute freedom necessarily means that human beings are absolutely and inescapably subject to God's will.

"prereflective" Sartre's term for that certain aspect of human existence that partakes of

the qualities of "being-in-itself"; that portion of our lives in which we carry out actions without being conscious of how or why we are doing them.

prescriptive imperative, commanding; a statement having the force of enjoining or compelling another person to act in a certain way or to accept the truth of a certain proposition. See **"ought."**

responsibility in common sense, the condition that exists when **normative** judgments, judgments of praise or blame, are validly attributed to one's actions. This common-sense notion presupposes that a person so judged could have acted otherwise than he actually did; so, a large and significant part of the way we think and speak about other people depends on the concept of the freedom of the will.

sin the state of humanity "fallen from grace," which Luther believed precludes the possibility that human volitions may determine the course of events. Arguing on strict scriptural grounds, Luther held that the expulsion of Adam and Eve from Paradise ended forever mankind's right to dominion and mastery over nature. For Calvin, this includes both original sin and the fallen, incapable state Luther describes.

will the faculty of preferring or desiring that something be the case; in Edwards's theory, that which predisposes us to act in accordance with the attainment of what we feel holds the highest positive value for us.

STUDY QUESTIONS

1. As you act, do you assume that you have at least some degree of freedom? If so, how could you justify this assumption?

2. How do you define freedom? Do you think that we agree about what freedom means?

3. What makes freedom a problem for Luther and Erasmus? Do you think the context in which we consider questions about freedom affects the outcome of the discussion?

4. How do you appraise Calvin's religious

reasons for the position he takes on the issue of freedom versus determinism?

5. What does it mean to say that Edwards is more philosophical about freedom than Luther or Calvin?

6. Does Edwards convince you that there is no essential conflict between necessity and liberty?

7. Schopenhauer appears to find contradictions in the idea of freedom. What are these, and do you agree with him?

8. Is James correct in thinking that neither determinism nor freedom can be conclusively demonstrated?

9. James suggests that it is impossible to have genuine morality and human responsibility without freedom. Is he correct?

10. Take both sides in a debate over freedom and determinism between James and Luther, James and Erasmus, James and Calvin, James and Edwards, James and Schopenhauer, or James and Sartre.

11. Sartre thinks we are "condemned to be free." Why, and what does his claim mean?

12. How does Sartre's analysis of human nature convince him that human beings are free? Do you agree?

NOTES

[1] Desiderius Erasmus, *On the Freedom of the Will*, ed. and trans. Philip S. Watson and B. Drewery, in *Luther and Erasmus: Free Will and Salvation* (Philadelphia: Westminster Press, 1969), p. 37.

[2] Martin Luther, *On the Bondage of the Will*, ed. and trans. E. Gordon Rupp and A. N. Marlow, in *Luther and Erasmus: Free Will and Salvation*, (Philadelphia: Westminster Press, 1969), p. 102.

[3] John Calvin, *Concerning the Eternal Predestination of God*, trans. J.K.S. Reid (London: James Clarke, 1961), p. 49.

[4] John Calvin, *Institutes of the Christian Religion*, 2 vols., trans. Henry Beveridge (London: James Clarke, 1962), 1:27.

[5] Jonathan Edwards, *Freedom of the Will*, ed. Paul Ramsey (New Haven: Yale University Press, 1957), p. 137. Used by permission.

[6] Martin Luther, *On the Bondage of the Will*, in *Luther and Erasmus: Free Will and Salvation*, pp. 118–19. (Vol. XVII: The Library of Christian Classics.) Copyright © MCMLXIX the Westminster Press. Reprinted and used by permission.

[7] Calvin, *Concerning the Eternal Predestination of God*, pp. 162–63 and 167–68.

[8] Edwards, *Freedom of the Will*, pp. 137–41.

[9] Arthur Schopenhauer, *Essay on the Freedom of the Will*, trans. Konstantin Kolenda (Indianapolis: Bobbs-Merrill, 1960), p. 3. Used by permission.

[10] William James, "The Dilemma of Determinism," in *The Will to Believe and Other Essays in Popular Philosophy* (New York: Dover, 1956), p. 151.

[11] William James, "On Some Hegelisms," in *The Will to Believe*, p. 269.

[12] William James, *The Letters of William James*, 2 vols., ed. by his son Henry James (New York: Atlantic Monthly Press, 1920), 1:147.

[13] William James, *Some Problems of Philosophy* (New York: Longmans, Green, 1911), p. 224.

[14]William James, *The Principles of Psychology,* 2 vols. (New York: Dover, 1950), 2:573.

[15]James, "The Dilemma of Determinism," pp. 159–63, 175–77.

[16]Jean-Paul Sartre, *Being and Nothingness,* trans. Hazel Barnes (New York: Philosophical Library, 1956), p. 615.

[17]Jean-Paul Sartre, "Existentialism Is a Humanism," trans. Philip Mairet, in *The Existentialist Tradition: Selected Writings,* ed. Nino Langiulli (Garden City, N.Y.: Doubleday Anchor Books, 1971), pp. 395–96, 403, 408–9. Used by permission of Nino Langiulli.

CHAPTER SEVEN

Do Rules Govern My Action?

*B*efore it makes much sense to decide what we should do, we need to know whether we are really free to act. So we began consideration of the basic question of Part II, "What should I do?", by discussing the freedom of the will. We discovered various views—they ranged from the extremes of self-determination with Sartre to the determinism of Luther or Schopenhauer. As long as opinion is divided, we concluded, the question is open and freedom remains a possibility. Now we move on to ask if **rules** govern our actions. We may be free to act, but are we anywhere told what we ought to do?

We begin with Plato's student, Aristotle, and his recommended **golden mean.** This mean is flexible, but Kant, to whom we will turn next, felt there are more stringent, universal imperatives we must obey. Closer to us `` time, the British philosopher John Stuart M`` offered an ethic based on rules about "utility." John Rawls, a contemporary American thinker, tries to build on and go beyond all three in developing a modern view of justice, which he regards as the **norm** for all action. Each of these four philosophers seeks rules to govern our actions. But the rules are not the same. We human beings evidently need to judge ourselves according to some norms. Which serve us best, however, is a question.

Aristotle and the Mean between Extremes

As you know from Chapter Four, Aristotle studied with Plato in Athens, eventually formed his own school there, and became justifiably famous in his own right. He wrote on every aspect of philosophy, but his *Nicomachean Ethics* is widely studied because it contains his most important thoughts on moral matters and is a cornerstone for all who consider norms for action. Plato believed in eternal Forms, but the highest, the one he called the Good, eluded final definition. Aristotle's theories are more down to earth. While agreeing with Plato that every action aims at some good, Aristotle held that "the highest of all goods achievable by action . . . is happiness," which is sufficient unto itself and does not require Plato's transcendent Forms.[1]

Happiness as the Good

Although **happiness** is our aim, Aristotle emphasized that people differ "with regard to what happiness is" (1095a, p. 937). To clarify the meaning of this crucial concept, Aristotle stressed that true happiness must be something that lasts: "For one swallow does not make a summer, nor does one day; and

ARISTOTLE 384–322 B.C.

so too one day, or a short time, does not make a man blessed and happy" (1098a, p. 943). It is here that the question of rules arises. For we all might find happiness at various moments by accident, but if we are going to sustain it for a lifetime, we must know and obey the rules of happiness. Otherwise our lives are governed by chance, and Aristotle hardly thinks that the best mode of life.

The rules of happiness, Aristotle explained, are essentially linked with **virtue**. In fact, his definition of "human good" is precisely that it is an "activity of soul in accordance with virtue, and if there be more than one virtue, in accordance with the best and most complete" (1098a, p. 943). In general, says Aristotle, virtue "is a state of character concerned with choice" (1106b, p. 959). It consists of two kinds: intellectual and moral. The former involves skill in such things as mathematics and philosophy. The latter—it includes courage and generosity, for example—focuses on action and "comes about as a result of habit" (1103a, p. 952). "Neither by nature," Aristotle adds, "nor contrary to nature do the virtues arise in us; rather we are adapted by nature to receive them, and they are made perfect by habit" (1103a, p. 952).

Moral virtues are learned habits; that is, we learn by practice how to act and deal with people. As Aristotle says: "We become just by doing just acts, temperate by doing temperate acts, brave by doing brave acts" (1103b, p. 952). In this sense, our training reveals the rules that guide our action, and how we are brought up makes all the difference. Part of our early training, moreover, must instill in us the ability to think critically about action, for Aristotle understands that "temperance and courage . . . are destroyed by excess and defect" (1104a, p. 954). Too much of this or too little of that and we miss the mark that virtue requires. Here we come upon Aristotle's notion of the mean, and you can see how naturally this idea arises when you are talking about virtue in action.

Virtue Is a Mean

Excessive athletic training can wear you out before the race. Too little makes you unable to win. Virtue is a matter of choice "lying in a mean" (1107a, p. 959). But, Aristotle adds, the mean must be "relative to us, this being determined by a rational principle, and by that principle by which the man of practical wisdom would determine it" (1107a, p. 959). He does not intend to set up some absolute standard. Norms are a matter of judgment. You will fail if you mechanically follow the same norm each time. To win the prize fight, Rocky must determine his opponent's strengths and weaknesses and then plan a training program for himself accordingly. The virtuous man or woman is the one with the good sense to size up the situation and find the middle way of action that cuts between excesses.

It is no easy task to find this middle ground. Energy that is excessive in one instance may be deficient in another. Also it needs to be said that in some cases the mean is not exactly a middle way at all. With respect to murder, for example, there is no middle path between "too much" and "too little." But many of life's decisions do involve finding the point of moderation. Who has courage, for instance? Courage, states Aristotle, "is a mean with regard to feelings of fear and confidence" (1115a, p. 974). The courageous person is not the one who is so foolish as to know no fear or to be overconfident but the one who finds the balance between these extremes. One must know fear to find the mean of courage. Having good role models is important for success in this regard, and, as the saying goes, "practice makes perfect." Therefore, "we must incline sometimes toward the excess, sometimes toward the deficiency, for so shall we most easily hit the mean and what is right" (1109b, p. 964). This is why Aristotle's notion of the mean as our rule to govern action is often referred to as the "golden mean," since "goodness is both rare and laudable and noble" (1109a, p. 963). It is no easy matter to learn the adjustable skill and to appraise every situation for what it requires, rather than simply repeating some previous plan. One person easily accepts your offer of a date for the party; another will do so only if you muster all your powers of persuasion.

Finding the Right Rule
for the Right Instance

Decision making would be easier if we could find one rule that fits every case. Aristotle does tell us that happiness depends on vir-

tue, and virtuous living depends on finding the mean. A basic rule for living is contained in those ideas, but they are not a simple recipe. It requires great skill and judgment to do right consistently. Temperance, Aristotle tells us, is a mean with regard to pleasures, but we all know that overindulgence is a common human failing. Happiness is the **good** we aim for, but to achieve it on a long-term basis requires first-rate training and skill. However, not everyone makes it a point to acquire these.

When Aristotle spoke of the "virtuous man," he offered the picture of a moral hero whose ways we would do well to imitate. Aristotle was surely aware that most of us tend to excess or defect in our actions, but he urged us to keep trying for the mean, lest happiness escape us. Do rules govern my actions? Yes, Aristotle says, and they should. We cannot do anything we please and expect to be happy, for happiness involves virtue. If virtue is absent, he believed, happiness will be, too. Since it is our nature to aim for what is good, and happiness is the good for human beings, Aristotle's contention is that we ought to be rule-governed. But the rules we need, he cautioned, may be as difficult to apply as they are important. Test that proposition as you read more from Aristotle's *Nicomachean Ethics*.

BOOK II

Virtue, then, being of two kinds, intellectual and moral, intellectual virtue in the main owes both its birth and its growth to teaching (for which reason it requires experience and time), while moral virtue comes about as a result of habit, whence also its name (ἠθική) is one that is formed by a slight variation from the word ἔθος (habit). From this it is also plain that none of the moral virtues arises in us by nature; for nothing that exists by nature can form a habit contrary to its nature. For instance the stone which by nature moves downwards cannot be habituated to move upwards, not even if one tries to train it by throwing it up ten thousand times; nor can fire be habituated to move downwards, nor can anything else that by nature behaves in one way be trained to behave in another. Neither by nature, then, nor contrary to nature do the virtues arise in us; rather we are adapted by nature to receive them, and are made perfect by habit.

Again, of all the things that come to us by nature we first acquire the potentiality and later exhibit the activity (this is plain in the case of the senses; for it was not by often seeing or often hearing that we got these senses, but on the contrary we had them before we used them, and did not come to have them by using them); but the virtues we get by first exercising them, as also happens in the case of the arts as well. For the things we have to learn before we can do them, we learn by doing them, e.g., men become builders by building and lyre-players by playing the lyre; so too we become just by doing just acts, temperate by doing temperate acts, brave by doing brave acts.

This is confirmed by what happens in states; for legislators make the citizens good by forming habits in them, and this is the wish of every legislator, and those who do not effect it miss their mark, and it is in this that a good constitution differs from a bad one.

Again, it is from the same causes and by the same means that every virtue is both produced and destroyed, and similarly every art; for it is from playing the lyre that both good and bad lyre-players are produced. And the corresponding statement is true of builders and of all the rest; men will be good or bad builders as a result of building well or badly. For if this were not so, there would have been no need of a teacher, but all men would have been born good or bad at their craft. This, then, is the case with the virtues also; by doing the acts that we do in our transactions with other men we become just or unjust, and by doing the acts that we do in the presence of danger, and being habituated to feel fear or confidence, we become

brave or cowardly. The same is true of appetites and feelings of anger; some men become temperate and good-tempered, others self-indulgent and irascible, by behaving in one way or the other in the appropriate circumstances. Thus, in one word, states of character arise out of like activities. This is why the activities we exhibit must be of a certain kind; it is because the states of character correspond to the differences between these. It makes no small difference, then, whether we form habits of one kind or of another from our very youth; it makes a very great difference, or rather *all* the difference.

Since, then, the present inquiry does not aim at theoretical knowledge like the others (for we are inquiring not in order to know what virtue is, but in order to become good, since otherwise our inquiry would have been of no use), we must examine the nature of actions, namely how we ought to do them; for these determine also the nature of the states of character that are produced, as we have said. Now, that we must act according to the right rule is a common principle and must be assumed—it will be discussed later, i.e., both what the right rule is, and how it is related to the other virtues. But this must be agreed upon beforehand, that the whole account of matters of conduct must be given in outline and not precisely, as we said at the very beginning that the accounts we demand must be in accordance with the subject-matter; matters concerned with conduct and questions of what is good for us have no fixity, any more than matters of health. The general account being of this nature, the account of particular cases is yet more lacking in exactness; for they do not fall under any art or precept but the agents themselves must in each case consider what is appropriate to the occasion, as happens also in the art of medicine or of navigation.

But though our present account is of this nature we must give what help we can. First, then, let us consider this, that it is the nature of such things to be destroyed by defect and excess, as we see in the case of strength and of health (for to gain light on things imperceptible we must use the evidence of sensible things); both excessive and defective exercise destroys the strength, and similarly drink or food which is above or below a certain amount destroys the health, while that which is proportionate both produces and increases and preserves it. So too is it, then, in the case of temperance and courage and the other virtues. For the man who flies from and fears everything and does not stand his ground against anything becomes a coward, and the man who fears nothing at all but goes to meet every danger becomes rash; and similarly the man who indulges in every pleasure and abstains from none becomes self-indulgent, while the man who shuns every pleasure, as boors do, becomes in a way insensible; temperance and courage, then, are destroyed by excess and defect, and preserved by the mean.

But not only are the sources and causes of their origination and growth the same as those of their destruction, but also the sphere of their actualization will be the same; for this is also true of the things which are more evident to sense, e.g., of strength; it is produced by taking much food and undergoing much exertion, and it is the strong man that will be most able to do these things. So too is it with the virtues; by abstaining from pleasures we become temperate, and it is when we have become so that we are most able to abstain from them. . . . (1103a–1104b, pp. 952–54.)

Next we must consider what virtue is. Since things that are found in the soul are of three kinds—passions, faculties, states of character, virtue must be one of these. By passions I mean appetite, anger, fear, confidence, envy, joy, friendly feeling, hatred, longing, emulation, pity, and in general the feelings that are accompanied by pleasure or pain; by faculties the things in virtue of which we are said to be capable of feeling these, e.g., of becoming angry or being pained or feeling pity; by states of character the things in virtue of which we stand well or badly with reference to the passions, e.g., with reference to anger we stand badly if we feel it violently or too weakly, and well if we

feel it moderately; and similarly with reference to the other passions.

Now neither the virtues nor the vices are *passions,* because we are not called good or bad on the ground of our passions, but are so called on the ground of our virtues and our vices, and because we are neither praised nor blamed for our passions (for the man who feels fear or anger is not praised, nor is the man who simply feels anger blamed, but the man who feels it in a certain way), but for our virtues and our vices we *are* praised or blamed.

Again, we feel anger and fear without choice, but the virtues are modes of choice or involve choice. Further, in respect of the passions we are said to be moved, but in respect of the virtues and the vices we are said not to be moved but to be disposed in a particular way.

For these reasons also they are not *faculties;* for we are neither called good nor bad, nor praised nor blamed, for the simple capacity of feeling the passions; again, we have the faculties by nature, but we are not made good or bad by nature; we have spoken of this before.

If, then, the virtues are neither passions nor faculties, all that remains is that they should be *states of character.*

Thus we have stated what virtue is in respect of its genus.

We must, however, not only describe virtue as a state of character, but also say what sort of state it is. We may remark, then, that every virtue or excellence both brings into good condition the thing of which it is the excellence and makes the work of that thing be done well; e.g., the excellence of the eye makes both the eye and its work good; for it is by the excellence of the eye that we see well. Similarly the excellence of the horse makes a horse both good in itself and good at running and at carrying its rider and at awaiting the attack of the enemy. Therefore, if this is true in every case, the virtue of man also will be the state of character which makes a man good and which makes him do his own work well.

How this is to happen . . . will be made

plain also by the following consideration of the specific nature of virtue. In everything that is continuous and divisible it is possible to take more, less, or an equal amount, and that either in terms of the thing itself or relatively to us; and the equal is an intermediate between excess and defect. By the intermediate in the object I mean that which is equidistant from each of the extremes, which is one and the same for all men; by the intermediate relatively to us that which is neither too much nor too little—and this is not one, nor the same for all. For instance, if ten is many and two is few, six is the intermediate, taken in terms of the object; for it exceeds and is exceeded by an equal amount; this is intermediate according to arithmetical proportion. But the intermediate relatively to us is not to be taken so; if ten pounds are too much for a particular person to eat and two too little, it does not follow that the trainer will order six pounds; for this also is perhaps too much for the person who is to take it, or too little—too little for Milo,* too much for the beginner in athletic exercises. The same is true of running and wrestling. Thus a master of any art avoids excess and defect, but seeks the intermediate and chooses this—the intermediate not in the object but relatively to us.

If it is thus, then, that every art does its work well—by looking to the intermediate and judging its works by this standard (so that we often say of good works of art that it is not possible either to take away or to add anything, implying that excess and defect destroy the goodness of works of art, while the mean preserves it; and good artists, as we say, look to this in their work), and if, further, virtue is more exact and better than any art, as nature also is, then virtue must have the quality of aiming at the intermediate. I mean moral virtue; for it is this that is concerned with passions and actions, and in these there is excess, defect, and the intermediate. For instance, both fear and confidence and appetite and anger and pity and in general pleasure and pain may be felt

*A famous wrestler.

both too much and too little, and in both cases not well; but to feel them at the right times, with reference to the right objects, towards the right people, with the right motive, and in the right way, is what is both intermediate and best, and this is characteristic of virtue. Similarly with regard to actions also there is excess, defect, and the intermediate. Now virtue is concerned with passions and actions, in which excess is a form of failure, and so is defect, while the intermediate is praised and is a form of success; and being praised and being successful are both characteristics of virtue. Therefore virtue is a kind of mean, since, as we have seen, it aims at what is intermediate.

Again, it is possible to fail in many ways (for evil belongs to the class of the unlimited, as the Pythagoreans conjectured, and good to that of the limited), while to succeed is possible only in one way (for which reason also one is easy and the other difficult—to miss the mark easy, to hit it difficult); for these reasons also, then, excess and defect are characteristic of vice, and the mean of virtue;

For men are good in but one way, but bad in many.

Virtue, then, is a state of character concerned with choice, lying in a mean, i.e., the mean relative to us, this being determined by a rational principle, and by that principle by which the man of practical wisdom would determine it. Now it is a mean between two vices, that which depends on excess and that which depends on defect; and again it is a mean because the vices respectively fall short of or exceed what is right in both passions and actions, while virtue both finds and chooses that which is intermediate. Hence in respect of its substance and the definition which states its essence virtue is a mean, with regard to what is best and right an extreme.

But not every action nor every passion admits of a mean; for some have names that already imply badness, e.g., spite, shamelessness, envy, and in the case of actions adultery, theft, murder; for all of these and suchlike things imply by their names that they are themselves bad, and not the excesses or deficiencies of them. It is not possible, then, ever to be right with regard to them; one must always be wrong. Nor does goodness or badness with regard to such things depend on committing adultery with the right woman, at the right time, and in the right way, but simply to do any of them is to go wrong. It would be equally absurd, then, to expect that in unjust, cowardly, and voluptuous action there should be a mean, an excess, and a deficiency; for at that rate there would be a mean of excess and of deficiency, an excess of excess, and a deficiency of deficiency. But as there is no excess and deficiency of temperance and courage because what is intermediate is in a sense an extreme, so too of the actions we have mentioned there is no mean nor any excess and deficiency, but however they are done they are wrong; for in general there is neither a mean of excess and deficiency, nor excess and deficiency of a mean. (1105b–1107a, pp. 956–59.)

That moral virtue is a mean, then, and in what sense it is so, and that it is a mean between two vices, the one involving excess, the other deficiency, and that it is such because its character is to aim at what is intermediate in passions and in actions, has been sufficiently stated. Hence also it is no easy task to be good. For in everything it is no easy task to find the middle, e.g., to find the middle of a circle is not for everyone but for him who knows; so, too, anyone can get angry—that is easy—or give or spend money; but to do this to the right person, to the right extent, at the right time, with the right motive, and in the right way, *that* is not for everyone, nor is it easy; wherefore goodness is both rare and laudable and noble.

Hence he who aims at the intermediate must first depart from what is the more contrary to it, as Calypso advises [in Homer's *Odyssey*]—

Hold the ship out beyond that surf and spray.

For of the extremes one is more erroneous, one less so; therefore, since to hit the mean is hard in the extreme, we must as a second best, as people say, take the least of the evils; and this will be done best in the way we describe.

But we must consider the things towards which we ourselves also are easily carried away; for some of us tend to one thing, some to another; and this will be recognizable from the pleasure and the pain we feel. We must drag ourselves away to the contrary extreme; for we shall get into the intermediate state by drawing well away from error, as people do in straightening sticks that are bent.

Now in everything the pleasant or pleasure is most to be guarded against; for we do not judge it impartially. We ought, then, to feel towards pleasure as the elders of the people felt towards Helen, and in all circumstances repeat their saying [from Homer's *Iliad*]; for if we dismiss pleasure thus we are less likely to go astray. It is by doing this, then (to sum the matter up), that we shall best be able to hit the mean.

But this is no doubt difficult, and especially in individual cases; for it is not easy to determine both how and with whom and on what provocation and how long one should be angry; for we too sometimes praise those who fall short and call them good-tempered, but sometimes we praise those who get angry and call them manly. The man, however, who deviates little from goodness is not blamed, whether he do so in the direction of the more or of the less, but only the man who deviates more widely; for *he* does not fail to be noticed. But up to what point and to what extent a man must deviate before he becomes blameworthy it is not easy to determine by reasoning, any more than anything else that is perceived by the senses; such things depend on particular facts, and the decision rests with perception. So much, then, is plain, that the intermediate state is in all things to be praised, but that we must incline sometimes towards the excess, sometimes towards the deficiency; for so shall we most easily hit the mean and what is right. (1109a–1109b, pp. 963–64.)

Immanuel Kant and the Categorical Imperative

Immanuel Kant began his *Foundations of the Metaphysics of Morals* (1785) by observing that "Ancient Greek philosophy was divided into three sciences: physics, ethics, and logic. This division conforms perfectly to the nature of the subject, and one can improve on it perhaps only by supplying its principle in order both to ensure its exhaustiveness and to define correctly the necessary subdivisions."[2] We met Kant in Chapter Two, where we learned how his attempts to preserve human knowledge led him to question whether we can know things in themselves. Aristotle would not have accepted Kant's doubts in that regard—he thought philosophy included metaphysics, the science of being itself—but this was not the only philosophical issue that divided them. For even though Kant praised the Greek philosophers, he did not find Aristotle's understanding of **ethics** and rule-governed action adequate. Where Aristotle stressed that the way to happiness is found in virtue that locates the mean between extremes, Kant developed a very different ethic based on duty. As we shall see, rules—Kant called them **imperatives**—proved essential in his outlook.

The Nature of Moral Experience

Recall that Kant was intrigued by the conditions that make human experience possible. Even the skeptical David Hume had to admit, for example, that our experience is organized so that we are convinced that cause-

IMMANUEL KANT 1724–1804

and-effect relationships are present. Hume had been unable to find a fully rational ground for that conviction, because no amount of empirical data could substantiate our belief that it is universally and necessarily the case that cause-and-effect patterns hold in our experience. But Hume's dilemma led Kant to an ingenious insight. Instead of supposing that human experience and knowledge must conform to the objects we encounter, he proposed that we ought to regard objects in experience as conforming to our capacities for perception and judgment. The cause-and-effect relationship, Kant argued, holds because the human mind structures our experience in such a way that this relationship is unavoidable in our observations.

Instead of thinking of the human mind as an instrument that duplicates an external world, Kant stated that the mind brings order and form to experience and knowledge. This outcome, however, means that the world as it appears in our experience cannot be equated with the world as it is in itself. Thus, Kant distinguished between a *noumenal* and a *phenomenal* reality, between things as they are in themselves and things as they appear to us. The result of that distinction was that human knowledge is restricted to the realm of phenomena and the conditions necessary to account for our experience there.

Kant realized that human reason has practical as well as theoretical interests; he prized scientific understanding, but our experience consists of much more. Artistic, religious, political, and ethical qualities were present as well. The latter especially concerned Kant. So he extended his analysis to show how moral experience is possible and what its nature involves. On the former issue, Kant took a position similar to William James's outlook on freedom.

When Kant stressed that human experience is structured in terms of cause-and-effect relations that make science possible, he recognized that this conclusion seemed to commit him to determinism. But he also believed that the reality of moral experience—which after all, is just as real as science—required something else, namely, human freedom. Morality tells us what we ought to do, but it is senseless to be told how to act in certain ways unless we are free to so act. Kant's solution to this problem was as follows: if freedom is ruled out of the phenomenal realm of existence, it can still be postulated as existing in the realm of things in themselves. Such a belief in freedom will have to be a matter

of faith, since we cannot have knowledge of things in themselves, but the belief is well warranted because it is a condition necessary for morality to make sense, which according to Kant it obviously does.

One can reasonably believe that freedom does exist, Kant argued, because it is an indispensable condition for making our moral experience possible. But, Kant also wanted to know, what is the nature of that experience? Kant's answer capitalized on what he took to be a basic fact: all of us organize our experience in terms of ideas about what we ought or ought not to do. In short, we experience a sense of **obligation** or **duty,** and this experience is the essence of morality. Granted, people do not always agree on the detail of this obligation, but the experience that we ultimately ought or ought not to do some things is a fundamental fact of our lives. Kant therefore took up the task of investigating the foundations of this experience, and his approach was similar to the one he had taken in analyzing the cause-and-effect relationship.

Kant was impressed that a sense of "ought" is something universal regardless of our empirical situation. It seemed to him that all persons experience a sense of moral obligation that cannot be simply derived from experience, for we can always ask whether any explicit sense of obligation is in fact what ought to be carried out. "Ought," reasoned Kant, must function like the category of cause and effect. It must be part of our inherent reasoning process, a power that dictates how we categorize experience, not something that is derived from empirical data. Appeals to experiences cannot provide an intelligible foundation for these qualities of obligation; they only tell us what is the case, not what ought to be the case. On the other hand, without a critique of the powers of reason, any rationalistic claim that particular obligations or rules are self-evident and any appeal to religious authority to ground norms of conduct are likely to be misleading. Kant wanted us to use the self-critical powers of reason alone to find out what we ought to do.

Duty and Law

When Kant stressed that a sense of obligation lies at the core of moral experience, he equated obligation with duty. If we feel that we ought to do something, he argued, we feel an obligation, and that obligation is a duty. Kant's moral philosophy is not limited to any particular duty but to a sense of duty that characterizes all moral experience. The premium Kant placed on duty, as well as the relation of duty to reason, is explained by his claim that "nothing in the world—indeed nothing even beyond the world—can possibly be conceived which could be called good without qualification except a *good will*" (p. 11). If we reflect, we will see that most things we call good are not so without qualification. Material wealth or mental brilliance, for instance, can be misused and hence become evil. But a **good will,** one that strives persistently to achieve goodness, is good without qualification. Kant is convinced that reason makes us all agree on what "good" means.

One's will is good insofar as it acts purely from a sense of what ought to be or, as Kant put it, for the sake of duty. This is our chief motive for action. The goodness of our will depends not on its success in achieving some proposed end but on its orientation in willing. Because we are finite, we may not succeed in accomplishing what ought to be done or will as we should, but a human will that always acts for the sake of duty is good without qualification. There is a difference, Kant went on to explain, between acting for the sake of duty and merely acting in accord with duty. In the latter instance, one may be motivated by considerations of self-interest or utility and still do what duty dictates. In such a case, however, the moral goodness of the action is compromised. Moral goodness depends only on the presence of a motive to act solely for duty's sake.

No philosopher has emphasized duty more than Kant. "Duty," he continued, "is the necessity of an action executed from respect for law" (p. 16). That principle, he contended, refers not to any particular law but to law in general. For instance, you may disagree with a particular traffic law but still acknowledge in general that such regulations are necessary to keep traffic moving smoothly. If we consider the idea of law in general, moreover, its fundamental feature is **universality;** it applies without exception to everyone who falls under its jurisdiction. The police, of course, do not catch everyone who speeds, but in principle all who break the speed limit are equally subject to arrest. **Law,** then, is applicable without exception.

Kant believed that morality arises from the fact that we are self-consciously capable of acting in terms of law, which means not considering ourselves as exceptions. This capacity, in turn, is at the heart of acting from duty. To act from the motive of duty, Kant said, implies a reverence for the concept of law as such. Thus, the moral goodness of a human action depends on its being done out of reverence for law. Although other motives may be present, an act is moral only insofar as it is done from a sense of duty.

The outcome of this analysis, Kant held, is that "I should never act in such a way that I could not always will that my maxim should be a universal law" (p. 18). That is, you are not acting from the motive of duty unless the rule that governs your action in a situation can be universalized—made applicable for everyone—without negating its effectiveness. For example, suppose that "It is all right for me to lie when I am in trouble" is your rule. Obviously if everyone lied when in trouble, the likelihood of anyone's being believed would be severely undercut. However, it is precisely the hope of being believed and, hence, being spared from undesirable consequences, that stands behind the original maxim. In short, according to Kant, you could not act on your original rule without destroying the basis of its universal effectiveness. But to do that would be to act immorally (that is, without reverence for law), and thus from a motive other than duty alone.

The principle that you ought to "act only according to that maxim by which you can at the same time will it should become a universal law" is another way that Kant formulated his **categorical imperative** (p. 39). As Kant explained this imperative in more personal terms, he said it meant that human beings should never be treated as the **means** to an **end**—as objects—but always as persons with inherent worth. By calling his fundamental moral rule a categorical imperative, Kant contrasted it with a **hypothetical imperative.** The latter declares that an action is required only if one has some other end in mind for which the action in question is a necessary condition. A categorical imperative, however, is unconditionally binding. It is enough by itself to prompt action, and, Kant believed, it binds us by virtue of our nature as rational beings.

Kant believed that his imperative is a demand of our own reason. Yet by the commonly understood definition of "demand," we have the implication that people do not always act in accord with reason and that they do not possess a holy will, that is, one that would never be inclined to do anything except to will the good. Obviously Kant's high standard makes it difficult for any of us to be smug about how morally good we are, for typically our wills are not "holy." For example, Kant would say that it is the duty of a merchant not to cheat the customers, but refusing to cheat is not particularly praiseworthy in its own right. You may not want to cheat because you understand that if you get caught it will be bad for business. If concerns of that kind enter into your calculations, you are acting from self-interest and

not from a sense of duty for its own sake. For Kant, cheating is wrong—period. That consideration alone should govern our action, not whether cheating might impoverish or enrich us in the long run.

In short, Kant sharply disagreed with Aristotle, who was wrong, he believed, to think that the rules of virtue and the rules of happiness are simply one and the same. We can work hard, accomplish much, achieve lasting happiness, and, according to Kant, still not act as the categorical imperative prescribes, because the rules that produce a good will are not necessarily identical with those that happiness requires. Kant conceded one thing to Aristotle, however. Human beings are more likely to be concerned about being happy than about being good. That moral shortcoming, Kant thought, is all too natural. In no way, however, does it reduce our obligation to conform to the categorical imperative.

We ought to be good, Kant insisted, and that demand means obedience to the moral law. Though we may repress or disobey it, Kant affirmed that a sense of obligation to heed the categorical imperative is found in every culture and in every individual's experience. That sense is a factor that makes moral experience possible, not a concept derived from experience. It thus gives us a firm basis to guide our action, if only we will heed it. See if Kant persuades you as you read more from his *Foundations of the Metaphysics of Morals.*

Nothing in the world—indeed nothing even beyond the world—can possibly be conceived which could be called good without qualification except a *good will.* Intelligence, wit, judgment, and the other talents of the mind, however they may be named, or courage, resoluteness, and perseverance as qualities of temperament, are doubtless in many respects good and desirable. But they can become extremely bad and harmful if the will, which is to make use of these gifts of nature and which in its special constitution is called character, is not good. It is the same with the gifts of fortune. Power, riches, honor, even health, general well-being, and the contentment with one's condition which is called happiness, make for pride and even arrogance if there is not a good will to correct their influence on the mind and on its principles of action so as to make it universally conformable to its end. It need hardly be mentioned that the sight of a being adorned with no feature of a pure and good will, yet enjoying uninterrupted prosperity, can never give pleasure to a rational impartial observer. Thus the good will seems to constitute the indispensable condition even of worthiness to be happy.

Some qualities seem to be conducive to this good will and can facilitate its action, but, in spite of that, they have no intrinsic unconditional worth. They rather presuppose a good will, which limits the high esteem which one otherwise rightly has for them and prevents their being held to be absolutely good. Moderation in emotions and passions, self-control, and calm deliberation not only are good in many respects but even seem to constitute a part of the inner worth of the person. But however unconditionally they were esteemed by the ancients, they are far from being good without qualification. For without the principle of a good will they can become extremely bad, and the coolness of a villain makes him not only far more dangerous but also more directly abominable in our eyes than he would have seemed without it.

The good will is not good because of what it effects or accomplishes or because of its adequacy to achieve some proposed end; it is good only because of its willing, i.e., it is good of itself. And, regarded for itself, it is to be esteemed incomparably higher than anything which could be brought about by it in favor of any inclination or even of the sum total of all inclinations. Even if it should happen that, by a particularly unfortunate fate or by the niggardly provision of a stepmotherly nature, this will should be wholly lacking in power to accomplish its purpose,

and if even the greatest effort should not avail it to achieve anything of its end, and if there remained only the good will (not as a mere wish but as the summoning of all the means in our power), it would sparkle like a jewel in its own right, as something that had its full worth in itself. Usefulness or fruitlessness can neither diminish nor augment this worth. Its usefulness would be only its setting, as it were, so as to enable us to handle it more conveniently in commerce or to attract the attention of those who are not yet connoisseurs, but not to recommend it to those who are experts or to determine its worth. (Pp. 11–13.)

To be kind where one can is duty, and there are, moreover, many persons so sympathetically constituted that without any motive of vanity or selfishness they find an inner satisfaction in spreading joy, and rejoice in the contentment of others which they have made possible. But I say that, however dutiful and amiable it may be, that kind of action has no true moral worth. It is on a level with [actions arising from] other inclinations, such as the inclination to honor, which, if fortunately directed to what in fact accords with duty and is generally useful and thus honorable, deserve praise and encouragement but no esteem. For the maxim lacks the moral import of an action done not from inclination but from duty. But assume that the mind of that friend to mankind was clouded by a sorrow of his own which extinguished all sympathy with the lot of others and that he still had the power to benefit others in distress, but that their need left him untouched because he was preoccupied with his own need. And now suppose him to tear himself, unsolicited by inclination, out of this dead insensibility and to perform this action only from duty and without any inclination—then for the first time his action has genuine moral worth. Furthermore, if nature has put little sympathy in the heart of a man, and if he, though an honest man, is by temperament cold and indifferent to the sufferings of others, perhaps because he is provided with special gifts of patience and fortitude and expects or even requires that others should have the same—and such a man would certainly not be the meanest product of nature—would not he find in himself a source from which to give himself a far higher worth than he could have got by having a good-natured temperament? This is unquestionably true even though nature did not make him philanthropic, for it is just here that the worth of the character is brought out, which is morally and incomparably the highest of all: he is beneficient not from inclination but from duty.

To secure one's own happiness is at least indirectly a duty, for discontent with one's condition under pressure from many cares and amid unsatisfied wants could easily become a great temptation to transgress duties. But without any view to duty all men have the strongest and deepest inclination to happiness, because in this idea all inclinations are summed up. But the precept of happiness is often so formulated that it definitely thwarts some inclinations, and men can make no definite and certain concept of the sum of satisfaction of all inclinations which goes under the name of happiness. It is not to be wondered at, therefore, that a single inclination, definite as to what it promises and as to the time at which it can be satisfied, can outweigh a fluctuating idea, and that, for example, a man with the gout can choose to enjoy what he likes and to suffer what he may, because according to his calculations at least on this occasion he has not sacrificed the enjoyment of the present moment to a perhaps groundless expectation of a happiness supposed to lie in health. But even in this case, if the universal inclination to happiness did not determine his will, and if health were not at least for him a necessary factor in these calculations, there yet would remain, as in all other cases, a law that he ought to promote his happiness, not from inclination but from duty. Only from this law would his conduct have true moral worth.

[Thus the first proposition of morality is that to have moral worth an action must be done from duty.] The second proposition is:

An action performed from duty does not have its moral worth in the purpose which is to be achieved through it but in the maxim by which it is determined. Its moral value, therefore, does not depend on the realization of the object of the action but merely on the principle of volition by which the action is done without any regard to the objects of the faculty of desire. From the preceding discussion it is clear that the purposes we may have for our actions and their effects as ends and incentives of the will cannot give the actions any unconditional and moral worth. Wherein, then, can this worth lie, if it is not in the will in relation to its hoped-for effect? It can lie nowhere else than in the principle of the will, irrespective of the ends which can be realized by such action. For the will stands, as it were, at the crossroads halfway between its a priori principle which is formal and its a posteriori incentive which is material. Since it must be determined by something, if it is done from duty it must be determined by the formal principle of volition as such since every material principle has been withdrawn from it.

The third principle, as a consequence of the two preceding, I would express as follows: Duty is the necessity of an action executed from respect for law. I can certainly have an inclination to the object as an effect of the proposed action, but I can never have respect for it precisely because it is a mere effect and not an activity of a will. Similarly, I can have no respect for any inclination whatsoever, whether my own or that of another; in the former case I can at most approve of it and in the latter I can even love it, i.e., see it as favorable to my own advantage. But that which is connected with my will merely as ground and not as consequence, that which does not serve my inclination but overpowers it or at least excludes it from being considered in making a choice—in a word, law itself—can be an object of respect and thus a command. Now as an act from duty wholly excludes the influence of inclination and therewith every object of the will, nothing remains which can determine the will objectively except the law, and nothing subjectively except pure respect for this practical law. This subjective element is the maxim* that I ought to follow such a law even if it thwarts all my inclinations.

Thus the moral worth of an action does not lie in the effect which is expected from it or in any principle of action which has to borrow its motive from this expected effect. For all these effects (agreeableness of my own condition, indeed even the promotion of the happiness of others) could be brought about through other causes and would not require the will of a rational being, while the highest and unconditional good can be found only in such a will. Therefore, the preeminent good can consist only in the conception of the law in itself (which can be present only in a rational being) so far as this conception and not the hoped-for effect is the determining ground of the will. This preeminent good, which we call moral, is already present in the person who acts according to this conception, and we do not have to look for it first in the result.† (Pp. 17–20.)

Everything in nature works according to laws. Only a rational being has the capacity of acting according to the conception of laws, i.e., according to principles. This capacity is will. Since reason is required for the derivation of actions from laws, will is nothing else than practical reason. If reason infallibly determines the will, the actions which such

a being recognizes as objectively necessary are also subjectively necessary. That is, the will is a faculty of choosing only that which reason, independently of inclination, recognizes as practically necessary, i.e., as good. But if reason of itself does not sufficiently determine the will, and if the will is subjugated to subjective conditions (certain incentives) which do not always agree with objective conditions; in a word, if the will is not of itself in complete accord with reason (the actual case of men), then the actions which are recognized as objectively necessary are subjectively contingent, and the determination of such a will according to objective laws is constraint. That is, the relation of objective laws to a will which is not completely good is conceived as the determination of the will of a rational being by principles of reason to which this will is not by nature necessarily obedient.

The conception of an objective principle so far as it constrains a will, is a command (of reason), and the formula of this command is called an *imperative*.

All imperatives are expressed by an "ought" and thereby indicate the relation of an objective law of reason to a will which is not in its subjective constitution necessarily determined by this law. This relation is that of constraint. Imperatives say that it would be good to do or to refrain from doing some-

---

*A maxim is the subjective principle of volition. The objective principle (i.e., that which would serve all rational beings also subjectively as a practical principle if reason had full power over the faculty of desire) is the practical law.

†It might be objected that I seek to take refuge in an obscure feeling behind the word "respect," instead of clearly resolving the question with a concept of reason. But though respect is a feeling, it is not one received through any [outer] influence but is self-wrought by a rational concept; thus it differs specifically from all feelings of the former kind which may be referred to inclination or fear. What I recognize directly as a law for myself I recognize with respect, which means merely the consciousness of the submission of my will to a law without the intervention of other influences on my mind. The direct determination of the will by the law and the consciousness of this determination is respect; thus respect

can be regarded as the effect of the law on the subject and not as the cause of the law. Respect is properly the conception of a worth which thwarts my self-love. Thus it is regarded as an object neither of inclination nor of fear, though it has something analogous to both. The only object of respect is the law, and indeed only the law which we impose on ourselves and yet recognize as necessary in itself. As a law, we are subject to it without consulting self-love; as imposed on us by ourselves, it is a consequence of our will. In the former respect it is analogous to fear and in the latter to inclination. All respect for a person is only respect for the law (of righteousness, etc.) of which the person provides an example. Because we see the improvement of our talents as a duty, we think of a person of talents as the example of a law, as it were (the law that we should by practice become like him in his talents), and that constitutes our respect. All so-called moral interest consists solely in respect for the law.

thing, but they say it to a will which does not always do something simply because it is presented as a good thing to do. Practical good is what determines the will by means of the conception of reason and hence not by subjective causes but, rather, objectively, i.e., on grounds which are valid for every rational being as such. It is distinguished from the pleasant as that which has an influence on the will only by means of a sensation from merely subjective causes, which hold only for the senses of this or that person and not as a principle of reason which holds for everyone.‡

A perfectly good will, therefore, would be equally subject to objective laws (of the good), but it could not be conceived as constrained by them to act in accord with them, because, according to its own subjective constitution, it can be determined to act only through the conception of the good. Thus no imperatives hold for the divine will or, more generally, for a holy will. The "ought" is here out of place, for the volition of itself is necessarily in unison with the law. Therefore imperatives are only formulas expressing the relation of objective laws of volition in general to the subjective imperfection of

‡The dependence of the faculty of desire on sensations is called inclination, and inclination always indicates a need. The dependence of a contingently determinable will on principles of reason, however, is called interest. An interest is present only in a dependent will which is not of itself always in accord with reason; in the divine will we cannot conceive of an interest. But even the human will can take an interest in something without thereby acting from interest. The former means the practical interest in the action; the latter, the pathological interest in the object of the action. The former indicates only the dependence of the will on principles of reason in themselves, while the latter indicates dependence on the principles of reason for the purpose of inclination, since reason gives only the practical rule by which the needs of inclination are to be aided. In the former case the action interests me, and in the latter the object of the action (so far as it is pleasant for me) interests me. In the first section we have seen that, in the case of an action performed from duty, no regard must be given to the interest in the object, but merely in the action itself and its principle in reason (i.e., the law).

the will of this or that rational being, e.g., the human will.

All imperatives command either hypothetically or categorically. The former present the practical necessity of a possible action as a means to achieving something else which one desires (or which one may possibly desire). The categorical imperative would be one which presented an action as of itself objectively necessary, without regard to any other end.

Since every practical law presents a possible action as good and thus as necessary for a subject practically determinable by reason, all imperatives are formulas of the determination of action which is necessary by the principle of a will which is in any way good. If the action is good only as a means to something else, the imperative is hypothetical, but if it is thought of as good in itself, and hence as necessary in a will which of itself conforms to reason as the principle of this will, the imperative is categorical.

The imperative thus says what action possible to me would be good, and it presents the practical rule in relation to a will which does not forthwith perform an action simply because it is good, in part because the subject does not always know that the action is good and in part (when he does know it) because his maxims can still be opposed to the objective principles of practical reason.

The hypothetical imperative, therefore, says only that the action is good to some purpose, possible or actual. In the former case it is a problematical, in the latter an assertorical, practical principle. The categorical imperative, which declares the action to be of itself objectively necessary without making any reference to a purpose, i.e., without having any other end, holds as an apodictical (practical) principle.

There is one end, however, which we may presuppose as actual in all rational beings so far as imperatives apply to them, i.e., so far as they are dependent beings; there is one purpose not only which they *can* have but which we can presuppose that they all *do* have by a necessity of nature. This purpose is happiness. The hypothetical imperative which represents the practical necessity of action as means to the promotion of happiness is an assertorical imperative. We may not expound it as merely necessary to an uncertain and a merely possible purpose, but as necessary to a purpose which we can a priori and with assurance assume for everyone because it belongs to his essence. Skill in the choice of means to one's own highest welfare can be called prudence[§] in the narrowest sense. Thus the imperative which refers to the choice of means to one's own happiness, i.e., the precept of prudence, is still only hypothetical; the action is not absolutely commanded but commanded only as a means to another end.

Finally, there is one imperative which directly commands a certain conduct without making its condition some purpose to be reached by it. This imperative is categorical. It concerns not the material of the action and its intended result but the form and the principle from which it results. What is essentially good in it consists in the intention, the result being what it may. This imperative may be called the imperative of morality. (Pp. 33–38.)

To see how the imperative of morality is possible is, then, without doubt the only question needing an answer. It is not hypothetical, and thus the objectively conceived necessity cannot be supported by any presupposition, as was the case with the hypothetical imperatives. But it must not be overlooked that it cannot be shown by any example (i.e., it cannot be empirically shown) whether or not there is such an imperative; it is rather to be suspected that all impera-

[§]The word "prudence" may be taken in two senses, and it may bear the name of prudence with reference to things of the world and private prudence. The former sense means the skill of a man in having an influence on others so as to use them for his own purposes. The latter is the ability to unite all these purposes to his own lasting advantage. The worth of the first is finally reduced to the latter, and of one who is prudent in the former sense but not in the latter we might better say that he is clever and cunning yet, on the whole, imprudent.

tives which appear to be categorical may yet be hypothetical, but in a hidden way. For instance, when it is said, "Thou shalt not make a false promise," we assume that the necessity of this avoidance is not a mere counsel for the sake of escaping some other evil, so that it would read, "Thou shalt not make a false promise so that, if it comes to light, thou ruinest thy credit"; we assume rather that an action of this kind must be regarded as of itself bad and that the imperative of the prohibition is categorical. But we cannot show with certainty by any example that the will is here determined by the law alone without any other incentives, even though this appears to be the case. For it is always possible that secret fear of disgrace, and perhaps also obscure apprehension of other dangers, may have had an influence on the will. Who can prove by experience the nonexistence of a cause when experience shows us only that we do not perceive the cause? But in such a case the so-called moral imperative, which as such appears to be categorical and unconditional, would be actually only a pragmatic precept which makes us attentive to our own advantage and teaches us to consider it.

There is, therefore, only one categorical imperative. It is: Act only according to that maxim by which you can at the same time will that it should become a universal law.

Now if all imperatives of duty can be derived from this one imperative as a principle, we can at least show what we understand by the concept of duty and what it means, even though it remain undecided whether that which is called duty is an empty concept or not.

The universality of law according to which effects are produced constitutes what is properly called nature in the most general sense (as to form), i.e., the existence of things so far as it is determined by universal laws. [By analogy], then, the universal imperative of duty can be expressed as follows: Act as though the maxim of your action were by your will to become a universal law of nature.

We shall now enumerate some duties, adopting the usual division of them into duties to ourselves and to others and into perfect and imperfect duties.

1. A man who is reduced to despair by a series of evils feels a weariness with life but is still in possession of his reason sufficiently to ask whether it would not be contrary to his duty to himself to take his own life. Now he asks whether the maxim of his action could become a universal law of nature. His maxim, however, is: For love of myself, I make it my principle to shorten my life when by a longer duration it threatens more evil than satisfaction. But it is questionable whether this principle of self-love could become a universal law of nature. One immediately sees a contradiction in a system of nature whose law would be to destroy life by the feeling whose special office is to impel the improvement of life. In this case it would not exist as nature; hence that maxim cannot obtain as a law of nature, and thus it wholly contradicts the supreme principle of all duty.

2. Another man finds himself forced by need to borrow money. He well knows that he will not be able to repay it, but he also sees that nothing will be loaned him if he does not firmly promise to repay it at a certain time. He desires to make such a promise, but he has enough conscience to ask himself whether it is not improper and opposed to duty to relieve his distress in such a way. Now, assuming he does decide to do so, the maxim of his action would be as follows: When I believe myself to be in need of money, I will borrow money and promise to repay it, although I know I shall never do so. Now this principle of self-love or of his own benefit may very well be compatible with his whole future welfare, but the question is whether it is right. He changes the pretension of self-love into a universal law and then puts the question: How would it be if my maxim became a universal law? He immediately sees that it could never hold as a universal law of nature and be consistent with itself; rather it must nec-

essarily contradict itself. For the universality of a law which says that anyone who believes himself to be in need could promise what he pleased with the intention of not fulfilling it would make the promise itself and the end to be accomplished by it impossible; no one would believe what was promised to him but would only laugh at any such assertion as vain pretense.

3. A third finds in himself a talent which could, by means of some cultivation, make him in many respects a useful man. But he finds himself in comfortable circumstances and prefers indulgence in pleasure to troubling himself with broadening and improving his fortunate natural gifts. Now, however, let him ask whether his maxim of neglecting his gifts, besides agreeing with his propensity to idle amusement, agrees also with what is called duty. He sees that a system of nature could indeed exist in accordance with such a law, even though man (like the inhabitants of the South Sea Islands) should let his talents rust and resolve to devote his life merely to idleness, indulgence, and propagation—in a word, to pleasure. But he cannot possibly will that this should become a universal law of nature or that it should be implanted in us by a natural instinct. For, as a rational being, he necessarily wills that all his faculties should be developed, inasmuch as they are given to him for all sorts of possible purposes.

4. A fourth man, for whom things are going well, sees that others (whom he could help) have to struggle with great hardships, and he asks, "What concern of mine is it? Let each one be as happy as heaven wills, or as he can make himself; I will not take anything from him or even envy him; but to his welfare or to his assistance in time of need I have no desire to contribute." If such a way of thinking were a universal law of nature, certainly the human race could exist, and without doubt even better than in a state where

everyone talks of sympathy and good will, or even exerts himself occasionally to practice them while, on the other hand, he cheats when he can and betrays or otherwise violates the rights of man. Now although it is possible that a universal law of nature according to that maxim could exist, it is nevertheless impossible to will that such a principle should hold everywhere as a law of nature. For a will which resolved this would conflict with itself, since instances can often arise in which he would need the love and sympathy of others, and in which he would have robbed himself, by such a law of nature springing from his own will, of all hope of the aid he desires. (Pp. 42–47.)

The question then is: Is it a necessary law for all rational beings that they should always judge their actions by such maxims as they themselves could will to serve as universal laws? If it is such a law, it must be connected (wholly a priori) with the concept of the will of a rational being as such. But in order to discover this connection we must, however reluctantly, take a step into metaphysics, although into a region of it different from speculative philosophy, i.e., into metaphysics of morals. In a practical philosophy it is not a question of assuming grounds for what happens but of assuming laws of what ought to happen even though it may never happen—that is to say, objective, practical laws. Hence in practical philosophy we need not inquire into the reasons why something pleases or displeases, how the pleasure of mere feeling differs from taste, and whether this is distinct from a general satisfaction of reason. Nor need we ask on what the feeling of pleasure or displeasure rests, how desires and inclinations arise, and how, finally, maxims arise from desires and inclination under the cooperation of reason. For all these matters belong to an empirical psychology, which would be the second part of physics if we consider it as philosophy of nature so far as it rests on empirical laws. But here it is a question of objectively practical laws and thus of the relation of a will to itself so far as it

determines itself only by reason; for everything which has a relation to the empirical automatically falls away, because if reason of itself alone determines conduct it must necessarily do so a priori. The possibility of reason thus determining conduct must now be investigated.

The will is thought of as a faculty of determining itself to action in accordance with the conception of certain laws. Such a faculty can be found only in rational beings. That which serves the will as the objective ground of its self-determination is an end, and, if it is given by reason alone, it must hold alike for all rational beings. On the other hand, that which contains the ground of the possibility of the action, whose result is an end, is called the means. The subjective ground of desire is the incentive, while the objective ground of volition is the motive. Thus arises the distinction between subjective ends, which rest on incentives, and objective ends, which depend on motives valid for every rational being. Practical principles are formal when they disregard all subjective ends; they are material when they have subjective ends, and thus certain incentives, as their basis. The ends which a rational being arbitrarily proposes to himself as consequences of his action are material ends and are without exception only relative, for only their relation to a particularly constituted faculty of desire in the subject gives them their worth. And this worth cannot, therefore, afford any universal principles for all rational beings or valid and necessary principles for every volition. That is, they cannot give rise to any practical laws. All these relative ends, therefore, are grounds for hypothetical imperatives only. (Pp. 50–51.)

John Stuart Mill and the Principle of Utility

Born in London, John Stuart Mill (1806–1873) was the son of the distinguished philosopher James Mill (1773–1836), who person-

JOHN STUART MILL   1806–1873

ally supervised the boy's rigorous education. A child prodigy, Mill had mastered the Greek and Latin classics in the original languages, as well as history, economics, logic, and mathematics, by the age of 14. In his early twenties, however, Mill suffered from acute depression, a condition he attributed to his intensive analytical training. Mill spent thirty-three years of his life working for the East India Company, rising to the position of director. Philosophy and social theory occupied him, too. In 1843 he published his *System of Logic,* which many scholars regard as his most profound work, and followed it with *Principles of Political Economy* (1848). A staunch believer in representative government, women's rights, and economic justice, Mill served briefly in Parliament, but his greatest contributions to politics came through writings such as *On Liberty* (1859) and *Utilitar-*

ianism (1861), which have influenced public policy around the world.

Mill's Quarrel with Kant

Kant's rules for moral action did not depend on particular circumstances and personal inclinations. Nor did he think that sound moral decisions were based on calculations about consequences. The results of decisions elude our complete control. It would not be sound to base moral praise or blame on consequences, for we can have the worst of motives and still, by chance, good may come of them—or vice versa. Kant claimed instead that ethical evaluations ought to rest on how we will, for that dimension of our lives remains in our control even when the consequences of our decisions do not. Thus, Kant contended that only the will itself can be good without qualification. The will meets that criterion if and only if its activity is governed by the categorical imperative that reason dictates. And when we act in that way, Kant went on to say, we are actually the most free, since we are acting in harmony with what reason itself says is right.

Philosophers call this approach to ethics **deontological,** a term derived from *dein,* the Greek word for duty. In morality, argued Kant, the key is to stress duties, not consequences; whether one sincerely tried to fulfill a moral obligation for its own sake is more important than whether the attempt succeeded or failed. Views such as Aristotle's ethics, which stresses the results of action and is therefore called **teleological** (from *telos,* the Greek word for purpose or goal), missed the point that one could be happy but fall short of having a "good will," at least as Kant understood that concept.

John Stuart Mill sized up Kant's position and thought it went awry. Specifically, either Kant did not pay enough attention to the consequences of actions, or, his claims to the contrary notwithstanding, Kant justified some intentions against others by considering their results. Here is how Mill objected to Kant:

> This remarkable man, whose system of thought will long remain one of the landmarks in the history of philosophical speculation, . . . [lays] down a universal first principle as the origin and ground of moral obligation; it is this: "So act that the rule on which thou actest would admit of being adopted as a law by all rational beings." But when he begins to deduce from this precept any of the actual duties of morality, he fails, almost grotesquely, to show that there would be any contradiction, any logical (not to say physical) impossibility, in the adoption by all rational beings of the most outrageously immoral rules of conduct. All he shows is that the *consequences* of their universal adoption would be such as no one would choose to incur.[3]

Mill wanted a clearer outcome, and it seemed to rest in a modified return to Aristotle's understanding that human happiness is the good at which ethics rightly aims.

The Rules of Utilitarianism

One result of Mill's quarrel with Kant was a book called *Utilitarianism* (1861). In brief, **utilitarianism** is a teleological ethic. It takes the consequences of actions to be the criteria of their moral worth. The view holds, moreover, that three basic rules should govern human conduct. First, people should act to promote the greatest balance of good over evil. Next, because goodness is best defined in terms of pleasure—utilitarianism is a form of **hedonism**—people should act to maximize the greatest balance of pleasure over pain. Third, individual self-satisfaction is not enough for morality, which requires us to act in ways that promote the greatest happiness for the greatest number of people. The latter

norm—sometimes called "the **benevolence principle**"—gives utilitarianism a distinctively social and political flavor. We cannot judge actions simply in terms of ourselves; their social impact is equally important.

In 1823 Mill formed the Utilitarian Society. He was the first to use the term "utilitarianism" to name an ethical theory, and he became the leader of the utilitarian movement. But Mill was not the originator of the position. That distinction went to another British thinker, Jeremy Bentham (1748—1832), who had looked for a single ethical principle that could simplify his country's legal system. Equating happiness with pleasure, he appealed to "the principle of utility" and took it to mean that whatever produces happiness is useful and whatever detracts from happiness is not.

Mill found Bentham's theory too simple, however. The problem was that his idea of pleasure was purely quantitative. You consider the various desires that people have—for what else can happiness be but fulfilled desire?—and then you sanction the combination of choices that will produce the most pleasure. Bentham was on the right track, Mill agreed, but his calculations badly underestimated the importance of qualitative distinctions. Mill succinctly summed up his correction as follows: "It is better to be a human being dissatisfied than a pig satisfied; better to be Socrates dissatisfied than a fool satisfied" (p. 10).

Competent Judges Are Needed to Decide Questions of Utility

Mill admitted that "questions of ultimate ends do not admit of proof" (p. 34). Nevertheless, that conclusion did not lead him to skepticism about our ability to judge what is good, because he reasoned that we start with the desire for happiness as given and inescapable. As a "first principle," it is not something one proves but rather something one reasons from. Yet there is an undeniable evidence in its favor as well. Here is how Mill explained the point:

> The utilitarian doctrine is that happiness is desirable, and the only thing desirable, as an end; . . . the sole evidence it is possible to produce that anything is desirable is that people actually do desire it. . . . No reason can be given why the general happiness is desirable, except that each person, so far as he believes it to be attainable, desires his own happiness. This, however, being a fact, we have not only all the proof which the case admits of, but all which it is possible to require, that happiness is a good, that each person's happiness is a good to that person, and the general happiness, therefore, a good to the aggregate of all persons. (P. 34.)

Kant would have protested that this analysis begs the question of what we ought to do. The fact that we desire X does make it "desirable" in the sense that we can and do desire it, but, Kant would contend, X may or may not be what we ought to desire irrespective of what our desires actually are. In short, Kant's view would be that Mill fallaciously derives what ought to be from what is in fact. If Kant is correct, what we ought to do may conflict much more with happiness—especially understood in terms of pleasure and pain—than Mill admitted. Another possible difficulty in Mill's position is his assumption that each person's desire for his or her own happiness would produce, if achieved, the general happiness of the greatest number of persons. Mill assumed that we will see that our own happiness is linked with that of others. That seems reasonable, but the issue is how far such awareness extends. If it honestly seems to us that our own happiness does not entail concern about "the greatest number," and thus we do not desire their happiness, then will Mill have to find some other basis—perhaps one

closer to Kant—to ground an obligation he thinks we ought to recognize?

Such problems left Mill undaunted, and he continued to feel that we can soundly calculate on the basis of "greatest happiness principle" (p. 7). But having introduced his qualitative concerns about higher and lower forms of pleasure, Mill wondered how to keep majority rule from being destructive and tyrannical. If we are going to rank pleasures as to their qualitative values, competent judges will be needed, because there will be differences of opinion to reconcile. Mill advanced the following solution to this problem:

> On a question of which is the best worth having of two pleasures, or which of two modes of existence is the most grateful to the feelings, apart from its moral attributes and from its consequences, the judgment of those who are qualified by knowledge of both, or, if they differ, that of the majority among them, must be admitted as final. (P. 11.)

If Mill thought Bentham's utilitarianism was too simple, the adjustments Mill advocated may have complicated matters more than he hoped, especially when we add in Mill's conviction that human liberty is essential. *On Liberty* took up the question of the power society can exercise over the individual. Mill wanted to safeguard individual freedom and so he argued that

> Protection . . . against the tyranny of the magistrate is not enough; there needs [to be] protection also against the tyranny of the prevailing opinion and feeling; against the tendency of society to impose, by other means than civil penalties, its own ideas and practices as rules of conduct on those who dissent from them; to fetter the development, and, if possible, prevent the formation, of any individuality not in harmony with its ways, and compel all characters to fashion themselves upon the model of its

own. There is a limit to the legitimate interference of collective opinion with individual independence: and to find that limit, and maintain it against encroachment, is as indispensable to a good condition of human affairs, as protection against political despotism.[4]

Mill wanted a balance, a "fitting adjustment between individual independence and social control" (p. 259). Such equilibrium, he recognized, is rarely a natural state of affairs. If we are to pursue our own goals while also advancing the greatest happiness for the greatest number, which has now got to include qualitative calculations, we will indeed need competent leaders and a citizenry well trained to follow them. The difficulty of achieving those goals will be considerable, Mill admitted, because intolerance is "so natural to mankind . . . in whatever they really care about" (p. 261).

Easy to State, Hard to Practice

Mill's utilitarian principles begin simply, but they end up complex. It is easy to affirm that we should strive for the greatest good of the greatest number. We may even agree that happiness is best defined in terms of pleasure, but how exactly do we measure it in quantity and quality? To implement utilitarianism, we must master a host of problems that involve qualitative distinctions about pleasure, the tyranny of the majority, the importance of liberty, and the need for competent judges, to mention just a few.

All those considerations suggest that defining "the greatest good" and whom "the greatest number" includes and excludes will put us in the middle of political as well as philosophical dilemmas. Although Mill thought Bentham's utilitarianism was oversimplified, he believed that his own more sophisticated version provided relatively clear

standards for judgment. Was he too optimistic?

Mill's theory sounds good "in principle," but can it sustain a consensus on specific issues? When disputes occur, Mill appeals to competent judges, but what if people disagree about who is qualified to judge? And when the judges do not concur, what assures that the opinion of the majority will produce a good outcome? Mill thought his utilitarianism was in better touch with human inclinations than Kant's rationalistic morality. In that judgment he may have been correct. Yet the consequences of utilitarian rules themselves may not warrant Mill's optimism that this theory is the key for distributing happiness agreeably. With those issues in mind, look in more detail at Mill's rules for governing our actions, as expressed in *Utilitarianism* and *On Liberty*.

The creed which accepts as the foundation of morals "utility" or the "greatest happiness principle" holds that actions are right in proportion as they tend to promote happiness; wrong as they tend to produce the reverse of happiness. By happiness is intended pleasure and the absence of pain; by unhappiness, pain and the privation of pleasure. To give a clear view of the moral standard set up by the theory, much more requires to be said; in particular, what things it includes in the ideas of pain and pleasure, and to what extent this is left an open question. But these supplementary explanations do not affect the theory of life on which this theory of morality is grounded—namely, that pleasure and freedom from pain are the only things desirable as ends; and that all desirable things (which are as numerous in the utilitarian as in any other scheme) are desirable either for pleasure inherent in themselves or as means to the promotion of pleasure and the prevention of pain.

Now such a theory of life excites in many minds, and among them in some of the most estimable in feeling and purpose, inveterate dislike. To suppose that life has (as they express it) no higher end than pleasure—no better and nobler object of desire and pursuit—they designate as utterly mean and groveling, as a doctrine worthy only of swine, to whom the followers of Epicurus were, at a very early period, contemptuously likened; and modern holders of the doctrine are occasionally made the subject of equally polite comparisons by its German, French, and English assailants.

When thus attacked, the Epicureans have always answered that it is not they, but their accusers, who represent human nature in a degrading light, since the accusation supposes human beings to be capable of no pleasures except those of which swine are capable. If this supposition were true, the charge could not be gainsaid, but would then be no longer an imputation; for if the sources of pleasure were precisely the same to human beings and to swine, the rule of life which is good enough for the one would be good enough for the other. The comparison of the Epicurean life to that of beasts is felt as degrading, precisely because a beast's pleasures do not satisfy a human being's conceptions of happiness. Human beings have faculties more elevated than the animal appetites and, when once made conscious of them, do not regard anything as happiness which does not include their gratification. I do not indeed, consider the Epicureans to have been by any means faultless in drawing out their scheme of consequences from the utilitarian principle. To do this in any sufficient manner, many Stoic, as well as Christian, elements require to be included. But there is no known Epicurean theory of life which does not assign to the pleasures of the intellect, of the feelings and imagination, and of the moral sentiments a much higher value as pleasures than to those of mere sensation. It must be admitted, however, that utilitarian writers in general have placed the superiority of mental over bodily pleasures chiefly in the greater permanency, safety, uncostliness, etc., of the former—that is, in their circumstantial advantages rather than in their intrinsic nature. And on all these points utilitarians have fully proved their case; but they might have taken the other and, as it may be called, higher ground with entire consistency. It is quite compatible with the principle of utility to recognize the fact that some kinds of pleasure are more desirable and more valuable than others. It would be absurd that, while in estimating all other things quality is considered as well as quantity, the estimation of pleasure should be supposed to depend on quantity alone.

If I am asked what I mean by difference of quality in pleasures, or what makes one pleasure more valuable than another, merely as a pleasure, except its being greater in amount, there is but one possible answer. Of two pleasures, if there be one to which all or almost all who have experience of both give a decided preference, irrespective of any feeling of moral obligation to prefer it, that is the more desirable pleasure. If one of the two is, by those who are competently acquainted with both, placed so far above the other that they prefer it, even though knowing it to be attended with a greater amount of discontent, and would not resign it for any quantity of the other pleasure which their nature is capable of, we are justified in ascribing to the preferred enjoyment a superiority in quality so far outweighing quantity as to render it, in comparison, of small account.

Now it is an unquestionable fact that those who are equally acquainted with and equally capable of appreciating and enjoying both do give a most marked preference to the manner of existence which employs their higher faculties. Few human creatures would consent to be changed into any of the lower animals for a promise of the fullest allowance of a beast's pleasures; no intelligent human being would consent to be a fool, no instructed person would be an ignoramus, no person of feeling and conscience would be selfish and base, even though they should be persuaded that the fool, the dunce, or the rascal is better satisfied with his lot than they are with theirs. They would not resign what they possess more than he for the most complete satisfaction of all the desires which they have in common with him. If they ever fancy they would, it is only in cases of unhappiness so extreme that to escape from it they would exchange their lot for almost any other, however undesirable in their own eyes. A being of higher faculties requires more to make him happy, is capable probably of more acute suffering, and certainly accessible to it at more points, than one of an inferior type; but in spite of these liabilities, he can never really wish to sink into what he feels to be a lower grade of existence. We may give what explanation we please of this unwillingness; we may attribute it to pride, a name which is given indiscriminately to some of the most and to some of the least estimable feelings of which mankind are capable; we may refer it to the love of liberty and personal independence, an appeal to which was with the Stoics one of the most effective means for the inculcation of it; to the love of power or to the love of excitement, both of which do really enter into and contribute to it; but its most appropriate appellation is a sense of dignity, which all human beings possess in one form or other, and in some, though by no means in exact, proportion to their higher faculties, and which is so essential a part of the happiness of those in whom it is strong that nothing which conflicts with it could be otherwise than momentarily an object of desire to them. Whoever supposes that this preference takes place at a sacrifice of happiness—that the superior being, in anything like equal circumstances, is not happier than the inferior—confounds the two very different ideas of happiness and content. It is indisputable that the being whose capacities of enjoyment are low has the greatest chance of having them fully satisfied; and a highly endowed being will always feel that any happiness which he can look for, as the world is constituted, is imperfect. But he can learn to bear its imperfections, if they are at all bearable; and they will not make him envy the being who is indeed unconscious of the imperfections, but only because he feels not at all the good which those imperfections qualify. It is better to be

a human being dissatisfied than a pig satisfied; better to be Socrates dissatisfied than a fool satisfied. And if the fool, or the pig, are of a different opinion, it is because they only know their own side of the question. The other party to the comparison knows both sides.

It may be objected that many who are capable of the higher pleasures occasionally, under the influence of temptation, postpone them to the lower. But this is quite compatible with a full appreciation of the intrinsic superiority of the higher. Men often, from infirmity of character, make their election for the nearer good, though they know it to be the less valuable; and this no less when the choice is between two bodily pleasures than when it is between bodily and mental. They pursue sensual indulgences to the injury of health, though perfectly aware that health is the greater good. It may be further objected that many who begin with youthful enthusiasm for everything noble, as they advance in years, sink into indolence and selfishness. But I do not believe that those who undergo this very common change voluntarily choose the lower description of pleasures in preference to the higher. I believe that, before they devote themselves exclusively to the one, they have already become incapable of the other. Capacity for the nobler feelings is in most natures a very tender plant, easily killed, not only by hostile influences, but by mere want of sustenance; and in the majority of young persons it speedily dies away if the occupations to which their position in life has devoted them, and the society into which it has thrown them, are not favorable to keeping that higher capacity in exercise. Men lose their high aspirations as they lose their intellectual tastes, because they have not time or opportunity for indulging them; and they addict themselves to inferior pleasures, not because they deliberately prefer them, but because they are either the only ones to which they have access or the only ones which they are any longer capable of enjoying. It may be questioned whether anyone who has remained equally susceptible to both classes of pleasures ever knowingly and calmly preferred the lower, though many, in all ages, have broken down in an ineffectual attempt to combine both.

From this verdict of the only competent judges, I apprehend there can be no appeal. On a question which is the best worth having of two pleasures, or which of two modes of existence is the most grateful to the feelings, apart from its moral attributes and from its consequences, the judgment of these who are qualified by knowledge of both, or, if they differ, that of the majority among them, must be admitted as final. And there needs be the less hesitation to accept this judgment respecting the quality of pleasures, since there is no other tribunal to be referred to even on the question of quantity. What means are there of determining which is the acutest of two pains, or the intensest of two pleasurable sensations, except the general suffrage of those who are familiar with both? Neither pains nor pleasures are homogeneous, and pain is always heterogeneous with pleasure. What is there to decide whether a particular pleasure is worth purchasing at the cost of a particular pain, except the feelings and judgment of the experienced? When, therefore, those feelings and judgment declare the pleasures derived from the higher faculties to be preferable *in kind*, apart from the question of intensity, to those of which the animal nature, disjoined from the higher faculties, is susceptible, they are entitled on this subject to the same regard.

I have dwelt on this point as being part of a perfectly just conception of utility or happiness considered as the directive rule of human conduct. But it is by no means an indispensable condition to the acceptance of the utilitarian standard; for that standard is not the agent's own greatest happiness, but the greatest amount of happiness altogether; and if it may possibly be doubted whether a noble character is always the happier for its nobleness, there can be no doubt that it makes other people happier, and that the world in general is immensely a gainer by it. Utilitarianism, therefore, could only

attain its end by the general cultivation of nobleness of character, even if each individual were only benefited by the nobleness of others, and his own, so far as happiness is concerned, were a sheer deduction from the benefit. But the bare enunciation of such an absurdity as this last renders refutation superfluous.

According to the greatest happiness principle, as above explained, the ultimate end, with reference to and for the sake of which all other things are desirable—whether we are considering our own good or that of other people—is an existence exempt as far as possible from pain, and as rich as possible in enjoyments, both in point of quantity and quality; the test of quality and the rule for measuring it against quantity being the preference felt by those who, in their opportunities of experience, to which must be added their habits of self-consciousness and self-observation, are best furnished with the means of comparison. This, being according to the utilitarian opinion the end of human action, is necessarily also the standard of morality, which may accordingly be defined "the rules and precepts for human conduct," by the observance of which an existence such as has been described might be, to the greatest extent possible, secured to all mankind; and not to them only, but, so far as the nature of things admits, to the whole sentient creation.[5]

. . . I regard utility as the ultimate appeal on all ethical questions; but it must be utility in the largest sense, grounded on the permanent interests of man as a progressive being. Those interests, I contend, authorize the subjection of individual spontaneity to external control, only in respect to those actions of each, which concern the interest of other people. If anyone does an act hurtful to others, there is a prima facie case for punishing him, by law or, where legal penalties are not safely applicable, by general disapprobation. There are also many positive acts for the benefit of others, which he may rightfully be compelled to perform; such as, to give evidence in a court of justice; to bear his fair share in the common defense, or in any other joint work necessary to the interest of the society of which he enjoys the protection; and to perform certain acts of individual beneficence, such as saving a fellow creature's life, or interposing to protect the defenseless against ill-usage, things which whenever it is obviously a man's duty to do, he may rightfully be made responsible to society for not doing. A person may cause evil to others not only by his actions but by his inaction, and in either case he is justly accountable to them for the injury. The latter case, it is true, requires a much more cautious exercise of compulsion than the former. To make anyone answerable for doing evil to others, is the rule; to make him answerable for not preventing evil, is, comparatively speaking, the exception. Yet there are many cases clear enough and grave enough to justify that exception. In all things which regard the external relations of the individual, he is *de jure* amenable to those whose interests are concerned, and if need be, to society as their protector. There are often good reasons for not holding him to the responsibility; but these reasons must arise from the special expediencies of the case: either because it is a kind of case in which he is on the whole likely to act better, when left to his own discretion, than when controlled in any way in which society have it in their power to control him; or because the attempt to exercise control would produce other evils, greater than those which it would prevent. When such reasons as these preclude the enforcement of responsibility, the conscience of the agent himself should step into the vacant judgment seat and protect those interests of others which have no external protection; judging himself all the more rigidly because the case does not admit of his being made accountable to the judgment of his fellow-creatures.

But there is a sphere of action in which society, as distinguished from the individual, has, if any, only an indirect interest; comprehending all that portion of a person's life and conduct which affects only himself, or if it also affects others, only with their free, voluntary, and undeceived consent and participation. When I say only himself, I mean directly, and in the first instance: for whatever affects himself, may affect others *through* himself; and the objection which may be grounded on this contingency, will receive consideration in the sequel. This, then, is the appropriate region of human liberty. It comprises, first, the inward domain of consciousness; demanding liberty of conscience, in the most comprehensive sense; liberty of thought and feeling; absolute freedom of opinion and sentiment on all subjects, practical or speculative, scientific, moral, or theological. The liberty of expressing and publishing opinions may seem to fall under a different principle, since it belongs to that part of the conduct of an individual which concerns other people; but, being almost of as much importance as the liberty of thought itself, and resting in great part on the same reasons, is practically inseparable from it. Secondly, the principle requires liberty of tastes and pursuits; of framing the plan of our life to suit our own character; of doing as we like, subject to such consequences as may follow, without impediment from our fellow-creatures, so long as what we do does not harm them, even though they should think our conduct foolish, perverse, or wrong. Thirdly, from this liberty of each individual, follows the liberty, within the same limits, of combination among individuals; freedom to unite, for any purpose not involving harm to others; the persons combining being supposed to be of full age, and not forced or deceived.

No society in which these liberties are not, on the whole, respected, is free, whatever may be its form of government, and none is completely free in which they do not exist absolute and unqualified. The only freedom which deserves the name, is that of pursuing our own good in our own way, so long as we do not attempt to deprive others of theirs, or impede their efforts to obtain it. Each is the proper guardian of his own health, whether bodily, or mental and spiritual. Mankind are greater gainers by suffering each other to live as seems good to themselves, than by compelling each to live as seems good to the rest. . . .

He who knows only his own side of the case, knows little of that. His reasons may be good, and no one may have been able to refute them. But if he is equally unable to refute the reasons on the opposite side; if he does not so much as know what they are, he has no ground for preferring either opinion. The rational position for him would be suspension of judgment, and unless he contents himself with that, he is either led by authority, or adopts, like the generality of the world, the side to which he feels most inclination. Nor is it enough that he should hear the arguments of adversaries from his own teachers, presented as they state them, and accompanied by what they offer as refutations. That is not the way to do justice to the arguments, or bring them into real contact with his own mind. He must be able to hear them from persons who actually believe them; who defend them in earnest, and do their very utmost for them. He must know them in their most plausible and persuasive form; he must feel the whole force of the difficulty which the true view of the subject has to encounter and dispose of; else he will never really possess himself of the portion of truth which meets and removes that difficulty. Ninety-nine in a hundred of what are called educated men are in this condition; even of those who can argue fluently for their opinions. Their conclusion may be true, but it might be false for anything they know: they have never thrown themselves into the mental position of those who think differently from them, and considered what such persons may have to say; and consequently they do not, in any proper sense of the word, know the doctrine which they themselves profess. They do not know those parts of it which explain and justify the remainder; the considerations which show that a fact which seemingly conflicts with another is reconcilable with it, or that, of two apparently

strong reasons, one and not the other ought to be preferred. All that part of the truth which turns the scale, and decides the judgment of a completely informed mind, they are strangers to; nor is it ever really known, but to those who have attended equally and impartially to both sides, and endeavored to see the reasons of both in the strongest light. So essential is this discipline to a real understanding of moral and human subjects, that if opponents of all important truths do not exist, it is indispensable to imagine them, and supply them with the strongest arguments which the most skilful devil's advocate can conjure up.[6]

John Rawls and Justice as Fairness

Studied by economists and political scientists as well as by philosophers, John Rawls's *A Theory of Justice* (1971) is one of the most influential philosophical works of the second half of the twentieth century. John Rawls (b. 1921) teaches at Harvard University. Drawing together ideas he had discussed in a series of important articles beginning with "Justice As Fairness" (1958), Rawls explained that his book would "generalize and carry to a higher order of abstraction the traditional theory of the social contract."[7] He argued that, as John Locke and others developed that theory, the best way to look at the formation of government is to conceive it as originating from agreements about rights and duties that are mutually reached by persons electing to join a social body. Stressing the importance of respect for individuals and his belief that no decision can be right unless it can be universalized, Kant also made important contributions to the social contract tradition in political philosophy. Rawls believed, however, that there was more to say on these matters. Specifically, he wanted to outline the ingredients essential to a contemporary society that is at once democratic and just.

The Veil of Ignorance

Rawls maintains that the concept of a **social contract** should draw attention to theoretical considerations more than to historical debates about how a particular society or form of government came to be. In particular, he contends that when we think about a social contract, we should be trying to discern "the principles that free and rational persons concerned to further their own interests would accept in an initial position of equality as defining the fundamental terms of their association" (p. 11). These principles, Rawls believes, are ones that would promote what he calls "justice as fairness." From a very early age, people are sensitive about being treated fairly or unfairly. So when Rawls speaks about "justice as fairness," he can be confident that his starting point relates to our common shared experiences. But not everyone agrees on what "fairness" means, and Rawls attempts to remedy that situation.

What Rawls wants us to consider is nothing less than the most fundamental rules we would choose to abide by—individually and collectively—if we acted rationally in a "hypothetical situation of equal liberty" (p. 12). What does this situation entail? For one thing, it calls on us to set aside our particular circumstances and to behave as if we were ignorant of them. The point is this: if we are going to arrive at decisions establishing principles of justice, we do well not to consider, at least for the moment, certain historical and social facts about our specific situation. Rather, Rawls argues, we ought to think as if "no one knows his place in society, his class position or social status, nor does any one know his fortune in the distribution of natural assets and abilities, his intelli-

gence, strength, and the like. . . . The principles of justice are chosen behind a **veil of ignorance**" (p. 12). That is, we start off as perfectly equal human persons.

If everybody is in the same position when the deliberations begin, there is fairness at that level. Rawls believes that a rational inquiry starting from that base will extend fairness further, because the persons who are making the decisions will naturally take into account the understanding that they will continue to desire fair treatment no matter what their place in society might turn out to be. According to Rawls, one especially attractive ingredient in this approach is that the parties to these deliberations can be highly self-regarding. That is, they can think in terms of their self-interest, which in this case does not result in a Hobbesian war of all against all, because no one knows in advance what his or her particular situation may turn out to be. On the contrary, in what Rawls calls the "**original position**," reflection about our self-interest will naturally lead to "justice as fairness" because each of us will want to maximize our own life chances.

What Are the Principles of Justice?

Many philosophers are swayed by Mill's utilitarianism. One way or another, they argue that the basic ethical principle is that we should do what produces the greatest good for the greatest number of persons. Rawls contends, however, that such a principle would not emerge from his "original position." In that situation, "since each desires to protect his interests, his capacity to advance his conception of the good, no one has a reason to acquiesce in an enduring loss for himself in order to bring about a greater balance of satisfaction" (p. 14). Expediency may dictate that some people must lose if others are to prosper, but Rawls's vision of **justice** requires personal and public decision making that results in gains for all. This does not mean, however, that it is unjust for some people to obtain greater benefits than others. The test is whether such inequalities enhance everyone's existence.

Here, Rawls emphasizes, we can see the connection between the theory of justice and the theory of rational choice. The latter entails that people will choose what is best for them. Rawls thinks, therefore, that people will want to have opportunities and, specifically, opportunities to advance their well-being. But a rational person will also recognize that human existence involves limits and constraints. Not everyone, for example, can actually be the richest or the most powerful of persons. It can also be true that some people might amass great wealth and power while many others are impoverished and miserable. Rational choices made from the "original position" would try to find a middle ground that maximizes both opportunities for individuals and benefits for all.

Rawls wants us to arrive at what he calls **"reflective equilibrium"** (p. 20). Even in the original position, he knows that much fine-tuning will be required to derive principles of justice to which all parties will gladly assent. But he hopes that we can achieve a mutual adjustment between a statement of basic principles and our considered judgments about what fair treatment does and does not entail. Rawls is not sure that everyone will agree with his findings, but after exploring several provisional formulations, he offers two fundamental rules, as follows:

1. Each person is to have an equal right to the most extensive system of equal liberties compatible with a similar system of liberty for all.

2. Social and economic inequalities are to be arranged so that they are both:
   a. to the greatest benefit of the least advantaged, consistent with the just savings principle, and
   b. attached to offices and positions open to all under conditions of fair equality or opportunity. (P. 302.)

Rawls accompanies these principles with two "priority rules." They indicate, first, that he places a premium on equal liberty. This is essential for human dignity and mutual respect and is not to be sacrificed except for the sake of life itself. But there is also a check on the inequalities that liberty will breed. It consists of the commitment that these differences must themselves ensure **fairness.** That is, Rawls's second priority rule explains that inequality of opportunity should enhance opportunity for those who have the least of it. Your advantage should help the disadvantaged; otherwise it cannot be just. Moreover, just as there must be savings to ensure life for future human generations—the savings principle—those same savings should also "on balance mitigate the burden of those bearing this hardship" (p. 303). In other words, efficiency in achieving the maximum welfare for the greatest number in the future does not simply take precedence over fair treatment for everyone now living.

What Does Rawls's Theory Accomplish?

John Rawls sums up his position with the following "general conception":

> All social primary goods—liberty and opportunity, income and wealth, and the bases of self-respect—are to be distributed equally unless an unequal distribution of any or all of these good is to the advantage of the least favored. (P. 303.)

With these formulations, Rawls makes good his desire "to generalize and carry to a higher order of abstraction the traditional theory of social contract" (p. viii). But something more has been accomplished, too. To see this, remember that Rawls admits that not everyone will agree with his precise formulations of the principles of justice or even with his portrayal of the "original position." Indeed, Rawls concludes *A Theory of Justice* by recalling that the hypothetical nature of the original position invites the criticism that it is so remote from the real world as to be irrelevant. His answer to that charge, however, is as bold as it is simple: "The conditions embodied in the description of this situation are ones that we do in fact accept. Or if we do not, then we can be persuaded to do so by philosophical considerations" (p. 587). What Rawls has done is to help us understand the conditions for moral choice, what it means to be rationally moral. Unless we strive in that direction, our likelihood of using philosophical considerations to make right decisions is severely undermined. Perhaps life seems farthest from being reasonable when we feel that things are not fair for us. Conversely, where fairness prevails, it is hard to contend that life is unreasonable. To find out what is rational and fair, Rawls believes, involves a mixture of perspectives.

Rawls closes by urging that the most important decision to make is to learn to look at the human situation from the perspective of eternity. What he means by that concept is not that we should try to stand outside the world or that we should try to assume God's view. Rather, we should try to "bring together into one scheme all individual perspectives and arrive together at regulative principles that can be affirmed by everyone as he lives by them, each from his own standpoint" (p. 587). Rawls is under no illusion that people will actually succeed in doing these things; but to the extent that they fail, the world is at risk. Thus, one way to make a **right** decision is to strive to do so as John Rawls suggests. He says of his human perspective on eternity that "purity of heart, if one could attain it, would be to see clearly and to act with grace and self-command from this point of view" (p. 587).

Rawls puts our moral consideration in the setting of society and the human community. The decisions societies make effect and limit the options that are open to us, as well as how and whether we are able to reach a practical decision. As we consider what rules to use to make our decisions, then, it is important to project how society (as well as God and our inner condition) will affect the outcome. As you debate with yourself over whether you should become, for example, a doctor or a poet or a banker, is part of your decision determined by how you think that choice of yours will affect society (or your family)? Or can your decision be a totally individual affair? Keep those questions in mind as you think further about John Rawls's rules for justice, as set down in 1971 in *A Theory of Justice*.

THE ROLE OF JUSTICE

Justice is the first virtue of social institutions, as truth is of systems of thought. A theory however elegant and economical must be rejected or revised if it is untrue: likewise laws and institutions no matter how efficient and well-arranged must be reformed or abolished if they are unjust. Each person possesses an inviolability founded on justice that even the welfare of society as a whole cannot override. For this reason justice denies that the loss of freedom for some is made right by a greater good shared by others. It does not allow that the sacrifices imposed on a few are outweighed by the larger sum of advantages enjoyed by many. Therefore in a just society the liberties of equal citizenship are taken as settled; the rights secured by justice are not subject to political bargaining or to the calculus of social interests. The only thing that permits us to acquiesce in an erroneous theory is the lack of a better one; analogously, an injustice is tolerable only when it is necessary to avoid an even greater injustice. Being first virtues of human activities, truth and justice are uncompromising.

These propositions seem to express our intuitive conviction of the primacy of justice. No doubt they are expressed too strongly. In any event I wish to inquire whether these contentions or others similar to them are sound, and if so how they can be accounted for. To this end it is necessary to work out a theory of justice in the light of which these assertions can be interpreted and assessed. I shall begin by considering the role of the principles of justice. Let us assume, to fix ideas, that a society is a more or less self-sufficient association of persons who in their relations to one another recognize certain rules of conduct as binding and who for the most part act in accordance with them. Suppose further that these rules specify a system of cooperation designed to advance the good of those taking part in it. Then, although a society is a cooperative venture for mutual advantage, it is typically marked by a conflict as well as by an identity of interests. There is an identity of interests since social cooperation makes possible a better life for all than any would have if each were to live solely by his own efforts. There is a conflict of interests since persons are not indifferent as to how the greater benefits produced by their collaboration are distributed, for in order to pursue their ends they each prefer a larger to a lesser share. A set of principles is required for choosing among the various social arrangements which determine this division of advantages and for underwriting an agreement on the proper distributive shares. These principles are the principles of social justice: they provide a way of assigning rights and duties in the basic institutions of society and they define the appropriate distribution of the benefits and burdens of social cooperation.

Now let us say that a society is well-ordered when it is not only designed to advance the good of its members but when it is also effectively regulated by a public conception of justice. That is, it is a society in which (1) everyone accepts and knows that the others accept the same principles of justice, and (2) the basic social institutions generally satisfy and are generally known to satisfy these principles. In this case while men may put forth excessive demands on one another, they nevertheless acknowl-

edge a common point of view from which their claims may be adjudicated. If men's inclination to self-interest makes their vigilance against one another necessary, their public sense of justice makes their secure association together possible. Among individuals with disparate aims and purposes, a shared conception of justice establishes the bonds of civic friendship; the general desire for justice limits the pursuit of other ends. One may think of a public conception of justice as constituting the fundamental charter of a well-ordered human association.

Existing societies are of course seldom well-ordered in this sense, for what is just and unjust is usually in dispute. Men disagree about which principles should define the basic terms of their association. Yet we may still say, despite this disagreement, that they each have a conception of justice. That is, they understand the need for, and they are prepared to affirm, a characteristic set of principles for assigning basic rights and duties and for determining what they take to be the proper distribution of the benefits and burdens of social cooperation. Thus it seems natural to think of the concept of justice as distinct from the various conceptions of justice and as being specified by the role which these different sets of principles, these different conceptions, have in common.* Those who hold different conceptions of justice can, then, still agree that institutions are just when no arbitrary distinctions are made between persons in the assigning of basic rights and duties and when the rules determine a proper balance between competing claims to the advantages of social life. Men can agree to this description of just institutions since the notions of an arbitrary distinction and of a proper balance, which are included in the concept of justice, are left open for each to interpret according to the principles of justice that he accepts. These principles single out which similarities and differences among persons are relevant in determining rights and duties and they

---

*Here I follow H.L.A. Hart, *The Concept of Law* (Oxford: Clarendon, 1961), pp. 155–59.

specify which division of advantages is appropriate. Clearly this distinction between the concept and the various conceptions of justice settles no important questions. It simply helps to identify the role of the principles of social justice.

Some measure of agreement in conceptions of justice is, however, not the only prerequisite for a viable human community. There are other fundamental social problems, in particular those of coordination, efficiency, and stability. Thus the plans of individuals need to be fitted together so that their activities are compatible with one another and they can all be carried through without anyone's legitimate expectations being severely disappointed. Moreover, the execution of these plans should lead to the achievement of social ends in ways that are efficient and consistent with justice. And finally, the scheme of social cooperation must be stable: it must be more or less regularly complied with and its basic rules willingly acted upon; and when infractions occur, stabilizing forces should exist that prevent further violations and tend to restore the arrangement. Now it is evident that these three problems are connected with that of justice. In the absence of a certain measure of agreement on what is just and unjust, it is clearly more difficult for individuals to coordinate their plans efficiently in order to ensure that mutually beneficial arrangements are maintained. Distrust and resentment corrode the ties of civility, and suspicion and hostility tempt men to act in ways they would otherwise avoid. So while the distinctive role of conceptions of justice is to specify basic rights and duties and to determine the appropriate distributive shares, the way in which a conception does this is bound to affect the problems of efficiency, coordination, and stability. We cannot, in general, assess a conception of justice by its distributive role alone, however useful this role may be in identifying the concept of justice. We must take into account its wider connections; for even though justice has a certain priority, being the most important virtue of institutions, it is still true that, other things equal, one conception of justice is preferable to another when its broader consequences are more desirable. (Pp. 3–6.)

THE MAIN IDEA OF THE THEORY OF JUSTICE

My aim is to present a conception of justice which generalizes and carries to a higher level of abstraction the familiar theory of the social contract as found, say, in Locke, Rousseau, and Kant. In order to do this we are not to think of the original contract as one to enter a particular society or to set up a particular form of government. Rather, the guiding idea is that the principles of justice for the basic structure of society are the object of the original agreement. They are the principles that free and rational persons concerned to further their own interests would accept in an initial position of equality as defining the fundamental terms of their association. These principles are to regulate all further agreements; they specify the kinds of social cooperation that can be entered into and the forms of government that can be established. This way of regarding the principles of justice I shall call justice as fairness.

Thus we are to imagine that those who engage in social cooperation choose together, in one joint act, the principles which are to assign basic rights and duties and to determine the division of social benefits. Men are to decide in advance how they are to regulate their claims against one another and what is to be the foundation charter of their society. Just as each person must decide by rational reflection what constitutes his good, that is, the system of ends which it is rational for him to pursue, so a group of persons must decide once and for all what is to count among them as just and unjust. The choice which rational men would make in this hypothetical situation of equal liberty, assuming for the present that this choice problem has a solution, determines the principles of justice.

In justice as fairness the original position of equality corresponds to the state of nature in the traditional theory of the social contract. This original position is not, of course, thought of as an actual historical state of affairs, much less as a primitive condition of culture. It is understood as a purely hypothetical situation characterized so as to lead to a certain conception of justice. Among the essential features of this situation is that no one knows his place in society, his class position or social status, nor does anyone know his fortune in the distribution of natural assets and abilities, his intelligence, strength, and the like. I shall even assume that the parties do not know their conceptions of the good or their special psychological propensities. The principles of justice are chosen behind a veil of ignorance. This ensures that no one is advantaged or disadvantaged in the choice of principles by the outcome of natural chance or the contingency of social circumstances. Since all are similarly situated and no one is able to design principles to favor his particular condition, the principles of justice are the result of a fair agreement or bargain. For given the circumstances of the original position, the symmetry of everyone's relations to each other, this initial situation is fair between individuals as moral persons, that is, as rational beings with their own ends and capable, I shall assume, of a sense of justice. The original position is, one might say, the appropriate initial status quo, and thus the fundamental agreements reached in it are fair. This explains the propriety of the name "justice as fairness": it conveys the idea that the principles of justice are agreed to in an initial situation that is fair. The name does not mean that the concepts of justice and fairness are the same, any more than the phrase "poetry as metaphor" means that the concepts of poetry and metaphor are the same.

Justice as fairness begins, as I have said, with one of the most general of all choices which persons might make together, namely, with the choice of the first principles of a conception of justice which is to regulate all subsequent criticism and reform of institutions. Then, having chosen a conception of justice, we can suppose that they are to choose a constitution and a legislature to enact laws, and so on, all in accordance with the principles of justice initially agreed upon. Our social situation is just if it is such that by this sequence of hypothetical agreements we would have contracted into the general system of rules which defines it. Moreover, assuming that the original position does determine a set of principles (that is, that a particular conception of justice would be chosen), it will then be true that whenever social institutions satisfy these principles those engaged in them can say to one another that they are cooperating on terms to which they would agree if they were free and equal persons whose relations with respect to one another were fair. They could all view their arrangements as meeting the stipulations which they would acknowledge in an initial situation that embodies widely accepted and reasonable constraints on the choice of principles. The general recognition of this fact would provide the basis for a public acceptance of the corresponding principles of justice. No society can, of course, be a scheme of cooperation which men enter voluntarily in a literal sense; each person finds himself placed at birth in some particular position in some particular society, and the nature of this position materially affects his life prospects. Yet a society satisfying the principles of justice as fairness comes as close as a society can to being a voluntary scheme, for it meets the principles which free and equal persons would assent to under circumstances that are fair. In this sense its members are autonomous and the obligations they recognize self-imposed. (Pp. 11–13.)

Summary

If we seek rules to guide our decisions and actions, we need to ask to what extent they will be universal (applicable to everyone without distinction) or individual (ours alone to determine for ourselves). Aristotle urged us to follow general rules of conduct because they are the route to happiness, but he recognized that virtuous action cannot be detailed in advance. There will be variations from person to person and from situation to situation. Although Kant based his rules on duty much more than Aristotle, the German philosopher also believed that there are universal rules for conduct. Again they do not specify action in advance of our reasoning about the problems we face, but we do have basic guidelines that we ought to follow in deciding what we should do.

John Stuart Mill wanted individual freedom of judgment, but when he advocated seeking the greatest happiness for the greatest number, he also recognized the need for expert opinion to solve disputes about how this ought to be achieved. Once more the moral theory developed by a philosopher does not decide cases for us automatically, but it does provide a way to think about what ought to occur. John Rawls has built on the views of Aristotle, Kant, and Mill but tries to go beyond them with his "original position," which he hopes will produce shared agreement about the basic rules we ought to heed. His theory spreads out the options with which we have to reckon.

All the philosophers considered in this chapter say "Yes, there are rules to govern our actions." They do so with good reason, too, because we cannot expect to live as human beings should unless we have sound moral guidance. But the complication is that the philosophers do not all agree about what the norms are and how they should work. So as we conclude this chapter, we need to face the problem posed in the one that follows: "How do I make right decisions?" For that question applies not only with respect to a given set of rules but also with respect to deciding which set of rules or combination of them best points in the right direction.

GLOSSARY

"benevolence principle" the principle of John Stuart Mill's **utilitarianism** that asserts that while pleasure or satisfaction is the fundamental aim of an ethical system, such a system is incomplete unless it also aims at the "greatest satisfaction for the greatest possible number." See also **hedonism, universality.**

categorical imperative Kant's term for the type of **imperative** that applies universally, regardless of the particular facts of a given case, and without reference to the particular interests of the participants in a given situation. Kant believes that the authority of such a principle derives from the essential nature of human beings as rational creatures, and his specific idea of the kind of proposition possessing such an unconditional authority echoes the Christian doctrine of "doing unto others as you would have them do unto

you." In Kant's terms, it is always our absolute **duty** to respect certain absolute **rights** of others; these absolute rights he expresses in terms of the right a person has not to be used as a **means** to an **end.**

deontological from the Greek *dein,* meaning "duty," a term describing a theory of ethics that takes the concept of **duty** to be central and indispensable; in such a theory the understanding of "good" reflects recognition of the duty to adhere to rational principles in deciding how to regulate our conduct.

duty an action that must be performed, either because a person has freely undertaken an **obligation** to do the action, or because a person accepts the authority of a **rule** prescribing that action. Our acceptance of the authority of a rule may be tacit, as in the case of the **social contract;** coerced, as when we follow a law out of the fear of punishment for disobedience; or free, explicit, and rational, as Kant believes must be true in the case of the categorical imperative.

end a thing or state of affairs considered as a practical objective, as an outcome that is desired; the purpose for which an action or series of actions is performed.

ethics from the Greek words incorporating the sense of moral or customary, the branch of philosophy concerned with principles, standards, norms, and ideals of conduct, and with concepts of good, bad, right, and wrong as they function to regulate and determine human behavior.

fairness the key aspect of justice in any given social order under the theory of John Rawls; the term denotes the goal of setting up a system for the distribution of such necessary goods, rights, and privileges as a society can bestow on its citizens as *equally* as possible, regardless of the identity of those who control the power and authority to make that distribution. For Rawls, this means setting up the system so that no particular persons will be able to satisfy their own self-interest simply because they occupy certain positions in the system, without deserving or earning the compensation and privileges that such positions bring. From this it follows that fairness implies *equality of opportunity,* such that people of differing degrees of talent can compete without unjustly imposed disadvantages for positions of different value within the system.

golden mean in Aristotle's ethical theory, the concept of an ideal balance among the various personal characteristics it is possible to have; the avoidance of both an excess and a deficiency of such characteristics so as to remain at harmony with oneself and one's fellow citizens.

good the ideal state of perfection, satisfaction, harmony, or justice, which ethical systems are aimed at bringing about within the sphere of human communal life. What distinguishes ethical theories from one another is often the content attributed to the notion of the "good": for Aristotle, this consists in the achievement of happiness, while for Kant it means the fulfillment of duties; for Mill it is a social ideal consisting of the maximum of pleasure and satisfaction provided for the majority of citizens, while for Rawls it means the fairest possible distribution of the rights, privileges, and commodities that are necessary for a life free from want and conducive to positive self-expression.

"good will" in Kant's theory, the ideal standard against which human conduct is measured, in which the intention or "will" lying behind actions, rather than the actions' actual consequences, is the proper object of moral concern and judgment. This notion of the content of ethical judgment is often contrasted with what are called *consequentialist* theories of ethics, of which **utilitarianism** is an example. In these theories, the outcome of actions is the primary object of moral judgment.

happiness the concept that Aristotle believed formed the contents of the "Good." Aristotle's theory of happiness defines it as the outcome of a life lived consistently with the **virtues.**

hedonism a type of ethical doctrine that equates what is *good* with what is simply pleasurable or gratifying to people and holds that the fundamental motivations of human life are the pursuit of pleasure and the avoidance of pain.

hypothetical imperative Kant's term for an **imperative** that is binding only in relation to the achievement of some particular end or purpose; a proposition expressing what ought to be done if a particular result is desired. Hypothetical imperatives form the majority of practical judgments but are inherently moral only insofar as they do not trespass on the absolute limit on action represented by the **categorical** imperative.

imperative Kant's term for a **prescriptive** proposition, ethical principle, law, or **rule** governing action, one that specifies what it is a person's duty to do in a given situation. Besides recognizing that such propositions exist in our language, Kant believed that some imperatives have the force of being necessarily binding on all rational agents because they are necessarily implied by the idea of human freedom, which makes the experience of a sense of moral responsibility possible. See also **categorical imperative, hypothetical imperative.**

justice a moral concept that concerns the actions of those responsible for governing a society. In Rawls's theory, the quality of justice is linked with being *fair,* with acting so as to preserve the equality of opportunity and the equal distribution of socially important rights and commodities in the constitution of the laws and legal practices of a given society.

law a customary practice, or **norm,** which is taken to be universally binding on all members of a community or social order as a condition of membership in that body. The social institution in which such customs are embodied, recorded, interpreted, and applied to particular cases concerning the conduct of citizens. In Kant's theory, respect for the idea of law *as such* is a necessary outcome of being a rational agent, and therefore the ground of the sense of obligation or duty in general. See also **obligation, universality.**

means a thing considered in its expediency, as a tool that might be useful in the process of attaining an **end** or desired outcome.

norm a standard of behavior or judgment consisting in the common beliefs and practices of a group of people and expressed in the form of *value* concepts ("good," "wrong," etc.).

obligation an action whose performance is felt by someone to be necessary, whose nonperformance is felt to be unthinkable or wrong. A duty to perform an action incurred by a promise or a debt.

"original position" in Rawls's theory of justice, a hypothetical point of view from which rational agents would deliberate about the way to set up a social system to maximize its fairness. In the "original position," rational agents are denied knowledge of any facts concerning their own position within the projected society, thus ensuring that their

deliberations are free of any bias connected with their desire to exploit that particular position.

reflective equilibrium in Rawls's theory, a term referring to an ideal state of mutual assent among members of a society over what principles will produce the highest degree of justice in practice. This notion corresponds to the ideal of universal assent in the theory of the **social contract.**

right morally proper or just, as in "that was the *right* thing to do"; in another sense, a justified claim to be permitted to act in a certain way, to pursue certain ends, or to expect certain behavior of others, as in "he has the *right* to do (or believe or expect) that thing."

rule a prescriptive guideline specifying what can or is to be done by a person under certain conditions, just as the rules of a game specify what each player is to do, and when they are to do it, during the course of play.

social contract a theory of the justification of the right of a state to govern, based on the assumption that citizens permit such authority by their explicit or tacit consent, and that such authority implies a reciprocal obligation of the state to recognize certain rights for its citizens.

teleological the type of ethical theory that, like Aristotle's theory, defines the good in ethics in terms of a human *telos,* or characteristic set of purposes and ends, and emphasizes the consequences of actions.

universality in Kant's theory and in Mill's utilitarianism, the property that moral principles require for their validity: namely, that they be applicable to all persons at all times without exception. Rawls's theory of justice is also mainly concerned with the problem of formulating principles that possess genuine universality.

utilitarianism the ethical doctrine, established by Bentham and elaborated by John Stuart Mill, that takes the object of moral judgment to be the consequences of actions, the contents of the good to be pleasure or satisfaction, and the aim of moral agency to be the production of the most pleasure among the largest possible number of persons.

"veil of ignorance" Rawls's term for the limitation on the types of knowledge available to rational agents in the "original position" so as to ensure that their decisions will apply the principle of fairness as universally as possible.

virtue in Aristotle's ethical theory, a quality of character, consisting of a settled, habitual way of responding to particular situations, that tends in the long run to lead to a state of harmony and moderation in human affairs.

STUDY QUESTIONS

1. Will we all agree on the nature of Aristotle's "mean" with respect to a specific action, or do you think that "the mean" is more ambiguous? Defend your position.

2. How easy or important is it to recognize outstandingly virtuous persons to be used as role models?

3. Do you agree with Kant that, despite our differences on life's particulars, we share universally a sense of "ought"?

4. Do you believe that you have a sense of obligation? If so, was it essentially learned from experience, or do you think Kant is correct to say that this sense is a "given" that structures all moral experience and makes possible an experience one perceives as "moral?"

5. Do you desire "the greatest happiness for the greatest number"? Why or why not?

6. What problems do you see in trying to put Mill's principle of utilitarianism into practice?

7. Would you agree to be a party to Rawls's "original position" and to let the decisions reached there be morally binding on you? Why or why not?

8. If you put yourself behind Rawls's "veil of ignorance," would you reason in the way he thinks you should?

9. Can Rawls's two principles of justice actually help you to decide what is right?

10. Can you state Rawls's theory of "justice as fairness" in your own terms? Do you accept this account?

11. Of the four theories discussed in this chapter, which appeals to you most? Why?

NOTES

[1] Aristotle, *Nicomachean Ethics* (1095a), trans. W. D. Ross, in *The Basic Works of Aristotle*, ed. Richard McKeon (New York: Random House, 1941), p. 937.

[2] Immanuel Kant, *Foundations of the Metaphysics of Morals*, trans. Lewis White Beck (Indianapolis: Bobbs-Merrill, 1978), p. 3. Copyright © 1978, 1985 by Macmillan Publishing Company. Reprinted by permission.

[3] John Stuart Mill, *Utilitarianism*, ed. George Sher (Indianapolis: Hackett, 1979), p. 4.

[4] John Stuart Mill, *On Liberty*, in *Essential Works of John Stuart Mill*, ed. Max Lerner (New York: Bantam Books, 1965), pp. 258–59.

[5] Mill, *Utilitarianism*, pp. 7–12.

[6] Mill, *On Liberty*, in *Essential Works*, pp. 264–66 and 287–88.

[7] John Rawls, *A Theory of Justice* (Cambridge, Mass.: Belknap Press of Harvard University Press, 1971), p. viii. © 1971 by the President and Fellows of Harvard College. Reprinted by permission of Harvard University Press and Oxford University Press.

CHAPTER EIGHT

How Do I Make Right Decisions?

*M*en and women involved in an active life often think philosophers are impractical and therefore not of much use in everyday decision making. In truth, philosophers are themselves divided on this question—just as they are on nearly every issue. Some, often called "idealists," think the business of the philosopher is to deal only with intellectual, speculative matters. Others, such as the American pragmatist, William James, feel very strongly that philosophy should speak to "real issues" and help people with the decisions they face in everyday life. In this chapter, we take a diverse group of authors and try to show how each deals with practical decision making.

Some of the philosophers we will discuss wrote about ethics and might therefore seem to be good candidates to instruct us on how to make a decision. Much to the disappointment of many beginning students in philosophy, however, ethical theory as a subject is often just that—theory, rather than an attempt to solve practical problems. Two of the philosophers we will present, Augustine and Kierkegaard, are also theologians. But wait and see how such dissimilar thinkers approach practical decision making. Perhaps their very diversity will illuminate the issue for you.

Basic to philosophy is the conviction that its primary task is to help clarify questions,

not necessarily to provide answers. Since the time of Socrates, philosophers have been convinced that one reason we have trouble making decisions—as all of us do at times—is that the questions we face have not been clearly defined and the crucial terms at issue are ambiguous. In Plato's *Republic*, for example, the argument is over how to secure justice in society. Plato wrote his dialogue to show that the various persons in the discussion disagree primarily because each uses a different meaning for "justice." Sound decisions, advised Plato, cannot be made until clarity about the meaning for that term is obtained. It is, of course, the aim of this whole book, not simply this chapter, to try to help the serious student clarify such troubling questions. Philosophy cannot always resolve these for you, but it may improve your decision making by showing you how to sort out the issues you face.

Epicurus and the Goodness of Pleasure

From the origin of Western philosophy, as part of their effort to answer the question "What should I do?", thinkers have raised the question "What is the good in life?" An early example is the Greek philosopher Epicurus (341–270 B.C.), whose teachings were

EPICURUS 341–270 B.C.

as "the state wherein the body is free from pain and the mind from anxiety," Epicurus did insist that pleasure is the highest good, but the way of living he recommended was actually much more austere than the popular label "epicurean" suggests (p. 57).

Anticipating David Hume, Epicurus argued that we should "use our sensations as the foundations of all our investigations."[2] In so doing, Epicurus and Lucretius found our world to be one of unceasing change, but they also noted repetitions of uniform patterns within which that change occurred. The limited nature of change suggested that nothing comes from nothing and nothing returns to nothing. To deny those propositions, they contended, would eliminate all boundaries and make the nature of change unintelligible. As for what does exist, Epicurus and Lucretius agreed that reality consists of **atoms** moving in a void. These varied atoms are in motion and account for the enduring quality of existence. Their movements produce interactions, creating the changes we experience. Human beings are also composed of atoms. A man or a woman comes into existence only when the necessary conditions have been met. Nature gives us life, and, although neither immortality nor a special destiny awaits us after death, we can learn to live well in the time that is ours. This account of the origin of all things is fundamental to Epicurean views on goodness and pleasure, as we shall see.

later spread abroad in the Roman world by Lucretius (99–55 B.C.). Lucretius wrote a major philosophical work in verse, *On the Nature of Things*. Most of the writings of Epicurus are lost, but we do know that he established a philosophical school in Athens where he stressed the value of human friendship and taught that the study of philosophy is "the means for securing happiness."[1] Sometimes we call a person fond of luxury and sensuous pleasure, especially eating and drinking, an **"epicurean."** Defining **pleasure**

The Bidding of Our Own Hearts

Epicurus taught that no event occurs unless other events precede it in a causal series. Together with the image of atoms falling through space in uniform patterns, that principle appears to lead to the conclusion that human life is determined as cause and effect follow upon each other in unbroken regularity. Epicurus was quite satisfied with such an outcome. It violated his sense of order to think that indeterminacy and chance could be part of our experience. But to escape complete determinism, he adopted the doctrine that atoms sometimes "swerve," thus breaking their regular patterns to allow us a sense of freedom. It fell to Lucretius to elaborate this suggestion. He proposed that some atoms, which are integral parts of human persons, have a self-controlling autonomy that enables conscious choice and moral judgment to be free. Lucretius put the issue this way:

> If all movement is always interconnected, the new arising from the old in a determinate order . . . what is the source of the free will possessed by living things . . . that will power snatched from the fates whereby we follow the path along which we are severally led by pleasure, swerving from our course at no set time or place but at the bidding of our own hearts?[3]

In addition to the impacts of atoms colliding in space, he concluded, there must be an "inborn power" that makes it possible for us to choose our goals in life and to make moral judgments.

Although Epicurus held that the universe "has always been such as it now is, and so it shall always be," neither he nor Lucretius asserted a complete determinism.[4] Their theories about swerving atoms, however, do not answer every question about our ability to choose the life we want. How, for instance, did Lucretius know that his "inborn power" was not itself determined so that one's feeling of freedom was nothing more than a feeling? He didn't. Nevertheless, Epicurus and Lucretius did recognize that we human beings possess a feeling of freedom and engage in a search for the good in life that must be reckoned with. Moreover, they raised many of the right questions in trying to explain what happens when we do "the bidding of our own hearts." Epicurus thought the first step was to train ourselves to evaluate the options before us carefully as we work for happiness in life.

Should Pleasure Be Our Guide?

The future, said Epicurus, "is neither ours nor wholly not ours."[5] Experience contains unexpected happenings that are fortuitous or undesirable, and we must cope with them. Philosophy comes to our aid by forcing us to take seriously some basic teachings about desire, pleasure, and pain. For example, Epicurus wrote:

> You must consider that of the desires some are natural, some are vain, and of those that are natural, some are necessary, others only natural. Of the necessary desires, some are necessary for happiness, some for the ease of the body, some for life itself. The man who has a perfect knowledge of this will know how to make his every choice or rejection tend toward gaining health of body and peace of mind, since this is the final end of the blessed life. For to gain this end, namely, freedom from pain and fear, we do everything. . . . For this reason we say that pleasure is the beginning and the end of the blessed life. We recognize pleasure as the first and natural good; starting from pleasure we accept or reject; and we return to this as we judge every good thing, trusting this feeling of pleasure as our guide. (P. 55.)

Now you should understand why Epicurus thinks we need first to know the laws that govern the natural world so that we can pursue the life of pleasure in the context of the natural laws governing our existence. Pleasure blindly pursued can be disastrous.

Where pleasure and pain are concerned, mastering the art of choosing well is, however, never easy. Not every pleasure, Epicurus went on to say, ought to be chosen. For example, the use of cocaine produces pleasure, but this drug is addictive and injurious and can be deadly. Likewise, although every pain is an evil, not all pain is to be avoided. Some is a necessary means to achieve the highest good. A toothache gives us a sign that we need to visit a dentist. To achieve our goal, Epicurus said, "We must not resist Nature but obey her."[6] We do this when we satisfy "the necessary desires and also those bodily desires that do not harm while sternly rejecting those that are harmful" (p. 67). Such prudence, he argued, reflects a wise use of the limited options we have. It also extends our pleasure by preventing enslavement to desires that will destroy our peace of mind.

"Freedom," Epicurus claimed, "is the greatest fruit of self-sufficiency" (p. 72). He warns us not to become enslaved by desire. However, one must also ask whether the equation of goodness with pleasure is sufficient to guide us. For instance, even with the distinctions Epicurus made, what would he do if someone disagreed with his analysis of a particular pleasure? If pleasure is the greatest good and I insist that some of the pleasures he calls unnatural are really essential for me, can Epicurus combat that claim on his own terms? Or must he set aside his pleasure criterion and argue from other standards? Moreover, are things such as truthtelling, justice, and courage to be pursued if and only if they give pleasure, and are they to be set aside if they give pain? One rejoinder could be that in the long run these virtues actually do give pleasure of the profoundest kind, and so pain endured for their sake is worth the cost. But that line of argument glosses over our difficulty in finding a neat fit between virtue and pleasure.

At times virtuous people suffer most, such as Job in the Bible, and Epicurus envisioned no life beyond death in which they might be compensated for their trouble. Epicurus and Lucretius start us on a quest for the good as pleasure, but insofar as they confine our goal within boundaries established by pleasure

and pain, they leave us to ask "Is pleasure a satisfactory criterion for the good life?" As you read Epicurus' "Letter to Menoeceus," see whether you agree that pleasure as the good, plus our knowledge of natural laws, offers us a sufficient guide to make the right decisions that lead to the best life.

INTRODUCTION

Epicurus to Menoeceus, greeting.

Let no young man delay the study of philosophy, and let no old man become weary of it; for it is never too early nor too late to care for the well-being of the soul. The man who says that the season for this study has not yet come or is already past is like the man who says it is too early or too late for happiness. Therefore, both the young and the old should study philosophy, the former so that as he grows old he may still retain the happiness of youth in his pleasant memories of the past, the latter so that although he is old he may at the same time be young by virtue of his fearlessness of the future. We must therefore study the means of securing happiness, since if we have it we have everything, but if we lack it we do everything in order to gain it.

BASIC TEACHINGS

The Gods THE GODS EXIST; BUT IT IS IMPIOUS TO ACCEPT THE COMMON BELIEFS ABOUT THEM. THEY HAVE NO CONCERN WITH MEN. Practice and study without ceasing that which I was always teaching you, being assured that these are the first principles of the good life. After accepting god as the immortal and blessed being depicted by popular opinion, do not ascribe to him anything in addition that is alien to immortality or foreign to blessedness, but rather believe about him whatever can uphold his blessed immortality. The gods do indeed exist, for our perception of them is clear; but they are not such as the crowd imagines them to be, for most men do not retain the picture of the gods that they first receive. It is not the man who destroys the gods of popular belief who is impious, but he who describes the gods in the terms accepted by the many. For the opinions of the many about the gods are not perceptions but false suppositions. According to these popular suppositions, the gods send great evils to the wicked, great blessings [to the righteous], for they, being always well disposed to their own virtues, approve those who are like themselves, regarding as foreign all that is different.

Death PHILOSOPHY, SHOWING THAT DEATH IS THE END OF ALL CONSCIOUSNESS, RELIEVES US OF ALL FEAR OF DEATH. A LIFE THAT IS HAPPY IS BETTER THAN ONE THAT IS MERELY LONG. Accustom yourself to the belief that death is of no concern to us, since all good and evil lie in sensation and sensation ends with death. Therefore the true belief that death is nothing to us makes a mortal life happy, not by adding to it an infinite time, but by taking away the desire for immortality. For there is no reason why the man who is thoroughly assured that there is nothing to fear in death should find anything to fear in life. So, too, he is foolish who says that he fears death, not because it will be painful when it comes, but because the anticipation of it is painful; for that which is no burden when it is present gives pain to no purpose when it is anticipated. Death, the most dreaded of evils, is therefore of no concern to us; for while we exist death is not present, and when death is present we no longer exist. It is therefore nothing either to the living or to the dead since it is not present to the living, and the dead no longer are.

But men in general sometimes flee death as the greatest of evils, sometimes [long for it] as a relief from [the evils] of life. [The wise man neither renounces life] nor fears its end; for living does not offend him, nor does he suppose that not to live is in any way an evil. As he does not choose the food that is most in quantity but that which is most pleasant, so he does not seek the enjoyment of the longest life but of the happiest.

He who advises the young man to live well, the old man to die well, is foolish, not only because life is desirable, but also because

the art of living well and the art of dying well are one. Yet much worse is he who says that it is well not to have been born, but

> once born, be swift to pass through Hades' gates [Theognis]

If a man says this and really believes it, why does he not depart from life? Certainly the means are at hand for doing so if this really be his firm conviction. If he says it in mockery, he is regarded as a fool among those who do not accept his teaching.

Remember that the future is neither ours nor wholly not ours, so that we may neither count on it as sure to come nor abandon hope of it as certain not to be.

THE MORAL THEORY

Pleasure as the Motive THE NECESSARY DESIRES ARE FOR HEALTH OF BODY AND PEACE OF MIND; IF THESE ARE SATISFIED, THAT IS ENOUGH FOR THE HAPPY LIFE. You must consider that of the desires some are natural, some are vain, and of those that are natural, some are necessary, others only natural. Of the necessary desires, some are necessary for happiness, some for the ease of the body, some for life itself. The man who has a perfect knowledge of this will know how to make his every choice or rejection tend toward gaining health of body and peace [of mind], since this is the final end of the blessed life. For to gain this end, namely freedom from pain and fear, we do everything. When once this condition is reached, all the storm of the soul is stilled, since the creature need make no move in search of anything that is lacking, nor seek after anything else to make complete the welfare of the soul and the body. For we only feel the lack of pleasure when from its absence we suffer pain; [but when we do not suffer pain,] we no longer are in need of pleasure. For this reason we say that pleasure is the beginning and the end of the blessed life. We recognize pleasure as the first and natural good; starting from pleasure we accept or reject; and we return to this as we judge every good thing, trusting this feeling of pleasure as our guide.

Pleasures and Pains PLEASURE IS THE GREAT-EST GOOD; BUT SOME PLEASURES BRING PAIN, AND IN CHOOSING, WE MUST CONSIDER THIS. For the very reason that pleasure is the chief and the natural good, we do not choose every pleasure, but there are times when we pass by pleasures if they are outweighed by the hardships that follow; and many pains we think better than pleasures when a greater pleasure will come to us once we have undergone the long-continued pains. Every pleasure is a good since it has a nature akin to ours; nevertheless, not every pleasure is to be chosen. Just so, every pain is an evil, yet not every pain is of a nature to be avoided on all occasions. By measuring and by look-ing at advantages and disadvantages, it is proper to decide all these things; for under certain circumstances we treat the good as evil, and again, the evil as good.

Self-Sufficiency THE TRULY WISE MAN IS THE ONE WHO CAN BE HAPPY WITH A LITTLE. We regard self-sufficiency as a great good, not so that we may enjoy only a few things, but so that, if we do not have many, we may be satisfied with the few, being firmly per-suaded that they take the greatest pleasure in luxury who regard it as least needed, and that everything that is natural is easily pro-vided, while vain pleasures are hard to obtain. Indeed, simple sauces bring a plea-sure equal to that of lavish banquets if once the pain due to need is removed; and bread and water give the greatest pleasure when one who is in need consumes them. To be accustomed to simple and plain living is conducive to health and makes a man ready for the necessary tasks of life. It also makes us more ready for the enjoyment of luxury if at intervals we chance to meet with it, and it renders us fearless against fortune.

True Pleasure THE TRUEST HAPPINESS DOES NOT COME FROM ENJOYMENT OF PHYSICAL PLEASURES BUT FROM A SIMPLE LIFE, FREE FROM ANXIETY, WITH THE NORMAL PHYSICAL NEEDS SATISFIED. When we say that pleasure is the end, we do not mean the pleasure of the profligate or that which depends on physi-cal enjoyment—as some think who do not

understand our teachings, disagree with them, or give them an evil interpretation—but by pleasure we mean the state wherein the body is free from pain and the mind from anxiety. Neither continual drinking and dancing, nor sexual love, nor the enjoyment of fish and whatever else the luxurious table offers brings about the pleasant life; rather, it is produced by the reason which is sober, which examines the motive for every choice and rejection, and which drives away all those opinions through which the greatest tumult lays hold of the mind.

Prudence PRUDENCE OR PRACTICAL WISDOM SHOULD BE OUR GUIDE. Of all this the begin-ning and the chief good is **prudence**. For this reason prudence is more precious than philosophy itself. All the other virtues spring from it. It teaches that it is not possible to live pleasantly without at the same time liv-ing prudently, nobly, and justly, [nor to live prudently, nobly, and justly] without living pleasantly; for the virtues have grown up in close union with the pleasant life, and the pleasant life cannot be separated from the virtues.

CONCLUSION

Panegyric on the Prudent Man Whom then do you believe to be superior to the prudent man: he who has reverent opinions about the gods, who is wholly without fear of death, who has discovered what is the high-est good in life and understands that the highest point in what is good is easy to reach and hold and that the extreme of evil is lim-ited either in time or in suffering, and who laughs at that which some have set up as the ruler of all things, [Necessity? He thinks that the chief power of decision lies within us, although some things come about by neces-sity,] some by chance, and some by our own wills; for he sees that necessity is irrespon-sible and chance uncertain, but that our actions are subject to no power. It is for this reason that our actions merit praise or blame. It would be better to accept the myth about the gods than to be a slave to the determin-ism of the physicists; for the myth hints at a hope for grace through honors paid to the gods, but the necessity of determinism is inescapable. Since the prudent man does not, as do many, regard chance as a god (for the gods do nothing in disorderly fashion) or as an unstable cause [of all things], he believes that chance does [not] give man good and evil to make his life happy or miserable, but that it does provide opportunities for great good or evil. Finally, he thinks it better to meet misfortune while acting with reason than to happen upon good fortune while acting senselessly; for it is better that what has been well-planned in our actions [should fail than that what has been ill-planned] should gain success by chance.

Final Words to Menoeceus Meditate on these and like precepts, by day and by night, alone or with a like-minded friend. Then never, either awake or asleep, will you be dismayed; but you will live like a god among men; for life amid immortal blessings is in no way like the life of a mere mortal.[7] (boldface added to identify glossary terms)

EPICTETUS c. 50–130

Epictetus and the Stoical Attitude

Although it differs substantially from Epicureanism, no philosophy took more seriously the task of making the right decisions than the ancient tradition of the Stoics. **Stoicism** emphasized freedom from passion, **equanimity** before the laws of nature, and, contrary to Epicurus, indifference to pleasure or pain. Apparently its perspective contains good advice, since still today we may commend anyone who faces life—especially adversity—with a "stoical attitude." Stoicism's counsel makes sense to every generation and remains useful as a guide to life's decisions.

Although Stoicism originated in Athens during the fourth century B.C., its greatest impact occurred within the Roman Empire.

Its outlook was particularly well suited to an age not unlike our own—one in which the extent and power of political regimes seemed to dwarf what an individual could control. Among the adherents of Stoicism one finds Marcus Aurelius (121–180), a gifted general and emperor, whose *Meditations* remains one of Stoicism's classic texts. If the mighty feel constrained by forces larger than they can command, the appeal of Stoicism to the average person must have been that much greater. Stoic elements later mingled with early Christian teachings. As a guide to life it is, however, in many ways an alternative to religion. The Stoic emphasis is on the power of reason to liberate us through an understanding of natural law; a Stoic sees philosophy as a way of preparation and self-redemption. In the modern world, philosophers such as Comte make the same recommendation, only they stress science as the avenue to right choice.

We can best discern the Stoic way by considering the teachings of Epictetus (c. 50–130). Unique among the philosophers we have met, Epictetus began life as a slave. While serving as his master's secretary, Epictetus received training in Stoic thought and when, eventually, he found his way to Rome and was granted freedom, he offered the same training to others. We know Epictetus today not because any of his writings survive, but because he left a deep impression on a young Roman student named Flavius Arrian. From Arrian's careful notes comes *The Enchiridion* (c. 120), or manual, which contains practical Stoic teachings and advice. Studied for centuries as a guide to making choices in life, *The Enchiridion* also includes in its counsel a picture of what the attitude of the philosopher should be and how philosophy can become your guide.

What Is within Our Power?

The opening lines of *The Enchiridion* keynote the fundamental assumption that supports Stoic advice about the right decisions.

> There are things which are within our power, and there are things which are beyond our power. Within our power are opinion, aim, desire, aversion, and, in one word, whatever affairs are our own. Beyond our power are body, property, reputation, office, and, in one word, whatever are not properly our own affairs.[8]

The Stoic way to a good life involves discerning the difference between things that are in our control and things that are not. As Epictetus sized up those differences, his emphasis fell on training our desires and attitudes. These factors we can control, but no person can guarantee what will happen to anything else in the world. We may improve our chances for good health by self-discipline, but the body is never immune from injury or disease. We can insure our property and still lose it. Our reputation depends on what others think, not simply on what we do. Its status is as precarious as any offices we hold, and the latter are subject to the

vicissitudes of business cycles and shifting political winds. Not least of all, death waits for each of us, and we rarely control its schedule. But self-control is possible; that is the crucial fact and is or should be the basis for every choice. If we train our attitudes and desires so that we can accept life's outcome—no matter what it is—with equanimity, then we are prepared as completely as anyone can be for the decisions that will face us.

Epictetus' teaching is more complex than it looks. Stoicism is actually a strenuous outlook, although some have thought of it as a **quietist** philosophy that advises us to attempt as little as possible. At one point, for example, *The Enchiridion* suggests that a good Stoic will "live as one seeking to be a Socrates" (p. 39). For Epictetus that counsel means that one will always try to improve and will seek perfection "following reason alone" (pp. 38–39). Using our critical capacities, we must discern what is best and let that vision be "an inviolable law" (p. 38) for our choices. True Stoics train themselves so that their highest desire is "to understand nature, and follow her" (p. 38).

The understanding of nature sought by the Stoics is not obtained simply by mastering the most up-to-date theories about the nature of the universe. But what needs to be stressed is that the universe is governed by rational laws. To put one's attitudes in conformity with the workings of those laws is the beginning of wisdom. The goal, suggests Epictetus, is to discern what he calls the **"will of Nature"** by, for example, observing closely what happens to people (p. 26). When we do this "stoically," we see that our lives are like those of actors "in a drama of such sort as the Author chooses—if short, then in a short one; if long, then in a long one. If it be his pleasure that you should enact a poor man, or a cripple, or a ruler, or a private citizen, see that you act it well. For this is your business—to act well the given part, but to choose it belongs to another" (p.

23). Playing the given part well is a matter of attitude and desire. Using our powers to their limit enhances the dignity of our roles and the order of the universe as a whole. As you can see, this is demanding advice. The choices it requires are hard ones because they involve so much self-discipline.

But how does one know his or her part? That discernment requires critical self-awareness, for nature may cast one in a direction but not specify all the details. Some people, for example, may be "born athletes"—they can simply run faster and jump farther than most of their peers. Are they necessarily destined, then, to compete in the Olympic Games? Epictetus considers that example to illustrate his point, and his conclusion is that we should "in every affair consider what precedes and what follows, and then undertake it" (p. 27). Consider what you must do to become an Olympian, urges Epictetus, and contemplate, too, what the various outcomes of that lot may be—"then, if it be for your advantage, engage in the affair" (p. 27). That is, you "engage in the affair" only if you can control your ability to accept the outcome calmly, whether success or failure. Much in our life is determined for us, the Stoic philosophy insists, but we specify the details and determine our response to them. It is our duty to strive to be the best in our roles. Doing so, however, requires calm deliberation and the cultivation of an attitude that is prepared to say: If something is beyond my power, it is nothing to me. That attitude, the Stoics believe, will lead us to make the right decisions, that is, decisions whose outcome we can accept.

What Disturbs Us?

Stoicism aims at inner tranquility. Yet it is an unsettling philosophy when we realize the great self-discipline it demands. For even if Stoic advice contains an element of common sense that many can appreciate, this philos-ophy is extremely rigorous and demanding. You can read Stoic teachings, even agree with them, and still be a long way from living "stoically." This philosophy offers you an initiation into a discipline. Disturbingly difficult at first, it seeks to calm troubled spirits by teaching us that people "are disturbed not by things, but by the views which they take of things" (p. 19).

Epictetus understood that in our present undisciplined state, our view is likely to be just the opposite. But we can acquire self-control through proper philosophical instruction and practice. We are likely to need substantial measures of both, for Epictetus knew that even in a world governed by rational laws, there will be plenty to upset us. Loved ones will die; wars will be lost; empires will be overthrown; and businesses will fail. Marriages will break up, and friends will betray. His stringent prescription is nonetheless to "demand not that events should happen as you wish; but wish them to happen as they do happen, and you will go on well" (p. 20). This, of course, is easier to do for small events than for catastrophes. In spite of how it may seem, the Stoic aim is not to take pleasure in tragedy or to find joy in sorrow. Nor is Epictetus telling us to do away with love, patriotism, and fidelity. In short, he is not saying "don't give a damn." His Stoicism urges us to "restrain desire," but that restriction is not incompatible with trying your hardest, if you remain free from an enslaving desire to change what cannot be altered.

Stoicism, says Epictetus, will put us in harmony with nature and give us peace with ourselves. Ironically, however, being a Stoic is not our natural condition. No one is born a Stoic. Yet if we try the Stoic way, Epictetus urges, we can progress. Whatever degree of control we achieve is a benefit, even if we fail to master ourselves perfectly. The crucial issue, in fact, is to realize that the perfect Stoic attitude, even if impossible to attain, is at least open for us to aim at. Even the conviction that such a degree of self-control is achievable may carry us a long way. It assures us, for instance, that nothing in the future needs to outstrip our powers of coping and acceptance. Certainly a great part of what unnerves us is our fear of the future and our possible inadequacies to deal with what may occur. With Stoic confidence that we can be the master of our responses, it is easier to make decisions with a confidence in our own powers of controlled response.

Should Evil and Death Be Nothing to Us?

The wisdom of Stoicism results largely from a distinction between things that are in our power and things that are not. But this distinction is probably less simple than Epictetus made it out to be, particularly if we live in a universe more subject to change and uncertainty than the Stoics envisioned. If death is absolutely the end of us, for example, no one should argue with Epictetus when he says that a man is merely foolish if he wants his children and his wife to live forever. But is that a foolish hope if the Stoics' views about the natural order are questionable?

Likewise, Epictetus urges us to see that our anguish over evil in the world is largely a function of our feelings and attitudes. But if our future is more open than Epictetus predicted, perhaps it is not so easy to remain "stoically" tranquil and to accept with equanimity whatever comes. What comes to us may be the result of decisions that lie less in natural law and more in the human will. It may be one thing to say that death is natural. It could be something else to confront a future armed with nuclear warheads and to say that whatever happens we will wish things to happen as they do, and that if we do so we will go on well. Stoic equanimity has much to commend it when we are dealing with "what comes naturally." But what if the most critical happenings do not simply fit "a plan of nature" in the future we happen to face?

Toward the end of *The Enchiridion*, Epictetus describes his ideal of the philosopher. Among other things, he stresses that this philosopher "restrains desire; he transfers his aversion to those things only which thwart the proper use of our own will; . . . and, in a word, he keeps watch over himself as over an enemy and one in ambush" (p. 37). The true Stoic philosopher is one who "looks to himself for all help or harm" (p. 37). If philosophy today advocates that Stoic character and imparts it to others, it can help us make the decisions we need to make with equanimity. In particular, philosophy can do this if it takes to heart the Stoic maxim that the proper use of the human will involves unstinting effort "to understand nature, and follow her" (p. 38). As we face the twenty-first century, however, we also need to consider whether "nature" is the same as the Stoics found it in Epictetus' day. Our sense of the humanly possible may exceed what Epictetus could have envisioned in his wildest dreams. To discover our destiny and to conform ourselves to it—that Stoic advice is still timely. But the question that follows is: How much of the earth's fate rests as yet undetermined in human hands? As you read more from Epictetus' *Enchiridion*, consider how human decisions affect the future and appraise whether Stoicism, valuable as its advice may be, is the best basis for conclusions about your life.

I

There are things which are within our power, and there are things which are beyond our power. Within our power are opinion, aim, desire, aversion, and, in one word, whatever affairs are our own. Beyond our power are body, property, reputation, office, and, in one word, whatever are not properly our own affairs. . . .

Seek at once, therefore, to be able to say to every unpleasing semblance, "You are but a semblance and by no means the real thing." And then examine it by those rules which you have; and first and chiefly by this: whether it concerns the things which are within our own power or those which are not; and if it concerns anything beyond our power, be prepared to say that it is nothing to you.

V

Men are disturbed not by things, but by the views which they take of things. Thus death is nothing terrible, else it would have appeared so to Socrates. But the terror consists in our notion of death, that it is terrible. When, therefore, we are hindered or disturbed, or grieved, let us never impute it to others, but to ourselves—that is, to our own views. It is the action of an uninstructed person to reproach others for his own misfortunes; of one entering upon instruction, to reproach himself; and one perfectly instructed, to reproach neither others nor himself.

VIII

Demand not that events should happen as you wish; but wish them to happen as they do happen, and you will go on well.

XIV

If you wish your children and your wife and your friends to live forever, you are foolish, for you wish things to be in your power which are not so, and what belongs to others to be your own. So likewise, if you wish your servant to be without fault, you are foolish, for you wish vice not to be vice but something else. But if you wish not to be disappointed in your desires, that is in your own power. Exercise, therefore, what is in your power. A man's master is he who is able to confer or remove whatever that man seeks or shuns. Whoever then would be free, let him wish nothing, let him decline nothing, which depends on others; else he must necessarily be a slave.

XV

Remember that you must behave as at a banquet. Is anything brought round to you? Put out your hand and take a moderate share. Does it pass by you? Do not stop it. Is it not yet come? Do not yearn in desire toward it, but wait till it reaches you. So with regard to children, wife, office, riches; and you will some time or other be worthy to feast with the gods. And if you do not so much as take the things which are set before you, but are able even to forego them, then you will not only be worthy to feast with the gods, but to rule with them also. For, by thus doing, Diogenes and Heraclitus, and others like them, deservedly became divine, and were so recognized.

XVII

Remember that you are an actor in a drama of such sort as the Author chooses—if short, then in a short one; if long, then in a long one. If it be his pleasure that you should enact a poor man, or a cripple, or a ruler, or a private citizen, see that you act it well. For this is your business—to act well the given part, but to choose it belongs to another.

XXVI

The will of nature may be learned from things upon which we are all agreed. As when our neighbor's boy has broken a cup, or the like, we are ready at once to say, "These are casualties that will happen"; be assured, then, that when your own cup is likewise broken, you ought to be affected just as when another's cup was broken. Now apply this to greater things. Is the child or wife of another dead? There is no one who would not say, "This is an accident of mortality." But if anyone's own child happens to die, it is immediately, "Alas! how wretched am I!" It should be always remembered how we are affected on hearing the same thing concerning others.

XXIX

In every affair consider what precedes and what follows, and then undertake it. Otherwise you will begin with spirit, indeed, careless of the consequences, and when these are developed, you will shamefully desist. "I would conquer at the Olympic Games." But consider what precedes and what follows, and then, if it be for your advantage, engage in the affair. You must conform to rules, submit to a diet, refrain from dainties; exercise your body, whether you choose it or not, at a stated hour, in heat and cold; you must drink no cold water, and sometimes no wine—in a word, you must give yourself up to your trainer as to a physician. Then, in the combat, you may be thrown into a ditch, dislocate your arm, turn your ankle, swallow an abundance of dust, receive stripes [for negligence], and, after all, lose the victory. When you have reckoned up all this, if your inclination still holds, set about the combat. Otherwise, take notice, you will behave like children who sometimes play wrestlers, sometimes gladiators, sometimes blow a trumpet, and sometimes act a tragedy, when they happen to have seen and admired these shows. Thus you too will be at one time a wrestler, and another a gladiator; now a philosopher, now an orator; but nothing in earnest. . . .

XLVI

Never proclaim yourself a philosopher, nor make much talk among the ignorant about your principles, but show them by actions. Thus, at an entertainment, do not discourse how people ought to eat, but eat as you ought. For remember that thus Socrates also universally avoided all ostentation. And when persons came to him and desired to be introduced by him to philosophers, he took them and introduced them; so well did he bear being overlooked. So if ever there should be among the ignorant any discussion of principles, be for the most part silent. For there is great danger in hastily throwing out what is undigested. And if anyone tells you that you know nothing, and you are not nettled at it, then you may be sure that you have really entered on your work. For sheep do not hastily throw up the grass to show the shepherds how much they have eaten, but, inwardly digesting their food, they pro-

duce it outwardly in wool and milk. Thus, therefore, do you not make an exhibition before the ignorant of your principles, but of the actions to which their digestion gives rise.

L

Whatever rules you have adopted, abide by them as laws, and as if you would be impious to transgress them; and do not regard what anyone says of you, for this, after all, is no concern of yours. How long, then, will you delay to demand of yourself the noblest improvements, and in no instance to transgress the judgments of reason? You have received the philosophic principles with which you ought to be conversant; and you have been conversant with them. For what other master, then, do you wait as an excuse for this delay in self-reformation? You are no longer a boy but a grown man. If, therefore, you will be negligent and slothful, and always add procrastination to procrastination, purpose to purpose, and fix day after day in which you will attend to yourself, you will insensibly continue to accomplish nothing and, living and dying, remain of vulgar mind. This instant, then, think yourself worthy of living as a man grown up and a proficient. Let whatever appears to be the best be to you an inviolable law. And if any instance of pain or pleasure, glory or disgrace, be set before you, remember that now is the combat, now the Olympiad comes on, nor can it be put off; and that by one failure and defeat honor may be lost or—won. Thus Socrates became perfect, improving himself by everything, following reason alone. And though you are not yet a Socrates, you ought, however, to live as one seeking to be a Socrates. (Pp. 17, 19, 20–23, 26–28, 36, 38–39.)

Augustine and His "Confessions"

Born in northern Africa, Saint Augustine (354–430) witnessed political upheavals and military disasters that hastened the fall of the

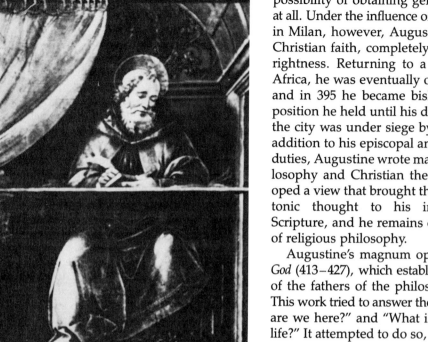

AUGUSTINE 354–430

Roman Empire. At the same time, Christianity's influence was rising. The Roman emperors had been Christian since Constantine's conversion some forty years earlier, and by 380 Christianity was decreed to be the empire's official religion. But there were still plenty of religions and philosophies competing for attention. Thus when Augustine, a distinguished academic, was teaching rhetoric in Rome and Milan, he was exposed to the conflicting "truths" of different schools of thought (including the Epicureans and Stoics). In addition, he experienced the dilemma of trying to reconcile Christian teachings concerning God's **omnipotence** and goodness with the presence of evil and suffering in the world. Although he had been raised a Christian, Augustine became skeptical about Christianity and even about the

possibility of obtaining genuine knowledge at all. Under the influence of Bishop Ambrose in Milan, however, Augustine resumed his Christian faith, completely convinced of its rightness. Returning to a monastic life in Africa, he was eventually ordained a priest, and in 395 he became bishop of Hippo, a position he held until his death in 430 when the city was under siege by the Vandals. In addition to his episcopal and administrative duties, Augustine wrote many books on philosophy and Christian theology. He developed a view that brought the insights of Platonic thought to his interpretation of Scripture, and he remains one of the giants of religious philosophy.

Augustine's magnum opus is *The City of God* (413–427), which established him as one of the fathers of the philosophy of history. This work tried to answer the questions "Why are we here?" and "What is the purpose of life?" It attempted to do so, however, not by focusing primarily on individual lives but by considering human history as a whole. Following the Bible's lead, Augustine interpreted history as a divine drama that unfolded in three basic acts: God's purposeful creation, humanity's "fall," and the **redemption** of the damage resulting from human sin so that God's original good purpose could be fulfilled.

This view of history was panoramic. But Augustine's sweeping approach is complemented by another that focused intently on the individual's place within God's cosmic play. Earlier, for example, Augustine's *Confessions* (400) traced his spiritual odyssey with the hope that, by sharing his personal experience, individuals could be helped to make the right decisions. Because human decisions occur in historical settings, we will discuss Augustine's advice by noting how he outlined history's development in *The City of God*. Then we explore how his *Confessions* can become a personal guide to life in that broad context.

A Tale of Two Cities

Roman tradition held that the empire was eternal, but in 410 Rome was sacked by the Visigoths. Obviously tradition was not fool-proof, and Augustine was led to reappraise the empire's role in God's providential plans. His reflections led him to contemplate "the glorious city of God" and in particular to affirm the following:

> . . . though there are very many and great nations all over the earth, whose rites and customs, speech, arms, and dress, are distinguished by marked differences, yet there are no more than two kinds of human society, which we may justly call two cities, according to the language of our Scriptures. The one consists of those who wish to live after the flesh, the other of those who wish to live after the spirit. . . .[9]

History exhibits vast variety, but according to Augustine, it is essentially composed of a conflict between two opposing forces. God's sovereignty is eternal and it will prevail, but the human abuse of the freedom God created has led to a rebellious earthly realm that opposes God's will. God cannot be disobeyed with impunity, however, and history's course unfolds a story of divine judgment and redemption.

The city of God ultimately transcends the earthly realm, but within the latter the heavenly city, as Augustine sometimes calls it, can also be discerned. As history unfolds, however, we cannot simply identify these cities with specific places. Certainly Los Angeles or New York could qualify as "earthly" on Augustine's terms, but his distinction between the two realms was more subtle. All human society bears the marks of corruption, Augustine believed, but within the earthly city—the fallen state that results from sin—there are those who belong to the everlasting city of God. Redeemed by God's grace, they live attuned to God and will obtain eternal life. As for those who remain in the fallen earthly city, never to escape its limits, they will perish there unredeemed. They have received their just desserts. According to Augustine, then, history conforms to God's nature and purpose. It testifies at once to the destructive consequences of disobeying God and to the grace of God that brings good out of evil through redemption.

Within history, argued Augustine, "the two cities, the heavenly and the earthly, . . . are mingled together from the beginning down to the end" (p. 668). Though our judgment is imperfect until God's final judgment separates the sheep from the goats, it is possible to detect whether a society or an individual inclines one way or the other. The test involves love. For the two cities, according to Augustine,

> have been formed by two loves: the earthly by the love of self, even to the contempt of God; the heavenly by the love of God, even to the contempt of self. The former, in a word, glories in itself, the latter in the Lord. For the one seeks glory from men; but the greatest glory of the other is God, the witness of conscience. The one lifts up its head in its own glory; the other says to its God, "Thou art my glory, and the lifter up of mine head." In the one, the princes and the nations it subdues are ruled by the love of ruling; in the other, the princes and the subjects serve one another in love, the latter obeying, while the former take thought for all. (P. 477.)

Augustine put his analysis in theological terms, but, as far as making right decisions is concerned, his basic point can be grasped by anyone: what and how we love are indeed issues that can fulfill or destroy our lives individually and collectively. Augustine recognized that in particular historical circumstances, we will not make those judgments perfectly. But he urged that we try our best to find the fulfillment offered by the city of God, which resists and transcends history's corruption.

The Confessions *as a Guide to Decision*

Augustine's *City of God* sets out the grand scheme within which our lives and our decisions are and should be made. Love perverted by pride caused the fall and began the corrupted earthly city in which we all live. But the love of God is not entirely dead in human hearts; it keeps the vision of the city of God alive in opposition to the secular city. Divine perfection meant that God foreknew all that would happen in human affairs, and God planned accordingly. That conviction left Augustine with the problem of reconciling God's control of events with the reality of human freedom. If Augustine never resolved that issue to everyone's satisfaction, he remained convinced that we possess the freedom to make decisions. For our present discussion, that is a key idea to keep in mind. It explains why Augustine wrote his *Confessions*, that is, to show how his own life embodied the struggle between the two cities and how he had journeyed from an unsatisfying earthly orientation to one that made his life increasingly worthwhile.

Confession, Augustine claimed, played a central role in this process. Much of the *Confessions* therefore dwells on Augustine's discovery that his concerns and commitments were for a long time not what they ought to have been. One of the most important "right decisions" that Augustine proposed is a soul-searching that asks: Am I on the right track? Am I living as I should? Augustine knew that our lives can become so misdirected that even asking such questions is extremely difficult. But what he found in his own experience was that, if we act in time, a basic personal restlessness prompts us to keep looking for a better way of life. Augustine put the point this way: "Thou [i.e., God] hast made us for Thee and our heart is unquiet till it finds its rest in Thee."[10] According to Augustine, what disturbs our life process and makes decision blind or difficult is that whether we are aware of it or not, we seek reconciliation with God and are discontent until we find it. If we let our own discontent orient us so that our soul is cleansed by confession, our capacities can be unblocked and we can live in more fulfilling ways. Augustine, of course, did see God at work in us throughout the whole process. But even if you do not concur with his theology, you can recognize that Augustine's psychology may be sound.

All that is good, affirmed Augustine, comes ultimately from God. Thus, whenever we seek the good in our lives, that yearning is a way of seeking God, little as we may realize it. Again, confession and reconciliation with God are of crucial importance to Augustine if we do not wish to remain confused and corrupted by sin, which in Augustine's view is a matter of willfully misplaced priorities.

According to Augustine, human existence is placed in the middle range of a **hierarchy** of being, which has God at the top and nonbeing at the bottom. Not only are we all dependent on God for our existence, but our natures are such that our well-being and fulfillment depend on a positive orientation toward God, one in which we recognize our dependence on God and respond to God's will in love and service to others (i.e., in obedience). Human fulfillment, thought Augustine, is constituted by the cultivation of one's relation to God. On the other hand, if one willfully turns away from God, a course of action follows that produces distortion in the self and plunges one toward the end of the hierarchy characterized by nonbeing. To turn from God is to turn away from the sustaining source of existence itself. Such an action leads to a loss of identity, that is, a lack of recognition of one's identity as a creature of God. The results are fragmentation and disintegration of the self and a corresponding lack of fulfillment.

Augustine contrasted these two styles of life in terms of concern and love for what is

eternal as opposed to what is **temporal**. What is eternal, he argued, is also the most real and of the greatest perfection. By orienting oneself toward the eternal features of existence (truth, for example), one draws near to the source of all power and meaning and hence allows for the fulfillment that is natural to us as God's creatures. To turn toward temporal things (for example, material wealth, political power, sensual pleasure) and to make them the focus of one's concerns is to preoccupy oneself with that which is changing and perishing and hence of less reality, value, and sustaining power. In these circumstances, we may lose ourselves to the pursuit of values that stand lower on the hierarchical scale. The loss that occurs in these cases is characterized by Augustine as a lack of being and an absence of good. One falls short of what he or she could be. We stand lower on the scale of being than we ought to, and this may lead to a disorientation for others as well.

Augustine did not recommend neglect of temporal concerns. The structure of our existence in the world requires us to attend to them. Our attention, however, should not be focused on the temporal to the exclusion or neglect of the eternal. Proper balance requires that **priority** be given to one's relationship to God. If this ordering is followed, temporal concerns will find their rightful place. On the other hand, Augustine argued, an orientation that gives primacy to temporal concerns will bring out the qualities of lack and deficiency, and they are the identifying marks of the evil that people do. To do evil is to create a lack or a deficiency in oneself or in others. It is to push oneself or others away from God and toward nonbeing.

Right decisions rest on the right ordering of priorities, and although we may not believe, with Augustine, that right ordering is divinely ordained, we can recognize that life does differentiate between the pursuits that provide lasting worth and those that do not. Again, not everyone will set up priori-

ties as Augustine did, but as the following reading from the *Confessions* suggests, he nonetheless leaves us with this insight: no decision is more important than the one that keeps us looking for the right priorities.

Great is the power of memory; its deep and boundless multiplicity is something fearful, O my God! And this is the mind, and I am this myself. What, then, am I, O my God? What is my nature? A life of many aspects and many ways, strikingly immeasurable.

Look into the fields, hollows, and innumerable caverns of my memory, filled beyond number with innumerable kinds of things, either by means of images as in the case of all bodies, or by means of their own presence as in the case of the arts, or by means of some sort of notions or impressions as in the case of the feelings of the mind (which the memory keeps even when the mind is not undergoing them, though whatever is in the memory is in the mind!). I run through all these things, and I flit here and there. I even go as deep as I can, yet there is no limit. So great is the power of memory, so great is the power of life in man who lives mortally!

What shall I do, Thou true Life of mine, O my God? I shall pass over even this power of mine which is called memory; I shall pass over it to reach Thee, sweet Light. What dost Thou say to me? Behold, going up through my mind to Thee, who dwellest above me, I shall even pass over this power of mine which is called memory, desiring to attain Thee where Thou canst be attained, and to cleave to Thee where it is possible to be in contact with Thee.

For, even beasts and birds have memory; otherwise, they could not find their lairs and nests, or the many other things to which they become accustomed. And they could not grow accustomed to any thing, unless through memory. Therefore, I shall even pass over memory to attain Him who has set me apart from the four-footed beasts and made me "wiser than the fowls of the air." I shall even pass over memory, so that I may find Thee—where, O truly good and serene Sweetness—where shall I find Thee? But, if I find Thee without memory, I am without remembrance of Thee. And how, indeed, may I find Thee, if I am without remembrance of Thee?

The woman who had lost her drachma and looked for it with a lamp [Luke 8:10] would not have found it, unless she retained some remembrance of it. For, when it had been found, how would she know whether it was the one, if she retained no remembrance of it? I remember many lost things which I have looked for and found. From this, I know that, when I was looking for one of them, and people would say to me: "Perhaps this is it? Maybe this one?" I would continue to say: "It is not," until the thing I was seeking was shown to me. Unless I had some remembrance of it, whatever it was, I should not have found it, even if it were shown to me, for I should not have recognized it. That is always the way it is, when we look for some lost thing and find it. Yet, of course, when by chance something is lost from sight, not from memory—any visible body, for example—its image is retained within, and it is sought until it comes back within view. And, when it is found, it is recognized from the image which is within. We do not say that we have found what we lost, if we do not recognize it, and we cannot recognize it, if we do not remember it. It disappeared, indeed, from before our eyes, but it was retained in memory.

What? When the memory itself loses something, as happens when we forget and try to remember, pray, where do we look for it, unless in the memory itself? And in it, if one thing is presented in place of another, we reject it until the thing we are looking for turns up. When it does turn up, we say: "This is it." We would not say that unless we recognized it, and we would not recognize it unless we remembered. Yet, we certainly had forgotten it.

Or, had it disappeared, not completely, but only in part? And is the other part sought, by means of that which is retained, because

the memory felt that its object of consideration was not as complete as usual, and, feeling the defect in a habit which was, as it were, defective in some part, it strove to get back what was missing?

For instance, if a man who is known comes before our eyes or into our thoughts, and we are trying to recall his name, which we have forgotten, then, any other name which occurs fails to be connected, because it has not been customary for our thought of him to go along with it; hence, it is rejected until that name occurs which our customary way of thinking of the man accepts as not inappropriate. And, from what source does it occur, if not from memory itself? For, when we recognize it, on being reminded by someone else, it is from there that it comes. So, we do not accept it as something new, but, in recalling it, we judge that what has been said is the right name. But, if it is entirely wiped out of mind, then we do not remember even when reminded. And, if we even remember that we have forgotten it, then we have not yet completely forgotten. Therefore, we would not be able to look for something that has been lost, if we had altogether forgotten it.

Now, how do I look for Thee, O Lord? When I look for Thee, my God, I am looking for the happy life. May I seek Thee, so that my soul may live. For, my body has life from my soul, and my soul has life from Thee. How, then, do I seek the happy life? It is not mine, until I can say: "Enough, there it is." Here, then, I ought to say how I do look for it, whether through remembrance, as though I had forgotten it and I still retained the fact that I had forgotten, or through a desire to learn it as something unknown, either something I never knew, or which I have so forgotten that I have no remembrance even that I have forgotten it. Surely, the happy life is this: what all men desire and [such that] there is absolutely no one who does not desire it? Where did they know it, this object which they desire in such a way? Where did they see it, to love it so? Certainly, we do possess it, but how I know not.

There is one certain way whereby each

man, when he possesses this object, is then happy, and there also are those who are happy in hope. The latter possess it in an inferior way, compared to those who are already really happy, yet they are better off than those others who are happy neither in reality nor in hope. Still, unless this third kind of people possessed it, in some way, they would not desire to be happy; that they have such a desire is most certain. Somehow or other they came to know it, and so they possess it in some kind or other of knowledge. My problem concerning this is whether it may be in the memory; for, if it is there, then we were at one time happy, either all individually, or all in that man who was the first to sin, in whom also we all died [1 Corinthians 15:22], from whom we are all born amidst unhappiness. I do not ask this question now, but I do ask whether the happy life is in the memory.

Now, we would not love it, unless we knew it. We hear this word and we all admit that we seek this thing, for we are not delighted merely by the sound. When a Greek hears this word in Latin, he is not delighted, for he does not know what has been said. Yet, we Latins are delighted, as he is, too, if he hears it in Greek, for the thing itself is neither Greek nor Latin, this thing which Greeks and Latins and men of every tongue yearn to obtain. So, it is known to all men who, if they could be asked whether they desire to be happy, would reply in one voice, without any hesitation, that they do. This would be impossible, unless the thing itself, of which this is the name, were kept in their memory.

Now, is this the same as the case of the man who, having seen Carthage, remembers it? No! The happy life is not seen with the eyes, since it is not a body.

Is it like the example of our remembering numbers? No! One who possesses these in knowledge does not seek to obtain further, but we possess the happy life in knowledge, and so we love it, yet wish to attain it further so that we may *be* happy.

Is it like the instance where we remember the art of oratory? No! For, though, when this word has been heard, people recall to mind the thing itself, even those who are not yet eloquent—and many do desire to be (whence it is apparent that eloquence exists in their knowledge), but, on the other hand, they have observed through the senses of the body that other people are eloquent and they are delighted and long to be likewise; they would not be delighted except from interior knowledge and they would not desire to be likewise unless they were so delighted. However, we do not have personal experience of the happy life in other people, through any sense of the body.

Is it like the way in which we remember joy? Perhaps so. For, I remember my joy even when sad, just as I do the happy life when I am unhappy, and I have never seen, or heard, or smelled, or tasted, or touched my joy by any sense of the body, but I have experienced it in my mind when I have been joyful. Its knowledge stuck in my memory, so that I am able to remember it, sometimes with contempt, sometimes with longing, depending on the difference between the things from which my joy came, as I remember it. For, I have been imbued with a certain joy arising from shameful things, and, as I now recall this, I feel disgust and curse it; at other times, it arises from good and virtuous things, and I recall it with longing, even though, perhaps, they are no longer available, and therefore I am saddened as I recall my former joy.

Where, then, and when did I experience my happy life that I should now remember, love, and desire it? Not just I alone, or in the company of a few people, but absolutely all people want to be happy. Unless we knew it with certain knowledge, we would not will it with such a certain act of will. But, how is this? If the question be asked of two men whether they wish to serve in the army, it is quite possible that one of them may reply that he wants to, the other that he does not. But, if they are asked whether they wish to be happy, both will say at once and without any hesitation that they do desire it. Nor is there any different reason why one wishes to enter military service and the other does not, than that they wish to be happy. One man, perhaps, finds his joy in one thing, another man in another? Even so, they agree that they all wish to be happy, just as they would agree, if asked the question, that they wish to possess joy. This joy they call the happy life. Even though one man attains it here, another there, still it is but one thing which all men strive to reach, so that they may be joyful. Now, since this is a thing which no man can deny experiencing, it is therefore recognized as found in the memory, when the name, happy life, is heard.

Far be it, O Lord, far be it from the heart of Thy servant who is confessing to Thee, far be it that I should consider myself happy by virtue of just any joy which I experience. For, there is a joy which is not given to the wicked, but rather to them who serve Thee for Thine own sake; for such people, Thou Thyself art Joy. And this is the happy life, to rejoice unto Thee, from Thee, on account of Thee: this it is and there is none other. They who think that there is another pursue a different joy, and not the true one. Yet, their will is not turned away from some representation of joy.

Is it, then, uncertain that all men wish to be happy, because those who do not wish to find their joy in Thee—and this is the only happy life—do not, in point of fact, desire the happy life? Or, do all desire this, but, because "the flesh lusts against the spirit, and the spirit against the flesh . . . so that they do not do what they wish" [Romans 7:18], they descend to that of which they are capable and are content with it, for they do not desire that for which they have insufficient capacity, to the extent that their desire would render them capable of it?

Now, I ask all men whether they would prefer to get their joy from truth rather than from falsity? They will hesitate as little to say that they prefer it from truth as they hesitate in saying that they wish to be happy. Indeed, the happy life is joy arising from truth. For, this is the joy coming from Thee, who art the Truth, O God; Thou art "my light," the salvation of my countenance, O my God. This happy life all men desire; this life, which

alone is happy, all men desire; the joy arising from truth all men desire. (Pp. 285–93.)

Søren Kierkegaard and "Either/Or"

Epicurus argued that pleasure is the good, and Epictetus urged people to evaluate what is within their power to control. Augustine experienced uncertainty about what he ought to do, but through his confessions felt he had found assurance about God and the priorities human beings should adopt. All these philosophers from the ancient world lived in difficult times; nonetheless each thought that making the right decisions could be a clear-cut matter. Centuries later, a Danish thinker, Søren Kierkegaard (1813–1855), was not so sure. The consideration of the pursuit of pleasure filled much of his life and writing, but pleasure, he concluded, was ambiguous and fickle. Although Kierkegaard loved to contemplate possibilities, he differed from Epictetus in finding that the boundaries between what is possible and what is not are anything but clear and distinct. Agreeing with Augustine that life's significance involves God, Kierkegaard discovered that our relationship to God raises as many questions as it answers.

In the process of wrestling with the issues of ambiguity and uncertainty, Kierkegaard offered counsel about making decisions. However, Kierkegaard did not see history so much as God's cosmic drama but rather as the setting in which individuals must struggle to find themselves. Historical circumstances might be different over the centuries, but Kierkegaard's interest focused less on whether those changes indicated progress and more on how the basic dilemmas of human existence remain the same. Outer circumstances tended to be unimportant for

SØREN AABYE KIERKEGAARD
1813–1855

Kierkegaard. He saw the individual self—not the masses of humanity—as the center of the struggle for decisive action.

Kierkegaard's short life began and ended in Copenhagen. The son of a wealthy merchant, he was brought up in a strict Christian home. In 1830 he entered university to study theology, but an increasing rebelliousness distracted him. Although we will not focus on it here, a religious passion dominated Kierkegaard's later thought, and he sometimes remarked that the life of a country parson might have suited him best. As a young man, however, he lived without a definite sense of direction. Then, in 1838, Kierkegaard experienced a religious conversion. Shortly thereafter he finished his degree in theology and became engaged to a teenager named Regine Olsen. Kierkegaard's life seemed to stabilize, but he broke the engagement in about a year. His explanation was that he had a religious task and marriage was incompatible with it. Whether that is the whole story remains unclear, but in any case Kierkegaard launched a distinctive writing project that included numerous books published pseudonymously. In these writings, Kierkegaard sketched the lifestyles that he called aesthetic, ethical, and religious. Convinced that each had distinctive appeals and that choosing one orientation over another was a matter of **"either/or"**—though never in such a way that the right decision was obvious—Kierkegaard pointed out the pros and cons of these different ways of life. Then, he insisted, the one key to authentic existence is to make a decisive choice.

The story of Kierkegaard's life entered directly into his philosophical views, and he thought that was how it should be. As the father of the philosophical outlook called "existentialism," he felt that philosophy had grown too distant from life's problems, too speculative, too rational. Life is not so neatly packaged, a point Kierkegaard drove home by injecting his writing with comments on his life and by keeping a journal intended for publication. He often discussed the "tragic events" that both changed his life and made him speak out, beginning with his broken engagement. Melancholy, said Kierkegaard, was his mistress. Ultimately he clashed with the established church, although he attended services regularly most of his life and knew Denmark's religious leaders personally. In addition to melancholy, he frequently wrote about **anxiety** and **dread,** which may seem strange because outwardly his existence appears to have been comfortable. Kierkegaard had an inheritance from his father and, except for his writing, publishing, and managing his private affairs, never had to work for a living; yet his life was full of turmoil. He was sure that life is inescapably that way. Thus, neither philosophy nor religion, he concluded, should lead to a life of comfort but instead should prod us to confront honestly life's hard, often paradoxical, decisions.

Pleasure, Repetition, and Boredom

Decisions in the scientific world may be perfectly logical and rational, but Kierkegaard believed that, in our personal lives, we often face an "either/or." That is, we must decide between incompatible ways of living. We have to choose, and there is often no way to reconcile the opposites. None of Kierkegaard's writings is more famous than *Either/Or* (1843), which illustrates this point by contrasting two lifestyles, the **aesthetic** and the **ethical**.

Kierkegaard presented this pseudonymous two-volume work as though it had been composed by two completely different men— one still young, the other older—whose styles of life were distinctly opposite. Suggesting that pleasure-seeking is the most natural way for us, *Either/Or* first takes up the aesthetic life. It seeks to enjoy existence by experiencing pleasure and resisting any lasting commitments: "No moment must be permitted so great a significance that it cannot be forgotten when convenient; each moment ought, however, to have so much significance that it can be recollected at will."[11] Don't get pinned down, the aesthetic way advises, "the whole secret lies in arbitrariness" (1:295).

Except for the choice to pursue pleasure, the aesthetic approach holds that any **decision** is to be made cautiously if at all. The reason is that "boredom is the root of all evil" (1:282). **Boredom** is the result of **repetition,** and a resolute **commitment** involves a lot of that. In *Repetition: An Essay in Experimental Psychology* (1843), Kierkegaard explored how life brings up the same circumstances again and again. Yet in some ways repetition can be an ally. We want friends we can count on, for example, and a life with too many surprises can be disastrous. But repetition can wear you down unless you find ways to escape it or to make it work on your behalf. We cannot escape repetition and so must learn to deal with it. Unless we do, the results of all decisions will be frustrating.

How to cope with repetition—that is a fascinating and important question, Kierkegaard tells us. A pleasure-seeking life may try what he called "the rotation method." No attempt to escape from boredom will be successful unless it is carefully planned. The advice that haphazard pleasure-seeking is sure to result in pain dates back at least to Epicurus. Thus, a plan that does not depend on a radical change of location and scene is in order. You change, as it were, the crop and the mode of cultivation in the same field, and then perhaps the happiness that depends on what is "interesting" and novel can be yours.

The problem, however, is that boredom may still intrude. The pursuit of pleasure itself may become boring, or you may become bored with yourself. In short, a life oriented by the pursuit of pleasure may drive one to despair. But this outcome is not entirely obvious. Although a jaded hedonist who has "tried everything" may admit that "pleasure disappoints," he or she may add "possibility never" (1:40). There is always the chance that things will go better next time. Arguments will not settle the matter; only decision can do so. To illustrate that point, Kierkegaard devotes the second volume of *Either/Or* to outlining an ethical lifestyle very different from the aesthetic approaches he described first.

Ethical Decisiveness

Kierkegaard uses the character he names Judge William to personify ethical decisiveness in *Either/Or.* "He who would define his life task ethically," the judge observes, "has ordinarily not so considerable a selection to choose from; on the other hand, the act of choice has far more importance for him" (2:171). Judge William discusses marriage at length. Contrary to the pleasure-seeker, who moves from one relationship to another, Judge William argues that a lasting marriage provides meaning that is much more precious. Marriage may reduce the "selection to choose from"; but it involves a decisive commitment, and without such decision, the judge continues, life will turn out empty. The highest pleasures, in fact, are found in the most lasting commitments. To that argument the judge adds that "an aesthetic choice is no choice" because it is the opposite of commitment. Aesthetic choices sample one event and then move on. They overlook that a self is to be won or lost by the choices one makes.

An ethical life recognizes the importance of commitment and the impact of its presence—or absence—on the personality. Kierkegaard feels that avoiding commitment may make life easy and pleasant, but it does little to create a decisive personality. We must meet life's demands for our decisions and in timely fashion, or else the decisions will be made for us. At one point, Kierkegaard casts life's dilemmas in the following way: "If you marry, you will regret it; if you do not marry, you will also regret it; if you marry or do not marry, you will regret both; whether you marry or do not marry, you will regret both" (1:37). Yet life demands that we decide and will not wait for some supposed solution that will wipe out its paradoxes. Thus decision consists simply of accepting a paradoxical situation and, with firm resolve, selecting a course of action, the paradoxes notwithstanding.

Although Kierkegaard apparently favors the resoluteness of the ethical life over the detachment of the aesthetic, the point of *Either/Or* is not that the ethical view is obviously better than the aesthetic one. For there is plenty of evidence on the other side. Commitments—especially marriages, for example—can be catastrophic. A detached life of pleasure-seeking has much to commend it by comparison. The issue, then, does come down to "either/or." But Kierkegaard does not decide this for his readers. In that way his analysis is a form of what he liked

to call "indirect communication." Kierkegaard sets the stage, hoping that we will see ourselves among the characters and dilemmas he describes. Then he leaves us to decide the outcome.

There are different ways of living, and they are not all reconcilable. The problem is that the arguments and evidence do not line up so that the right decision is obvious. Kierkegaard's advice is that we must expect to confront options that are clearly different but not so clearly right or wrong. And within that setting, he tells us, life elicits a choice one way or the other: "As truly as there is a future," says Judge William, "just so truly is there an either/or" (2:177). Kierkegaard recommends that we choose lucidly, self-consciously. Only by doing so will we genuinely seize our opportunities to determine the future and come to know who we are because we have defined our self by our choices.

The Incompleteness of Truth and the Impossibility of Finality

Although the *Confessions* of Augustine was anguished, their author was convinced that we can know truth with certainty. That belief made Augustine sure that he could discern history's course with some finality. Kierkegaard, on the other hand, returned to the notion of "Socratic ignorance." The more we learn, the more we will realize how much we do not know and how little we are able to assert with finality. "How far does the Truth admit of being learned?" asked Kierkegaard.[12] The answer, in *Philosophical Fragments* (1844), is "not very much."

We ask questions, but often we do not even know what can have led us to ask them, let alone produce final answers. In such a situation, one is not likely to pronounce on the ultimate course of life. Socrates may have thought that all we learn is recalled from an earlier age, but Kierkegaard disagreed. Far from our minds containing hidden knowledge that is drawn out by questioning, we hardly know in which direction to turn at the start. Time is no advantage to us either, according to Kierkegaard, because all men and women start at essentially the same place regardless of historical circumstances. It does not matter where we start in the world's history. As we investigate our status as learners, awareness of our ignorance is crucial if we are to approach truth. Accepting this situation, counseled Kierkegaard, provides the only realistic context for the choices life prods us to make.

Those who see history as progressing often see the past as being determined. You may argue that history has a fixed goal and is proceeding toward it, but if the course is not a necessary one, history could turn out different from your expectations. It is the philosopher's account of the past that gives him or her the confidence to predict the course of the future, but Kierkegaard short-circuited that process by claiming that the past is not necessary; it did not have to be. Thus, examination of the past cannot be relied on to predict the future with assurance, nor can it determine decisions about our personal lives.

In his *Philosophical Fragments*, Kierkegaard argued that we should take the uncertainty we feel over the future and use it as a model to understand the past. That is, as we look at the future we feel a sense of possibility, uncertainty, and even uneasiness. The past is what is, but that does not mean that events could not have come out otherwise. The past is no more necessary than the future; both are contingent.

One of Kierkegaard's most intriguing arguments against any necessity controlling life is his belief that no plan is ever enacted as it is laid out in theory. As a plan is put into action, it undergoes change. Suffering is involved in the effort to move from possibility to actuality. This fact affects the out-

come in unpredictable ways. "If a plan in coming into existence is in itself changed," wrote Kierkegaard, "it is not this plan that comes into being" (p. 90). By coming into existence, he added, things show that they are not necessary, for if they were necessary they would already be. What has happened has happened and cannot be undone, but Kierkegaard also contended that "all coming into existence takes place with freedom, not by necessity" (p. 93). If we develop a false sense of immutability about life's course, our basis for making decisions is sure to be thrown off.

Understanding comes in retrospect, but Kierkegaard reminds us not to forget that we live forward. For example, you decide with great determination that you will earn A's in all your courses this term. You are not vague about this; you lay out a definite plan, scheduling your time and plotting your approach to each course in detail. When the first paper comes due, however, you find that writing it is not as easy as you had hoped. You have an outline, but working out the detail proves difficult. Under pressure, your outline and perhaps even your central ideas change, because they will not go down on paper exactly as you had conceived them. You suffer, as you well know, in this creative process. The paper does not go as predicted, but your struggle may bring something new to birth. In any case, only after the task is done will you understand what you have been through. Even then the comprehension is unlikely to be complete, for every account of our past possesses the same elusiveness that characterizes the future.

Even this awareness is insufficient to give us certainty about the future, because the future has too many contingencies and uncertainties to make such simplicity possible. Thus, Kierkegaard stressed that the right decision is to accept the fact that life has elements of unpredictability that cannot be overcome. We should decide to live with that recognition. Decisions are harder to come by when fixity is lacking, but, rather than thwarting our attempts to reach firm decisions about life, accepting uncertainty provides the only realistic basis for decision making. Explore more of Kierkegaard's thought in the selections that follow. The first is part of his pseudonymous preface to *Either/Or*; the second a portion from his *Philosophical Fragments*. See if you decide the same.

. . . I had best proceed in order and explain how I came into possession of these papers. It is now about seven years since I first noticed at a merchant's shop here in town a secretary which from the very first moment I saw it attracted my attention. It was not of modern workmanship, had been used a good deal, and yet it fascinated me. It is impossible for me to explain the reason for this impression, but most people in the course of their lives have had some similar experience. My daily path took me by this shop, and I never failed a single day to pause and feast my eyes upon it. I gradually made up a history about it; it became a daily necessity for me to see it, and so I did not hesitate to go out of my way for the sake of seeing it, when an unaccustomed route made this necessary. And the more I looked at it, the more I wanted to own it. I realized very well that it was a peculiar desire, since I had no use for such a piece of furniture, and it would be an extravagance for me to buy it. But desire is a very sophisticated passion. I made an excuse for going into the shop, asked about other things, and as I was leaving, I casually made the shopkeeper a very low offer for the secretary. I thought possibly he might accept it; then chance would have played into my hands. It was certainly not for the sake of the money I behaved thus, but to salve my conscience. The plan miscarried, the dealer was uncommonly firm. I continued to pass the place daily, and to look at the secretary with loving eyes. "You must make up your mind," I thought, "for suppose it is sold, then it will be too late. Even

if you were lucky enough to get hold of it again, you would never have the same feeling about it." My heart beat violently; then I went into the shop. I bought it and paid for it. "This must be the last time," thought I, "that you are so extravagant; it is really lucky that you bought it, for now every time you look at it, you will reflect on how extravagant you were; a new period of your life must begin with the acquisition of the secretary." Alas, desire is very eloquent, and good resolutions are always at hand.

The secretary was duly set up in my apartment, and as in the first period of my enamorment I had taken pleasure in gazing at it from the street, so now I walked back and forth in front of it at home. Little by little I familiarized myself with its rich economy, its many drawers and recesses, and I was thoroughly pleased with my secretary. Still, things could not continue thus. In the summer of 1836 I arranged my affairs so that I could take a week's trip to the country. The postilion was engaged for five o'clock in the morning. The necessary baggage had been packed the evening before, and everything was in readiness. I awakened at four, but the vision of the beautiful country I was to visit so enchanted me that I again fell asleep, or into a dream. My servant evidently thought he would let me sleep as long as possible, for he did not call me until half-past six. The postilion was already blowing his horn, and although I am not usually inclined to obey the mandates of others, I have always made an exception in the case of the postboy and his musical theme. I was speedily dressed and already at the door, when it occurred to me, Have you enough money in your pocket? There was not much there. I opened the secretary to get at the money drawer to take what money there was. Of course the drawer would not move. Every attempt to open it failed. It was all as bad as it could possibly be. Just at this moment, while my ears were ringing with the postboy's alluring notes, to meet such difficulties! The blood rushed to my head, I became angry. As Xerxes ordered the sea to be lashed, so I resolved to take a terrible revenge. A hatchet was fetched. With it I dealt the secretary a shattering blow, shocking to see. Whether in my anger I struck the wrong place, or the drawer was as stubborn as myself, the result of the blow was not as anticipated. The drawer was closed, and the drawer remained closed. But something else happened. Whether my blow had struck exactly the right spot, or whether the shock to the whole framework of the secretary was responsible, I do not know, but I do know that a secret door sprang open, one which I had never before noticed. This opened a pigeonhole that I naturally had never discovered. Here to my great surprise I found a mass of papers, the papers which form the content of the present work. My intention as to the journey remained unchanged. At the first station we came to I would negotiate a loan. A mahogany case in which I usually kept a pair of pistols was hastily emptied and the papers were placed in it. Pleasure had triumphed, and had become even greater. In my heart I begged the secretary for forgiveness for the harsh treatment, while my mind found its doubt strengthened, that the external is not the internal, as well as my empirical generalization confirmed, that luck is necessary to make such discoveries possible.

I reached Hillerød in the middle of the forenoon, set my finances in order, and got a general impression of the magnificent scenery. The following morning I at once began my excursions, which now took on a very different character from that which I had originally intended. My servant followed me with the mahogany case. I sought out a romantic spot in the forest where I should be as free as possible from surprise, and then took out the documents. Mine host, who noticed these frequent excursions in company with the mahogany case, ventured the remark that I must be trying to improve my marksmanship. For this conjecture I was duly grateful, and left him undisturbed in his belief.

A hasty glance at the papers showed me that they were made up of two collections whose external differences were strongly marked. One of them was written on a kind of vellum in quarto, with a fairly wide margin. The handwriting was legible, sometimes even a little elegant, in a single place, careless. The other was written on full sheets of foolscap with ruled columns, such as is ordinarily used for legal documents and the like. The handwriting was clear, somewhat spreading, uniform and even, apparently that of a business man. The contents also proved to be very dissimilar. One part consisted of a number of aesthetic essays of varying length, the other was composed of two long inquiries and one shorter one, all with an ethical content, as it seemed, and in the form of letters. This dissimilarity was completely confirmed by a closer examination. The second series consists of letters written to the author of the first series.

But I must try to find some briefer designation to identify the two authors. I have examined the letters very carefully, but I have found little or nothing to the purpose. Concerning the first author, the aesthete, the papers yield absolutely nothing. As for the second, the letter writer, it appears that his name was William, and that he was a magistrate, but of what court is not stated. If I were to confine myself strictly to this data, and decide to call him William, I should lack a corresponding designation for the first author, and should have to give him an arbitrary name. Hence I have preferred to call the first author A, the second B.

In addition to the longer essays, I have found among the papers a number of slips of paper on which were written aphorisms, lyrical effusions, reflections. The handwriting indicated A as the author, and the nature of the contents confirmed my conjecture.

Then I tried to arrange the papers as well as I could. In the case of those written by B this was fairly easy. Each of these letters presupposes the one preceding, and in the second letter there is a quotation from the first; the third letter presupposes the other two.

The arranging of A's papers was not so simple. I have therefore let chance determine the order, that is to say, I have left them in the order in which I found them, without being able to decide whether this order has any chronological value or ideal-significance. The slips of paper lay loose in the pigeonhole, and so I have had to allot them a place. I have placed them first because it seemed to me that they might best be regarded as provisional glimpses of what the longer essays develop more connectedly. I have called them *Diapsalmata,* and have added as a sort of motto: *ad se ipsum.* This title and this motto are in a manner mine, and yet not altogether so. They are mine insofar as they are applied to the whole collection, but they also belong to A, for the word *Diapsalmata* was written on one of the slips of paper, and on two of them, the phrase, *ad se ipsum.* A little French verse which was found above one of the aphorisms, I have placed on the inside of the title page, a common practice with A himself. Since many of the aphorisms have a lyric form, it seemed proper to use the word *Diapsalmata* as the principal title. If the reader should consider this choice unfortunate, then I must acknowledge that this was my own device, and that the word was certainly in good taste as used by A himself for the aphorism over which it is found. I have left the arrangement of the individual aphorisms to chance. That these individual expressions often contradict one another seemed quite natural, since each one of them belongs precisely to an essential mood. I did not think it worthwhile to adopt an arrangement that would make these contradictions less striking. I followed chance, and it is also chance that has directed my attention to the fact that the first and the last aphorisms correspond to one another, as the one is touched by the suffering that lies in being a poet, while the other enjoys the satisfaction which lies in always having the laugh on its side.

As to A's aesthetic essays, I have nothing to emphasize concerning them. They were found all ready for printing, and insofar as they contain any difficulties, they must be permitted to speak for themselves. For my part I may state that I have added a translation of the Greek quotations scattered through the essays, which is taken from one of the better German translations.

The last of A's papers is a story entitled *Diary of the Seducer.* Here we meet with new difficulties, since A does not acknowledge himself as author, but only as editor. This is an old trick of the novelist, and I should not object to it, if it did not make my own position so complicated, as one author seems to be enclosed in another, like the parts in a Chinese puzzle box. Here is not the place to explain in greater detail the reasons for my opinion. I shall only note that the dominant mood in A's preface in a manner betrays the poet. It seems as if A had actually become afraid of his poem, as if it continued to terrify him, like a troubled dream when it is told. If it were an actual occurrence which he had become privy to, then it seems strange that the preface shows no trace of A's joy in seeing the realization of the idea which had so often floated before his mind. The idea of the seducer is suggested in the essay on the *Immediate-Erotic* as well as in the *Shadowgraphs,* namely, the idea that the analogue to Don Juan must be a reflective seducer who comes under the category of the interesting, where the question is not about how many he seduces, but about how he does it. I find no trace of such joy in the preface, but rather, as was said, a certain horror and trembling, which might well have its cause in his poetical relationship to this idea. Nor am I surprised that it affected A thus; for I, who have simply nothing to do with this narrative, I who am twice removed from the original author, I, too, have sometimes felt quite strange when, in the silence of the night, I have busied myself with these papers. It was as if the Seducer came like a shadow over the floor, as if he fixed his demoniac eye upon me, and said: "Well, so you are going to publish my papers! It is quite unjustifiable in you; you arouse anxiety in the dear little lassies. Yet obviously, in return you would make me and my kind harmless. There you are mistaken; for I need only change the method, and my circumstances become more favorable than before. What a stream of lassies I see running straight into my arms when they hear that seductive name: a seducer! Give me half a year and I shall provide a story which will be more interesting than all I have hitherto experienced. I imagine a young, vigorous girl of spirit who conceives the extraordinary idea of avenging her sex upon me. She thinks to coerce me, to make me feel the pangs of unrequited love. That is just the girl for me. If she does not herself strike deeply enough, then I shall come to her assistance. I shall writhe like the eel of the Wise Men of Gotham. And then when I have brought her to the point I wish, then is she mine!"

But perhaps I have already abused my position as editor in burdening the reader with my reflections. The occasion must provide the excuse. It was on account of the awkwardness of my position, occasioned by A's calling himself only the editor, not the author of this story, that I let myself be carried away.

What more I have to say about this story shall be exclusively in my role as editor. I think that I have perhaps found something in it that will determine the time of its action. The Diary has a date here and there, but the year is always omitted. This might seem to preclude further inquiry, but by studying the individual dates, I believe I have found a clue. Of course every year has a seventh of April, a third of July, a second of August, and so forth; but it is not true that the seventh of April falls every year upon Monday. I have therefore made certain calculations, and have found that this combination fits the year 1834. I cannot tell whether A had thought of this or not, but probably not, since then he would not have used so much caution as he has. Nor does the Diary read, Monday the seventh of April, and so on, but merely April 7. Even on the seventh of April, the entry begins thus: "Consequently on Monday"—whereby the reader's attention is distracted; but by reading through the entry under this date, one sees that it must have been written on Monday. As far as this story is concerned, I now have a definite date. But every attempt to utilize it in determining the time of the other essays has failed. I might have made this story the third in the collection, but, as I said above, I preferred to leave

it to chance, and everything is in the sequence in which I found it.

As far as B's papers are concerned, these arrange themselves easily and naturally. In their case I have permitted myself an alteration, and have provided them with a title, since their epistolary style prevented the author from using a title. Should the reader, therefore, after having become familiar with the contents, decide that the titles are not well chosen, I shall have to reconcile myself to the disappointment of having done something poorly that I wished to do well.

Here and there I found a remark set down in the margin. These I have made into footnotes, so as not to interrupt the even flow of the text.

As regards B's manuscript, I have allowed myself no alterations, but have scrupulously treated it as a finished document. I might perhaps have easily corrected an occasional carelessness, such as is explicable when one remembers that the author is merely a letter writer. I have not wished to do this because I feared that I might go too far. When B states that out of every hundred young men who go astray, ninety-nine are saved by women, and one by divine grace, it is easy to see that he has not been very rigid in his reckoning, since he provides no place at all for those who are actually lost. I could easily have made a little modification in the reckoning, but there seemed to me something far more beautiful in B's miscalculation. In another place he mentions a Greek wise man by the name of Myson, and says of him that he enjoyed the rare distinction of being reckoned among the Seven Sages, when their number is fixed at fourteen. I wondered at first where B could have got this information, and also what Greek author it was that he cited. My suspicion at once fell on Diogenes Laertius, and . . . I found a reference to him. B's statement might perhaps need correction; the case is not quite as he puts it, since there was some uncertainty among the ancients as to who the Seven Sages were. But I have not thought it worthwhile to make any corrections, since it seemed to me that while his statement is not quite accurate historically, it might have another value.

The point I have now reached, I had arrived at five years ago. I had arranged the papers as at present, had decided to publish them, but thought best to postpone it for a time. Five years seemed long enough. The five years are now up, and I begin where I left off. I need not assure the reader that I have tried in every conceivable way to find some trace of the authors. The dealer, like most of his kind, kept no books; he did not know from whom he had bought the secretary; he thought it might have been at public auction. I shall not attempt to describe the many fruitless attempts I have made to identify the authors, attempts which have taken so much of my time, since the recollection gives me no pleasure. As to the result, however, I can describe it to the reader very briefly, for the result was simply nil.

As I was about to carry out my decision to have the papers published, one more scruple awakened within me. Perhaps the reader will permit me to speak frankly. It occurred to me that I might be guilty of an indiscretion toward the unknown authors. However, the more familiar I became with the papers, the more these scruples disappeared. The papers were of such a nature that since my most painstaking investigations had failed to throw any light upon them, I was confident that no reader would be able to do so, for I dare compare myself with any such reader, not in taste and sympathy and insight, but in tirelessness and industry. For supposing the anonymous authors were still living, that they lived in this town, that they came unexpectedly upon their own papers, still if they themselves kept silent, there would be no consequences following the publication. For in the strictest sense of the word, these papers do what we sometimes say of all printed matter—they keep their own counsel.

One other scruple that I have had was in itself of less significance and fairly easy to overcome, and has been overcome in even an easier way than I had anticipated. It occurred to me that these papers might be financially lucrative. It seemed proper that I should receive a small honorarium for my editorial services; but an author's royalty would be too much. As the honest Scotch farmers in *The White Lady* decided to buy and cultivate the family estate, and then restore it to the Counts of Avenel if they should ever return, so I decided to put the entire returns at interest, so that when the authors turned up, I could give them the whole amount with compound interest. If the reader has not already, because of my complete ineptitude, assured himself that I am neither an author nor a professional literary man who makes publishing his profession, then the naïveté of this reasoning must establish it indisputably. My scruples were probably more easily overcome because in Denmark an author's royalty is by no means a country estate, and the authors would have to remain away a long time for their royalties, even at compound interest, to become a financial object.

It remained only to choose a title. I might call them Papers, Posthumous Papers, Found Papers, Lost Papers, and so forth. A number of variants could be found, but none of these titles satisfied me. In selecting a title I have therefore allowed myself a liberty, a deception, for which I shall try to make an accounting. During my constant occupation with the papers, it dawned upon me that they might be looked at from a new point of view, by considering all of them as the work of one man. I know very well everything that can be urged against this view, that it is unhistorical, improbable, unreasonable, that one man should be the author of both parts, although the reader might easily be tempted to the play on words, that he who says A must also say B. However, I have not yet been able to relinquish the idea. Let us imagine a man who had lived through both of these phases, or who had thought upon both. A's papers contain a number of attempts to formulate an aesthetic philosophy of life. A single, coherent, aesthetic view of life can scarcely be carried out. B's papers contain an ethical view of life. As I let this thought sink into my soul, it became clear to me that

I might make use of it in choosing a title. The one I have selected precisely expresses this. The reader cannot lose very much because of this title, for while reading the book he may perfectly well forget the title. Then, when he has read the book, he may perhaps reflect upon the title. This will free him from all finite questions as to whether A was really convinced of his error and repented, whether B conquered, or if it perhaps ended by B's going over to A's opinion. In this respect, these papers have no ending. If anyone thinks this is not as it should be, one is not thereby justified in saying that it is a fault, for one must call it a misfortune. For my own part I regard it as fortunate. One sometimes chances upon novels in which certain characters represent opposing views of life. It usually ends by one of them convincing the other. Instead of these views being allowed to speak for themselves, the reader is enriched by being told the historical result, that one has convinced the other. I regard it as fortunate that these papers contain no such information. Whether A wrote his aesthetic essays after having received B's letters, whether his soul continued to be tossed about in wild abandon, or whether it found rest, I cannot say, since the papers indicate nothing. Nor is there any clue as to how things went with B, whether he had strength to hold to his convictions or not. When the book is read, then A and B are forgotten, only their views confront one another, and await no finite decision in particular personalities.

I have nothing further to say except that the honored authors, if they were aware of my project, might possibly wish to accompany their papers with a word to the reader. I shall therefore add a few words with them holding and guiding the pen. A would probably interpose no objection to the publication; he would probably warn the reader: read them or refuse to read them, you will regret both. What B would say is more difficult to decide. He would perhaps reproach me, especially with regard to the publication of A's papers. He would let me feel that he had no part in them, that he washed his hands of responsibility. When he had done this, then he would perhaps turn to the book with these words: "Go out into the world then; escape if possible the attention of critics, seek a single reader in a favorable hour, and should you meet a feminine reader, then would I say: 'My fair reader, you will perhaps find in this book something you ought not to know; other things you might well profit from knowing; may you so read the first that having read it, you may be as one who has not read it; may you read the other so that having read it, you may be as one who cannot forget it.' " I, as editor, only add the wish that the book may meet the reader in an auspicious hour, and that the fair reader may succeed in following B's well-meant advice.

The Editor[13]

COMING INTO EXISTENCE

. . . The change of coming into existence is a transition from possibility to actuality.

Can the necessary come into existence? Coming into existence is a change, but the necessary cannot be changed, since it always relates itself to itself and relates itself to itself in the same way. All coming into existence is a *suffering,* and the necessary cannot suffer; it cannot undergo the suffering of the actual, which is that the possible (not only the excluded possibility but also the accepted possibility) reveals itself as nothing in the moment it becomes actual, for the possible is made into nothing by the actual. Everything which comes into existence proves precisely by coming into existence that it is not necessary, for the only thing which cannot come into existence is the necessary, because the necessary *is.*

Is not necessity then a synthesis of possibility and actuality? What could this mean? Possibility and actuality do not differ in essence but in being; how could there from this difference be formed a synthesis constituting necessity, which is not a determination of being but a determination of essence, since it is the essence of the necessary to be. If possibility and actuality could be united to become necessity, they would become an absolutely different essence, which is not a kind of change; and in becoming necessity or the necessary, they would become that which alone of all things excludes coming into existence, which is just as impossible as it is self-contradictory. (Compare the Aristotelian principle: "it is possible," "it is possible that not," "it is not possible."—The theory of true and false propositions—Epicurus—tends only to confuse the issue here, since essence and not being is reflected upon, and in this way no help is given with respect to the characterization of the future.)

The necessary is a category entirely by itself. Nothing ever comes into existence with necessity; likewise the necessary never comes into existence and something by coming into existence never becomes the necessary. Nothing whatever exists because it is necessary, but the necessary exists because it is necessary or because the necessary is. The actual is no more necessary than the possible, for the necessary is absolutely different from both. (Compare Aristotle's doctrine of the two kinds of possibility in relationship to the necessary. His mistake lies in his beginning with the principle that everything necessary is possible. In order to avoid having to assert contradictory and even self-contradictory predicates about the necessary, he helps himself out by two kinds of possibility, instead of discovering that his first principle is incorrect, since possibility cannot be predicated of the necessary.)

The change involved in coming into existence is actuality; the transition takes place with freedom. No coming into existence is necessary. It was not necessary before the coming into existence, for then there could not have been the coming into existence, nor after the coming into existence, for then there would not have been the coming into existence.

All coming into existence takes place with freedom, not by necessity. Nothing comes into existence by virtue of a logical ground, but only by a cause. Every cause terminates in a freely effecting cause. The illusion occasioned by the intervening causes is that the coming into existence seems to be necessary; the truth about intervening causes is that just as they themselves have come into existence they point back ultimately to a freely effecting cause. Even the possibility of deducing consequences from a law of nature gives no evidence for the necessity of any coming into existence, which is clear as soon as one reflects definitively on coming into existence. The same is the case with manifestations of freedom, provided we do not let ourselves be deceived by the manifestations of freedom but reflect upon the coming into existence.

The Historical Everything that has come into existence is *eo ipso* historical. For even if it accepts no further historical predicate, it nevertheless accepts the one decisive historical predicate: it has come into existence. That whose coming into existence is a simultaneous coming into existence (*Nebeneinander,* Space) has no other history than this. But even when viewed in this light (*en masse*), and abstracting from what an ingenious speculation calls the history of nature in a special sense, nature has a history.

But the historical is the past (for the present pressing upon the confines of the future has not yet become historical). How then can it be said that nature, though immediately present, is historical, except in the sense of the said ingenious speculation? The difficulty comes from the fact that nature is too abstract to have a dialectic with respect to time in the stricter sense. This is nature's imperfection, that it has no history in any other sense; but it is a perfection in nature that it nevertheless has this suggestion of a history, namely that it has come into existence. (This constitutes its past, the fact that it exists is its present.) On the other hand, it is the perfection of the Eternal to have no history, and of all that is, the Eternal alone has absolutely no history.

However, coming into existence may present a reduplication, i.e., the possibility of a second coming into existence within the first coming into existence. Here we have the historical in the stricter sense, subject to a dialectic with respect to time. The coming into existence which in this sphere is identical with the coming into existence of nature is a possibility, a possibility which for nature is its whole reality. But this historical coming into existence in the stricter sense is a coming into existence within a coming into existence, which should constantly be kept in mind. The more specifically historical coming into existence occurs by the operation of a relatively freely effecting cause, which in turn points ultimately to an absolutely freely effecting cause.

The Past What has happened has happened, and cannot be undone; in this sense it does not admit of change (Chrysippus the Stoic—Diodorus the Megarian). Is this immutability identical with the immutability of the necessary? The immutability of the past has been brought about by a change, namely the change of coming into existence; such an immutability does not exclude all change, since it did not exclude this change. All change is excluded (subjecting the concept to a temporal dialectic) only by being excluded in every moment. If the past is conceived as necessary, this can happen only by virtue of forgetting that it has come into existence; is such forgetfulness perhaps also necessary?

What has happened has happened as it happened; in this sense it does not admit of change. But is this immutability identical with the immutability of the necessary? The immutability of the past consists in the fact that its actual "thus" cannot become different; but does it follow from this that its possible "how" could not have been realized in a different manner? The immutability of the necessary, on the contrary, consists in its constant relating itself to itself, and in its relating itself to itself always in the same manner, excluding every change. It is not content with the immutability that belongs to the past, which as we have shown is not merely subject to a dialectic with respect to a prior change from which it emerges, but must even suffer a dialectic with respect to a higher change which annuls it. (Repentance, for example, which seeks to annul an actuality.)

The future has not yet happened. But it is not *on that account* less necessary than the past, since the past did not become necessary by coming into existence, but on the contrary proved by coming into existence that it was not necessary. If the past had become necessary it would not be possible to infer the opposite about the future, but it would rather follow that the future also was necessary. If necessity could gain a foothold at a single point, there would no longer be any distinguishing between the past and the future. To assume to predict the future (prophesy) and to assume to understand the necessity of the past are one and the same thing, and only custom makes the one seem more plausible than the other to a given generation. The past has come into existence; coming into existence is the change of actuality brought about by freedom. If the past had become necessary it would no longer belong to freedom; i.e., it would no longer belong to that by which it came into existence. Freedom would then be in a sorry case, both an object of laughter and deserving of tears, since it would be responsible for what did not belong to it, being destined to bring offspring into the world for necessity to devour. Freedom itself would be an illusion, and coming into existence no less so; freedom would be witchcraft and coming into existence a false alarm.[14]

Summary

All the philosophers discussed in this chapter are concerned to help people make right decisions, but only rarely do they prescribe exactly what someone should do. This is as it should be where philosophy is concerned, for at its core stands the Socratic conviction that men and women must first come to know themselves. Of course, individual thinkers do take strong positions. They want to convince you about many things. But it is important to remember that philosophy is more than the thought of any single thinker. Each individual alerts us to things we ignore at our peril. Yet the scope of philosophy tells us that no theory contains the whole truth or the last word. Guides to help us make the right decisions are available; but in the end, decision making leaves us to wrestle with ourselves.

As that wrestling occurs, however, several practical hints about good decision making emerge from the writers presented in this chapter. First, Epicurus and Epictetus urge us to consider the extent and limits of our freedom—Considering what is possible and what is not, and evaluating both what nature requires of us and what the limits of our powers are. These steps of deliberation do not guarantee wise choices, but without them decisions are unlikely to be sound. Augustine stresses the need for getting straight about the priorities among higher and lower values. Kierkegaard wants us to be aware of the paradoxes life presents and of the need to recognize that there are times when we must be decisive even though our alternatives are not entirely clear. As for learning about ourselves, he suggests that we may discover the most about ourselves after a decisive act and not before. Finding out what is most important to us, as Augustine and Kierkegaard both knew as well, is not a matter best decided in haste. This is partly because what we value as individuals has immense social implications. We shall consider aspects of that topic in the next chapter.

GLOSSARY

aesthetic having to do with sensation, enjoyment, and appreciation. In Kierkegaard's philosophy, the aesthetic is one term of the **"either/or"** dichotomy having to do with fundamentally opposite attitudes toward the conduct of life; the aesthetic mode is one in which the gratification of immediate desires takes precedence over decisions that commit a person to a determinate course of action in the future.

anxiety apprehension, fearful anticipation; in Kierkegaard, the state of mind stemming from the uncertainty of the future, which prompts us to make decisions and commitments aimed at lending a definite, predictable, repetitive structure to our lives.

atom in the materialist philosophy of Epicurus and Lucretius, the smallest irreducible particle of material reality. Faced with the problem of determinism and free choice, Lucretius suggested that some atoms change according to determinate patterns, while others are capable of "swerving" or introducing randomness and unpredictability, the condition of the possibility of choice, into material nature.

boredom *ennui*, a state of restlessness and weariness in the face of the predictability of life. In Kierkegaard, boredom is "the root of all evil" and a fundamental condition of life; it compels us to depart from our commitments in adopting the worship of novelty that characterizes the aesthetic mode of life, and finally leads us to despair when this pursuit of momentary pleasure also proves ineffective against itself.

commitment the adherence to one's promises and duties that defines the **ethical** mode of life; ethical consistency, *noblesse oblige*; in Kierkegaard, the antithesis of the "arbitrariness" that characterizes the aesthetic mode of life.

confession a direct and forthright revelation of personal beliefs, concerns, and actions, often used in the religious sense of "baring one's soul," as to God. For Augustine and Kierkegaard, confession forms an important mode of philosophizing in which the philosopher's own experience forms the basis and the subject matter of his works.

decision the act of choosing, of narrowing down the possibilities for action to one which we will actually adopt. In Kierkegaard, the act of decision is unavoidable in a fundamental sense even in the aesthetic mode, which bases itself on "arbitrariness"; the force of anxiety and boredom necessitates at least the fundamental choice of the mode of life we will follow.

dread See **anxiety.**

"either/or" term used in the title of Kierkegaard's most well-known work, denoting the fundamental ambiguity and uncertainty of human life, and the unavoidability of decision making that gives human existence its distinctive quality.

epicurean referring to the philosophy of Epicurus, or in general to philosophies or lifestyles that focus on pleasure and sensuality. Epicurus' philosophy merges the position that all knowledge is gained through the senses with the ethical position that sensual pleasure and pain are the most basic good and evil, since they are the good and evil that we can know most directly and unambiguously.

equanimity the term in Stoical philosophy for the state of mind aimed at by the practical discipline of philosophy, the state of remaining undisturbed by that which has no genuine importance. See **quietist.**

eternal the sphere of unchanging truth occupied by an omnipotent God, which Augustine contrasts with the world of change and uncertainty occupied by fallible human beings. See **temporal.**

ethical having to do with principle, duty, honor, etc. The mode of living Kierkegaard opposed to the aesthetic, in which acts of choice and commitment take precedence over the pursuit of momentary pleasures and the attempt to live as arbitrarily as possible.

hierarchy an ordering by rank, priority, or degree of fundamentality; Augustine conceived of Being as being so ordered, with

God occupying the realm of absolute being and human life occupying a middle ground between God and the realm of absolute nonbeing.

omnipotence the absolute ability to control events, which is possessed by God and is contrasted by Augustine with the finite capacity of human beings to control their own destinies.

panegyric a eulogy, or formal rhetorical mode of praise; for example, the "Panegyric on the Prudent Man" that concludes the reading by Epicurus.

pleasure the idea of what is gratifying to our most immediate or natural desires, often treated as an ethical theme in conjunction with sensual gratification, in contrast with "higher" pleasures or satisfactions.

priority the concept Augustine uses to express the superiority of the divine (or "City of God") over the temporal. Since earthly existence is a lower form in the hierarchy of being, Augustine believes that all truly valuable endeavors are aimed at that which is higher in priority, that is, toward the realization of the divine in the temporal.

prudence self-restraint, caution, practical wisdom in the attainment of one's purposes.

quietist a philosophical viewpoint that advocates doing as little as possible as a means to achieving equanimity, since all actions are ultimately fruitless. This term is often used, inaccurately, to describe the Stoical philosophy.

redemption the transformation of evil into good that, in Augustine's view, stems from the benevolent grace of God, and the power by which persons dwelling in the earthly "city" may escape its boundaries and find everlasting life in the "City of God."

repetition in Kierkegaard, the constant recurrence of the same events in human life, which often leads us to boredom and dissatisfaction with our lives.

Stoicism the ancient school of philosophy represented by Epictetus and Marcus Aurelius, which advocated the effort to attain a harmonious state of mind through attention to the laws of nature and to the distinction between what we can and cannot control. For the Stoics, living in accordance with the laws of nature entailed a willful disciplining of the more immediate desires, which often cause us to value what is practically valueless from the philosophical point of view and to seek what is not within our capacity to obtain.

temporal as opposed to eternal, that which changes and is not permanent; the human realm where we can fail as God cannot.

"will of Nature" the aim of Stoic understanding; the complete expression of the order of nature and its laws, with which the Stoics believed a person ought to try to harmonize his or her life.

STUDY QUESTIONS

1. If the good is pleasure, as Epicurus says, does that mean that making the right decisions is easy? In what sense yes; in what senses no?

2. How does Epictetus determine what is within our power and what is not? Do you agree with his analysis?

3. Augustine stresses that confession is an important ingredient in making right decisions. Does his conviction square with your experience?

4. Does Augustine's theory about the "two cities" make sense to you? To what extent do you agree with the way Augustine outlines the priorities we ought to have?

5. Kierkegaard presents demanding and paradoxical situations in which logic and reason cannot produce a decision. Do you find yourself in situations like that from time to time? What can or should you do about it?

6. What seems to you to be the most important insight that Kierkegaard offers concerning decision making?

7. The thinkers discussed in this chapter urge you to consider what is most important to you. What would you say in response to that issue, and how would your answer affect your understanding of what is involved in making decisions that are right?

NOTES

[1] Epicurus, "Letter to Menoeceus," in *Letters, Principle Doctrines, and Vatican Sayings*, trans. Russel M. Greer (Indianapolis: Bobbs-Merrill, 1964), p. 53. Reprinted with permission of Macmillan Publishing Company. Copyright © 1985, 1964 by Macmillan Publishing Company.

[2] Epicurus, "Letter to Herodotus," in *Letters, Principal Doctrines, and Vatican Sayings*, p. 9.

[3] Lucretius, *The Nature of the Universe*, trans. Ronald Latham (Baltimore: Penguin Books, 1960), p. 67.

[4] Epicurus, "Letter to Herodotus," p. 10.

[5] Epicurus, "Letter to Menoeceus," p. 55.

[6] Epicurus, "The Vatican Sayings," in *Letters, Principle Doctrines, and Vatican Sayings*, p. 67.

[7] Epicurus, "Letter to Menoeceus," pp. 53–59.

[8] Epictetus, *The Enchiridion*, trans. Thomas W. Higginson (Indianapolis: Bobbs-Merrill, 1977), p. 17. © 1985 by Macmillan Publishing Company. Reprinted by permission.

[9] Saint Augustine, *The City of God*, trans. Marcus Dods (New York: Modern Library, 1950), pp. 1, 441.

[10]Saint Augustine, *Confessions*, trans. Vernon J. Bourke (New York: Fathers of the Church, 1953), p. 3. Used by permission.

[11]Søren Kierkegaard, *Either/Or*, trans. David F. Swenson and Lillian Marvin Swenson. (Princeton, N.J.: Princeton University Press, 1971), 1:289. Copyright 1944, © 1972 renewed by Howard A. Johnson. Reprinted by permission of Princeton University Press.

[12]Søren Kierkegaard, *Philosophical Fragments*, trans. David Swenson and Howard V. Hong (Princeton, N.J.: Princeton University Press, 1967), p. 11.

[13]Kierkegaard, *Either/Or*, 1:4–15.

[14]Kierkegaard, *Philosophical Fragments*, pp. 91–96.

CHAPTER NINE

Do I Have Rights in Society?

*A*ll of us think we possess or ought to possess certain rights. We should be able to do certain things and refuse to do others, either because we are citizens of a particular state or simply because we are human. As we think about such beliefs, we discover that **rights** are linked to **duties.** If we all have rights, presumably we also have a responsibility to honor those rights. Moreover, it may even be true that rights are derived from duties, for at times you may have a right to expect certain treatment *from* me only if you also have a duty to behave in a certain manner *toward* me.

As we discuss these issues, which are a concern for us all, we will again present a variety of approaches. Some philosophers have dealt with questions about rights by appealing to a **state of nature** from which all societies have come, one in which there were no civil laws. They try to show how our present political circumstances arose from those origins. Thomas Hobbes is famous for this approach. John Locke also refers to a "state of nature," but his model contains a greater ethical structure than was observed by Hobbes. Because Hobbes and Locke do not agree about the qualities of a "state of nature," their theories about rights do not come out the same either.

Political leaders have a stake in these issues at least as much as philosophers. Thomas

Jefferson is a good example, and we will explore his use of "self-evident" truths about life, liberty, and the pursuit of happiness. Jean-Jacques Rousseau is another influential thinker when the question is "Do I have rights in society?" He stresses the idea of a **social contract** in which people reason together about the rights and rules that should govern them. Vital questions about which prerogatives belong to individuals and which belong to the body politic emerge from his discussions. More recently, Ayn Rand has championed the rights of individuals against an increasing governmental domination. Her Objectivist perspective on individualism does not satisfy everyone, however, and some of the reasons are illustrated effectively by the American pragmatist, John Dewey.

These thinkers will diverge and disagree, but they have much in common, too. They are convinced, for example, that human rights can withstand tyrannical forces only if attention is paid to education. Think about it: If nobody ever taught you, or if you could not learn, what would life be like? At the very least, existence would be crude, and there probably would be no human civilization. We teach so that people can develop and care for themselves, earn a living, provide food and shelter for their families. But our broad educational goals are more complex. Education is a social enterprise; it involves the well-being of groups as well as individuals. Education, power, and rights—political and economic—have much to do with each other. Although the nation with the best-educated leadership and populace will not necessarily be the most powerful and free, it is no accident that those qualities flourish in societies that excel in education. The education we provide and the rights and duties we possess are closely intertwined.

Most of the thinkers we meet in this chapter were influenced by the movement we call the Enlightenment. This began as a reaction against what was considered the "faith orientation" of Medieval philosophy. As the writings of the Greek and Roman philosophers were rediscovered, intellectual leaders became fascinated with the idea of eliminating superstition from human thinking and freeing all human society to reach its full potential through independent, critical, rational exploration of all phenomena and ideas.

Thomas Hobbes and the State of Nature

Thomas Hobbes (1588–1679) felt that we can understand our moral and political life only by returning to examine its origins. He sought to educate us by presenting a supposed state of nature where no codes and laws existed. Hobbes was not concerned with the historical question of when civil societies emerged; he asked, rather, how civil society developed and what it ought to be. Unlike some thinkers who believe that we would be better off if we could be liberated from governmental authority and return to more "natural" conditions, Hobbes did not regard the state of nature as a desirable place to live. For instance, he denied that people are sympathetic socially by nature. Instead, he thought they are motivated primarily by a desire for power and by a fear of others. The natural condi-

THOMAS HOBBES 1588–1679

tion of humanity is virtually a state of war, asserted Hobbes, in the following famous passage.

> In such condition [i.e., the state of nature] there is no place for industry, because the fruit thereof is uncertain: and consequently no culture of the earth, no navigation nor use of the commodities that may be imported by sea; no commodious building; no instruments of moving and removing such things as require much force; no knowledge of the face of the earth; no account of time; no arts, no letters; no society; and, which is worst of all, continual fear and danger of violent death; and the life of man solitary, poor, nasty, brutish, and short.[1]

Given these inauspicious origins, Hobbes contended that peace and order are what people most need and should desire. He intended his political theory, and in particular his outlook about rights and duties, to help achieve those ends. Opinion about the wisdom of Hobbes's political philosophy is mixed, however, and some critics regard him as the father of modern totalitarianism.

Born near Malmesbury, England, Hobbes was educated at Oxford and served for a time as Francis Bacon's assistant. He was much intrigued by Galileo's writings on physics, which helped convince him that only matter exists and that every happening can in principle be predicted in terms of precise scientific laws. Hobbes was also profoundly influenced by the English Civil War (1642–49). The "Roundheads," mostly the Puritan followers of Parliament, successfully battled the royalist "Cavaliers," and on January 30, 1649, Charles I was beheaded. England became a republic, but not for long, because Oliver Cromwell soon established a virtual dictatorship. That reign did not last either. By 1660 Charles II was on the throne, and England had a limited monarchy. Hobbes observed much of this civil upheaval from a distance, having fled to France in 1640 when civil war was clearly impending. There he composed his great work on political theory, *Leviathan, or the Matter, Form, and Power of a Commonwealth, Ecclesiastical and Civil* (1651). It advanced the views that Hobbes felt the English Civil War confirmed, namely, that humanity's inhumanity made a powerful sovereign government essential.

Is Our Natural Situation in Life Secure?

Sometimes we take our governments and our moral codes for granted. We think we ought to have political stability as a natural condition. But is our situation one that is only sometimes disturbed by personal threats or revolutions? Hobbes felt that humanity's state of nature was quite different from what we take for granted. It was rife with instability, and the result was that the prime need of all human beings was and is to find both security in a moral code and peace under a stable government. Hobbes thought that the struc-ture of the required government would have to fit human nature, and so he set himself the task of deducing political principles from what he took to be the fundamental inclinations of men and women.

"Everything," contended Hobbes, "is best understood by its constitutive causes."[2] If so, we must first go back and attempt to determine what human nature would be like in its unfettered state rather than as we may find it today in society. Devoid of social restraints, argued Hobbes, our natural condition is to distrust and dread each other. Following what he called "the right of nature," people will assert themselves as they think necessary to avoid violent death and to preserve their lives. Living in accord with this natural right, people are essentially equal but not necessarily happy. For in "a condition of war of everyone against everyone—in which case everyone is governed by his own reason and there is nothing he can make use of that may not be a help unto him in preserving his life against his enemies—it follows that in such a condition every man has a right to everything, even to one another's body."[3]

In the state of nature, Hobbes also believed, individual desire determines what is good or bad, and in this condition there will inevitably be strife as people try to get what they want. The intolerability of this situation, however, causes an awakening that leads to life within the boundaries of **natural law**. Hobbes defined a law of nature as "a precept or general rule, found out by reason, by which a man is forbidden to do that which is destructive of his life or takes away the means of preserving the same and to omit that by which he thinks it may best be preserved" (p. 109). The first three natural laws Hobbes identified are as follows:

1. We should "seek peace and follow it"; but when we cannot obtain peace, we should

use "all means we can to defend ourselves."

2. For the sake of peace and self-preservation we should be willing, "when others are too, . . . to lay down [our] right to all things, and be contented with so much liberty against other men as [we] would allow other men against [ourselves]."

3. We should carry out the contracts to which we agree; otherwise "covenants are in vain and but empty words, and, the right of all men to all things remaining, we are still in the condition of war." (Pp. 110, 119.)

In sum, people should and do agree to establish a civil society, a **commonwealth.** They surrender the natural right of self-assertion, form a compact, and bow to the **sovereign** they empower. Note that Hobbes felt that our moral codes and governments result from a very practical necessity. We are virtually forced to give up our natural right to seize whatever we want because of the chaos such anarchy causes and because we fear retaliation if our powers fail. Thus, we are not naturally civil creatures but come to abide by **civil law** only out of forced convenience and fear about what will happen if we try to live without restraining social structures. The rights we have in society and the laws we live under are therefore human constructions aimed at securing peace and stability.

The Sovereign's Power

Hobbes portrayed a state of nature in which individuals basically do not get along. Recognizing how disastrous that situation will be, they eventually come together out of necessity and agree to establish a higher authority to govern them. As Hobbes described this pact, his emphasis fell on the importance of individuals agreeing to let a sovereign rule. According to his notion,

therefore, the social contract binds the individuals who agree to let a sovereign rule, but the contract is between the citizens themselves, not between the sovereign and the **citizens.**

The sovereign can be either an individual or an assembly. But whatever its form, the sovereignty ought to be complete and not directly subject to the wishes of the citizens. True, the sovereign would have to have citizens' interests at heart and allow for liberty, lest his power perish through rebellion, but the sovereign could hardly tolerate disobedience that disturbed the public peace and stability. The sovereign, then, would establish the law and enforce it; the citizens, in turn, had a duty to obey.

According to Hobbes, the sovereign's law was the measure of justice. Strictly speaking, there could not be an unjust law, because the law defines justice. A law could be bad insofar as it failed to ensure the safety of the people. Decisions on that score, however, were not reserved to the people, since that path would lead to anarchy. Instead, Hobbes relied on the conscientious judgment of the sovereign to do what is best.

Do I have rights in society? In Hobbes's view, a natural right to life and self-preservation exists, but we have given up the right to do anything that we think necessary to fulfill those ends. Such an individualistic pursuit would put everyone at risk, and it is reasonable to let a sovereign rule for the sake of the public peace and stability we need and crave. Within the legal structure established by the sovereign, civil rights can have their place, but their content and extent will be only as the sovereign decrees. Hobbes claimed that he had both provided a description of the emergence of civil society and articulated a persuasive account of how human rights in society should be understood. Does his story ring true? Think about that as your reading from *Leviathan* continues.

OF THE NATURAL CONDITION OF MANKIND AS CONCERNING THEIR FELICITY AND MISERY

Nature has made men so equal in the faculties of the body and mind as that, though there be found one man sometimes manifestly stronger in body or of quicker mind than another, yet, when all is reckoned together, the difference between man and man is not so considerable as that one man can thereupon claim to himself any benefit to which another may not pretend as well as he. For as to the strength of body, the weakest has strength enough to kill the strongest, either by secret machination or by confederacy with others that are in the same danger with himself.

And as to the faculties of the mind, setting aside the arts grounded upon words, and especially that skill of proceeding upon general and infallible rules called science—which very few have and but in few things, as being not a native faculty born with us, nor attained, as prudence, while we look after somewhat else—I find yet a greater equality among men than that of strength. For prudence is but experience, which equal time equally bestows on all men in those things they equally apply themselves unto. That which may perhaps make such equality incredible is but a vain conceit of one's own wisdom, which almost all men think they have in a greater degree than the vulgar—that is, than all men but themselves and a few others whom, by fame or for concurring with themselves, they approve. For such is the nature of men that howsoever they may acknowledge many others to be more witty or more eloquent or more learned, yet they will hardly believe there be many so wise as themselves; for they see their own wit at hand and other men's at a distance. But this proves rather that men are in that point equal than unequal. For there is not ordinarily a greater sign of the equal distribution of anything than that every man is contented with his share.

From this equality of ability arises equality of hope in the attaining of our ends. And therefore if any two men desire the same thing, which nevertheless they cannot both enjoy, they become enemies; and in the way to their end, which is principally their own conservation, and sometimes their delectation only, endeavor to destroy or subdue one another. And from hence it comes to pass that where an invader has no more to fear than another man's single power, if one plant, sow, build, or possess a convenient seat, others may probably be expected to come prepared with forces united to dispossess and deprive him, not only of the fruit of his labor, but also of his life or liberty. And the invader again is in the like danger of another.

And from this diffidence of one another there is no way for any man to secure himself so reasonable as anticipation—that is, by force or wiles to master the persons of all men he can, so long till he see no other power great enough to endanger him; and this is no more than his own conservation requires, and is generally allowed. Also, because there be some that take pleasure in contemplating their own power in the acts of conquest, which they pursue farther than their security requires, if others that otherwise would be glad to be at ease within modest bounds should not by invasion increase their power, they would not be able, long time, by standing only on their defense, to subsist. And by consequence, such augmentation of dominion over men being necessary to a man's conservation, it ought to be allowed him.

Again, men have no pleasure, but on the contrary a great deal of grief, in keeping company where there is no power able to overawe them all. For every man looks that his companion should value him at the same rate he sets upon himself; and upon all signs of contempt or undervaluing naturally endeavors, as far as he dares (which among them that have no common power to keep them in quiet is far enough to make them destroy each other), to extort a greater value from his contemners by damage and from others by the example.

So that in the nature of man we find three principal causes of quarrel: first, competition; second, diffidence; thirdly, glory.

The first makes men invade for gain, the second for safety, and the third for reputation. The first use violence to make themselves masters of other men's persons, wives, children, and cattle; the second, to defend them; the third, for trifles, as a word, a smile, a different opinion, and any other sign of undervalue, either direct in their persons or by reflection in their kindred, their friends, their nation, their profession, or their name.

Hereby it is manifest that, during the time men live without a common power to keep them all in awe, they are in that condition which is called war, and such a war as is of every man against every man. . . .

OF THE FIRST AND SECOND NATURAL LAWS, AND OF CONTRACTS

The right of nature, which writers commonly call *jus naturale*, is the liberty each man has to use his own power, as he will himself, for the preservation of his own nature—that is to say, of his own life—and consequently of doing anything which, in his own judgment and reason, he shall conceive to be the aptest means thereunto.

By liberty is understood, according to the proper signification of the word, the absence of external impediments; which impediments may oft take away part of a man's power to do what he would, but cannot hinder him from using the power left him according as his judgment and reason shall dictate to him.

A law of nature, *lex naturalis*, is a precept or general rule, found out by reason, by which a man is forbidden to do that which is destructive of his life or takes away the means of preserving the same and to omit that by which he thinks he may be best preserved. For though they that speak of this subject use to confound *jus* and *lex*, *right* and *law*, yet they ought to be distinguished; because right consists in liberty to do or to forbear, whereas law determines and binds to one of them; so that law and right differ as much as obligation and liberty, which in one and the same matter are inconsistent. And because the condition of man . . . is a

condition of war of everyone against everyone—in which case everyone is governed by his own reason and there is nothing he can make use of that may not be a help unto him in preserving his life against his enemies—it follows that in such a condition every man has a right to everything, even to one another's body. And therefore, as long as this natural right of every man to everything endures, there can be no security to any man, how strong or wise soever he be, of living out the time which nature ordinarily allows men to live. And consequently it is a precept or general rule of reason *that every man ought to endeavor peace, as far as he has hope of obtaining it; and when he cannot obtain it, that he may seek and use all helps and advantages of war.* The first branch of which rule contains the first and fundamental law of nature, which is *to seek peace and follow it.* The second, the sum of the right of nature, which is, *by all means we can to defend ourselves.*

From this fundamental law of nature, by which men are commanded to endeavor peace, is derived this second law: *that a man be willing, when others are so too, as far forth as for peace and defense of himself he shall think it necessary, to lay down this right to all things, and be contented with so much liberty against other men as he would allow other men against himself.* For as long as every man holds this right of doing anything he likes, so long are all men in the condition of war. But if other men will not lay down their right as well as he, then there is no reason for anyone to divest himself of his, for that were to expose himself to prey, which no man is bound to, rather than to dispose himself to peace. This is that law of the gospel: *whatsoever you require that others should do to you, that do ye to them.* . . .

OF THE CAUSES, GENERATION, AND DEFINITION OF A COMMONWEALTH

The final cause, end, or design of men, who naturally love liberty and dominion over others, in the introduction of that restraint upon themselves in which we see them live in commonwealths is the foresight of their own preservation, and of a more contented life thereby—that is to say, of getting themselves out from that miserable condition of war which is necessarily consequent . . . to the natural passions of men when there is no visible power to keep them in awe and tie them by fear of punishment to the performance of their covenants and observation of those laws of nature set down [elsewhere in the *Leviathan*].

For the laws of nature—as *justice, equity, modesty, mercy,* and, in sum, *doing to others as we would be done to*—of themselves, without the terror of some power to cause them to be observed, are contrary to our natural passions, that carry us to partiality, pride, revenge, and the like. And covenants without the sword are but words, and of no strength to secure a man at all. Therefore, notwithstanding the laws of nature (which everyone has then kept when he has the will to keep them, when he can do it safely), if there be no power erected, or not great enough for our security, every man will—and may lawfully—rely on his own strength and art for caution against all other men. And in all places where men have lived by small families, to rob and spoil one another has been a trade, and so far from being reputed against the law of nature that the greater spoils they gained, the greater was their honor; and men observed no other laws therein but the laws of honor—that is, to abstain from cruelty, leaving to men their lives and instruments of husbandry. And as small families did then, so now do cities and kingdoms, which are but greater families, for their own security enlarge their dominions upon all pretenses of danger and fear of invasion or assistance that may be given to invaders, and endeavor as much as they can to subdue or weaken their neighbors by open force and secret arts, for want of other caution, justly; and are remembered for it in after ages with honor.

Nor is it the joining together of a small number of men that gives them this security, because in small numbers small additions on the one side or the other make the advantage of strength so great as is sufficient to carry the victory, and therefore gives encouragement to an invasion. The multitude sufficient to confide in for our security is not determined by any certain number but by comparison with the enemy we fear, and is then sufficient when the odds of the enemy is not of so visible and conspicuous moment to determine the event of war as to move him to attempt.

And be there never so great a multitude, yet if their actions be directed according to their particular judgments and particular appetites, they can expect thereby no defense nor protection, neither against a common enemy nor against the injuries of one another. For being distracted in opinions concerning the best use and application of their strength, they do not help but hinder one another, and reduce their strength by mutual opposition to nothing; whereby they are easily not only subdued by a very few that agree together, but also, when there is no common enemy, they make war upon each other for their particular interest. For if we could suppose a great multitude of men to consent in the observation of justice and other laws of nature without a common power to keep them all in awe, we might as well suppose all mankind to do the same; and then there neither would be, nor need to be, any civil government or commonwealth at all, because there would be peace without subjection.

Nor is it enough for the security which men desire should last all the time of their life that they be governed and directed by one judgment for a limited time, as in one battle or one war. For though they obtain a victory by their unanimous endeavor against a foreign enemy, yet afterwards, when either they have no common enemy or he that by one part is held for an enemy is by another part held for a friend, they must needs, by the difference of their interests, dissolve and fall again into a war among themselves.

It is true that certain living creatures, as bees and ants, live sociably one with another—which are therefore by Aristotle numbered among political creatures—and yet have no other direction than their particular judgments and appetites, nor speech whereby one of them can signify to another what he thinks expedient for the common benefit; and therefore some man may perhaps desire to know why mankind cannot do the same. To which I answer:

First, that men are continually in competition for honor and dignity, which these creatures are not; and consequently among men there arises on that ground envy and hatred and finally war, but among these not so.

Secondly, that among these creatures the common good differs not from the private; and being by nature inclined to their private, they procure thereby the common benefit. But man, whose joy consists in comparing himself with other men, can relish nothing but what is eminent.

Thirdly, that these creatures—having not, as man, the use of reason—do not see nor think they see any fault in the administration of their common business; whereas among men there are very many that think themselves wiser and abler to govern the public better than the rest, and these strive to reform and innovate, one this way, another that way, and thereby bring it into distraction and civil war.

Fourthly, that these creatures, though they have some use of voice in making known to one another their desires and other affections, yet they want that art of words by which some men can represent to others that which is good in the likeness of evil, and evil in the likeness of good, and augment or diminish the apparent greatness of good and evil, discontenting men and troubling their peace at their pleasure.

Fifthly, irrational creatures cannot distinguish between *injury* and *damage*, and therefore, as long as they be at ease, they are not offended with their fellows; whereas man is then most troublesome when he is most at ease, for then it is that he loves to show his wisdom and control the actions of them that govern the commonwealth.

Lastly, the agreement of these creatures is natural, that of men is by covenant only, which is artificial; and therefore it is no wonder if there be somewhat else required besides

covenant to make their agreement constant and lasting, which is a common power to keep them in awe and to direct their actions to the common benefit.

The only way to erect such a common power as may be able to defend them from the invasion of foreigners and the injuries of one another, and thereby to secure them in such sort as that by their own industry and by the fruits of the earth they may nourish themselves and live contentedly, is to confer all their power and strength upon one man, or upon one assembly of men that may reduce all their wills, by plurality of voices, unto one will; which is as much as to say, to appoint one man or assembly of men to bear their person, and everyone to own and acknowledge himself to be author of whatsoever he that so bears their person shall act or cause to be acted in those things which concern the common peace and safety, and therein to submit their wills every one to his will, and their judgments to his judgment. This is more than consent or concord; it is a real unity of them all in one and the same person, made by covenant of every man with every man, in such manner as if every man should say to every man, *I authorize and give up my right of governing myself to this man, or to this assembly of men, on this condition, that you give up your right to him and authorize all his actions in like manner.* This done, the multitude so united in one person is called a commonwealth, in Latin *civitas*. This is the generation of that great Leviathan (or rather, to speak more reverently, of that *mortal god*) to which we owe, under the *immortal God*, our peace and defense. For by this authority, given him by every particular man in the commonwealth, he has the use of so much power and strength conferred on him that, by terror thereof, he is enabled to form the wills of them all to peace at home and mutual aid against their enemies abroad. And in him consists the essence of the commonwealth, which, to define it, is *one person, of whose acts a great multitude, by mutual covenants one with another, have made themselves every one the author, to the end he may use the strength and means of them all as he shall think expedient for their peace and common defense.* And he that carries this person is called sovereign and said to have *sovereign power;* and everyone besides, his subject. . . . (Pp. 104–107, 109–110, 139–43.)

John Locke and the Limits of Government

In Chapter Two we met John Locke (1632–1704) and examined his empirical approach for gaining knowledge. We noted that Locke's most important contribution may have been in political philosophy, and now we can explore that possibility further. Like Hobbes, Locke was an Englishman who knew about political turmoil, but he treated this knowledge very differently. Although Cromwell's rule had been followed by the Restoration (of the hereditary monarchy) in 1660, the reign of Charles II did not sustain the peace and order that Hobbes advocated. By the late 1670s, England was again bitterly divided into two main factions, the Tories supporting the king and the Whigs opposing him. When Charles was succeeded by his brother James II in 1685, the situation became even more unstable, since James was an ardent Roman Catholic who did not have the support of the Tories. Soon a bloodless coup occurred; James fled the country, and William of Orange was called to the British throne, together with his wife Mary, who was the daughter of James. Parliament affirmed basic civil liberties, including religious toleration. These events in England of 1688–89 were soon known as the "Glorious Revolution."

Hobbes died nearly a decade before 1688. Had he lived longer, it is unlikely that "glorious" would have been his description for the arrival of a more limited government than he had advocated. John Locke took a differ-

JOHN LOCKE 1632–1704

ent view. Suspected earlier of undermining the rule of Charles II, he had gone into exile in Holland, but Locke returned to England with William and Mary, bringing with him two of his most famous writings, the *Essay Concerning Human Understanding* and *Two Treatises of Government* (1690).

These works revealed an outlook at odds with that of Thomas Hobbes. Both philosophers referred to a state of nature, but in Locke's view human beings were "naturally" much more "civilized" than Hobbes found them. According to Hobbes, people were driven by a restless desire for power that left them pitted against each other until they recognized the necessity of a sovereign to establish law and order. In contrast, Locke's state of nature was much more tranquil. Human sympathy could be said to be natural, and it was motivated by an early recognition of, and a mutual respect for, basic rights. In short, Locke found human nature much more benign than did Hobbes. Government, therefore, was needed not to establish law and order from scratch but rather to maximize the opportunity to exercise rights that were in fact acknowledged in the state of nature. Though it might be too much for Locke to describe the events of 1688 as either glorious or revolutionary, he believed that they had produced steps in the right direction.

How Should Human Nature Be Understood?

Our initial discussion of Locke in Chapter Two emphasized his mistrust of claims for certainty based on appeals to innate ideas or religious authority. For Locke, knowledge claims were less likely to be matters of certainty than of probability, and they did need to be tested empirically. Even then, people's judgments might still disagree, but Locke did not see the danger in such circumstances that Hobbes perceived. The reason is that Locke found human beings to be more benevolent toward each other, more reasonable, than Hobbes thought was the case.

The Lockean state of nature, for example, "has a law of nature to govern it, which obliges everyone; and reason, which is that law, teaches all mankind who will but consult it that, being all equal and independent, no one ought to harm another in his life, health, liberty, or possessions. . . . "[4] Hobbes, too, had referred to the law of nature, and at times his description of it was close to Locke's. But Locke was much more confident than Hobbes that people were naturally inclined to obey what reason teaches. Locke's suspicion of authority, moreover, made him

doubt that having a Hobbesian absolute sovereign was a desirable way to eliminate obstacles to human happiness. Such a sovereign would more likely compound them. Locke wrote:

> I easily grant that civil government is the proper remedy for the inconveniences of the state of nature, which must certainly be great where men may be judges in their own case; since it is easy to be imagined that he who was so unjust as to do his brother an injury will scarcely be so just as to condemn himself for it; but I shall desire those who make this objection to remember that absolute monarchs are but men, and if government is to be the remedy of those evils which necessarily follow from men's being judges in their own cases, and the state of nature is therefore not to be endured, I desire to know what kind of government that is, and how much better it is than the state of nature, where one man commanding a multitude has the liberty to judge in his own case, and may do to all his subjects whatever he pleases, without the least liberty to anyone to question or control those who execute his pleasure, and in whatsoever he does, whether led by reason, mistake, or passion, must be submitted to? Much better it is in the state of nature, wherein men are not bound to submit to the unjust will of another; and if he that judges, judges amiss in his own or any other case, he is answerable for it to the rest of mankind. (Pp. 9–10.)

Locke saw the state of nature as one of "perfect freedom," one in which people "order their actions and dispose of their possessions and persons as they think fit, within the bounds of the law of nature, without asking leave or depending upon the will of any other man" (p. 4). Again this view seems to resemble that of Hobbes, and Locke concurred with him in saying that there is a basic equality among people. Yet Locke did not conclude that a war of all against all would follow. Admittedly there are the "inconveniences" of the state of nature, but Locke could settle for that relatively mild term, because he believed that "calm reason and conscience" exert an influence even before the establishment of formal governments.

Life, Liberty, and Property

"Men living together according to reason, without a common superior on earth with authority to judge between them," said Locke, "is properly the state of nature" (p. 13). Once more disputing Hobbes, Locke further explained that there is a "plain difference between the state of nature and the state of war which, however some men have confounded, are as far distant as a state of peace, good-will, mutual assistance, and preservation, and a state of enmity, malice, violence, and mutual destruction are one from another" (pp. 12–13). Nevertheless, what is properly the state of nature does not always exist as such. Thus, governments are necessary to make life better, Locke affirmed, but their powers must be limited to ensure that rights are preserved.

Locke held that the law of nature enjoined people to respect mutually the rights of life, liberty, and property. His position on **property** is especially interesting because he employed the term in more than one sense. Sometimes Locke used "property" inclusively to mean people's "lives, liberty and estates, which I call by the general name, 'property' " (p. 71). On other occasions he restricted the meaning to the products of one's labor. Particularly with regard to the latter meaning, Locke contested Hobbes's position again. Hobbes took this sort of property rights to exist only after a legal order had been established, but Locke believed the relationship worked the other way around: private property precedes civil law, because the right to property is part of the (natural) **moral law.**

Locke's argument went as follows. We have a right to self-preservation, and thus we also have a right to that which is necessary to sustain our lives. To obtain what we need in this regard requires us to labor. Our labor belongs to us, and thus when our labor removes things from the state of nature where they belonged to no one in particular, those things become our own. According to Locke, however, there is also a limit to the amount of property one may accumulate: "As much as anyone can make use of to any advantage of life before it spoils, so much he may by his labor fix a property in; whatever is beyond this is more than his share and belongs to others. Nothing was made by God for man to spoil or destroy" (p. 19).

Although the right to property is a natural right in both Locke's broad and narrower meanings, Locke knew that nature alone does not secure it. Thus, using the term inclusively, he argued that "the chief and great end . . . of men's uniting into commonwealths and putting themselves under government is the preservation of their property" (p. 71). This "uniting," Locke believed, must rest on the mutual **consent** of those who form a compact. Again, Hobbes had said something similar, but Locke added a major qualification. Locke's sense of consent did not result in the establishment of an absolute sovereign. On the contrary, the consent was only to have laws made and enforced to confirm the rights people have by nature. A division of legislative, executive, and judicial power, coupled with majority rule, is the most likely way to achieve these ends, Locke believed. The function of the state should be limited to the protection and nurturing of the people's natural rights. Failure to do so could result in a justified rebellion.

Similar Beginnings, Different Results

Locke wanted to educate people to realize that oppression results when governments forget that the chief function of government is to protect the basic rights of its citizens.

We hold these rights naturally; no government confers them. But we need to remember that Hobbes, no less than Locke, thought that he had an accurate understanding of human nature and the political life that best suited it. These English philosophers used many of the same terms in discussing the issues: for example, the state of nature and the law of nature. The resulting theories, however, were not only different but in sharp disagreement. For instance, to the question "Do I have rights in society?" Hobbes would answer "Yes, but primarily they are the civil rights that the sovereign confers." Locke's response would also be affirmative, but in quite a different sense, because his emphasis fell on the natural rights that we retain and have a right to expect a limited government to respect.

The conflict between these two thinkers means that both views cannot be completely true. But where we are dealing with minds of the calibre of Hobbes's and Locke's, it would be implausible to conclude that one theory is simply right, the other simply wrong. The issue is to educate ourselves by trying to discern where the insights of each are on or off the target. One way to start is to ask whether you find Hobbes's pessimistic view of human nature or Locke's optimistic account more persuasive as a context for considering issues about your rights in society. Carry on that process by considering more of Locke's *Second Treatise of Government*.

OF POLITICAL OR CIVIL SOCIETY

87. Man, being born, as has been proved, with a title to perfect freedom and uncontrolled enjoyment of all the rights and privileges of the law of nature equally with any other man or number of men in the world, has by nature a power not only to preserve his property—that is, his life, liberty, and estate—against the injuries and attempts of other men, but to judge of and punish the breaches of that law in others as he is persuaded the offense deserves, even with death itself in crimes where the heinousness of the fact in his opinion requires it. But because no political society can be, nor subsist, without having in itself the power to preserve the property and, in order thereunto, punish the offenses of all those of that society, there and there only is political society where every one of the members has quitted his natural power, resigned it up into the hands of the community in all cases that exclude him not from appealing for protection to the law established by it. And thus all private judgment of every particular member being excluded, the community comes to be umpire by settled standing rules, indifferent and the same to all parties, and by men having authority from the community for the execution of those rules decides all the differences that may happen between any members of that society concerning any matter of right, and punishes those offenses which any member has committed against the society with such penalties as the law has established; whereby it is easy to discern who are, and who are not, in political society together. Those who are united into one body and have a common established law and judicature to appeal to, with authority to decide controversies between them and punish offenders, are in civil society one with another; but those who have no such common appeal, I mean on earth, are still in the state of nature, each being, where there is no other, judge for himself and executioner, which is, as I have before shown it, the perfect state of nature.

88. And thus the commonwealth comes by a power to set down what punishment shall belong to the several transgressions which they think worthy of it committed amongst the members of that society—which is the power of making laws—as well as it has the power to punish any injury done unto any of its members by any one that is not of it—which is the power of war and peace—and all this for the preservation of the property of all the members of that soci-

ety as far as is possible. But though every man who has entered into civil society and is become a member of any commonwealth has thereby quitted his power to punish offenses against the law of nature in prosecution of his own private judgment, yet, with the judgment of offenses which he has given up to the legislative in all cases where he can appeal to the magistrate, he has given a right to the commonwealth to employ his force for the execution of the judgments of the commonwealth, whenever he shall be called to it; which, indeed, are his own judgments, they being made by himself or his representative. And herein we have the original of the legislative and executive power of civil society, which is to judge by standing laws how far offenses are to be punished when committed within the commonwealth, and also to determine, by occasional judgments founded on the present circumstances of the fact, how far injuries from without are to be vindicated; and in both these to employ all the force of all the members when there shall be need.

89. Whenever, therefore, any number of men are so united into one society as to quit every one his executive power of the law of nature and to resign it to the public, there and there only is a political or civil society. And this is done wherever any number of men, in the state of nature, enter into society to make one people, one body politic, under one supreme government, or else when anyone joins himself to, and incorporates with, any government already made; for hereby he authorizes the society or, which is all one, the legislative thereof to make laws for him as the public good of the society shall require, to the execution whereof his own assistance, as to his own decrees, is due. And this puts men out of a state of nature into that of a commonwealth by setting up a judge on earth, with authority to determine all the controversies and redress the injuries that may happen to any member of the commonwealth; which judge is the legislative, or magistrates appointed by it. And wherever there are any number of men, however associated, that have no such decisive power

to appeal to, there they are still in the state of nature.

90. Hence it is evident that absolute monarchy, which by some men is counted the only government in the world, is indeed inconsistent with civil society, and so can be no form of civil government at all; for the end of civil society [is] to avoid and remedy these inconveniences of the state of nature which necessarily follow from every man being judge in his own case, by setting up a known authority to which everyone of that society may appeal upon any injury received or controversy that may arise, and which everyone of the society ought to obey. Wherever any persons are who have not such an authority to appeal to for the decision of any difference between them, there those persons are still in the state of nature; and so is every absolute prince, in respect of those who are under his dominion. . . .

OF THE BEGINNING OF POLITICAL SOCIETIES

95. Men being, as has been said, by nature all free, equal, and independent, no one can be put out of this estate and subjected to the political power of another without his own consent. The only way whereby anyone divests himself of his natural liberty and puts on the bonds of civil society is by agreeing with other men to join and unite into a community for their comfortable, safe, and peaceable living one amongst another, in a secure enjoyment of their properties and a greater security against any that are not of it. This any number of men may do, because it injures not the freedom of the rest; they are left as they were in the liberty of the state of nature. When any number of men have so consented to make one community or government, they are thereby presently incorporated and make one body politic wherein the majority have a right to act and conclude the rest.

96. For when any number of men have, by the consent of every individual, made a community, they have thereby made that community one body, with a power to act as one body, which is only by the will and

determination of the majority; for that which [animates] any community being only the consent of the individuals of it, and it being necessary to that which is one body to move one way, it is necessary the body should move that way whither the greater force carries it, which is the consent of the majority; or else it is impossible it should act or continue one body, one community, which the consent of every individual that united into it agreed that it should; and so everyone is bound by that consent to be concluded by the majority. And therefore we see that in assemblies impowered to act by positive laws, where no number is set by that positive law which impowers them, the act of the majority passes for the act of the whole and, of course, determines, as having by the law of nature and reason the power of the whole.

97. And thus every man, by consenting with others to make one body politic under one government, puts himself under an obligation to everyone of that society to submit to the determination of the majority and to be concluded by it; or else this original compact, whereby he with others incorporates into one society, would signify nothing, and be no compact, if he be left free and under no other ties than he was in before in the state of nature. For what appearance would there be of any compact? What new engagement if he were no further tied by any decrees of the society than he himself thought fit and did actually consent to? This would be still as great a liberty as he himself had before his compact, or anyone else in the state of nature has who may submit himself and consent to any acts of it if he thinks fit.

98. For if the consent of the majority shall not in reason be received as the act of the whole and conclude every individual, nothing but the consent of every individual can make anything to be the act of the whole; but such a consent is next to impossible ever to be had if we consider the infirmities of health and avocations of business which in a number, though much less than that of a commonwealth, will necessarily keep many away from the public assembly. To which, if we add the variety of opinions and contrariety of interests which unavoidably happen in all collections of men, the coming into society upon such terms would be only like Cato's coming into the theater only to go out again. Such a constitution as this would make the mighty leviathan of a shorter duration than the feeblest creatures, and not let it outlast the day it was born in; which cannot be supposed till we can think that rational creatures should desire and constitute societies only to be dissolved; for where the majority cannot conclude the rest, there they cannot act as one body, and consequently will be immediately dissolved again.

99. Whosoever, therefore, out of a state of nature unite into a community must be understood to give up all the power necessary to the ends for which they unite into society to the majority of the community, unless they expressly agreed in any number greater than the majority. And this is done by barely agreeing to unite into one political society, which is all the compact that is, or needs be, between the individuals that enter into or make up a commonwealth. And thus that which begins and actually constitutes any political society is nothing but the consent of any number of freemen capable of a majority to unite and incorporate into such a society. And this is that, and that only, which did or could give beginning to any lawful government in the world. . . .

OF THE ENDS OF POLITICAL SOCIETY AND GOVERNMENT

123. If man in the state of nature be so free, as has been said, if he be absolute lord of his own person and possessions, equal to the greatest, and subject to nobody, why will he part with his freedom, why will he give up his empire and subject himself to the dominion and control of any other power? To which it is obvious to answer that though in the state of nature he has such a right, yet the enjoyment of it is very uncertain and constantly exposed to the invasion of others; for all being kings as much as he, every man his equal, and the greater part no strict observers of equity and justice, the enjoy-

ment of the property he has in this state is very unsafe, very unsecure. This makes him willing to quit a condition which, however free, is full of fears and continual dangers; and it is not without reason that he seeks out and is willing to join in society with others who are already united, or have a mind to unite, for the mutual preservation of their lives, liberties, and estates, which I call by the general name "property."

124. The great and chief end, therefore, of men's uniting into commonwealths and putting themselves under government is the preservation of their property. To which in the state of nature there are many things wanting:

First, there wants an established, settled, known law, received and allowed by common consent to be the standard of right and wrong and the common measure to decide all controversies between them; for though the law of nature be plain and intelligible to all rational creatures, yet men, being biased by their interest as well as ignorant for want of studying it, are not apt to allow of it as a law binding to them in the application of it to their particular cases.

125. Secondly, in the state of nature there wants a known and indifferent judge with authority to determine all differences according to the established law; for everyone in that state being both judge and executioner of the law of nature, men being partial to themselves, passion and revenge is very apt to carry them too far and with too much heat in their own cases, as well as negligence and unconcernedness to make them too remiss in other men's.

126. Thirdly, in the state of nature there often wants power to back and support the sentence when right, and to give it due execution. They who by any injustice offend will seldom fail, where they are able, by force, to [get away with] their injustice; such resistance many times makes the punishment dangerous and frequently destructive to those who attempt it.

127. Thus mankind, notwithstanding all the privileges of the state of nature, being

but in an ill condition while they remain in it, are quickly driven into society. Hence it comes to pass that we seldom find any number of men live any time together in this state. The inconveniences that they are therein exposed to by the irregular and uncertain exercise of the power every man has of punishing the transgressions of others make them take sanctuary under the established laws of government and therein seek the preservation of their property. It is this makes them so willingly give up every one his single power of punishing, to be exercised by such alone as shall be appointed to it amongst them; and by such rules as the community, or those authorized by them to that purpose, shall agree on. And in this we have the original right of both the legislative and executive power, as well as of the governments and societies themselves.

128. For in the state of nature, to omit the liberty he has of innocent delights, a man has two powers:

The first is to do whatsoever he thinks fit for the preservation of himself and others within the permission of the law of nature, by which law, common to them all, he and all the rest of mankind are one community, make up one society, distinct from all other creatures. And, were it not for the corruption and viciousness of degenerate men, there would be no need of any other, no necessity that men should separate from this great and natural community and by positive agreements combine into smaller and divided associations.

The other power a man has in the state of nature is the power to punish the crimes committed against that law. Both these he gives up when he joins in a private, if I may so call it, or particular politic society and incorporates into any commonwealth separate from the rest of mankind.

129. The first power, viz., of doing whatsoever he thought fit for the preservation of himself and the rest of mankind, he gives up to be regulated by laws made by the society, so far forth as the preservation of himself and the rest of that society shall require;

which laws of the society in many things confine the liberty he had by the law of nature.

130. Secondly, the power of punishing he wholly gives up, and engages his natural force—which he might before employ in the execution of the law of nature by his own single authority, as he thought fit—to assist the executive power of the society, as the law thereof shall require; for being now in a new state, wherein he is to enjoy many conveniences from the labor, assistance, and society of others in the same community as well as protection from its whole strength, he is to part also with as much of his natural liberty, in providing for himself, as the good, prosperity, and safety of the society shall require, which is not only necessary, but just, since the other members of the society do the like.

131. But though men when they enter into society give up the equality, liberty, and executive power they had in the state of nature into the hands of the society, to be so far disposed of by the legislative as the good of the society shall require, yet it being only with an intention in everyone the better to preserve himself, his liberty and property— for no rational creature can be supposed to change his condition with an intention to be worse—the power of the society, or legislative constituted by them, can never be supposed to extend farther than the common good, but is obliged to secure everyone's property by providing against those three defects above-mentioned that made the state of nature so unsafe and uneasy. And so whoever has the legislative or supreme power of any commonwealth is bound to govern by established standing laws, promulgated and known to the people, and not by extemporary decrees; by indifferent and upright judges who are to decide controversies by those laws; and to employ the force of the community at home only in the execution of such laws, or abroad to prevent or redress foreign injuries, and secure the community from inroads and invasion. And all this to be directed to no other end but the peace, safety, and public good of the people. (Pp. 48–51, 54–56, 70–73.)

Thomas Jefferson and the Pursuit of Happiness

Thomas Hobbes and John Locke helped to initiate political changes that permanently altered history, and their impact reached beyond Europe. In fact, it was in the New World, specifically in the British colonies of North America, that their theories—especially Locke's—were put into practice most extensively. Promoting an Enlightenment based on observation and reason's role in improving society, the colonists were convinced that the universe was governed by reasonable natural laws. Those laws, in turn, granted rights and duties to us all. But Hobbes, Locke, and their Continental counterparts were not always successful in implementing the political consequences of their views. Established powers rarely yield easily to the innovative social ideas of philosophers. Yet, as Thomas Paine, the exuberant champion of the American Revolution, put it in 1776: "The birthday of a new world [was] at hand."[5]

Being of a similar mind, Thomas Jefferson (1743–1826) devoted himself to a form of political activity that would vindicate Paine's hope. In a wide-ranging career, he served as governor of Virginia, ambassador to France, secretary of state under George Washington, and vice president under John Adams. As the third president of the United States, 1801–1809, he engineered the purchase of the vast Louisiana Territory, which did so much to nourish an American sense of opportunity. This man of practical affairs, however, is best remembered for the Declaration of Independence and in particular for the statement: "We hold these truths to be

THOMAS JEFFERSON 1743–1826

self-evident, that all men are created equal, that they are endowed by their Creator with certain unalienable Rights, that among these are Life, Liberty, and the pursuit of Happiness."[6] Finding himself in a situation that permitted philosophy to be put into practice, Jefferson influenced "the course of human events" in ways few thinkers have matched.

In thinking of Jefferson as a "philosopher," it is worth noting the breadth of his activities. We have mentioned his elective offices and the diplomatic and administrative services he performed for his country, but Jefferson also left us with the gift of a classic architectural style. He was truly "a Renaissance man," who excelled simultaneously in many fields of endeavor. Few philosophers have matched Jefferson's diverse accomplishments, but it is important to see that a person can combine effective public action with clear philosophical writing.

Self-Evident Truths

In the Declaration of Independence, Jefferson stressed "self-evident" truths. Since his famous statements about equality and human rights depended on this concept, it bears special significance. What did Jefferson mean in holding that at least some truths, in this case politically crucial ones, are "self-evident"? Apparently this claim involved his conviction that by the examination of a proposition, we may see that it is unquestionably true. But how does that procedure work, especially when the propositions under examination are bound to be controversial because they make claims about political powers, cultural traditions, and individual prerogatives?

Jefferson's appeal to self-evident truths drew on views developed by Locke. Locke himself did not believe that *innate* truth exists, fearing that if basic truths were simply implanted in our minds at birth, we might be discouraged from questioning our assumptions and from taking up the empirical investigations necessary to advance knowledge. Locke did, however, want truth to be *self-evident*. Self-evidence exists, he felt, when critical inquiry uncovers irresistible propositions. We can affirm such propositions without hesitation or doubt, since to deny them would violate our best intuition. As examples, Locke asked us to consider truths such as black is not white, a triangle is not a square.

However, the Declaration of Independence deals with nothing as simple as color or as obvious as geometry. Even if self-evident truth exists in those cases, does that necessarily mean it also exists in the political arena? Locke answered yes, and Jefferson agreed. Of course, any such proposition would have to be judged on its merits. The critical test would be whether an analysis of the idea in question, and the evidence for or against it, resulted in the rationally irresistible and undeniable conviction that the truth has to be so. "We hold these truths to be self-evident," said Jefferson. But what happens if there are some who disagree? What happens if people fail to concur on what truths are self-evident? Jefferson trusted that a proper use of reason would create agreement, and he hoped it would result in acceptance of the truths he himself found to be self-evident. The problem was to get the opposition to inquire anew, to educate them to see the truth, and to recognize that only a perverse form of self-interest could cause people to deny what reason made plain when rightly used. Obviously, Jefferson lived in an age self-confident about its use of reason. Plato, Aristotle, Spinoza, and Descartes were also confident about discovering ultimate truth. Jefferson's trust had a long tradition behind it.

Jefferson realized that his claims might encounter opposition. He knew that not everyone would automatically discern what he held to be self-evident, for this would require a clear understanding of concepts and an examination of experience. Since only a few would have the intellectual preparation needed to see the truth, Jefferson's philosophy was not without elitist aspects. But on the whole he was more trustful of "the people" than some of the other Founding Fathers—Alexander Hamilton and James Madison, for example. Believing that God had endowed every human mind with moral sensitivity, Jefferson argued that once individuals are free to inquire and think for themselves, sound moral insight and political policy will emerge. "Truth is great," he contended, "and will prevail if left to herself; . . . she is the proper and sufficient antagonist to error."[7]

Human Equality and Unalienable Rights

"All men are created equal." Never did a person write more troublesome words. Yet this was the first among Jefferson's self-evident truths. It is not true, however, let alone self-evident, that all men are created with equal physical strength, intellectual ability, or social status. It would be closer to fact to say that all men are created *unequal* in most respects. Jefferson would not have denied this. He recognized that there are many varieties of human character and performance; some deserve honor and power, others not. What, then, did he have in mind when he asserted human **equality**?

The phrase "created equal," Jefferson believed, means that we all belong to the same species. God created that species and its members, women and men, essentially the same. Our chances for success may differ, but all of us are alike in having life bestowed on us. Additionally, Jefferson said, each of us is born with a desire for happiness. None of us dissents on that score, although we will seek and pursue, find or lose, happiness in diverse ways. If we are equal in these senses, Jefferson suggested, we are essentially alike. No one automatically has the **prerogative** to dominate another. To be created equal entails the right to liberty.

A right use of reason, contended Jefferson, will show that "all men are created equal" is a self-evident truth. Furthermore, this truth leads to others, namely, that men are endowed by God "with certain unalienable Rights" including the rights to preserve life, sustain liberty, and pursue happiness. Those rights, Jefferson asserted, are not merely legal privileges that governments grant or withhold as they please. Rather, such rights are natural. As part and parcel of what is meant by being human, they belong equally to all men and are not violated with impunity. Nonetheless, the sense in which rights are unalienable is elusive, since Jefferson's Declaration later states that "to secure these rights Governments are instituted among men." Apparently unalienable rights are not invulnerable to challenge; but if they are not invulnerable, in what way are they unalienable?

A strict interpretation of "unalienable" suggests that the rights in question belong to each of us uniquely. An unalienable right can be taken away, for life and liberty and the pursuit of happiness can be snuffed out like a candle. Jefferson argued that nonetheless, such rights are unalienable in the sense that they are nontransferable. Strictly speaking, we cannot give them up to anyone, nor should we take them away from anyone. We are endowed with the rights to preserve life, maintain liberty, and pursue happiness, Jefferson thought, and therefore, we also have a responsibility to respect those rights. That responsibility is a duty mandated by our Creator. No good comes from trying to flee from these rights and duties; down that road lies the domination of others over us. Nor should we be tempted to give them up to others; down that path lies the tyranny of a ruler who assumes too much power. Governments can and should be formed to ensure that human rights are not violated, but people should also take responsibility for their lives and governments. Hence, Jefferson thought that all government must have a democratic base. A right to rebellion also exists whenever a government extends its power too far. The motto Jefferson chose for his seal—"Rebellion to tyrants is obedience to God"—summed up his views precisely.

Is Jefferson's Political Philosophy a Self-Evident Truth?

Thomas Jefferson regarded our basic human rights as a gift from God. Nature and reason, it followed, should testify to a universal moral structure that underwrites them. But what if there is no God? What if nature is amoral? What if reason insists that the most self-evident truth of all is that history shows us the constant violation of human rights? Are unalienable rights not worth the paper they are written on "in history" unless political might protects them? In the late twentieth century, we may sense that Hobbes was right. It is no longer difficult to suggest that nothing other than human power secures a person's rights. And if rights depend on human power alone, can they still be natural and unalienable? They may exist even when not supported by human power, but today it seems increasingly hard to have these rights recognized as independent of power. Today few people would speak as comfortably as Jefferson did about his self-evident truths, an outcome that is partly an unintended consequence of Jefferson's own philosophy.

In his *Notes on the State of Virginia* (1785), Jefferson affirmed that "our rulers can have authority over such natural rights only as we have submitted to them. The rights of conscience we never submitted, we could not submit. We are answerable for them to our God."[8] No one was more explicit or emphatic than Jefferson about the fundamental, sacred quality of conscience. This gives us both the right and the duty to make judgments in accord with the best evidence we can find and the soundest moral insight we can obtain. He hoped that such an appeal would fit with the self-evident truths he set forth, although he recognized that these might be more apparent to some persons than to others. His democratic leanings, however, leave us with an atmosphere of relativity rather than with a certainty of moral and political rationalism.

In our world, political and economic systems differ, nor are right and wrong the same in every culture. To claim self-evidence for one's particular perspective may seem arrogant and inexpedient, since doing so tends to brand every other view erroneous, regardless of how much support the other views can muster. Yet it is equally dangerous to give up Jefferson's confidence. He was ready to call some views false and some practices wrong because they violated his convictions. Jefferson's emphasis on human rights remains important, since hardly any of us want to give up the belief that we do have rights that must not be compromised or usurped. But again: What is the foundation of that conviction?

Jefferson offered God, human nature, a morally structured universe, and an appropriate form of government. If we cannot assent to all his propositions or agree when he called them self-evident, we face a challenge. We can move toward the position that "might makes right," or we can try to justify our political beliefs with new reasons for might to respond to right. To call any solution to our current problems self-evident may go too far, but every student of philosophy ought to think long and hard about this dilemma and its possible resolutions.

As we look back on Jefferson's day, we can see that his own thinking about human equality, for example, may have been less than self-evident. Jefferson owned slaves. The issue of their equal rights to life, liberty, and the pursuit of happiness perplexed him, and the legacy of that problem still haunts the United States. Jefferson said "men" were created equal. Scholars remain divided about the degree to which he intended to use the term generically, including both sexes of the species. In any case, struggles about equal rights for women, prompted in part by Jefferson's rhetoric, resound across the world. Additionally, the current arguments about abortion provide a significant example of the kind of situation Jefferson inadvertently helped to create. Holding that individuals have unalienable rights by nature, Jefferson makes us consider who is an individual. And if we conclude that both an unborn child and its mother qualify, we are left to wrestle with a possible conflict over their respective rights

to life, liberty, and the pursuit of happiness. The debate extends beyond the individuals directly involved. It reaches out to touch the society at large and raises again the issue of whether it is government that actually decides what our unalienable rights shall be. The answers to these tough questions may not be as self-evident as we could wish, but Jefferson's thought continues to provide a context for their consideration. To illustrate that point for yourself, examine Jefferson's Declaration of Independence (1776), concentrating on both the answers it provides and the questions it raises when the issue is "Do I have rights in society?"

When in the Course of human events it becomes necessary for one people to dissolve the political bands which have connected them with another, and to assume among the powers of the earth, the separate and equal station to which the Laws of Nature and of Nature's God entitle them, a decent respect to the opinions of mankind requires that they should declare the causes which impel them to the separation.

We hold these truths to be self-evident, that all men are created equal, that they are endowed by their Creator with certain unalienable Rights, that among these are Life, Liberty, and the pursuit of Happiness.—That to secure these rights, Governments are instituted among Men, deriving their just powers from the consent of the governed.— That whenever any Form of Government becomes destructive of these ends, it is the Right of the People to alter or to abolish it, and to institute new Government, laying its foundation on such principles, and organizing its powers in such form, as to them shall seem most likely to effect their Safety and Happiness. Prudence, indeed, will dictate that Governments long established should not be changed for light and transient causes; and accordingly all experience hath shown, that mankind are more disposed to suffer, while evils are sufferable, than to right themselves by abolishing the forms to which they are accustomed. But when a long train of abuses and usurpations, pursuing invariably the same Object, evinces a design to reduce them under absolute Despotism, it is their right, it is their duty, to throw off such Government, and to provide new Guards for their future security.—Such has been the patient sufferance of these Colonies; and such is now the necessity which constrains them to alter their former Systems of Government. The history of the present King of Great Britain is a history of repeated injuries and usurpations, all having in direct object the establishment of an absolute Tyranny over these States. To prove this, let Facts be submitted to a candid world.

He has refused his Assent to Laws, the most wholesome and necessary for the public good.

He has forbidden his Governors to pass Laws of immediate and pressing importance, unless suspended in their operation till his Assent should be obtained; and when so suspended, he has utterly neglected to attend to them.

He has refused to pass other Laws for the accommodation of large districts of people, unless those people would relinquish the right of Representation in the Legislature, a right inestimable to them and formidable to tyrants only.

He has called together legislative bodies at places unusual, uncomfortable, and distant from the depository of their public Records, for the sole purpose of fatiguing them into compliance with his measures.

He has dissolved Representative Houses repeatedly, for opposing with manly firmness his invasions on the rights of the people.

He has refused for a long time, after such dissolutions, to cause others to be elected; whereby the Legislative powers, incapable of Annihilation, have returned to the People at large for their exercise; the State remaining in the mean time exposed to all the dangers of invasion from without, and convulsions within.

For suspending our own Legislatures, and declaring themselves invested with power to legislate for us in all cases whatsoever.

He has abdicated Government here, by declaring us out of his Protection and waging War against us.

He has plundered our seas, ravaged our Coasts, burnt our towns, and destroyed the lives of our people.

He is at this time transporting large Armies of foreign Mercenaries to complete the works of death, desolation, and tyranny, already begun with circumstances of Cruelty and perfidy scarcely paralleled in the most barbarous ages, and totally unworthy of the Head of a civilized nation.

He has constrained our fellow Citizens taken Captive on the high Seas to bear Arms against their Country, to become the executioners of their friends and Brethren, or to fall themselves by their Hands.

He has excited domestic insurrections amongst us, and has endeavored to bring on the inhabitants of our frontiers; the merciless Indian Savages, whose known rule of warfare, is an undistinguished destruction of all ages, sexes, and conditions.

In every stage of these Oppressions We have Petitioned for Redress in the most humble terms: Our repeated Petitions have been answered only by repeated injury. A Prince, whose character is thus marked by every act which may define a Tyrant, is unfit to be the ruler of a free people.

Nor have We been wanting in attentions to our British brethren. We have warned them from time to time of attempts by their legislature to extend an unwarrantable jurisdiction over us. We have reminded them of the circumstances of our emigration and settlement here. We have appealed to their native justice and magnanimity, and we have conjured them by the ties of our common kindred to disavow these usurpations, which would inevitably interrupt our connections and correspondence. They too have been deaf to the voice of justice and of consanguinity. We must, therefore, acquiesce in the necessity, which denounces our Separation, and hold them, as we hold the rest of mankind, Enemies in War, in Peace Friends.

We, therefore, the Representatives of the United States of America, in General Congress, Assembled, appealing to the Supreme Judge of the world for the rectitude of our intentions, do, in the Name, and by Authority of the good People of these Colonies solemnly publish and declare, That these United Colonies are, and of Right ought to be Free and Independent States; that they are Absolved from all Allegiance to the British Crown, and that all political connection between them and the State of Great Britain, is and ought to be totally dissolved; and that as Free and Independent States, they have full Power to levy War, conclude Peace, contract Alliances, establish Commerce, and to do all other Acts and Things which Independent States may of right do.

And for the support of this Declaration, with a firm reliance on the protection of divine Providence, we mutually pledge to each other our Lives, our Fortunes, and our sacred Honor. (Pp. 3–7.)

JEAN-JACQUES ROUSSEAU 1712–1778

Jean-Jacques Rousseau and the Social Contract

"Everything is good as it leaves the hands of the Author of things," wrote Jean-Jacques Rousseau (1712–1778), "but everything degenerates in the hands of man."[9] Determined to correct this deterioration, Rousseau offered his distinctive political philosophy in works such as *Emile* and the well-known *The Social Contract*. Both these works appeared in 1762; each contributed decisively to the French Revolution, which broke out in 1789. Rousseau believed that people are not thoroughly social beings by nature. In a state of nature, people are basically good, and they tend to be benign toward each other. But these conditions do not last, and indeed people need to live in society to become fully

human. Rousseau wanted to educate people to form a society well. Ironically, these concerns reflected needs that Rousseau himself felt intensely, for it would be an understatement to say that his life was unsettled. He has been called a perfect example of an outsider in society.

Rousseau was born in Geneva, Switzerland. His mother died while he was an infant, and his upbringing was chaotic. He lacked formal education, traveled restlessly, and tried first one profession and then another, apparently without enough discipline to fend off failure. He lived with numerous women and fathered five children who ended up in a home for abandoned boys and girls because Rousseau did not care for them properly. He switched from Protestantism to Roman Catholicism, then back again, as expediency dictated. Yet in the midst of these unsettled ways, Rousseau remained convinced that he was a genius with important things to say. His appraisal was not wrong, but his views on politics, religion, and education aroused hostile reactions on the Continent, for Rousseau was no friend of established institutions. Thus, he accepted David Hume's invitation to go to England. But when Rousseau's capricious behavior led to an irreparable falling out with his British friend, he returned to Paris and died in France a short time later.

Born Free

"Man was born free," asserted Rousseau, "and he is everywhere in chains."[10] His theories of politics and education sought to make people free again. Rousseau knew that we could not permanently return to a state of nature that was essentially good. Nor would we necessarily want to do this, because civil society offered desirable improvements. Unfortunately, those improvements were not the whole story. The evolution of human societies had shackled people because men and women paid insufficient attention to what human relations ought to be. Rousseau's educational theory therefore aimed to train people to be good and not merely powerful. His political theory aimed at creating an environment in which what is right dictates how might is employed, rather than letting the desire to maintain power prescribe what must be done. Humanity had needlessly compromised its own goodness, argued Rousseau, and thus it was time to think carefully about the social contract that ought to relate us through mutual rights and duties.

"Since no man has any natural authority over his fellows," argued Rousseau, "and since force alone bestows no right, all legitimate authority among men must be based on covenants" (p. 53). In the society that ought to exist, he contended, moral and political considerations never would be divorced.

Instead of being bound together by force, people should be linked by a social contract, a pact resulting in a political order to which reasonable persons would freely and willingly give their allegiance.

According to Rousseau, freedom is so essential to human life that "to renounce freedom is to renounce one's humanity, one's rights as a man and equally one's duties" (pp. 54–55). Although "men are not naturally enemies" in the state of nature, in spite of their natural freedom people find that "the obstacles to their preservation in a state of nature prove greater than the strength that each man has to preserve himself in that state" (pp. 55, 59). They unite to deal with these circumstances, but in doing so freedom has been lost and persons have been dehumanized. Thus, what especially intrigued Rousseau was: "How to find a form of association which will defend the person and goods of each member with the collective force of all, and under which each individual, while uniting himself with the others, obeys no one but himself, and remains as free as before" (p. 60). The solution, Rousseau believed, was a proper social contract, as described above.

Rousseau did not envision a collection of autonomous individuals, each striving to protect his or her prerogatives against those of every other. Instead, he proposed a social contract that entailed "the total alienation by each associate of himself and his rights to the whole community" (p. 60). In this contract, Rousseau continued,

> [S]ince each man gives himself to all, he gives himself to no one; and since there is no associate over whom he does not gain the same rights as others gain over him, each man recovers the equivalent of everything he loses, and in the bargain acquires more power to preserve what he has. . . . What man loses by the social contract is his natural liberty and the absolute right to anything that tempts him and that he can take; what he gains by the social contract is civil liberty and the legal

right of property in what he possesses. (Pp. 61, 65.)

In one respect, Rousseau sided with Hobbes because he favored the idea of giving up one's natural rights. But he abhorred the Hobbesian notion that these rights should be given up to an absolute sovereign who was not a fully participating partner in the social contract. For Rousseau there was a sovereign, but the sovereign was the people themselves. The natural rights of individuals were given up to form a "public person." All parties to the contract are aspects of that **body politic,** and those who are thus "associated in it take collectively the name of *a people,* and call themselves individually *citizens,* insofar as they share in the sovereign power, and *subjects,* insofar as they put themselves under the laws of the state" that results from the social contract (pp. 61–62.)

The "**general will,**" as Rousseau called it, replaces the individual will as normative. Indeed, it may even have to coerce individuals to be truly human and free in Rousseau's sense of those terms, for, argued Rousseau,

> [T]he general will alone can direct the forces of the state in accordance with that end which the state has been established to achieve— the common good; for if conflict between private interests has made the setting up of civil societies necessary, harmony between those same interests has made it possible. It is what is common to those different interests which yields the social bond; if there were no point on which separate interests coincided, then society could not conceivably exist. And it is precisely on the basis of this common interest that society must be governed. (P. 69.)

On this basis, genuine human equality and respect are ensured, because securing the essential good for all parties to the contract will take priority. Men and women thereby become the social, political, and moral beings nature makes it possible for them to be. Their freedom and happiness are enhanced as natural liberty is replaced by civil liberty. The idealistic Rousseau was realistic enough, however, to recognize that the general will might differ radically from *the will of all,* which aims less at the public good and more at "private interest, and is indeed no more than the sum of individual desires" (p. 72).

The problem, claimed Rousseau, is that "we always want what is advantageous but we do not always discern it. The people is never corrupted, but it is often misled; and only then does it seem to will what is bad" (p. 72). Hence, even a majority rule can be tyrannical unless it is governed by the general will, which, Rousseau assured us, "is always rightful and always tends to the public good" (p. 72). The general will ought to be sovereign, and it would be sovereign in a truly enlightened republic, which Rousseau took to be the ideal type of state. There people experience the highest form of freedom, namely, that of living under laws freely chosen and of their own making. But until education is perfected, there will be differences between the general will and the will of all, and this remains a problem. Indeed, until everyone is sufficiently enlightened, even the general will itself may need further focusing. Rousseau suggested that in the interim a specially qualified individual or group might act in a legislative capacity to discern and implement what the general will required. Without proper training and education, of course, such leaders might become tyrants. The success of Rousseau's political idealism hinges on good education. Rousseau recognized that fact and devoted much of his writing to pedagogical concerns.

Start with the Child

"We begin to instruct ourselves when we begin to live," wrote Rousseau.[11] Hence, Rousseau's philosophy gave birth to a fictitious orphan boy named Emile, who served as an instance of human nature and as a case study to show what good education for society ought to be. As Emile's teacher, Rousseau claimed, "living is the job I want to teach him. On leaving my hands, he will, I admit, be neither magistrate nor soldier nor priest. He will, in the first place, be a man. All that a man should be, he will in case of need know how to be as well as anyone" (pp. 41–42). Entrusting himself to raise the infant Emile, Rousseau analyzed what it takes to make a man.

"Cities," he noted, "are the abyss of the human species" (p. 59). That terse appraisal summed up much of the criticism Rousseau directed against what he took to be the unfortunate course of human events. Cities jam people together in close quarters, usually for the purpose of pursuing selfish economic desires, divisive political ambitions, and vain pleasures. They spawn inequality, hypocrisy, and idleness. Especially within the institutions and "civilized" ways that are inseparable from the rise of modern cities, Rousseau suggested, "man's breath is deadly to his kind. This is no less true in the literal sense than the figurative" (p. 59).

Rousseau pictured a state of nature as far more benign. He did not say that this "state of nature" had actually existed, but his description expressed a primitive ideal that good education and politics should keep in mind. As Rousseau described it, the state of nature was a kind of utopia. To be sure, the individuals in this state of nature, governed essentially by instincts, were limited. But their lives were happy, because they were essentially equal and independent. They knew how to live in accord with their basic natural needs, which could be fulfilled by nature's bounty. If unimpeded by desires to dominate and if nurtured by innate feelings of sympathy, human freedom could be as innocent as it was real. Some of the highest forms of this natural existence, Rousseau believed,

occurred within families and the early communities that sprang up around them. Since they lived self-sufficiently within a natural and not an urban environment, primitive men and women had not missed perfection by much.

They had not, however, achieved perfection fully. The relative isolation of individuals, in which each one is valuable for his or her own sake, characterized Rousseau's early ideal state of nature. But life unavoidably brings people more and more together. Eventually they are set at odds. For example, as Rousseau's contemporary Adam Smith observed, the desire to "truck, barter, and exchange" appears. People begin to worry about property, to contest what is "mine" or "yours," "ours" or "theirs." Divisions appear between the rich and the poor. As the powerful and the weak are separated, inequality worsens. Social systems emerge that build on and even entrench those power relations. Chains are forged and used to bind people without their consent.

To support his belief that education could liberate us, Rousseau pictured Emile first in a country setting. His goal was not to turn the clock back to some ideal stage that might never have existed. Emile already belonged to a modern society and would never dwell in either a primitive state of nature or an ideal political order. Rousseau insisted that the right questions are: What should Emile's society be? What ought to be the nature of a political order, modern or not? What kind of education best brings what is and what ought to be closer together for our society?

The Education of Nature

Rousseau agreed with Aristotle that the virtue of a citizen and the virtue of a man or woman may not be identical. If those virtues are to coincide, Rousseau maintained, education must have priority. Specifically, what

Emile needed was what Rousseau called the **education of nature,** an upbringing that maximizes the importance of the child's natural development. Since Emile was born physically helpless, the first emphasis should be on doing what is necessary to encourage his own activity. At this level nature and experience are the primary teachers. What counts most is that the child learn to do things for itself. Care must be taken to ensure not only that Emile's health is robust but also that the child never acquires the feeling that he can in any way command others to do his bidding. The goal, Rousseau summarized, is to help Emile to do more for himself and to require less from others. He must be loved and taught in a way that makes him free.

As Emile passes into boyhood, increasingly he becomes an individual person, self-conscious of his own happiness or distress. At this stage, Rousseau placed great value on the importance of play. Such pleasure is good; it is unwise to live as if existence were a stern preparation for some future happiness that may never arrive. More importantly, in wholesome play Emile may achieve an **equilibrium** between his own desires and his natural capacities. We must train people to realize that such an equilibrium is essential for the individual's good and for society, since freedom is found in that equilibrium. Rousseau offered this advice:

> Your child ought to get a thing not because he asks for it but because he needs it, and do a thing not out of obedience but only out of necessity. Thus the words *obey* and *command* will be proscribed from his lexicon, and even more so *duty* and *obligation*. But *strength, necessity, impotence,* and *constraint* should play a great role in it. (P. 59.)

The objective was to make Emile neither domineering nor subservient. Rather, he should become aware of his own worth by attaining a sense of self-confidence and self-sufficiency within limits not imposed artificially by human might but naturally through his own experience and abilities. Such lessons will lay the foundation for an even more important one, namely, that it is wrong to disregard any person's natural freedom.

As Emile enters his teens, Rousseau places more emphasis on the acquisition of knowledge. Still he does not force formal learning on his student. Having argued that naturally aroused desire provides the auspicious time to teach Emile to read, Rousseau feels that an awakening curiosity about nature itself will stir his understanding. Advantage should be taken of Emile's own interests. Questions should be posed for him but few answers given. Let the young man seek, inquire, and find out for himself. This learning will bring him pleasure and stimulate his desire to know even more powerfully. In addition, Emile should learn to work with his hands. Since European society was so far removed from what ought to be, it would be plunged into crisis and revolution, and Rousseau wanted Emile to be equipped to earn a living. Possession of a trade skill seemed the best insurance.

Though raised in the country, Emile would likely be a city-dweller, exposed to all manner of corruption, vice, and immorality but also to the beauty of its art, music, and theater. Therefore, it would also be crucial to hone Emile's aesthetic sensibilities and his moral perceptions, especially at a time when his own sexual impulses would awaken strongly. Born with instincts for self-love and attachment to those who responded to him with care, Emile could be brought to awareness that others have similar feelings and an equal right to them. Moreover, since human life unavoidably involves interdependence, an awareness that human well-being depends on cooperation, mutual respect, fair treatment, and just laws should characterize a well-taught person, even if in practice human society failed to give those qualities the honor they deserve. Nothing human would be foreign to Emile. He would know the good and the evil as well as the grace and the ugliness that human beings produce. But the education of nature would make him so love justice, peace, and beauty that he would do what promotes them most. Reinforced religiously, these same sentiments would also channel the young man's sexual drives toward their best natural expression, namely marriage, for "it is not good for man to be alone" (p. 357).

As to the woman who is right for Emile—Rousseau named her Sophie—nature bestowed as much perfection on her as on Emile. Each was proportioned properly according to their sexual differences. Those differences must not be ignored. Rousseau thought that men "ought to be active and strong," women passive and weak. One must "necessarily will and be able; it suffices that the other put up little resistance. . . . Woman is made specially to please man" (p. 358). Sophie's education, therefore, should make her a sensitive wife and an intelligent mother. Rousseau believed that men and women are equal by being complementary members of the same species. Their differences make them unequal, too, but these inequalities enhance their complementarity. For example, Rousseau claimed that "woman has more wit, man more genius; women observes and man reasons. From this conjunction results the clearest insight and the most complete science regarding itself that the human mind can acquire—in a word, the surest knowledge of oneself and others available to our species" (p. 387).

The education of Emile created a gentleman. Born naturally good, given an environment that allowed his capacities to grow neither too soon nor too late, trained in ways that steeled him against the vice and corruption of modern social institutions, Emile acquired the strength of intellect, will, and spirit that enabled him to be what Rousseau thought an individual man ought to be. Such persons could transmute the individual wills and the will of all into the general will. They could perfect Rousseau's social contract.

The philosophy of a Thomas Hobbes was far too pessimistic for Rousseau, and Rousseau's idealism challenges us to reconsider how we can close the gap between what is and what ought to be. To what extent are his educational and political prescriptions compatible with what actually can be done? If "ought" implies "can," are Rousseau's ideals practically or only logically possible? To what degree can a twentieth-century world contain Emiles and Sophies and a benign general will of the kind Rousseau desired? Such questions should sharpen the focus as you read from *The Social Contract*.

WHETHER THE GENERAL WILL CAN ERR

It follows from what I have argued that the general will is always rightful and always tends to the public good; but it does not follow that the decisions of the people are always equally right. We always want what is advantageous but we do not always discern it. The people is never corrupted, but it is often misled; and only then does it seem to will what is bad.

There is often a great difference between the will of all [what all individuals want] and the general will; the general will studies only the common interest while the will of all studies private interest, and is indeed no more than the sum of individual desires. But if we take away from these same wills, the pluses and minuses which cancel each other out, the sum of the difference is the general will.*

*"Every interest," says the Marquis d'Argenson, "has its different principles. Harmony between two interests is created by opposition to that of a third." He might have added that the harmony of all interests is created by opposition to those of each. If there were no different interests, we should hardly be conscious of a common interest, as there would be no resistance to it; everything would run easily of its own accord, and politics would cease to be an art.

From the deliberations of a people properly informed, and provided its members do not have any communication among themselves, the great number of small differences will always produce a general will and the decision will always be good. But if groups, sectional associations are formed at the expense of the larger association, the will of each of these groups will become general in relation to its own members and private in relation to the state; we might then say that there are no longer as many votes as there are men but only as many votes as there are groups. The differences become less numerous and yield a result less general. Finally, when one of these groups becomes so large that it can dominate the rest, the result is no longer the sum of many small differences, but one great divisive difference; then there ceases to be a general will, and the opinion which prevails is no more than a private opinion.

Thus if the general will is to be clearly expressed, it is imperative that there should be no sectional associations in the state, and that every citizen should make up his own mind for himself[†]—such was the unique and sublime invention of the great Lycurgus. But if there are sectional associations, it is wise to multiply their number and to prevent inequality among them, as Solon, Numa, and Servius did. These are the only precautions which can ensure that the general will is always enlightened and the people protected from error.

THE LIMITS OF SOVEREIGN POWER

If the state, or the nation, is nothing other than a legal person the life of which consists in the union of its members and if the most important of its cares is its own preservation, it must have a universal and compelling power to move and dispose of each part in whatever manner is beneficial to the whole. Just as nature gives each man an absolute power over all his own limbs, the social pact gives the body politic an absolute power over all its members; and it is this same power which, directed by the general will, bears . . . the name of sovereignty.

However, we have to consider beside the public person those private persons who compose it, and whose life and liberty is naturally independent of it. Here we have to distinguish clearly the respective rights of the citizen and of the sovereign,[‡] and distinguish those duties which the citizens have as subjects from the natural rights which they ought to enjoy as men.

We have agreed that each man alienates by the social pact only that part of his power, his goods, and his liberty which is the concern of the community; but it must also be admitted that the sovereign alone is judge of what is of such concern.

Whatever services the citizen can render the state, he owes whenever the sovereign demands them; but the sovereign, on its side, may not impose on the subjects any burden which is not necessary to the community; the sovereign cannot, indeed, even will such a thing, since according to the law of reason no less than to the law of nature nothing is without a cause.

The commitments which bind us to the social body are obligatory only because they are mutual; and their nature is such that in fulfilling them a man cannot work for others without at the same time working for himself. How should it be that the general will is always rightful and that all men constantly wish the happiness of each but for the fact that there is no one who does not take that word "each" to pertain to himself and in voting for all think of himself? This proves that the equality of rights and the notion of justice which it produces derive

---

[†]"Divisions," says Machiavelli, "sometimes injure and sometimes aid a republic. The injury is done by cabals and factions; the service is rendered by a party which maintains itself without cabals and factions. Since, therefore, it is impossible for the founder of a republic to provide against enmities, he must make the best provision he can against factions." *History of Florence*, Book VII.

[‡]Please, attentive reader, do not hasten to accuse me of contradiction. I cannot avoid a contradiction of words, because of the poverty of language; but wait.

from the predilection which each man has for himself and hence from human nature as such. It also proves that the general will, to be truly what it is, must be general in its purpose as well as in its nature; that it should spring from all and apply to all; and that it loses its natural rectitude when it is directed towards any particular and circumscribed object—for in judging what is foreign to us, we have no sound principle of equity to guide us.

For, indeed, whenever we are dealing with a particular fact or right, on a matter which has not been settled by an earlier and general agreement, that question becomes contentious. It is a conflict in which private interests are ranged on one side and the public interest on the other; and I can see neither the law which is to be followed nor the judge who is to arbitrate. It would be absurd in such a dispute to seek an express decision of the general will; for a decision could only be a conclusion in favor of one of the contending parties, and it would be regarded by the other party as an alien, partial will, a will prone to error and liable in such circumstances to fall into injustice. So we see that even as a private will cannot represent the general will, so too the general will changes its nature if it seeks to deal with an individual case; it cannot as a *general* will give a ruling concerning any one man or any one fact. When the people of Athens, for example, appointed or dismissed its leaders, awarding honors to one, inflicting penalties on another, and by a multitude of particular decrees indiscriminately exercised all the functions of an administration, then the people of Athens no longer had what is correctly understood as a general will and ceased to act as sovereign and acted instead as magistrate. All this may seem at variance with commonly accepted notions; but I must be given time to expound my own.

It should nevertheless be clear from what I have so far said that the general will derives its generality less from the number of voices than from the common interest which unites them—for the general will is an institution in which each necessarily submits himself to the same conditions which he imposes on others; this admirable harmony of interest and justice gives to social deliberations a quality of equity which disappears at once from the discussion of any individual dispute precisely because in these latter cases there is no common interest to unite and identify the decision of the judge with that of the contending parties.

Whichever way we look at it, we always return to the same conclusion: namely that the social pact establishes equality among the citizens in that they all pledge themselves under the same conditions and must all enjoy the same rights. Hence by the nature of the compact, every act of sovereignty, that is, every authentic act of the general will, binds or favors all the citizens equally, so that the sovereign recognizes only the whole body of the nation and makes no distinction between any of the members who compose it. What then is correctly to be called an act of sovereignty? It is not a covenant between a superior and an inferior, but a covenant of the body with each of its members. It is a legitimate covenant, because its basis is the social contract; an equitable one, because it is common to all; a useful one, because it can have no end but the common good; and it is a durable covenant because it is guaranteed by the armed forces and the supreme power. So long as the subjects submit to such covenants alone, they obey nobody but their own will; and to ask how far the respective rights of the sovereign and the citizen extend is to ask how far these two can pledge themselves together, each to all and all to each.

From this it is clear that the sovereign power, wholly absolute, wholly sacred, wholly inviolable as it is, does not go beyond the limits of the general covenants; and thus that every man can do what he pleases with such goods and such freedom as is left to him by these covenants; and from this it follows that the sovereign has never any right to impose greater burdens on one subject than on another, for whenever that happens a private grievance is created and the sovereign's power is no longer competent.

Granted these distinctions, it becomes manifestly false to assert that individuals make any real renunciation by the social contract; indeed, as a result of the contract they find themselves in a situation preferable in real terms to that which prevailed before; instead of an alienation, they have profitably exchanged an uncertain and precarious life for a better and more secure one; they have exchanged natural independence for freedom, the power to destroy others for the enjoyment of their own security; they have exchanged their own strength which others might overcome for a right which the social union makes invincible. Their very lives, which they have pledged to the state, are always protected by it; and even when they risk their lives to defend the state, what more are they doing but giving back what they have received from the state? What are they doing that they would not do more often, and at greater peril, in the state of nature, where every man is inevitably at war and at the risk of his life, defends whatever serves him to maintain life? Assuredly, all must now fight in case of need for their country, but at least no one has any longer to fight for himself. And is there not something to be gained by running, for the sake of the guarantee of safety, a few of those risks we should each have to face alone if we were deprived of that assurance?

ON LAW

We have given life and existence to the body politic by the social pact; now it is a matter of giving it movement and will by legislation. For the primitive act by which the body politic is formed and united does not determine what it shall do to preserve itself.

What is good and in conformity with order is such by the very nature of things and independently of human agreements. All justice comes from God, who alone is its source; and if only we knew how to receive it from that exalted fountain, we should need neither governments nor laws. There is undoubtedly a universal justice which springs from reason alone, but if that justice is to be admitted among men it must be reciprocal. Humanly speaking, the laws of natural justice, lacking any natural sanction, are unavailing among men. In fact, such laws merely benefit the wicked and injure the just, since the just respect them while others do not do so in return. So there must be covenants and positive laws to unite rights with duties and to direct justice to its object. In the state of nature, where everything is common, I owe nothing to those to whom I have promised nothing, and I recognize as belonging to others only those things that are of no use to me. But this is no longer the case in civil society, where all rights are determined by law.

Yet what, in the last analysis, is law? If we simply try to define it in terms of metaphysical ideas, we shall go on talking without reaching any understanding; and when we have said what natural law is, we shall still not know what the law of the state is.

I have already said that the general will cannot relate to any particular object. For such a particular object is either within the state or outside the state. If it is outside, then a will which is alien to it is not general with regard to it: if the object is within the state, it forms a part of the state: Then there comes into being a relationship between the whole and the part which involves two separate entities, the part being one, and the whole, less that particular part, being the other. But a whole less a particular part is no longer a whole; and so as long as this relationship exists there is no whole but only two unequal parts, from which it follows that the will of the one is no longer general with respect to the other.

But when the people as a whole makes rules for the people as a whole, it is dealing only with itself; and if any relationship emerges, it is between the entire body seen from one perspective and the same entire body seen from another, without any division whatever. Here the matter concerning which a rule is made is as general as the will which makes it. And *this* is the kind of act which I call a law.

When I say that the province of the law is always general, I mean that the law considers all subjects collectively and all actions in the abstract; it does not consider any individual man or any specific action. Thus the law may well lay down that there shall be privileges, but it may not nominate the persons who shall have those privileges; the law may establish several classes of citizen, and even specify the qualifications which shall give access to those several classes, but it may not say that this man or that shall be admitted; the law may set up a royal government and an hereditary succession, but it may not elect a king or choose a royal family—in a word, no function which deals with the individual falls within the province of the legislative power.

On this analysis, it is immediately clear that we can no longer ask *who* is to make laws, because laws are acts of the general will; no longer ask if the prince is above the law, because he is a part of the state; no longer ask if the law can be unjust, because no one is unjust to himself; and no longer ask how we can be both free and subject to laws, for the laws are but registers of what we ourselves desire.

It is also clear that since the law unites universality of will with universality of the field of legislation, anything that any man, no matter who, commands on his own authority is not a law; even what the sovereign itself commands with respect to a particular object is not a law but a decree, not an act of sovereignty but an act of government.

Any state which is ruled by law I call a "republic," whatever the form of its constitution; for then, and then alone, does the public interest govern and then alone is the "public thing"—the *res publica*—a reality. All legitimate government is "republican."§ . . .

Laws are really nothing other than the conditions on which civil society exists. A

§By this word I understand not only an aristocracy or democracy, but generally any government directed by the general will, which is law. If it is to be legitimate, the government must not be united with the sovereign, but must serve it as its ministry. So even a monarchy can be a republic. . . .

people, since it is subject to laws, ought to be the author of them. The right of laying down the rules of society belongs only to those who form the society; but how can they exercise it? Is it to be by common agreement, by a sudden inspiration? Has the body politic an organ to declare its will? Who is to give it the foresight necessary to formulate enactments and proclaim them in advance, and how is it to announce them in the hour of need? How can a blind multitude, which often does not know what it wants, because it seldom knows what is good for it, undertake by itself an enterprise as vast and difficult as a system of legislation? By themselves the people always will what is good, but by themselves they do not always discern it. The general will is always rightful, but the judgment which guides it is not always enlightened. It must be made to see things as they are, and sometimes as they should be seen; it must be shown the good path which it is seeking, and secured against seduction by the desires of individuals; it must be given a sense of situation and season, so as to weigh immediate and tangible advantages against distant and hidden evils. Individuals see the good and reject it; the public desires the good but does not see it. Both equally need guidance. Individuals must be obliged to subordinate their will to their reason; the public must be taught to recognize what it desires. Such public enlightenment would produce a union of understanding and will in the social body, bring the parts into perfect harmony, and lift the whole to its fullest strength. Hence the necessity of a lawgiver.[12]

Ayn Rand and the Objectivist Approach

Hobbes and Rousseau defined social contracts by virtue of which people momentarily give up basic rights expecting to receive them back from society with greater security than before. Locke and Jefferson stressed a

A Y N   R A N D   1905–1982

different approach. Fundamental human rights, they said, are unalienable. Nothing should preempt them. According to Locke and Jefferson, any theory suggesting that we relinquish these rights, however momentarily, is extremely dangerous. It puts the individual at the mercy of society.

Disagreeing with Hobbes and Rousseau, Ayn Rand (1905–1982) supported Locke and Jefferson, whose philosophy, she thought, had its deepest roots in Aristotle:

> It took centuries of intellectual, philosophical development to achieve political freedom. It was a long struggle, stretching from Aristotle to John Locke to the Founding Fathers. The system they established was not based on unlimited majority rule, but on its opposite: on individual rights, which were not to be alienated by majority vote or minority plotting. The individual was not left at the mercy of his neighbors or his leaders: the Constitutional system of checks and balances was scientifically devised to protect him from both.[13]

Born in a Russian city, St. Petersburg (now Leningrad), Rand immigrated to the United States in 1926 and became an American citizen five years later. Love for her new country found expression in the belief that "the United States of America is the greatest, the noblest, and, in its original founding principles, the *only* moral country in the history of the world."[14]

Rand feared that the founding principles of the United States were endangered. Twentieth-century totalitarianism and genocide offered too much evidence that individual human rights were far from unalienable. As she defended individual rights, Rand articulated her philosophy in best-selling novels, which illustrates that the style of philosophical writing can be as diverse as philosophy's questions. In *We the Living* (1936) and *Anthem* (1938), she reflected on Soviet life and dissented against socialist government. Better known are *The Fountainhead* (1943) and *Atlas Shrugged* (1957). These novels explore a moral and economic philosophy emphasizing individualism and self-interest. Disciplined, rational, and active, Rand's heroes resist communal pressures that restrict personal advancement or rob people of individual **liberty**. In a speech that Rand regarded as containing the essence of her thought, the protagonist of *Atlas Shrugged*, John Galt, asserts that

> *Rights* are conditions of existence required by man's nature for his proper survival. If man is to live on earth, it is *right* for him to use his mind, it is *right* to act on his own free judgment, it is *right* to work for his values and to keep the product of his work. If life on earth is his purpose, he has a *right* to live as a rational being: nature forbids him to be irrational. Any group, any gang, any nation that attempts to negate man's rights, is *wrong*, which means: is evil, which means: is anti-life.[15]

Ideas influence human existence tremendously, but Rand thought that Western philosophy was a mixed blessing because some of its major strands were enemies of human rights. The remedy was not to abandon philosophy, which is essential to our rational existence, but to defend true philosophy against deception. Rand accepted that challenge in her novels and also in many essays she reasserted her confidence that "if you accept the importance of philosophy and the task of examining it critically, it is *my* philosophy that you will come to accept."[16]

The "Essentials"

Ayn Rand called her philosophy **Objectivism.** One reason for the name was that she regarded so much of Western philosophy as "subjectivism." The main culprit, she felt, was Immanuel Kant. Under his influence for more than two hundred years, "the dominant trend of philosophy has been directed to a single goal: the destruction of man's mind, of his confidence in the power of reason" (pp. 6–7). Rand aimed to reinstate that confidence, which meant rejecting Kant's view that we cannot know things in themselves and that the mind puts us in touch directly only with a phenomenal world largely of its own making.

Objectivism, Rand explained, possesses the following "essentials":

> in metaphysics, *the Law of Identity*—in epistemology, *the supremacy of reason*—in ethics, *rational egoism*—in politics, *individual rights* (i.e., capitalism)—in aesthetics, *metaphysical values.* (P. 22.)

This outlook entails the existence of the universe independently of and with primacy over consciousness. Moreover, the Law of Identity—A is A and Man is Man, she liked to say—holds that "things are what they are" (p. 14). In chess, for example, a queen is a queen. She has an identity; the queen can do certain things and only certain things because that is her nature. All of reality is like that, according to Rand, and there are several corollaries with respect to our knowledge.

The nature of consciousness is to perceive what exists—the **metaphysically given,** as Rand called it. Although sense experience is our "only direct cognitive contact with reality" (p. 90), once consciousness is prompted by the senses, it can conceptualize the information they provide. Concepts, in turn, permit language. With its help we obtain knowledge and science, which can exist because the nature of a thing is identifiable when we use reason—the essential identifying property of human existence—to evaluate experience logically. Of course human beings are neither omniscient nor infallible, but truth is available by using reason to determine whether our judgments "correspond to or contradict the facts of reality" (p. 27). According to Rand, one application of that principle shows that the "subjectivism" unleashed by Kant is far less reasonable than he and his followers have claimed. His theory amounts to saying that things are never what we ordinarily find them to be. Since nobody lives by that conclusion, it deserves rejection, she claimed.

The Virtue of Selfishness

Rand found Kant's epistemology and metaphysics unfortunate enough, but she went on to argue that Kant used them as the means to an even more undesirable end. In brief, Kant compounded his attack on common sense by claiming, in Rand's words, that "an action is moral *only* if you perform it out of a sense of duty and derive no benefit from it of any kind, neither material nor spiritual; if you derive any benefit, your action is not moral any longer" (p. 65). Rand dubbed Kant's moral philosophy **altruism.** Its basic principle, she stated, "is that man has no right to exist for his own sake, that service to others is the only justification of his existence, and that self-sacrifice is his highest moral duty, virtue, and value" (p. 61). Objectivism abhors altruism, finding it not only contrary to human nature but also irrational. This opinion does not mean, however, that Rand was uncharitable; nor does it mean that her morality says "Anything goes" and "Do your own thing." It does advocate "**rational egoism,**" or, to use the title of one of her best-known books, *The Virtue of Selfishness*.

Far from referring to the pursuit of one's whims at any cost, selfishness rightly understood means *"concern with one's own interests."*[17] Insofar as it is rational, selfishness is virtuous, a conviction Rand elaborated by discussing the importance of ethics. Nature offers us a fundamental choice. We can choose or decline to exist as human persons. If the latter choice is ours, we either die or become less than human, and ethics has no place because it is the science that objectively details the right goals for a human being to pursue. Thus, if we choose to be human, ethics becomes "an *objective, metaphysical necessity of man's survival*" (p. 23). Rand expanded her point as follows:

> The standard of value of the Objectivist ethics—the standard by which one judges what is good or evil—is *man's life,* or: that which is required for man's survival *qua* man. . . . "Man's survival *qua* man" means the terms, methods, conditions, and goals required for the survival of a rational being through the whole of his lifespan—in all those aspects of existence which are open to his choice. . . . Since reason is man's basic means of survival, that which is proper to the life of a rational being is the good; that which negates, opposes, or destroys it is the evil. (Pp. 23–24.)

Rational beings, Rand contended, recognize that life is an end in itself and in particular that every living human person shares the dignity of that status. Additionally, they understand that the achievement of one's own happiness is the highest moral purpose for an individual. Happiness entails self-esteem, which means that one does not "desire the unearned" but rather gives "value for value" (p. 31). In short, rational beings understand that there are objective metaphysical values. Specifically, we recognize human rights and we defend the liberty they provide. When these things are done, the virtue of selfishness becomes apparent.

The Libertarian Appeal

As a political philosophy, Objectivism becomes **libertarianism,** which one of its proponents defines as "the doctrine that every person is the owner of his own life, and that no one is the owner of anyone else's life: and that consequently every human being has the right to act in accordance with his own choices, unless those actions infringe on the equal liberty of other human beings to act in accordance with their choices."[18] Rand joins libertarians in emphasizing *rights* where freedom is concerned.

In general, a right is a moral principle that stakes out and justifies a person's freedom to act in a social setting. According to Rand, rights pertain primarily to individuals. Groups, which Rand understands to be formed always by individuals, can obtain prerogatives by contractual agreement among persons, but those prerogatives never legitimate coercion. The most basic right is a person's right to life. There are others—for example, the right to pursue happiness, but not the right to happiness. Following Locke, Rand gave a special priority to the right to property, without which "no other rights are possible."[19] It is next to life itself, Rand asserted, because we must sustain ourselves as human persons, and we cannot do that unless we retain ownership of the products of our own efforts.

Rights ensure us the room to act because their existence entails "freedom from physical compulsion, coercion, or interference" (p. 94). We are obliged not to interfere in the rightful freedom of others, and they are obliged to refrain from infringing on ours. From a moral point of view, failure to heed these boundaries constitutes criminal behavior. Governments exist to thwart potential violators of human rights; their primary, if not sole, responsibility is to thwart and punish initial acts of coercion. But any government must also be watched and checked, lest its tendency to tyrannize eradicate the very liberty it should protect. Included in that liberty is economic activity, which Rand equated with free-enterprise capitalism. Thus her philosophy is vehemently anticommunist. Beyond the restrictions of noninterference with the rightful liberty of persons, individuals incur no obligations except those they accept voluntarily. Certainly these do not involve any self-sacrificing altruism, which Rand finds "incompatible with freedom, with capitalism, and with individual rights" (p. 95).

Are Things Black and White or Gray?

Ayn Rand titled one of her essays "The Cult of Moral Grayness." Gray was not her favorite color. She equated it with uncertainty about our achieving knowledge. "Gray" also included ethical positions that dissented from her claim that "morality is a code of black and white" and specifically one of enlightened selfishness (p. 79). Rand's philosophy appeals to some because it promises clarity not ambiguity, certainty not just probability, direct truth about reality not interpretations, and a morality that legitimates self-interest. In short, she offers answers not just more questions. For those reasons, one may wonder whether she removed grayness quite as much as she thought.

Naturally we all want clarity, certainty, and the certification that we know reality as it is and that our self-interest is good. Everyone wants to be right. Life is simpler when it is not gray. Rand puts philosophy in the service of what comes naturally. The unintended irony in her doing so, however, is that this approach does raise more

questions than it answers. We would like certainty, but, if the history of human thought suggests anything, it is that the quest for certainty is continually frustrated. Rand, of course, disagreed. Indeed she would find the approach of this book—which stresses that no single theory is obviously true over all the others—fundamentally misguided. Her theory remains an option. It is an important one because it takes such a determined stand against much of philosophy past and present.

Describing rights as "moral principles which define and protect a man's freedom of action, but impose no obligations on other men," she believed that human conflict would recede insofar as people acted within their rights (p. 97). But is that forecast accurate? Are rights destined to be a bone of contention just because their status and effect are less than perfectly clear? To decide—a key word—involves doing what the author says: observe, reason, judge, test. If we do those things properly, Rand thought, we will agree with her. If we do not agree with her, either we have unwittingly botched the process of rational deliberation or we are being perverse. Rand never hesitated to say that her philosophical opponents were guilty on one or both counts, and few rivaled her as a polemicist. According to Rand, for instance, those she called "the theoreticians of altruism"—John Rawls and John Dewey along with Kant—knowingly distorted selfishness in attacking it. In fact, they were really bent on destroying "reason, intelligence, ability, merit, self-confidence, self-esteem."[20] Whether such charges enhance Rand's credibility is a problem in its own right.

Disagreements on fundamental matters do occur among reasonable men and women who are neither mistaken nor perverse. When that happens, what can a philosopher like Ayn Rand do? Short of changing her position, she could reiterate that those who do not agree with her are *wrong*. Beyond that, she could argue that holding "wrong" views leads to other errors, and by pointing them out presumably her case would be strengthened. But calling an outlook wrong does not make it so, and social criticism is no different from a theory of knowledge: rational persons of good will and sound judgment can and do disagree about what is right as well as about what we can know. Inquiry can and should continue, but the history of philosophy tells us that a point can be reached at which further argument is not persuasive. Reason can prevail, and still our differences may be irreconcilable.

Although such disagreement does not mean that every judgment is equally valid or invalid, it does suggest that Objectivism is not as obvious as Rand hoped her readers would find it. Of course that outcome does not falsify Rand's approach. Instead, as she stressed, the need remains to exercise rationally the right to make voluntary, uncoerced decisions. Try weighing those factors as you consider whether the following selection from *The Virtue of Selfishness* is a matter of black and white.

If one wishes to advocate a free society— that is, capitalism—one must realize that its indispensable foundation is the principle of individual rights. If one wishes to uphold individual rights, one must realize that capitalism is the only system that can uphold and protect them. And if one wishes to gauge the relationship of freedom to the goals of today's intellectuals, one may gauge it by the fact that the concept of individual rights is evaded, distorted, perverted, and seldom discussed, most conspicuously seldom by the so-called conservatives.

"Rights" are a moral concept—the concept that provides a logical transition from the principles guiding an individual's actions to the principles guiding his relationship with others—the concept that preserves and protects individual morality in a social context—the link between the moral code of a man and the legal code of a society, between ethics and politics. *Individual rights are the means of subordinating society to moral law.*

Every political system is based on some code of ethics. The dominant ethics of mankind's history were variants of the altruist–collectivist doctrine which subordinated the individual to some higher authority, either mystical or social. Consequently, most political systems were variants of the same statist tyranny, differing only in degree, not in basic principle, limited only by the accidents of tradition, of chaos, of bloody strife and periodic collapse. Under all such systems, morality was a code applicable to the individual, but not to society. Society was placed *outside* the moral law, as its embodiment or source or exclusive interpreter—and the inculcation of self-sacrificial devotion to social duty was regarded as the main purpose of ethics in man's earthly existence.

Since there is no such entity as "society," since society is only a number of individual men, this meant, in practice, that the rulers of society were exempt from moral law; subject only to traditional rituals, they held total power and exacted blind obedience—on the implicit principle of: "the good is that which is good for society (or for the tribe, the race, the nation), and the ruler's edicts are its voice on earth."

This was true of all statist systems, under all variants of the altruist–collectivist ethics, mystical or social. "The divine right of kings" summarizes the political theory of the first— "*Vox populi, vox dei*" of the second. As witness: the theocracy of Egypt, with the Pharaoh as an embodied god—the unlimited majority rule or *democracy* of Athens—the welfare state run by the emperors of Rome— the Inquisition of the late Middle Ages—the absolute monarchy of France—the welfare state of Bismarck's Prussia—the gas chambers of Nazi Germany—the slaughterhouse of the Soviet Union.

All these political systems were expressions of the altruist–collectivist ethics—and their common characteristic is the fact that society stood above the moral law, as an omnipotent, sovereign whim worshiper. Thus, politically, all these systems were variants of an *amoral* society.

The most profoundly revolutionary achievement of the United States of America was *the subordination of society to moral law.*

The principle of man's individual rights represented the extension of morality into the social system—as a limitation on the power of the state, as man's protection against the brute force of the collective, as the subordination of *might* to *right*. The United States was the first *moral* society in history.

All previous systems had regarded man as a sacrificial means to the ends of others, and society as an end in itself. The United States regarded man as an end in himself, and society as a means to the peaceful, orderly, *voluntary* coexistence of individuals. All previous systems had held that man's life belongs to society, that society can dispose of him in any way it pleases, and that any freedom he enjoys is his only by favor, by the *permission* of society, which may be revoked at any time. The United States held that man's life is his by *right* (which means: by moral principle and by his nature), that a right is the property of an individual, that society as such has no rights, and that the only moral purpose of a government is the protection of individual rights.

A "right" is a moral principle defining and sanctioning a man's freedom of action in a social context. There is only *one* fundamental right (all the others are its consequences or corollaries): a man's right to his own life. Life is a process of self-sustaining and self-generated action; the right to life means the right to engage in self-sustaining and self-generated action—which means: the freedom to take all the actions required by the nature of a rational being for the support, the furtherance, the fulfillment, and the enjoyment of his own life. (Such is the meaning of the right to life, liberty, and the pursuit of happiness.)

The concept of a "right" pertains only to action—specifically, to freedom of action. It means freedom from physical compulsion, coercion, or interference by other men.

Thus, for every individual, a right is the moral sanction of a *positive*—of his freedom to act on his own judgment, for his own goals, by his own *voluntary, uncoerced* choice. As to his neighbors, his rights impose no obligations on them except of a *negative* kind: to abstain from violating his rights.

The right to life is the source of all rights—and the right to property is their only implementation. Without property rights, no other rights are possible. Since man has to sustain his life by his own effort, the man who has no right to the product of his effort has no means to sustain his life. The man who produces while others dispose of his product is a slave.

Bear in mind that the right to property is a right to action, like all the others: it is not the right *to an object*, but to the action and the consequences of producing or earning that object. It is not a guarantee that a man *will* earn any property, but only a guarantee that he will own it if he earns it. It is the right to gain, to keep, to use, and to dispose of material values.

The concept of individual rights is so new in human history that most men have not grasped it fully to this day. In accordance with the two theories of ethics, the mystical or the social, some men assert that rights are a gift of God—others, that rights are a gift of society. But, in fact, the source of rights is man's nature.

The Declaration of Independence stated that men "are endowed by their Creator with certain unalienable rights." Whether one believes that man is the product of a Creator or of nature, the issue of man's origin does not alter the fact that he is an entity of a specific kind—a rational being—that he cannot function successfully under coercion, and that rights are a necessary condition of his particular mode of survival.

"The source of man's rights is not divine law or congressional law, but the law of identity. A is A—and Man is Man. *Rights* are conditions of existence required by man's nature for his proper survival. If man is to live on earth, it is *right* for him to use his mind, it is *right* to act on his own free judgment, it is *right* to work for his values and to keep the product of his work. If life on earth is his purpose, he has a *right* to live as a rational being: nature forbids him the irrational." (*Atlas Shrugged*)

To violate man's rights means to compel him to act against his own judgment, or to expropriate his values. Basically, there is only one way to do it: by the use of physical force. There are two potential violators of man's rights: the criminals and the government. The great achievement of the United States was to draw a distinction between these two—by forbidding to the second the legalized version of the activities of the first.

The Declaration of Independence laid down the principle that "to secure these rights, governments are instituted among men." This provided the only valid justification of a government and defined its only proper purpose: to protect man's rights by protecting him from physical violence.

Thus the government's function was changed from the role of ruler to the role of servant. The government was set to protect man from criminals—and the Constitution was written to protect man from the government. The Bill of Rights was not directed against private citizens, but against the government—as an explicit declaration that individual rights supersede any public or social power.

The result was the pattern of a civilized society which—for the brief span of some hundred and fifty years—America came close to achieving. A civilized society is one in which physical force is banned from human relationships—in which the government, acting as a policeman, may use force *only* in retaliation and *only* against those who initiate its use.[21]

John Dewey and Democracy

Along with Charles Peirce and William James, two philosophers we have met previously, John Dewey (1859–1952) started the move-

ment known as American pragmatism. To distinguish his version of it from those of Peirce and James, Dewey called his philosophy "instrumentalism." The name appealed to him because he liked to think of human intelligence as the probing instrument men and women must use to deal with life's personal and social problems. Frequently habitual responses are sufficient, but Dewey was especially impressed by the ways in which life challenges custom and tradition. Fresh inquiry is often called for, he stressed, and his philosophy sought to organize human intelligence to meet such challenges, particularly as they appeared in our social and political existence.

These concerns made Dewey a staunch defender of **democracy**. In fact, as the following passage suggests, Dewey looked on democracy as a moral ideal:

> Democracy as compared with other ways of life is the sole way of living which believes wholeheartedly in the process of experience as end and as means; as that which is capable of generating the science which is the sole dependable authority for the direction of further experience and which releases emotions, needs, and desires so as to call into being the things that have not existed in the past. For every way of life that fails in its democracy limits the contacts, the exchanges, the communications, the interactions by which experience is steadied while it is also enlarged and enriched. The task of this release and enrichment is one that has to be carried on day by day. Since it is one that can have no end till experience itself comes to an end, the task of democracy is forever that of the creation of a freer and more humane experience in which all share and to which all contribute.[22]

Born in Burlington, Vermont, Dewey taught in New England schools before completing his doctoral studies at Johns Hopkins University. There Peirce was one of his teachers, and Dewey's dissertation focused on the philosophy of Kant. After ten years of teach-

JOHN DEWEY 1859–1952

ing at the University of Michigan, Dewey went to the University of Chicago. He helped to found a famous laboratory school and also became much involved in social issues provoked by urbanization, technological advances, and the arrival of increasing numbers of immigrants in the United States. In 1904 Dewey left Chicago for New York City and Columbia University, where he taught until his retirement. A prolific author, in works such as *Democracy and Education* (1916), *Reconstruction in Philosophy* (1920), *Human Nature and Conduct* (1922), and *Experience and Nature* (1925), he argued that human existence is fundamentally an ongoing social

process that enjoins us to use a scientific method of inquiry, which Dewey regarded as "the final arbiter of all questions of fact, existence, and intellectual assent."[23]

Individualism Old and New

Already we have noted Ayn Rand's antipathy toward Dewey. The issue between them boiled down to a difference of opinion about "human nature and conduct." Rand stressed rights belonging to individuals and wanted individuals to be left alone to exercise them. Dewey could not accept such an outlook because it underplayed the interrelatedness of our existence. Thus, his philosophy did not accentuate the notion of rights held privately by independent persons. Dewey did believe that individuals are real and that they possess freedom that is rightly theirs to exercise democratically. But a person is a social reality, and the development of democracy in the modern world convinced him that human well-being required us to rethink the notion of **individualism** and the rights and duties it should involve.

Dewey's experience led him to *Individualism Old and New* (1929–30). Writing during the Great Depression, he saw that the long-standing American emphasis on individualism—rooted in the thought of Jefferson and Locke—provided a pivotal issue for the nation and the world. In the United States, argued Dewey, individualism has a natural history. If the outcome of that history is now uncertain, the ideal neither can nor should be excised. American identity depends on it. Therefore, Dewey's effort was to reinterpret individualism so that it would not be a hindrance but a help.

Always somewhat mythological, old-style American individualism, contended Dewey, had been modeled after the image of self-reliant, self-made pioneers. They saw opportunities for personal fortunes and set out to win them on their own. Dewey believed that circumstances were threatening that ideal. A basic reason was that America was increasingly organized in huge corporations. Ironically, that had occurred because the old individualism was once an effective dream. It spurred people to build amazing businesses and industrial plants, but this very success had burst the bubble. Though individuals remained, more and more they were becoming cogs in wheels that turned out products collectively. People were becoming incorporated; most lacked the opportunity to "make it" on their own.

According to Dewey, a dangerous exception to this analysis did exist. Old individualism could still take the form of measuring success in terms of money. Even within the corporate structure, such individualism could yet find expression in grabs for all-that-one-can-get. Dewey believed, too, that Americans had learned new ways to argue collectively so that management and labor, even government and people, seated themselves repeatedly at a table of hard bargains. In most cases, though, Dewey sensed that the individual remained the loser. As the old individualism persisted, alienation and frustration rose. Even if the old ideal dissolved in one person, its presence in others took its toll as the rounds of competition spiraled on—right into a crash.

Dewey assumed that no return to a preindustrial, precorporate America was possible. Indeed, if such a reversal had been possible, he would not have favored it. Even in the midst of an economic slump, he saw the increase in knowledge and technological power as vindicating the potential for good that use of scientific method can bring to life. His point was that human intelligence must be used more extensively and rigorously than ever to harness that potential and to channel it so that humanizing benefits accrue to all. Instead of encouraging the practical rationality of cost-effectiveness to become the tail that wags the dog, Dewey thought that

Americans must rally ingenuity to discern a strengthened and renewed understanding of what the initiatives of individualism ought to entail.

Too many people live "in a situation which is so incomplete that it cannot be admitted into the affections and yet is so pervasive that it cannot be escaped: a situation which defines an individual divided within himself."[24] The basic problem, he added, was one "of forming a new psychological and moral type" (p. 83). For example, Dewey's "new" individual would be scientifically oriented, at least in terms of an education that would provide him or her with a critical method for tackling life's problems. In addition, this individual's concern would focus on the social utility of action and planning, on the broad range of effects that policies have on national and international life. While recognizing that we must build on rather than tear down our existing industrial, scientific, and technological base, Dewey's individual would have an awareness tempered by understanding that economic concerns are appropriate just to the degree that they serve civil quality. That concern, Dewey argued, favored a strong role for government in fostering social and economic development. It also suggested that the individual's pursuit of happiness would best find its fulfillment in working for the well-being of society. If those efforts sometimes required persons to oppose established policies, Dewey hoped their attitudes would nonetheless seek to overcome alienation between individuals and society, labor and management, government and people.

Education and Democracy

Dewey's concern about individualism reflected his belief that sound education is essential for a thriving democracy:

A democracy is more than a form of government; it is primarily a mode of associated living, of conjoint communicated experience. . . . Obviously a society to which stratification into separate classes would be fatal, must see to it that intellectual opportunities are accessible to all on equable and easy terms. A society marked off into classes need be specially attentive only to the education of its ruling elements. A society which is mobile, which is full of channels for the distribution of a change occurring anywhere, must see to it that its members are educated to personal initiative and adaptability. Otherwise, they will be overwhelmed by the changes in which they are caught and whose significance or connections they do not perceive."[25]

For Dewey all philosophy involved educational issues, and throughout his writings he described the kind of education he thought democracy requires. In *The Quest for Certainty* (1929), for example, Dewey argued that in the past we had dealt with a world of hazards by "supplication, sacrifice, ceremonial rite, and magical cult."[26] The course he recommended was "to invent arts and by their means turn the powers of nature to account. . . . This is the method of changing the world through action, as the other is the method of changing the self in emotion and idea" (p. 3). Philosophy needs to be changed, but obviously so does education. "The depreciation of action, of doing and making, has been cultivated by philosophers" (p. 4). All that must go.

Dewey strongly believed that there was too sharp a division between theory and practice. This led to the famous maxim associated with Dewey's name: "learning by doing." This was not an appeal to antiintellectualism but rather a call to take advantage of the fact that people—especially the young—are active, curious, and ready to explore. Dewey's pragmatism has often been called the experimental method in education and philosophy. It was not enough for Dewey to consider theories; we must see what they produce in action. Part of Dewey's proposal

was based on his dislike for generalization. He felt that we deal with individualized and unique situations that are never exactly duplicable and about which no complete assurance is possible. Thus, we need to be prepared to experiment anew each time a problem arises.

Dewey held that Greek philosophy had separated knowledge from action with disastrous consequences. "The realm of the practical," he said, "is the region of change, and change is always contingent" (p. 19). If we recognize the radical nature of the changing character of the world we live in, we must educate for that. He opposed the **spectator theory of knowledge** and abhorred a quest for certainty that separates "theory and practice, knowledge and action" (pp. 23–24). Our job is to integrate these elements. Yet experience can furnish us only with contingent probability, which means that education must supply us with the tools to learn experimentally. Certainty becomes impossible. Yet to accomplish much is not easy. "Doing is always subject to peril, to the danger of frustration" (p. 33). Thus, Dewey added,

> . . . The problem of philosophy concerns the *interaction* of our judgments about ends to be sought with knowledge of the means for achieving them. . . . There is thus no a priori test or rule for the determination of the operations which define ideas. They are themselves experimentally developed in the course of actual inquiries. (Pp. 37, 124.)

These statements taken together outline Dewey's theories on education. It is pointless to teach abstract, formal knowledge. We must present actual problems that demand solution and try to see if practical action can be worked out. Formal training has little value in itself and may miss the point.

Nothing any longer can be called abstractly true, Dewey thought, because "the validity of the object of thought depends upon the *consequences* of the operations which define the object of thought" (p. 129). We must always ask: What are the practical results of an idea? "Ideas are worthless except as they pass into actions which rearrange and reconstruct in some way, be it little or large, the world in which we live," Dewey concluded (p. 138). Education cannot be judged successful by the abstract knowledge memorized, but only by the changes that result from it. Education once took its model from classical literature; now it must turn to the methods of science. We must remember that when Dewey recommended that our new educational models be adapted from science, he thought of science primarily as a method of experiment, not as a fixed body of knowledge to be learned. Dewey was well aware of the vast amount of factual data available in the natural sciences. But he felt that the success of modern science lay in its flexible method of experiment. Education ought to take its cues from that approach.

As for the question of what schools should be like, Dewey's first answer was that they should be places where theory is put into practice. Next, Dewey tied the experimental theory in education closely to preparation for democracy. School life should reflect the environment; it should not be a world apart. Since such education is only partly provided in the conventional classroom, schools must be opened out to the world. The aim should also be the growth of natural capacities, with which Dewey feels we are endowed at birth. We must build by trying "to teach a child what is of use to him as a child," Dewey tells us.[27] Our initial attention, then, should be on the needs of the child, not on the needs of the adult world or on some world of abstract learning.

Dewey stressed "the tools of learning" and their mastery. The child must be stimulated, not forced. The teacher should "present situations that make pupils hungry to acquire additional knowledge" (p. 12). Cultivating critical and creative attitudes of inquiry should

be among education's main goals. "What the pupil really needs is not exact information about topography," Dewey said by way of illustration, "but to have to find out for himself" (p. 13). Dewey deplored educational regimentation. In the ideal situation: "No individual child is forced to a task that does not appeal" (p. 19). Some of Rousseau's romantic optimism remains alive in the view of human nature that lies behind Dewey's theories.

"Democracy," held Dewey, "is itself an educational principle."[28] He took the idea of democracy to be opposed to any conception of aristocracy. "Every individual must be consulted in such a way, actively not passively, that he himself becomes a part of the process of authority, of the process of social control" (p. 35). But the problem is complicated because we must not simply pass on the education or values of the past. "The educational problem today is . . . infinitely more difficult because it has to face all of the problems of the modern world" (p. 42). Yet Dewey remained hopeful: "The foundation of democracy is faith in the capacities of human nature" (p. 59). That faith made him place the highest premium on education. "Since freedom of mind and freedom of expression are the root of all freedom," he concluded, "to deny freedom in education is a crime against democracy" (p. 78). As you read from Dewey's "Pedagogic Creed" (1897), see if you agree with what he suggests about the link among individual rights and duties, democracy, and education.

I BELIEVE THAT

Education is the fundamental method of social progress and reform.

All reforms which rest simply upon the enactment of law, or the threatening of certain penalties, or upon changes in mechanical or outward arrangements, are transitory and futile.

Education is a regulation of the process of coming to share in the social consciousness; and that the adjustment of individual activity on the basis of this social consciousness is the only sure method of social reconstruction.

This conception has due regard for both the individualistic and socialistic ideals. It is duly individual because it recognizes the formation of a certain character as the only genuine basis of right living. It is socialistic because it recognizes that this right character is not to be formed by merely individual precept, example, or exhortation, but rather by the influence of a certain form of institutional or community life upon the individual, and that the social organism through the school, as its organ, may determine ethical results.

In the ideal school we have the reconciliation of the individualistic and the institutional ideals.

The community's duty to education is, therefore, its paramount moral duty. By law and punishment, by social agitation and discussion, society can regulate and form itself in a more or less haphazard and chance way. But through education society can formulate its own purposes, can organize its own means and resources, and thus shape itself with definiteness and economy in the direction in which it wishes to move.

When society once recognizes the possibilities in this direction, and the obligations which these possibilities impose, it is impossible to conceive of the resources of time, attention, and money which will be put at the disposal of the educator.

It is the business of everyone interested in education to insist upon the school as the primary and most effective interest of social progress and reform in order that society may be awakened to realize what the school stands for, and aroused to the necessity of endowing the educator with sufficient equipment properly to perform his task.

Education thus conceived marks the most perfect and intimate union of science and art conceivable in human experience.

The art of thus giving shape to human powers and adapting them to social service is the supreme art; one calling into its service the best of artists; that no insight, sympathy, tact, executive power, is too great for such service.

With the growth of psychological service, giving added insight into individual structure and laws of growth; and with growth of social science, adding to our knowledge of the right organization of individuals, all scientific resources can be utilized for the purposes of education.

When science and art thus join hands the most commanding motive for human action will be reached, the most genuine springs of human conduct aroused, and the best service that human nature is capable of guaranteed.

The teacher is engaged, not simply in the training of individuals, but in the formation of the proper social life.

Every teacher should realize the dignity of his calling: that he is a social servant set apart for the maintenance of proper social order and the securing of the right social growth.

In this way the teacher always is the prophet of the true God and the usherer in of the true kingdom of God.[29]

Summary

All the philosophers in this chapter—Hobbes, Locke, Jefferson, Rousseau, Rand, and Dewey—have left a profound impact on contemporary political life partly because they answered "yes" to the question "Do I have rights in society?" But this result also comes from their different and conflicting views about the source, nature, and destiny of our rights. Hobbes and Locke clashed over human nature. Hobbes contended that people would be in a state of war until they gave up their natural rights and allowed a sovereign the exclusive authority to govern them. Believing that people are more naturally benevolent, Locke insisted that we must never give up our natural rights, although we need governments to protect them. Even ordinary people, thought Jefferson, could be rational enough to discern the self-evident truths that his philosophy defended. Despite their good intentions, Rousseau countered, people might not be sufficiently perceptive to know what is good for them. Until the proper education prevailed, an authoritative lawgiver would be needed to promote their own good. Both Rand and Dewey harbored suspicions about such appeals to authority, but even as they affirmed democratic principles, their philos-ophies clashed. Dewey's democracy was too socialistic for Rand; Rand's democracy was too individualistic for Dewey.

All these outlooks have persuasive power. Each has had a large following. Confronted by the differences, what should we do? Dewey's emphasis on critical inquiry commends itself as one response that deserves a high priority. Making the best-informed judgments possible, we need to ask: What have been or will be the practical consequences if we follow the teachings of Hobbes, Rousseau, Rand, or any of the others? As we try that pragmatic test, we may start to learn which views are preferable and why. That same process of self-education can also help us to see what is needed—and what we might do—to make society better, which is the topic of the next chapter.

GLOSSARY

altruism the idea of a human capacity to act in the interests of others, setting self-interest aside. Philosophers have differed radically over whether such a capacity exists and what its role is.

body politic in Rousseau, the "public person" or collective entity formed when a number of individuals give their consent to the **social contract,** hence substituting the "general will" for the will of each individual as the basis of normative judgments.

citizens the people considered as the subjects of a sovereign state or nation, each one possessing the rights and duties that belong to him or her in this capacity.

civil law in Hobbes and Locke, the form of law that replaces the "law of nature" or the "moral law" when a people submit themselves to the sovereignty of a government; in Hobbes, the civil law functions to prevent the endless conflict that characterizes the "state of nature"; for Locke it is an outgrowth of the natural moral law, in particular of the natural rights of property.

commonwealth the domain of mutual interest that, once recognized by individuals, forms the basis of the formal **social contract.** Hobbes defined commonwealth as the subsumption of a multitude of persons, as subjects, under the authority of one person or legislative body, as **sovereign.**

consent the mutual agreement of all parties to the **social contract;** in Rousseau, that which legitimates the authority given to the government to act on behalf of the **general will.**

democracy the form of government in which authority is vested in the people, acting through elected representatives.

duties the obligations to respect and not interfere with others; in classical political theory, duties are complementary to rights, the obligations of others to respect and not interfere with oneself.

"education of nature" in Rousseau's *Emile,* the form of nurturing that stresses the natural course of human development and the cultivation of natural human virtues, to maximize the role of independence of judgment and self-reliance that would lead a person so instructed to be suited to participate in the social contract, with its implications of public trust.

equality the key concept of Jefferson's political philosophy, which held that all citizens of a commonwealth should enjoy the same rights and the same degree of liberty, based on what Jefferson considered to be the inviolable natural rights of man.

equilibrium in Rousseau, a state of balance between a person's desires and natural capacities, not unlike Aristotle's "golden mean," which results from an **"education of nature"** and forms the essential condition of freedom as Rousseau sees it.

"general will" for Rousseau, the concept that replaces the individual will as the source of social norms when individuals incorporate themselves into a society by means of the **social contract,** and representing the basis of the notion of a whole people as the **sovereign** of a state. Rousseau contrasts the general will with the "will of all," which represents the universal tendency to seek the goals of pure self-interest.

individualism the political doctrine that the fundamental unit of a society is the individual, and that certain natural rights accrue to each individual. In the **Objectivism** of Ayn Rand, the interests of the individual take precedence over the dictates of the state, while Dewey's individualism stresses the degree to which individuals are formed by social processes that inevitably tie their identity to the social order to which they belong.

libertarian the political doctrine that personal liberty is the highest political value, and that states should interfere as little as possible in the sphere of individual rights. In the **Objectivism** of Ayn Rand, "rational egoism," or the pursuit of self-interest, is seen as taking a natural precedence over altruism, or the subjugation of self-interest to a respect for the interests of others.

liberty freedom, the absence of constraint on the exercise of a person's natural rights, instincts, and aims.

"metaphysically given" in Rand's philosophy, the reality with which our consciousness is immediately in contact. Rand uses this notion to reject the "subjectivism" of philosophers like Kant, and the moral doctrines this "subjectivism" supports.

moral law the system of normative beliefs Locke saw operating in the "state of nature," which for Locke provides that basis for civil law. In particular, Locke saw the moral basis for civil law to be the natural rights of **property.**

natural law in Hobbes, a principle of reason that forbids a person to do anything to endanger his own life or prosperity. It is from this conception of what is rational to do under natural circumstances that Hobbes derives his conception of the **state of nature** as "a war of all against all," each person serving only the interest of self-preservation.

Objectivism the title Ayn Rand gives to her philosophy, which is intended to oppose what Rand considers the "subjectivism" of most of modern Western philosophy. "Rational egoism," or the pursuit of self-interest, is seen as taking a natural precedence over altruism, or the subjugation of self-interest to a respect for the interests of others.

prerogative a special right, or privilege, a term Jefferson used in discussing the power of a **sovereign** over his subjects and the basis of his right to govern. Jefferson believed that any such prerogative entailed corresponding obligations.

property what belongs to a person, that of which a person has a right to claim possession. In Locke's theory of property rights, things become property when they are transformed by labor, and the rights of possession of property belong to the persons whose labor has produced the property in question.

"rational egoism" Rand's term for the ethical branch of her "Objectivist" philosophy. Like Hobbes, Rand sees the pursuit of self-interest as fundamentally rational and natural, since reason is a characteristic adaptation to the environment made by the human organism to secure its own survival.

rights where there exist morally or legally sanctioned limits on one person's interference with another person's freedom (of action, speech, belief, etc.), the person whose freedom is protected is said to have a right to engage in the sanctioned activities. By implication, a corresponding duty to recognize a right is imposed by the same authority that sanctions the right itself.

social contract an agreement or covenant to which the state and its citizens are envisioned as parties, which specifies the reciprocal rights and obligations of each party and is entered into voluntarily for mutual benefit. Rousseau and Locke based their notions of the legitimacy of the authority of government on the assumption that such an agreement is implicit in a rightfully constituted body politic.

sovereign Hobbes's term for the person or group standing at the head of a government and ruling over its citizens.

spectator theory of knowledge Dewey's term for the philosophical theories he believed made too sharp a division between theory and practice; Dewey believed that rejecting such theories in favor of a pragmatic theory emphasizing the interrelation of the theoretical and practical components of knowledge was an essential step in planning an educational program that would support democratic values.

state of nature a hypothetical condition of human beings prior to their being brought under the administration of a sovereign state, a notion used by many political philosophers of the age of Hobbes and Locke. Hobbes viewed the state of nature as a realm of unqualified conflict between persons, and he saw the state as a way of mediating those conflicts. Locke, on the other hand, thought that certain restraining moral laws, like those governing the rights of property, were inherent in the state of nature. For Locke, then, the recognition of rights and duties provides the germ from which civil laws are to be derived, representing as it does characteristic features of human nature, not conditions that must be imposed by the state.

STUDY QUESTIONS

1. Do you think a "state of nature" ever existed? Why and how do Hobbes, Locke, and Rousseau use that idea?

2. Whose theory of rights is more persuasive to you, Hobbes's or Locke's? Why?

3. Do we have a natural right to property, as Locke believed, or are property rights primarily established by civil law, as Hobbes asserted?

4. If you had to live in a society governed by Hobbes's principles or by Locke's, which would you choose, and why?

5. Do you believe that there are "self-evident truths"? If not, why not? If so, do they include moral and political claims, as Thomas Jefferson believed?

6. In view of the obvious inequalities in the world, how do you interpret and evaluate Jefferson's claim that "all men are created equal"?

7. Do you think that Rousseau's theory about the social contract provides an adequate basis for discerning our rights and duties in society?

8. Can you distinguish between Rousseau's "will of all" and his "general will"? Are these concepts useful in delineating what ought to happen in society?

9. Does Ayn Rand convince you that we know things as they are in themselves? Would your answer have any implications for understanding human rights?

10. When "selfishness" is rightly grasped, will we all construe it in Ayn Rand's way?

11. What does Dewey mean when he says that democracy is a moral ideal? Do you agree with him?

12. Is Dewey too optimistic about what education and scientific method can accomplish, particularly where democracy is concerned? If not, why? If so, what alternative to his theory would you propose?

NOTES

[1] Thomas Hobbes, *Leviathan*, ed. Herbert W. Schneider (Indianapolis: Bobbs-Merrill, 1958), p. 107.

[2] Thomas Hobbes, *The Citizen* (New York: Appleton-Century-Crofts, 1949), p. 10.

[3] Hobbes, *Leviathan*, p. 110.

[4] John Locke, *The Second Treatise of Government*, ed. Thomas P. Peardon (Indianapolis: Bobbs-Merrill, 1952), p. 5.

[5] Thomas Paine, *Common Sense*, in *Common Sense and Other Political Writings*, ed. Nelson F. Adkins (Indianapolis: Bobbs-Merrill, 1953), p. 51.

[6] Thomas Jefferson, "The Declaration of Independence," in *The Political Writings of Thomas Jefferson*, ed. Edward Dumbauld (Indianapolis: Bobbs-Merrill, 1955), pp. 3–4.

[7] From Jefferson's draft of the Statute of Virginia for Religious Freedom. See *The Political Writings of Thomas Jefferson*, p. 35.

[8] See *The Political Writings of Thomas Jefferson*, p. 36.

[9] Jean-Jacques Rousseau, *Emile or On Education*, trans. Allan Bloom (New York: Basic Books, 1979), p. 37.

[10] Jean-Jacques Rousseau, *The Social Contract*, trans. Maurice Cranston (Baltimore: Penguin Books, 1971), p. 49. Reprinted by permission of A. D. Peters & Co. Ltd.

[11] Rousseau, *Emile*, p. 42.

[12] Rousseau, *The Social Contract*, pp. 72–78, 80–83.

[13] Ayn Rand, "Theory and Practice," in Ayn Rand et al., *Capitalism: The Unknown Ideal* (New York: New American Library, 1967), pp. 138–39.

[14] Ayn Rand, *Philosophy: Who Needs It* (New York: New American Library, 1984), p. 10.

[15] Ayn Rand, *Atlas Shrugged*, cited in Ayn Rand, *For the New Intellectual: The Philosophy of Ayn Rand* (New York: Random House, 1961), p. 229.

[16] Rand, *Philosophy: Who Needs It*, p. 10.

[17] Ayn Rand, *The Virtue of Selfishness* (New York: New American Library, 1964), p. vii. Copyright © 1961, 1964 by Ayn Rand. Reprinted by arrangement with New American Library, New York, New York, with the permission of the Estate of Ayn Rand.

[18] John Hospers, "What Libertarianism Is," in *Morality in Practice*, ed. James P. Sterba (Belmont, Calif.: Wadsworth, 1984), p. 17.

[19] Rand, *The Virtue of Selfishness*, p. 94.

[20] Rand, *Philosophy: Who Needs It*, p. 51.

[21] Rand, *The Virtue of Selfishness*, pp. 92–95.

[22] John Dewey, "Creative Democracy—The Task Before Us," in *Classic American Philosophers*, ed. Max H. Fisch (New York: Appleton-Century-Crofts, 1951), p. 394.

[23] John Dewey, *A Common Faith* (New Haven: Yale University Press, 1934), p. 31.

[24] John Dewey, *Individualism Old and New* (New York: Capricorn Books, 1962), p. 50.

[25] John Dewey, *Democracy and Education: An Introduction to the Philosophy of Education* (New York: Macmillan, 1922), pp. 101–2.

[26] John Dewey, *The Quest for Certainty* (New York: G. P. Putnam's, 1960), p. 3.

[27] John Dewey and Evelyn Dewey, *Schools of Tomorrow* (New York: E. P. Dutton, 1962), p. 2.

[28] John Dewey, *Problems of Men* (New York: Philosophical Library, 1946), p. 34.

[29] John Dewey, "My Pedagogic Creed" (1897), in *The Philosophy of John Dewey*, 2 vols., ed. John J. McDermott (New York: G. P. Putnam's, 1973), 2:452–54.

CHAPTER TEN

Can I Make Society Better?

A prominent American corporation has proclaimed: "Progress is our most important product." People, too, speak about **progress,** in school, in a career, or in building a reputation. We may seek progress in extending human rights, in achieving more peaceful relations among nations, or in eradicating cancer. Progress can be defined in ways that are value-free. We can speak of it simply as a more advanced development of a process. We might say, for instance, that there has been progress in the twentieth century in perfecting ever more powerful nuclear weapons. But often we attach value to the term. In those cases, "progress" implies a condition better than the one that preceded it. When we think about progress in that way, usually we equate it with an improvement in the quality of life.

Can I make society better? The answer seems to be yes, and yet the "yes" cannot be simple, because it raises questions about how society should be improved and about the obstacles to this goal. When philosophers raise such questions about society's betterment, they sometimes wonder how far a study of history reveals an improvement in the quality of life, especially in its ethical dimensions. They want to know whether today we are better off in pursuing happiness or in accomplishing what we ought to do than our ancestors were. As we consider the varied responses philosophers produce, we see once more that philosophy as a whole offers a mixed report. That observation should help us to understand how complex the issue is when "Can I make society better?" becomes one of the questions of philosophy.

As we try to decide whether we can make society better, we will first encounter the proposals of Niccolò Machiavelli, a hardheaded realist who aimed at making society

NICCOLÒ MACHIAVELLI 1469–1527

better for rulers, though not necessarily for the ruled. Based on principles of political **expediency**, Machiavelli's counsel has been taken to heart by the practitioners of power politics. Thus, if one is to make society better, this philosopher's teachings must be reckoned with. Thomas Malthus is quite different in his outlook. His name is associated with economics more than with philosophy, but he had much to say about the demographic problems that thwart social betterment. Particularly, he calculated the immense prices to be paid for the world's exploding population growth. No philosopher has had greater impact on the contemporary world than Karl Marx, the next thinker we discuss. The key to human betterment, he believed, was through a communist revolution that would displace capitalism's exploitive ways. Marx thought history was inevitably moving in that direction. This process would be charged by using violence, and the result would be a vastly improved human society. Looking back on what Marxist and other revolutionary regimes accomplished, Hannah Arendt is far less optimistic about the good that results from political revolution. She joins the previous three in believing that it is possible for society to improve, but she urges us to beware of proposals that presume progress to be inevitable, unambiguous, and within the control of our human plans.

Niccolò Machiavelli and the Art of War

During the Western world's Renaissance, the Italian philosopher Niccolò Machiavelli (1469–1527) considered how society could best be regulated. His deliberations grew out of the political intrigue of his home city, Florence, and from a concern to give prudent counsel to the leadership of that city-state.

He recorded these reflections in *The Prince* (1512–13). This work, along with *The Discourses* (1517), established Machiavelli as one of the most controversial yet realistic political theorists of the modern world.

Machiavelli was a statesman who played a prominent role in the republican government that came to power when the Medici family was overthrown in 1494, but his political career abruptly terminated when the republic fell and Lorenzo de' Medici assumed control in 1512. He dedicated *The Prince* to the new Medici ruler, but the book never brought its author the major political appointments he coveted. Instead, the Medici line was displaced again, and Machiavelli died soon after. His views, however, came to possess the authority Machiavelli was unable to obtain in his lifetime. They are about power, and they rest on the following principle:

> A prince should . . . have no other aim or thought, nor take up any other thing for his study, but war and its organization and discipline; for that is the only art that is necessary for one who commands. . . .[1]

Dealing with the Affairs of the World

Machiavelli's aim was to share "all that long experience and assiduous research have taught me of the affairs of the world."[2] But his practical counsel was not intended for everyone. It was only for political leaders, especially those at the top. His was an era, claimed Machiavelli, when people were "ungrateful, voluble, dissemblers, anxious to avoid danger, and covetous of gain."[3] If only the human masses were less stupid and irrational, he lamented, the climate in which a republican government could make progress would be much improved. He valued popular successes in self-rule, and he hoped such occasions would arise again. But Machiavelli was deeply skeptical that human nature or society as he observed it could be sufficiently improved. Nor could it be said that his aim was to show how a leader can control unruly citizens in a way that serves the best interests of the latter. What he observed of the world made Machiavelli more realistic, and more pessimistic, than that. If Plato was an idealist, Machiavelli made it clear that he based his views on historical experience, a perspective he had acquired through long observation of modern events and a constant study of the past.

The art of war, Machiavelli reported, is not restricted to battlefields of armed conflict. At every turn, we find, life is a conflict of forces, a fight for survival, a **power** struggle. To maintain himself in such a world, a political leader must guard his strength. Machiavelli wanted to provide guidance on staying in power. The question of ends for which power should be used is obscured by the question of how to secure and extend a ruler's control. As political expediency leaps to the fore, power becomes an end in itself. Since Machiavelli assumed that the self-interest of a prince and the well-being of his subjects were not necessarily one and the same (though he denied they were opposites), most of *The Prince* and much of *The Discourses* consider only how to maintain power. If a leader seeks an improved position in that regard, what advice should be followed?

The Rules of Conduct

Noting that "many have imagined republics and principalities which have never been seen or known to exist in reality," Machiavelli observed that

> . . . how we live is so far removed from how we ought to live, that he who abandons what is done for what ought to be done, will rather learn to bring about his own ruin than his preservation. A man who wishes to make a

profession of goodness in everything must necessarily come to grief among so many who are not good. (P. 56.)

Machiavelli's teachings stress what is useful in the "real" world, not the "ideal" world. Any prince who wants to survive cannot afford to be too virtuous, he asserted. Far from being totally honest, completely fair, wholly truthful, consistently just, and so on, Machiavelli's wise ruler must learn how *not* to be good while always "appearing" to be so. It is not that the traditional virtues are bad. However, the prince must learn when it is expedient to be virtuous and when not. It follows that he must also school himself in new "virtues"—cunning and deceit, unscrupulousness and ruthlessness. These qualities may be necessary to save the state and with it the ruler's power. The right mixture of traits in the prince is fundamental, and so is the timing of their use. In addition, one must anticipate the consequences of acting in one way or another. This means that the skillful prince must understand his subjects, those who are not his subjects (i.e., foreigners), and himself. Otherwise he might become trapped in the illusion that his best interests necessarily lie in acting in accordance with what moral traditions and religions have taught.

The ruler exists in the dangerous realm of power politics. Thus, a prince's training must produce a stark understanding of power. The examinations he must pass include questions such as: "[Is it] better to be loved more than feared, or feared more than loved?" (p. 61). He must take the correct answer to heart, which according to Machiavelli is that being both loved and feared is most advantageous. But "as it is difficult for the two to go together, it is much safer to be feared than loved, if one of the two has to be wanting" (p. 61). To graduate from this school is more difficult than it looks, however. The fear one instills must breed neither hatred nor contempt, for either would threaten a ruler's security.

The Lion and the Fox

The prince must learn from beasts as well as from men and women. There are two ways of winning and securing power: by law, the way proper to human beings, and by force, the way proper to beasts. The beasts to emulate, Machiavelli reports, are the lion and the fox. Lions are vulnerable to traps; foxes anticipate such dangers and are forewarned. Foxes, in turn, are vulnerable to wolves, but the latter are terrified by lions. The use of force is a fact of political life, and lying and betrayal are forms of force no less than slings and arrows. One should expect political agreements to be made and then broken, and the prince's leonine qualities should prepare him to strike back effectively. The prince should be foxlike, too. "Therefore," as Machiavelli prescribed,

> [a] prudent ruler ought not to keep faith when by so doing it would be against his interest, and when the reasons which made him bind himself no longer exist. If men were all good, this precept would not be a good one; but as they are bad, and would not observe their faith with you, so you are not bound to keep faith with them. (P. 64.)

Nothing is gained if one's lying and deceit become obvious. Machiavelli pointed out that, fortunately, such misfortune can be avoided by learning well the arts of disguise. Then one can appear to be "all mercy, faith, integrity, humanity, and religion" even when one is not (p. 65). No prince should "deviate from what is good, if possible, but be able to do evil if constrained" (p. 65). Thus, a shrewd ruler will utilize violence efficiently, speedily, and without remorse when the need arises. But since persuasion is less wasteful, he will try that first whenever possible. Even

smart ruler will infuse his persuasive rhetoric with allusions to religion and to divinity. The impression that one's policies are sanctioned by religion always affects the masses favorably, Machiavelli thought, although moral scruples stemming from religious beliefs might inhibit a prince's effectiveness. Politicians should invoke God's name to support their cause. Decisiveness and resolution are essential, too. The prudent ruler will seek counsel and listen well, but he will make his own decisions and carry them out with conviction and dispatch.

The Lesser Evil

To his credit, Machiavelli did not take lightly the implications of his political realism:

> Let no state believe that it can always follow a safe policy, rather let it think that all are doubtful. This is found in the nature of things, that one never tries to avoid one difficulty without running into another, but prudence consists in being able to know the nature of the difficulties, and taking the least harmful as good. (Pp. 84–85.)

Lorenzo de' Medici and the Florentine city-state disappeared long ago. Today political authority rarely rests in the hands of princes such as Machiavelli described. Yet as one contemplates the advice he gave, it seems clear that much of the world's power is wielded by leaders who have learned Machiavelli's lessons all too well. To our sorrow, we honor him by referring to the **"Machiavellian"** quality of much political life in recent centuries. Some scholars call Machiavelli the father of modern political theory. As he explored the nature of political sovereignty, he downplayed what ought to be and concentrated instead on the realities of politics as a power struggle. Divine authority and moral sanctions are functionally absent in that struggle; the ability to win competitions between rival political forces is all-important. It can hardly be denied that his descriptions apply widely today. To the extent that we sanction Machiavelli's conduct for rulers, all of us are affected, since we are then obliged to accept lies, deceitful deeds, and the appearance of virtue without the substance. Or, we must learn to be accomplices in policies that foist such actions on others. These are some of the realities that must be faced if we are to answer yes when the question is: Can I make society better? Will the activities of Machiavelli's prince improve the lot of mankind? Consider those questions as you read on, and if the answer to the second question is no, ask yourself what forms of alternative political action are open to us.

Niccolò Machiavelli to Lorenzo the Magnificent:

It is customary for those who wish to gain the favor of a prince to endeavor to do so by offering him gifts of those things which they hold most precious, or in which they know him to take especial delight. In this way princes are often presented with horses, arms, cloth of gold, gems, and such-like ornaments worthy of their grandeur. In my desire however, to offer to Your Highness some humble testimony of my devotion, I have been unable to find among my possessions anything which I hold so dear or esteem so highly as that knowledge of the deeds of great men which I have acquired through a long experience of modern events and a constant study of the past.

With the utmost diligence I have long pondered and scrutinized the actions of the great, and now I offer the results to Your Highness within the compass of a small volume: and although I deem this work unworthy of Your Highness' acceptance, yet my confidence in your humanity assures me that you will receive it with favor, knowing that it is not in my power to offer you a greater gift than that of enabling you to understand in a very short time all those things which I have learned at the cost of privation and

danger in the course of many years. I have not sought to adorn my work with long phrases or high-sounding words or any of those superficial attractions and ornaments with which many writers seek to embellish their material, as I desire no honor for my work but such as the novelty and gravity of its subject may justly deserve. . . .

THE VARIOUS KINDS OF GOVERNMENT AND THE WAYS BY WHICH THEY ARE ESTABLISHED

All states and dominions which hold or have held sway over mankind are either republics or monarchies. Monarchies are either hereditary in which the rulers have been for many years of the same family, or else they are of recent foundation. The newly founded ones are either entirely new, as was Milan to Francesco Sforza, or else they are, as it were, new members grafted on to the hereditary possessions of the prince that annexes them, as is the kingdom of Naples to the King of Spain. The dominions thus acquired have either been previously accustomed to the rule of another prince, or else have been free states, and they are annexed either by force of arms of the prince himself, or of others, or else fall to him by good fortune or special ability.

OF HEREDITARY MONARCHIES

I will not here speak of republics, . . . I will deal only with monarchies, and will discuss how the various kinds described above can be governed and maintained. . . .

THE DUTIES OF A PRINCE WITH REGARD TO THE MILITIA

A prince should . . . have no other aim or thought, nor take up any other thing for his study, but war and its organization and discipline, for that is the only art that is necessary to one who commands, and it is of such virtue that it not only maintains those who are born princes, but often enables men of private fortune to attain to that rank. And one sees, on the other hand, that when princes think more of luxury than of arms, they lose their state. The chief cause of the loss of states, is the contempt of this art, and the way to acquire them is to be well versed in the same.

Francesco Sforza, through being well armed, became, from private status, Duke of Milan; his sons, through wishing to avoid the fatigue and hardship of war, from dukes became private persons. For among other evils caused by being disarmed, it renders you contemptible; which is one of those disgraceful things which a prince must guard against. . . . Because there is no comparison whatever between an armed and a disarmed man; it is not reasonable to suppose that one who is armed will obey willingly one who is unarmed; or that any unarmed man will remain safe among armed servants. For one being disdainful and the other suspicious, it is not possible for them to act well together. And therefore a prince who is ignorant of military matters . . . cannot be esteemed by his soldiers, nor have confidence in them.

He ought, therefore, never to let his thoughts stray from the exercise of war; and in peace he ought to practise it more than in war, which he can do in two ways: by action and by study. As to action, he must, besides keeping his men well disciplined and exercised, engage continually in hunting, and thus accustom his body to hardships; and meanwhile learn the nature of the land, how steep the mountains are, how the valleys debouch, where the plains lie, and understand the nature of rivers and swamps. To all this he should devote great attention. This knowledge is useful in two ways. In the first place, one learns to know one's country, and can the better see how to defend it. Then by means of the knowledge and experience gained in one locality, one can easily understand any other that it may be necessary to observe; for the hills and valleys, plains and rivers of Tuscany, for instance, have a certain resemblance to those of other prov-

inces, so that from a knowledge of the country in one province one can easily arrive at a knowledge of others. And that prince who is lacking in this skill is wanting in the first essentials of a leader; for it is this which teaches how to find the enemy, take up quarters, lead armies, plan battles and lay siege to towns with advantage.

Philopoemen, prince of the Achaei, among other praises bestowed on him by writers, is lauded because in times of peace he thought of nothing but the methods of warfare, and when he was in the country with his friends, he often stopped and asked them: If the enemy were on that hill and we found ourselves here with our army, which of us would have the advantage? How could we safely approach him maintaining our order? If we wished to retire, what ought we to do? If they retired, how should we follow them? And he put before them as they went along all the contingencies that might happen to an army, heard their opinion, gave his own, fortifying it by argument; so that thanks to these constant reflections there could never happen any incident when actually leading his armies for which he was not prepared.

But as to exercise for the mind, the prince ought to read history and study the actions of eminent men, see how they acted in warfare, examine the causes of their victories and defeats in order to imitate the former and avoid the latter, and above all, do as some men have done in the past, who have imitated some one, who has been much praised and glorified, and have always kept his deeds and actions before them, as they say Alexander the Great imitated Achilles, Caesar Alexander, and Scipio Cyrus. And whoever reads the life of Cyrus written by Xenophon, will perceive in the life of Scipio how gloriously he imitated the former, and how, in chastity, affability, humanity, and liberality Scipio conformed to those qualities of Cyrus as described by Xenophon.

A wise prince should follow similar methods and never remain idle in peaceful times, but industriously make good use of them, so that when fortune changes she may find him prepared to resist her blows, and to prevail in adversity.

OF THE THINGS FOR WHICH MEN, AND ESPECIALLY PRINCES, ARE PRAISED OR BLAMED

It now remains to be seen what are the methods and rules for a prince as regards his subjects and friends. And as I know that many have written of this, I fear that my writing about it may be deemed presumptuous, differing as I do, especially in this matter, from the opinions of others. But my intention being to write something of use to those who understand, it appears to me more proper to go to the real truth of the matter than to its imagination; and many have imagined republics and principalities which have never been seen or known to exist in reality; for how we live is so far removed from how we ought to live, that he who abandons what is done for what ought to be done, will rather learn to bring about his own ruin than his preservation. A man who wishes to make a profession of goodness in everything must necessarily come to grief among so many who are not good. Therefore it is necessary for a prince, who wishes to maintain himself, to learn how not to be good, and to use this knowledge and not use it, according to the necessity of the case.

Leaving on one side, then, those things which concern only an imaginary prince, and speaking of those that are real, I state that all men, and especially princes, who are placed at a greater height, are reputed for certain qualities which bring them either praise or blame. Thus one is considered liberal, another *misero* or miserly . . .; one a free giver, another rapacious; one cruel, another merciful; one a breaker of his word, another trustworthy; one effeminate and pusillanimous, another fierce and high-spirited; one humane, another haughty; one lascivious, another chaste; one frank, another astute; one hard, another easy; one serious, another frivolous; one religious, another an unbeliever, and so on. I know that every one will

admit that it would be highly praiseworthy in a prince to possess all the above-named qualities that are reputed good, but as they cannot all be possessed or observed, human conditions not permitting of it, it is necessary that he should be prudent enough to avoid the scandal of those vices which would lose him the state, and guard himself if possible against those which will not lose it him, but if not able to, he can indulge them with less scruple. And yet he must not mind incurring the scandal of those vices, without which it would be difficult to save the state, for if one considers well, it will be found that some things which seem virtues would, if followed, lead to one's ruin, and some others which appear vices result in one's greater security and wellbeing.

OF LIBERALITY AND NIGGARDLINESS

Beginning now with the first qualities above named, I say that it would be well to be considered liberal; nevertheless liberality such as the world understands it will injure you, because if used virtuously and in the proper way, it will not be known, and you will incur the disgrace of the contrary vice. But one who wishes to obtain the reputation of liberality among men, must not omit every kind of sumptuous display, and to such an extent that a prince of this character will consume by such means all his resources, and will be at last compelled, if he wishes to maintain his name for liberality, to impose heavy taxes on his people, become extortionate, and do everything possible to obtain money. This will make his subjects begin to hate him, and he will be little esteemed being poor, so that having by this liberality injured many and benefited but few, he will feel the first little disturbance and be endangered by every peril. If he recognizes this and wishes to change his system, he incurs at once the charge of niggardliness.

A prince, therefore, not being able to exercise this virtue of liberality without risk if it be known, must not, if he be prudent, object to be called miserly. In course of time he will be thought more liberal, when it is seen that by his parsimony his revenue is sufficient, that he can defend himself against those who make war on him, and undertake enterprises without burdening his people, so that he is really liberal to all those from whom he does not take, who are infinite in number, and niggardly to all to whom he does not give, who are few. In our times we have seen nothing great done except by those who have been esteemed niggardly; the others have all been ruined. Pope Julius II, although he had made use of a reputation for liberality in order to attain the papacy, did not seek to retain it afterwards, so that he might be able to wage war. The present King of France has carried on so many wars without imposing an extraordinary tax, because his extra expenses were covered by the parsimony he had so long practised. The present King of Spain, if he had been thought liberal, would not have engaged in and been successful in so many enterprises.

For these reasons a prince must care little for the reputation of being a miser, if he wishes to avoid robbing his subjects, if he wishes to be able to defend himself, to avoid becoming poor and contemptible, and not to be forced to become rapacious; this niggardliness is one of those vices which enable him to reign. If it is said that Caesar attained the empire through liberality, and that many others have reached the highest positions through being liberal or being thought so, I would reply that you are either a prince already or else on the way to become one. In the first case, this liberality is harmful; in the second, it is certainly necessary to be considered liberal. Caesar was one of those who wished to attain the mastery over Rome, but if after attaining it he had lived and had not moderated his expenses, he would have destroyed that empire. And should any one reply that there have been many princes, who have done great things with their armies, who have been thought extremely liberal, I would answer by saying that the prince may either spend his own wealth and that of his subjects or the wealth of others. In the first case he must be sparing, but for the rest

he must not neglect to be very liberal. The liberality is very necessary to a prince who marches with his armies, and lives by plunder, sack and ransom, and is dealing with the wealth of others, for without it he would not be followed by his soldiers. And you may be very generous indeed with what is not the property of yourself or your subjects, as were Cyrus, Caesar, and Alexander; for spending the wealth of others will not diminish your reputation, but increase it, only spending your own resources will injure you. There is nothing which destroys itself so much as liberality, for by using it you lose the power of using it, and become either poor and despicable, or, to escape poverty, rapacious and hated. And of all things that a prince must guard against, the most important are being despicable or hated, and liberality will lead you to one or other of these conditions. It is, therefore, wiser to have the name of a miser, which produces disgrace without hatred, than to incur of necessity the name of being rapacious, which produces both disgrace and hatred.

OF CRUELTY AND CLEMENCY, AND WHETHER IT IS BETTER TO BE LOVED OR FEARED

Proceeding to the other qualities before named, I say that every prince must desire to be considered merciful and not cruel. He must, however, take care not to misuse this mercifulness. Cesare Borgia was considered cruel, but his cruelty had brought order to the [northern district of] Romagna, united it, and reduced it to peace and fealty. If this is considered well, it will be seen that he was really much more merciful than the Florentine people, who, to avoid the name of cruelty, allowed Pistoia to be destroyed. A prince, therefore, must not mind incurring the charge of cruelty for the purpose of keeping his subjects united and faithful; for, with a very few examples, he will be more merciful than those who, from excess of tenderness, allow disorders to arise, from whence spring bloodshed and rapine; for these as a rule injure the whole community, while the executions carried out by the prince injure only individuals. And of all princes, it is impossible for a new prince to escape the reputation of cruelty, new states being always full of dangers. Wherefore Virgil through the mouth of Dido says:

Res dura, et regni novitas me talia cogunt
Moliri, et late fines custode tueri.*

Nevertheless, he must be cautious in believing and acting, and must not be afraid of his own shadow, and must proceed in a temperate manner with prudence and humanity; so that too much confidence does not render him incautious, and too much diffidence does not render him intolerant.

From this arises the question whether it is better to be loved more than feared, or feared more than loved. The reply is, that one ought to be both feared and loved, but as it is difficult for the two to go together, it is much safer to be feared than loved, if one of the two has to be wanting. For it may be said of men in general that they are ungrateful, voluble, dissemblers, anxious to avoid danger, and covetous of gain; as long as you benefit them, they are entirely yours; they offer you their blood, their goods, their life, and their children, . . . when the necessity is remote; but when it approaches, they revolt. And the prince who has relied solely on their words, without making other preparations, is ruined; for the friendship which is gained by purchase and not through grandeur and nobility of spirit is bought but not secured, and at a pinch is not to be expended in your service. And men have less scruple in offending one who makes himself loved than one who makes himself feared; for love is held by a chain of obligation which, men being selfish, is broken whenever it serves their purpose; but fear is maintained by a dread of punishment which never fails.

Still, a prince should make himself feared in such a way that if he does not gain love, he at any rate avoids hatred; for fear and the absence of hatred may well go together, and will be always attained by one who abstains from interfering with the property of his citizens and subjects or with their women. And when he is obliged to take the life of any one, let him do so when there is a proper justification and manifest reason for it; but above all he must abstain from taking the property of others, for men forget more easily the death of their father than the loss of their patrimony. Then also pretexts for seizing property are never wanting, and one who begins to live by rapine will always find some reason for taking the goods of others, whereas causes for taking life are rarer and more fleeting.

But when the prince is with his army and has a large number of soldiers under his control, then it is extremely necessary that he should not mind being thought cruel; for without this reputation he could not keep an army united or disposed to any duty. Among the noteworthy actions of Hannibal is numbered this, that although he had an enormous army, composed of men of all nations and fighting in foreign countries, there never arose any dissension either among them or against the prince, either in good fortune or in bad. This could not be due to anything but his inhuman cruelty, which together with his infinite other virtues, made him always venerated and terrible in the sight of his soldiers, and without it his other virtues would not have sufficed to produce that effect. Thoughtless writers admire on the one hand his actions, and on the other blame the principal cause of them.

And that it is true that his other virtues would not have sufficed may be seen from the case of Scipio (famous not only in regard to his own times, but all times of which memory remains), whose armies rebelled against him in Spain, which arose from nothing but his excessive kindness, which allowed more license to the soldiers than was consonant with military discipline. He was

*"Harsh pressures and the newness of my reign / Compel me to these steps; I must maintain / My borders against foreign foes. . . . " (*Aeneid*, II, 563–64). [*Editor's translation.*]

reproached with this in the senate by Fabius Maximus, who called him a corrupter of the Roman militia. Locri having been destroyed by one of Scipio's officers was not revenged by him, nor was the insolence of that officer punished, simply by reason of his easy nature; so much so, that someone wishing to excuse him in the senate, said that there were many men who knew rather how not to err, than how to correct the errors of others. This disposition would in time have tarnished the fame and glory of Scipio had he persevered in it under the empire, but living under the rule of the senate this harmful quality was not only concealed but became a glory to him.

I conclude, therefore, with regard to being feared and loved, that men love at their own free will, but fear at the will of the prince, and that a wise prince must rely on what is in his power and not on what is in the power of others, and he must only contrive to avoid incurring hatred, as has been explained.

IN WHAT WAY PRINCES MUST KEEP FAITH

How laudable it is for a prince to keep good faith and live with integrity, and not with astuteness, every one knows. Still the experience of our times shows those princes to have done great things who have had little regard for good faith, and have been able by astuteness to confuse men's brains, and who have ultimately overcome those who have made loyalty their foundation.

You must know, then, that there are two methods of fighting, the one by law, the other by force: the first method is that of men, the second of beasts; but as the first method is often insufficient, one must have recourse to the second. It is therefore necessary for a prince to know well how to use both the beast and the man. This was covertly taught to rulers by ancient writers, who relate how Achilles and many others of those ancient princes were given to Chiron the centaur to be brought up and educated under his discipline. The parable of this semi-animal,

semi-human teacher is meant to indicate that a prince must know how to use both natures, and that the one without the other is not durable.

A prince being thus obliged to know well how to act as a beast must imitate the fox and the lion, for the lion cannot protect himself from traps, and the fox cannot defend himself from wolves. One must therefore be a fox to recognize traps, and a lion to frighten wolves. Those that wish to be only lions do not understand this. Therefore, a prudent ruler ought not to keep faith when by so doing it would be against his interest, and when the reasons which made him bind himself no longer exist. If men were all good, this precept would not be a good one; but as they are bad, and would not observe their faith with you, so you are not bound to keep faith with them. Nor have legitimate grounds ever failed a prince who wished to show colorable excuse for the non-fulfillment of his promise. Of this one could furnish an infinite number of modern examples, and show how many times peace has been broken, and how many promises rendered worthless, by the faithlessness of princes, and those that have been best able to imitate the fox have succeeded best. But it is necessary to be able to disguise this character well, and to be a great feigner and dissembler; and men are so simple and so ready to obey present necessities, that one who deceives will always find those who allow themselves to be deceived.

I will only mention one modern instance. [Pope] Alexander VI did nothing else but deceive men, he thought of nothing else, and found the occasion for it; no man was ever more able to give assurances, or affirmed things with stronger oaths, and no man observed them less; however, he always succeeded in his deceptions, as he well knew this aspect of things.

It is not, therefore, necessary for a prince to have all the above-named qualities, but it is very necessary to seem to have them. I would even be bold to say that to possess them and always to observe them is dangerous, but to appear to possess them is useful. Thus it is well to seem merciful, faithful, humane, sincere, religious, and also to be so; but you must have the mind so disposed that when it is needful to be otherwise you may be able to change to the opposite qualities. And it must be understood that a prince, and especially a new prince, cannot observe all those things which are considered good in men, being often obliged, in order to maintain the state, to act against faith, against charity, against humanity, and against religion. And, therefore, he must have a mind disposed to adapt itself according to the wind, and as the variations of fortune dictate, and, as I said before, not deviate from what is good, if possible, but be able to do evil if constrained.

A prince must take great care that nothing goes out of his mouth which is not full of the above-named five qualities, and, to see and hear him, he should seem to be all mercy, faith, integrity, humanity, and religion. And nothing is more necessary than to seem to have this last quality, for men in general judge more by the eyes than by the hands, for everyone can see, but very few have to feel. Everybody sees what you appear to be, few feel what you are, and those few will not dare to oppose themselves to the many, who have the majesty of the state to defend them; and in the actions of men, and especially of princes, from which there is no appeal, the end justifies the means. Let a prince therefore aim at conquering and maintaining the state, and the means will always be judged honorable and praised by everyone, for the vulgar is always taken by appearances and the issue of the event; and the world consists only of the vulgar, and the few who are not vulgar are isolated when the many have a rallying point in the prince. A certain prince of the present time . . . never does anything but preach peace and good faith, but he is really a great enemy to both, and either of them, had he observed them, would have lost him state or reputation on many occasions. (Pp. 3–5, 53–66.)

Thomas Malthus and Surplus People

Machiavelli showed that the question "Can I make society better?" is linked to the issue of what constitutes permissible conduct for political leaders. Thomas Malthus (1766–1834) pointed out something else: that the quality of social life also depends on how many people exist. Born to an upper-middle-class English family, Malthus studied mathematics at Cambridge University. Although he devoted most of his life to an academic career in economics—many of his students became important leaders in the powerful East India Company—Malthus was also an ordained clergyman, and his economic theories reflect Christian concerns. Malthus's economic interests were also philosophical because the former persuaded him that humanity faces a dilemma revolving around the question, "Can I make society better?"

Earlier in the eighteenth century, Adam Smith, the economist–philosopher we met in Chapter Three, assumed that population would grow only insofar as there was enough economic development to ensure a subsistence level for human life. He thought there would never be less than an equilibrium between population and a subsistence level for human life. Malthus was not so optimistic. His terse critique of Smith's population theory, and of the even more hopeful forecasts about human betterment that were enthusiastically discussed in his day, appeared in a short book with a long title: *An Essay on the Principle of Population as It Affects the Future Improvement of Society, with Remarks on the Speculations of Mr. Godwin, M. Condorcet, and Other Writers.* As widely read as it was controversial, this book, which first appeared in 1798, went through six more editions, the last one in 1826. The problem Malthus saw and his analysis of what ought to be done about it still challenge us today.

THOMAS ROBERT MALTHUS 1766–1834

A Dismal Science

Economics is sometimes called the dismal science. Malthus helped validate that label, arguing that population growth and the economic base needed to sustain it do not go together harmoniously. In fact, he was sure that it was not possible that they could. The increase in the number of people brought about by an industrialized, modernized economy would dramatically outstrip the means for subsistence, he predicted. Far from being a path toward progress that benefits everyone, the course of human events in the West would increasingly turn human existence into a struggle to avoid death. Not sur-

prisingly, Malthus's theory was unpopular, especially among those who were convinced that the world had experienced a hopeful Enlightenment. Malthus argued not only that the human species was propagating itself too abundantly, a liability and not an asset in the long run, but also that charity and well-intentioned legislation were only cruelty in disguise because they encourage such activity. Malthus envisioned a *laissez-faire* economy much more grim than Adam Smith's. Rather than favoring sympathetic intentions, which would only prolong the agony of **surplus** people, Malthus preferred to let nature's unremitting checks and balances put people out of their misery sooner rather than later. Malthus's outlook sounded a melancholy note: vast numbers of men and women will lead miserable lives. Obviously this is the greatest problem stalling society's betterment.

Although Malthus saw that some people amassed great fortunes and that spectacular advances occurred in some cycles of business, he was skeptical about overall progress in improving human conditions. His skepticism was based on careful calculations. Malthus emphasized that two factors about human life are undeniable: food is necessary for survival, and passion between the sexes has immense power. Living when contraceptive methods were neither diverse nor morally acceptable, he reasoned that these two pressures meant misfortune, since "the power of population is indefinitely greater than the power in the earth to produce subsistence for man."[4]

The Great Difficulty

Consulting the available **demographic** data, as well as his intuitions about sexual passion, Malthus calculated a doubling of human population every twenty-five years. Natural conditions—disease, inadequate food, and the like—might reduce that number, but, ironically, any progress toward checking those conditions would contribute to the likelihood that the human population would actually multiply in geometrical progression. Malthus argued that meanwhile the amount of land convertible to food production could be increased only arithmetically, one unit at a time. This, he lamented, would be sufficient neither to meet the need nor to prevent the conception of children. Taken together, these elements formed what Malthus called "the great difficulty that to me appears insurmountable in the way to the perfectibility of society" (p. 20).

No painless solution seemed available. As Malthus appraised the situation, "to prevent the recurrence of misery is, alas!, beyond the power of man" (p. 44). The poor, who are the least fitted economically to compete in the battle for scarce resources, would be those condemned to suffer most. Moreover, it seemed to Malthus, "the superior power of population cannot be checked without producing misery or vice" (p. 26). The most concerted efforts to provide relief for the poor would debase human life by making it dependent on the charity of individuals or governments. In addition, the available funds would be insufficient, and their use would further depress others into the impoverished class. It is better, thought Malthus, that population growth "should be checked from a foresight of the difficulties attending a family and the fear of dependent poverty than that it should be encouraged, only to be repressed afterwards by want and sickness" (p. 41). But if human reason can remove the need for charity only by exercising foresight, the odds are against that happening. Passion between the sexes, Malthus maintained, tends to prevail over planning, some of which Malthus rejected anyway since he thought contraception was wrong. "Famine," he concluded, "seems to be the last, the most dreadful resource of nature" (p. 56). When all else fails, its force will check population without remorse.

The Severe Touch of Truth

Although Adam Smith was on Malthus's mind, the main targets of Malthus's pessimism were those who argued that **utopia** was within humanity's grasp, if only people and institutions would function as they should. Malthus believed that such dreams were fantastic; they rest on the faulty assumption of "attributing almost all the vices and misery that are seen in civil society to human institutions" (p. 66). Social improvement is foiled by deeper obstacles than those. "The severe touch of truth," as Malthus called it (p. 70), makes plain that roadblocks to progress are built into the very nature of existence itself. It was no accident that the biblical Garden of Eden became polluted. No original or planned utopia can sustain itself, unless the basic conditions of human existence are altered.

Drawing a distinction between "an unlimited progress and a progress where the limit is merely undefined," Malthus said that "no person can deny the importance of improving the happiness of the human species. Even the least advance in this respect is highly valuable" (pp. 63, 94). Benevolence toward others is of crucial importance, but Malthus wanted people to think about what true benevolence entails. Our intentions and our sympathies sometimes mislead us; we try to sustain lives only to find people suffering further. On the other hand, harsher policies leave people in misery, too, and they infest our character with a calloused selfishness. "If no man were to allow himself to act till he had completely determined that the action he was about to perform was more conducive than any other to the general good," surmised Malthus, "the most enlightened minds would hesitate in perplexity and amazement" (p. 100). Nonetheless, we must put our best principles into action, for the unenlightened will not be so hesitant and all of us will pay a high price for their blundering mistakes. The question that remains, however, is whether Malthus's principles and the best ones are the same.

The Gracious Designs of Providence

Malthus, you recall, was a clergyman as well as an economist and a philosopher. His Christian convictions left him unable to let matters rest without considering our present life to be only a part, and not the whole, of reality. Although he argued the futility of asking why things are not other than they are and urged that we concentrate instead on accounting for the circumstances that actually do exist, he went on to pose the following question:

> And unless we wish to exalt the power of God at the expense of his goodness, ought we not to conclude that even to the Great Creator, Almighty as he is, a certain process may be necessary, a certain time (or at least what appears to us as time) may be requisite, in order to form beings with those exalted qualities of mind which fit them for his high purposes? (P. 117.)

Malthus answered by asserting that life is structured "for the creation and formation of mind, a process necessary to awaken inert, chaotic matter into spirit" (p. 117). Therefore, he claimed, "evil exists in the world not to create despair but activity" (p. 130). Misfortune, want, and suffering are the means to a greater good.

"The gracious designs of **Providence**," Malthus held, ordain that "population should increase much faster than food," for that extremity spurs on "the full cultivation of the earth" (p. 120). Furthermore, sorrow and distress often make us sympathetic as nothing else can, and God has ordained that the universe should run by general laws. Otherwise people would wait for God's special acts to save them; they would become lax in advancing their intellectual and spiritual potentialities. If "it is impossible that this law can operate and produce the effects apparently intended by the Supreme Being without occasioning partial evil," as Malthus went on to claim, nonetheless "we have every reason to think that there is no more evil in the world than what is absolutely necessary as one of the ingredients in the mighty process" (pp. 121, 128–29). That mighty process will result in a blessed, eternal life for those who endure and persevere with righteousness against life's stiff odds. Rejecting the notion that a merciful and just God could condemn anyone to eternal torment, Malthus settled upon eternal death, a consignment to oblivion, as a sufficient and equitable reward for those who added to human misery without repentance.

Is Society's Improvement Impossible?

Malthus at first took a dim view of the prospects for improving our conditions in society, but before he finished his reflections he asserted that God was in his heaven, and, if all was not right with the world in the short run, everything would be well eventually. Even within history, Malthus suggested, we can take some comfort from knowing that the factors that leave human misery beyond our control are themselves necessary. They could not be otherwise if God's good purposes are to be accomplished. Moreover, as Malthus reworked his original essay and produced a second edition, retitled *An Essay on the Principle of Population, or a View of Its Past and Present Effects on Human Happiness, with an Inquiry into Our Prospects Respecting the Future Removal or Mitigation of the Evils Which It Occasions* (1803), he placed greater stress on moral restraint as a way to remedy the disease of poverty. The poor have no right to guaranteed support, Malthus still maintained. Yet some improvement can be achieved by effective campaigns mounted by religious and governmental agencies to encourage no person to marry until he or she has the means to support any children who might be born.

Indeed, unless one simply accepts the laws of necessity as Malthus set them down on the basis of his observations, the boundary between despair and hope may be more flexible than he imagined. Yet other philosophers whom we have met, and some we will meet, reach different conclusions from their observations. Theologically, for example, Malthus's apologies for God are credible only if one affirms a radically limited God, one who can achieve goals only by working within inescapable conditions. Economically, there is an argument that Malthus simply underestimated human ingenuity and its ability to produce food in abundance while at the same time curtailing birth rates.

However, Malthus has some counterarguments. Theologically speaking, if the basic structures of existence are not necessary conditions within which God must work to fulfill his aims, and if those structures produce massive misery, how can we sustain any hope in God's essential goodness? Even if there is more room to maneuver than Malthus's early estimates about food production could foresee or his sexual ethics could condone, have human beings found an effective way to organize the world's economy and to moderate population growth so that society's problem of surplus people can be solved? Whether we attribute our shortcomings in this field to immutable structural conditions or to a failure of intelligence, conscience, and will, Malthus's philosophy is far from obsolete. "It is hoped," said Malthus of his outlook, "that the general result of the inquiry is such as not to make us give up the improvement of human society in despair" (p. 139). As you study more of his *Essay*, ask

yourself again "What can—and should—I do to make society better?"

It is an acknowledged truth in philosophy that a just theory will always be confirmed by experiment. Yet so much friction and so many minute circumstances occur in practice, which it is next to impossible for the most enlarged and penetrating mind to foresee, that on few subjects can any theory be pronounced just that has not stood the test of experience. But an untried theory cannot fairly be advanced as probable, much less as just, till all the arguments against it have been maturely weighed and clearly and consistently refuted.

I have read some of the speculations on the perfectibility of man and of society with great pleasure. I have been warmed and delighted with the enchanting picture which they hold forth. I ardently wish for such happy improvements. But I see great, and, to my understanding, unconquerable difficulties in the way to them. These difficulties it is my present purpose to state, declaring, at the same time, that so far from exulting in them, as a cause of triumph over the friends of innovation, nothing would give me greater pleasure than to see them completely removed.

The most important argument that I shall adduce is certainly not new. The principles on which it depends have been explained in part by Hume, and more at large by Dr. Adam Smith. It has been advanced and applied to the present subject, though not with its proper weight, or in the most forcible point of view, . . . and it may probably have been stated by many writers that I have never met with. I should certainly therefore not think of advancing it again, though I mean to place it in a point of view in some degree different from any that I have hitherto seen, if it had ever been fairly and satisfactorily answered.

The cause of this neglect on the part of the advocates for the perfectibility of mankind is not easily accounted for. I cannot doubt the talents of such men as Godwin and Condorcet. I am unwilling to doubt their candor. To my understanding, and probably to that of most others, the difficulty appears insurmountable. Yet these men of acknowledged ability and penetration scarcely deign to notice it, and hold on their course in such speculations, with unabated ardor and undiminished confidence. I have certainly no right to say that they purposely shut their eyes to such arguments. I ought rather to doubt the validity of them, when neglected by such men, however forcibly their truth may strike my own mind. Yet in this respect it must be acknowledged that we are all of us too prone to err. If I saw a glass of wine repeatedly presented to a man, and he took no notice of it; I should be apt to think that he was blind or uncivil. A juster philosophy might teach me rather to think that my eyes deceived me and that the offer was not really what I conceived it to be.

In entering upon the argument I must premise that I put out of the question, at present, all mere conjectures, that is, all suppositions, the probable realization of which cannot be inferred upon any just philosophical grounds. A writer may tell me that he thinks man will ultimately become an ostrich. I cannot properly contradict him. But before he can expect to bring any reasonable person over to his opinion, he ought to show that the necks of mankind have been gradually elongating, that the lips have grown harder and more prominent, that the legs and feet are daily altering their shape, and that the hair is beginning to change into stubs of feathers. And till the probability of so wonderful a conversion can be shown, it is surely lost time and lost eloquence to expatiate on the happiness of man in such a state; to describe his powers, both of running and flying, to paint him in a condition where all narrow luxuries would be contemned, where he would be employed only in collecting the necessaries of life, and where, consequently, each man's share of labor would be light, and his portion of leisure ample.

I think I may fairly make two postulata.

First, That food is necessary to the existence of man.

Secondly, That the passion between the sexes is necessary and will remain nearly in its present state.

These two laws, ever since we have had any knowledge of mankind, appear to have been fixed laws of our nature, and, as we have not hitherto seen any alteration in them, we have no right to conclude that they will ever cease to be what they now are, without an immediate act of power in that Being who first arranged the system of the universe, and for the advantage of his creatures, still executes, according to fixed laws, all its various operations.

I do not know that any writer has supposed that on this earth man will ultimately be able to live without food. But Mr. Godwin has conjectured that the passion between the sexes may in time be extinguished. As, however, he calls this part of his work a deviation into the land of conjecture, I will not dwell longer upon it at present than to say that the best arguments for the perfectibility of man are drawn from a contemplation of the great progress that he has already made from the savage state and the difficulty of saying where he is to stop. But towards the extinction of the passion between the sexes, no progress whatever has hitherto been made. It appears to exist in as much force at present as it did two thousand or four thousand years ago. There are individual exceptions now as there always have been. But, as these exceptions do not appear to increase in number, it would surely be a very unphilosophical mode of arguing, to infer merely from the existence of an exception, that the exception would, in time, become the rule, and the rule the exception.

Assuming then, my postulata as granted, I say that the power of population is indefinitely greater than the power in the earth to produce subsistence for man.

Population, when unchecked, increases in a geometrical ratio. Subsistence increases only in an arithmetical ratio. A slight acquaintance with numbers will show the immensity of the first power in comparison of the second.

By that law of our nature which makes food necessary to the life of man, the effects of these two unequal powers must be kept equal.

This implies a strong and constantly operating check on population from the difficulty of subsistence. This difficulty must fall somewhere and must necessarily be severely felt by a large portion of mankind.

Through the animal and vegetable kingdoms, nature has scattered the seeds of life abroad with the most profuse and liberal hand. She has been comparatively sparing in the room and the nourishment necessary to rear them. The germs of existence contained in this spot of earth, with ample food and ample room to expand in, would fill millions of worlds in the course of a few thousand years. Necessity, that imperious all-pervading law of nature, restrains them within the prescribed bounds. The race of plants and the race of animals shrink under this great restrictive law. And the race of man cannot, by any efforts of reason, escape from it. Among plants and animals its effects are waste of seed, sickness, and premature death. Among mankind, misery and vice. The former, misery, is an absolutely necessary consequence of it. Vice is a highly probable consequence, and we therefore see it abundantly prevail, but it ought not, perhaps, to be called an absolutely necessary consequence. The ordeal of virtue is to resist all temptation to evil.

This natural inequality of the two powers of population and of production in the earth and that great law of our nature which must constantly keep their effects equal form the great difficulty that to me appears insurmountable in the way to the perfectibility of society. All other arguments are of slight and subordinate consideration in comparison of this. I see no way by which man can escape from the weight of this law which pervades all animated nature. No fancied equality, no agrarian regulations in their utmost extent, could remove the pressure of it even for a single century. And it appears, therefore, to be decisive against the possible existence of a society, all the members of which should live in ease, happiness, and comparative leisure, and feel no anxiety about providing the means of subsistence for themselves and families. (Pp. 18–21.)

Karl Marx and the History of Class Struggles

Born twenty years after Malthus published his first edition of the *Essay on the Principle of Population*, Karl Marx (1818–1883) was sure that the British philosopher had underestimated greatly what could be done to eliminate suffering. Indeed, Marx thought that Malthus apologized too much for the status quo. Moreover, since he regarded religion as "the opium of the people," Marx believed that a critique of religion was fundamental to our understanding of any society and its goals.[5] Malthus's theories about God and evil struck Marx as exploitive and abhorrent because they might lead people to think that their suffering was inevitable. "The philosophers," Marx charged, "have only interpreted the world, in various ways; the point is to change it."[6]

Although Marx affirmed that there had been, is, and would be social improvement, he himself died in poverty. German by birth, Marx lived most of his adult life in London. His financial support came mostly from his friend and collaborator, Friedrich Engels (1820–1895), whom he first met in Paris during the 1840s. They made an unlikely team. Of Jewish origins, Marx was university-trained as a specialist in philosophy. Engels, the eldest son of a prominent German textile manufacturer, came from a family with strong Christian leanings, was educated for the commercial world, and was intrigued primarily by economic issues. What brought them together was the conviction that capitalistic society in the West exploited and

KARL MARX 1818–1883

wasted human life for the purpose of economic profit. Motivated to correct that situation, they developed the theory of **communism** so influential today. At times they wrote together; on other occasions each spoke for himself. Engels survived Marx and got the last word, but the greater genius belonged to Marx.

Marx seemed destined neither to be happy nor to achieve much fame during his lifetime. He was constantly plagued by financial problems and moved about the Continent and England. He studied and worked in obscurity in the British Museum in London, and there he produced some of his most influential works. He wrote for newspapers for a time and often attacked theories and people with whom he differed. He was attracted by the United States because he thought the American revolution fitted the Communist theory of history as moving toward increasing democratic revolutions led by the workers and all those who suffered economic repression.

A World to Win

In 1848 Marx put the finishing touches on a brief but explosive statement he and Engels had drafted together, the *Communist Manifesto*. It rivaled Thomas Jefferson's Declaration of Independence in its historical impact, offering a critique of **capitalism,** an interpretation of **history,** and a call for **revolution.** It culminated in a solemn warning and a ringing exhortation: "Let the ruling classes tremble at a Communistic revolution. The proletarians have nothing to lose but their chains. They have a world to win. WORKING MEN OF ALL COUNTRIES, UNITE!"[7]

As Marx viewed it, history is essentially social history rather than a process directed by isolated individuals. Moreover, he thought that social history "is the history of class struggles" (p. 473). In different eras, class divisions had assumed different forms. For example, if the Roman world was divided into social ranks that included patricians, plebians, and slaves, the medieval period had its feudal lords, vassals, guildmasters, journeymen, apprentices, and serfs. Capitalism emerged from the ruins of feudalism, but **class antagonisms** remained. According to Marx, the basic division in modern times became that between the **bourgeoisie** and the **proletariat.** The former owned the means of production and employed labor; the latter had to sell its labor power to live.

To understand how Marx appraised the long history that produced these developments, we must note one of his fundamental philosophical principles: "It is not the consciousness of men that determines their being but, on the contrary, their social being that determines their consciousness."[8] In addition, Marx went on to say, "the nature of individuals . . . depends on the material conditions determining their production."[9] That is, how you earn your living in the material world guides how you will think. Marx did not feel that human thought is powerless or philosophers meaningless; they exert vast influence. It is just that our ways of thinking and acting are natural, social, and historical products. More than that, a certain general consciousness comes to life in particular economic settings. Labor is essential to human existence. "As individuals express their life, so are they. What they are, therefore, coincides with their production, both with *what* they produce and with *how* they produce" (p. 161; Marx's italics).

As Marx dissected capitalism, a task to which he devoted most of his life, he located the roots of its power in the emergence of a new society in late medieval Europe. Industrialization, which ultimately destroyed medieval society, produced new forces of production involving machines, not individual skilled workers alone. Economic interest was the driving force behind this society, which sought freedom from religious and political restrictions. The discovery of new lands and the opening of new markets meant that men could "truck, barter, and exchange" far more extensively than before. That stimulus spurred the division of labor, technological development, large-scale production, and rationalized techniques of management. The Industrial Revolution, then, was not the beginning of capitalism but part of capitalism's progress. Life itself directed human activity to seek fulfillment in certain economic ways. The crucial need that emerged, which spurred the progress of capitalism, was profit-making. But profits were not needed simply to line the pockets of individuals. They were needed to amass capital and to promote investment that stimulated further economic growth.

Capitalism's historical development gave some persons great power; others were reduced to a wage-labor status little better than slavery. As Marx put it, the bourgeoisie, baptized "in the icy water of egotistical calculation, . . . has resolved personal worth into exchange value, and in place of the numberless indefeasible chartered freedoms, has set up that single unconscionable freedom—Free Trade."[10] The latter term, contended Marx, is a euphemism for naked, shameless, direct, brutal exploitation veiled by religious and political illusions. Though Marx did not always write such impassioned prose, these feelings were characteristic of the attack he considered necessary to bring about a time when society might leave behind the limited outlook of the bourgeoisie and "inscribe on its banners: from each according to his ability, to each according to his needs!"[11]

Marx believed that capitalism's history revealed a logic. It is an ordered development in which each basic stage is the necessary outcome of preceding conditions. His hope was that progress toward desirable ends would occur. Marx believed that the rise of the bourgeoisie had simplified the class struggle, so that now two great hostile camps, the bourgeoisie and the proletariat, were pitted against each other. In that situation, Marx went on to say, social existence would continue to determine consciousness. Marx was convinced that the outcome would ensure the dawning of a brighter day.

But Things Must Get Worse before They Get Better

Marx never denied the amazing accomplishments of bourgeois society. Its power brought people together in cities, advanced the means of production, concentrated property in the hands of a few, and engineered the centralized political control that produced the modern state. Indeed, the scientific and technological progress of bourgeois life is vital to Marx's communist society. That society was inevitable, Marx proclaimed. Despite the vast power residing in bourgeois capitalism, the logic at work within that power pressed bourgeois society toward its own negation. Capitalism, Marx claimed, is plagued by self-contradictions. For example, he observed, "the condition for capital is wage-labor."[12] Labor creates value, according to Marx. Capital can be accumulated because the value of the goods produced by labor enables them to be sold for more than it costs to produce them. But wage labor is also a critical factor in this process, because the rate of profit depends on squeezing wages down to a minimum. That objective can be reached partly by relying on cost-effective machines and partly by assuring the existence of a surplus pool of workers, which causes competition for jobs. Then the law of supply and demand takes over, and wages can be paid at the lowest rates compatible with subsistence. However, this process is less efficient than it looks. It leads to overproduction, because the capitalist must use his machines at top capacity to reap a profit, regardless of the demand. Too many goods become available and not enough are bought. That outcome, in turn, leads capitalists into competition with each other through price-cutting and consequent depressions or through attempts to expand and monopolize markets. Such competition drives some capitalists out of business, which situates capital in the hands of still fewer. But since the success of capitalism depends on growth, the vicious cycle goes around again.

Marx thought that capitalism would collapse of its own weight, because the repetition of business cycles would eventually bring the economy past the point of no return. But an even more certain and speedy demise was ensured, Marx thought, because in addition to forging—literally as well as figuratively—the weapons that would bring about its death, the bourgeoisie "has also called into existence the men who are to wield those weapons—the modern working-class—the proletarians" (p. 226). The revolutionary urge

comes about because these workers are increasingly alienated. Forced to sell themselves piecemeal, turned into little more than appendages of machines, able to exert scant control over the **means of production** or the products of their work, paid barely enough to survive and bear children whose fate it is to follow in their dreary footsteps, these workers could muster little respect from others or for themselves. They had been reduced to animals.

Human life, however, is crushed neither easily nor with impunity. Already the nineteenth century had witnessed the reactions of the proletariat to their misfortune. Here and there individuals and groups had protested, risen up, and fought back. Unemployment and bad living and working conditions led to riots and to the formation of labor unions. However, the targets were often misplaced. In their rage the workers destroyed machines or attacked individual owners. According to Marx, however, they did not go to the root of the matter, namely, the bourgeois conditions of production. But now the proletariat was growing. The scale of modern industry drove out small tradespeople and shopkeepers, thus adding to the proletariat's numbers. The proletariat would eventually become a majority and not a minority movement. But for the time being the working people lacked a clear sense of their identity as a class. With Marx's help, however, social existence would produce such a consciousness. In his *Manifesto*, he summarized the point:

> The advance of industry, whose involuntary promoter is the bourgeoisie, replaces the isolation of the laborers, due to competition, by their revolutionary combination, due to association. The development of Modern Industry, therefore, cuts from under its feet the very foundation on which the bourgeoisie produces and appropriates products. What the bourgeoisie, therefore, produces, above all, are its own grave-diggers. Its fall

and the victory of the proletariat are equally inevitable. (P. 231.)

The Victory of the Proletariat

Communists, Marx explained, have the best interests of the proletariat at heart. Since they are of the proletariat themselves, their avowed concern is to advance "the common interests of the entire proletariat, independently of all nationality" (p. 231). Resolutely pushing forward the cause of all working class parties, the communists "have over the great mass of the proletariat the advantage of clearly understanding the line of march, the conditions, and the ultimate general results of the proletarian movement" (p. 231). This includes forming the proletariat into one class conscious of itself, waging a successful revolution against bourgeois power, and achieving political control. In short, wrote Marx, the communist goal is equated with the proletariat's goal rightly understood. It is: "abolition of private property" (p. 232).

Few workers own anything of consequence, Marx said. The private property that he meant is capital and the means of production. It is the ownership of this property, specifically its ownership by a few, which constitutes the division between bourgeoisie and proletariat. Therefore, abolition of this kind of private property and its attendant forms of consciousness is the goal of communism, for only through such a development can the struggle between the two classes be resolved. The victory of the proletariat entails its elimination as a separate class. This means that the bourgeois class must disappear, too.

The elimination of private property, Marx argued, is entirely fitting, because capital and the means of production are actually social realities, not individual possessions. Since capital is generated collectively, it is not the conversion of personal property into social property that is at stake in the communist

cause. Rather, it is the elimination of a class character from the already social character of capital. The effort to achieve this goal will meet stiff resistance from the bourgeoisie. It will not be easy to organize the political struggles required to bring about such basic changes. A successful outcome, however, will bring liberation to all, including the bourgeoisie, if only they would see the light. As the oppressed proletariat finds freedom from alienation, so does the bourgeois class, since it has itself been dehumanized in a pursuit for capital that has led it to turn other human persons into things. Instead of "classes and class antagonisms," Marx promised political action that would genuinely act for universal human ends so that "we shall have an association in which the free development of each is the condition for the free development of all" (p. 238).

Is the Process Inevitable?

Marx had no timetable to predict exactly when or how his communist revolution would come about. Conditions vary from place to place. At times, gradual political steps could advance the cause, but Marx's *Manifesto* also emphasizes that its "ends can be attained only by the forcible overthrow of all existing social conditions" (p. 246). A complete transformation of society and its consciousness is the goal. In spite of the historical differences that had to be taken into account, Marx insisted that the communist revolution would ultimately be characterized by its universal qualities. More than that, he insisted that the victory for the international proletariat is inevitable, and with it universal emancipation.

We might dismiss such language as a rhetorical flourish, but its purpose is to encourage the communist cause, to urge people to seize every opportunity to overcome the class struggle between the bourgeoisie and the proletariat. Its effect is to say: "The proletariat is going to win. Join us!" What happens, though, if further support is not forthcoming, or if something else happens that seems to disconfirm the idea that the victory of the proletariat is at hand? Two options suggest themselves. First, "inevitable" might be a rhetorical flourish, perhaps one that Marx thought justified but not to be taken in the strict sense of meaning "certain, unavoidable, bound to happen no matter what." Or, it might be that "inevitable" was exactly the term intended. The victory of the proletariat really is in the cards, even if progress toward that goal seems temporarily stalled. If we try to pin down which of those options fits Marx's outlook best, the evaluation is tricky. The fairest answer is probably that Marx vacillated, that he was ambivalent.

Marx disclaimed the role of prophet. He was quite vague about the exact details of his communist dream. He emphasized that more than one path existed to bring humankind to that goal. On the other hand, he strongly believed that history was on his side. History is not, he claimed, a random configuration of events. It has a logic and so does the economic life that goes on within it. Friedrich Engels interpreted that logic much more mechanistically and deterministically than Marx was inclined to do. Nonetheless, Marx had few reservations about the success of the communist cause. Compare his view with Malthus's belief in the limits of population. Each wants change for society, although it is not agreed which change will be for the better.

The famous line that opens the *Communist Manifesto* announces: "A specter is haunting Europe—the specter of Communism" (p. 221). But today it is unclear that the "specter" of the proletariat victory is inevitable, let alone near. Not least among the reasons for this is that Marxism and Marx are not identical. Most Communist regimes today are several times removed from Marx's philosophy, which has been extensively modified

by Lenin, Stalin, Mao, and others. Although Marx recognized that any historical situation can evolve in more than one way, he thought that the broad patterns of history would unfold with less flexibility than may have been exhibited. Hence, he tended to underestimate the resiliency of capitalism, as well as the ability of the bourgeoisie and the proletariat to locate common interests that make their divisions less rigid and less brutal.

One View of History or Many?

As we try to assess Marx's role in the betterment of society and to decide if his predictions will come out as projected, we need to take a step back from Marx and consider G.W.F. Hegel (1770–1831), the German philosopher from whom Marx learned the most. We will discuss Hegel more fully in Chapter Twelve, but here it is important to note that he inspired Marx by developing an interpretation of history that emphasized points such as the following:

1. History is not a collection of discrete, unrelated facts; rather, it is a universal process in which everything is related.

2. Although it is full of destruction and negative elements, history is moving progressively.

3. This movement is governed by **dialectical logic**.

As far as history was concerned, Hegel's view of dialectic was that positive and negative forces, moving in tension and conflict, oppose each other and then finally resolve the clash by achieving a higher resolution. The pattern, he sometimes said, is that of thesis, antithesis, and synthesis. Within this pattern, Hegel believed that Spirit, as he called history's governing force, controlled material events. Marx felt that Hegel's dialectical analysis was basically sound, but it had erred fundamentally as well. Material forces and especially those of economic production, Marx believed, were history's controlling factor. They determined the character of thought, culture, politics—all the aspects Hegel saw as manifestations of Spirit. Thus, it is sometimes said that Marx stood Hegel's theory on its head. Marx's conviction, however, was that Hegel was the one who had things upside-down. The communist account put matters right-side up.

Hegel's *Phenomenology of Mind* (1807) explained how Spirit develops and what stages it goes through. When Hegel spoke this way, he was actually talking about God, who is manifested in history and achieves ever higher levels of awareness as history works out its dialectical movements. Religion itself is a step in this process, according to Hegel. When Marx reversed Hegel's way of interpreting dialectic and gave material forces priority over those of Spirit, he was naturally led away from religion and God, although he staunchly affirmed that a society's problems and prospects for improvement depended on a critical analysis of its religious outlook.

In *Lectures on the Philosophy of History*, first published in 1837, Hegel further explained how history develops as a dialectical process. This development, Hegel acknowledged, may not be immediately apparent. It is revealed clearly only after the proper philosophical interpretation has been applied to history's course. Hegel believed that his philosophy provided the necessary perspective, but his claim leads us to question whether there is one framework for viewing history or many. Hegel and Marx concurred that philosophy had reached a point of being able to see clearly the nature and destiny of humankind. But the irony is that having agreed on that much, they departed from each other radically when they fleshed out their shared outline. Each thought he knew the truth about history, but what they took truth to be was very different. They agreed that dialectic is the key for

understanding, but they were in conflict about the motive force behind history's movement, its leading participants, and its direction.

From particular national histories we have reached the stage of universal history, they agreed, at which race and national distinctions will fall away. But Marx's stress on worldwide class conflict was quite different from Hegel's view. For both, events may seem irrational, but behind the confusion an ultimate logic prevails. There the agreement ended, however, as the two went on to describe that logic in conflicting ways. Hegel and Marx both thought in terms of necessity, and yet both stressed freedom, too. But the uses to which they put these terms are not the same. There are leaders in history's development, Hegel and Marx agreed, and all persons are by no means equal in discerning the necessary future direction or the next dialectical stage. For Hegel, those who have such foresight are world historical figures under the direction of Spirit; for Marx, those individuals are the cadre of the Communist Party, who lead the proletariat to an expanded consciousness. Struggle is essential for advancing development, and there will be individual loss in the name of social progress. On these points, Hegel and Marx also saw eye to eye. But then the outlooks diverged again—Hegel's toward the idea that history is God's activity; Marx's toward a classless society. When we recognize Hegel behind Marx, we can better appreciate their joint contention that there is one and only one way to interpret history properly and only one way to lead to its betterment. But the singularity of their views eventually breaks down and leaves us to wonder how we can choose between a competing variety of interpretive frameworks.

Can we make society better? Marx and Hegel provide two distinct views. Marx saw history as ready for a revolutionary class struggle led by those who grasped what his theory of dialectical materialism proposes. They can advance history by discerning its structure and cooperating with it. Hegel, too, thought society was advancing, but his approach was governed less by socioeconomic categories and more by the conviction that God's embodiment in history enhances our consciousness of freedom in existence. Although these outlooks share much, they are not one and the same and perhaps neither can be carried out as programmed.

As we consider Marx and Hegel, two immensely powerful theoreticians, we need to remember the other philosophers taken up in this chapter. They help us to recognize the variety of interpretations that are possible. If we can declare no one theory as ultimately true, we face various proposals to improve the human lot. No one of them by itself may be able to transform the path of all societies, but each proposal may have some forcefulness in that regard. Neither Marx nor Hegel may be completely correct, especially insofar as each hoped to achieve a final philosophical view. But that outcome does not deny that both can be insightful in helping us to appraise how society can be made better. Turn, then, to read more of Karl Marx's *Communist Manifesto*, and see if you can find ways in which he hit as well as missed the target.

A specter is haunting Europe—the specter of Communism. All the powers of old Europe have entered into a holy alliance to exorcise this specter: pope and czar, Metternich and Guizot, French Radicals and German police-spies.

Where is the party in opposition that has not been decried as Communistic by its opponents in power? Where the Opposition that has not hurled back the branding reproach of Communism, against the more advanced opposition parties, as well as against its reactionary adversaries?

Two things result from this fact.

1. Communism is already acknowledged by all European powers to be itself a power.

2. It is high time that Communists should openly, in the face of the whole world, publish their views, their aims, their tendencies, and meet this nursery tale of the Specter of Communism with a manifesto of the party itself.

To this end, Communists of various nationalities have assembled in London and sketched the following manifesto, to be published in the English, French, German, Italian, Flemish, and Danish languages.

BOURGEOIS AND PROLETARIANS

The history of all hitherto existing society is the history of class struggles.

Freeman and slave, patrician and plebeian, lord and serf, guild-master and journeyman—in a word, oppressor and oppressed, stood in constant opposition to one another, carried on an uninterrupted, now hidden, now open fight, a fight that each time ended either in a revolutionary reconstitution of society at large or in the common ruin of the contending classes.

In the earlier epochs of history, we find almost everywhere a complicated arrangement of society into various orders, a manifold gradation of social rank. In ancient Rome we have patricians, knights, plebeians, slaves; in the Middle Ages, feudal lords, vassals, guild-masters, journeymen, apprentices, serfs; in almost all of these classes, again, subordinate gradations.

The modern bourgeois society that has sprouted from the ruins of feudal society has not done away with class antagonisms. It has but established new classes, new conditions of oppression, new forms of struggle in place of the old ones.

Our epoch, the epoch of the bourgeoisie, possesses, however, this distinctive feature: it has simplified the class antagonisms. Society as a whole is more and more splitting up into two great hostile camps, into two great classes directly facing each other: bourgeoisie and proletariat.

From the serfs of the Middle Ages sprang the chartered burghers of the earliest towns. From these burgesses the first elements of the bourgeoisie were developed.

The discovery of America, the rounding of the Cape, opened up fresh ground for the rising bourgeoisie. The East Indian and Chinese markets, the colonization of America, trade with the colonies, the increase in the means of exchange and in commodities generally, gave to commerce, to navigation, to industry, an impulse never before known, and thereby, to the revolutionary element in the tottering feudal society, a rapid development.

The feudal system of industry, under which industrial production was monopolized by closed guilds, now no longer sufficed for the growing wants of the new markets. The manufacturing system took its place. The guild-masters were pushed on one side by the manufacturing middle class; division of labor between the different corporate guilds vanished in the face of division of labor in each single workshop.

Meantime the markets kept ever growing, the demand ever rising. Even manufacture no longer sufficed. Thereupon, steam and machinery revolutionized industrial production. The place of manufacture was taken by the giant, Modern Industry, the place of the industrial middle class, by industrial millionaires, the leaders of whole industrial armies, the modern bourgeois.

Modern industry has established the world market, for which the discovery of America paved the way. This market has given an immense development to commerce, to navigation, to communication by land. This development has, in its turn, reacted on the extension of industry; and in proportion as industry, commerce, navigation, railways extended, in the same proportion the bourgeoisie developed, increased its capital, and pushed into the background every class handed down from the Middle Ages.

We see, therefore, how the modern bourgeoisie is itself the product of a long course of development, of a series of revolutions in the modes of production and of exchange.

Each step in the development of the bourgeoisie was accompanied by a corresponding political advance of that class. An oppressed class under the sway of the feudal nobility, an armed and self-governing association in the medieval commune; here independent urban republic (as in Italy and Germany), there taxable "third estate" of the monarchy (as in France), afterwards, in the period of manufacture proper, serving either the semifeudal or the absolute monarchy as a counterpoise against the nobility, and, in fact, cornerstone of the great monarchies in general, the bourgeoisie has at last, since the establishment of modern industry and of the world market, conquered for itself, in the modern representative state, exclusive political sway. The executive of the modern state is but a committee for managing the common affairs of the whole bourgeoisie.

The bourgeoisie, historically, has played a most revolutionary part.

The bourgeoisie, wherever it has got the upper hand, has put an end to all feudal, patriarchal, idyllic relations. It has pitilessly torn asunder the motley feudal ties that bound man to his "natural superiors," and has left remaining no other nexus between man and man than naked self-interest, than callous "cash payment." It has drowned the most heavenly ecstasies of religious fervor, of chivalrous enthusiasm, of philistine sentimentalism, in the icy water of egotistical calculation. It has resolved personal worth into exchange value, and in place of the numberless indefeasible chartered freedoms, has set up that single, unconscionable freedom—Free Trade. In one word, for exploitation, veiled by religious and political illusions, it has substituted naked, shameless, direct, brutal exploitation.

The bourgeoisie has stripped of its halo every occupation hitherto honored and looked up to with reverent awe. It has converted the physician, the lawyer, the priest, the poet, the man of science into its paid wage-laborers.

The bourgeoisie has torn away from the

family its sentimental veil, and has reduced the family relation to a mere money relation.

The bourgeoisie has disclosed how it came to pass that the brutal display of vigor in the Middle Ages, which Reactionists so much admire, found its fitting complement in the most slothful indolence. It has been the first to show what man's activity can bring about. It has accomplished wonders far surpassing Egyptian pyramids, Roman aqueducts, and Gothic cathedrals; it has conducted expeditions that put in the shade all former Exoduses of nations and crusades.

The bourgeoisie cannot exist without constantly revolutionizing the instruments of production, and thereby the relations of production, and with them the whole relations of society. Conservation of the old modes of production in unaltered form, was, on the contrary, the first condition of existence for all earlier industrial classes. Constant revolutionizing of production, uninterrupted disturbance of all social conditions, everlasting uncertainty and agitation distinguish the bourgeois epoch from all earlier ones. All fixed, fast-frozen relations, with their train of ancient and venerable prejudices and opinions, are swept away, all newformed ones become antiquated before they can ossify. All that is solid melts into air, all that is holy is profaned, and man is at last compelled to face with sober senses, his real conditions of life, and his relations with his kind.

The need of a constantly expanding market for its products chases the bourgeoisie over the whole surface of the globe. It must nestle everywhere, settle everywhere, establish connections everywhere.

The bourgeoisie has through its exploitation of the world market given a cosmopolitan character to production and consumption in every country. To the great chagrin of Reactionists, it has drawn from under the feet of industry the national ground on which it stood. All old-established national industries have been destroyed or are daily being destroyed. They are dislodged by new industries, whose introduction becomes a life-and-death question for all civilized nations, by industries that no longer work up indigenous raw material, but raw material drawn from the remotest zones; industries whose products are consumed, not only at home, but in every quarter of the globe. In place of the old wants, satisfied by the productions of the country, we find new wants, requiring for their satisfaction the products of distant lands and climes. In place of the old local and national seclusion and self-sufficiency, we have intercourse in every direction, universal interdependence of nations. And as in material, so also in intellectual production. The intellectual creations of individual nations become common property. National one-sidedness and narrow-mindedness become more and more impossible, and from the numerous national and local literatures, there arises a world literature.

The bourgeoisie, by the rapid improvement of all instruments of production, by the immensely facilitated means of communication, draws all, even the most barbarian, nations into civilization. The cheap prices of its commodities are the heavy artillery with which it batters down all Chinese walls, with which it forces the barbarians' intensely obstinate hatred of foreigners to capitulate. It compels all nations, on pain of extinction, to adopt the bourgeois mode of production; it compels them to introduce what it calls civilization into their midst, i.e., to become bourgeois themselves. In one word, it creates a world after its own image.

The bourgeoisie has subjected the country to the rule of the towns. It has created enormous cities, has greatly increased the urban population as compared with the rural, and has thus rescued a considerable part of the population from the idiocy of rural life. Just as it has made the country dependent on the towns, so it has made barbarian and semibarbarian countries dependent on the civilized ones, nations of peasants on nations of bourgeois, the East on the West.

The bourgeoisie keeps more and more doing away with the scattered state of the population, of the means of production, and of property. It has agglomerated population, centralized means of production, and has concentrated property in a few hands. The necessary consequence of this was political centralization. Independent or but loosely connected provinces, with separate interests, laws, governments, and systems of taxation, became lumped together into one nation, with one government, one code of laws, one national class-interest, one frontier, and one customs-tariff.

The bourgeoisie, during its rule of scarcely one hundred years, has created more massive and more colossal productive forces than have all preceding generations together. Subjection of Nature's forces to man, machinery, application of chemistry to industry and agriculture, steam navigation, railways, electric telegraphs, clearing of whole continents for cultivation, canalization of rivers, whole populations conjured out of the ground—what earlier century had even a presentiment that such productive forces slumbered in the lap of social labor?

We see then that the means of production and of exchange, on whose foundation the bourgeoisie built itself up, were generated in feudal society. At a certain stage in the development of these means of production and of exchange, the conditions under which feudal society produced and exchanged, the feudal organization of agriculture and manufacturing industry, in one word, the feudal relations of property become no longer compatible with the already developed productive forces; they became so many fetters. They had to be burst asunder; they were burst asunder.

Into their place stepped free competition, accompanied by a social and political constitution adapted to it, and by the economical and political sway of the bourgeois class.

A similar movement is going on before our own eyes. Modern bourgeois society with its relations of production, of exchange, and of property, a society that has conjured up such gigantic means of production and of exchange, is like the sorcerer who is no longer able to control the powers of the nether world which he has called up by his spells. The history of industry and commerce for many

a decade past is but the history of the revolt of modern productive forces against modern conditions of production, against the property relations that are the conditions for the existence of the bourgeoisie and of its rule. It is enough to mention the commercial crises that by their periodical return put on trial, each time more threateningly, the existence of the entire bourgeois society. In these crises a great part not only of the existing products, but also of the previously created productive forces, are periodically destroyed. In these crises there breaks out an epidemic that, in all earlier epochs, would have seemed an absurdity—the epidemic of overproduction. Society suddenly finds itself put back into a state of momentary barbarism; it appears as if a famine, a universal war of devastation, has cut off the supply of every means of subsistence; industry and commerce seem to be destroyed; and why? Because there is too much civilization, too much means of subsistence, too much industry, too much commerce. The productive forces at the disposal of society no longer tend to further the development of the conditions of bourgeois property; on the contrary, they have become too powerful for these conditions, by which they are fettered, and so soon as they overcome these fetters, they bring disorder into the whole of bourgeois society, endanger the existence of bourgeois property. The conditions of bourgeois society are too narrow to comprise the wealth created by them. And how does the bourgeoisie get over these crises? On the one hand by enforced destruction of a mass of productive forces; on the other, by the conquest of new markets, and by the more thorough exploitation of the old ones. That is to say, by paving the way for more extensive and more destructive crises, and by diminishing the means whereby crises are prevented.

The weapons with which the bourgeoisie felled feudalism to the ground are now turned against the bourgeoisie itself.

But not only has the bourgeoisie forged the weapons that bring death to itself; it has also called into existence the men who are to wield those weapons—the modern working class—the proletarians.

In proportion as the bourgeoisie, i.e., capital, is developed, in the same proportion is the proletariat, the modern working class, developed—a class of laborers, who live only so long as they find work, and who find work only so long as their labor increases capital. These laborers, who must sell themselves piecemeal, are a commodity, like every other article of commerce, and are consequently exposed to all the vicissitudes of competition, to all the fluctuations of the market.

Owing to the extensive use of machinery and to division of labor, the work of the proletarians has lost all individual character, and, consequently, all charm for the workman. He becomes an appendage of the machine, and it is only the most simple, most monotonous, and most easily acquired knack, that is required of him. Hence, the cost of production of a workman is restricted, almost entirely, to the means of subsistence that he requires for his maintenance, and for the propagation of his race. But the price of a commodity, and therefore also of labor, is equal to its cost of production. In proportion, therefore, as the repulsiveness of the work increases, the wage decreases. Nay more, in proportion as the use of machinery and division of labor increases, in the same proportion the burden of toil also increases, whether by prolongation of the working hours, by increase of the work exacted in a given time or by increased speed of the machinery, etc.

Modern industry has converted the little workshop of the patriarchal master into the great factory of the industrial capitalist. Masses of laborers, crowded into the factory, are organized like soldiers. As privates of the industrial army they are placed under the command of a perfect hierarchy of officers and sergeants. Not only are they slaves of the bourgeois class, and of the bourgeois state; they are daily and hourly enslaved by the machine, by the overlooker, and, above all, by the individual bourgeois manufacturer himself. The more openly this despo-

tism proclaims gain to be its end and aim, the more petty, the more hateful, and the more embittering it is.

The less the skill and exertion of strength implied in manual labor, in other words, the more modern industry becomes developed, the more is the labor of men superseded by that of women. Differences of age and sex have no longer any distinctive social validity for the working class. All are instruments of labor, more or less expensive to use, according to their age and sex.

No sooner is the exploitation of the laborer by the manufacturer, so far, at an end, and he receives his wages in cash, than he is set upon by the other portions of the bourgeoisie, the landlord, the shopkeeper, the pawnbroker, etc.

The lower strata of the middle class—the small tradespeople, shopkeepers, and retired tradesmen generally, the handicraftsmen and peasants—all these sink gradually into the proletariat, partly because their diminutive capital does not suffice for the scale on which modern industry is carried on and is swamped in the competition with the large capitalists, partly because their specialized skill is rendered worthless by new methods of production. Thus the proletariat is recruited from all classes of the population.

The proletariat goes through various stages of development. With its birth begins its struggle with the bourgeoisie. At first the contest is carried on by individual laborers, then by the workpeople of a factory, then by the operatives of one trade, in one locality, against the individual bourgeois who directly exploits them. They direct their attacks not against the bourgeois conditions of production, but against the instruments of production themselves; they destroy imported wares that compete with their labor, they smash to pieces machinery, they set factories ablaze, they seek to restore by force the vanished status of the workman of the Middle Ages.

At this stage the laborers still form an incoherent mass scattered over the whole country, and broken up by their mutual competition. If anywhere they unite to form more compact bodies, this is not yet the consequence of their own active union, but of the union of the bourgeoisie, which class, in order to attain its own political ends, is compelled to set the whole proletariat in motion, and is moreover yet, for a time, able to do so. At this stage, therefore, the proletarians do not fight their enemies, but the enemies of their enemies, the remnants of absolute monarchy, the landowners, the nonindustrial bourgeois, the petty bourgeoisie. Thus the whole historical movement is concentrated in the hands of the bourgeoisie; every victory so obtained is a victory for the bourgeoisie.

But with the development of industry the proletariat not only increases in number; it becomes concentrated in greater masses, its strength grows, and it feels that strength more. The various interests and conditions of life within the ranks of the proletariat are more and more equalized, in proportion as machinery obliterates all distinctions of labor, and nearly everywhere reduces wages to the same low level. The growing competition among the bourgeois, and the resulting commercial crises, make the wages of the workers ever more fluctuating. The unceasing improvement of machinery, ever more rapidly developing, makes their livelihood more and more precarious; the collisions between individual workmen and individual bourgeois take more and more the character of collisions between two classes. Thereupon the workers begin to form combinations (trades' unions) against the bourgeois; they club together in order to keep up the rate of wages; they found permanent associations in order to make provision beforehand for these occasional revolts. Here and there the contest breaks out into riots.

Now and then the workers are victorious, but only for a time. The real fruit of their battles lies, not in the immediate result, but in the ever-expanding union of the workers. This union is helped on by the improved means of communication that are created by modern industry and that place the workers of different localities in contact with one another. It was just this contact that was needed to centralize the numerous local struggles, all of the same character, into one national struggle between classes. But every class struggle is a political struggle. And that union, to attain which the burghers of the Middle Ages, with their miserable highways, required centuries, the modern proletarians, thanks to railways, achieve in a few years.

This organization of the proletarians into a class, and consequently into a political party, is continually being upset again by the competition between the workers themselves. But it ever rises up again, stronger, firmer, mightier. It compels legislative recognition of particular interests of the workers, by taking advantage of the divisions among the bourgeoisie itself. Thus the ten-hours' bill in England was carried.

Altogether, collisions between the classes of the old society further in many ways the course of development of the proletariat. The bourgeoisie finds itself involved in a constant battle. At first with the aristocracy; later on, with those portions of the bourgeoisie itself whose interests have become antagonistic to the progress of industry; at all times, with the bourgeoisie of foreign countries. In all these battles it sees itself compelled to appeal to the proletariat, to ask for its help, and thus to drag it into the political arena. The bourgeoisie itself, therefore, supplies the proletariat with its own elements of political and general education, in other words, it furnishes the proletariat with weapons for fighting the bourgeoisie.

Further, as we have already seen, entire sections of the ruling classes are, by the advance of industry, precipitated into the proletariat, or are at least threatened in their conditions of existence. These also supply the proletariat with fresh elements of enlightenment and progress.

Finally, in times when the class struggle nears the decisive hour, the process of dissolution going on within the ruling class, in fact within the whole range of old society, assumes such a violent, glaring character, that a small section of the ruling class cuts itself adrift, and joins the revolutionary class, the class that holds the future in its hands.

Just as, therefore, at an earlier period, a section of the nobility went over to the bourgeoisie, so now a portion of the bourgeoisie goes over to the proletariat, and in particular, a portion of the bourgeois ideologists, who have raised themselves to the level of comprehending theoretically the historical movement as a whole.

Of all the classes that stand face to face with the bourgeoisie today, the proletariat alone is a really revolutionary class. The other classes decay and finally disappear in the face of modern industry; the proletariat is its special and essential product.

The lower middle class, the small manufacturer, the shopkeeper, the artisan, the peasant, all these fight against the bourgeoisie, to save from extinction their existence as fractions of the middle class. They are therefore not revolutionary, but conservative. Nay more, they are reactionary, for they try to roll back the wheel of history. If by chance they are revolutionary, they are so only in view of their impending transfer into the proletariat; they thus defend not their present, but their future interests, they desert their own standpoint to place themselves at that of the proletariat.

The "dangerous class," the social scum, that passively rotting mass thrown off by the lowest layers of old society, may, here and there, be swept into the movement by a proletarian revolution; its conditions of life, however, prepare it far more for the part of a bribed tool of reactionary intrigue.

In the conditions of the proletariat, those of old society at large are already virtually swamped. The proletarian is without property; his relation to his wife and children has no longer anything in common with the bourgeois family relations; modern industrial labor, modern subjection to capital, the same in England as in France, in America as in Germany, has stripped him of every trace of national character. Law, morality, religion are to him so many bourgeois prejudices, behind which lurk in ambush just as many bourgeois interests.

All the preceding classes that got the upper hand, sought to fortify their already acquired status by subjecting society at large to their conditions of appropriation. The proletarians cannot become masters of the productive forces of society, except by abolishing their own previous mode of appropriation, and thereby also every other previous mode of appropriation. They have nothing of their own to secure and to fortify; their mission is to destroy all previous securities for, and insurances of, individual property.

All previous historical movements were movements of minorities, or in the interests of minorities. The proletarian movement is the self-conscious, independent movement of the immense majority, in the interests of the immense majority. The proletariat, the lowest stratum of our present society, cannot stir, cannot raise itself up, without the whole superincumbent strata of official society being sprung into the air.

Though not in substance, yet in form, the struggle of the proletariat with the bourgeoisie is at first a national struggle. The proletariat of each country must, of course, first of all settle matters with its own bourgeoisie.

In depicting the most general phases of the development of the proletariat, we traced the more or less veiled civil war, raging within existing society, up to the point where that war breaks out into open revolution, and where the violent overthrow of the bourgeoisie lays the foundation for the sway of the proletariat.

Hitherto, every form of society has been based, as we have already seen, on the antagonism of oppressing and oppressed classes. But in order to oppress a class, certain conditions must be assured to it under which it can, at least, continue its slavish existence. The serf, in the period of serfdom, raised himself to membership in the commune, just as the petty bourgeois, under the yoke of feudal absolutism, managed to develop into a bourgeois. The modern laborer, on the contrary, instead of rising with the progress of industry, sinks deeper and deeper below the conditions of existence of his own class. He becomes a pauper, and pauperism develops more rapidly than population and wealth. And here it becomes evident, that the bourgeoisie is unfit any longer to be the ruling class in society, and to impose its conditions of existence upon society as an overriding law. It is unfit to rule because it is incompetent to assure an existence to its slave within his slavery, because it cannot help letting him sink into such a state that it has to feed him, instead of being fed by him. Society can no longer live under this bourgeoisie, in other words, its existence is no longer compatible with society.

The essential condition for the existence, and for the sway of the bourgeois class, is the formation and augmentation of capital; the condition for capital is wage-labor. Wage labor rests exclusively on competition between the laborers. The advance of industry, whose involuntary promoter is the bourgeoisie, replaces the isolation of the laborers, due to competition, by their revolutionary combination, due to association. The development of modern industry, therefore, cuts from under its feet the very foundation on which the bourgeoisie produces and appropriates products. What the bourgeoisie, therefore, produces, above all, is its own grave-diggers. Its fall and the victory of the proletariat are equally inevitable.

PROLETARIANS AND COMMUNISTS

In what relation do the Communists stand to the proletarians as a whole?

The Communists do not form a separate party opposed to other working-class parties.

They have no interests separate and apart from those of the proletariat as a whole.

They do not set up any sectarian principles of their own, by which to shape and mould the proletarian movement.

The Communists are distinguished from the other working-class parties by this only: (1) In the national struggles of the proletarians of the different countries, they point out and bring to the front the common interests of the entire proletariat, independently of all nationality. (2) In the various stages of development which the struggle of the

working class against the bourgeoisie has to pass through, they always and everywhere represent the interests of the movement as a whole.

The Communists, therefore, are on the one hand, practically, the most advanced and resolute section of the working-class parties of every country, that section which pushes forward all others; on the other hand, theoretically, they have over the great mass of the proletariat the advantage of clearly understanding the line of march, the conditions, and the ultimate general results of the proletarian movement.

The immediate aim of the Communists is the same as that of all the other proletarian parties: formation of the proletariat into a class, overthrow of the bourgeois supremacy, conquest of political power by the proletariat.

The theoretical conclusions of the Communists are in no way based on ideas or principles that have been invented, or discovered, by this or that would-be universal reformer.

They merely express, in general terms, actual relations springing from an existing class struggle, from a historical movement going on under our very eyes. The abolition of existing property relations is not at all a distinctive feature of Communism.

All property relations in the past have continually been subject to historical change consequent upon the change in historical conditions.

The French Revolution, for example, abolished feudal property in favor of bourgeois property.

The distinguishing feature of Communism is not the abolition of property generally, but the abolition of bourgeois property. But modern bourgeois private property is the final and most complete expression of the system of producing and appropriating products, that is based on class antagonisms, on the exploitation of the many by the few.

In this sense, the theory of the Communists may be summed up in the single sentence: abolition of private property.

We Communists have been reproached with the desire of abolishing the right of personally acquiring property as the fruit of a man's own labor, which property is alleged to be the groundwork of all personal freedom, activity, and independence.

Hard-won, self-acquired, self-earned property! Do you mean the property of the petty artisan and of the small peasant, a form of property that preceded the bourgeois form? There is no need to abolish that; the development of industry has to a great extent already destroyed it, and is still destroying it daily.

Or do you mean modern bourgeois private property?

But does wage-labor create any property for the laborer? Not a bit. It creates capital, i.e., that kind of property which exploits wage-labor, and which cannot increase except upon condition of begetting a new supply of wage-labor for fresh exploitation. Property, in its present form, is based on the antagonism of capital and wage-labor. Let us examine both sides of this antagonism.

To be a capitalist is to have not only a purely personal, but a social, status in production. Capital is a collective product, and only by the united action of many members, nay, in the last resort, only by the united action of all members of society, can it be set in motion.

Capital is, therefore, not a personal, it is a social power.

When, therefore, capital is converted into common property, into the property of all members of society, personal property is not thereby transformed into social property. It is only the social character of the property that is changed. It loses its class character.

Let us now take wage-labor.

The average price of wage-labor is the minimum wage, i.e., that quantum of the means of subsistence which is absolutely requisite to keep the laborer in bare existence as a laborer. What, therefore, the wage-laborer appropriates by means of his labor merely suffices to prolong and reproduce a bare existence. We by no means intend to abolish this personal appropriation of the products of labor, an appropriation that is made for the maintenance and reproduction of human life, and that leaves no surplus wherewith to command the labor of others. All that we want to do away with is the miserable character of this appropriation, under which the laborer lives merely to increase capital, and is allowed to live only insofar as the interest of the ruling class requires it.

In bourgeois society, living labor is but a means to increase accumulated labor. In Communist society, accumulated labor is but a means to widen, to enrich, to promote the existence of the laborer.

In bourgeois society, therefore, the past dominates the present; in Communist society, the present dominates the past. In bourgeois society capital is independent and has individuality, while the living person is dependent and has no individuality.

And the abolition of this state of things is called by the bourgeois abolition of individuality and freedom! And rightly so. The abolition of bourgeois individuality, bourgeois independence, and bourgeois freedom is undoubtedly aimed at.

By freedom is meant, under the present bourgeois conditions of production, free trade, free selling and buying.

But if selling and buying disappears, free selling and buying disappears also. This talk about free selling and buying, and all the other "brave words" of our bourgeoisie about freedom in general, have a meaning, if any, only in contrast with restricted selling and buying, with the fettered traders of the Middle Ages, but have no meaning when opposed to the Communistic abolition of buying and selling, of the bourgeois conditions of production, and of the bourgeoisie itself.

You are horrified at our intending to do away with private property. But in your existing society, private property is already done away with for nine-tenths of the population; its existence for the few is solely due to its nonexistence in the hands of those nine-tenths. You reproach us, therefore, with intending to do away with a form of property, the necessary condition for whose existence is the nonexistence of any property for the immense majority of society.

In one word, you reproach us with intending to do away with your property. Precisely so; that is just what we intend.

From the moment when labor can no longer be converted into capital, money, or rent, into a social power capable of being monopolized, i.e., from the moment when individual property can no longer be transformed into bourgeois property, into capital, from that moment, you say, individuality vanishes.

You must, therefore, confess that by "individual" you mean no other person than the bourgeois, than the middle-class owner of property. This person must, indeed, be swept out of the way, and made impossible.

Communism deprives no man of the power to appropriate the products of society; all that it does is to deprive him of the power to subjugate the labor of others by means of such appropriation. . . .

In short, the Communists everywhere support every revolutionary movement against the existing social and political order of things.

In all these movements they bring to the front, as the leading question in each, the property question, no matter what its degree of development at the time.

Finally, they labor everywhere for the union and agreement of the democratic parties of all countries.

The Communists disdain to conceal their views and aims. They openly declare that their ends can be attained only by the forcible overthrow of all existing social conditions. Let the ruling classes tremble at a Communistic revolution. The proletarians have nothing to lose but their chains. They have a world to win.

WORKING MEN OF ALL
COUNTRIES, UNITE!
(Pp. 221–33, 246.)

Hannah Arendt and Revolution

"If Marx helped in liberating the poor, then it was not by telling them that they were the living embodiments of some historical or other necessity, but by persuading them that poverty itself is a political, not a natural phenomenon, the result of violence and violation rather than of scarcity."[13] That analysis comes from *On Revolution* (1963), an important book by Hannah Arendt (1906–1975). Her point was not that Karl Marx had obviously spoken the whole truth on this or any other subject. For Arendt's career as a political philosopher gave her firsthand knowledge of the mixed results that come from revolutionary attempts to answer the question "Can I make society better?"

The only child of Jewish parents, Arendt was born in Hannover, Germany. She studied philosophy at the University of Heidelberg, writing a dissertation on "The Concept of Love in St. Augustine" and receiving her doctorate at the age of 22. When Hitler took power in 1933, Arendt emigrated to France. She was interned there after World War II began because she was a German national, but in 1941 she reached the United States, becoming an American citizen in 1950. Arendt taught in numerous universities, including the University of Chicago, Princeton, and the New School for Social Research, a New York center made famous by intellectuals like herself who fled Europe's totalitarian revolutions. Her most controversial book was *Eichmann in Jerusalem: A Report on the Banality of Evil* (1963), which resulted from her coverage of the trial of Adolf Eichmann as a Nazi war criminal. Her other influential works include *The Origins of Totalitarianism* (1951) and *The Human Condition* (1958). In these writings, Arendt used what she had learned from history to interpret the human propensity to employ violent revolution in attempting political change. During the

HANNAH ARENDT 1906–1975

summer of 1950, for example, Arendt had reached the following conclusion:

> Never has our future been more unpredictable, never have we depended so much on political forces that cannot be trusted to follow the rules of common sense and self-interest—forces that look like sheer insanity if judged by the standards of other centuries. It is as though mankind had divided itself between those who believe in human omnipotence (who think that everything is possible if one knows how to organize masses for it) and those for whom powerlessness has become the major experience of their lives.[14]

She tried to discern a middle way between these extremes, one that might make society better by cutting between the twentieth century's "reckless optimism and reckless despair" (p. vii).

Revolution as a Modern Phenomenon

"Wars and revolutions" observed Arendt, "have thus far determined the physiognomy of the twentieth century."[15] The nineteenth century's commitments to nationalism, capitalism, imperialism, communism, and other ideologies endangered the world, but twentieth-century developments have produced even greater peril: "a constellation that poses the threat of total annihilation through war against the hope for the emancipation of all mankind through revolution" (p. 1). The fate of the earth hangs in the balance.

Although wars and revolutions share violence in common, they are not always identical. Revolution is more modern, according to Arendt, and it is distinguished from war primarily because revolution is "bound up with the notion of freedom" (p. 2). Traditionally, freedom has not figured prominently in the justifications offered for war. Today that idea may be used to bolster justification for a nuclear arms race, but Arendt's view is that "the idea of freedom was introduced into the debate of the war question only after it had become quite obvious that we had reached a stage of technical development where the means of destruction were such as to exclude their rational use. In other words, freedom has appeared in this debate like a *deus ex machina* to justify what on rational grounds has become unjustifiable" (p. 2).

Freedom, however, has been an essential thrust behind the phenomenon of revolution, and this especially concerned Arendt. The power of the idea, and the possibility that freedom can be won through revolution, is such, Arendt believed, that "even if we should succeed in changing the physiognomy of this century to the point where it would no longer be a century of wars, it most certainly will remain a century of revolutions" (p. 8). An evaluation of revolution, then, must take into account whether and how revolution promotes freedom. But the problem is that "freedom" has multiple meanings, not just one. Before we can agree about revolution, we need to reflect on freedom as well.

What Arendt called "the modern concept of revolution" emerged in eighteenth-century America and France. It is, she wrote, "inextricably bound up with the notion that the course of history suddenly begins anew, that an entirely new story, a story never known or told before, is about to unfold" (p. 21). War produces change, but "revolutions . . . are not mere changes" (p. 13). They are both the effect and the cause of a conviction that fundamentally inhibiting conditions in society are neither necessary nor inevitable. The stage was set for revolution when "men began to doubt that poverty is inherent in the human condition, to doubt that the distinction between the few, who through circumstances or strength or fraud had succeeded in liberating themselves from the shackles of poverty, and the laboring poverty-stricken multitude was inevitable and eternal" (p. 15).

The new experience in history was the conviction that people had the power and the freedom to bring a new social order into being and no longer had to endure existing human conditions. The term "revolution" had been used before, but its previous meanings highlight Arendt's contention. Earlier, revolution signified cyclical movement, the recurrence of an established pattern. Even in the American revolution, the emphasis was on a similar theme, namely, restoration of lost rights. But the broad social and economic impact of the American and French revolutions advanced the idea that radically new conditions and freedoms were possible and even irresistible. New images, says Arendt, began "to cluster around the old metaphor and an entirely new vocabulary [was] introduced into political language" (p. 42).

Revolutions and the Goal of Freedom

The French Revolution captured world attention more than the American, a fact that Arendt lamented because the former "ended in disaster" (p. 49). The French Revolution lost its focus on freedom; in particular its leaders failed to give sufficient care to establishing forms of government that could sustain the liberty they espoused. Conscientious attention to that concern was the hallmark of the founding of the United States. But unfortunately such political details did not grip human imagination as much as the notion that revolution is an inevitably progressive drive. Marx's philosophy emphasized the latter theme, urging that revolution was part of a dialectical necessity that would result in human liberation. But, Arendt went on to observe, as Marx offered his view, the goals of revolution were redefined: "The role of revolution was no longer to liberate men from the oppression of their fellow men, let alone to found freedom, but to liberate the life process of society from the fetters of scarcity so that it could swell into a stream of abundance. Not freedom but abundance became now the aim of revolution" (p. 58). Marx, of course, might contest Arendt's interpretation, for he thought that freedom had everything to do with the eradication of scarcity. Here we see again how our understanding of crucial terms colors questions that quite literally may become matters of life and death.

Human life has always been plagued by poverty, and Arendt did not deplore Marx's passion to change that situation. She was convinced, however, that revolution was at best a problematic solution. "No revolution," she wrote, "has ever solved the 'social question' and liberated men from the predicament of want" (p. 108). More likely, the historical record shows, "every attempt to solve the social question with political means leads into terror, and . . . it is terror which sends revolutions to their doom" (p. 108). It is only a beginning, but a step beyond this dilemma can be taken, Arendt believed, if we will distinguish carefully between liberation and freedom and also between rebellion and revolution. Liberation from oppression and its impoverishment may not be possible without rebellion, an action that throws off established power. But "there is nothing more futile than rebellion and liberation unless they are followed by the constitution of the newly won freedom" (p. 141). This is where revolution, "the foundation of freedom" as Arendt called it, must do its work to establish the conditions that make liberty real.

Unfortunately, Arendt suggested, most revolutions ignore these distinctions. They aim not at the constitution of freedom but at liberation from oppressive socioeconomic conditions via a forced political solution. She recognized, however, that this thrust is understandable, for human motivation seems to be such that "liberation from necessity, because of its urgency, will always take precedence over the building of freedom" (p. 108). Nonetheless the building of freedom—preceded by careful thought about what freedom means—is precisely what must be accomplished if revolutionary means are to make society better. "In the contest that divides the world today and in which so much is at stake," Arendt summarized, "those will probably win who understand revolution" (p. 8). As you continue studying Arendt's views, in the following selection from *On Revolution*, see if you understand why she said that and whether you think events will prove her correct.

If there was a single event that shattered the bonds between the New World and the countries of the old Continent, it was the French Revolution, which, in the view of its contemporaries, might never have come to pass without the glorious example on the other side of the Atlantic. It was not the fact of revolution but its disastrous course and the collapse of the French republic which eventually led to the severance of the strong spiritual and political ties between America and Europe that had prevailed all through the seventeenth and eighteenth centuries. Thus, Condorcet's *Influence de la Révolution d'Amérique sur l'Europe*, published three years before the storming of the Bastille, was to mark, temporarily at least, the end and not the beginning of an Atlantic civilization. One is tempted to hope that the rift which occurred at the end of the eighteenth century is about to heal in the middle of the twentieth century, when it has become rather obvious that Western civilization has its last chance of survival in an Atlantic community; and among the signs to justify this hope is perhaps also the fact that since the Second World War historians have been more inclined to consider the Western world as a whole than they have been since the early nineteenth century.

Whatever the future may hold in store for us, the estrangement of the two continents after the eighteenth-century revolutions has remained a fact of great consequence. It was chiefly during this time that the New World lost its political significance in the eyes of the leading strata in Europe, that America ceased to be the land of the free and became almost exclusively the promised land of the poor. To be sure, the attitude of Europe's upper classes toward the alleged materialism and vulgarity of the New World was an almost automatic outgrowth of the social and cultural snobbism of the rising middle classes, and as such of no great importance. What mattered was that the European revolutionary tradition in the nineteenth century did not show more than a passing interest in the American Revolution or in the development of the American republic. In conspicuous contrast to the eighteenth century, when the political thought of the *philosophes*, long before the outbreak of an American Revolution, was attuned to events and institutions in the New World, revolutionary political thought in the nineteenth and twentieth centuries has proceeded as though there never had occurred a revolution in the New World and as though there never had been any American notions and experiences in the realm of politics and government worth thinking about.

In recent times, when revolution has become one of the most common occurrences in the political life of nearly all countries and continents, the failure to incorporate the American Revolution into the revolutionary tradition has boomeranged upon the foreign policy of the United States, which begins to pay an exorbitant price for worldwide ignorance and for native oblivion. The point is unpleasantly driven home when even revolutions on the American continent speak and act as though they knew by heart the texts of revolutions in France, in Russia, and in China, but had never heard of such a thing as an American Revolution. Less spectacular perhaps, but certainly no less real, are the consequences of the American counterpart to the world's ignorance, her own failure to remember that a revolution gave birth to the United States and that the republic was brought into existence by no "historical necessity" and no organic development, but by a deliberate act: the foundation of freedom. Failure to remember is largely responsible for the intense fear of revolution in this country, for it is precisely this fear that attests to the world at large how right they are to think of revolution only in terms of the French Revolution. Fear of revolution has been the hidden *leitmotif* of postwar American foreign policy in its desperate attempts at stabilization of the status quo, with the result that American power and prestige were used and misused to support obsolete and corrupt political regimes that long since had become objects of hatred and contempt among their own citizens.

Failure to remember and, with it, failure to understand have been conspicuous whenever, in rare moments, the hostile dialogue with Soviet Russia touched upon matters of principle. When we were told that by freedom we understood free enterprise, we did very little to dispel this monstrous falsehood, and all too often we have acted as though we too believed that it was wealth and abundance which were at stake in the postwar conflict between the "revolutionary" countries in the East and the West. Wealth and economic well-being, we have asserted, are the fruits of freedom, while we should have been the first to know that this kind of "happiness" was the blessing of this country prior to the Revolution, and that its cause was natural abundance under "mild government," and neither political freedom nor the unchained, unbridled "private initiative" of capitalism, which in the absence of natural wealth has led everywhere to unhappiness and mass poverty. Free enterprise, in other words, has been an unmixed blessing only in this country, and it is a minor blessing compared with the truly political freedoms, such as freedom of speech and thought, of assembly and association, even under the best conditions. Economic growth may one day turn out to be a curse rather than a good, and under no conditions can it either lead into freedom or constitute a proof for its existence. A competition between America and Russia, therefore, with regard to production and standards of living, trips to the moon and scientific discoveries, may be very interesting in many respects; its outcome may even be understood as a demonstration of the stamina and gifts of the two nations involved, as well as of the value of their different social manners and customs. There is only one question this outcome, whatever it may be, will never be able to decide, and that is which form of government is better, a tyranny or a free republic. Hence, in terms of the American Revolution, the response to the Communist bid to equal and surpass the Western countries in production of consumer goods and economic growth should have been to rejoice over the new good prospects opening up to the people of the Soviet Union and its satellites, to be relieved that at least the conquest of poverty on a worldwide scale could constitute an issue of common concern, and then to remind our opponents that serious conflicts would not rise out of the disparity between two economic systems but only out of the conflict between freedom and tyranny, between the institutions of liberty, born out of the triumphant victory of a revolution, and the various forms of domination (from Lenin's one-party dictatorship to Stalin's totalitarianism to Khrushchev's attempts at an enlightened despotism) which came in the aftermath of a revolutionary defeat.

Finally, it is perfectly true, and a sad fact indeed, that most so-called revolutions, far from achieving the *constitutio libertatis*, have not even been able to produce constitutional guarantees of civil rights and liberties, the blessings of "limited government," and there is no question that in our dealings with other nations and their governments we shall have to keep in mind that the distance between tyranny and constitutional, limited government is as great as, perhaps greater than, the distance between limited government and freedom. But these considerations, however great their practical relevance, should be no reason for us to mistake civil rights for political freedom, or to equate these preliminaries of civilized government with the very substance of a free republic. For political freedom, generally speaking, means the right "to be a participator in government," or it means nothing. (Pp. 217–21.)

Summary

This chapter concludes Part II, which has focused on the question "What should I do?" That topic led us to ask about our freedom to act and the place of rules in decision making. It also made us consider other factors—attitudes and rights, for example—that affect the ways we do and ought to act. Finally we addressed the issue of whether we can make society better. The diverse thinkers we encountered in this chapter think that society can be improved, but some are more cautious than others about how to implement

that affirmation. If we take the four as a group, the collective response to our question might be: "Yes, society can be improved, but this is much easier said than done." The intent behind that response is not to discourage attempts to improve society, nor is it to deny that we ought to make an effort in that direction. But the warning is to avoid thinking that there is some obvious and direct path for healing society's ills.

Machiavelli helps us understand power politics. Whether we judge his advice to be cynical, pessimistic, or simply realistic, he presents factors to reckon with if society is to improve. Malthus alerts us to the magnitude of social problems. Not only is this a function of the sheer number of people who exist, but we need to recognize that good intentions can have undesirable consequences. In this group of four, Karl Marx is the most optimistic. His program for political change and human betterment has affected the world immensely, but we must balance its obvious accomplishments by an assessment of the degree to which we think it has actually made life better. As we do so, the constant philosophical problem of how to define key terms—freedom, happiness, justice, and so on—and how to cope with disagreements about their meanings looms up again. Finally, Hannah Arendt suggests that failure to think clearly about these issues is partly what makes revolutions go awry. They lapse into terror when they try to force human society into a preconceived socioeconomic mold rather than promoting liberty against tyranny of every kind.

Can I make society better? That still is the question, and at the end of the chapter we are back at the beginning. The thinkers we have studied here give a variety of responses. More than answering the question finally, however, they restate it for your further reflection. One of philosophy's roles, as we have noted before, is to make us reconsider and constantly revise what we think is possible. What comes next may modify your reactions further, for it is time to move on to Part III and to ask "What may I hope?" After all, if philosophy is to be more than abstract inquiry, we want it to lead us somewhere, to give us some help as we work to do something about our future. If it can assist us in that way, we will understand more about philosophy's worth.

GLOSSARY

bourgeoisie in Marx's political philosophy, the social class that controls capital and the means of economic production, and thereby controls the conditions of life for the working classes. Marx said that the bourgeoisie exploit the labor of the **proletariat** and that the two "classes" are natural enemies.

capitalism the type of economic system composed of privately owned enterprises in competition in a free market, supported by investments of capital from financial backers and depending on the labor power of a working class to produce the actual goods. In the Marxist analysis, labor power is purchased for a price (i.e., wages) dictated by the market value of the product and the interest of business owners in maximizing profits for themselves and for their investors. According to Marx, this arrangement tends to drive wages down to subsistence level.

"class antagonism" in Marx's revolutionary theory, the natural antipathy between the bourgeoisie and the proletariat, as the former exploits the labor of the latter.

communism Marx's proposal for a classless society, consisting of a powerful centralized state that would own all the means of production in the name of the working classes and would ensure the fair distribution of goods and services to all its citizens, thereby eliminating the conditions of exploitation and privilege that sustain class antagonism.

demographic relating to the statistical study of human aggregates or collectives, of which Malthus is a significant early figure.

"deus ex machina" an element, often specious, that is introduced into an argument to explain away what had appeared to be an insurmountable difficulty; Arendt comments that the notion of freedom serves just such a function in modern justifications of warfare.

dialectical logic the logical model of historical progress taken over from Hegel by Marx and Engels: The schematic outline of such a logic is that a particular object, event, or state of affairs (the "thesis") calls forth its own denial, negation, or opposite (the "antithesis"), and the tension between thesis and antithesis is resolved by a "synthesis," which provides a new thesis for the next phase of the logical progression. Marx substituted the structure of class antagonism into this formula to show how history was composed of a perpetual clash along socioeconomic lines, whose synthesis or resolution would be the establishment of the communist state.

expediency the principle that "the end justifies any means," which Machiavelli believed should form the basis of the practical deliberations of a person in political power; that is, the calculation of how a given state of affairs might serve as a means to the ruler's aim of increasing and consolidating his own power.

history the chronological development of human societies, which Hegel and Marx believed followed a regular, comprehensible pattern of evolution. See **dialectical logic.**

"Machiavellian" referring to the doctrines of the Italian philosopher Niccolò Machiavelli, or to any point of view resembling his. Machiavelli believed that the world of political administration is one characterized by a naked struggle for power at any cost and by any means, so that the art of politics must include the arts of deception and manipulation and its practice must be characterized by the quality of ruthlessness.

"means of production" in Marxist economic theory, the material, tools, real estate, and capital investments that are necessary for the production of goods and commodities. Marx believed that social injustice arises whenever a large class of people, being excluded from sharing in the ownership and control of these means, must themselves become part of the means of production by selling their labor power to the owners.

power the ability to influence and control the course of events and the behavior of others. For Marx this consists in a monopoly over the means of production. For Machiavelli, power was the ultimate aim of any ruler, an end that justified any means.

progress the concept of the betterment of the human condition through the process of history. Marx held that progress toward a communist utopia was inevitable, while Malthus believed that the problem of population provided a perhaps insurmountable obstacle to human advancement.

proletariat in Marx's analysis of economic class antagonism, the working class, or those excluded from ownership of the means of production.

Providence the theological principle introduced by Malthus to explain how the difficulties for the betterment of the human condition entailed by his theory of population could be consistent with the existence of a benevolent God. God has built this difficulty into the relation between humankind and the world, Malthus believed, to motivate human ingenuity and industry in cultivating and making the fullest use of the natural resources people find around them.

quantify to bring under the category of quantity, to render in mathematical terms for the purposes of measurement and analysis. Demographics, for instance, represents the quantification of sociological data.

revolution the phenomenon of political upheaval and the displacement of existing political orders, often violent, as Arendt notes, and motivated by the ideal of greater freedom for a greater number than was possible under the old regime.

surplus overproduction, surfeit, a larger amount than necessary or desirable; Malthus's demographic theory held that human societies tend to produce a surplus of human beings, and he traced many fundamental issues of philosophy to this purported fact.

utopia a fictional, ideal state, society, or means of organizing social life that effects the ideal aims of universal harmony, universal satisfaction, and so on.

violence the use of physical force by one person or group against another. For Arendt, the justification of violence is a crucial philosophical problem facing the revolutionary.

STUDY QUESTIONS

1. Is Machiavelli cynical or merely realistic when he advises leaders about the means and ends of politics?

2. Can Machiavelli's advice help you to make society better? If so, how? If not, why?

3. Is Malthus's theory about population still valid, or have recent developments outmoded it?

4. How does your response to Malthus affect your thinking on how we might improve society?

5. Do you think that the obviously wide impact of Marx's thought on political history proves that his views are correct?

6. How do you assess the greatest strengths and greatest weaknesses of Marx's outlook?

7. Do you agree with Arendt on the importance of revolution as a force in the modern world? On the whole, do you think that revolutions have improved the human situation?

8. What is Arendt's view about the relationship between freedom and revolution? How do you define those terms and their connections?

9. If you could do one thing to make society better, what would it be and how would you defend your decision?

10. As you survey the philosophers discussed in this chapter, do you detect any changes in your own thought about whether or how you can make society better?

11. Having reached the end of Part II in this book, how do you respond to the question, "What should I do?"

NOTES

[1] Niccolò Machiavelli, *The Prince*, trans. Luigi Ricci, rev. E. R. P. Vincent (New York: Modern Library, 1940), p. 53.

[2] Niccolò Machiavelli, *The Discourses*, trans. Christian E. Detmold (New York: Modern Library, 1940), p. 101.

[3] Machiavelli, *The Prince*, p. 61.

[4] Thomas Robert Malthus, *An Essay on the Principle of Population*, ed. Philip Appleman (New York: W. W. Norton, 1976) p. 20.

[5] Karl Marx, "Towards a Critique of Hegel's *Philosophy of Right: Introduction*," in *Karl Marx: Selected Writings*, ed., David McLellan (Oxford: Oxford University Press, 1977), p. 64. All quotations from Marx are in this edition.

[6] Karl Marx, "Theses on Feuerbach," p. 158.

[7] Karl Marx and Friedrich Engels, *Communist Manifesto*, p. 246.

[8] Karl Marx, "Preface to *A Critique of Political Economy*, p. 389.

[9] Karl Marx, *The German Ideology*, p. 161.

[10] Marx, *Communist Manifesto*, p. 223.

[11] Karl Marx, "Critique of the Gotha Programme," p. 569.

[12] Marx, *Communist Manifesto*, pp. 230–31.

[13] Hannah Arendt, *On Revolution* (New York: Viking Press, 1971), p. 57. Copyright © 1963 by Hannah Arendt. Reprinted by permission of Viking Penguin, Inc.

[14] Hannah Arendt, *The Origins of Totalitarianism*, rev. ed. (New York: Harcourt Brace Jovanovich, 1973), p. vii.

[15] Arendt, *On Revolution*, p. 1. Copyright © 1963 by Hannah Arendt. Reprinted by permission of Viking Penguin, Ltd.

III

WHAT MAY I HOPE?

It was by seeking, by probing, silence that I began to discover the perils and power of the word.

ELIE WIESEL
"Why I Write"

CHAPTER ELEVEN

Does God Exist?

When I ask "Do I have rights in society?" or "Can I make society better?" or many of the other questions of philosophy, a natural response is "I hope so." To hope for something is to want it. At times **hope** involves the anticipation or expectation that we will get what we want, but we also realize that hope is different from certainty. You may hope to be successful in business, but your hope indicates that you understand that you may not be. What does occur may be so contrary to your desire that you reach the point of "hoping against hope," which means that you are sustaining your desire even though the likelihood of fulfillment is remote. But when circumstances turn far enough against desire, we may reach a point of hopelessness.

When Immanuel Kant identified "What may I hope?" as one of philosophy's fundamental questions, he recognized a decisive feature of human existence. Humanity possesses purposeful awareness. We exist in the present and with a past, but we also move into the future. A sense of possibility is an essential part of our lives, but mere possibility is a fickle companion. Even if we are free to act, we neither know nor completely control what comes to be. The future attracts; it also makes us anxious. This makes us beings who hope, creatures who long for things that we may never obtain.

What we hope for can vary tremendously. Sometimes we hope for the very concrete: a better job, for example, or a new car or a good grade on a philosophy paper. Even when these hopes are fulfilled, however, they are rarely ends in themselves. Typically we hope for particular things because they are the means to fulfill a larger, if less articulated, aim. Where hope is concerned, Kant and other philosophers are especially interested in the larger dimensions of hope, which involve questions such as "Can my life make sense?" and "How should I deal with evil and death?" and "Does God exist?" What is at stake is the degree to which we are entitled to trust that human existence is significant.

We know that the questions that concern human beings cover a vast area. They range from a curiosity about life's details to reflection about the nature of the universe. We come to realize that some things appear and disappear while others last. We note how many ways of life there are, some more powerful, important, and valuable than others. What is ultimately real and lasting? How did this world of ours come to be? How do our lives fit into the scheme of things? The motives behind such questions vary considerably, but they give rise to the issue of God's existence. This emerges from our desire for understanding and our hope to fathom the nature of reality.

Most people do not consider philosophy when they think about God. Usually they are attracted or repelled by some religious tradition; they form their opinions about God from that experience, or they may be indifferent to religion, not caring to argue about God. Because philosophers are interested in discovering not only what we can know and what we ought to do but also what the reasonable boundaries of hope may be, they often analyze religious claims and test beliefs about God. Such an inquiry frequently asks whether there is a valid proof for God's existence. Whether the answer is positive, negative, or undecided, the issue of hope intertwines with the issue of God.

In considering the question of God's existence, we begin with Anselm and his controversial **ontological argument.** Staying within the medieval tradition, in which the question of the existence of **God** was central to philosophy, we turn next to Thomas Aquinas and his alternative to Anselm's argument. From their disagreement, we learn that not all philosophers who affirm God are of one mind. When we encounter Friedrich Nietzsche, the last philosopher to be discussed in this chapter, we enter a very different world. Nietzsche was radically skeptical about God's existence, but he nevertheless took the issue of God to be crucial. His views might not have been possible without the hard questions that David Hume had raised before him. If the medieval age generally accepted God, Hume (and others) eroded that conventional wisdom. One point to note in this variety of views is that none of the four philosophers would be rendered speechless by the others. They recognize the existence, even the necessity, of different points of view. Collectively, then, their alternative views should help us be more precise about the question "Does God exist?" and perhaps they can help you to form a more satisfying answer to that question as well.

Anselm and the Ontological Argument

Saint Anselm (1033–1109) was born in Aosta, a town in northern Italy. At an early age he decided to give his life to the Christian faith, and he did not swerve from his plan. Disciplined and bright, he entered the Benedictine order in 1060 and in 1078 became the leader of the monastery at Bec in Normandy, which was one of the great centers for learning at the time. Later Anselm went to England, where he became the Archbishop of Canterbury in 1093, serving in that position until his death. Throughout his career as a church leader, Anselm wrote influential works in philosophy and theology. In fact, he is best known because he tried to formulate "a single argument which would require no other for its proof than itself alone, and alone would suffice to demonstrate that God truly exists."[1] This argument is known as "the ontological argument," because it does not start by pointing out some aspect of our world or our experience. It simply begins by considering God's nature. Anselm's formulation intrigued philosophers and theologians for centuries, and it still does today. Others, such as Descartes and Spinoza, offered new versions of this argument in later eras. But Anselm began it all by claiming that if we consider God's nature carefully, we will see that God must exist. Specifically, he held that we will see that God necessarily exists if we inspect the following definition of God: "Thou art a being than which nothing greater can be conceived" (p. 7).

No one literally sees God, for God differs from all objects in the world. Thus, our questions include: What is God like? How can we approach God? Is there any way to prove that God either does or does not exist? Others besides Anselm formulated arguments for God's existence, but Anselm, Augustine, and those in this Platonic tradition are unique in asserting that if we merely reflect on the idea

ANSELM   1033–1109

Everything except God can be conceived not to exist, but the definition of a being "than which nothing greater can be conceived" cannot be fulfilled unless God exists. It follows, Anselm claims, that "no one who understands what God is can conceive that God does not exist" (p. 10).

In other words, you can claim that you do not understand the idea of God. But if you claim to understand the idea, you cannot deny God's existence. To possess real existence is part of the very idea of "that than which nothing greater can be conceived." If you understand that God is that being than which nothing greater exists, you cannot conceive of God as not existing. Having recognized the special qualities of God's nature, Anselm moves on to consider God in relation to time. Since nothing is greater than God, no time or place can contain him. In fact, God is the truth and light through whom all things are understood. Following this meditation, Anselm actually shifts his definition. God becomes "not only that than which a greater cannot be conceived but thou art a being greater than which nothing can be conceived" (p. 22). Anselm first attempts to prove God's existence by considering the special qualities that make God unique. But as he does so, he discovers that God's nature not only entails God's existence but also places God beyond the limits of our finite comprehension. God has neither past nor future existence, for example, but only present existence. If we grant this characteristic of God, is such a God really the kind of being our minds can fully comprehend?

Anselm's Reply to Gaunilo

Anselm's ontological argument was controversial from the outset. Some of the most significant criticisms brought against it came from one of Anselm's contemporaries, a monk named Gaunilo. If Anselm's argument were sound, objected Gaunilo, presumably we

of God, on what God is like, such an effort alone will convince us that God must exist. Some critics argue that our ability to think about God proves only that the idea of God exists in our minds, not that God exists in fact. Anselm disagrees. He argues that in God's case alone, you do not first think about God and then decide whether God exists outside your thoughts as well. God, argues Anselm, "cannot be conceived not to exist" (p. 8). God must exist both in our understanding and in reality. Albert Camus, as we will see, takes a quite different approach and denies God's existence. But it is important to note that Anselm's argument hinges on his definition of God:

> That than which nothing greater can be conceived, cannot exist in the understanding alone. For, suppose it exists in the understanding alone: then it can be conceived to exist in reality, which is greater. (P. 8.)

could prove the existence of many things—a perfect island, for example—merely by thinking about them. For nothing, according to this "logic," could be perfect unless it existed. But such reasoning would be absurd, Gaunilo argued, for there is a fundamental difference between an idea of some thing and that thing's existence. Having stated his ontological argument in a work entitled *Proslogium*, (c. 1078) Anselm added an "Appendix" that included Gaunilo's response "In Behalf of the Fool" (the fool is one who has the idea of God and yet denies God's existence) plus Anselm's answer to Gaunilo's objections. Crucial to this debate was the issue of whether the idea of God can exist in the mind if the object does not exist in reality. Speaking for "the fool," Gaunilo noted that "I have in my understanding all manner of unreal objects, having absolutely no existence in themselves."[2] For instance, Superman is universally recognized and understood, but that does not mean that he exists except as a fictional character. Anselm disputed Gaunilo's objection, but whether we accept that rejoinder depends on whether we agree that God alone is so unique that the concept of God and the existence of God cannot be separated as can concept and existence in the case of all other objects. The idea of God alone, writes Anselm, is such that:

> I cannot conceive of it in another way than by understanding it, that is, by comprehending in my knowledge its existence in reality. (P. 146.)

Real objects are one thing, and the understanding itself by which objects are grasped is another, Anselm admits. But what is special about God is that this distinction does not apply. *If* you understand God, then to conceive of God is enough to prove to you that God must exist in reality and cannot exist as an idea alone. Hence, any object you can conceive to exist but which does not exist in fact cannot be the being than which a greater

cannot be conceived. The latter must exist in reality, says Anselm, for "if such a being can be conceived to exist, necessarily it does exist" (p. 154). Conversely, if it can be conceived not to exist, it is not God. But now the major question arises: Is it really possible to conceive of God fully?

We hear statements of all kinds about God. At least to that extent, a "being than which a greater cannot be conceived" can be in our understanding. Still, do you fully understand what you hear? If you did conceive of God completely, you would understand that God has to exist. But just how full is your understanding of God? Most unreal objects can be understood without assuming their existing in fact. Anselm never denies that. But if "understanding," as Anselm defines it, means comprehending in knowledge an object's real existence, then there are many questions to ask about whether we understand the idea of God fully or only to a certain degree. Anselm settles on a compromise.

> So, when one says, "that than which nothing greater is conceivable," undoubtedly what is heard is conceivable and intelligible, although that being itself, than which a greater is inconceivable, cannot be conceived or understood. (P. 168.)

Anselm modifies the early formulation of his argument for God's existence into a challenge. Whoever denies that God exists must claim to understand fully and to conceive of "that than which a greater is inconceivable" (God). But this is a being whose nonexistence is impossible and also a being who, in the last analysis cannot be fully conceived or completely understood. Thus, you may say that you cannot conceive of God fully, which Anselm admits. But you cannot claim to have understood fully the phrase "that being than which nothing greater can exist" and still deny God's existence. That conclusion holds, Anselm reiterates, partly because in this case alone the very idea of "that than which nothing greater can be conceived" involves necessary existence. However, as his argument progresses, Anselm's conclusion also rests on his decision that God's uniqueness, which makes God's existence necessary, is also that which makes it impossible to comprehend God fully. Ideas of God are in our minds, and necessary existence may be included as part of one of those concepts. But it is impossible for anyone to claim a full comprehension of God.

Normally, of course, we have no trouble conceiving of objects. But as we consider God, Anselm wants us to realize that we face special, even unique, problems. God is said to be infinite, outside time and space, perfect, or even changeless. But the things we normally think about are finite objects, objects that move in space and time, subject to flaws or imperfections, constantly changing. Since our minds are not suited to comprehend such unusual attributes as God possesses, it is hard to say that we conceive of God if God's exceptional nature makes divinity different from all other objects. We may know some things about God, then, but it is difficult if not impossible to claim that we have fully conceived of such a divinity.

What Did Anselm Prove?

Philosophers are still arguing over just what, if anything, Anselm's argument "proves." That the debate still rages indicates that Anselm's argument is not the indubitable proof he hoped it would be. On the other hand, his own analysis of the argument concludes that God is beyond full comprehension. So you might say that Anselm did show that one cannot disprove God's existence easily, because "the greatest being that can be conceived" in fact transcends final conception. If Anselm's argument has demonstrated only this much, it has shown us something. We know more about God at the end of the discussion than we did at the beginning. The only real fool is the one who thinks it is easy to disprove God's existence, because he or she has not realized how God transcends our final conception.

What about our original question "Does God exist?" We began by saying that people believe in God's existence or nonexistence for many reasons. Some have personal experiences that convince them to accept one conclusion or the other. Others become involved in religions or groups whose devotees or doctrines persuade them. Nothing is illegitimate about such processes, as long as individuals state the grounds for their personal beliefs or disbeliefs. But philosophers are interested in whether there are any "valid arguments" that form a universally convincing proof for all who consider them. As far as evidence and logical validity go, can we be certain of God's existence as a matter of general knowledge?

In the final analysis, Anselm suggests something like this: you may take the idea of God and consider it in your mind. As you do so, you should notice that it is not like other ideas. The more you consider the characteristics that God must have in order to be "that than which a greater cannot be conceived," the more you should realize that God will elude full human comprehension. Our minds can think about God, but they cannot completely comprehend such a divinity. To learn how difficult it is for our minds to deal with God is to learn something significant about God, as well as about the limits of human understanding. And if Anselm has not silenced the doubter, at least he has shown that it is no easy matter to deny God's existence. In fact, the same difficulties that make it hard to prove God's existence make it equally impossible to disprove God's existence with any certainty. Anselm's proof may not be conclusive, but see if your insight is not expanded by considering it. Where God is concerned, this may be all we can ask.

The following selections come from

Anselm's *Proslogium* and take their cue from the biblical theme, "The fool hath said in his heart there is no God." Anselm wants to ask if this denial is possible.

TRULY THERE IS A GOD, ALTHOUGH THE FOOL HATH SAID IN HIS HEART, "THERE IS NO GOD." And so, Lord, do thou, who dost give understanding to faith, give me, so far as thou knowest it to be profitable, to understand that thou art as we believe; and that thou art that which we believe. And, indeed, we believe that thou art a being than which nothing greater can be conceived. Or is there no such nature, since the fool hath said in his heart, there is no God? (Psalms 14:1). But, at any rate, this very fool, when he hears of this being of which I speak—a being than which nothing greater can be conceived—understands what he hears, and what he understands is in his understanding; although he does not understand it to exist.

For, it is one thing for an object to be in the understanding, and another to understand that the object exists. When a painter first conceives of what he will afterward perform, he has it in his understanding, but he does not yet understand it to be, because he has not yet performed it. But after he has made the painting, he both has it in his understanding and he understands that it exists, because he has made it.

Hence, even the fool is convinced that something exists in the understanding, at least, than which nothing greater can be conceived. For, when he hears of this, he understands it. And whatever is understood, exists in the understanding. And assuredly that, than which nothing greater can be conceived, cannot exist in the understanding alone. For, suppose it exists in the understanding alone: then it can be conceived to exist in reality; which is greater.

Therefore, if that, than which nothing greater can be conceived, exists in the understanding alone, the very being, than which nothing greater can be conceived, is one, than which a greater can be conceived.

But obviously this is impossible. Hence, there is no doubt that there exists a being, than which nothing greater can be conceived, and it exists both in the understanding and in reality.

GOD CANNOT BE CONCEIVED NOT TO EXIST.— GOD IS THAT, THAN WHICH NOTHING GREATER CAN BE CONCEIVED.—THAT WHICH CAN BE CONCEIVED NOT TO EXIST IS NOT GOD. And it assuredly exists so truly, that it cannot be conceived not to exist. For, it is possible to conceive of a being which cannot be conceived not to exist; and this is greater than one which can be conceived not to exist. Hence, if that, than which nothing greater can be conceived, can be conceived not to exist, it is not that, than which nothing greater can be conceived. But this is an irreconcilable contradiction. There is, then, so truly a being than which nothing greater can be conceived to exist, that it cannot even be conceived not to exist; and this being thou art, O Lord, our God.

So truly, therefore, dost thou exist, O Lord, my God, that thou canst not be conceived not to exist; and rightly. For, if a mind could conceive of a being better than thee, the creature would rise above the Creator; and this is most absurd. And, indeed, whatever else there is, except thee alone, can be conceived not to exist. To thee alone, therefore, it belongs to exist more truly than all other beings, and hence in a higher degree than all others. For, whatever else exists does not exist so truly, and hence in a less degree it belongs to it to exist. Why, then, has the fool said in his heart, there is no God (Psalms 14:1), since it is so evident, to a rational mind, that thou dost exist in the highest degree of all? Why, except that he is dull and a fool?

HOW THE FOOL HAS SAID IN HIS HEART WHAT CANNOT BE CONCEIVED.—A THING MAY BE CONCEIVED IN TWO WAYS: (1) WHEN THE WORD SIGNIFYING IT IS CONCEIVED; (2) WHEN THE THING ITSELF IS UNDERSTOOD. AS FAR AS THE WORD GOES, GOD CAN BE CONCEIVED NOT TO EXIST; IN REALITY HE CANNOT. But how has the fool said in his heart what he could not conceive; or how is it that he could not conceive what he said in his heart? since it is the same to say in the heart, and to conceive.

But, if really, nay, since really, he both conceived, because he said in his heart; and did not say in his heart, because he could not conceive; there is more than one way in which a thing is said in the heart or conceived. For, in one sense, an object is conceived, when the word signifying it is conceived; and in another, when the very entity, which the object is, is understood.

In the former sense, then, God can be conceived not to exist; but in the latter, not at all. For no one who understands what fire and water are can conceive fire to be water, in accordance with the nature of the facts themselves, although this is possible according to the words. So, then, no one who understands what God is can conceive that God does not exist; although he says these words in his heart, either without any, or with some foreign, signification. For, God is that than which a greater cannot be conceived. And he who thoroughly understands this, assuredly understands that this being so truly exists, that not even in concept can it be nonexistent. Therefore, he who understands that God so exists, cannot conceive that he does not exist.[3]

IN BEHALF OF THE FOOL (A REPLY TO ANSELM BY GAUNILO)

1. If one doubts or denies the existence of a being of such a nature that nothing greater than it can be conceived, he receives this answer:

The existence of this being is proved, in the first place, by the fact that he himself, in his doubt or denial regarding this being, already has it in his understanding; for in hearing it spoken of he understands what is spoken of. It is proved, therefore, by the fact that what he understands must exist not only in his understanding, but in reality also.

And the proof of this is as follows. It is a greater thing to exist both in the understanding and in reality than to be in the understanding alone. And if this being is in the understanding alone, whatever has even in the past existed in reality will be greater than this being. And so that which was greater than all beings will be less than some being, and will not be greater than all: which is a manifest contradiction.

And hence, that which is greater than all, already proved to be in the understanding, must exist not only in the understanding, but also in reality: for otherwise it will not be greater than all other beings.

2. The fool might make this reply:

This being is said to be in my understanding already, only because I understand what is said. Now could it not with equal justice be said that I have in my understanding all manner of unreal objects, having absolutely no existence in themselves, because I understand these things if one speaks of them, whatever they may be?

Unless indeed it is shown that this being is of such a character that it cannot be held in concept like all unreal objects, or objects whose existence is uncertain: and hence I am not able to conceive of it when I hear of it, or to hold it in concept; but I must understand it and have it in my understanding; because, it seems, I cannot conceive of it in any other way than by understanding it, that is, by comprehending in my knowledge its existence in reality.

But if this is the case, in the first place there will be no distinction between what has precedence in time—namely, the having of an object in the understanding—and what is subsequent in time—namely, the understanding that an object exists; as in the example of the picture, which exists first in the mind of the painter, and afterward in his work.

Moreover, the following assertion can hardly be accepted: that this being, when it is spoken of and heard of, cannot be conceived not to exist in the way in which even God can be conceived not to exist. For if this is impossible, what was the object of this argument against one who doubts or denies the existence of such a being?

Finally, that this being so exists that it cannot be perceived by an understanding convinced of its own indubitable existence, unless this being is afterward conceived of—this should be proved to me by an indisputable argument, but not by that which you have advanced: namely, that what I understand, when I hear it, already is in my understanding. For thus in my understanding, as I still think, could be all sorts of things whose existence is uncertain, or which do not exist at all, if someone whose words I should understand mentioned them. And so much the more if I should be deceived, as often happens, and believe in them: though I do not yet believe in the being whose existence you would prove.

3. Hence, your example of the painter who already has in his understanding what he is to paint cannot agree with this argument. For the picture, before it is made, is contained in the artificer's art itself; and any such thing, existing in the art of an artificer, is nothing but a part of his understanding itself. A joiner, St. Augustine says, when he is about to make a box in fact, first has it in his art. The box which is made in fact is not life; but the box which exists in his art is life. For the artificer's soul lives, in which all these things are, before they are produced. Why, then, are these things life in the living soul of the artificer, unless because they are nothing else than the knowledge or understanding of the soul itself?

With the exception, however, of those facts which are known to pertain to the mental nature, whatever, on being heard and thought out by the understanding, is perceived to be real, undoubtedly that real object is one thing, and the understanding itself, by which the object is grasped, is another. Hence, even if it were true that there is a being than which a greater is inconceivable: yet to this being, when heard of and understood, the not-yet-created picture in the mind of the painter is not analogous.

4. Let us notice also the point touched on above, with regard to this being which is greater than all which can be conceived, and which, it is said, can be none other than God himself. I, so far as actual knowledge of the object, either from its specific or general character, is concerned, am as little able to conceive of this being when I hear of it, or to have it in my understanding, as I am to conceive of or understand God himself: whom, indeed, for this very reason I can conceive not to exist. For I do not know that reality itself which God is, nor can I form a conjecture of that reality from some other like reality. For you yourself assert that that reality is such that there can be nothing else like it.

For, suppose that I should hear something said of a man absolutely unknown to me, of whose very existence I was unaware. Through that special or general knowledge by which I know what man is, or what men are, I could conceive of him also, according to the reality itself, which man is. And yet it would be possible, if the person who told me of him deceived me, that the man himself, of whom I conceived, did not exist; since that reality according to which I conceived of him, though a no less indisputable fact, was not that man, but any man.

Hence, I am not able, in the way in which I should have this unreal being in concept or in understanding, to have that being of which you speak in concept or in understanding, when I hear the word *God* or the words, *a being greater than all other beings.* For I can conceive of the man according to a fact that is real and familiar to me: but of God, or a being greater than all others, I could not conceive at all, except merely according to the word. And an object can hardly or never be conceived according to the word alone.

For when it is so conceived, it is not so much the word itself (which is, indeed, a real thing—that is, the sound of the letters and syllables) as the signification of the word, when heard, that is conceived. But it is not conceived as by one who knows what is generally signified by the word; by whom, that is, it is conceived according to a reality and in true conception alone. It is conceived as by a man who does not know the object, and conceives of it only in accordance with the movement of his mind produced by hearing the word, the mind attempting to image for itself the signification of the word that is heard. And it would be surprising if in the reality of fact it could ever attain to this.

Thus . . . this being is also in my understanding, when I hear and understand a person who says that there is a being greater than all conceivable beings. So much for the assertion that this supreme nature already is in my understanding. . . .

6. For example: it is said that somewhere in the ocean is an island, which, because of the difficulty, or rather the impossibility, of discovering what does not exist, is called the lost island. And they say that this island has an inestimable wealth of all manner of riches and delicacies in greater abundance than is told of the Islands of the Blest; and that having no owner or inhabitant, it is more excellent than all other countries, which are inhabited by mankind, in the abundance with which it is stored.

Now if someone should tell me that there is such an island, I should easily understand his words, in which there is no difficulty. But suppose that he went on to say, as if by a logical inference: "You can no longer doubt that this island which is more excellent than all lands exists somewhere, since you have no doubt that it is in your understanding. And since it is more excellent not to be in the understanding alone, but to exist both in the understanding and in reality, for this reason it must exist. For if it does not exist, any land which really exists will be more excellent than it; and so the island already understood by you to be more excellent will not be more excellent."

If a man should try to prove to me by such reasoning that this island truly exists, and that its existence should no longer be doubted, either I should believe that he was jesting, or I know not which I ought to regard as the greater fool: myself, supposing that I should allow this proof; or him, if he should suppose that he had established with any certainty the existence of this island. For he ought to show first that the hypothetical excellence of this island exists as a real and indubitable fact, and in no wise as any unreal object, or one whose existence is uncertain, in my understanding.

7. This . . . is the answer the fool could make to the arguments urged against him. When he is assured in the first place that this being is so great that its nonexistence is not even conceivable, and that this in turn is proved on no other ground than the fact that otherwise it will not be greater than all things, the fool may make the same answer, and say:

When did I say that any such being exists in reality, that is, a being greater than all others?—that on this ground it should be proved to me that it also exists in reality to such a degree that it cannot even be conceived not to exist? Whereas in the first place it should be in some way proved that a nature which is higher, that is, greater and better, than all other natures, exists; in order that from this we may then be able to prove all attributes which necessarily the being that is greater and better than all possesses.

Moreover, it is said that the nonexistence of this being is inconceivable. It might better be said, perhaps, that its nonexistence, or the possibility of its nonexistence, is unintelligible. For according to the true meaning of the word, unreal objects are unintelligible. Yet their existence is conceivable in the way in which the fool conceived of the nonexistence of God. I am most certainly aware of my own existence; but I know, nevertheless, that my nonexistence is possible. As to that supreme being, moreover, which God is, I understand without any doubt both his existence, and the impossibility of his nonexistence. Whether, however, so long as I am most positively aware of my existence, I can conceive of my nonexistence, I am not sure. But if I can, why can I not conceive of the nonexistence of whatever else I know with the same certainty? If, however, I cannot, God will not be the only being of which it can be said, it is impossible to conceive of his nonexistence.[4]

ANSELM'S REPLY TO GAUNILO

It was a fool against whom the argument of my Proslogium was directed. Seeing, however, that the author of these objections is by no means a fool, and is a Catholic, speaking in behalf of the fool, I think it sufficient that I answer the Catholic.

A GENERAL REFUTATION OF GAUNILO'S ARGUMENT. IT IS SHOWN THAT A BEING THAN WHICH A GREATER CANNOT BE CONCEIVED EXISTS IN REALITY. You say—whosoever you may be, who say that a fool is capable of making these statements—that a being than which a greater cannot be conceived is not in the understanding in any other sense than that in which a being that is altogether inconceivable in terms of reality, is in the understanding. You say that the inference that this being exists in reality, from the fact that it is in the understanding, is no more just than the inference that a lost island most certainly exists, from the fact that when it is described the hearer does not doubt that it is in his understanding.

But I say: if a being than which a greater is inconceivable is not understood or conceived, and is not in the understanding or in concept, certainly either God is not a being than which a greater is inconceivable, or else he is not understood or conceived, and is not in the understanding or in concept. But I call on your faith and conscience to attest that this is most false. Hence, that than which a greater cannot be conceived is truly understood and conceived, and is in the understanding and in concept. Therefore either the grounds on which you try to controvert me are not true, or else the inference which you think to base logically on those grounds is not justified.

But you hold, moreover, that supposing that a being than which a greater cannot be conceived is understood, it does not follow that this being is in the understanding; nor, if it is in the understanding, does it therefore exist in reality.

In answer to this, I maintain positively: if that being can be even conceived to be, it must exist in reality. For that than which a greater is inconceivable cannot be conceived except as without beginning. But whatever can be conceived to exist, and does not exist, can be conceived to exist through a beginning. Hence what can be conceived to exist, but does not exist, is not the being than which a greater cannot be conceived. Therefore, if such a being can be conceived to exist, necessarily it does exist.

Furthermore: if it can be conceived at all, it must exist. For no one who denies or doubts the existence of a being than which a greater is inconceivable, denies or doubts that if it did exist, its nonexistence, either in reality or in the understanding, would be impossible. For otherwise it would not be a being than which a greater cannot be conceived. But as to whatever can be conceived, but does not exist—if there were such a being, its nonexistence, either in reality or in the understanding, would be possible. Therefore if a being than which a greater is inconceivable can be even conceived, it cannot be nonexistent.

But let us suppose that it does not exist, even if it can be conceived. Whatever can be conceived, but does not exist, if it existed, would not be a being than which a greater is inconceivable. If, then, there were a being a greater than which is inconceivable, it would not be a being than which a greater is inconceivable: which is most absurd. Hence, it is false to deny that a being than which a greater cannot be conceived exists, if it can be even conceived; much the more, therefore, if it can be understood or can be in the understanding.[5]

Thomas Aquinas and the Five Ways

Saint Thomas Aquinas (1225–1274) harmonized Christian theology with Aristotelian philosophy, and his writings form part of the intellectual base for the teachings of the Roman Catholic Church. Aquinas neatly summarized and subtly defended arguments for God's existence, which still spark debate and are considered classic models. But the future Saint's religious profession was not easy for him. Born near Aquino, between

THOMAS AQUINAS 1225–1274

Rome and Naples, Thomas Aquinas began his education in a Benedictine school. But when he wanted to join the Dominican order in 1243, his parents objected and locked him up in a castle. After he gained his freedom, Thomas went to Paris and Cologne to study theology. One of his teachers was Albertus Magnus, the great Dominican intellectual who was a follower of Aristotle. Aquinas had trouble gaining his license to teach, but when he succeeded he taught and wrote with distinction at monasteries in Italy as well as in Paris.

Anselm's philosophical heritage was Platonic; he employed an introspective approach in which the observation of nature was less important than reflection on the eternal truths discovered by the intellect alone. By contrast, an emphasis on the empirical observation of nature characterized Aristotle's philosophical method, and Aquinas found this attractive. But the conflict of Aristotle's thought with Christian doctrines caused Aquinas some uneasiness. As he sought to synthesize Aristotle's philosophy and Christian teachings in the *Summa Theologica* (c.

1265–74) and in the *Summa Contra Gentiles* (the summary of theology written expressly for non-Christian readers, 1258–60), Aquinas defined the relationship between philosophy and theology. He wanted to show how people can—and cannot—have knowledge about God.

Theology and Philosophy, Faith and Reason

Since Aristotle was a philosopher but not a Christian, Aquinas asserts that there are some fundamental differences between philosophy and **theology**: the philosopher begins and ends with that which can be known through reason; the theologian works within the context of **revelation** and speaks about God and other issues in religion, using reason within revealed principles that are accepted on authority and faith. One can use philosophical arguments to counter what is said against revelation and to interpret what faith means, but such use of philosophy is not sufficient to make philosophers out of theologians, since the theologian still operates in the context of revealed truth.

Aquinas holds that some truths (Christian teachings about the Trinity, for example) are solely within the domain of revelation. One can use them to argue and show that they are not contrary to reason, but to prove their truth through reason is not possible. Other truths are genuinely philosophical. They are not directly revealed by God but are discoverable and demonstrable through rational inquiry alone. There is, however, a third group of truths, and here philosophy and theology overlap. These truths, including the existence of God, are revealed but are also capable of being established by reason. Thus, although philosophy and theology have fundamental differences, they come together on important points. The name that Aquinas gives to this area of overlap is "natural theology."

Ultimately, according to Aquinas, philosophy and theology will never be in conflict, but he also contended that philosophical understanding alone cannot fully meet human needs. Revelation and faith are needed to supplement reason. Human fulfillment and the quest for meaning require a relationship to God and an understanding of God's nature that are fully possible only through revelation and faith. God's grace and a person's faith, argues Aquinas, complete and perfect what can be known through the rational investigations of nature. The limits of human reason, however, do not leave God's existence in doubt. It is interesting to compare the reliance of Aquinas on reason to Hegel's. Both stress the importance of reason, but Hegel takes reason as a complete guide, eliminating any final need for faith. For Hegel, the dialectic of reason naturally ends in an absolute, which is God. Not so for Thomas Aquinas.

Aquinas's Alternatives to Anselm's Ontological Argument

Philosophers do not disagree only concerning their conclusions. Methods of analysis and styles of argument separate them just as much. Anselm and Aquinas provide an example. They agreed that God's existence could be rationally demonstrated, but Aquinas mistrusted Anselm's ontological argument. Unswayed by Anselm's subtle distinctions, Aquinas was convinced that his predecessor had fallen prey to a faulty first principle, namely, that there may be an exception to the rule that a conception in the mind is never sufficient by itself to guarantee existence beyond the mind. It is better not to admit any exceptions to that rule, Aquinas contends, and thus, "It remains . . . that man is to reach the knowledge of God through reasoning by way of the likenesses of God found in His effects."[6] Inferences based on empirical observations, says Aquinas, not conclusions drawn from meditating on an idea, even of God, are the proper philosophical path to take in demonstrating God's existence.

In the *Summa Theologica*, Aquinas argues for God's existence in five ways.[7] Each argument starts from something perceptible to us in the natural world, but they share other important features as well. First, all rely on a **principle of sufficient reason.** As Aquinas states it, this principle means that there must be a final stopping point in any chain of explanation, which is to say that an **infinite regress** of causes or explanatory principles cannot be accepted. Moreover, the arguments also depend on the idea that the final point of rest cannot lie within the natural series one is attempting to account for. Rather, this point must be outside the series and different in nature from it or from any of its members. Finally, each argument arrives at an ultimate reality (for instance, a first efficient cause or an absolutely necessary being). Aquinas asserts that each of these ultimate factors, which we need to account for natural phenomena, is actually a manifestation of one and the same God.

God Must Be First

The initial argument starts with our experiences of motion or change. Following Aristotle, Aquinas interprets motion or change in terms of the transformation of potentiality into actuality. A thing cannot be moved unless it has a potential for movement. If this potential is to be actualized, something actual must set the thing in motion. In addition, nothing can set itself in motion, since it is impossible for one thing to be simultaneously actual and not actual in the same respect. For instance, something cannot actually be hot and not hot in the same respect at the same time; or you cannot be actually sitting and not sitting in the same respect simultaneously. It is apparent that "whatever is moved must be moved by another" (1:22). Moreover, if that by which something is moved is in turn itself moved, as is the case in all our experience, then a third mover must be posited, and so on ad infinitum. An infinite regress of these moved movers, however, is unintelligible. But we must reject this as an adequate explanation of movement. Thus, Aquinas concludes, our experience pushes us to assert that there must be a first, **unmoved mover,** which can be called God.

When Aquinas argues that an infinite regress is unintelligible, he is stating the fact that all relationships of dependency must have a stopping point. That is, there must be something on which other beings are dependent that itself is not dependent on anything else. Thus, the unmoved mover is *first* in the sense that everything is dependent on it and it is dependent on nothing. By placing the emphasis in this way, Aquinas does not restrict "firstness" to the temporal dimension. In fact, he admits that the existence of a series of moved movers going back infinitely into the past is possible. That is, it cannot be demonstrated by reason alone either that the past is finite or that there was a time in the past when no moved movers existed. Instead, Aquinas accepts on faith the Christian teaching that the world has not always existed. In this case, Aquinas thinks that the series of moved movers, whether finite or infinite, requires something beyond itself to explain its existence. A first unmoved mover is needed, that is, a creator who is ultimate, independent, and whose existence is necessary. Aquinas here borrows Aristotle's cosmology as his model, and his arguments for a "first mover" are quite similar.

Aquinas's second argument concentrates on cause-and-effect relationships. The natural world functions in terms of efficient causality. That is, everything we encounter in the natural order is an effect of a cause that produced it. For nothing in the natural order can be the cause of itself. To meet the conditions necessary to be cause of itself, a thing would have to exist prior to itself, which is an absurdity. On the other hand, it is not intellectually acceptable (satisfying) to stop with an infinite series of efficient causes in the natural order. An ultimate grounding is required, Aquinas argues. Hence there must be a first efficient cause, which, again, can be recognized as God. God stands as the ultimate and necessary source of all the cause-and-effect relationships we know.

Two Types of Existence

A third argument distinguishes between necessary and **contingent** existence. In the natural order, things come into existence and they perish. Such beings are contingent. If we assert, however, that a contingent existence like ours is the only kind, we find ourselves in trouble. Anything that is contingent, and therefore capable of nonexistence, has also come into being and hence at some juncture did not exist. Aquinas supplements this claim by asserting that if it is possible for every individual thing not to exist, there must have been a time when nothing was in existence. If this were true, however, there would be nothing in existence now, because nonexistent beings cannot generate their own existence. But clearly things do exist now, which means that there must be some beings that exist necessarily. Furthermore, one of these must cause the others to exist. This conclusion is generated by the fact that any necessary being either has its necessary existence caused by another necessary being or it does not. However, just as was the case with efficient causes, an infinite regress of necessary beings is impossible. Therefore, we must acknowledge the existence of one necessary being, God, that causes the existence of all others but is not itself caused.

The intriguing component in this third argument is Aquinas's assertion that if it is possible for everything not to exist, then at some time there was nothing in existence. Earlier in the proof, when Aquinas speaks of the possible nonexistence of things, the implication is that he is speaking about particular entities or things. But when he argues that if it is possible for everything not to exist then at some point there would have been nothing in existence, he has shifted from a consideration of individual things to a consideration of all individual things whose nonexistence is possible if taken together. It is also possible for the totality of individual things whose nonexistence is possible not to exist. Coupling this possibility with the principle that something is capable of nonexistence only if there is a point at which it did not exist, Aquinas concludes that if every existent thing is contingent, there must have been a time when nothing existed. In this view, if there ever were a time when nothing existed, nothing would exist now. By virtue of the fact that contingent beings now do exist, we know that there must be necessary beings, one of which makes all the others exist.

Value Judgments and the Teleological Argument

Aquinas's fourth argument, which is sometimes called the **cosmological** argument, moves to God from the degrees of truth, goodness, and like properties of things in the natural order. When we judge things comparatively with respect to such positive characteristics, argues Aquinas, we do so in terms of something that is the maximum of the quality of perfection in question. That which is the maximum of the quality we are considering, Aquinas asserts, must be the cause of the quality in all the things that possess it. Contingent possession of a quality of any kind (goodness, or hotness, for example) requires some other being that possesses that quality essentially (e.g., fire is "essentially" hot). Plato stressed the impor-

tance of the principle or form of the Good, and Aquinas follows Platonism here. Moreover, Aquinas contends that whatever is supreme in goodness or truth is also supreme in Being, and whatever is supreme in Being is the cause of the being in all things that exist. If this relationship does not hold, we have eliminated the conditions required to make basic comparative judgments intelligible, because there is a real hierarchy among existing beings. But such judgments are intelligible. Aquinas's conclusion, therefore, is that we are pushed to acknowledge one ultimate source of goodness, truth, and all being, and this is God.

All these versions of the cosmological argument for the existence of God depend on the idea that there must be a first cause or ultimate reason for the existence of the cosmos. In contrast, the last major argument for God's existence that Aquinas presents in the *Summa Theologica* is often called the **teleological argument** or the argument from design. In our world even things that lack knowledge (natural bodies, for example) still function in patterned and ordered ways. As Aquinas puts it, "they act for an end" (1:23). Moreover, this order occurs with such regularity that it is unthinkable that it is due to chance. The presence of pattern or design in that which lacks knowledge points to the reality of a transcendent directing intelligence. That which lacks knowledge cannot be said to move itself toward an end or toward the fulfillment of a purpose. Some intelligent being must exist through whom "all natural things are directed to their end; and this being we call God" (1:23).

In the *Summa Contra Gentiles* there is also an argument from design, but it is cast differently from the one in the *Summa Theologica*. Aquinas argues that things that are "contrary and discordant" cannot be maintained through time as parts of a single order unless there is a governing intelligence whose plan makes their coexistence possible. In our world we find that things of widely diverse natures do exist and that they exist together in one order. Aquinas concludes: "There must therefore be some being by whose providence the world is governed. This we call God."[8]

What Do Aquinas's Arguments Accomplish?

If Aquinas's arguments work, he has shown that there is (1) a first, unmoved mover, (2) a first efficient cause of all that exists, (3) one ultimate necessary being, (4) an ultimate source of being and all perfections, and (5) an intelligence that governs the universe. Additionally, he thinks that each argument points to the existence of a single reality, who should be acknowledged to be God. Within the demonstrations themselves, however, Aquinas does not offer any proof that all the arguments point to one and the same God. When he does take up this issue, he does so from the conclusion of his third argument, namely, that contingent beings cannot account for themselves and therefore require a necessary being. Thus, there is one ultimate necessary being and people will recognize this being to be God. The qualities noted in the conclusions of all the other arguments, Aquinas holds, will be found in the necessary being of the third proof. Hence, all the arguments can be taken as pointing to one God.

If we start with God as the ultimate necessary being, we can assert that such a being will contain no unactualized potentiality. To deny this, Aquinas claims, would be to assert that God could be other than God. Aquinas takes the introduction of any contingency to be equivalent to denying the original claim that God is the ultimate necessary being. If God could become other than God, there is a sense in which God's existence is not necessary. This conclusion entails either that God is presently less than the ultimate necessary being or that God possesses the capacity to become less than the ultimate necessary being, which is a defect that is incompatible with the nature of God.

God is **pure actuality;** that is, God's nature can contain no unactualized potential. Aquinas understood that assertion to mean that there is no difference between God's essence and God's existence, since divinity contains no potentiality or contingency, whereas we do. That is, we cannot speak of God's nature without implying that God exists, for God's essence is to exist fully. Moreover, if a being is fully actual, this means that it is perfection itself, since if it lacked any perfection this would involve the potentiality of being greater or of having something added to it. In addition to being the first unmoved mover and the first efficient cause of all that exists, God's perfection, which is the ultimate source and norm for all other manifestations of perfection (for example, goodness, truth), also entails the power required for the governance of the universe. This notion makes God the focus of all Platonic ideals or forms. Thus, the existence of God as the ultimate necessary being, which is the conclusion reached in Aquinas's third argument, implies that the qualities designated in all the other arguments are united in one being. Aquinas takes this implication to be sufficient evidence for asserting that each argument points to one and the same God.

Students of religion have objected to Aquinas's rationalism and said that there is a big difference between the God of the philosophers and "the God of Abraham, Isaac, and Jacob." That is to say, there is a gap between the analysis of Thomas Aquinas and the religious faith and practice of those who are less philosophically inclined. Aquinas, however, wanted faith to be enriched by understanding. His philosophical arguments about God's existence and nature, therefore, are attempts to figure out what the concept of God really means and what God must be like to account for the experiences men and women actually have.

Where his demonstrations for God's existence are concerned, Aquinas starts with fundamental human experiences. Everywhere we see motion and change, but how are they to be explained? Patterns of cause and effect are discernible time and again. What ultimately accounts for those relationships? Most things come into existence and perish. In the final analysis, how and why do these things exist? Nature is amazingly ordered and structured. What accounts for nature's design? For Aquinas, all those experiences and questions are paths that lead to God's existence. The problem, however, is that the same experiences and questions do not lead everyone to the same conclusion.

Aquinas's arguments ultimately rest on the premise that an infinite regress of causes or reasons is unintelligible and hence ultimately impossible. If one questions that assumption, his arguments become problematic. By advancing his version of the principle of sufficient reason, Aquinas thought he was on firm ground. For what could make better sense than to suppose that there is a rationally satisfactory answer for every sensible question a person can ask? By putting a stop to a regress of questions, causes, and explanations, God occupies the position of satisfying our reason's demand for finality. But what about the objections of those to whom an infinite regress does not seem as irrational and unintelligible as it did to Aquinas? What if some of our questions elude answers that are rational and satisfactory to all who inquire critically? What if God—or whatever is ultimate, if anything is—should turn out to be different from what Aquinas's theory suggests?

Aquinas sometimes anticipated such questions, and he tried to answer them. The problem is that those answers always seem to be subject to another round of questions, so that finality and certainty are more scarce than Aquinas hoped. Yet if his arguments for the existence of God fail to be universally convincing proofs, they rest on experiences that to this day prompt people to consider whether some being is ultimate, which is exactly what Aquinas wanted. See if the following arguments from the *Summa Theologica* keep the question of God's existence open, even if unresolved.

WHETHER THE EXISTENCE OF GOD IS SELF-EVIDENT?

Objection 1. It seems that the existence of God is self-evident. For those things are said to be self-evident to us the knowledge of which exists naturally in us, as we can see in regard to first principles. But as Damascene says, "the knowledge of God is naturally implanted in all." Therefore the existence of God is self-evident.

Obj. 2. Further, those things are said to be self-evident which are known as soon as the terms are known, which the Philosopher [Aristotle] says is true of the first principles of demonstration. Thus, when the nature of a whole and of a part is known, it is at once recognized that every whole is greater than its part. But as soon as the signification of the name *God* is understood, it is at once seen that God exists. For by this name is signified that thing than which nothing greater can be conceived. But that which exists actually and mentally is greater than that which exists only mentally. Therefore, since as soon as the name *God* is understood it exists mentally, it also follows that it exists actually. Therefore the proposition *God exists* is self-evident.

Obj. 3. Further, the existence of truth is self-evident. For whoever denies the existence of truth grants that truth does not exist: and, if truth does not exist, then the proposition *Truth does not exist* is true: and if there is anything true, there must be truth. But God is truth itself: "I am the way, the truth, and the life" (John 14:6). Therefore *God exists* is self-evident.

On the contrary, no one can mentally admit the opposite of what is self-evident, as the Philosopher states concerning the first principles of demonstration. But the opposite of the proposition *God is* can be mentally admitted: "The fool [says] in his heart, There is no God" [Psalms 14:1]. Therefore, that God exists is not self-evident.

I answer that, A thing can be self-evident in either of two ways: on the one hand, self-evident in itself, though not to us; on the other, self-evident in itself, and to us. A proposition is self-evident because the predicate is included in the essence of the subject: e.g., *Man is an animal,* for animal is contained in the essence of man. If, therefore, the essence of the predicate and subject be known to all, the proposition will be self-evident to all; as is clear with regard to the first principles of demonstration, the terms of which are certain common notions that no one is ignorant of, such as being and nonbeing, whole and part, and the like. If, however, there are some to whom the essence of the predicate and subject is unknown, the proposition will be self-evident in itself, but not to those who do not know the meaning of the predicate and subject of the proposition. Therefore, it happens, as Boethius says, that there are some notions of the mind which are common and self-evident only to the learned, as that incorporeal substances are not in space. Therefore I say that this proposition, *God exists,* of itself is self-evident, for the predicate is the same as the subject, because God is His own existence as will be hereafter shown. Now because we do not know the essence of God, the proposition is not self-evident to us, but needs to be demonstrated by things that are more known to us, though less known in their nature—namely, by His effects.

Reply Obj. 1. To know that God exists in a general and confused way is implanted in us by nature, inasmuch as God is man's beatitude. For man naturally desires happiness, and what is naturally desired by man is naturally known by him. This, however, is not to know absolutely that God exists; just as to know that someone is approaching is not the same as to know that Peter is approaching, even though it is Peter who is approaching; for there are many who imagine that man's perfect good, which is happiness, consists in riches, and others in pleasures, and others in something else.

Reply Obj. 2. Perhaps not everyone who hears this name *God* understands it to signify something than which nothing greater can be thought, seeing that some have believed God to be a body. Yet, granted that everyone understands that by this name *God* is signified something than which nothing greater can be thought, nevertheless, it does not therefore follow that he understands that what the name signifies exists actually, but only that it exists mentally. Nor can it be argued that it actually exists, unless it be admitted that there actually exists something than which nothing greater can be thought; and this precisely is not admitted by those who hold that God does not exist.

Reply Obj. 3. The existence of truth in general is self-evident, but the existence of a Primal Truth is not self-evident to us.

WHETHER IT CAN BE DEMONSTRATED THAT GOD EXISTS?

Objection 1. It seems that the existence of God cannot be demonstrated. For it is an article of faith that God exists. But what is of faith cannot be demonstrated, because a demonstration produces scientific knowledge, whereas faith is of the unseen, as is clear from the Apostle [Paul] (Heb. 11:1). Therefore it cannot be demonstrated that God exists.

Obj. 2. Further, essence is the middle term of demonstration. But we cannot know in what God's essence consists, but solely in what it does not consist, as Damascene says. Therefore we cannot demonstrate that God exists.

Obj. 3. Further, if the existence of God were demonstrated, this could only be from His effects. But His effects are not proportioned to Him, since He is infinite and His effects are finite, and between the finite and infinite there is no proportion. Therefore, since a cause cannot be demonstrated by an effect not proportioned to it, it seems that the existence of God cannot be demonstrated.

On the contrary, the Apostle says: "The invisible things of Him are clearly seen, being understood by the things that are made" (Rom. 1:20). But this would not be unless the existence of God could be demonstrated through the things that are made; for the first thing we must know of anything is whether it exists.

I answer that, Demonstration can be made in two ways: One is through the cause, and is called *propter quid,* and this is to argue from what is prior absolutely. The other is through the effect, and is called a demonstration *quia;* this is to argue from what is prior relatively only to us. When an effect is better known to us than its cause, from the effect we proceed to the knowledge of the cause. And from every effect the existence of its proper cause can be demonstrated, so long as its effects are better known to us; because, since every effect depends upon its cause, if the effect exists, the cause must preexist. Hence the existence of God, insofar as it is not self-evident to us, can be demonstrated from those of His effects which are known to us.

Reply Obj. 1. The existence of God and other like truths about God, which can be known by natural reason, are not articles of faith, but are preambles to the articles; for faith presupposes natural knowledge, even as grace presupposes nature and perfection the perfectible. Nevertheless, there is nothing to prevent a man, who cannot grasp a proof, from accepting, as a matter of faith, something which in itself is capable of being scientifically known and demonstrated.

Reply Obj. 2. When the existence of a cause is demonstrated from an effect, this effect takes the place of the definition of the cause in proving the cause's existence. This is especially the case in regard to God, because, in order to prove the existence of anything, it is necessary to accept as a middle term the meaning of the name, and not its essence, for the question of its essence follows on the question of its existence. Now the names

given to God are derived from His effects, as will be later shown. Consequently, in demonstrating the existence of God from His effects, we may take for the middle term the meaning of the name *God.*

Reply Obj. 3. From effects not proportioned to the cause no perfect knowledge of that cause can be obtained. Yet from every effect the existence of the cause can be clearly demonstrated, and so we can demonstrate the existence of God from His effects; though from them we cannot know God perfectly as He is in His essence.

WHETHER GOD EXISTS?

Objection 1. It seems that God does not exist; because if one of two contraries be infinite, the other would be altogether destroyed. But the name *God* means that He is infinite goodness. If, therefore, God existed, there would be no evil discoverable; but there is evil in the world. Therefore God does not exist.

Obj. 2. Further, it is superfluous to suppose that what can be accounted for by a few principles has been produced by many. But it seems that everything we see in the world can be accounted for by other principles, supposing God did not exist. For all natural things can be reduced to one principle, which is nature; and all voluntary things can be reduced to one principle, which is human reason, or will. Therefore there is no need to suppose God's existence.

On the contrary, it is said in the person of God: "I am Who am" (Exod. 3:14).

I answer that, The existence of God can be proved in five ways.

The first and more manifest way is the argument from motion. It is certain, and evident to our senses, that in the world some things are in motion. Now whatever is moved is moved by another, for nothing can be moved except it is in potentiality to that toward which it is moved; whereas a thing moves inasmuch as it is in act. For motion is nothing else than the reduction of something from potentiality to actuality. But nothing can be reduced from potentiality to actuality, except by something in a state of actuality. Thus that which is actually hot, as fire, makes wood, which is potentially hot, to be actually hot, and thereby moves and changes it. Now it is not possible that the same thing should be at once in actuality and potentiality in the same respect, but only in different respects. For what is actually hot cannot simultaneously be potentially hot; but is it simultaneously potentially cold. It is therefore impossible that in the same respect and in the same way a thing should be both mover and moved, i.e., that it should move itself. Therefore, whatever is moved must be moved by another. If that by which it is moved be itself moved, then this also must needs be moved by another, and that by another again. But this cannot go on to infinity, because then there would be no first mover, and, consequently, no other mover, seeing that subsequent movers move only inasmuch as they are moved by the first mover; as the staff moves only because it is moved by the hand. Therefore it is necessary to arrive at a first mover, moved by no other; and this everyone understands to be God.

The second way is from the nature of efficient cause. In the world of sensible things we find there is an order of efficient causes. There is no case known (neither is it, indeed, possible) in which a thing is found to be the efficient cause of itself; for so it would be prior to itself, which is impossible. Now in efficient causes it is not possible to go on to infinity, because in all efficient causes following in order, the first is the cause of the intermediate cause, and the intermediate is the cause of the ultimate cause, whether the intermediate cause be several, or one only. Now to take away the cause is to take away the effect. Therefore, if there be no first cause among efficient causes, there will be no ultimate, nor any intermediate, cause. But if in efficient causes it is possible to go on to infinity, there will be no first efficient cause, neither will there be an ultimate effect, nor any intermediate efficient causes; all of which is plainly false. Therefore it is necessary to admit a first efficient cause, to which everyone gives the name of God.

The third way is taken from possibility and necessity, and runs thus. We find in nature things that are possible to be and not to be, since they are found to be generated, and to be corrupted, and consequently, it is possible for them to be and not to be. But it is impossible for these always to exist, for that which can not-be at some time is not. Therefore, if everything can not-be, then at one time there was nothing in existence. Now if this were true, even now there would be nothing in existence, because that which does not exist begins to exist only through something already existing. Therefore, if at one time nothing was in existence, it would have been impossible for anything to have begun to exist; and thus even now nothing would be in existence—which is absurd. Therefore, not all beings are merely possible, but there must exist something the existence of which is necessary. But every necessary thing either has its necessity caused by another, or not. Now it is impossible to go on to infinity in necessary things which have their necessity caused by another, as has been already proved in regard to efficient causes. Therefore we cannot but admit the existence of some being having of itself its own necessity, and not receiving it from another, but rather causing in others their necessity. This all men speak of as God.

The fourth way is taken from the gradation to be found in things. Among beings there are some more and some less good, true, noble, and the like. But *more* and *less* are predicated of different things according as they resemble in their different ways something which is the maximum, as a thing is said to be hotter according as it more nearly resembles that which is hottest; so that there is something which is truest, something best, something noblest, and, consequently, something which is most being, for those things that are greatest in truth are greatest in being, as it is written in [Aristotle's] *Metaphysics* II. Now the maximum in any genus is the cause of all in that genus, as fire, which is the maximum of heat, is the cause of all hot things, as is said in the same book. Therefore there must also be something which is to all beings the cause of their being, goodness, and every other perfection; and this we call God.

The fifth way is taken from the governance of the world. We see that things which lack knowledge, such as natural bodies, act for an end, and this is evident from their acting always, or nearly always, in the same way, so as to obtain the best result. Hence it is plain that they achieve their end, not fortuitously, but designedly. Now whatever lacks knowledge cannot move toward an end, unless it be directed by some being endowed with knowledge and intelligence; as the arrow is directed by the archer. Therefore some intelligent being exists by whom all natural things are directed to their end; and this being we call God.

Reply Obj. 1. As Augustine says: "Since God is the highest good, He would not allow any evil to exist in His works, unless His omnipotence and goodness were such as to bring good even out of evil" (*Enchiridion*, XI). This is part of the infinite goodness of God, that He should allow evil to exist, and out of it produce good.

Reply Obj. 2. Since nature works for a determinate end under the direction of a higher agent, whatever is done by nature must be traced back to God as to its first cause. So likewise whatever is done voluntarily must be traced back to some higher cause other than human reason and will, since these can change and fail; for all things that are changeable and capable of defect must be traced back to an immovable and self-necessary first principle, as has been shown.[9]

David Hume and Natural Religion

"I do not seek to understand that I may believe," wrote Anselm, "but I believe in order to understand. For this also I believe—that unless I believed, I should not understand."[10] Anselm did not think that proof of

DAVID HUME   1711–1776

God's existence was a prerequisite for religious faith. Rather he argued that what he accepted on faith was also rationally demonstrable. In similar fashion, Thomas Aquinas stated that although faith revealed some things reason could not attain, still there was no conflict between them. Indeed, the proofs for God stood on purely rational grounds. The skeptical David Hume—we have met him in Chapters Two and Three—dissented from the tradition that saw reason and religious faith as mutually supportive. Anselm and Thomas Aquinas felt that existence could not make sense unless God was real. Hume, too, hoped that existence was rational, but he was less sure. In particular he harbored suspicion about truth claims based on revelation and faith commitments alone, because they dogmatically supported too many conflicting opinions. He was dubious about the power of reason or experience to demonstrate religion's beliefs.

Hume's *Enquiry Concerning Human Understanding,* for example, devoted a section to miracles. Many religions report such occurrences and hold that miracles offer decisive evidence to support religious belief. Hume rejected this outlook. His skepticism had to allow for the possibility that our normal expectations about experience might be radically subverted, but to prove that a **miracle**—by definition a violation of nature's regularity—had happened also struck Hume as conceptually incoherent. Demonstrations depend on regularities in experience. If you claim that a miracle has occurred, what can possibly constitute the proof? A miracle can be demonstrated, replied Hume, if the falsity of the testimony for it would be an even greater miracle—a more radical improbability than the phenomenon reported initially. When a miracle is reported, one may have happened; but Hume contended that the regularity of experience suggests the greater likelihood to be that the person making such a claim is mistaken.

Convinced that religious claims based on revelation, faith experience, or purportedly rational demonstrations had produced conflict and strife at least as much as they had improved the human condition, Hume suspected that reason and faith were at odds. Rather than "believing in order to understand," Hume mounted a critique of belief in God's existence that exposed what he took to be religion's lack of rational foundations. The result was not to disprove religious claims, but simply to show that the authority claimed for them was questionable. Hume carried on this investigation most thoroughly in *Dialogues Concerning Natural Religion*. The dialogue form of the work made it difficult to know for sure whether the various characters stated Hume's views explicitly. Nevertheless upon the advice of friends who were concerned about the book's contents, which were controversial if not radical in their day, Hume withheld the *Dialogues* from publication. Under a provision of his will, they were published posthumously in 1779.

Human Experience and Natural Religion

Anselm and Thomas Aquinas thought that the testimony of human experience and reason could show the truth of essential religious claims, including the existence of God. **Natural religion** is what Hume called this outlook, which claims not to presuppose faith but to demonstrate the truth of faith by appeals to the natural order and our experience. Hume took seriously the notion that we are entitled to believe what tested experience shows. Where religion is concerned, contended Hume, the outcome of that process does not yield much positive content. Thus the *Dialogues Concerning Human Experience* raises fundamental objections to claims that we can conclusively demonstrate God's existence and the positive qualities of God's nature by appeals to a priori principles or to experiences. On the other hand, the *Dialogues* do not claim to demonstrate that God does not exist or that God can be known with absolute finality not to have particular attributes. What emerges instead is a skepticism with respect to all claims for genuine knowledge in these areas.

The *Dialogues* consist of discussions between three characters: (1) Demea is a religiously orthodox man who believes that God's existence is self-evident, but he affirms the primacy of faith in any attempt to understand God's nature and opposes the view that people can comprehend and demonstrate God's attributes through reason. If people could do that, God's sovereignty and majesty would be compromised. (2) Philo, a skeptic, agrees that reason is severely limited in assisting us to know the nature of God; indeed, he goes on to deny the validity of human claims to know conclusively that God exists. (3) Cleanthes, an advocate of natural religion, thinks that God's existence can be known conclusively by reasoning from experience and nature. Hume did not specifically identify himself with any one figure in the *Dialogues*, but it is generally thought that the arguments of Philo most closely represent his position.

An Attack on the
Argument from Design

The central issue of the *Dialogues* focuses on Cleanthes' assertion not only that the existence of God can be demonstrated by an appeal to experience and the natural world, but also that such an appeal enables us to obtain genuine knowledge concerning God's nature. To prove his point, Cleanthes presents a version of the argument from design. Anyone who looks at the world will see that it is one great machine, which can be broken down into an infinite number of smaller machines. These parts are adjusted to each other so as to function harmoniously. These harmonious relationships include an adaptation of means to ends. That is, there is a manifestation of purpose and planning in the universe. Moreover, says Cleanthes, this "curious adapting of means to ends, throughout all nature, resembles exactly, though it much exceeds, the productions of human contrivance; of human design, thought, wisdom, and intelligence."[11] Since the effects (that is, natural objects and human artifacts) resemble each other so closely, we infer by analogy that the natural objects are like the human artifacts in having a cause and that the causes must closely resemble each other. In this way, holds Cleanthes, we can prove both the existence of God and the fact that God has a mind and a will not unlike ours.

This approach, Philo retorts, leaves one at best with an ambiguous outcome that does not adequately ground the religious position Cleanthes wants to support. Philo's criticism concentrates on two aspects of Cleanthes'

argument: its use of analogical reasoning and its use of the cause-and-effect relationship. The validity of Cleanthes' argument, which is based on an analogy, depends on the closeness of similarity between the effects under examination. Here both the parts and the whole of nature are taken to be like human products or works of art, thus requiring a divine artisan not unlike a human creator. Such reasoning, Philo argues, rests on an unsound foundation.

First, the resemblance between the effects being compared is not as elaborate as Cleanthes supposes. The natural world differs in many respects from a machine or a human product such as a house or a work of art. Experience shows, moreover, that "thought, design, intelligence, such as we discover in men and other animals, is no more than one of the springs and principles of the universe, as well as heat or cold, attraction or repulsion, and a hundred others, which fall under daily observation" (p. 147). It is not certain that these other principles of order require active intelligence as their source, and it is not impossible that intelligence can be the product of some other principle. To argue that all order reveals the existence of intelligence at its base is to attribute the qualities of a small part of the universe to the whole. Such inferences are always questionable.

In addition, our idea of cause-and-effect relationships actually rests on the experience of constant conjunction—a view of Hume's discussed in Chapter Two—and the resemblance between the universe and the products of human intelligence is slight. This severely undercuts the possibility of making conclusive judgments concerning the cause or causes of the universe. If we are dealing with a particular member of a class of things, we may be able to make sound judgments concerning its cause or causes. From the existence of a particular house, for example, you can infer the existence of a builder on the basis of the experience you have had of other houses whose builders you know. But this situation does not hold with respect to the universe. Not only is it considerably different from the products of human intelligence, but it is not a member of any group of things that we know. Thus, since we have no experience of the production of other universes and no direct access to the causes that may have produced this universe, we are left in a position of ambiguity with respect to our knowledge of the source of our universe.

The Debate Continues

Unconvinced by Philo's objections, Cleanthes stresses the naturalness of our belief in an intelligent creator of the universe. He also clings to the view that we can know causes from effects, even in the case of the universe, and that the universe reveals its cause to be a good and almighty God who creates a world of purpose, beauty, and harmony. Now Demea joins the fray, pointing out still other dangers in arguing from effects to causes. For instance, if we obtain knowledge about God through analogy with human existence, how are we to cope with the fact that the human mind is finite and often subject to confusion, change, and emotional disturbance? If we say that the effects reveal the cause, we may end by affirming that the cause is also subject to confusion, change, and emotional disturbance, which is clearly contrary to orthodox teaching about God. On the other hand, if we deny that God is this way, in what sense does the effect reveal the cause, and what are we to say about the origin of possible defects in human existence?

Philo adds fuel to the fire by arguing that Cleanthes' claims are vacuous, for so many alternative accounts are equally possible and probable. The effects (that is, the parts and the whole of the universe) are sufficiently ambiguous to call into question any claims to move from them to clear knowledge of God's nature. If Cleanthes' claims are maintained in the face of this ambiguity, they reveal themselves to be not only anthropomorphic but also selectively anthropomorphic in a way that is ungrounded.

To illustrate, Philo points out that the universe does not allow us to affirm very clearly anything about God's perfection. We lack familiarity with a series of constructions of various universes that is sufficient to measure the perfection of this universe. Moreover, we cannot be sure that this universe was created by only one God. Perhaps a plurality of deities, none of them perfect, was involved. Or maybe transcendent deities are not involved at all. The world might be the product of a metabolic process such as we see when seeds grow into plants without an outside designer introducing their order. Or it may even be that the world is simply the result of a chance arrangement of atomic particles. In short, concludes Philo, we lack sufficient data to corroborate any particular theory about the origin, structure, and order of the universe. No particular system of religious belief can be demonstrated on the basis of appeals to experience and the natural order. Religious belief remains possible, but it is more a matter of faith than some of its proponents would like to admit.

Demea's Difficulties

Demea, as well as Cleanthes, is troubled by the preceding suggestions, for Philo apparently questions the very existence of a sovereign, creating God. Demea believes that the existence of such a God is self-evident, even though he holds that one cannot rationally comprehend God's nature. Starting from the principle that all that exists has a reason or a cause grounding its existence, Demea asserts that there must be a first cause that exists necessarily. Even if the sequence of causes occurring in the world is infinite, something will be needed to account for the existence of the series of causes in the world. The only being that is capable of accounting for the existence of such a series, whether finite or infinite, is an ultimate necessary being, who cannot be conceived not to exist without contradiction. This being is God.

Cleanthes, rather than Philo, takes exception to this line of thought, which has some similarities to Anselm's. Matters of fact, objects Cleanthes, cannot be demonstrated a priori. Anything we can conceive as existent, we can also conceive as nonexistent without contradiction. Where it is possible to conceive of alternatives without contradiction, final demonstration is impossible. According to Cleanthes, an a priori proof of God's existence such as that attempted by Demea will not work because "the words . . . *necessary existence,* have no meaning; or, which is the same thing, none that is consistent" (p. 190). In addition, Cleanthes points out that Demea's a priori proof, even if it could be used legitimately, does not necessarily give us a transcendent creator. The ultimate necessary being and source of change and movement could just as well be matter itself.

Philo adds that a priori arguments usually leave people uneasy, and it is unlikely that such demonstrations have ever had much power in religious life. Demea concurs: religious life does not develop primarily from proofs and demonstrations but as a response to the experiences of finitude, destruction, and suffering that human life contains. Primarily our need of help and security turns us toward God.

Practical Religion?

At first, Philo seems sympathetic to this practical approach to religion. But he qualifies his feeling by stressing that the features of human existence noted by Demea conflict with the emphasis placed by traditional theology and religion on the perfection of God (that is, God's absolute goodness and power).

It is difficult to see that the positing of such qualities is rationally grounded. We have no a priori grasp of God's nature, and the empirical data before us do not necessarily imply God's absolute perfection, since they indicate that existence is a mixture of good and evil. If we possessed a clear comprehension of God's nature and all existence, we might see the perfection of God's total plan for the universe. But we lack such comprehension. Thus, for example, Philo would not find it acceptable to say that we have good grounds for believing that this life, in which evil occurs, is merely a small but perhaps necessary interlude in a broader existence in which pure goodness triumphs. In addition, it will not do to say that evil is illusory and everything is actually good. Evil stands as a brute fact. For Philo, it is a serious obstacle to the soundness of the claim that God's perfection is absolute.

Philo summarized his position with respect to the moral qualities of the possible first cause or causes of the universe. There are four main options. The first cause or causes could be (1) absolutely good, (2) absolutely evil, (3) both good and evil, or (4) really indifferent to good and evil. The first two options are unlikely. Moreover, the steadiness and regularity of things argues against the third. No conflict of interests or powers is indicated in the ultimate foundations of existence, according to Philo, since the mixture of good and evil in existence does not alter very much one way or the other. In addition, the indifference of the first cause or causes to good and evil seems more likely than a mere standoff or balance between conflicting interests or powers in the first cause or causes. For Philo, then, the fourth option seems the most likely.

Demea recognizes that Philo is truly a skeptic and not a man of orthodox religious faith. Revelation and religious commitment, which are valid and crucially important in Demea's thinking, do not have a positive place in Philo's orientation. Demea leaves, but Cleanthes and Philo stay on for more discussion. Philo dominates the final exchange, although he is more mellow than before. He admits that he likes to play the skeptic, but adds that Cleanthes is right to stress the idea of design in the universe and the naturalness of thinking in terms of an intelligent creator as its source. Moreover, Philo is prepared to admit that Cleanthes is right in asserting that there are some likenesses between the works of nature and the products of human activity. He is not, however, ready to agree that the likenesses are sufficient to permit us to draw any precise analogies between human and divine intelligence. Nor are the likenesses sufficient to ground our claims to have a clear comprehension of the nature of the cause or causes of order in the world. This is particularly true with respect to claims concerning the moral qualities and interests of the cause or causes. The most that natural religion will allow us to say on these matters, suggests Philo, is *"that the cause or causes of order in the universe probably bear some remote analogy to human intelligence"* (p. 227). Thus, even if religion has some positive utilitarian value for society, which Philo doubts because he believes that the sources and practical effects of religion are largely fear and terror, it cannot really be said to have a firm, rational grounding.

Hume and Religion in the Modern World

At the end of the *Dialogues* Philo says, "To be a philosophical skeptic is, in a man of letters, the first and most essential step toward being a sound, believing Christian" (p. 228). Some find this statement ironic, but it fits Hume's basic philosophical view quite well. Hume's is a mitigated skepticism. He does not take doubt as a final resting place. He only urges us not to claim more validity or certainty for our beliefs than experience war-

rants. Thus, being skeptical about one's convictions is a first step in trying to sort out what one will believe on the basis of empirical data and rational argument or reference to other grounds of belief.

We do not live in the worlds in which Aristotle proved the existence of an unmoved mover or Anselm and Thomas Aquinas offered their arguments for God's existence. Hume is evidence for that, because he drove a wedge between the compatibility of faith and reason, theology and philosophy, on which Anselm and Thomas Aquinas banked. If Hume's critique shows that religion is not entirely natural, however, it probably opens up more options than it closes. For the key finding of Hume's skepticism is that no one is bound to accept any particular view as finally binding. Its challenge remains: Develop your own theory—religious or not— if you want, but seek to make it as believable as possible by trying to mold it closely to experience. This is precisely what Hume himself attempted to do. His efforts led him to conclude that religion would not fare well in this process, but since Hume's appeal is to experience and not to an outcome fixed in advance, the issues of religion and God remain topics for dialogue. As you read the following selections from the *Dialogues Concerning Natural Religion*, see where the challenge of Hume's skepticism leads you with respect to the question "Does God exist?"

I must own, Cleanthes, said Demea, that nothing can more surprise me than the light in which you have all along put this argument. By the whole tenor of your discourse, one would imagine that you were maintaining the Being of a God against the cavils of atheists and infidels, and were necessitated to become a champion for that fundamental principle of all religion. But this, I hope, is not by any means a question among us. No man, no man at least of common sense, I am persuaded, ever entertained a serious doubt with regard to a truth so certain and self-evident. The question is not concerning the *being* but the *nature* of God. This I affirm, from the infirmities of human understanding, to be altogether incomprehensible and unknown to us. The essence of that supreme Mind, his attributes, the manner of his existence, the very nature of his duration—these and every particular which regards so divine a Being are mysterious to men. Finite, weak, and blind creatures, we ought to humble ourselves in his august presence, and, conscious of our frailties, adore in silence his infinite perfections which eye hath not seen, ear hath not heard, neither hath it entered into the heart of man to conceive. They are covered in a deep cloud from human curiosity; it is profaneness to attempt penetrating through these sacred obscurities, and, next to the impiety of denying his existence, is the temerity of prying into his nature and essence, decrees and attributes.

But lest you should think that my *piety* has here got the better of my *philosophy*, I shall support my opinion, if it needs any support, by a very great authority. I might cite all the divines, almost from the foundation of Christianity, who have ever treated of this or any other theological subject; but I shall confine myself, at present, to one equally celebrated for piety and philosophy. It is Father [Nicholas] Malebranche [French follower of Descartes, 1638–1715] who, I remember, thus expresses himself. "One ought not so much," says he, "to call God a spirit in order to express positively what he is, as in order to signify that he is not matter. He is a Being infinitely perfect—of this we cannot doubt. But in the same manner as we ought not to imagine, even supposing him corporeal, that he is clothed with a human body, as the anthropomorphites asserted, under color that that figure was the most perfect of any, so neither ought we to imagine that the spirit of God has human ideas or bears any resemblance to our spirit, under color that we know nothing more perfect than a human mind. We ought rather to believe that as he comprehends the perfections of matter without being material . . .

he comprehends also the perfections of created spirits without being spirit, in the manner we conceive spirit: that his true name is *He that is,* or, in other words, Being without restriction, All Being, the Being infinite and universal."

After so great an authority, Demea, replied Philo, as that which you have produced, and a thousand more which you might produce, it would appear ridiculous in me to add my sentiment or express my approbation of your doctrine. But surely, where reasonable men treat these subjects, the question can never be concerning the *being* but only the *nature* of the Deity. The former truth, as you well observe, is unquestionable and self-evident. Nothing exists without a cause; and the original cause of this universe (whatever it be) we call God, and piously ascribe to him every species of perfection. Whoever scruples this fundamental truth deserves every punishment which can be inflicted among philosophers, to wit, the greatest ridicule, contempt, and disapprobation. But as all perfection is entirely relative, we ought never to imagine that we comprehend the attributes of this divine Being, or to suppose that his perfections have any analogy or likeness to the perfections of a human creature. Wisdom, thought, design, knowledge—these we justly ascribe to him because these words are honorable among men, and we have no other language or other conceptions by which we can express our adoration of him. But let us beware lest we think that our ideas anywise correspond to his perfections, or that his attributes have any resemblance to these qualities among men. He is infinitely superior to our limited view and comprehension, and is more the object of worship in the temple than of disputation in the schools.

In reality, Cleanthes, continued he, there is no need of having recourse to that affected skepticism so displeasing to you in order to come at this determination. Our ideas reach no farther than our experience. We have no experience of divine attributes and operations. I need not conclude my syllogism, you can draw the inference yourself. And it is a pleasure to me (and I hope to you, too) that just reasoning and sound piety here concur in the same conclusion, and both of them establish the adorably mysterious and incomprehensible nature of the Supreme Being.

Not to lose any time in circumlocutions, said Cleanthes, addressing himself to Demea, much less in replying to the pious declamations of Philo, I shall briefly explain how I conceive this matter. Look round the world, contemplate the whole and every part of it: you will find it to be nothing but one great machine, subdivided into an infinite number of lesser machines, which again admit of subdivisions to a degree beyond what human senses and faculties can trace and explain. All these various machines, and even their most minute parts, are adjusted to each other with an accuracy which ravishes into admiration all men who have ever contemplated them. The curious adapting of means to ends, throughout all nature, resembles exactly, though it much exceeds, the productions of human contrivance—of human design, thought, wisdom, and intelligence. Since therefore the effects resemble each other, we are led to infer, by all the rules of analogy, that the causes also resemble, and that the Author of nature is somewhat similar to the mind of man, though possessed of much larger faculties, proportioned to the grandeur of the work which he has executed. By this argument a posteriori, and by this argument alone, do we prove at once the existence of a Deity and his similarity to human mind and intelligence.

I shall be so free, Cleanthes, said Demea, as to tell you that from the beginning I could not approve of your conclusion concerning the similarity of the Deity to men, still less can I approve of the mediums by which you endeavor to establish it. What! No demonstration of the Being of God! No abstract arguments! No proofs a priori! Are these which have hitherto been so much insisted on by philosophers all fallacy, all sophism? Can we reach no farther in this subject than experience and probability? I will not say that this is betraying the cause of a Deity; but surely, by this affected candor, you give advantages to atheists which they never could obtain by the mere dint of argument and reasoning.

What I chiefly scruple in this subject, said Philo, is not so much that all religious arguments are by Cleanthes reduced to experience, as that they appear not to be even the most certain and irrefragable of that inferior kind. That a stone will fall, that fire will burn, that the earth has solidity, we have observed a thousand and a thousand times; and when any new instance of this nature is presented, we draw without hesitation the accustomed inference. The exact similarity of the cases gives us a perfect assurance of a similar event, and a stronger evidence is never desired nor sought after. But wherever you depart, in the least, from the similarity of the cases, you diminish proportionably the evidence, and may at last bring it to a very weak *analogy*, which is confessedly liable to error and uncertainty. After having experienced the circulation of the blood in human creatures, we make no doubt that it takes place in Titius and Maevius; but from its circulation in frogs and fishes it is only a presumption, though a strong one, from analogy that it takes place in men and other animals. The analogical reasoning is much weaker when we infer the circulation of the sap in vegetables from our experience that the blood circulates in animals; and those who hastily followed that imperfect analogy are found, by more accurate experiments, to have been mistaken.

If we see a house, Cleanthes, we conclude, with the greatest certainty, that it had an architect or builder because this is precisely that species of effect which we have experienced to proceed from that species of cause. But surely you will not affirm that the universe bears such a resemblance to a house that we can with the same certainty infer a similar cause, or that the analogy is here entire and perfect. The dissimilitude is so striking that the utmost you can here pretend to is a guess, a conjecture, a presumption concerning a similar cause; and how that pretension will be received in the world, I leave you to consider.

It would surely be very ill received, replied Cleanthes; and I should be deservedly blamed and detested did I allow that the proofs of a Deity amounted to no more than a guess or conjecture. But is the whole adjustment of means to ends in a house and in the universe so slight a resemblance? the economy of final causes? the order, proportion, and arrangement of every part? Steps of a stair are plainly contrived that human legs may use them in mounting; and this inference is certain and infallible. Human legs are also contrived for walking and mounting; and this inference, I allow, is not altogether so certain because of the dissimilarity which you remark; but does it, therefore, deserve the name only of presumption or conjecture?

Good God! cried Demea, interrupting him, where are we? Zealous defenders of religion allow that the proofs of a Deity fall short of perfect evidence! And you, Philo, on whose assistance I depended in proving the adorable mysteriousness of the Divine Nature, do you assent to all these extravagant opinions of Cleanthes? For what other name can I give them? or, why spare my censure when such principles are advanced, supported by such an authority, before so young a man as Pamphilus?

You seem not to apprehend, replied Philo, that I argue with Cleanthes in his own way, and, by showing him the dangerous consequences of his tenets, hope at last to reduce him to our opinion. But what sticks most with you, I observe, is the representation which Cleanthes has made of the argument a posteriori; and, finding that that argument is likely to escape your hold and vanish into air, you think it so disguised that you can scarcely believe it to be set in its true light. Now, however much I may dissent, in other respects, from the dangerous principle of Cleanthes, I must allow that he has fairly represented that argument, and I shall endeavor so to state the matter to you that you will entertain no further scruples with regard to it.

Were a man to abstract from everything which he knows or has seen, he would be altogether incapable, merely from his own ideas, to determine what kind of scene the universe must be, or to give the preference to one state or situation of things above another. For as nothing which he clearly conceives could be esteemed impossible or implying a contradiction, every chimera of his fancy would be upon an equal footing; nor could he assign any just reason why he adheres to one idea or system, and rejects the others which are equally possible.

Again, after he opens his eyes and contemplates the world as it really is, it would be impossible for him at first to assign the cause of any one event, much less of the whole of things, or of the universe. He might set his fancy a rambling, and she might bring him in an infinite variety of reports and representations. These would all be possible, but, being all equally possible, he would never of himself give a satisfactory account for his preferring one of them to the rest. Experience alone can point out to him the true cause of any phenomenon.

Now, according to this method of reasoning, Demea, it follows (and is, indeed, tacitly allowed by Cleanthes himself) that order, arrangement, or the adjustment of final causes, is not of itself any proof of design, but only so far as it has been experienced to proceed from that principle. For aught we can know a priori, matter may contain the source or spring of order originally within itself, as well as mind does; and there is no more difficulty in conceiving that the several elements, from an internal unknown cause, may fall into the most exquisite arrangement, than to conceive that their ideas, in the great universal mind, from a like internal unknown cause, fall into that arrangement. The equal possibility of both these suppositions is allowed. But, by experience, we find (according to Cleanthes) that there is a difference between them. Throw several pieces of steel together, without shape or form, they will never arrange themselves so as to compose a watch. Stone and mortar and wood, without an architect, never erect a house. But the ideas in a human mind, we see, by an unknown, inexplicable economy, arrange themselves so as to form the plan of a watch or house. Experience, therefore, proves that there is an original principle of order in mind, not in matter. From similar effects we infer similar causes. The adjustment of means to ends is alike in the universe, as in a machine of human contrivance. The causes, therefore, must be resembling.

I was from the beginning scandalized, I must own, with this resemblance which is asserted between the Deity and human creatures, and must conceive it to imply such a degradation of the Supreme Being as no sound theist could endure. With your assistance, therefore, Demea, I shall endeavor to defend what you justly call the adorable mysteriousness of the Divine Nature, and shall refute this reasoning of Cleanthes, provided he allows that I have made a fair representation of it.

When Cleanthes had assented, Philo, after a short pause, proceeded in the following manner.

That all inferences, Cleanthes, concerning fact are founded on experience, and that all experimental reasonings are founded on the supposition that similar causes prove similar effects, and similar effects similar causes, I shall not at present much dispute with you. But observe, I entreat you, with what extreme caution all just reasoners proceed in the transferring of experiments to similar cases. Unless the cases be exactly similar, they repose no perfect confidence in applying their past observation to any particular phenomenon. Every alteration of circumstances occasions a doubt concerning the event; and it requires new experiments to prove certainly that the new circumstances are of no moment or importance. A change in bulk, situation, arrangement, age, disposition of the air, or surrounding bodies—any of these particulars may be attended with the most unexpected consequences. And unless the objects be quite familiar to us, it is the highest temerity to expect with assurance, after any of these changes, an event similar to that which before fell under our observation. The slow and deliberate steps of philosophers here, if anywhere, are distinguished from the precipitate march of the vulgar, who, hurried on by the smallest similitude, are incapable of all discernment or consideration.

But can you think, Cleanthes, that your usual phlegm and philosophy have been preserved in so wide a step as you have taken when you compared to the universe houses, ships, furniture, machines, and, from their similarity in some circumstances, inferred a similarity in their causes? Thought, design, intelligence, such as we discover in men and other animals, is no more than one of the springs and principles of the universe, as well as heat or cold, attraction or repulsion, and a hundred others which fall under daily observation. It is an active cause by which some particular parts of nature, we find, produce alterations on other parts. But can a conclusion, with any propriety, be transferred from parts to the whole? Does not the great disproportion bar all comparison and inference? From observing the growth of a hair, can we learn anything concerning the generation of a man? Would the manner of a leaf's blowing, even though perfectly known, afford us any instruction concerning the vegetation of a tree?

But allowing that we were to take the *operations* of one part of nature upon another for the foundation of our judgment concerning the *origin* of the whole (which never can be admitted), yet why select so minute, so weak, so bounded a principle as the reason and design of animals is found to be upon this planet? What peculiar privilege has this little agitation of the brain which we call *thought,* that we must thus make it the model of the whole universe? Our partiality in our own favor does indeed present it on all occasions, but sound philosophy ought carefully to guard against so natural an illusion.

So far from admitting, continued Philo, that the operations of a part can afford us any just conclusion concerning the origin of the whole, I will not allow any one part to form a rule for another part if the latter be very remote from the former. Is there any reasonable ground to conclude that the inhabitants of other planets possess thought, intelligence, reason, or anything similar to these faculties in men? When nature has so extremely diversified her manner of operation in this small globe, can we imagine that she incessantly copies herself throughout so immense a universe? And if thought, as we may well suppose, be confined merely to this narrow corner and has even there so limited a sphere of action, with what propriety can we assign it for the original cause of all things? The narrow views of a peasant who makes his domestic economy the rule for the government of kingdoms is in comparison a pardonable sophism.

But were we ever so much assured that a thought and reason resembling the human were to be found throughout the whole universe, and were its activity elsewhere vastly greater and more commanding than it appears in this globe, yet I cannot see why the operations of a world constituted, arranged, adjusted, can with any propriety be extended to a world which is in its embryo state, and is advancing toward that constitution and arrangement. By observation we know somewhat of the economy, action, and nourishment of a finished animal, but we must transfer with great caution that observation to the growth of a fetus in the womb, and still more to the formation of an animalcule in the loins of its male parent. Nature, we find, even from our limited experience, possesses an infinite number of springs and principles which incessantly discover themselves on every change of her position and situation. And what new and unknown principles would actuate her in so new and unknown a situation as that of the formation of a universe, we cannot, without the utmost temerity, pretend to determine.

A very small part of this great system, during a very short time, is very imperfectly discovered to us; and do we thence pronounce decisively concerning the origin of the whole?

Admirable conclusion! Stone, wood, brick, iron, brass, have not, at this time, in this minute globe of earth, an order or arrangement without human art and contrivance; therefore, the universe could not originally attain its order and arrangement without something similar to human art. But is a part of nature a rule for another part very wide of the former? Is it a rule for the whole? Is a very small part a rule for the universe? Is nature in one situation a certain rule for nature in another situation vastly different from the former?

And can you blame me, Cleanthes, if I here imitate the prudent reserve of Simonides, who, according to the noted story, being asked by Hiero, *What God was?* desired a day to think of it, and then two days more; and after that manner continually prolonged the term, without ever bringing in his definition or description? Could you even blame me if I had answered, at first, *that I did not know,* and was sensible that this subject lay vastly beyond the reach of my faculties? You might cry out skeptic and rallier, as much as you pleased; but, having found in so many other subjects much more familiar the imperfections and even contradictions of human reason, I never should expect any success from its feeble conjectures in a subject so sublime and so remote from the sphere of our observation. When two *species* of objects have always been observed to be conjoined together, I can *infer,* by custom, the existence of one wherever I *see* the existence of the other; and this I call an argument from experience. But how this argument can have place where the objects, as in the present case, are single, individual, without parallel or specific resemblance, may be difficult to explain. And will any man tell me with a serious countenance that an orderly universe must arise from some thought and art like the human because we have experience of it? To ascertain this reasoning it were requisite that we had experience of the origin of worlds; and it is not sufficient, surely, that we have seen ships and cities arise from human art and contrivance.

Philo was proceeding in this vehement manner, somewhat between jest and earnest, as it appeared to me, when he observed some signs of impatience in Cleanthes, and then immediately stopped short. What I had to suggest, said Cleanthes, is only that you would not abuse terms, or make use of popular expressions to subvert philosophical reasonings. You know that the vulgar often distinguish reason from experience, even where the question relates only to matter of fact and existence, though it is found, where that *reason* is properly analyzed, that it is nothing but a species of experience. To prove by experience the origin of the universe from mind is not more contrary to common speech than to prove the motion of the earth from the same principle. And a caviller might raise all the same objections to the Copernican system which you have urged against my reasonings. Have you other earths, might he say, which you have seen to move? Have . . .

Yes! cried Philo, interrupting him, we have other earths. Is not the moon another earth, which we see to turn round its center? Is not Venus another earth, where we observe the same phenomenon? Are not the revolutions of the sun also a confirmation, from analogy, of the same theory? All the planets, are they not earths which revolve about the sun? Are not the satellites moons which move round Jupiter and Saturn, and along with these primary planets round the sun? These analogies and resemblances, with others which I have not mentioned, are the sole proofs of the Copernican system; and to you it belongs to consider whether you have any analogies of the same kind to support your theory.

In reality, Cleanthes, continued he, the modern system of astronomy is now so much received by all inquirers, and has become so essential a part even of our earliest education, that we are not commonly very scrupulous in examining the reasons upon which it is founded. It is now become a matter of mere curiosity to study the first writers on that subject who had the full force of prejudice to encounter, and were obliged to turn their arguments on every side in order to render them popular and convincing. But if we peruse Galileo's famous *Dialogues* concerning the system of the world, we shall find that that great genius, one of the sublimest that ever existed, first bent all his endeavors to prove that there was no foundation for the distinction commonly made between elementary and celestial substances. The schools, proceeding from the illusions of sense, had carried this distinction very far; and had established the latter substances to be ingenerable, incorruptible, unalterable, impassible; and had assigned all the opposite qualities to the former. But Galileo, beginning with the moon, proved its similarity in every particular to the earth: its convex figure, its natural darkness when not illuminated, its density, its distinction into solid and liquid, the variations of its phases, the mutual illuminations of the earth and moon, their mutual eclipses, the inequalities of the lunar surface, etc. After many instances of this kind, with regard to all the planets, men plainly saw that these bodies became proper objects of experience, and that the similarity of their nature enabled us to extend the same arguments and phenomena from one to the other.

In this cautious proceeding of the astronomers you may read your own condemnation, Cleanthes, or rather may see that the subject in which you are engaged exceeds all human reason and inquiry. Can you pretend to show any such similarity between the fabric of a house and the generation of a universe? Have you ever seen nature in any such situation as resembles the first arrangement of the elements? Have worlds ever been formed under your eye, and have you had leisure to observe the whole progress of the phenomenon, from the first appearance of order to its final consummation? If you have, then cite your experience and deliver your theory. (Pp. 141–51.)

Friedrich Nietzsche and the Death of God

As we have seen, some philosophers deny that God's existence can be proved. Others go further by insisting that religion and a belief in God are detrimental to human life.

No Western thinker had a greater impact on the latter score than Friedrich Nietzsche (1844–1900), who was born in the Prussian town of Röcken. Like Kierkegaard, Nietzsche rebelled against a strict Christian upbringing. Unlike Kierkegaard, however, he never achieved a positive reconciliation with the past. For a time Nietzsche thought he would follow his father into the Lutheran ministry, but he gave up that idea to study linguistics. His academic career was interrupted by service in the ambulance corps of the German army during the Franco-Prussian War. Illnesses contracted during his military duty left him weakened, and in 1879 poor health forced him to quit teaching. His next decade was marked by a search for medical help and by a series of brilliant philosophical writings. Early in 1889, however, Nietzsche suffered a serious mental breakdown from which he never recovered.

Nietzsche's Style

Nietzsche's rebellious spirit found expression in the style of his writing. He had little patience for attempts at the rigorous definition of terms, sustained logical analysis, and proofs about the ultimate nature of things, all of which in his view typified previous philosophy. Flashes of insight, aphoristic expressions, and proclamations are characteristic of his work. His ideas often appear to be nonsystematic and disconnected, characterized by conflict and even contradiction. Nietzsche did not try to explain away these tensions to make things easy for his readers. Connections do exist between the disparate assertions, but he provokes you to figure out the appropriate links for yourself.

Nietzsche's philosophical style is a miniature of the world he experienced. This world had some pattern and structure, but it did not form a rational system connected at every turn by the principle of sufficient reason. Nietzsche tries to describe the features of

FRIEDRICH WILHELM NIETZSCHE
1844–1900

existence as he sees them. He offers interpretations of broad trends in the development of morality and religion, and he does so partly by announcing the death of God.

Self-Deception and the Will to Power

"We are unknown to ourselves, we men of knowledge—and with good reason."[12] Thus begins *On the Genealogy of Morals* (1887). Nietzsche's theme was that even though people may regard themselves as well-informed, sophisticated, and knowledgeable, their lack of courage has kept them from uncovering what lies at the foundation of human existence and morality. Previous attempts to speak to such issues reveal more about the decadence of Western civilization than they do about how things really are. Nietzsche's hope was to eradicate this plague of self-delusion. He worked to lay bare facts people had suppressed and hidden, envisioning himself as a therapist who could free his readers from the cultural restrictions that stifle excellence. But the freedom that emerges might be overwhelming. "Independence is for the very few," said Nietzsche; "it is a privilege of the strong."[13] For the few who resist retreating into the security illusions provide, this twilight of the idols of conventional morality and religion is the dawn of a new hope.

Some philosophers take the **reductionist** view. One principle, not many, governs their interpretations. God is used by some as the ultimate source of explanation. However, Nietzsche felt that it is self-deception not to admit honestly that "life simply *is* will to power" (p. 203). He was no advocate of the democratic ideal of human equality. Such a doctrine, he thought, only levels the quality of life toward mediocrity. Individuals vary greatly in their talents and abilities, and there are basic qualitative differences that leave us unequal as persons. Nevertheless, according to Nietzsche, each individual will do what he or she can to assert power. Each will strive to achieve and hold a position of dominance. This tendency means that struggle is a basic fact of life. There is fierce competition for the top positions of power. If anyone falters at the top, someone else takes over.

Beyond Good and Evil

As Nietzsche interpreted the course of human history, Western culture has been dominated by an unfortunate distinction between "good" and "evil," a distinction that the Christian religion in particular has done much to encourage. Spurred by a deep hatred of aristocratic ways they could not emulate, the masses of humanity, often supported by religious leaders, have indulged in a revenge-motivated negation of the qualities of an aristocratic life. As Nietzsche saw things, the "good" of the good–evil distinction has emphasized equality, selflessness, meekness, humility, sympathy, pity, and other qualities of weakness. It has castigated the noble, aristocratic qualities—self-assertion, daring creativity, passion, and desire for conquest—by calling them evil. The prevalence of this concept of evil, Nietzsche contended, is responsible for weakness and mediocrity among those in dominant positions. It has annihilated the qualities that are essential for excellence in life. For Nietzsche, the low state of contemporary society indicated that not much had been done to fulfill these needs for excellence.

Human existence, however, need not end on this dismal note. If Nietzsche sometimes regards himself as a voice crying in the wilderness, he also thought human life could redeem itself by going "beyond good and evil."

> Must the ancient fire not some day flare up much more terribly, after much longer preparation? More: must one not desire it with all one's might? even will it? even promote it?[14]

The spirit of nobility—affirmation of life, struggle, and conquest, and a passionate desire to excel—these characteristics need to be uplifted. Our aim is not to duplicate the past but to bring these essential qualities back into contemporary life.

A Revaluation of Values

The proclamation of the death of God is an essential ingredient in the revaluation of values Nietzsche advocates. This rests on his conviction that slave morality and the existence of God, especially as the latter is understood in Christianity, are inextricably tied together. Nothing has done more than Christianity to entrench the slave morality in human consciousness. In Nietzsche's view, for example, the Christian emphasis on love is simply a way of extolling qualities of weakness. Christianity urges that it is our responsibility to cultivate those attributes, not because of an abstract concept of duty, but because it is God's will that we do so. As this conception develops, Nietzsche argues, it binds people in debilitating guilt. It also leads them to an escapist tendency to seek for fulfillment beyond this world.

Although one-sided, Nietzsche's critique was loud and clear: Christianity, with its conception of a transcendent, omnipotent, omniscient, just, and loving God, denies and negates all that is valuable in this world. Institutionalized by church and state, Christian theology and morality have made prisoners of Western humanity. Christianity claims that true freedom exists in serving God, but it denies a genuinely creative freedom by asserting that the world and its value structure are fixed by the will of God. It claims to offer people release from sin and guilt, but it does so at the expense of reducing them to mediocrity. Christianity advances a doctrine of love and charity, but this teaching actually rests on a feeling of hatred and revenge directed toward the qualities of nobility. Nietzsche does not deny that the long dominance of the Christian faith is a real manifestation of the **will to power** and that certain individuals have revealed unusual qualities of strength in establishing Christianity's authority. But he is convinced that the result has been to place an inferior breed in control of life. By proving that God is dead, Nietzsche believed that the underpinning of Christian morality could be eliminated, thus making it less difficult to move beyond our present system of good and evil.

Nietzsche thought the question of God's existence was more psychological than metaphysical. That is, Nietzsche thought that belief in God is simply an additional tool used by the slave mentality to distort the facts of life, and to attack and to bring to submission individuals of noble character. His aim was not so much to prove or disprove the existence of God but to show that belief in God can create a sickness. He wanted to convince people that the highest achievements in human life depend on the elimination of this belief. Nietzsche, then, assumed that God does not exist and concentrated on the psychotherapeutic task of freeing people from the idea that they are dependent on God.

The Madman

If one argues that Nietzsche's philosophy begs the question of God's existence, he is not without a powerful rebuttal. His is not a logical disproof of God's reality but an appraisal of human experience, which notes that, from a functional point of view, the credibility of God's existence is crumbling. Nietzsche advanced this "argument" in *The Gay* [joyful] *Science* (1882). There he spoke of "a madman" who runs into a marketplace crying, "I seek God! I seek God!"[15] This action provokes laughter from the men in the marketplace, who, Nietzsche reports, do not believe in God. In jest, they ask the madman whether God is lost, hiding, or traveling on a voyage. But with a penetrating glance, the madman confronts his tormenters with this announcement: "God is dead. God remains dead. And we have killed him" (p. 181).

It is significant that Nietzsche's story involves people who do not believe in God and the claim that people have killed God. Although nineteenth-century Europe was still dominated by Christian concepts, Nietzsche believed that the strength of Christianity was far less than it had been. People professed to be Christians and to have faith in God, but their confessions were habitual responses that lacked depth and authenticity. With Europe lost in mediocrity, Nietzsche found that developments in science and technology had eroded the idea of human dependence on God. They had displaced that conception with a new trust in human power and the possibility of progress through human efforts alone. Philosophical critiques of theological arguments and the ever-present conflict between the presence of unmerited suffering and the assertion of God's omnipotence and goodness took their toll. Thus, a combination of factors turned our attention away from God toward humanity and its world. Functionally speaking, this change of outlook constituted the death of God in Western civilization.

Nietzsche's view was that people in the nineteenth century already lived in a world largely devoid of God but did not realize it. Those who hear the madman's announcement stare at him in astonishment. These men, who are really Nietzsche's contemporaries, do not give God a place of importance. They have put God to death, but they lack an awareness of this fact and its significance. The madman puts it this way:

> Lightning and thunder require time, the light of the stars requires time, deeds require time even after they are done, before they can be seen and heard. This deed is still more distant from them than the most distant stars— *and yet they have done it themselves.* (P. 182.)

The madman believes that he has come before his time. People have killed God, but they are not yet ready to confront this fact and its importance.

The death of God is a critical matter, as Nietzsche's madman understands when he asks, "What did we do when we unchained this earth from its sun?" (p. 181). In a series of rhetorical questions, he suggests that the death of God leaves us disoriented and in darkness.

> Is there any up or down left? Are we not straying as through an infinite nothing? Do we not feel the breath of empty space? Has it not become colder? Is not night and more night coming on all the while? Must not lanterns be lit in the morning? (P. 181.)

Nietzsche's final appraisal, though, was not that this dizzying instability should be the occasion for despair and sorrow. On the contrary, the death of God is an occasion to affirm life. It signifies a release, a new awareness of freedom and responsibility, and an opportunity for creative action. The situation, Nietzsche acknowledged, is full of uncertainties. It is not clear how people will react when made to understand the fact that God is dead. There is no guarantee that they will take advantage of the new freedom and opportunities for creativity available in a world where God's control is absent. Nevertheless, Nietzsche retained a guarded optimism.

> At long last the horizon appears free again to us, even granted that it is not bright; at last our ships may venture out again, venture out to face any danger; all the daring of the lover of knowledge is permitted again; the sea, *our* sea, lies open again; perhaps there has never yet been such an "open sea." (P. 280.)

Is Nietzsche a Modern Prophet of Atheism?

Anselm and Thomas Aquinas might have applauded two lines of graffiti that report the following brief exchange: "God is dead" (signed Nietzsche) and "Nietzsche is dead" (signed God). Nietzsche's philosophy could hardly be more at odds with theirs. For while these church fathers would argue that the highest quality of human existence comes with faith in God, Nietzsche's basic conviction is that belief in God's existence debilitates and corrupts the human spirit. Moreover, these thinkers are in fundamental disagreement about the nature of existence. If Anselm and Aquinas understand existence as a rationally ordered creation, Nietzsche holds that "we invented the concept 'purpose.' In reality purpose is *lacking*."[16] Life is not without rhyme or reason. But, according to Nietzsche, human consciousness largely creates that meaning, and consciousness exists for no purpose that transcends itself. Contrary to what Anselm and Aquinas believed, our ability to philosophize is less a search for objective truth and more a reflection of a will to power that seeks to impose its own beliefs on reality. Nietzsche, then, offers us the ideal of the tragic hero who affirms existence in spite of and even because of the fact that he or she finds it ultimately absurd.

We have noted that it was not Nietzsche's philosophical style to try to prove his case by arguing for it directly. Instead he worked more like an artist, painting a picture of human existence as he saw it. Nowhere, for example, did he offer a disproof of God's existence that would parallel in form or tone the arguments that Anselm and Aquinas mounted to show that God is real. He distrusted the power of human reason to accomplish what is wanted in the proofs for God's existence. Thus, even though Nietzsche believed that there is no God, he also believed that it would be counterproductive to try to show conclusively that God does not exist. He used metaphorical language about the death of God and focused attention on what the consequences are if people do not believe God exists.

One can debate Nietzsche's conclusion about God, but it can hardly be denied that his psychological approach to philosophy and religion undermines the quest for certainty reflected in Anselm's and Aquinas's attempts to prove that God exists. The mass destruction we have witnessed in twentieth-century life supports Nietzsche's pessimism in one way, and yet it might also cause us to doubt the optimistic claims about human potentiality that he nevertheless expressed. Given persistent reports of religious experiences, the death of God as reported by Nietzsche is not a fait accompli. Still, it is less easy to discover God since Hume and Nietzsche arrived on the scene. Nietzsche's claim that God is dead must be taken more tentatively than the tone of his pronouncements suggest, but Nietzsche's work shows that an affirmative answer to the question "Does God exist?" cannot escape the threat of doubt. Consider that situation as you read the following selections from *The Gay Science*, and ask again "What may I hope?"

THE MADMAN

Have you not heard of that madman who lit a lantern in the bright morning hours, ran to the marketplace, and cried incessantly: "I seek God! I seek God!"—As many of those who did not believe in God were standing around just then, he provoked much laughter. Has he got lost? asked one. Did he lose his way like a child? asked another. Or is he hiding? Is he afraid of us? Has he gone on a voyage? emigrated?—Thus they yelled and laughed.

The madman jumped into their midst and pierced them with his eyes. "Whither is God?" he cried: "I will tell you. *We have killed him*—you and I. All of us are his murderers. But how did we do this? How could we drink up the sea? Who gave us the sponge to wipe away the entire horizon? What were we doing when we unchained this earth from its sun? Whither is it moving now? Whither are we moving? Away from all suns? Are we not plunging continually? Backward, sideward, forward, in all directions? Is there still any up or down? Are we not straying as through an infinite nothing? Do we not feel the breath of empty space? Has it not become colder? Is not night continually closing in on us? Do we not need to light lanterns in the morning? Do we hear nothing as yet of the noise of the gravediggers who are burying God?

Do we smell nothing as yet of the divine decomposition? Gods, too, decompose. God is dead. God remains dead. And we have killed him.

"How shall we comfort ourselves, the murderers of all murderers? What was holiest and mightiest of all that the world has yet owned has bled to death under our knives: who will wipe this blood off us? What water is there for us to clean ourselves? What festivals of atonement, what sacred games shall we have to invent? Is not the greatness of this deed too great for us? Must we ourselves not become gods simply to appear worthy of it? There has never been a greater deed; and whoever is born after us—for the sake of this deed he will belong to a higher history than all history hitherto."

Here the madman fell silent and looked again at his listeners; and they, too, were silent and stared at him in astonishment. At last he threw his lantern on the ground, and it broke into pieces and went out. "I have come too early," he said then; "my time is not yet. This tremendous event is still on its way, still wandering; it has not yet reached the ears of men. Lightning and thunder require time; the light of the stars requires time; deeds, though done, still require time to be seen and heard. This deed is still more distant from them than the most distant stars—*and yet they have done it themselves.*"

It has been related further that on the same day the madman forced his way into several churches and there struck up his *requiem aeternam deo.* Led out and called to account, he is said always to have replied nothing but: "What after all are these churches now if they are not the tombs and sepulchers of God?"

THE MEANING OF OUR CHEERFULNESS

The greatest recent event—that "God is dead," that the belief in the Christian god has become unbelievable—is already beginning to cast its first shadows over Europe. For the few at least, whose eyes—the *suspicion* in whose eyes is strong and subtle enough for this spectacle, some sun seems to have set and some ancient and profound trust has been turned into doubt; to them our old world must appear daily more like evening, more mistrustful, stranger, "older." But in the main one may say: The event itself is far too great, too distant, too remote from the multitude's capacity for comprehension even for the tidings of it to be thought of as having *arrived* as yet. Much less may one suppose that many people know as yet *what* this event really means—and how much must collapse now that this faith has been undermined because it was built upon this faith, propped up by it, grown into it; for example, the whole of our European morality. This long plenitude and sequence of breakdown, destruction, ruin, and cataclysm that is now impending—who could guess enough of it today to be compelled to play the teacher and advance proclaimer of this monstrous logic of terror, the prophet of a gloom and an eclipse of the sun whose like has probably never yet occurred on earth?

Even we born guessers of riddles who are, as it were, waiting on the mountains, posted between today and tomorrow, stretched in the contradiction between today and tomorrow, we firstlings and premature births of the coming century, to whom the shadows that must soon envelop Europe really *should* have appeared by now—why is it that even we look forward to the approaching gloom without any real sense of involvement and above all without any worry and fear for *ourselves?* Are we perhaps still too much under the impression of the *initial consequences* of this event—and these initial consequences, the consequences for *ourselves,* are quite the opposite of what one might perhaps expect: They are not at all sad and gloomy but rather like a new and scarcely describable kind of light, happiness, relief, exhilaration, encouragement, dawn.

Indeed, we philosophers and "free spirits" feel, when we hear the news that "the old god is dead," as if a new dawn shone on us; our heart overflows with gratitude, amazement, premonitions, expectation. At long last the horizon appears free to us again, even if it should not be bright; at long last our ships may venture out again, venture out to face any danger; all the daring of the lover of knowledge is permitted again; the sea, *our* sea, lies open again; perhaps there has never yet been such an "open sea."[17]

Summary

We first responded to the question "Does God exist?" by exploring Anselm's attempt to find one conclusive argument that would prove God's reality. His effort to move from the concept of God to the reality of God went too far for Thomas Aquinas, who divided his own quest for certainty into five paths, each

locating the same God by reflecting on one feature of the natural world. Hume believed that neither human reason nor any experience of the natural world could provide the religious authority that Anselm and Thomas Aquinas wanted. A century later, Nietzsche proclaimed the death of God.

Nevertheless, the question "Does God exist?" continues to provoke a wide array of responses. Where it will lead any individual is uncertain, but the posing of the query itself is closely related to the hope that life can make good sense. People do not agree about the role of God and religious belief, but insofar as we are beings who hope, the issue of God remains alive among the questions of philosophy.

GLOSSARY

atheism the philosophical position that holds that there exist no supernatural beings such as God or gods.

contingent the term used by Aquinas for the type of existence that is defined by its impermanence, that is, by the fact that it comes into being out of nonbeing and in time passes back into nonbeing. Aquinas contrasts this situation with that of necessary existences, which must exist in order to serve as the causes of contingent beings' coming to be. Since there cannot be an **infinite regress** of beings causing one another, we must suppose that God, which causes other things to exist but is itself uncaused, necessarily exists.

cosmological argument one of Aquinas's three main arguments for the existence of God, which asserts that God's existence is required to prevent ordinary judgments from becoming entangled in an **infinite regress** like that of the chain of causes. Since we are able to make intelligible judgments about beings, goodness, and truth, there must be some being that exemplifies these qualities in their most supreme form, or we would have no ultimate reason or cause to believe that

our judgments can be true. See also **teleological argument, unmoved mover.**

God the deity of the Judeo–Christian tradition, to whom is attributed the creation of the universe. In the philosophical tradition, attempts to prove the existence of God lead from purely scriptural to more intellectual conceptions of this deity, such as Aquinas's identification of God with the **unmoved mover,** or Anselm's description of God as absolute perfection.

hope an attitude of desire toward some outcome, coupled with the expectation that this outcome will actually follow even in the absence of evidence to support that supposition.

infinite regress a sequence, as of causes or explanations, that continues without terminating (that is, has no final point). Aquinas used Aristotle's judgment that this type of sequence is an intellectual absurdity in the cosmological proof of God, positing God as the point of termination in such a sequence.

miracle an event that defies the usual laws of nature and is taken as evidence for the existence of a supreme and omnipotent being. In his *Enquiry Concerning Human Understanding,* Hume asserted that the overwhelming regularity of nature makes it always more likely than not that a person witnessing a "miracle" is mistaken or misled about what he is experiencing than that he is actually witnessing a counterexample to the laws of nature.

"natural religion" Hume's term for the theological attempt to establish the existence of God by appeal to human experience, which he explores in the *Dialogue Concerning Natural Religion.*

ontological argument the argument for the existence of God set forth by Anselm, whose strategy is to assert that the very meaning of the concept of God is such that there can be no doubt about God's existence. God is absolutely perfect; in order to be perfect, a thing must be, or exist; therefore, God exists.

principle of sufficient reason the principle, common to all five of Aquinas's proofs of God, that **infinite regress** in a series of explanations is a sign of absurdity, so that there must be some supreme explanatory principle sufficient to bring this chain to an end.

"pure actuality" Aquinas's notion that to serve as the **principle of sufficient reason,** God must be a kind of being that contains no unactualized potential, unlike **contingent** beings, which always must contain such potential.

reductionist the tendency in philosophy, which Nietzsche diagnosed, to boil all reality or existence down to a single concept or scheme, in which things of particular kinds are to be seen as the modalities.

revelation knowledge gained from a divine source; in Aquinas, a source of knowledge that along with faith, is needed to complete the task of acquiring knowledge for which reason alone is insufficient.

teleological argument the 'argument from design,' the proof of the existence of God that depends on the systematic order we find in nature. Such an order, the argument runs, would not be possible without supposing that some creator had imposed this order on its own creation.

theology in the work of Aquinas, a discipline that intersects with and supplements philosophy in important ways; the areas in which the two disciplines intersect Aquinas terms "natural theology."

unmoved mover the notion in Aristotle's *Metaphysics* of a cause that is itself uncaused, taken over by Aquinas in the cosmological argument for the existence of God.

"will to power" Nietzsche's conception of the source of all ideas, especially the idea of God; inasmuch as all human life is an expression of a desire to dominate and control the world with which one is confronted, ideas form part of our means to this end. Nietzsche saw the idea of God as having the primary function of exerting control over other human beings through the "slave morality," which is upheld by the religious institutions that are founded on such an idea.

STUDY QUESTIONS

1. Does Anselm's ontological argument lead all his readers where he wants them to go? What conclusion do you think he intended them to reach?

2. Do you find the idea of God both as easy and as difficult to grasp as Anselm thought you should? Why?

3. Do the arguments of Thomas Aquinas lead him—and you—to rational belief in one God, as he intended, without the necessity of relying on faith?

4. Do you find the need for an ultimate starting point or a final answer as compelling as Aquinas thinks you should?

5. Following up on Hume's *Dialogues,* how do you appraise the chances of grounding religious belief on the natural world and on common human experience? Are there other sound ways in which such belief could be grounded?

6. Religiously speaking, how important or unimportant are "proofs" for the existence of God?

7. Do you understand the source of Nietzsche's radical critique of religion? What effect do you think he wanted to achieve?

8. Why did Nietzsche proclaim the death of God? Do you find his proclamation convincing?

9. How would you describe and evaluate the relations between human hope and the existence of God?

NOTES

[1] Anselm, *Proslogium,* in *Basic Writings,* trans. Sidney Norton Deane (La Salle, Ill.: Open Court, 1958), p. 6. Reprinted by permission of Open Court Publishing Company.

[2] Anselm/Gaunilo, "Appendix: In Behalf of the Fool," in *Basic Writings,* p. 146.

[3] Anselm, *Proslogium,* in *Basic Writings,* pp. 7–10.

[4] Anselm/Gaunilo, "Appendix: In Behalf of the Fool," in *Basic Writings,* pp. 145–52.

[5] Anselm, "Appendix: Reply to Gaunilo," in *Basic Writings,* pp. 153–55.

[6] Thomas Aquinas, *Summa Contra Gentiles* (I, ch. 11), trans. Anton C. Pegis (Garden City, N.Y.: Doubleday Image Books, 1955), p. 83.

[7] Thomas Aquinas, *Summa Theologica* (I, Ques. 2, Art. 3), in *Basic Writings of Saint Thomas Aquinas,* 2 vols., ed. and trans. Anton C. Pegis (New York: Random House, 1945), 1:22–23. Reprinted by permission of the A. C. Pegis Estate.

[8] Aquinas, *Summa Contra Gentiles,* (I, ch. 13), p. 96.

[9] Aquinas, *Summa Theologica* (I, Ques. 2, Arts. 1–3), in *Basic Writings of Saint Thomas Aquinas,* 1:18–24.

[10] Anselm, *Proslogium,* in *Basic Writings,* p. 7.

[11] David Hume, *Dialogues Concerning Natural Religion,* ed. Norman Kemp Smith (Indianapolis: Bobbs-Merrill, 1947), p. 143.

[12] Friedrich Nietzsche, *On the Genealogy of Morals,* trans. Walter Kaufmann and R. J. Hollingdale (New York: Vintage Books, 1967), p. 15.

[13] Friedrich Nietzsche, *Beyond Good and Evil,* trans. Walter Kaufmann (New York: Vintage Books, 1966), p. 41.

[14] Nietzsche, *On the Genealogy of Morals,* p. 54.

[15] Friedrich Nietzsche, *The Gay Science,* trans. Walter Kaufmann (New York: Vintage Books, 1974), pp. 181–82. Copyright © 1974 by Random House, Inc. Reprinted by permission of the publisher.

[16] Friedrich Nietzsche, *Twilight of the Idols,* trans. R. J. Hollingdale, (Baltimore: Penguin Books, 1971), p. 54. Nietzsche's italics.

[17] Nietzsche, *The Gay Science,* pp. 181–82, 279–80.

CHAPTER TWELVE

Can My Life Make Sense?

When Kant asked, "What may I hope?" he was especially intrigued by the observation that human hope extends beyond the acquisition of physical possessions. Most philosophers share his fascination about our propensity to develop hopes that involve moral goals, metaphysical visions, and religious promises. Do you hope, for instance, that life makes sense, that it is ultimately reasonable, purposeful, and intelligible in a way that takes account of your own existence? Usually people do have such hopes, philosophers among them, even though life is obviously filled with a variety of patterns and plans, purposes and projects. Ironically, the very fact that life does make so much sense provides one reason for people to hope. For unless life made some sense, it would be hopeless—literally. You go to class, exams come, there is a party this weekend, and your family plans a vacation—all these events fill your life and they do make sense. Yet in the midst of such everyday plans, you still may ask: Is this all worthwhile? Where is it getting me?

We fill our days with obvious plans and purposes, even if they are aimed at nothing more than a meal we need or a movie we would like to see. But sometimes this does not satisfy us, even when the plans are carried out. We hope for more than life's routine. Friendship, love, work, play—all those realities give us good reasons for living. One difficulty is that those elements are not the only ones we experience. Untimely death stalks us. Love and friendship cannot always resist the onslaughts that threaten them. Apparently senseless accidents intrude; natural and man-made violence reduces our fondest accomplishments to rubble. Seemingly without rhyme or reason, our best-laid plans come to naught. True, if we study such events they often make a kind of sense. They do not take place in a vacuum but are the outcomes of certain causes and effects. Nonetheless some events may strike us as catastrophes, leaving us to feel that life lacks the overall sense it ought to possess. Humanity's place in the scheme of things, let alone that of an individual person, seems immensely fragile. Life may be swallowed up eventually by a void that reduces everything to empty silence. Can my life make sense? For human beings that question is as natural as the hope that its answer is "Yes." To answer in the affirmative, however, takes **courage,** a theme emphasized by Paul Tillich, the last of the five philosophers we will encounter in this chapter. He coined the phrase "the courage to be," but watch to see how that idea also underlies the thought of Blaise Pascal, G. W. F. Hegel, Henry David Thoreau, and Albert Camus.

Blaise Pascal and His Forced Wager

Meditating on the thought of René Descartes, his older French contemporary, Blaise Pascal (1623–1662) remarked: "All philosophy is not worth one hour of pain."[1] On another occasion he concluded that "to make light of philosophy is to be a true philosopher" (p. 3). Nearly all philosophers have been dissatisfied with philosophy's past. Many are uneasy about its future as well. Yet few would share Pascal's scathing assessments. You might wonder whether a person who said such things could really be a philosopher. Pascal counts as one nonetheless, partly because he studied the question "Can my life make sense?" His *Pensées* (1670) was intended to answer questions about Christian doctrine. Unfinished, the book has a fragmentary form, which gives it the flavor of an intellectual–spiritual diary. In trying to fathom life's meaning, Pascal probably wrote as much for himself as for a public audience, but his aphoristic style makes him a memorable and eminently quotable thinker.

Pascal's life was as brilliant as it was brief. Accomplished in mathematics and geometry, he was a pioneer in probability theory. He made important contributions in physics. He also invented a computer. Although by our present standards, of course, the device was extremely simple—merely a way to process numbers efficiently—it is impressive that he had the concept so long ago. These feats brought Pascal fame in his own day, and they secure his place as one of history's greatest mathematicians and scientists. His profoundly religious experience, however, made him a "living thinker" in ways that his other discoveries could not.

Because his life was a mixture of social prominence and spiritual intensity, Pascal has been called a man of the world among ascetics and an ascetic among men of the world.

BLAISE PASCAL 1623–1662

Belonging to a devout Catholic family, Pascal experienced a spiritual awakening on November 23, 1654. On that occasion he wrote what is now referred to as his "Memorial," and he kept it with him always. At his death, it was found sewn into the lining of his coat.

FIRE

> God of Abraham, God of Isaac, God of Jacob,
> Not of the philosophers and scholars.
> Certitude. Joy. Certitude. Emotion. Sight. Joy.
> Forgetfulness of the world and of all outside God.
> The world has not known Thee, but I have known Thee.
> Joy! joy! joy! Tears of joy.
> My God, wilt thou leave me?
> Let me not be separated from Thee for ever.[2]

Pascal's *Pensées* followed these sentiments, often reflecting the theological themes found among his heterodox friends at Port-Royal, the Jansenists, an austere, seventeenth-century Catholic order influenced by the Protestant thought of John Calvin. In defending Christianity, Pascal's reflections also contain insight about life in general, because Pascal found that the human condition was one of finitude, uncertainty, and considerable misery. Those convictions also account for his suspicion of philosophy. It may be doing what is natural in catering to our yearning for certainty, he argued, but philosophy also misleads us by suggesting that reason alone can provide the stability life needs.

Asking the Right Questions

When we ask "Can my life make sense?" Pascal is an excellent author to study because he grasps the moods that bring questions to the fore, states only what is essential, and leaves the rest to the reader to elaborate. One of his themes is the significance of death. Most of us would rather not think about death, Pascal admits, and we become experts at fending it off. But death remains before us, as Pascal suggests in the following scene:

> Let us imagine a number of men in chains, and all condemned to death, where some are killed each day in the sight of the others, and those who remain see their own fate in that of their fellows and wait their turn, looking at each other sorrowfully and without hope. It is an image of the condition of men.[3]

Our condition raises other issues, too. At one point, for example, Pascal writes in this vein:

> When I consider the short duration of my life, swallowed up in the eternity before and after, the little space which I fill, and even can see, engulfed in the infinite immensity of spaces of which I am ignorant, and which know me not, I am frightened, and am astonished at being here rather than there,

why now rather than then. Who has put me here? By whose order and direction have this time and place been allotted to me? (P. 61.)

These passages suggest how the insights of mathematical and scientific reason may combine with an existential concern and lead us to appropriate the hope religion offers.

The Necessity of the Wager

Pascal's best-known contribution to philosophy is called "**Pascal's wager.**" In the section of his *Pensées* devoted to it, he speaks about the search for God. For Pascal that search *is* the quest for meaning in life, because God provides the hope that we can be redeemed from misery and death. The question of the soul's immortality is of particularly great consequence. If only death awaits even the noblest lives, we will possess no lasting satisfaction. To have only doubt is a great burden where such questions are concerned, but failure to move beyond that condition is even worse. As Pascal's "Memorial" suggests, religious experience can convey a kind of certitude, at least in the moment of its happening. But he also recognized that life goes on and is never completely immune to doubt and uncertainty. Where the meaning of life is at stake, we are dealing with faith, which means taking the risk of making and sustaining a commitment.

Pascal argues that we ought to bet that life does make sense. That wager, he underscores, is about God's existence and purposes. For if God does not exist, life's meaning will at best be tragic and at worst simply annihilated. We ought to wager that God exists and live accordingly. To do so, he contends, is not irrational but exactly the opposite. In our human situation it is not given to us to demonstrate that God exists, and yet an analysis of our predicament suggests that faith in God is sensible. The importance of this claim is clarified when Pascal writes that "Man is but a reed, the most feeble thing in nature; but he is a thinking reed. . . . Thought constitutes the greatness of man" (p. 97). Pascal believes that reason is limited, but it ought not to be disparaged for "all our dignity consists . . . in thought" (p. 97). For Pascal, religious faith is a further expression of human dignity. The thoughtful person, Pascal believes, will see that the wager makes sense:

> Let us weigh the gain and the loss in wagering that God is. Let us estimate these two chances. If you gain, you gain all; if you lose, you lose nothing. Wager, then, without hesitation that He is. (P. 67.)

The clincher in this argument, Pascal believes, is that this wager is forced. Not to choose is also a choice, for the decision is made by refusing to try, to enter in, to venture. This situation has the either/or quality Kierkegaard noted. Lack of belief excludes one from the benefits of faith. But the most important point is that we must choose; an either/or situation offers no middle ground.

The God of Pascal's Wager

We know that Pascal distinguished between the God of philosophers and scholars and the God of Abraham, Isaac, and Jacob. In conjunction with the wager, note some other remarks that Pascal made about God and God's relation to us. As a Christian, Pascal affirms that his religion teaches two essential truths: "That there is a God whom men can know, and that there is a corruption in their nature which renders them unworthy of Him" (p. 153). God is "a God of love," adds Pascal, and God will "fill the soul and heart of those whom He possesses" (p. 154). These are not rationally demonstrable claims. On the contrary, religion often places us in a precarious position, saying that people "are in darkness and estranged from God, that He has hidden Himself from their knowledge, that this is in fact the name which He gives Himself in the Scriptures, *Deus absconditus*" (p. 53). Thus, as far as reason is concerned,

> [i]t is incomprehensible that God should exist, and it is incomprehensible that He should not exist; that the soul should be joined to the body, and that we should have no soul; that the world should be created, and that it should not be created, etc.; that original sin should be, and that it should not be. (Pp. 64–65.)

But, Pascal asserts in one of his most famous lines, "The heart has its reasons, which reason does not know" (p. 78). He goes on to say: "It is the heart which experiences God, and not the reason. This is faith: God felt by the heart, not by the reason" (p. 78).

Pascal's Fundamental Point

As Pascal saw it, your decision as to whether life makes sense does not depend on reason alone but more on your willingness to act when confronted by a forced wager. This is Pascal's fundamental point. He argues that such a situation does not offend the concept of reason. Indeed, defining life as meaningful is no greater affront to reason than the opposite decision. At least in the long run you have everything to gain and nothing to lose by believing. An eternity of happiness is at stake. In fact, when forced to gamble, the paradox is that the reasonable action is to let choice transcend reason in order to allow oneself to be possessed by God. Those who demand certainty prior to commitment fail to understand the human situation. If you object that religion is too uncertain and God too difficult, while sufficient meaning can be found without entanglement in the vagaries of either, remember that Pascal thinks the issue of life beyond death is crucial where life's significance is concerned. It is hard to conceive that death is not the end for us, unless God does exist.

"To deny, to believe, and to doubt well," Pascal thought, "are to a man what the race is to a horse" (p. 76). Pascal likens life to a game, but one that should be played out earnestly. To do so takes us beyond reason, for "the last proceeding of reason is to recognize that there is an infinity of things beyond it" (p. 77). Played well, the game of life teaches reason to trust the heart. Yet that result can occur only when we give reason its due as well. Each has its own order. In searching for meaning in life, Pascal recommends that we must be careful not to confuse the two or to try to reduce one to the other. Life might be simpler if we could do the latter, but Pascal insists that this is impossible. There are two levels, two ways of proceeding. They can supplement each other, but they do not always blend. We must learn to live with both and discount neither. It is this paradox that forces us to wager about the meaning of life.

How to Make Sense

When we ask "Can my life make sense?" is our answer: "Not of itself and not on its own?" Life does not come with built-in answers for the questions of philosophy, in spite of our hope that it might. But for Pascal that does not mean that life has no meaning in itself. Nor does it follow, as some philosophers assert, that all meaning is dependent on us and varies with each individual. Pascal thinks that life has meaning in itself, but our awareness of it is not assured unless we gamble. We must make the wager first; then the purpose of life may become clear.

As you consider Pascal's argument, you will find it similar to other philosophers (e.g., the existentialists or the American pragmatists). All were reacting against the security of a rational system that seemed to make all things plain. Pascal and others saw the inev-

itable risk in all existence. As opposed to the positivist, August Comte, for example, who felt that all problems could be handled with scientific precision if not certainty, Pascal asserts the precarious uncertainty of human existence in the face of scientific advance. Like Augustine, he views our earthly city as one related to a city of God, but one that in our uncertain situation reflects the heavenly city only imperfectly. Read on from the *Pensées* and ask yourself whether you are willing to make Pascal's wager, and why.

. . . Let man then contemplate the whole of nature in her full and grand majesty, and turn his vision from the low objects which surround him. Let him gaze on that brilliant light, set like an eternal lamp to illumine the universe; let the earth appear to him a point in comparison with the vast circle described by the sun; and let him wonder at the fact that this vast circle is itself but a very fine point in comparison with that described by the stars in their revolution round the firmament. But if our view be arrested there, let our imagination pass beyond; it will sooner exhaust the power of conception than nature that of supplying material for conception. The whole visible world is only an imperceptible atom in the ample bosom of nature. No idea approaches it. We may enlarge our conceptions beyond all imaginable space; we only produce atoms in comparison with the reality of things. It is an infinite sphere, the center of which is everywhere, the circumference nowhere. In short it is the greatest sensible mark of the almighty power of God, that imagination loses itself in that thought.

Returning to himself, let man consider what he is in comparison with all existence; let him regard himself as lost in this remote corner of nature; and from the little cell in which he finds himself lodged, I mean the universe, let him estimate at their true value the earth, kingdoms, cities, and himself. What is a man in the Infinite?

But to show him another prodigy equally astonishing, let him examine the most delicate things he knows. Let a mite be given him, with its minute body and parts incomparably more minute, limbs with their joints, veins in the limbs, blood in the veins, humors in the blood, drops in the humors, vapors in the drops. Dividing these last things again, let him exhaust his powers of conception, and let the last object at which he can arrive be now that of our discourse. Perhaps he will think that here is the smallest point in nature. I will let him see therein a new abyss. I will paint for him not only the visible universe, but all that he can conceive of nature's immensity in the womb of this abridged atom. Let him see therein an infinity of universes, each of which has its firmament, its planets, its earth, in the same proportion as in the visible world; in each earth animals, and in the last mites, in which he will find again all that the first had, finding still in these others the same thing without end and without cessation. Let him lose himself in wonders as amazing in their littleness as the others in their vastness. For who will not be astounded at the fact that our body, which a little ago was imperceptible in the universe, itself imperceptible in the bosom of the whole, is now a colossus, a world, or rather a whole, in respect of the nothingness which we cannot reach? He who regards himself in this light will be afraid of himself, and observing himself sustained in the body given him by nature between those two abysses of the Infinite and Nothing, will tremble at the sight of these marvels; and I think that, as his curiosity changes into admiration, he will be more disposed to contemplate them in silence than to examine them with presumption.

For in fact what is man in nature? A Nothing in comparison with the Infinite, an All in comparison with the Nothing, a mean between nothing and everything. Since he is infinitely removed from comprehending the extremes, the end of things and their beginning are hopelessly hidden from him in an impenetrable secret; he is equally incapable of seeing the Nothing from which he was made, and the Infinite in which he is swallowed up. (Pp. 16–18.)

. . . Let us now speak according to natural lights.

If there is a God, He is infinitely incomprehensible, since, having neither parts nor limits, He has no affinity to us. We are then incapable of knowing either what He is or if He is. This being so, who will dare to undertake the decision of the question? Not we, who have no affinity to Him.

Who then will blame Christians for not being able to give a reason for their belief, since they profess a religion for which they cannot give a reason? They declare, in expounding it to the world, that it is a foolishness, *stultitiam*; and then you complain that they do not prove it! If they proved it, they would not keep their word; it is in lacking proofs, that they are not lacking in sense. "Yes, but although this excuses those who offer it as such, and takes away from them the blame of putting it forward without reason, it does not excuse those who receive it." Let us then examine this point, and say, "God is, or He is not." But to which side shall we incline? Reason can decide nothing here. There is an infinite chaos which separated us. A game is being played at the extremity of this infinite distance where heads or tails will turn up. What will you wager? According to reason, you can do neither the one thing nor the other; according to reason, you can defend neither of the propositions.

Do not then reprove for error those who have made a choice; for you know nothing about it. "No, but I blame them for having made, not this choice, but a choice; for again both he who chooses heads and he who chooses tails are equally at fault, they are both in the wrong. The true course is not to wager at all."

Yes; but you must wager. It is not optional. You are embarked. Which will you choose then? Let us see. Since you must choose, let us see which interests you least. You have two things to lose, the true and the good; and two things to stake, your reason and your will, your knowledge and your happiness; and your nature has two things to shun, error and misery. Your reason is no more shocked in choosing one rather than the other, since you must of necessity choose. This is one point settled. But your happiness? Let us weigh the gain and the loss in wagering that God is. Let us estimate these two chances. If you gain, you gain all; if you lose, you lose nothing. Wager, then, without hesitation that He is.—"That is very fine. Yes, I must wager; but I may perhaps wager too much."—Let us see. Since there is an equal risk of gain and of loss, if you had only to gain two lives, instead of one, you might still wager. But if there were three lives to gain, you would have to play (since you are under the necessity of playing), and you would be imprudent, when you are forced to play, not to chance your life to gain three at a game where there is an equal risk of loss and gain. But there is an eternity of life and happiness. And this being so, if there were an infinity of chances, of which one only would be for you, you would still be right in wagering one to win two, and you would act stupidly, being obliged to play, by refusing to stake one life against three at a game in which out of an infinity of chances there is one for you, if there were an infinity of an infinitely happy life to gain. But there is here an infinity of an infinitely happy life to gain, a chance of gain against a finite number of chances of loss, and what you stake is finite. It is all divided; wherever the infinite is and there is not an infinity of chances of loss against that of gain, there is no time to hesitate, you must give all. And thus, when one is forced to play, he must renounce reason to preserve his life, rather than risk it for infinite gain, as likely to happen as the loss of nothingness.

For it is no use to say it is uncertain if we will gain, and it is certain that we risk, and that the infinite distance between the *certainty* of what is staked and the *uncertainty* of what will be gained, equals the finite good which is certainly staked against the uncertain infinite. It is not so, as every player stakes a certainty to gain an uncertainty, and yet he stakes a finite certainty to gain a finite uncertainty, without transgressing against reason. There is not an infinite distance

between the certainty staked and the uncertainty of the gain; that is untrue. In truth, there is an infinity between the certainty of gain and the certainty of loss. But the uncertainty of the gain is proportioned to the certainty of the stake according to the proportion of the chances of gain and loss. Hence it comes that, if there are as many risks on one side as on the other, the course is to play even; and then the certainty of the stake is equal to the uncertainty of the gain, so far is it from fact that there is an infinite distance between them. And so our proposition is of infinite force, when there is the finite to stake in a game where there are equal risks of gain and of loss, and the infinite to gain. This is demonstrable; and if men are capable of any truths, this is one.

If we must not act save on a certainty, we ought not to act on religion, for it is not certain. But how many things we do on an uncertainty, sea voyages, battles! I say then we must do nothing at all, for nothing is certain, and that there is more certainty in religion than there is as to whether we may see tomorrow; for it is not certain that we may see tomorrow, and it is certainly possible that we may not see it. We cannot say as much about religion. It is not certain that it is; but who will venture to say that it is certainly possible that it is not? Now when we work for tomorrow, and so on an uncertainty, we act reasonably; for we ought to work for an uncertainty according to the doctrine of chance which was demonstrated above.

Saint Augustine has seen that we work for an uncertainty, on sea, in battle, etc. But he has not seen the doctrine of chance which proves that we should do so. Montaigne has seen that we are shocked at a fool, and that habit is all-powerful; but he has not seen the reason of this effect.

All these persons have seen the effects, but they have not seen the causes. They are, in comparison with those who have discovered the causes, as those who have only eyes are in comparison with those who have intellect. For the effects are perceptible by sense, and the causes are visible only to the intellect. And although these effects are seen by the mind, this mind is, in comparison with the mind which sees the causes, as the bodily senses are in comparison with the intellect. (Pp. 66–68.)

The heart has its reasons, which reason does not know. We feel it in a thousand things. I say that the heart naturally loves the Universal Being, and also itself naturally, according as it gives itself to them; and it hardens itself against one or the other at its will. You have rejected the one, and kept the other. Is it by reason that you love yourself?

It is the heart which experiences God, and not the reason. This, then, is faith: God felt by the heart, not by the reason. (P. 78.)

G. W. F. Hegel and the Cunning of Reason

Philosophers are not of one mind when they ask "Can life make sense?" Nor do they agree about how to interpret our hope that the answer is yes. Some affirm their belief that life makes perfect sense but doubt that we can obtain enough knowledge to validate this hope completely. A second group maintains that philosophy can demonstrate the thoroughly rational nature of existence, thus replacing the need for hope with the satisfaction of knowledge. A third contingent emphasizes a gap between what is and what ought to be. They want to transform hope into an action that bridges this gulf. Others affirm the need to bridge the gulf while insisting that it will remain forever. To hope otherwise is self-deception, they say. And still others contend that within the courage to hope for meaning in spite of absurdity, undeceived glimpses of an undergirding purpose for human existence can be obtained. Watch to see how each of the philosophers

GEORG WILHELM FRIEDRICH HEGEL
1770–1831

discussed in this chapter typifies one of these orientations.

If Pascal exemplifies the first kind of thinker, the German philosopher Georg Wilhelm Friedrich Hegel (1770–1831) represents the second group. Succeeding Kant as the most influential philosopher in continental Europe, from 1818 until his death Hegel held a prestigious professorship at the University of Berlin. His bold and far-reaching mind mightily influenced Karl Marx and many existential thinkers despite their disagreements with him. Hegel wrote about history, religion, art, politics, and ethics as well as logic and epistemology. The result was an elaborate metaphysical system affirming that life makes perfect sense, though it is not without many twists and turns. Failure to interpret those turns properly, Hegel argued, will leave us mistakenly convinced that existence is threatened by the negation of meaning. But if we explore existence adequately, the cunning of reason, as Hegel called it, becomes apparent and reveals itself to be part of an overall scheme in which "what is rational is actual and what is actual is rational."[4]

The Rational and the Real

Convinced that philosophy's job is to clarify the rational and the real, Hegel had to do nothing less than account for the nature of all that exists. What struck him most profoundly was that all that exists is dynamic and alive. Everything in the world moves in stages, he thought, the perishing of one producing the new conditions of another. Change negates what is but carries forward something of the past into what comes next. We find advance; we find reversal; but both fit together into a pattern, although it is not apparent at first. Existence moves so that one stage, owing to its own incompleteness, eventually contradicts itself and tends to become its opposite. This pattern repeats so that the opposition is transmuted into a third stage, which brings the first two together. The new outcome is different from what preceded it; yet clearly it is the result of what went before as well.

Hegel called this continuous negation and affirmation *dialectic*. The dialectical movement of existence, in turn, involved the **triadic** pattern just now noted, which he sometimes described as moving from a **thesis,** to an **antithesis,** and then to a **synthesis** of the two. For example, we assert that absolute democracy is the best modern political system (thesis). But when it is tried, disagreement and chaos threaten to destroy the ideal, and we

see that some form of authority and privilege must be granted to a few (antithesis). But if this tends to create a totalitarian and repressive state, we may compromise on federalism, a balance of powers, and a representational democratic voice (synthesis).

These dialectical movements are fundamental to Hegel's account of the nature of life itself. He believed that the history of the world can be understood adequately only if we recognize that it reflects a developing rational mind acting to make itself ever more concrete, aware of itself, and thus free. Three basic stages characterize the development of reality, which Hegel often called God, the **Absolute,** or **Reason.** Initially, Hegel stated, Being's form is that of "**Idea-in-itself,**" an awareness that is self-contained but abstract and lacking in particularity and concreteness. Naturally impelled to realize itself, the "Idea-in-itself" overcomes its incompleteness, although only in part, by a self-negation in which it becomes the "**Idea-outside-itself**" or, more simply, **Nature.** Nature exhibits order and pattern. It is rational just as the "Idea-in-itself" was logical. Rationality within "Idea-in-itself" was necessary for Nature to be possible. But Nature was necessary, too, because otherwise what was only possible in the "Idea-in-itself" could not become real. Nature, moreover, is in process, too. As it develops, human consciousness evolves. For history, though it is impossible without Nature, is more than Nature. In history the stage of **Spirit** is reached. Spirit is also necessary because it involves self-consciousness, the "Idea-as-conscious-of-itself." Only in the realm of Spirit can history's quest for concreteness, awareness, and freedom move toward culmination.

Human existence has a decisive role in that quest, since our history is essential to the life of Spirit. Through you and me, your culture and mine, the absolute itself becomes free and self-aware. According to Hegel, this historical process is neither random nor unintelligible. There is Reason in history, which reveals order no less than Nature and logic no less than the "Idea-in-itself." In multiple ways and levels, dialectical and triadic relationships are present as history moves from one era to another.

Consider, for instance the dialectical development of the modern political state. Its early origins are found in the family, which is an organic unity. But the family contains its own antithesis, for individuals within it eventually grow up, leave, and carry out their own purposes in civil society. The state emerges as the synthesis of the family and civil society. Within it elements of family unity and of the individuality of civil society can be found, but they have been transmuted into a new form of what Hegel called unity-in-difference. In sum, Hegel saw in history movement that involves the negation of what is, in favor of another stage that tends toward an opposite situation but without the total destruction of what had gone before. Then another growth follows, bringing the previous stages into a relationship in which neither is the same and yet both are present, transformed in the circumstances that now exist.

The Philosophy of World History

Human persons exist because they are necessary for the Absolute to become aware of itself. As Hegel explained that proposition, he also held that "Reason is the law of the world and that, therefore, in world history, things have come about rationally."[5] But Hegel acknowledged that history must be taken empirically. If history wastes human life, that reality cannot be glossed over any more than we should discount anything that affirms our most idealistic hopes. In all cases, he stressed, "If you look at the world rationally the world looks rationally back" (p. 12). Hegel denied that the world will always confront us in exactly the ways we would like. Much of the

time, he thought, it would not do so. But he held that the world is both intelligible and good if we think about it rationally as we look around us.

Hegel called his approach "a theodicy, a justification of God" (p. 18). As noted earlier, he sometimes used God as a synonym for Being or the Absolute. His claim was that we should look at history to see how it contributes to God's life—in which we live and move and have our being—and particularly to God's awareness and freedom. Hence, referring to the present stage, Hegel wrote:

> The essence of Spirit—its substance—is Freedom. Following this abstract definition it may be said that world history is the exhibition of Spirit striving to attain knowledge of its own nature. . . . World history is the progress of the consciousness of freedom. . . . The actualization of this Freedom is the final purpose of the world. (Pp. 22–24.)

Yet Hegel never shied away from the fact that his justification of God, his emphasis on self-consciousnesses and freedom, might contain a terrible truth.

History, said Hegel, could be called "the slaughter-bench at which the happiness of peoples, the wisdom of states, and the virtue of individuals have been sacrificed" (p. 27). Human life is used and abused. As Hegel put it, "The cunning of reason sets the passions to work for itself, while that through which it develops itself pays the penalty and suffers the loss" (p. 44). Human individuals and groups carry forward the experience of Being itself, but they neither control nor fully understand all the detail of how and where Reason works out its own destiny through them. We pursue intended consequences, but the unintended ones, often to our sorrow more than to our joy, may make the greater impact. Thus, argued Hegel,

> . . . in speaking of purpose in and for itself, the so-called prosperity or misfortune of this or that isolated individual cannot be regarded

as an essential element in the rational order of the universe. . . . The universal law is not designed for individuals as such, who indeed may find themselves very much the losers. But by the term "ideal" we also understand the ideal of Reason, of the good and true. (P. 45.)

The expansion of freedom moves from the oriental stage (where one is free), to the classical (where a few are free), to the modern (where all are free). For Hegel in this way Reason moves its way out in history. We must be careful to see, however, that "freedom" does not mean individual license but only an expansion of consciousness of our place in the world scheme.

The conclusion we should draw, Hegel pleaded, is not that human beings are merely insignificant pawns, cannon fodder in the bloody unfolding of the process. Instead, because men and women can know and appreciate the ideal of Reason and because they advance that ideal as they struggle with their own acts of good and evil, human persons are ends in themselves. Their lives are the life of God. Through them that Absolute life makes sense by creating more life and by exhibiting an order and a purpose that are intelligible and good. Therefore, Hegel affirmed, "The actual world is as it ought to be, . . . the truly good, the universal divine Reason is the power capable of actualizing itself" (p. 47).

This self-actualizing process, admitted Hegel, is at war with itself. It must march from one experience to another if it is to express its freedom and know itself concretely and completely. It follows, Hegel reasoned, that "The history of the world moves on a higher level than . . . proper morality" (p. 82). He meant that history does not conform to any particular human conception of good and evil. Those conceptions are natural and valid for the people who hold them. They may even be necessary stages in the life of reason, but the overall scheme relativizes

them. It is not true, though, that history is completely beyond good and evil. In all its episodes and epochs it carries forward the sifted experience of good and evil that history accumulates and thereby advances the freedom and self-actualization of all. In that advance we find the goodness that justifies God and our lives.

Hegel believed that "ruin is at the same time emergence of new life. . . . Spirit is essentially the result of its own activity. Its activity is transcending the immediately given, negating it, and returning into itself" (pp. 88, 94). As this process continues, it will be governed more and more by Reason's appreciation of its own perfectibility. That norm, contended Hegel, moves history toward ever greater realization of a form of goodness that maximizes justice, beauty, and love.

Does Hegel Answer Our Question?

Few philosophies can match the panoramic quality of Hegel's speculative interpretation of existence. Much of his theory does make sense, and in particular his description of history as a slaughter-bench is all too accurate. His reference to the cunning of reason fits some of our experience, and so does his reminder that we ought not to expect the processes of life to make our wishes come true. We are only finite, if crucial, elements in a dialectical scheme of infinite dimension and complexity. When Hegel tells us that existence is a process, we find some supporting evidence in the age of science. In addition, some of that process can be interpreted along his dialectical and triadic lines. Nor is it difficult to agree that history does not conform to our morality but runs on a higher level, at least in the sense that history transcends our schemes of good and evil. Repeatedly, moreover, new life does spring from ruins, sometime enhancing self-awareness and freedom. Even Hegel's most sweeping claim—that the life of God consists of a movement from Idea to Nature to Spirit—is plausible, although his arguments may not convince us that it must be so. In your judgment, for instance, has history in fact moved to bring about greater freedom in Hegel's sense, and even if so, does this expansion justify the losses it entails?

After giving Hegel his due, a question still needs to be asked: Does Hegel's view make final sense? The problem is that his grisly picture of history as a slaughter-bench leaves us doubting whether the rational is real and whether the actual world is as it ought to be. Hegel tried to explain this difficulty away by saying that he did not mean that every single detail in reality is just as it ought to be. Rather, by "the rational is real and the real is rational," Hegel meant that the essential and the necessary are what are truly real, and the truly real is what is essential and necessary. Such distinctions leave some events as accidental and contingent; they did not have to be as they are. Presumably some of life's destruction, waste, and suffering, which we rightly call irrational, would fall into the latter categories. Not that those happenings are illusory or unreal, for they have undeniable power. The point is that some aspects of the process are more real—essential, required, lasting, even better—than others.

Yet did Hegel's solution solve our problem? He emphasized that history is a process, that the form of that process consists of the dialectical interconnectedness and interdependence of all that exists, and that Spirit is at war with itself. So how could Hegel pick and choose between the accidental and the essential, the contingent and the necessary, in denying that every horror in existence is just as it ought to be? One criterion would be to consider the factors that endure and the ones that tend to disappear, regarding the former as essential and necessary. But in the development of Hegel's Spirit, because nothing endures unchanged or disappears

without a trace, it is not easy to make such a distinction. Nor is it clear that such discriminations would enable us to rule out the necessity of many evils, unless we accept another questionable assumption, namely, that history reveals progress toward moral reasonableness.

If everything is as it ought to be, we have to rest content with history's blood-drenched slaughter-bench. If not every detail is just as it ought to be, we must discern a clear difference between what is essential and what is accidental, or else be left unconvinced that things are quite as rational as Hegel said. Hegel might claim that the difference is clear for anyone who looks at the world rationally, but the dissenters against his claims have been many, especially the existentialists and pragmatists. To dismiss them all as irrational would be far more arrogant than the attitude Hegel despised when he observed men and women insisting that reality ought to conform to their ideals. Hegel can show us that life makes more sense than we imagine. But as you study his theory in the passages that follow—they come from *Reason in History* and Hegel's *Philosophy of Right*—ask yourself whether you think his reach exceeded his grasp where history's meaning is concerned.

The sole thought which philosophy brings to the treatment of history is the simple concept of *Reason*: that Reason is the law of the world and that, therefore, in world history, things have come about rationally. This conviction and insight is a presupposition of history as such; in philosophy itself it is not presupposed. Through its speculative reflection philosophy has demonstrated that Reason—and this term may be accepted here without closer examination of its relation to God—is both *substance and infinite power*, in itself the infinite material of all natural and spiritual life as well as the *infinite form*, the actualization of itself as content. It is *substance*, that is to say, that by which and in which all reality has its being and subsistence. It is infinite *power*, for Reason is not so impotent as to bring about only the ideal, the ought, and to remain in an existence outside of reality—who knows where—as something peculiar in the heads of a few people. It is the infinite *content* of all essence and truth, for it does not require, as does finite activity, the condition of external materials, of given data from which to draw nourishment and objects of its activity; it supplies its own nourishment and is its own reference. And it is infinite *form*, for only in its image and by its fiat do phenomena arise and begin to live. It is its own exclusive pre-supposition and absolutely final purpose, and itself works out this purpose from potentiality into actuality, from inward source to outward appearance, not only in the natural but also in the spiritual universe, in world history. That this *Idea* or *Reason* is the True, the Eternal, the Absolute Power and that it and nothing but it, its glory and majesty, manifests itself in the world—this, as we said before, has been proved in philosophy and is being presupposed here as proved.

Those among you . . . who are not yet acquainted with philosophy, could perhaps be asked to come to these lectures on world history with the belief in Reason, with a desire, a thirst for its insight. It is indeed this desire for rational insight, for cognition, and not merely for a collection of various facts, which ought to be presupposed as a subjective aspiration in the study of the sciences. For even though one were not approaching world history with the thought and knowledge of Reason, at lest one ought to have the firm and invincible faith that there is Reason in history and to believe that the world of intelligence and of self-conscious willing is not abandoned to mere chance, but must manifest itself in the light of the rational Idea. Actually, however, I do not have to demand such belief in advance. What I have said here provisionally, and shall have to say later on, must, even in our branch of science, be taken as a summary view of the whole. It is not a presupposition of study; it is a *result* which happens to be known to myself because I already know the whole. Therefore, only the study of world history itself can show that it has proceeded rationally, that it represents the rationally necessary course of the World Spirit, the Spirit whose nature is indeed always one and the same, but whose one nature unfolds in the course of the world. This, as I said, must be the result of history. History itself must be taken as it is; we have to proceed historically, empirically. . . .

As our first condition we must therefore state that we apprehend the historical faithfully. In such general terms, however, as "faithfully" and "apprehend" lies an ambiguity. Even the average and mediocre historian, who perhaps believes and pretends that he is merely receptive, merely surrendering himself to the data, is not passive in his thinking. He brings his categories with him and sees the data through them. In everything that is supposed to be scientific, Reason must be awake and reflection applied. To him who looks at the world rationally the world looks rationally back. The relation is mutual. (Pp. 11–13.)

WHAT IS RATIONAL IS ACTUAL AND WHAT IS ACTUAL IS RATIONAL

On this conviction the plain man like the philosopher takes his stand, and from it philosophy starts in its study of the universe of mind as well as the universe of nature. If reflection, feeling, or whatever form subjective consciousness may take, looks upon the present as something vacuous and looks beyond it with the eyes of superior wisdom, it finds itself in a vacuum, and because it is actual only in the present, it is itself mere vacuity. If on the other hand the Idea passes for "only an Idea," for something represented in an opinion, philosophy rejects such a view and shows that nothing is actual except the Idea. Once that is granted, the great thing is to apprehend in the show of the temporal and transient the substance which is immanent and the eternal which is present. For since rationality (which is synonymous with the Idea) enters upon external existence simultaneously with its actualization, it emerges with an infinite wealth of forms, shapes, and appearances. Around its heart it throws a motley covering with which consciousness is at home to begin with, a covering which the concept has first to penetrate before it can find the inward pulse and feel it still beating in the outward appearances. But the infinite variety of circumstance which is developed in this externality by the light of the essence glinting in it— this endless material and its organization— this is not the subject matter of philosophy. To touch this at all would be to meddle with things to which philosophy is unsuited; on such topics it may save itself the trouble of giving good advice. . . .

. . . To comprehend what is, this is the task of philosophy, because what is, is reason. Whatever happens, every individual is a child of his time; so philosophy too is its own time apprehended in thoughts. It is just as absurd to fancy that a philosophy can transcend its contemporary world as it is to fancy that an individual can overleap his own age, jump over Rhodes. If his theory really goes beyond the world as it is and builds an ideal one as it ought to be, that world exists indeed, but only in his opinions, an unsubstantial element where anything you please may, in fancy, be built. . . .

One word more about giving instruction as to what the world ought to be. Philosophy in any case always comes on the scene too late to give it. As the thought of the world, it appears only when actuality is already there cut and dried after its process of formation has been completed. The teaching of the concept, which is also history's inescapable lesson, is that it is only when actuality is mature that the ideal first appears over against the real and that the ideal apprehends this same real world in its substance and builds it up for itself into the shape of an intellectual realm. When philosophy paints its gray in gray, then has a shape of

life grown old. By philosophy's gray in gray it cannot be rejuvenated but only understood. The owl of Minerva spreads its wings only with the falling of the dusk.[6]

Henry David Thoreau and Life without Principle

While Hegel developed his philosophy in Berlin, Henry David Thoreau (1817–1862) was growing up in the American village of Concord, Massachusetts. He found much to agree with in Hegel's claim that the actual world is as it should be, but he also felt keenly the gap between the purpose we hope to find and what life turns out to be. His desire to narrow that gap prompted his friend and fellow transcendentalist Ralph Waldo Emerson (1803–1882) to eulogize Thoreau as "a born protestant." Educated at Harvard College, Thoreau found academic philosophy stuffy. Supporting himself by working in the family pencil-making business and by surveying land, he took his greatest satisfaction from careful observation of life in the fields and rivers of New England. A skilled essayist and lecturer, in writings such as *Walden, or Life in the Woods* (1854) Thoreau developed an outlook that focused as much on the individual as Hegel's concentrated on the universal. Although Thoreau is not always listed among the professional philosophers, he provided a guide to life based on simplicity and retreat that many read and emulate.

Thoreau's State of Mind

Emerging partly out of impulses loosely derived from post-Kantian German philosophy, "American **transcendentalism**" was less an intellectual system than a state of mind shared by numerous nineteenth-century

HENRY DAVID THOREAU 1817–1862

established institutions, traditional practices, and humanity's blindness and lethargy stifling for individuality and excellence. Shades of Rousseau's romanticism colored this profile. Traces of Hegel's high estimate of humanity's role in making sense of life appeared as well.

Thoreau embodied all the foregoing characteristics. Unlike many transcendentalists, however, he not only talked about nature but was intimately acquainted with it. Although he deplored more than Hegel the slaughter-bench qualities of history, Thoreau reveled in nature's wildness. He welcomed the beauty he saw:

> . . . Nature is so rife with life that myriads can be afforded to be sacrificed and suffered to prey on one another; that tender organizations can be so serenely squashed out of existence like pulp—tadpoles which herons gobble up, and tortoises and toads run over in the road; and sometimes it has rained flesh and blood![7]

Thoreau's exuberance was not a morbid celebration of suffering and destruction but rather a confession of his wonder and awe about life's creative energy. Nature taught him that the individual participates in a unified, inexhaustible organic process. Even its seemingly negative features were actually contributions to an unsurpassed splendor. Yet this romantic outlook did not prevent Thoreau from being puzzled by existence in a way that Hegel was not. "Why," asked this American, "do precisely these objects which we behold make a world? Why has man just these species of animals for his neighbors; as if nothing but a mouse could have filled this crevice?" (P. 471.) Thoreau posed the questions but did not answer them, except by implying that God created the world because it is beautiful and good. Tantalizing and problematic in its simplicity, this response is reminiscent of Hegel's thought. Thoreau, however, showed little interest in complex

writers. Although the movement eludes simple definition, it did involve a specific set of concerns, among them an exaltation of the human spirit, which it linked with divinity, and an insistence on the authority of individual conscience. The discovery of truth through firsthand experience was a priority, especially when experience produced undeniable intuitions that were possible when feeling, imagination, and action—as well as reason—reacted creatively with nature. In addition, there was an emphasis on nature's dynamic life and on its capacity to symbolize moral truth, as well as a belief that all existence is alive and fundamentally good—organically interrelated, not inevitably torn by discord. Finally, the transcendentalists had a proclivity for social criticism that found dialectical demonstrations of the sort Hegel loved.

Quiet Desperation

Thoreau was not a metaphysician who tried to prove that life makes sense. Intuitively, life did make sense to him, but he felt that life was full of unresolved problems, too. In particular, his study of American life suggested to him that "the mass of men lead lives of quiet desperation" (p. 263). Failing to understand where true goodness lies, they pursue happiness frantically but achieve very little of it. Trapped in their own confusion, imprisoned by social structures, economic cravings, and technological accomplishments not of their own making, their lives make less sense than they should. These conditions create desperation because people cannot find the happiness they seek. This result also leaves them quiet, because they do not know where to turn next. Thoreau's social critique outlined human shortcomings but prescribed practices to correct them. Too often, he counseled, "When the farmer has got his house, he may not be the richer but the poorer for it, and it be the house that has got him" (p. 288). Or, with technology and "modern conveniences" in mind, he urged that the problem is that "We do not ride on the railroad; it rides on us" (p. 345). Since life's sense is "frittered away by detail," the objective should be: "Simplify, simplify" (p. 344).

If Hegel's metaphysics was too grandiose for Thoreau, the American could appreciate how the cunning of reason might plunge people into quiet desperation by enticing them to live a "Life without Principle." In an essay with that title, Thoreau viewed the central question "How do Americans spend their lives?" as an economic issue in more senses than the term "economic" at first suggests. The world, wrote Thoreau, is a place of business and busyness—so much so that

Thoreau protested he could not find a notebook to write in because they were all ruled to record dollars and cents. A man who walks in the woods, he observed wryly, may be regarded as loafing, but if he cuts down the woods for profit, "he is esteemed an industrious and enterprising citizen."[8] Principle, lamented Thoreau, has been perverted, if not lost altogether. Americans are living life without principle because they take life with principle too seriously. If they lived with less concern for finance, the meaning of their lives would be richer.

The problem, Thoreau insisted, is that "The ways by which you may get money almost without exception lead downward" (p. 634). Writing when gold had been discovered in the American West, Thoreau believed that "The rush to California . . . and the attitude, not merely of merchants, but of philosophers and prophets, so-called, in relation to it, reflects the greatest disgrace on mankind" (p. 638). Nor was Thoreau simply denouncing the lure of wealth. Too much depended on luck in striking it rich: "Did God direct us so to get our living," complained Thoreau, "digging where we never planted—and He would, perchance, reward us with lumps of gold? . . . We select granite for the underpinning of our houses and barns. We build fences of stone; but we do not ourselves rest on an underpinning of granitic truth" (p. 644).

One place to find granitic truth was in the woods, Thoreau affirmed. So in 1845 he had gone to live on Emerson's land at Walden Pond. Although he kept to himself, Thoreau ventured in and out of Concord, as necessary. In addition, he was jailed briefly for refusal to pay a tax to support America's war with Mexico, which he saw as an attempt to add slave territory to the United States. As Thoreau looked back on his life in the woods, he did not recommend that everyone do what he had done. It was more important, he felt, that each person "be very careful to find out and pursue *his own* way, and not his father's or his mother's or his neighbor's"—or that of any philosopher instead, he might have added.[9] Struggling to carve out a career, each student may take Thoreau's course to heart: your decisions must finally be yours.

Doing What I Think Is Right

The political implications of Thoreau's optimism were apparent to him. Indeed, in an earlier essay on **civil disobedience** (1849), he had already made them explicit. The most basic principle in Thoreau's political philosophy was the following: "It is not desirable to cultivate a respect for the law, so much as for the right. The only obligation which I have a right to assume, is to do at any time what I think right."[10] Law and justice, noted Thoreau, are not necessarily identical. The two frequently conflict. In such cases respect for law must not become an end in itself if life is to make sense. Thoreau was no anarchist. He knew that governments and laws are necessary, but he considered them expedients only. A sense of justice must judge and reform them. Whenever they proved inexpedient, rebellion that goes beyond the law may be required.

How does one know what is right and what is wrong? Ultimately, Thoreau argued, we must and should depend on what we individually think is right. But in stressing the personal dimensions of decision making, Thoreau never intended to encourage a radical subjectivism: life cannot make sense if everything that people think right is actually right. In that case existence would be irrationally riddled with conflicting desires and contradictory ideals. Still, Thoreau knew that what one thinks is right is an ultimate court of appeal that is decisive for that person. Thus, the problem is how to adjust one's thinking so that what is thought to be right and what actually is right are one and the same for that individual.

Action, felt Thoreau, was no less important than theory in dealing with that dilemma. Specifically, he advocated nonviolent civil disobedience as an effective way for an individual or a minority to show that governmental policies or majority opinions were wrong. Thoreau's chief targets were slavery, war, imperialism, government's failure to live up to American ideals, and economic practices that hindered self-reliance and drove people to desperation instead. Thoreau could see no reason to doubt that his views were right. In addition, his assumption was that a minority could reform society, because, at least in America, the state would sooner change its ways than keep just men and women in prison. Such optimism, however, did not lead Thoreau to think that sufficient reforms could be achieved by "adopting the ways which the State has provided for remedying the evil." Impatiently, Thoreau proclaimed, "I know not of such ways. They take too much time, and a man's life will be gone. I have other affairs to attend to" (p. 120). As for the objection that civil disobedience—even if it is based on a willingness to accept punishment—breeds a dangerous loss of respect for law and thus plays into the hands of violence and instability, Thoreau rejoined simply that staying within legal boundaries can lead to an even more severe injustice. The law is not immune to corruption. Its procedures can be too slow, too subject to deceitful compromises and devious manipulations.

The Essential Facts of Life

Thoreau summed up his Walden Pond experience by saying, "I went to the woods because I wished to live deliberately, to front only the essential facts of life, and see if I could not learn what it had to teach, and not, when I came to die, discover that I had not lived."[11] His essential facts included living in harmony with a self-critical conscience that knew the difference between right and wrong. Life would make the most sense when lived that way. One's actions and thoughts would be synchronized; they would be as right as it is possible for them to be. In propounding these points, however, Thoreau too easily overlooked another. In the statement that the only obligation he could assume was to do what he thought right, Thoreau's principle becomes radically subjective and is not easily squared with another premise he held dear, namely, that thinking one is right and actually being right are not always the same.

Ultimately, Thoreau's appeal was to properly refined conscience. But in his case that appeal either begs the question of what "properly refined" should mean or requires us to accept Thoreau's own moral judgments as authoritative. The latter outcome seems unlikely, because appeals to conscience notoriously produce disagreement not agreement. Indeed, such appeals are often made precisely when one knows that an intransigent opposition exists. If communal harmony is needed to make sense of life, Thoreau's political philosophy is not as well suited to closing the gap between sense and nonsense as he thought. Nonetheless, he did see clearly another essential factor: Thoreau despised hypocrisy more than anything else. He knew that neither individual nor community life can achieve wholeness in the absence of an honest relationship between thought and action.

In calling on men and women to simplify their lives, Thoreau meant that people should concentrate on the essentials, not becoming distracted by fleeting details. This, he believed, would promote a morally sound human community. Here Thoreau's approach has similarities with Hegel's attempt to distinguish the necessary and the accidental in accounting for what is real and rational. But if Hegel's view contained a hidden snare because the complexities of the dialectical unfolding made it difficult to draw such lines, Thoreau's outlook suffers from oversimpli-

fication. Nature does not always speak with one voice, if it speaks at all; nor does intuition or conscience. Thoreau is clearest when he speaks as a critic, and few people would quarrel with his convictions that slavery, war, imperialism, and corruption are wrong. Having found agreement on those points, however, it does not follow that the Good is always as obvious as Thoreau made out. He came closest to sensing that point when he recognized that his own principle—to do only what he thought right—needed qualification if it were not to become a license that would legitimize any behavior. As we confront life's hardest problems, the best courses of action are rarely obvious. We are left to sort out the relationships between thinking we are right and being right. Consider how Thoreau might help you to do so as your reading from "Life without Principle" continues.

Let us consider the way in which we spend our lives.

This world is a place of business. What an infinite bustle! I am awaked almost every night by the panting of the locomotive. It interrupts my dreams. There is no sabbath. It would be glorious to see mankind at leisure for once. It is nothing but work, work, work. I cannot easily buy a blank-book to write thoughts in; they are commonly ruled for dollars and cents. An Irishman, seeing me making a minute in the fields, took it for granted that I was calculating my wages. If a man was tossed out of a window when an infant, and so made a cripple for life, or scared out of his wits by the Indians, it is regretted chiefly because he was thus incapacitated for—business! I think that there is nothing, not even crime, more opposed to poetry, to philosophy, ay, to life itself, than this incessant business.

There is a coarse and boisterous money-making fellow in the outskirts of our town, who is going to build a bank-wall under the hill along the edge of his meadow. The powers have put this into his head to keep him out of mischief, and he wishes me to spend three weeks digging there with him. The result will be that he will perhaps get some more money to hoard, and leave for his heirs to spend foolishly. If I do this, most will commend me as an industrious and hard-working man; but if I choose to devote myself to certain labors which yield more real profit, though but little money, they may be inclined to look on me as an idler. Nevertheless, as I do not need the police of meaningless labor to regulate me, and do not see anything absolutely praiseworthy in this fellow's undertaking any more than in many an enterprise of our own or foreign governments, however amusing it may be to him or them, I prefer to finish my education at a different school.

If a man walk in the woods for love of them half of each day, he is in danger of being regarded as a loafer; but if he spends his whole day as a speculator, shearing off those woods and making earth bald before her time, he is esteemed an industrious and enterprising citizen. As if a town had no interest in its forests but to cut them down! . . .

The ways by which you may get money almost without exception lead downward. To have done anything by which you earned money *merely* is to have been truly idle or worse. If the laborer gets no more than the wages which his employer pays him, he is cheated, he cheats himself. If you would get money as a writer or lecturer, you must be popular, which is to go down perpendicularly. Those services which the community will most readily pay for, it is most disagreeable to render. You are paid for being something less than a man. The State does not commonly reward a genius any more wisely. . . .

The aim of the laborer should be, not to get his living, to get "a good job," but to perform well a certain work; and, even in a pecuniary sense, it would be economy for a town to pay its laborers so well that they would not feel that they were working for low ends, as for a livelihood merely, but for

scientific, or even moral ends. Do not hire a man who does your work for money, but him who does it for love of it. . . . [12]

It is remarkable that there is little or nothing to be remembered written on the subject of getting a living; how to make getting a living not merely honest and honorable, but altogether inviting and glorious; for if *getting* a living is not so, then living is not. One would think, from looking at literature, that this question had never disturbed a solitary individual's musings. Is it that men are too much disgusted with their experience to speak of it? The lesson of value which money teaches, which the Author of the Universe has taken so much pains to teach us, we are inclined to skip altogether. As for the means of living, it is wonderful how indifferent men of all classes are about it, even reformers, so called—whether they inherit, or earn, or steal it. I think that Society has done nothing for us in this respect, or at least has undone what she has done. Cold and hunger seem more friendly to my nature than those methods which men have adopted and advise to ward them off.

The title *wise* is, for the most part, falsely applied. How can one be a wise man, if he does not know any better how to live than other men? If he is only more cunning and intellectually subtle? Does Wisdom work in a treadmill? Or does she teach how to succeed *by her example?* Is there any such thing as wisdom not applied to life? Is she merely the miller who grinds the finest logic? It is pertinent to ask if Plato got his *living* in a better way or more successfully than his contemporaries—or did he succumb to the difficulties of life like other men? Did he seem to prevail over some of them merely by indifference, or by assuming grand airs? Or find it easier to live, because his aunt remembered him in her will? The ways in which most men get their living, that is, live, are mere make-shifts, and a shirking of the real business of life—chiefly because they do not know, but partly because they do not mean, any better.

The rush to California, for instance, and the attitude, not merely of merchants, but of philosophers and prophets, so called, in relation to it, reflect the greatest disgrace on mankind. That so many are ready to live by luck, and so get the means of commanding the labor of others less lucky, without contributing any value to society! And that is called enterprise! I know of no more startling development of the immortality of trade, and all the common modes of getting a living. The philosophy and poetry and religion of such a mankind are not worth the dust of a puffball. The hog that gets his living by rooting, stirring up the soil so, would be ashamed of such company. If I could command the wealth of all the worlds by lifting my finger, I would not pay *such* a price for it. Even Mahomet knew that God did not make this world in jest. It makes God to be a moneyed gentleman who scatters a handful of pennies in order to see mankind scramble for them. The world's raffle! A subsistence in the domains of Nature a thing to be raffled for! What a comment, what a satire, on our institutions! The conclusion will be, that mankind will hang itself upon a tree. And have all the precepts in all the Bibles taught men only this? And is the last and most admirable invention of the human race only an improved muck-rake? Is this the ground on which Orientals and Occidentals meet? Did God direct us so to get our living, digging where we never planted—and He would, perchance, reward us with lumps of gold? (Pp. 637–39.)

To speak impartially, the best men that I know are not serene, a world in themselves. For the most part, they dwell in forms, and flatter and study effect only more finely than the rest. We select granite for the underpinning of our houses and barns; we build fences of stone; but we do not ourselves rest on an underpinning of granitic truth, the lowest primitive rock. Our sills are rotten. What stuff is the man made of who is not coexistent in our thought with the purest and subtilest truth? I often accuse my finest acquaintances of an immense frivolity; for, while there are manners and compliments we do not meet, we do not teach one another the lessons of honesty and sincerity that the brutes do, or of steadiness and solidity that the rocks do. The fault is commonly mutual, however; for we do not habitually demand any more of each other. (Pp. 644–45.)

We should treat our minds, that is, ourselves, as innocent and ingenuous children, whose guardians we are, and be careful what objects and what subjects we thrust on their attention. Read not the Times. Read the Eternities. Conventionalities are at length as bad as impurities. Even the facts of science may dust the mind by their dryness, unless they are in a sense effaced each morning, or rather rendered fertile by the dews of fresh and living truth. Knowledge does not come to us by details, but in flashes of light from heaven. Yes, every thought that passes through the mind helps to wear and tear it, and to deepen the ruts, which, as in the streets of Pompeii, evince how much it has been used. How many things there are concerning which we might well deliberate whether we had better know them—had better let their peddling-carts be driven, even at the slowest trot or walk, over that bridge of glorious span by which we trust to pass at last from the farthest brink of time to the nearest shore of eternity! Have we no culture, no refinement—but skill only to live coarsely and serve the Devil? To acquire a little worldly wealth, or fame, or liberty, and make a false show with it, as if we were all husk and shell, with no tender and living kernel to us? Shall our institutions be like those chestnut-burs which contain abortive nuts, perfect only to prick the fingers?

America is said to be the arena on which the battle of freedom is to be fought; but surely it cannot be freedom in a merely political sense that is meant. Even if we grant that the American has freed himself from a political tyrant, he is still the slave of an economical and moral tyrant. Now that the republic—the *res-publica*—has been settled, it is time to look after *res-privata*—the private state—to see, as the Roman senate charged its consuls, *"ne quid res-*PRIVATA *detrimenti caperet,"* that the *private* state receive no detriment.

Do we call this the land of the free? What is it to be free from King George and continue the slaves of King Prejudice? What is it to be born free and not to live free? What is the value of any political freedom, but as a means to moral freedom? Is it a freedom to be slaves, or a freedom to be free, of which we boast? We are a nation of politicians, concerned about the outmost defenses only of freedom. It is our children's children who may perchance be really free. We tax ourselves unjustly. There is a part of us which is not represented. It is taxation without representation. We quarter troops, we quarter fools and cattle of all sorts upon ourselves. We quarter our gross bodies on our poor souls, till the former eat up all the latter's substance.

With respect to a true culture and manhood, we are essentially provincial still, not metropolitan—mere Jonathans. We are provincial, because we do not find at home our standards; because we do not worship truth, but the reflection of truth; because we are warped and narrowed by an exclusive devotion to trade and commerce and manufactures and agriculture and the like, which are but means, and not the end. (Pp. 649–50.)

Those things which now most engage the attention of men, as politics and the daily routine, are, it is true, vital functions of human society, but should be unconsciously performed, like the corresponding functions of the physical body. They are *infra-human*, a kind of vegetation. I sometimes awake to a half-consciousness of them going on about me, as a man may become conscious of some of the processes of digestion in a morbid state, and so have the dyspepsia, as it is called. It is as if a thinker submitted himself to be rasped by the great gizzard of creation. Politics is, as it were, the gizzard of society, full of grit and gravel, and the two political parties are its two opposite halves—sometimes split into quarters, it may be, which grind on each other. Not only individuals, but states, have thus a confirmed dyspepsia, which expresses itself, you can imagine by what sort of eloquence. Thus our life is not altogether a forgetting, but also, alas! to a great extent, a remembering, of that which we should never have been conscious of, certainly not in our waking hours. Why should we not meet, not always as dyspeptics, to tell our bad dreams, but sometimes as *eupeptics*, to congratulate each other on the ever-glorious morning? I do not make an exorbitant demand, surely. (Pp. 644–45.)

Albert Camus and the Absurd

Philosophers are more likely to be ignored than given awards. Albert Camus (1913–1960) is an exception. Among his credits is the 1957 Nobel Prize for literature. Although Camus was hardly fond of being called an existentialist, the writings that made him a Nobel laureate did much to popularize that philosophical movement. Novelist, playwright, and essayist, Camus was born and educated in Algeria, where he founded a theater group for which he wrote and produced plays. In 1940 he moved to Paris, became active in the French resistance against the Nazis occupation, and later practiced journalism. He was friendly with Jean-Paul Sartre, but the two had a falling out and became philosophical rivals, even though many of their views were similar.

Camus was not an academic philosopher. Living in difficult times when existence could not be taken for granted, he set aside the technicalities of epistemology and metaphysics to assay life's meaning. Owing to World War II and its aftermath, it seemed to Camus that traditional values and ways of life had collapsed. He dramatized that situation in plays and novels such as *The Stranger*

tal who challenged fate. Sisyphus would not submit to the authoritarian gods, and the gods retaliated by requiring him to push a huge boulder up a hill only to see it roll down again, throughout eternity. Endless repetitions of this task, apparently, gained him nothing. We have not progressed beyond the mythical condition of Sisyphus, Camus argued. Setting the stage with that insight, he began as follows:

> There is but one truly serious philosophical problem, and that is **suicide.** Judging whether life is or is not worth living amounts to answering the fundamental question of philosophy.[13]

Unlike Pascal, Camus did not think that God or religious faith can provide what we need to resolve this problem. His quest, Camus reports in a preface to the *Myth* penned in 1955, is to live "without the aid of eternal values" (p. v). He felt that an appeal to God and religion is no longer credible. He was sure that we live in an era different from that of Pascal, Hegel, or Thoreau. In our time, "the **absurd**" has center stage.

What Is the Absurd?

Absurdity comes to us in a feeling that can strike a person "at any streetcorner" (p. 9). One "feels alien, a stranger"—even to oneself (p. 5). This feeling arises as a function of an encounter between the world and the demands we make as rational beings. Specifically, absurdity arises from the confrontation between "human need and the unreasonable silence of the world" (p. 21). We ask a thousand "whys" that lack answers. We want solutions, but we stir up absurdity, because no sooner does thought assert something than it seems to negate what is affirmed. "The absurd," writes Camus, "depends as much on man as on the world" (p. 16). Thus, when we ask the question of life's meaning, we realize that our demand

ALBERT CAMUS 1913–1960

(1942) and *The Plague* (1947) and reflected on it philosophically in essays that asked, "Does life make sense?" His demise leaves the answer in suspense, for Camus died suddenly. A lover of fast cars, he lost his life in a crash.

Life as a Modern Myth

With its penchant for scientific precision and mathematical clarity, much modern philosophy has sought to do away with mythical forms of expression. Yet few philosophical works in the twentieth century have exerted greater popular appeal than *The Myth of Sisyphus* (1942). Camus adopted a theme from ancient tales about Greek gods and heros because he was attracted to **Sisyphus,** a mor-

for answers gives rise to the feeling of absurdity as much as any characteristic of the world itself.

Yet Camus believes that the yearning to find answers that satisfy us neither can nor should go away. It makes us what we are. If human awareness did not exist, the absurd would not either. Note, too, that the absurd is not the elimination of meaning. In fact, it would not exist without our plans and purposes. The problem is that the meaning we take for granted can crumble almost before we know it.

> It happens that the stage sets collapse. Rising, streetcar, four hours of work, meal, sleep, and Monday, Tuesday, Wednesday, Thursday, Friday, and Saturday according to the same rhythm—this path is easily followed most of the time. But one day the "why" arises and everything begins in that weariness tinged with amazement. (P. 10.)

The feeling of absurdity, Camus goes on to explain, is not "the notion of the absurd" (p. 21). That feeling comes to us because "the absurd is essentially a divorce" (p. 22). It is what results when human consciousness and the world collide.

Does the Absurd Dictate Death?

Convinced that he cannot escape the absurd as long as he lives, Camus insists that existence implies "a total absence of hope" (p. 23). He can see nothing that could make it possible for him to transcend the absurd. Death, however, would put an end to it. Hence, suicide is an option. Indeed, since absurdity infests existence so painfully, would it not make sense to say that the absurd invites us to die, even dictates that we should? Camus's answer is an emphatic "no." Far from solving any problem, suicide is the ultimate cop-out. In fact, it is the unforgivable existential sin: "It is essential to die unreconciled and not of one's own free will" (p. 41). Sui-

cide compounds the negation of meaning by making it impossible to capitalize on the recognition that "the absurd has meaning only insofar as it is not agreed to" (p. 24). Absurdity will not go away if we say that we refuse to die. On the contrary, it will remain. But Camus thinks we should let it remain in order to defy it. Indeed, he even advises that we should make a point of contemplating the absurd, because "Life will be lived all the better if it has no meaning" (p. 40). Defiance of the absurd maximizes life's intensity in a way that would not be possible if some transcendent God guaranteed life's significance. Camus makes that wager to counter Pascal's.

Camus argued that there is a logic that makes sense in the face of the absurd. "I want to know," he wrote, "whether I can live with what I know and with that alone. . . . I don't know whether this world has a meaning that transcends it. But I know that I do not know that meaning and that it is impossible for me just now to know it" (pp. 30, 38). Thus, to hope that there is a way beyond the absurd in this life is philosophical suicide. One cannot remain honest if one has succumbed to the temptation offered by that hope. But at the same time Camus understood that reason alone will not be enough to persuade us that he is right. Willing is required to draw the conclusions Camus wanted from his logic of the absurd. Among other things, we will have to decide what it means that "there is so much stubborn hope in the human heart" (p. 76).

The Absurd Hero

Sisyphus is Camus's absurd hero. He loves life and hates death. His passions have condemned him, but the grandeur of Sisyphus is that he never gives up and is never dishonest. He accepts his fate only to defy it. Thereby he gives meaning to existence, meaning that cannot negate absurdity but refuses to succumb to its impact. Sisyphus is a creator who makes sense in circumstances that apparently rob human life of significance. Camus wants us all to find a way to live like Sisyphus. He speaks at length about how artistic creativity can move us in that direction, but his point, like Thoreau's, is that each individual must find his or her own way.

It is important to note the picture of Sisyphus with which the *Myth* ends. Although it would be natural to focus on Sisyphus as he pushes his rock up the hill, Camus asks us to reflect on Sisyphus when he reaches the top. He knows the rock will roll down, and it does. But as Sisyphus heads down to retrieve it, he does not despair. He surmounts his fate by scorning it, stronger than the rock. "We must," Camus concludes, "imagine Sisyphus happy" (p. 91). Sisyphus sees clearly; he has ceased to hope for release. But by giving up hope and facing absurdity squarely, he has created meaning. Life has meaning if we make it so by our activity, although existence in itself can never satisfy us.

The Rebel

Camus drew three consequences from the existence of the absurd: "my revolt, my freedom, and my passion" (p. 47). Decision was his, and his love of life led him to defy the absurd. In *The Myth of Sisyphus,* Camus drew those consequences from a reflection on suicide. In a sequel, *The Rebel* (1951), Camus expanded on his earlier themes. This time murder provoked him. The twentieth century was proving Hegel correct once more: history is a slaughter-bench, overflowing with disease, injustice, and especially man-made death. The absurd does not dictate suicide, but does it legitimize murder?

Camus again answers "no." If the absurd implies that everything is permitted, it does not follow that nothing is forbidden. Building on the insight that the most authentically human response to absurdity is to protest against it, Camus emphasized that such defiance does and should have a social component. Absurdity enters existence not so much because my own private needs go unmet, but because conditions exist that waste our lives and rob human relationships of significance. Hence, far from dictating suicide or legitimizing murder, the absurd should lead to rebellion in the name of justice and human solidarity. "I rebel," Camus says, modifying the Cartesian formula, "therefore we exist."[14]

Here, like Sisyphus, we face an uphill climb, because the **rebellion** Camus advocates is characterized by moderation. By moderation, Camus does not mean to say that our actions should be hesitant, dispassionate, or weak. But he does not want the rebel to become the revolutionary who so often destroys life under the pretense of redeeming it.

> The logic of the rebel is to want to serve justice so as not to add to the injustice of the human condition, to insist on plain language so as not to increase the universal falsehood, and to wager, in spite of human misery, for happiness. (P. 285.)

Recall that Camus's roots were in Algeria, and in many ways he found the independence movement of the 1950s an impossible situation, at least as far as realizing one's hopes and desires was concerned. Camus was no pacifist. He knew that the logic of the rebel might even require the rebel to kill. But a true rebel will never say or do anything "to legitimize murder, because rebellion, in principle, is a protest against death" (p. 285).

As if the task of rebellion were not difficult enough, Camus once more reminds us that the rebel can never expect to escape the fate of Sisyphus:

> Man can master in himself everything that should be mastered. He should rectify in creation everything that can be rectified. And after he has done so, children will still die

unjustly even in a perfect society. Even by his greatest effort man can only propose to diminish arithmetically the sufferings of the world. (P. 303.)

Perhaps things would have been different if the world had been ours to create. But at least "Man is not entirely to blame; it was not he who started history" (p. 297). On the other hand, neither "is he entirely innocent, since he continues it" (p. 297). Thus, when we question "Can my life make sense?", the task before us, Camus concluded, is "to learn to live and to die, and, in order to be a man, to refuse to be a god" (p. 306). As you read the selections that follow from *The Myth of Sisyphus,* see if you agree with their author's answer to the question "Can my life make sense?"

ABSURDITY AND SUICIDE

There is but one truly serious philosophical problem, and that is suicide. Judging whether life is or is not worth living amounts to answering the fundamental question of philosophy. All the rest—whether or not the world has three dimensions, whether the mind has nine or twelve categories—comes afterward. These are games; one must first answer. And if it is true, as Nietzsche claims, that a philosopher, to deserve our respect, must preach by example, you can appreciate the importance of that reply, for it will precede the definitive act. These are facts the heart can feel; yet they call for careful study before they become clear to the intellect.

If I ask myself how to judge that this question is more urgent than that, I reply that one judges by the actions it entails. I have never seen anyone die for the ontological argument. Galileo, who held a scientific truth of great importance, abjured it with the greatest ease as soon as it endangered his life. In a certain sense, he did right.*

*From the point of view of the relative value of truth. On the other hand, from the point of view of virile behavior, this scholar's fragility may well make us smile.

That truth was not worth the stake. Whether the earth or the sun revolves around the other is a matter of profound indifference. To tell the truth, it is a futile question. On the other hand, I see many people die because they judge that life is not worth living. I see others paradoxically getting killed for the ideas or illusions that give them a reason for living (what is called a reason for living is also an excellent reason for dying). I therefore conclude that the meaning of life is the most urgent of questions. How to answer it? On all essential problems (I mean thereby those that run the risk of leading to death or those that intensify the passion of living) there are probably but two methods of thought: the method of La Palice and the method of Don Quixote. Solely the balance between evidence and lyricism can allow us to achieve simultaneously emotion and lucidity. In a subject at once so humble and so heavy with emotion, the learned and classical dialectic must yield, one can see, to a more modest attitude of mind deriving at one and the same time from common sense and understanding.

Suicide has never been dealt with except as a social phenomenon. On the contrary, we are concerned here, at the outset, with the relationship between individual thought and suicide. An act like this is prepared within the silence of the heart, as is a great work of art. The man himself is ignorant of it. One evening he pulls the trigger or jumps. Of an apartment-building manager who had killed himself I was told that he had lost his daughter five years before, that he had changed greatly since, and that that experience had "undermined" him. A more exact word cannot be imagined. Beginning to think is beginning to be undermined. Society has but little connection with such beginnings. The worm is in man's heart. That is where it must be sought. One must follow and understand this fatal game that leads from lucidity in the face of existence to flight from light.

There are many causes for a suicide, and generally the most obvious ones were not the most powerful. Rarely is suicide committed (yet the hypothesis is not excluded) through reflection. What sets off the crisis is almost always unverifiable. Newspapers often speak of "personal sorrows" or of "incurable illness." These explanations are plausible. But one would have to know whether a friend of the desperate man had not that very day addressed him indifferently. He is the guilty one. For that is enough to precipitate all the rancors and all the boredom still in suspension.

But if it is hard to fix the precise instant, the subtle step when the mind opted for death, it is easier to deduce from the act itself the consequences it implies. In a sense, and as in melodrama, killing yourself amounts to confessing. It is confessing that life is too much for you or that you do not understand it. Let's not go too far in such analogies, however, but rather return to everyday words. It is merely confessing that that "is not worth the trouble." Living, naturally, is never easy. You continue making the gestures commanded by existence for many reasons, the first of which is habit. Dying voluntarily implies that you have recognized, even instinctively, the ridiculous character of that habit, the absence of any profound reason for living, the insane character of that daily agitation, and the uselessness of suffering.

What, then, is that incalculable feeling that deprives the mind of the sleep necessary to life? A world that can be explained even with bad reasons is a familiar world. But, on the other hand, in a universe suddenly divested of illusions and lights, man feels an alien, a stranger. His exile is without remedy since he is deprived of the memory of a lost home or the hope of a promised land. This divorce between man and his life, the actor and his setting, is properly the feeling of absurdity. All healthy men having thought of their own suicide, it can be seen, without further explanation, that there is a direct connection between this feeling and the longing for death.

The subject of this essay is precisely this relationship between the absurd and suicide, the exact degree to which suicide is a solution to the absurd. The principle can be established that for a man who does not cheat, what he believes to be true must determine his action. Belief in the absurdity of existence must then dictate his conduct. It is legitimate to wonder, clearly and without false pathos, whether a conclusion of this importance requires forsaking as rapidly as possible an incomprehensible condition. I am speaking, of course, of men inclined to be in harmony with themselves.

Stated clearly, this problem may seem both simple and insoluble. But it is wrongly assumed that simple questions involve answers that are no less simple and that evidence implies evidence. A priori and reversing the terms of the problem, just as one does or does not kill oneself, it seems that there are but two philosophical solutions, either yes or no. This would be too easy. But allowance must be made for those who, without concluding, continue questioning. Here I am only slightly indulging in irony: this is the majority. I notice also that those who answer "no" act as if they thought "yes." As a matter of fact, if I accept the Nietzschean criterion, they think "yes" in one way or another. On the other hand, it often happens that those who commit suicide were assured of the meaning of life. These contradictions are constant. It may even be said that they have never been so keen as on this point where, on the contrary, logic seems so desirable. It is a commonplace to compare philosophical theories and the behavior of those who profess them. But it must be said that of the thinkers who refused a meaning to life none except Kirilov [the madman in Dostoyevski's novel, *The Possessed*] who belongs to literature, Peregrinos who is born of legend,[†] and Jules Lequier who belongs to hypothesis, admitted his logic to the point of refusing that life. Schopenhauer is often cited, as a fit subject for laughter, because

[†]I have heard of an emulator of Peregrinos, a postwar writer who, after having finished his first book, committed suicide to attract attention to his work. Attention was in fact attracted, but the book was judged no good.

he praised suicide while seated at a well-set table. This is no subject for joking. That way of not taking the tragic seriously is not so grievous, but it helps to judge a man.

In the face of such contradictions and obscurities must we conclude that there is no relationship between the opinion one has about life and the act one commits to leave it? Let us not exaggerate in this direction. In a man's attachment to life there is something stronger than all the ills in the world. The body's judgment is as good as the mind's, and the body shrinks from annihilation. We get into the habit of living before acquiring the habit of thinking. In that race which daily hastens us toward death, the body maintains its irreparable lead. In short, the essence of that contradiction lies in what I shall call the act of eluding because it is both less and more than diversion in the Pascalian sense. Eluding is the invariable game. The typical act of eluding, the fatal evasion that constitutes the third theme of this essay, is hope. Hope of another life one must "deserve" or trickery of those who live not for life itself but for some great idea that will transcend it, refine it, give it a meaning, and betray it.

Thus everything contributes to spreading confusion. Hitherto, and it has not been wasted effort, people have played on words and pretended to believe that refusing to grant a meaning to life necessarily leads to declaring that it is not worth living. In truth, there is no necessary common measure between these two judgments. One merely has to refuse to be misled by the confusions, divorces, and inconsistencies previously pointed out. One must brush everything aside and go straight to the real problem. One kills oneself because life is not worth living, that is certainly a truth—yet an unfruitful one because it is a truism. But does that insult to existence, that flat denial in which it is plunged come from the fact that it has no meaning? Does its absurdity require one to escape it through hope or suicide— this is what must be clarified, hunted down, and elucidated while brushing aside all the rest. Does the Absurd dictate death? This

problem must be given priority over others, outside all methods of thought and all exercises of the disinterested mind. Shades of meaning, contradictions, the psychology that an "objective" mind can always introduce into all problems have no place in this pursuit and this passion. It calls simply for an unjust—in other words, logical—thought. That is not easy. It is always easy to be logical. It is almost impossible to be logical to the bitter end. Men who die by their own hand consequently follow to its conclusion their emotional inclination. Reflection on suicide gives me an opportunity to raise the only problem to interest me: Is there a logic to the point of death? I cannot know unless I pursue, without reckless passion, in the sole light of evidence, the reasoning of which I am here suggesting the source. This is what I call an absurd reasoning. Many have begun it. I do not yet know whether or not they kept to it.

When Karl Jaspers, revealing the impossibility of constituting the world as a unity, exclaims: "This limitation leads me to myself, where I can no longer withdraw behind an objective point of view that I am merely representing, where neither I myself nor the existence of others can any longer become an object for me," he is evoking after many others those waterless deserts where thought reaches its confines. After many others, yes indeed, but how eager they were to get out of them! At that last crossroad where thought hesitates, many men have arrived and even some of the humblest. They then abdicated what was most precious to them, their life. Others, princes of the mind, abdicated likewise, but they initiated the suicide of their thought in its purest revolt. The real effort is to stay there, rather, insofar as that is possible, and to examine closely the odd vegetation of those distant regions. Tenacity and acumen are privileged spectators of this inhuman show in which absurdity, hope, and death carry on their dialogue. The mind can then analyze the figures of that elementary yet subtle dance before illustrating them and reliving them itself.

ABSURD WALLS

Like great works, deep feelings always mean more than they are conscious of saving. The regularity of an impulse or a repulsion in a soul is encountered again in habits of doing or thinking, is reproduced in consequences of which the soul itself knows nothing. Great feelings take with them their own universe, splendid or abject. They light up with their passion an exclusive world in which they recognize their climate. There is a universe of jealousy, of ambition, of selfishness, or of generosity. A universe—in other words, a metaphysic and an attitude of mind. What is true of already specialized feelings will be even more so of emotions basically as indeterminate, simultaneously as vague and as "definite," as remote and as "present" as those furnished us by beauty or aroused by absurdity.

At any streetcorner the feeling of absurdity can strike any man in the face. As it is, in its distressing nudity, in its light without effulgence, it is elusive. But that very difficulty deserves reflection. It is probably true that a man remains forever unknown to us and that there is in him something irreducible that escapes us. But *practically* I know men and recognize them by their behavior, by the totality of their deeds, by the consequences caused in life by their presence. Likewise, all those irrational feelings which offer no purchase to analysis. I can define them *practically*, appreciate them *practically*, by gathering together the sum of their consequences in the domain of the intelligence, by seizing and noting all their aspects, by outlining their universe. It is certain that apparently, though I have seen the same actor a hundred times, I shall not for that reason know him any better personally. Yet if I add up the heroes he has personified and if I say that I know him a little better at the hundredth character counted off, this will be felt to contain an element of truth. For this apparent paradox is also an apologue. There is a moral to it. It teaches that a man defines himself by his make-believe as well as by his sincere impulses. There is thus a lower key of feelings, inaccessible in the heart but partially disclosed by the acts they imply and the attitudes of mind they assume. It is clear that in this way I am defining a method. But it is also evident that that method is one of analysis and not of knowledge. For methods imply metaphysics; unconsciously they disclose conclusions that they often claim not to know yet. Similarly, the last pages of a book are already contained in the first pages. Such a link is inevitable. The method defined here acknowledges the feeling that all true knowledge is impossible. Solely appearances can be enumerated and the climate make itself felt.

Perhaps we shall be able to overtake that elusive feeling of absurdity in the different but closely related worlds of intelligence, of the art of living, or of art itself. The climate of absurdity is in the beginning. The end is the absurd universe and that attitude of mind which lights the world with its true colors to bring out the privileged and implacable visage which that attitude has discerned in it.

All great deeds and all great thoughts have a ridiculous beginning. Great works are often born on a streetcorner or in a restaurant's revolving door. So it is with absurdity. The absurd world more than others derives its nobility from that abject birth. In certain situations, replying "nothing" when asked what one is thinking about may be pretense in a man. Those who are loved are well aware of this. But if that reply is sincere, if it symbolizes that odd state of soul in which the void becomes eloquent, in which the chain of daily gestures is broken, in which the heart vainly seeks the link that will connect it again, then it is as it were the first sign of absurdity.

It happens that the stage sets collapse. Rising, streetcar, four hours in the office or the factory, meal, streetcar, four hours of work, meal, sleep, and Monday Tuesday Wednesday Thursday Friday and Saturday according to the same rhythm—this path is easily followed most of the time. But one day the "why" arises and everything begins in that weariness tinged with amazement.

"Begins"—this is important. Weariness comes at the end of the acts of a mechanical life, but at the same time it inaugurates the impulse of consciousness. It awakens consciousness and provokes what follows. What follows is the gradual return into the chain or it is the definitive awakening. At the end of the awakening comes, in time, the consequence: suicide or recovery. In itself weariness has something sickening about it. Here, I must conclude that it is good. For everything begins with consciousness and nothing is worth anything except through it. There is nothing original about these remarks. But they are obvious; that is enough for a while, during a sketchy reconnaissance in the origins of the absurd. Mere "anxiety," as Heidegger says, is at the source of everything.

Likewise and during every day of an unillustrious life, time carries us. But a moment always comes when we have to carry it. We live on the future: "tomorrow," "later on," "when you have made your way," "you will understand when you are old enough." Such irrelevancies are wonderful, for, after all, it's a matter of dying. Yet a day comes when a man notices or says that he is thirty. Thus he asserts his youth. But simultaneously he situates himself in relation to time. He takes his place in it. He admits that he stands at a certain point on a curve that he acknowledges having to travel to its end. He belongs to time, and by the horror that seizes him, he recognizes his worst enemy. Tomorrow, he was longing for tomorrow, whereas everything in him ought to reject it. That revolt of the flesh is the absurd.[‡]

A step lower and strangeness creeps in: perceiving that the world is "dense," sensing to what a degree a stone is foreign and irreducible to us, with what intensity nature or a landscape can negate us. At the heart of all beauty lies something inhuman, and these hills, the softness of the sky, the outline of these trees at this very minute lose the illusory meaning with which we had clothed them, henceforth more remote than a lost paradise. The primitive hostility of the world rises up to face us across millennia. For a second we cease to understand it because for centuries we have understood in it solely the images and designs that we had attributed to it beforehand, because henceforth we lack the power to make use of that artifice. The world evades us because it becomes itself again. That stage scenery masked by habit becomes again what it is. It withdraws at a distance from us. Just as there are days when under the familiar face of a woman, we see as a stranger her we had loved months or years ago, perhaps we shall come even to desire what suddenly leaves us so alone. But the time has not yet come. Just one thing: that denseness and that strangeness of the world is the absurd.

Men, too, secrete the inhuman. At certain moments of lucidity, the mechanical aspect of their gestures, their meaningless pantomime makes silly everything that surrounds them. A man is talking on the telephone behind a glass partition; you cannot hear him, but you see his incomprehensible dumb show: you wonder why he is alive. This discomfort in the face of man's own inhumanity, this incalculable tumble before the image of what we are, this "nausea," as [Sartre] calls it, is also the absurd. Likewise the stranger who at certain seconds comes to meet us in a mirror, the familiar and yet alarming brother we encounter in our own photographs is also the absurd.

I come at last to death and to the attitude we have toward it. On this point everything has been said and it is only proper to avoid pathos. Yet one will never be sufficiently surprised that everyone lives as if no one "knew." This is because in reality there is no experience of death. Properly speaking, nothing has been experienced but what has been lived and made conscious. Here, it is barely possible to speak of the experience of others' deaths. It is a substitute, an illusion, and it never quite convinces us. That melancholy convention cannot be persuasive.

[‡]But not in the proper sense. This is not a definition, but rather an enumeration of the feelings that may admit of the absurd. Still, the enumeration finished, the absurd has nevertheless not been exhausted.

The horror comes in reality from the mathematical aspect of the event. If time frightens us, this is because it works out the problem and the solution comes afterward. All the pretty speeches about the soul will have their contrary convincingly proved, at least for a time. From this inert body on which a slap makes no mark the soul has disappeared. This elementary and definitive aspect of the adventure constitutes the absurd feeling. Under the fatal lighting of that destiny, its uselessness becomes evident. No code of ethics and no effort are justifiable a priori in the face of the cruel mathematics that command our condition.[15]

Let us insist again on the method: it is a matter of persisting. At a certain point on his path the absurd man is tempted. History is not lacking in either religions or prophets, even without gods. He is asked to leap. All he can reply is that he doesn't fully understand, that it is not obvious. Indeed, he does not want to do anything but what he fully understands. He is assured that this is the sin of pride, but he does not understand the notion of sin; that perhaps hell is in store, but he has not enough imagination to visualize that strange future; that he is losing immortal life, but that seems to him an idle consideration. An attempt is made to get him to admit his guilt. He feels innocent. To tell the truth, that is all he feels—his irreparable innocence. This is what allows him everything. Hence, what he demands of himself is to live *solely* with what he knows, to accommodate himself to what is, and to bring in nothing that is not certain. He is told that nothing is. But this at least is a certainty. And it is with this that he is concerned: he wants to find out if it is possible to live *without appeal*. (P. 39.)

Before encountering the absurd, the everyday man lives with aims, a concern for the future or for justification (with regard to whom or what is not the question). He weighs his chances, he counts on "someday," his retirement or the labor of his sons. He still thinks that something in his life can

be directed. In truth, he acts as if he were free, even if all the facts make a point of contradicting that liberty. But after the absurd, everything is upset. That idea that "I am," my way of acting as if everything has a meaning (even if, on occasion, I said that nothing has)—all that is given the lie in vertiginous fashion by the absurdity of a possible death. Thinking of the future, establishing aims for oneself, having preferences—all this presupposes a belief in freedom, even if one occasionally ascertains that one doesn't feel it. But at that moment I am well aware that that higher liberty, that freedom *to be*, which alone can serve as basis for a truth, does not exist. Death is there as the only reality. After death the chips are down. I am not even free, either, to perpetuate myself, but a slave, and, above all, a slave without hope of an eternal revolution, without recourse to contempt. And who without revolution and without contempt can remain a slave? What freedom can exist in the fullest sense without assurance of eternity?

But at the same time the absurd man realizes that hitherto he was bound to that postulate of freedom on the illusion of which he was living. In a certain sense, that hampered him. To the extent to which he imagined a purpose to his life, he adapted himself to the demands of a purpose to be achieved and became the slave of his liberty. Thus I could not act otherwise than as the father (or the engineer or the leader of a nation, or the post-office subclerk) that I am preparing to be. I think I can choose to be that rather than something else. I think so unconsciously, to be sure. But at the same time I strengthen my postulate with the beliefs of those around me, with the presumptions of my human environment (others are so sure of being free, and that cheerful mood is so contagious!). However far one may remain from any presumption, moral or social, one is partly influenced by them and even, for the best among them (there are good and bad presumptions), one adapts one's life to them. Thus the absurd man realizes that he was not really free. To speak clearly, to the extent to which I hope, to which I worry about a truth that might be individual to me, about a way of being or creating, to the extent to which I arrange my life and prove thereby that I accept its having a meaning, I create for myself barriers between which I confine my life. I do like so many bureaucrats of the mind and heart who only fill me with disgust and whose only vice, I now see clearly, is to take man's freedom seriously.

The absurd enlightens me on this point: there is no future. Henceforth this is the reason for my inner freedom. I shall use two comparisons here. Mystics, to begin with, find freedom in giving themselves. By losing themselves in their god, by accepting his rules, they become secretly free. In spontaneously accepted slavery they recover a deeper independence. But what does that freedom mean? It may be said, above all, that they *feel* free with regard to themselves, and not so much free as liberated. Likewise, completely turned toward death (taken here as the most obvious absurdity), the absurd man feels released from everything outside that passionate attention crystallizing in him. He enjoys a freedom with regard to common rules. It can be seen at this point that the initial themes of existential philosophy keep their entire value. The return to consciousness, the escape from everyday sleep represent the first steps of absurd freedom. But it is existential *preaching* that is alluded to, and with it that spiritual leap which basically escapes consciousness. In the same way (this is my second comparison), the slaves of antiquity did not belong to themselves. But they knew that freedom which consists in not feeling responsible.[§] Death, too, has patrician hands which, while crushing, also liberate.

Losing oneself in that bottomless certainty, feeling henceforth sufficiently remote from one's own life to increase it and take a broad view of it—this involves the principle

§I am concerned here with a factual comparison, not with an apology of humility. The absurd man is the contrary of the reconciled man.

of a liberation. Such new independence has a definite time limit, like any freedom of action. It does not write a check on eternity. But it takes the place of the illusions of *freedom*, which all stopped with death. The divine availability of the condemned man before whom the prison doors open in a certain early dawn, that unbelievable disinterestedness with regard to everything except for the pure flame of life—it is clear that death and the absurd are here the principles of the only reasonable freedom: that which a human heart can experience and live. This is a second consequence. The absurd man thus catches sight of a burning and frigid, transparent and limited universe in which nothing is possible but everything is given, and beyond which all is collapse and nothingness. He can then decide to accept such a universe and draw from it his strength, his refusal to hope, and the unyielding evidence of a life without consolation.

But what does life mean in such a universe? Nothing else for the moment but indifference to the future and a desire to use up everything that is given. Belief in the meaning of life always implies a scale of values, a choice, our preferences. Belief in the absurd, according to our definitions, teaches the contrary. But this is worth examining.

Knowing whether or not one can live *without appeal* is all that interests me. I do not want to get out of my depth. This aspect of life being given me, can I adapt myself to it? Now, faced with this particular concern, belief in the absurd is tantamount to substituting the quantity of experiences for the quality. If I convince myself that this life has no other aspect than that of the absurd, if I feel that its whole equilibrium depends on that perpetual opposition between my conscious revolt and the darkness in which it struggles, if I admit that my freedom has no meaning except in relation to its limited fate, then I must say that what counts is not the best living but the most living. It is not up to me to wonder if this is vulgar or revolting, elegant or deplorable. Once and for all, value judgments are discarded here in favor of factual judgments. I have merely to draw the conclusions from what I can see and to risk nothing that is hypothetical. Supposing that living in this way were not honorable, then true propriety would command me to be dishonorable.

The most living; in the broadest sense, that rule means nothing. It calls for definition. It seems to begin with the fact that the notion of quantity has not been sufficiently explored. For it can account for a large share of human experience. A man's rule of conduct and his scale of values have no meaning except through the quantity and variety of experiences he has been in a position to accumulate. Now, the conditions of modern life impose on the majority of men the same quantity of experiences and consequently the same profound experience. To be sure, there must also be taken into consideration the individual's spontaneous contribution, the "given" element in him. But I cannot judge of that, and let me repeat that my rule here is to get along with the immediate evidence. I see, then, that the individual character of a common code of ethics lies not so much in the ideal importance of its basic principles as in the norm of an experience that it is possible to measure. To stretch a point somewhat, the Greeks had the code of their leisure just as we have the code of our eight-hour day. But already many men among the most tragic cause us to foresee that a longer experience changes this table of values. They make us imagine that adventurer of the everyday who through mere quantity of experiences would break all records (I am purposely using this sports expression) and would thus win his own code of ethics. Yet let's avoid romanticism and just ask ourselves what such an attitude may mean to a man with his mind made up to take up his bet and to observe strictly what he takes to be the rules of the game.

Breaking all the records is first and foremost being faced with the world as often as possible. How can that be done without contradictions and without playing on words? For on the one hand the absurd teaches that all experiences are unimportant, and on the other it urges toward the greatest quantity of experiences. How, then, can one fail to do as so many of those men I was speaking of earlier—choose the form of life that brings us the most possible of that human matter, thereby introducing a scale of values that on the other hand one claims to reject?

But again it is the absurd and its contradictory life that teaches us. For the mistake is thinking that that quantity of experiences depends on the circumstances of our life when it depends solely on us. Here we have to be oversimple. To two men living the same number of years, the world always provides the same sum of experiences. It is up to us to be conscious of them. Being aware of one's life, one's revolt, one's freedom, and to the maximum, is living, and to the maximum. . . .

Thus I draw from the absurd three consequences, which are my revolt, my freedom, and my passion. By the mere activity of consciousness I transform into a rule of life what was an invitation to death—and I refuse suicide. (Pp. 42–47.)

The gods had condemned Sisyphus to ceaselessly rolling a rock to the top of a mountain, whence the stone would fall back of its own weight. They had thought with some reason that there is no more dreadful punishment than futile and hopeless labor.

If one believes Homer, Sisyphus was the wisest and most prudent of mortals. According to another tradition, however, he was disposed to practice the profession of highwayman. I see no contradiction in this. Opinions differ as to the reasons why he became the futile laborer of the underworld. To begin with, he is accused of a certain levity in regard to the gods. He stole their secrets. Aegina, the daughter of Aesopus, was carried off by Jupiter. The father was shocked by that disappearance and complained to Sisyphus. He, who knew of the abduction, offered to tell about it on condition that Aesopus would give water to the citadel of Corinth. To the celestial thunderbolts he preferred the benediction of water.

He was punished for this in the underworld. Homer tells us also that Sisyphus had put Death in chains. Pluto could not endure the sight of his deserted, silent empire. He dispatched the god of war, who liberated Death from the hands of her conqueror.

It is said also that Sisyphus, being near to death, rashly wanted to test his wife's love. He ordered her to cast his unburied body into the middle of the public square. Sisyphus woke up in the underworld. And there, annoyed by an obedience so contrary to human love, he obtained from Pluto permission to return to earth in order to chastise his wife. But when he had seen again the face of this world, enjoyed water and sun, warm stones and the sea, he no longer wanted to go back to the infernal darkness. Recalls, signs of anger, warnings were of no avail. Many years more he lived facing the curve of the gulf, the sparkling sea, and the smiles of earth. A decree of the gods was necessary. Mercury came and seized the impudent man by the collar and, snatching him from his joys, led him forcibly back to the underworld, where his rock was ready for him.

You have already grasped that Sisyphus is the absurd hero. He *is*, as much through his passions as through his torture. His scorn of the gods, his hatred of death, and his passion for life won him that unspeakable penalty in which the whole being is exerted toward accomplishing nothing. This is the price that must be paid for the passions of this earth. Nothing is told us about Sisyphus in the underworld. Myths are made for the imagination to breathe life into them. As for this myth, one sees merely the whole effort of a body straining to raise the huge stone, to roll it and push it up a slope a hundred times over; one sees the face screwed up, the cheek tight against the stone, the shoulder bracing the clay-covered mass, the foot wedging it, the fresh start with arms outstretched, the wholly human security of two earth-clotted hands. At the very end of his long effort measured by skyless space and time without depth, the purpose is achieved. Then Sisyphus watches the stone rush down in a few moments toward that lower world whence he will have to push it up again toward the summit. He goes back down to the plain.

It is during that return, that pause, that Sisyphus interests me. A face that toils so close to stones is already stone itself! I see that man going back down with a heavy yet measured step toward the torment of which he will never know the end. That hour like a breathing-space which returns as surely as his suffering, that is the hour of consciousness. At each of those moments when he leaves the heights and gradually sinks toward the lairs of the gods, he is superior to his fate. He is stronger than his rock.

If this myth is tragic, that is because its hero is conscious. Where would his torture be, indeed, if at every step the hope of succeeding upheld him? The workman of today works every day in his life at the same tasks, and this fate is no less absurd. But it is tragic only at the rare moments when it becomes conscious. Sisyphus, proletarian of the gods, powerless and rebellious, knows the whole extent of his wretched condition: it is what he thinks of during his descent. The lucidity that was to constitute his torture at the same time crowns his victory. There is no fate that cannot be surmounted by scorn.

If the descent is thus sometimes performed in sorrow, it can also take place in joy. This word is not too much. Again I fancy Sisyphus returning toward his rock, and the sorrow was in the beginning. When the images of earth cling too tightly to memory, when the call of happiness becomes too insistent, it happens that melancholy rises in man's heart: this is the rock's victory, this is the rock itself. The boundless grief is too heavy to bear. These are our nights of Gethsemane. But crushing truths perish from being acknowledged. Thus, Oedipus at the outset obeys fate without knowing it. But from the moment he knows, his tragedy begins. Yet at the same moment, blind and desperate, he realizes that the only bond linking him to the world is the cool hand of a girl. Then a tremendous remark rings out: "Despite so many ordeals, my advanced age and the nobility of my soul make me conclude that all is well." Sophocles' Oedipus, like Dostoyevsky's Kirilov, thus gives the recipe for the absurd victory. Ancient wisdom confirms modern heroism.

One does not discover the absurd without being tempted to write a manual of happiness. "What! by such narrow ways—?" There is but one world, however. Happiness and the absurd are two sons of the same earth. They are inseparable. It would be a mistake to say that happiness necessarily springs from the absurd discovery. It happens as well that the feeling of the absurd springs from happiness. "I conclude that all is well," says Oedipus, and that remark is sacred. It echoes in the wild and limited universe of man. It teaches that all is not, has not been, exhausted. It drives out of this world a god who had come into it with dissatisfaction and a preference for futile sufferings. It makes of fate a human matter, which must be settled among men.

All Sisyphus' silent joy is contained therein. His fate belongs to him. His rock is his thing. Likewise, the absurd man, when he contemplates his torment, silences all the idols. In the universe suddenly restored to its silence, the myriad wondering little voices of the earth rise up. Unconscious, secret calls, invitations from all the faces, they are the necessary reverse and price of victory. There is no sun without shadow, and it is essential to know the night. The absurd man says yes and his effort will henceforth be unceasing. If there is a personal fate, there is no higher destiny, or at least there is but one which he concludes is inevitable and despicable. For the rest, he knows himself to be the master of his days. At that subtle moment when man glances backward over his life, Sisyphus returning toward his rock, in that slight pivoting he contemplates that series of unrelated actions which becomes his fate, created by him, combined under his memory's eye and soon sealed by his death. Thus, convinced of the wholly human origin of all that

is human, a blind man eager to see who knows that the night has no end, he is still on the go. The rock is still rolling.

I leave Sisyphus at the foot of the mountain! One always finds one's burden again. But Sisyphus teaches the higher fidelity that negates the gods and raises rocks. He too concludes that all is well. This universe henceforth without a master seems to him neither sterile nor futile. Each atom of that stone, each mineral flake of that night-filled mountain, in itself forms a world. The struggle itself toward the heights is enough to fill a man's heart. One must imagine Sisyphus happy. (Pp. 88–91.)

Paul Tillich and the Courage to Be

"The decisive event which underlies the search for meaning and the despair of it in the 20th century," observed Paul Tillich (1886–1965), "is the loss of God in the 19th century."[16] Although agreeing with much of Camus's analysis of the human predicament, Tillich tried to develop a credible religious alternative in response to the question "Can my life make sense?" Born in Germany, Tillich served as an army chaplain in World War I. He then taught theology and philosophy in German universities, but he was opposed to Nazism and when Hitler came to power in 1933, Tillich immigrated to the United States. From 1933 to 1956 he taught at Union Theological Seminary in New York City, and from 1956 until his death, he was a professor at Harvard University and the University of Chicago.

Although Tillich's thinking was much influenced by living and writing in the United States, the existential movement impressed him even more. Religion and God had often been used as a way to affirm life's meaning, but Tillich understood that the insights of

PAUL TILLICH 1886–1965

Feuerbach, Kierkegaard, Nietzsche, Sartre, and Camus had introduced the challenge of modern skepticism and pessimism where traditional values were concerned. Tillich's response was to develop a novel philosophical theology. It pivoted around the theme found in the title of one of his most important books, *The Courage to Be* (1952).

The Meaning of Courage

Focusing on courage as a human virtue, Tillich believed that this trait is not rooted merely in human nature but can be traced to something beyond. In a way that echoed Camus's defiance of absurdity, he defined courage as "self-affirmation 'in-spite-of,' that is in spite of that which tends to prevent the self from affirming itself" (p. 32). As finite beings for example, we cannot escape the anxiety that threatens to overcome us because we are afraid of inevitable death. While that anxiety may become intensified to the point of despair, human beings nevertheless possess resources in battling such threats. Anxiety will turn to courage, Tillich believed, if for no other reason than that the alternative is despair. But if we do gain the courage we need, Tillich thought, it proves to be a matter of religious "grace" (p. 85). This is where God enters the picture. Each of us can acquire courage by joining some organized group or political movement, but none of these, Tillich felt, satisfactorily accounts for the existence of courage. God is the issue in our struggle to acquire courage and to avoid despair.

Sometimes it seems that human existence is meaningless, but Tillich argued that we should not accept such absurd experiences as final. Rather, he believed that we can discover God, not in abstract thought and argument, but in the struggle with anxiety, despair, and meaninglessness. One path to discovery is through the experience of courage itself. Because we are threatened with non-existence, courage always includes a risk, Tillich claimed—that is, if we are going to face the challenge and not abandon life. We do not enter religious faith with certainty but with uncertainty and a challenge similar to the one Pascal offered us earlier.

> One can only become confident about one's existence after ceasing to base one's confidence on oneself. On the other hand the courage of confidence is in no way based on anything finite besides oneself, not even in the Church. It is based on God and solely on God, who is experienced in a unique and personal encounter. (P. 163.)

In this passage, Tillich was talking specifically about the spirit of the Protestant Reformation, but the sentiment holds good for his analysis of the ultimate origins of courage as well.

Although not everyone will immediately interpret the experience of courage in the way Tillich suggests, his approach makes religious belief possible. He said that "faith is the state of being grasped by the power of being itself." The term "being itself" is the name Tillich prefers to use for God (p. 172). Ordinary experiences, Tillich urged, put us in touch with power that transcends the ordinary. God can be discerned in such encounters. As we experience the most radical threat, death, we discover the power that makes it possible for us to face death. Even the experience of meaninglessness depends on the experience of meaning, so that the ultimacy of meaning is the basis for the experience of meaninglessness and forms a basis for confidence. In short, the courage to continue to be in spite of despair is Tillich's key to God. Courage has a revelatory character. For Tillich: "There are no valid arguments for the existence of God, but there are acts of courage in which are affirmed the power of being, whether we know it or not" (p. 181).

Courage is a human act. We may see death sweep over millions as, for example, in the Holocaust. And yet some who survived—though by no means all—reported that the courage to face death brought them closer to a sense of God's presence rather than further away. Such glimpses of God as the ultimate source of courage do not "prove" God's existence, but for Tillich they ultimately serve as the basis for belief. Psychological facts may be more important than all the logical arguments that purport to demonstrate God's existence from the nature of the world. Yet Tillich emphasized that this outcome does not lead to the usual comfortable, supportive God of ordinary religion. The ultimate source of the courage to be, he argued, is the "God above God" (p. 182).

The relation between God and life's meaning, admitted Tillich, is not easily found, and Tillich's quest leads beyond any standard ideas about God we may have inherited. For instance, Tillich held that "the courage to be is rooted in the God who appears when God has disappeared in the anxiety of doubt" (p. 190). Sitting quietly in the classroom thinking about God's existence will not do the trick; more risk is needed to discover the God above God. We must first turn away from rational thought and explore our psychological moods of anxiety and despair. But if we find ourselves seized by courage as the result of a grace granted to us from beyond ourselves, the God who is beyond the early God we lost may appear and provide us with the ground for courage to continue life's struggles.

Coping with Uncertainty

Does Tillich's analysis of human experience form any kind of "proof" for God's existence? Does it offer any assurance that life makes sense? Certainly Tillich intended his interpretation of experience to be universally valid. His analysis makes an appeal that goes beyond abstract argument and logical necessity and urges us to see our own experience in a new light. Such an "argument" will not work for one who finds it impossible to match Tillich's interpretation of experience with what he or she is actually living through. But for those who can feel the "fit" between what Tillich is saying and what they experience, Tillich's analysis may become psychologically compelling. If Tillich is correct, moreover, we can discover what lies at the heart of human existence by finding the courage to take the risks required to uncover it. Still, can those who risk the venture of self-examination be sure that meaning will emerge from the venture? Not entirely. Since Tillich thinks uncertainty and anxiety, as well as courage, are part of the structure of our existence, no experience can immunize us from our doubts about God's reality and life's meaning.

Uncertainty and anxiety are unavoidable if one seeks God. Tillich realized that many may not want to assume such risks, and no one be compelled to do so. But Tillich was also convinced that some form of despair lies hidden in all human existence. Thus, the challenge is to explore this situation to find the meaning that may be within it. In *The Myth of Sisyphus,* Camus considered the absurd as a starting point. It was not the conclusion of an inquiry but a reality to begin with. In addition, he thought that religious responses to render the absurd less than ultimate would be dishonest escapes from life's facts. Tillich recognized the courage in Camus's stance but also wanted us to have the courage not to conclude too soon that the absurd is an ultimate. God, he agreed, is no more certain than human experience, which is always permeated by uncertainty. Nevertheless the claim that God exists can be found in the courage to be that is available to us as we face despair. For Tillich, the search for God and for meaning in life are one and the same.

Speaking as a theologian, Tillich wrote: "The basic theological question is the question of God."[17] He thought it important to describe God as fully as possible in terms understandable by contemporary men and women. Again, Tillich began with an exploration of courage, since that psychological approach is familiar today. The fact that we are finite and face a limited existence, he contends, drives us to the question of God (1:165). It is just because human existence is riddled with questions about its meaningfulness that it is possible for us to find God. This leads Tillich to describe God, not as necessary in the way that Anselm did but in a more Pascalian manner, as containing an element of ultimate indeterminacy (1:168). If God's nature involves indeterminacy, that affects our attempts to answer the question "Can my life make sense?" For a God whose nature is not fixed may elude all "conclusive" arguments for or against life's meaning.

If we reach a knowledge of God, argues Tillich, it is not because God falls within our frameworks of rational demonstration. That would make God too much into an object like every other we encounter. As a result, Tillich does not say much about God directly. He points to the divine only indirectly, by focusing on the human condition. He does not believe in arguments that try to prove God's existence by examining some fact about the world, for "If we derive God from the world, he cannot be that which transcends the world infinitely" (1:205). But Tillich likes the question about God's existence, because it can give us an answer about life. "The question of God is possible because an awareness of God is present in the question of God" (1:206).

Ultimate Concern

"God," says Tillich, "is the name for that which concerns us ultimately" (1:211). This proposition means that "whatever concerns a man ultimately becomes God for him, and, conversely, it means that a man can be concerned ultimately only about that which is God for him" (1:206). Thus, to ask the question "Can my life make sense?" is to ask if anything concerns us ultimately. To the extent that such a concern involves us, God exists whether we are aware of it or not. This seems reminiscent of the definitional strategies adopted by Anselm in his ontological argument, but Tillich expounds his idea of ultimate concern so that we are directed to examine our own quest for meaning and courage. Although we are tempted to invest many of our concerns with ultimacy, not every concern can qualify as ultimate. We often do raise up idols, but in doing so we should realize that they are finite gods. Only "the holy," concludes Tillich, "is the *quality* of that which concerns man ultimately" (1:215).

Many religious traditions speak of a personal God. This, Tillich thought, indicates the concreteness of humanity's ultimate concern (1:223). Religiously, we need to speak about God as living, but Tillich cautioned us to think of such terms as symbolic, not literal. The end result is that his arguments can lead us to the symbols we need to approach God properly, although they may not lead directly to God. Our experience of existing as limited beings in the world points us to God, whom Tillich defines as the ground and the destiny of all finite existence, as our ultimate concern and thus our ground of meaning. Of course, we can decide that death is not our ultimate concern, but Tillich feels that you will merely substitute some finite end or object as your ultimate concern, whereas only God deserves such attention. Some theologians deny that there is suffering in God, but Tillich's "ultimate ground" (or God) participates in all forms of human experience, including our painful struggles to make sense of life.

Therefore, just to the extent that we understand our human situation, we are capable of discerning how God is involved in it and provides the courage that gives life meaning. That should make us realize that words cannot encompass God completely and that our questions about life's meaning cannot adequately be put into sentences. But that realization also opens the way to develop a symbolic way of speaking that enlarges our grasp of what lies beyond our capacity for literal description. We find the symbols we need to talk about God and decide which ones work best. We can also realize why we cannot come closer than to describe God symbolically. We can still say we are "certain" of life's meaning, that we have found courage, but we must be careful not to claim more for such a conviction than is warranted by its basis in our uncertain experience. As human beings, we may instinctively search for certainty. But if God is seen as the ground of human experience and life's meaning, we know that certainty is not found there. Yet in ways similar to but also different from those of Camus, Tillich thinks we can obtain the

courage to face absurdity so that life makes sense. Now read some of *The Courage to Be* and see whether Tillich speaks to you more persuasively than Pascal, Hegel, Thoreau, or Camus as you wrestle with the issue "Can my life make sense?"

Courage is the self-affirmation of being in spite of the fact of nonbeing. It is the act of the individual self in taking the anxiety of nonbeing upon itself by affirming itself either as part of an embracing whole or in its individual selfhood. Courage always includes a risk, it is always threatened by nonbeing, whether the risk of losing oneself and becoming a thing within the whole of things or of losing one's world in an empty self-relatedness. Courage needs the power of being, a power transcending the nonbeing which is experienced in the anxiety of fate and death, which is present in the anxiety of emptiness and meaninglessness, which is effective in the anxiety of guilt and condemnation. The courage which takes this threefold anxiety into itself must be rooted in a power of being that is greater than the power of oneself and the power of one's world. Neither self-affirmation as a part nor self-affirmation as oneself is beyond the manifold threat of nonbeing. Those who are mentioned as representatives of these forms of courage try to transcend themselves and the world in which they participate in order to find the power of being-itself and a courage to be which is beyond the threat of nonbeing. There are no exceptions to this rule; and this means that every courage to be has an open or hidden religious root. For religion is the state of being grasped by the power of being-itself. In some cases the religious root is carefully covered, in others it is passionately denied; in some it is deeply hidden and in others superficially. But it is never completely absent. For everything that is participates in being-itself, and everybody has some awareness of this participation, especially in the moments in which he experiences the threat of nonbeing. This leads us to a final consideration, the double question: How is the courage to be rooted in being-itself, and how must we understand being-itself in the light of the courage to be? The first question deals with the ground of being as source of the courage to be, the second with courage to be as key to the ground of being.[18]

THE GOD ABOVE GOD AND THE COURAGE TO BE

The ultimate source of the courage to be is the "God above God"; this is the result of our demand to transcend theism. Only if the God of theism is transcended can the anxiety of doubt and meaninglessness be taken into the courage to be. The God above God is the object of all mystical longing, but mysticism also must be transcended in order to reach him. Mysticism does not take seriously the concrete and the doubt concerning the concrete. It plunges directly into the ground of being and meaning, and leaves the concrete, the world of finite values and meanings, behind. Therefore it does not solve the problem of meaninglessness. In terms of the present religious situation this means that Eastern mysticism is not the solution of the problems of Western Existentialism, although many people attempt this solution. The God above the God of theism is not the devaluation of the meanings which doubt has thrown into the abyss of meaninglessness; he is their potential restitution. Nevertheless absolute faith agrees with the faith implied in mysticism in that both transcend the theistic objectivation of a God who is a being. For mysticism such a God is not more real than any finite being, for the courage to be such a God has disappeared in the abyss of meaninglessness with every other value and meaning.

The God above the God of theism is present, although hidden, in every divine–human encounter. Biblical religion as well as Protestant theology are aware of the paradoxical character of this encounter. They are aware that if God encounters man God is neither object nor subject and is therefore above the scheme into which theism has forced him. They are aware that personalism with respect to God is balanced by a transpersonal presence of the divine. They are aware that forgiveness can be accepted only if the power of acceptance is effective in man—biblically speaking, if the power of grace is effective in man. They are aware of the paradoxical character of every prayer, of speaking to somebody to whom you cannot speak because he is not "somebody," of asking somebody of whom you cannot ask anything because he gives or gives not before you ask, of saying "thou" to somebody who is nearer to the I than the I is to itself. Each of these paradoxes drives the religious consciousness toward a God above the God of theism.

The courage to be which is rooted in the experience of the God above the God of theism unites and transcends the courage to be as a part and the courage to be as oneself. It avoids both the loss of oneself by participation and the loss of one's world by individualization. The acceptance of the God above the God of theism makes us a part of that which is not also a part but is the ground of the whole. Therefore our self is not lost in a larger whole, which submerges it in the life of a limited group. If the self participates in the power of being-itself it receives itself back. For the power of being acts through the power of the individual selves. It does not swallow them as every limited whole, every collectivism, and every conformism does. This is why the Church, which stands for the power of being-itself or for the God who transcends the God of the religions, claims to be the mediator of the courage to be. A church which is based on the authority of the God of theism cannot make such a claim. It inescapably develops into a collectivist or semicollectivist system itself. . . .

Absolute faith, or the state of being grasped by the God beyond God, is not a state which appears beside other states of the mind. It never is something separated and definite, an event which could be isolated and described. It is always a movement in, with, and under other states of the mind. It is the situation on the boundary of man's possibilities. It *is* this boundary. Therefore it is both the courage of despair and the courage in and above every courage. It is not a place where one can live, it is without the safety of words and concepts, it is without a name, a church, a cult, a theology. But it is moving in the depth of all of them. It is the power of being, in which they participate and of which they are fragmentary expressions.

One can become aware of it in the anxiety of fate and death when the traditional symbols, which enable men to stand the vicissitudes of fate and the horror of death have lost their power. When "providence" has become a superstition and "immortality" something imaginary that which once was the power in these symbols can still be present and create the courage to be in spite of the experience of a chaotic world and a finite existence. The Stoic courage returns but not as the faith in universal reason. It returns as the absolute faith which says Yes to being without seeing anything concrete which could conquer the nonbeing in fate and death.

And one can become aware of the God above the God of theism in the anxiety of guilt and condemnation when the traditional symbols that enable men to withstand the anxiety of guilt and condemnation have lost their power. When "divine judgment" is interpreted as a psychological complex and forgiveness as a remnant of the "father-image," what once was the power in those symbols can still be present and create the courage to be in spite of the experience of an infinite gap between what we are and what we ought to be. The Lutheran courage returns but not supported by the faith in a judging and forgiving God. It returns in terms of the absolute faith which says Yes although there is no special power that conquers guilt. The courage to take the anxiety of meaninglessness upon oneself is the boundary line up to which the courage to be can go. Beyond it is mere nonbeing. Within

it all forms of courage are reestablished in the power of the God above the God of theism. *The courage to be is rooted in the God who appears when God has disappeared in the anxiety of doubt.* (Pp. 186–90.)

Summary

Camus disagreed with Hegel: "The real is not entirely rational, nor is the rational entirely real."[19] Pascal and Thoreau did not see eye to eye with Hegel either. Each was a rebel on the question of life's meaning. The acceptance of things as they are, they agreed, is not enough to sustain hope. A significant life depends on defying the odds. It requires spending life actively so that life makes sense. Hegel was content to follow the logic of reason in its development, since he thought reason governed history and gave it purpose. Camus thought individuals could give meaning and purpose to life, but more for themselves than for societies or for hisory as a whole. To do that much is difficult, but Camus believed that rebellion against absurdity provides our only legitimate hope. Up to a point Tillich agreed with Camus. In the courage to be that we experience, however, he located new glimpses of the God-beyond-God that makes it possible to affirm a religious response when we ask "Can my life make sense?"

In discussing whether life makes sense, we began with Pascal's aim to force us to gamble on life and its meaning. Actually, he does not think we have choice. We see Hegel as the supreme rationalist, who finds meaning and progress in every event—not when taken individually but when seen in history's world-scale dialectical progression. Thoreau emerges with a quiet answer. Life can make sense if you simplify your lifestyle, seek a certain calm in the midst of busyness, and concentrate on ordinary events to give life significance. Camus is more radical: life is absurd taken in itself. Meaning is not to be found objectively. Life makes sense only if we have the strength to rebel against absurdity. We must take responsibility ourselves to give meaning to what otherwise might appear as endless repetition. Tillich returns to the question of God but not in a traditional sense. Searching for God is the same as searching for meaning in life and requires courage in the face of uncertainty. Here, then, are five views of how life does and does not make sense. Yet perhaps we cannot hope to make sense of life unless we can find a way to cope with evil and death. We turn to that task in the next chapter.

GLOSSARY

absolute the ultimate goal of the Hegelian dialectic. See **Reason**.

absurd as Camus describes it, the pointless, hopeless, meaningless character that human life sometimes assumes for some people, which presents philosophy with its most concrete problem, that of justifying the value of human existence.

antithesis the second stage of the Hegelian dialectic, in which what was asserted in the thesis is negated, contradicted, or denied.

civil disobedience Thoreau's term for a non-violent method of opposing the power of the State. Unlike Kant, Thoreau believed that individual conscience should take precedence over a "respect for law as such," and where the two clashed, a person should follow his or her conscience rather than the letter of the law, in disregard of the legal sanctions that might be brought against him or her.

courage in Tillich's theology, the chief among human virtues, because courage is required for the bold act of self-assertion that is necessary for human beings to continue to live in the face of all the absurdity and chaos in the world that threaten to thwart human self-expression.

"Idea-in-itself" the first stage of Hegel's account of historical development, that of a rational construct that is self-contained but unrealized in any concrete way.

"Idea-outside-itself" the second stage in Hegel's theory of historical development, in which the **"Idea-in-itself"** finds concrete expression and comes to constitute what we know as the order of Nature.

Nature Hegel uses this term close to its ordinary meaning, as the world in front of us; but it comes to be what it is as a result of the process he describes.

"Pascal's wager" Pascal's famous argument for the rationality of belief in God: namely, that although a wrong belief in the existence of God could do no harm, a wrong disbelief could result in our losing the opportunity to live a life rich in religious significance. Therefore, it is more rational to make the "wager" that God *does* exist, even though we have no evidence either for or against such a proposition.

Reason in Hegel, the goal of the dialectical development of human consciousness, which he also called God or the **Absolute.** This goal is reached by a progressive synthesis of the **Idea-in-itself** and the **Idea-for-itself,** the rational and the real.

rebellion in Camus's philosophy, "a protest against death," the assertion of oneself through the act of rebelling against the absurdity of existence, against both murder and suicide.

Sisyphus figure in classical mythology whose task for eternity was to roll a huge stone up a hill, only to have the stone roll down again at each completion of the upward roll. Camus's philosophy turns on the image of Sisyphus courageously refusing to be broken by this task and continuing with the task in spite of its absurd and frustrating nature.

Spirit Hegel's third stage of historical development, that of the "Idea-as-conscious-of-itself," that collective human consciousness which expresses itself in the process of history, and which in its attempt to come to know its own nature provides history with its dialectical structure.

suicide the deliberate act of killing oneself, the possibility of which Camus saw as constituting a fundamental philosophical problem.

synthesis the final stage in Hegel's dialectic, in which the opposition between **antithesis** and **thesis** is resolved.

thesis the first stage of Hegel's dialectic, in which a thing comes to be or is asserted as a being-in-itself.

transcendentalism a philosophical movement in nineteenth-century New England whose principal figures included Ralph Waldo Emerson and Henry David Thoreau. The American transcendentalists combined Kantian idealistic epistemological concerns with a strong element of romanticism. Thoreau's writings in particular are preoccupied with the autonomy of the individual, with ethics as an expression and extension of natural order, and with a radical opposition to the state.

triadic a term describing the logical structure of Hegel's dialectic, which concerns the relations and transformations among three terms, **thesis, antithesis,** and **synthesis.**

STUDY QUESTIONS

1. Do you agree with Pascal that life forces us to wager? Can you see a way to avoid his particular gamble about God?

2. Does God's existence seem as important to you as it does to Pascal? Is it a matter demanding your decision?

3. From what you know of world history, can you see the pattern of rational dialectical development that Hegel observed?

4. Do you think that Hegel imposes sense on the world, or that he finds it there?

5. As you read Thoreau's recommendations on how to live, where do you agree or disagree? In your judgment does he qualify as a "philosopher"?

6. What would happen if we all withdrew, as Thoreau did? Can those who must be in the middle of political/social struggles still find the meaning and calm that he achieved in the isolation of Walden?

7. Does Camus's attitude on "absurdity" seem too radical a view to you, or do you find it justified in your own experience?

8. If the world's silent response to our demands for meaning renders life absurd, do you agree with Camus that each of us can give meaning to life by willing rebellion?

9. Are you persuaded by Tillich's attempt to link the search for meaning with the experience of courage and the reality of God?

10. If Tillich's "God-beyond-God" is beyond rational conceptualization, can such a God provide an acceptable support as you search for meaning in life?

11. How do you respond to the question "Can my life make sense?" and why?

NOTES

[1]Blaise Pascal, *Pensées*, trans. W. F. Trotter (New York: E. P. Dutton, 1958), p. 23.

Reprinted by permission of J. M. Dent & Sons Ltd. (Everyman's Library series).

[2]Quoted from Geddes MacGregor, *Philosophical Issues in Religious Thought* (Boston: Houghton Mifflin, 1973), p. 273.

[3]Pascal, *Pensées*, p. 60.

[4]G.W.F. Hegel, *Philosophy of Right*, trans. T. M. Knox (New York: Oxford University Press, 1967), p. 10. Reprinted by permission.

[5]G.W.F. Hegel, *Reason in History*, trans. Robert S. Hartman (Indianapolis: Bobbs-Merrill, 1953), p. 11. Reprinted with permission of Macmillan Publishing Company. Copyright © 1953, 1985 by Macmillan Publishing Company. Renewed 1981 by Rita S. Hartman.

[6]Hegel, *Philosophy of Right*, pp. 10–13.

[7]Henry David Thoreau, *Walden*, in *The Portable Thoreau*, ed. Carl Bode (New York: Viking, 1964), pp. 557–58. Copyright 1947, © 1962, 1964 by the Viking Press, Inc. Copyright renewed © 1975 by the Viking Press, Inc. Reprinted by permission of Viking Penguin, Inc.

[8]Henry David Thoreau, "Life without Principle," in *The Portable Thoreau*, p. 633.

[9]Thoreau, *Walden*, p. 325.

[10]Henry David Thoreau, "On the Duty of Civil Disobedience," in *The Portable Thoreau*, p. 111.

[11]Thoreau, *Walden*, p. 343.

[12]Thoreau, "Life without Principle," pp. 632–35.

[13]Albert Camus, *The Myth of Sisyphus and Other Essays*, trans. Justin O'Brien (New York: Vintage Books, 1955), p. 3. Copyright © 1955 by Alfred A. Knopf, Inc. Reprinted by permission of the publisher.

[14]Albert Camus, *The Rebel*, trans. Anthony Bower (New York: Vintage Books, 1956), p. 22.

[15]Camus, *The Myth of Sisyphus*, pp. 3–12.

[16]Paul Tillich, *The Courage to Be* (New Haven: Yale University Press, 1960), p. 142. Copyright 1960 by Yale University Press. Reprinted by permission.

[17]Paul Tillich, *Systematic Theology*, 3 vols. (Chicago: University of Chicago Press, 1951–63), 1:163.

[18]Tillich, *The Courage to Be*, pp. 155–56.

[19]Camus, *The Rebel*, p. 295.

CHAPTER THIRTEEN

How Should I Deal with Evil and Death?

S eventy million human beings uprooted, enslaved, or killed in the twentieth century alone: Albert Camus made that estimate when he published *The Rebel* in 1951. We can only guess what the figure would be today. What happened to those victims? Is death—utter annihilation—their end? How should we think about such destruction of human life? Considering such questions as these causes many to reflect on the significance of evil and whether we human beings can hope to withstand its onslaught. Why does evil exist? How should evil be understood? Where does it end? Can we realistically hope that it will ultimately be overcome? Nearly everyone wonders about these issues, and some philosophers regard them as the most important ones we can raise. All who grieve over the loss are likely to agree.

Human existence forces every person to cope in solitude with tragedy and sorrow, with suffering, injustice, and death. However, philosophers understand that these experiences need to be shared as well. They search for ways to deal with, if not to understand, the presence of evil and death. As with all the questions we study, philosophers do not speak with one voice when they inquire about these realities. In this instance particularly, they may offer words to aid understanding and even to nurture hope, but it remains for each of us to determine what answers make the most sense.

Some of you may be content to think about life and leave the question of death for a later time. Life is not easily explained, however; oddly enough, being forced to face the issue of death may actually help you understand life. Life and death, as some Eastern philosophers have argued, may need to be understood together, and perhaps one cannot be understood apart from the other. We can avoid facing the problems of evil and death for a time, but never indefinitely. It might help us to succeed in life if we were prepared to deal with them.

In this chapter, Leibniz stands as a prime example of the rationalistic optimist who is sure that ultimately there is a good reason for everything that happens. He argues that we live in "the best of all possible worlds," which if true offers a certain amount of comfort. Bertrand Russell is a rationalist in his approach, too, but he differs from Leibniz by rejecting religious solutions to the problems of evil and death. Instead Russell is the humanist who is content to deal with these problems on a purely here-and-now basis. Martin Luther King, Jr., is known for his opposition to racial discrimination, but his writings also show him to be a philosopher who develops a theory about how to face evil. Elie Wiesel, a Jewish survivor of Ausch-witz, writes about evil from firsthand experience of its extreme forms. Far less optimistic than any of the other three, he nonetheless refuses to succumb to despair. In the beginning of this book we stressed that our discussions would not be restricted to those who belong in the typical annals of philosophy. Leibniz and Russell fit the conventional models. King and Wiesel do not, and yet the writings they produced in response to their practical dealings with evil and death are profoundly philosophical in outlook. King and Wiesel help us to remember that the questions of philosophy are much too important to be confined to the studies of professors and the classrooms of academic life.

Gottfried Wilhelm von Leibniz and the Best of All Possible Worlds

Gottfried Wilhelm von Leibniz (1646–1716) thought that we live in the best of all **possible worlds**. He drew that conclusion not by ignoring the reality of evil and death but by taking both with the utmost seriousness. Like Descartes and Spinoza, this German philosopher was a seventeenth-century rationalist who believed that a proper use of reason could demonstrate the true answer for every question of philosophy. This led him to some optimistic conclusions.

Leibniz worked on the cutting edge in many different fields, distinguishing himself not only as a philosopher but also as scientist, mathematician, historian, and diplomat. The seventeenth century saw a flowering of science and mathematics in the work of Galileo, Newton, and others. Leibniz knew and corresponded with most of the leading scientific theorists of his day and in the process

GOTTFRIED WILHELM VON LEIBNIZ
1646–1716

made his own significant contributions. Striving to develop a coherent metaphysical foundation for the newly emerging sciences, he discovered a form of the differential calculus. Newton claimed that his findings in this field came first, but controversy continues over whether that honor should go to Leibniz.

Leibniz was the son of a professor, although he himself did not teach. He was a counselor in the court of the duke of Brunswick, and he performed diplomatic missions while in the service of the archbishop of Mainz. Many of his important writings were not published in his lifetime because he was usually too busy to attend to the details of publication. Leibniz was certainly interested in the problem of **evil,** but among Leibniz's other projects were efforts to unify Protestants and Catholics and to unite the states of Europe politically. In the midst of this activity, his philosophical work continued, much of it contained in the lengthy letters he sent to his patrons and colleagues. Today Leibniz's writings fill some forty volumes. None are better known than those on evil.

What Is Theodicy?

The only large book Leibniz published during his lifetime was written for his friend, Sophie Charlotte, the queen of Prussia. Its title, *Theodicy* (1710), utilized a term that indicates how Leibniz sized up the problem of evil. A **theodicy** is a theory that explains God's relation to human life with specific reference to God's justice in ordaining or permitting evil. Usually a theodicy defends God and vindicates God's relation to evil. This was Leibniz's approach, too. It required him to treat questions that are as intriguing as they are difficult. What kinds of evil are there? Why is the world ordered as it is, if a just and benevolent God is its creator? Is evil avoidable?

Not every philosopher who writes about evil sets up the questions in Leibniz's way. Some even question the basic assumptions that operate in a theodicy, for the existence of evil does not necessarily entail the existence of God. Yet Leibniz's path remains a perennial one in Western thought. Evil's presence commonly raises religious issues. When God enters a picture that contains cruelty, suffering, and death, we wonder how and why divinity could be involved. Why do bad things happen, especially—as they frequently do—to good people? In accounting for God's ways, evil is the chief question that troubles us. What, if anything, will God do to change things for the better? Can we give an account that justifies evil in God's design? Leibniz thought he could.

The Principles of Reason

As a rationalist and a logician, Leibniz believed that two great principles manifest themselves in all reality, God included. First is the **principle of noncontradiction.** It mandates that both a proposition or state of affairs and its exact negation cannot be true at once. Thus, asserted Leibniz, there are truths of reason that are characterized by their logical necessity. They cannot be denied without contradiction. One example is that "two truths cannot contradict each other."[1] That claim is important in Leibniz's theodicy, because while he believed that there is revealed truth as well as truth that can be discerned by reason alone, the former will never be in ultimate conflict with the latter. If revelation witnesses that God's ways are justifiable, which Leibniz took to be the case, reason can go far in vindicating them, too.

Second, there is the **principle of sufficient reason.** Nothing, argued Leibniz, exists or happens by accident. On the contrary, there is an ultimate and final justification for everything. Contemporary physicists may disagree, but in the seventeenth century necessity held greater sway. Some things are the way they are because they could not logically be otherwise. Conceptually, for instance, an equilateral triangle is going to be a triangle no matter what. But a host of things do not fit within Leibniz's category of logically necessary facts. Your existence would be a case in point; others can think of a world without you and not face a contradiction. In a world governed by the principle of sufficient reason, however, the existence of contingent beings—those like you, whose reality is both possible and yet in principle deniable without contradiction—is determined by "moral necessity" (p. 10). In a word, they exist because they are fit to exist.

Whether we can fulfill it now or not, the postulate is that for every event a reason sufficient to explain its existence can be found. Leibniz elaborates by noting that we see nature functioning in terms of physical laws. But it is reasonable to ask why these laws exist. His answer is that they exist because they ought to. This fitness, moreover, is not determined in isolation. According to Leibniz, it depends on God who alone "has the privilege of existing necessarily" and without whom "there would not only be nothing existing, but nothing even possible."[2] This God, Leibniz continues, creates a universe of preestablished harmony, one that combines the greatest possible variety of beings and the greatest possible order.

The Best of All Possible Worlds

It would be self-contradictory, said Leibniz, for God not to act in accordance with the principle of sufficient reason. Hence, he affirms that "nothing can come from God that is not altogether consistent with goodness, justice, and holiness."[3] That judgment, however, complicated matters when Leibniz affirmed the reality of evil. By his reckoning, evil exists in three forms: "Evil may be taken metaphysically, physically, and morally. *Metaphysical evil* consists in mere imperfection, *physical evil* in suffering, and *moral evil* in sin" (p. 40). Some imperfection is inevitable in the created order. Only God is truly perfect and God cannot create himself; to do so would be contradictory. Physical evil, on the other hand, is usually the result of moral evil, the latter existing through human freedom.

Since he was committed to the principle of sufficient reason, Leibniz affirmed that God "cannot but have chosen the best" (p. 35). Ours must be the best of all possible worlds, according to Leibniz, for "if there were not the best among all possible worlds, God would not have produced any" (p. 35). He specified "world" to mean not only planet earth but "the whole succession and the whole agglomeration of all existent things" (p. 35). However, Leibniz recognized that these judgments are not likely to ring true at first glance. If this were the case, there would have been no need to write his philosophy. So he moved ahead by considering God's options in creating. God's creation involves choosing one from an infinity of possible worlds. Possibility, Leibniz notes, is limited only by the principle of contradiction. Thus, he tells us, "God wills *antecedently* the good and *consequently* the best" (p. 41).

First, God grasps every conceivable possibility. He would actualize them all insofar as each is good. But even for God there are impossibilities. Not every good can exist simultaneously; some are mutually contradictory. He cannot, for example, create us all artistically sensitive and at the same time impervious to pain and loss. God had to make a selection. Consequently, he created the best world: the one that contains the least defective combination of goods. "Nothing better could have been created," writes Leibniz, "than what God created."[4] But the best of all possible worlds is not to be confused with a perfect world. Indeed, Leibniz underscores, the best of all possible worlds—our world—clearly does contain evil.

We have already mentioned Leibniz's belief that metaphysical evil is inherent in any world that God could create. God, held Leibniz, must permit it in order to bring the best of all possible worlds into being. Physical and moral evil, however, are in principle avoidable. So, what is God's relationship to them? First, Leibniz states that "God wills moral evil not at all, and physical evil or suffering he does not will absolutely."[5] The latter, Leibniz adds, God often wills "as a penalty owing to guilt, and often also as a means to an end, that is, to prevent greater evils or to obtain greater good" (p. 41). That kind of evil is part of God's response to moral evil, whose source is human freedom. Human freedom, we know, can have unfortunate results. God also permits the results of freedom to appear, though moral evil never has "the function of a means," and he keeps it from being final by ensuring that his justice prevails.[6] In due course God will set everything right in the best of all possible worlds.

Leibniz never denied the prominence of evil, but he did see it in an optimistic light. In principle, God could have created a world with far less evil than ours exhibits. But that world would not have been the best one possible. In the final analysis, God's reason and will would not incline to create any other. In fact, despite the emphasis Leibniz placed on the contingency of physical and moral evil, it turns out that "if the smallest evil that comes to pass in the world were missing in it, it would no longer be this world; which, with nothing omitted and all allowance made, was found the best by the Creator who chose it."[7]

Is God Bound to Evil?

Leibniz frequently spoke about God's choices in creating and about the vast array of possibilities from which God could select. But the more one inspects closely what Leibniz's theodicy entails, the more it becomes clear that the best of all possible worlds and its God are really bound by necessity. Neither the world nor God can avoid evil. In one way or another, it is a consequence of God's perfection. The best of all possible worlds requires evil and apparently its particular instances, too. The compensation is that this tight metaphysical package also allows Leibniz to be assured that evil and death do not have the last word.

That outcome can be comforting, but the amount of evil logically or morally necessitated may be a price higher than some want to pay. In any case, a critical question remains, which is whether God must be as Leibniz portrays his divinity. The rationalist Leibniz makes God a rationalist, too. Accepting what Leibniz takes to be the laws of reason, it becomes inconceivable that God would not create the best of all possible worlds—as Leibniz defines that concept—and our world would have to be the one that fits it. But why can't God act outside Leibniz's rules of reason?

Leibniz stressed that we cannot understand all the ways of God. Where the problem of evil is concerned, he added, one of the difficulties is that we cannot enlarge our view of the universe enough. We see the evils in human affairs, and we forget how insignificant they may be in comparison to the greater goods produced in the whole universe that God's wisdom governs. Still, Leibniz thought he had identified enough about how God's wisdom works to permit him to justify evil's destructive presence in our lives. Leibniz's view makes evil seem tame. On the other hand, Camus's recounting of atrocity makes us wonder about ourselves, the world, and God, just as Elie Wiesel will.

Unless we are convinced that we do live in the best of all possible worlds, we will need to reconsider what God is like—if God exists at all—and to look for other theodicies. But in dealing with other suggestions, we need to keep in mind Leibniz's concept of the best of all possible worlds. Is there such a thing as *the* best of all possible worlds— even for God? Does reason commit us to a single standard that specifies every detail of goodness and existence? How would we change the world, if we could, and what constraints would we face if we assumed God's role in creation? Should we want such an assurance that evil and death can be explained positively, if we believe that the only way to get that comfort entails the necessary evil Leibniz puts into his best of all possible worlds?

Questions such as these may help us decide what we want to say about evil, death, and God. In particular, is God bound in the ways Leibniz describes God's choices? If God has genuine—not merely logical—alternatives and can choose whichever he wants, his decisions become more free and less predictable. This makes God responsible for creating a world that is perhaps not as rationally ordered as Leibniz's terms dictate. That outlook might fit our senses of freedom and openness better, and it might account for the uncertainties of evil at the same time. It would not, however, enable us to answer in Leibniz's optimistic way the question of whether evil and death are justified. For if evil and death are not necessary aspects of the best of all possible worlds, God's justification—if there is one—remains suspended in the future. Do we live in a world of such ultimate uncertainty? Should we decide to live in a world without God, or opt for a God who is different from the one Leibniz portrayed? What possible explanations are open to us? Let those questions guide your further reading of Leibniz's philosophy, as expressed in the essay "A Vindication of God's Justice Reconciled with His Other Perfections and All His Actions" (1710). See where the reflection leads you.

---

1. The apologetic examination of the cause of God not only enhances the divine glory, but also serves our own advantage. It may move us to honor his greatness, that is, his power and wisdom, as well as to love his goodness and the perfections which derive from it, namely, his justice and holiness, and to imitate them as much as it is in our power. This apology contains two parts, of which the first may be considered as rather preparatory and the second as the principal. The first part studies, separately, *the greatness and the goodness of God*; the second, what pertains to these two perfections taken together, including the **providence** which he extends to all creatures, and the *government* which he exercises over the creatures endowed with intelligence, particularly in all matters concerning piety and salvation.

2. Theologians of excessive rigor have taken into account his greatness at the expense of his goodness, while those of greater laxity have done the opposite. True orthodoxy would consist in paying equal respect to both perfections. One may designate as **anthropomorphism** the error of those who neglect his greatness, and as **despotism** the error of those who disregard his goodness.

3. The *greatness of God* has to be studiously defended, particularly against the Socinians and some semi-Socinians.* . . . This greatness can be considered under two main headings, God's omnipotence and his omniscience.

4. The **omnipotence** implies God's independence from everything else, as well as the dependence of everything upon him.

5. The *independence of God* manifests itself in his existence as well as in his actions: in his existence since he is a necessary and eternal being and, as it is commonly expressed, an *Ens a se*. Hence it follows also that he is beyond measure.

6. In his actions he is independent both naturally and morally. He is naturally independent, since he is absolutely free, and determined to action only by himself. He is morally independent since he . . . has no superior. [Leibniz used the Greek word *anupeuthunos*.]

7. The *dependence of everything on God* extends to all that is possible, that is, to all that does not imply contradiction, as well as to all that is actual.

8. The *possibility* of things, even of those that have no actual existence, has itself a reality founded in the divine existence. For if God did not exist, nothing would be possible, and the possibles are from eternity in the ideas of the divine intellect.

9. *Actual* beings depend upon God for their existence as well as for their actions, and depend not only upon his intellect but also upon his will. Their existence depends upon God, since all things have been freely

---

* . . . the majority of Socinians . . . denied the foreknowledge of God, and particularly that He foresaw the acts of free creatures.

created by God and are maintained in existence by him. There is a sound doctrine which teaches that this divine preservation in existence is a continued creation—comparable to the rays continually emitted by the sun—although the creatures do not emanate from the divine essence nor emanate necessarily.

10. *In their actions* all things depend upon God, since God concurs in their actions insofar as these actions have some degree of perfection, which must always come from God.

11. God's *concurrence* (even the ordinary, nonmiraculous, concurrence) is at the same time immediate and special. It is *immediate* since the effect depends upon God not only for the reason that its cause originates in God, but also for this other reason, that God concurs no less nor more indirectly in producing this effect than in producing its cause.

12. The concurrence is *special* because it aims not only at the existence of the thing and its actions, but also at the mode and qualities of this existence insofar as there is inherent in them some degree of perfection, which always flows from God, the father of light and dispenser of all good.

13. So far we have dealt with the divine power. Let us now proceed to his wisdom, which, because of its immensity, is called *omniscience*. Since this wisdom is the most perfect possible (just as is his omnipotence), it comprehends every idea and every truth, that is, everything, simple or complex, which can be an object of the understanding. It comprehends equally everything possible and everything actual.

14. His knowledge of the *possibles* constitutes what is called the *science of simple intelligence*. Its objects are the things as well as their relationships, and, in respect to both, their necessity or contingency.

15. *Contingent possibles* can be considered either separately or as all correlated in an infinity of entire possible worlds, each of which is perfectly known to God, though only one among them has been produced into existence. It is indeed useless to invent a plurality of actual worlds since a single universe comprehends for us the totality of created things in all times and places; in this sense we use here the term *world*.

16. His knowledge of actual things, that is, of the world produced into existence and of all past, present, and future states of the world, is called *science of vision*. It differs from the science of simple intelligence of this same world considered as merely possible only in that it contains, added to the latter, the reflexive knowledge whereby God knows his decree to produce it into actual existence. Nothing more is needed as a foundation for the divine foreknowledge.

17. The *science* commonly called intermediate is contained in the science of simple intelligence if the latter is taken in the sense we have expounded above. If, however, one wants a science midway between the science of simple intelligence and the science of vision one could conceive both the science of simple intelligence and the intermediate science differently from the common usage. In this case one could assign to the intermediate science not only the knowledge of conditional future events but, generally, the knowledge of all contingent possibles. Thus the science of simple intelligence would be taken in a more restricted sense, namely, as dealing with possible and necessary truths, while the science of vision would deal with contingent and actual truths. The intermediate science and the science of simple intelligence would have this in common, that they both deal with possible truths, while the intermediate science and the science of vision would both deal with contingent truths.

18. So far we have considered the divine greatness; now we shall deal with the *divine goodness*. Just as wisdom or knowledge of truth is a perfection of the understanding, so goodness or striving for the good is a perfection of the will. All will, indeed, has as its object the good, be it but an apparent good; but the divine will has no object which would not be both good and true.

19. We shall study, therefore, both the will and its object, namely, good and evil, which

provide the reasons for willing and rejecting. As to the will, we will study its nature and its species.

20. The *nature* of the will requires *freedom*, which consists in this: that the voluntary action be spontaneous and deliberate, and therefore exclude that necessity which suppresses deliberation.

21. Freedom excludes *metaphysical necessity*, the opposite of which is impossible, that is, implies contradiction. However, it does not exclude *moral* necessity, the opposite of which is unfit. For although God cannot fall into error in choosing, and therefore always chooses what is most fitting, this is so little opposed to his freedom that it rather renders it more perfect. It would be incompatible with his freedom if there were only one possible objective of the will, that is, if only one aspect of the universe were possible. For in this case there would no longer be any choice nor any possibility of praising the wisdom and goodness of Him who acts.

22. Therefore, those who maintain that only the actual—what God actually has chosen—is possible are mistaken, or at least express themselves awkwardly. This was the error of Diodorus the Stoic, according to Cicero, and among Christian thinkers that of Abelard, Wycliff, and Hobbes. I shall deal with freedom more elaborately later on, when human freedom will have to be defended.

23. So much about the nature of will. We come now to the **division of will**. For our present purpose we must introduce two divisions: on the one hand, the distinction of antecedent will and consequent will, and, on the other hand, the distinction between productive and permissive will.

24. The *first division* distinguishes between acts of will which are antecedent or prior and those which are consequent or final; or, which comes to the same, the will either inclines or decrees. In the first case it is incomplete; in the second, complete or absolute. Some authors, however, explain differently this division (at least the first). They maintain that the antecedent will of God (for instance, that all men be saved) precedes the consideration of the actions of

the creatures, while the consequent will (for instance, that some be damned) is posterior to this consideration. But the first also precedes and the second also follows other acts of the divine will. For the very consideration of the actions of the creatures is not only presupposed by certain acts of the divine will, but also presupposes in its turn certain acts of the divine will without which actions of the creatures could not occur. This is why St. Thomas [Aquinas] . . . and others understand this division in the same sense in which we do, namely, that the antecedent will is directed toward some particular good in itself, in proportion to its degree of goodness, so that this will is only a relative will (*secundum quid*). The consequent will, on the contrary, aims at the whole and contains the ultimate determination whence it issues in an absolute decree. Since we are speaking of the divine will, it always obtains its full effect. For the rest, if anyone refuses to accept our explanation, we will not quarrel with him about words and if he prefers he may substitute for *antecedent* and *consequent*, *prior* and *final*.

25. The **antecedent will** is entirely serious and pure and ought not to be confused with velleity (which consists in this: that one would will if one were able, and would wish to be able), which does not exist in God; nor is it to be confused with conditional will, with which we do not deal here. The antecedent will of God tends toward actualizing all good and repelling all evil, as such, and in proportion to the degree of goodness and evil. How serious this will is, God himself confirmed when he so firmly asserted that he did not want the death of the sinner, that he wanted all men to be saved, and that he hated sin.

26. The **consequent will** arises from the concurrence of all antecedent acts of will. When the effects of all antecedent acts of will cannot be carried out together, the maximum effect which can be obtained by wisdom and power will be obtained. This will is also commonly called *decree*.

27. Hence it is evident that even the antecedent acts of will are not altogether vain,

but have their own kind of efficacy. For though they produce effects, these effects are not always full, but are restricted by the concurrence of other antecedent acts of will. However, the decisive act of will, which results from all inclining acts of will, always produces its full effect, provided the power is adequate to the will, which it certainly is in the case of God. Only with regard to this decisive act of will is this axiom valid: who has the power and the will does what he wills. For since this power is supposed to imply also the knowledge required for action, nothing intrinsic or extrinsic can be thought of as lacking for action. And it cannot be said that the felicity and perfection of God *qua* will is in any way diminished by the fact that not all his acts of will produce their full effects. For he wills what is good only according to the degree of goodness which is inherent in it, and his will is the more satisfied the better the result obtained.

28. According to the *second division*, the will is either **productive** when it determines the actions of the agent himself, or **permissive** when it regards the actions of others. Sometimes one may permit (that is, not prevent) actions which one has not the right to commit, as for instance, acts of sin; on this, more later. The proper object of permissive will is not the permitted action but the permission itself.

29. So far we have dealt with the will; now we shall study the *reasons for willing*, namely, *good* and *evil*. Either of these is of three kinds: metaphysical, physical, and moral.

30. *Metaphysical* good or evil, in general, consists in the perfection or imperfection of all creatures, even those not endowed with intelligence. The heavenly Father, according to Christ's own words, takes care of the lilies of the field and of the sparrows; and according to Jonah, God watches over the animals [Matt. 6:28–30, 10:29; Luke 12:6; Jonah 4:11].

31. *Physical* good or evil is understood as applying especially to the advantage or disadvantage of intelligent substances. An example of this is the *evil of punishment*.

32. *Moral* good or evil is attributed to the virtuous or vicious actions of these substances, for example, the evil of guilt. In this sense physical evil ordinarily is the effect of moral evil, although the two do not always occur in the same subjects. This may seem to be devious, but the deviation is later redressed with such profit that even the innocents would not wish not to have suffered. See also below, article 55.

33. God wills what is good per se, at least antecedently. He wills in general the perfection of all things and particularly the felicity and virtue of all intelligent substances; and as has already been pointed out, he wills each good according to its degree of goodness.

34. Evils are not the object of God's antecedent will unless this will tends to suppress them. They are, however, though indirectly, the objects of his consequent will. For sometimes greater goods could not be obtained if these evils were eliminated. In this case the removal of the evil would evidently not produce the desired effect. Thus, though the suppression is consistent with the antecedent will, it is not taken over into the consequent will. This is why Thomas Aquinas, following St. Augustine, was right in saying that God permits certain evils to occur lest many goods be prevented.

35. Sometimes metaphysical and physical evils (e.g., imperfections in things and the evils of punishment in persons) become subsidiary goods, namely as means for greater goods.

36. Moral evil or the evil of guilt has never, however, the function of a means. For, as the Apostle [Paul] admonishes, evil ought not to be done so that good may ensue [Rom. 3:8]. At the most, moral evil sometimes has the function of the kind of condition called *sine qua non*, that is, of an indispensable and concomitant condition without which the desired good could not be obtained. For the desired good implies also the desired suppression of the evil. At any rate, the admission of some evil does not follow from the principle of absolute necessity, but from the principle of fitness. There must, indeed, be a reason for God to permit the evil rather

than not to permit it; but no reason of the divine will can be determined by anything but the good.

37. Moreover, the evil of guilt is never the object of God's productive will, but only sometimes of his permissive will, since he himself never commits a sin, but, at the most, in certain cases permits it to be committed.

38. Concerning the permission to sin, there is a general rule common to God and man, namely, that nobody ought to permit another man to sin unless by preventing it he would himself commit an evil action. In one word, it is always *illicit* to permit another man to sin unless duty demands this permission. . . .

39. Thus, among the objectives of the divine will, the ultimate end is the best, while any good may be a subaltern end, and indifferent events, such as the evil of punishment, may often be means. But the evil of guilt is an end only as the condition *sine qua non* for something which for other reasons ought to be. In this sense, as Christ has said, "It is impossible but that offenses will come" [Matt. 18:7; Luke 17:1].

40. So far we have dealt with the divine greatness and goodness separately, as far as is necessary for the preparatory part of this apology. Now we shall study what pertains to the two perfections taken together. Now, *common to greatness and goodness* is everything which presupposes not goodness alone, but also greatness (that is, wisdom and power). For greatness makes it possible for goodness to attain its effect. Goodness, in turn, refers either to all created things or especially to intelligences. Joined to greatness, goodness constitutes, in the first case, providence in the creation and government of the universe, and in the second case, justice in ruling, particularly over the substances which are endowed with reason.

41. The divine wisdom directs the divine goodness which extends to the totality of created things. Therefore the *divine providence* manifests itself in the total series of the universe. It follows that among the infinite number of possible series God has selected the best, and that consequently this best universe is that which actually exists. For all things in the universe are in mutual harmony and the truly wise will therefore never decide without having taken the whole into consideration, nor will his judgment bear on anything but the whole. With regard to the parts taken separately, the divine will may have been antecedent; with regard to the whole, it must be understood as a decree.

42. Hence, to speak rigorously, there is no necessity for a succession of divine decrees, but one may say that there has been one decree of God only, which decree has produced into existence the present series of the universe, all the elements of this series having been considered beforehand and compared with the elements entering into other series.

43. This is why the divine decree is also immutable, since all reasons which might be opposed to it have already been considered. But therefrom no other *necessity* arises than the necessity of the consequence, or the so-called *hypothetical* necessity. This is the kind of necessity which arises from the prevision and preordination attributed to God. This necessity is not absolute; it does not make that which follows (*consequens*) absolutely necessary, since another order of the universe was equally possible, both as to the parts and as to the whole, and since God by his choice of this contingent series has not abolished its contingency.

44. Despite the certainty of the events in this universe, our prayers and labors are not useless for the obtaining of those future goods which we desire. For when God contemplated in his mind the representation of this actual series before deciding to create it, this representation contained also the prayers which, if this series were chosen, would figure in it, just as the representation contained all the other causes of all the effects which the series would comprehend. These prayers and these other causes, therefore, have contributed their due weight to the choice of this series and of the events figuring in it. And the reasons which now move

God to action or permission had already moved him at that time to decide how he would act and what he would permit.

45. We have already remarked above that events, though determined by the divine foreknowledge and providence, are not thereby determined absolutely to occur whatever you do or do not do, but that they are determined by their causes and reasons. Therefore, if one called prayers or effort and labor useless, he would indulge in that *Sophism* which the ancients already called *lazy*. . . .

46. Thus the infinite wisdom of the Almighty allied with his boundless goodness has brought it about that nothing better could have been created, everything taken into account, than what God has created. As a consequence all things are in perfect harmony and conspire in the most beautiful way: the formal causes or souls with the material causes or bodies, the efficient or natural causes with the final or moral causes, and the realm of grace with the realm of nature.

47. Whenever, therefore, some detail of the work of God appears to us reprehensible, we should judge that we do not know enough about it and that according to the wise who would understand it, nothing better could even be desired.

48. Hence it follows, furthermore, that there is no greater felicity than to serve so good a master, and that we should therefore love God above everything else and trust him without reservation.

49. The strongest reason for the choice of the best series of events (namely, our world) was Jesus Christ, God become Man, who as a creature represents the highest degree of perfection. He had, therefore, to be contained in that series, noblest among all, as a part, indeed the head, of the created universe. To him also all power has been granted in heaven and on earth, in him all the peoples were to be blessed, and through him every creature will be freed from servitude and corruption to enjoy the liberty and glory of the children of God.

50. So far we have dealt with general providence. Goodness, with special reference to intelligent creatures, together with wisdom, constitutes *justice*, of which the highest degree is *holiness*. Taken in this very wide sense, justice comprehends not only strict law but also equity, and therefore also laudable mercy.

51. Justice, taken in a general sense, can be divided into justice in a more *special* sense and holiness. *Justice in the special sense* is concerned with physical good and evil, namely, that of intelligent beings; holiness, with moral good and evil.

52. *Physical good and evil* occur in this life as well as in life hereafter. There is much complaint that *in this life* human nature is exposed to so many evils. Those who feel this way fail to consider that a great part of this evil is the effect of human guilt. In fact, they do not recognize with sufficient gratitude the divine goods of which we are the beneficiaries, and pay more attention to our sufferings than to our blessings.

53. Others are particularly dissatisfied with the fact that physical good and evil are not distributed in proportion to moral good and evil, or in other words, that frequently the just are miserable while the unrighteous prosper.

54. To these complaints there are two answers: the first, given by the Apostle, namely, that the afflictions of this life are nothing compared with the future glory, which will be revealed to us [2 Cor. 4:17]. The second, which Christ Himself has suggested, in an admirable parable: If the grain falling to the soil did not die, it would not bear fruit [John 12:24].

55. Thus our afflictions not only will be largely compensated, but they will serve to increase our felicity. These evils are not only profitable, but indispensable. See also article 32.

56. A still greater difficulty arises with regard to *future life*. For there, too, it is objected, evil by far prevails over good, since few are elected. It is true that Origen has absolutely denied the eternity of damnation; some of the ancient authors, among

them [the fourth-century Christian Latin poet] Prudentius, have believed that only few would be damned for eternity. Some others have thought that eventually all Christians would be saved, and Jerome seems sometimes to have shared this opinion.

57. But there is no reason to resort to these paradoxes which are to be rejected. The true answer is that the whole amplitude of the celestial realm must not be evaluated according to our inadequate knowledge. For the Vision of God can give to the blessed such a glory that the sufferings of all the damned cannot be compared to such a good. Moreover, the scripture acknowledges an incredible multitude of *blessed Angels*, and nature itself shows us a great *variety of creatures*, as new inventions bring to evidence. Thus it is easier for us than it was for St. Augustine and other ancients to defend the predominance of good over evil.[8] [Boldface added to identify glossary terms.]

BERTRAND ARTHUR WILLIAM RUSSELL
1872–1970

Bertrand Russell and a Free Man's Worship

Few philosophers have attracted wider audiences in their day than Bertrand Russell (1872–1970), an eloquent spokesman for people who found views like Leibniz's incredible. Russell was a dissenter who frequently attacked religion to advance a nonsectarian **humanism,** a "free man's worship," as he called it. Russell addressed the problem of evil very differently from philosophers who give God a central role.

Although Leibniz and Russell disagreed about God and religion, they were in many respects intellectual brothers. Indeed, in an early work *A Critical Exposition of the Philosophy of Leibniz* (1900), Russell praised Leibniz for developing "an unusually complete and coherent system," but concluded that "the best parts of his philosophy are the most abstract, and the worst those which most nearly concern human life."[9] Russell placed

Leibniz's theodicy in the latter category, his work on logic and epistemology in the former. That he found those parts of Leibniz's philosophy enlightening was significant, for Russell himself was a giant in the development of logical theory.

Born in Wales, Russell went to Cambridge University in England and later taught at Cambridge until pacifist activities led to his dismissal in 1916. On three occasions he ran for Parliament, each time unsuccessfully. Russell supported himself by public lecturing and prolific writing until, in 1938, he moved to the United States. He taught briefly at the University of Chicago and UCLA and he planned to go to the City College of New York in 1940, but his appointment was blocked out of fear that Russell's liberal moral views would corrupt his students. He returned to Cambridge in 1944, and after World War II became increasingly involved in defending unpopular causes. Russell took seriously the Socratic tradition that likens the philosopher to a gadfly. He was awarded the Nobel Prize for literature in 1950.

Russell wrote extensively on subjects familiar and esoteric. His *Principia Mathematica* (1910–13), coauthored with Alfred North Whitehead, is a *tour de force* in the philosophy of mathematics that is accessible only to specialists. But such popular and controversial works as *Marriage and Morals* (1929) were equally accomplished and are much more widely read. All his many writings about religion carry a similar message. While religion "has made some contributions to civilization," he nonetheless regarded it "as a disease born of fear and as a source of untold misery to the human race."[10] Russell was not sure whether he should be called an atheist or an agnostic, but he didn't worry much about it. As a humanist, he wanted people to be self-reliant and to live by their own standard, without fear of eternal punishment or hope for heavenly rewards. A chief reason cited by Russell when asked why he could not be a Christian was that "There is one very serious defect in Christ's moral character, and that is that He believed in hell."[11] Where virtue is concerned, Russell rated Socrates higher than Jesus. To put it mildly, Bertrand Russell was an independent thinker.

Accepting the World as It Is

Where the problem of evil is concerned, one could hardly imagine a view more opposed to Leibniz's than Russell's. This radical opposition is intriguing because both Leibniz and Russell prided themselves on developing a philosophy of religion that was in harmony with science. But if Leibniz thought that such complementarity with science makes this the best of all possible worlds, one in which evil actually enhances the good, Russell offered a very different picture. The scientific world, he contends, entails:

> That man is the product of causes which had no prevision of the end they were achieving; that his origin, his growth, his hopes and fears, his loves and his beliefs, are but the outcome of accidental collocations of atoms; that no fire, no heroism, no intensity of thought and feeling, can preserve an individual life beyond the grave; that all the labors of the ages, all the devotion, all the inspiration, all the noonday brightness of human genius, are destined to extinction in the vast death of the solar system, and that the whole temple of man's achievement must inevitably be buried beneath the debris of a universe in ruins—all these things, if not quite beyond dispute, are yet so nearly certain that no philosophy which rejects them can hope to stand.[12]

If Leibniz's theodicy was optimistic, Russell's sketch is its devastatingly pessimistic antithesis. And yet Russell hoped to find an encouraging response to this bleakness, for "amid such a world, if anywhere, our ideals henceforward must find a home" (p. 107).

In a sense, Russell's answer to the question of whether we must consider evil and death as final is a tragic but resounding yes. Yet in getting us to accept the world as he thinks it is, Russell urged us not to accept evil but to oppose it when we can. For human beings, the conflict between good and evil exists. But since it does exist, neither God nor any other supernatural power ensures that the good will prevail in Russell's less-than-the-best of all possible worlds. Human energy will not transcend the demise of our universe either. The message Russell wanted to drive home, however, is that we should not be discouraged. Rather, we should face life honestly and make the best of it. "In spite of death," he insisted, "man is yet free, during his brief years, to examine, to criticize, to know, and in imagination to create" (p. 107). For Russell, those hopes must be enough, just as they were for Sartre and Camus, although their perspective is different from his.

A Hoping Self Must Die

Russell hoped conventional religious belief would die. In describing his "free man's worship," he echoed themes that are surprisingly similar to the "dark night of the soul" that figures so centrally in the report of mystics. That is, we must go through a difficult period before hope can be seen. "We must learn," says Russell, "that the world was not made for us" (p. 111). But this is a tortuous lesson to take to heart. To learn it we must enter a cavern of despair whose "floor is paved with the gravestones of abandoned hopes. There self must die; there the eagerness, the greed of untamed desire, must be slain" (p. 112).

This death of the self must occur so that we can be liberated from enslavement to misdirected hopes. On that point hinges Russell's critique of religion. He believed that all religious experience is tainted by an attitude that bestows undeserved honor on a power that is at once indifferent to us and beyond our control. That is how the concept of God functions, Russell holds. Whether God is idealized or merely idolized, the result is the same: human freedom is imprisoned by hoping in—and thereby becoming subservient to—Fate.

Finding the Right Kind of Worship

Though the self must die in the sense of abandoning religious hope, Russell did not advocate the abolition of **worship.** What is needed instead is to practice the right kind. If "the nonhuman world is unworthy of our worship," humanity itself has qualities that should attract our deepest respect and allegiance (p. 112). These qualities, it should be pointed out, shine forth brilliantly because they are fragile, even doomed, in an uncaring universe. But from time to time they prevail, and when they do, the grandeur of humanity is revealed.

"To abandon the struggle for private happiness," writes Russell, "to expel all eagerness of temporary desire, to burn with passion for eternal things—this is emancipation, and this is the free man's worship" (p. 114). Russell's "eternal things" include intelligence, self-control, sympathy, and the insight that "the good life must be lived in a good society and is not fully possible otherwise."[13] Love and freedom are high on the list as well. At their best, the human expression of these qualities is no less awesome than the power of nature that eventually consumes us. In the drama that recounts their meeting, we should bow to honor human worth and not glorify the forces that put it to waste. Some of those forces are human. In fact, Russell thinks, evil is kept alive largely because we care more about punishing enemies than about serving friends. The purging of hate through love is essential to a free man's worship.

What Are the Alternatives to Religion?

Russell thought religion caused far more troubles than it eliminated because religion depended too much on unexamined experience and was essentially opposed to intelligence. Revelation, tradition, and authority were its mainstays, and at one point or another all these preempted critical inquiry. If religion appealed to the heart, that was no advance; Russell would take Descartes's proof for God's existence before he would accept Pascal's sentimentality. Mystical insight, with its reports of an intense and immediate illumination, might have commendable elements insofar as it helps cultivate a renunciation of naive hopes. It might indicate a strong conviction about the nature of the universe, too. But Russell was loathe to grant mystical experience a higher status than humanism. For **mysticism,** according to Russell, tended to regard all evil as mere appearance, something that will disappear in a broader perspective. A religious approach tries to supersede the importance of ever-critical, inquiring intelligence.

We will be more free, said Russell, and have a greater chance of solving problems that are within our control, if we liberate ourselves from belief in God and trust human intelligence as it works scientifically. We will then live without illusion, and yet we will find that worship has its place. Clearly, Russell sized up the problem of evil differently from Leibniz. In a way, evil and death are not problems for Russell. Neither the reality of the former nor human awareness of the latter would exist without our subjective emotion and reflective consciousness. They are there as facts that will not go away. Nothing does or can justify them. Our task is simply to cope with evil and death in the best ways intelligence can find.

"Only more and wiser intelligence can make a happier world," Russell concluded.[14] The question is to what extent this can and will happen. One issue is whether a religiously motivated hope may contribute more than Russell thinks if it enables us to respond positively to the world's ills. If Russell found vulnerable points in Leibniz's philosophy, does that make Russell's philosophy of religion preferable? As free men and women with critical intelligence, keep that question open as you study more of Russell's arguments in the following selection from "A Free Man's Worship."

To Dr. Faustus in his study Mephistophelis told the history of the Creation, saying,

The endless praises of the choirs of angels had begun to grow wearisome; for, after all, did he not deserve their praise? Had he not given them endless joy? Would it not be more amusing to obtain undeserved praise, to be worshiped by beings whom he tortured? He smiled inwardly, and resolved that the great drama should be performed.

For countless ages the hot nebula whirled aimlessly through space. At length it began to take shape, the central mass threw off planets, the planets cooled, boiling seas and burning mountains heaved and tossed, from black masses of cloud hot sheets of rain deluged the barely solid crust. And now the first germ of life grew in the depths of the ocean and developed rapidly in the fructifying warmth into vast forest trees, huge ferns springing from the damp mold, sea monsters breeding, fighting, devouring, and passing away. And from the monsters, as the play unfolded itself, Man was born, with the power of thought, the knowledge of good and evil, and the cruel thirst for worship. And Man saw that all is passing in this mad, monstrous world, that all is struggling to snatch, at any cost, a few brief moments of life before Death's inexorable decree. And Man said, "There is a hidden purpose, could we but fathom it, and the purpose is good; for we must reverence something, and in the visible world there is nothing worthy of reverence." And Man stood aside from the struggle, resolving that God intended harmony to come out of chaos by human efforts. And when he followed the instincts which God had transmitted to him from his ancestry of beasts of prey, he called it Sin, and asked God to forgive him. But he doubted whether he could be justly forgiven, until he invented a divine Plan by which God's wrath was to have been appeased. And seeing the present was bad, he made it yet worse, that thereby the future might be better. And he gave God thanks for the strength that enabled him to forgo even the joys that were possible. And God smiled; and when he saw that Man had become perfect in renunciation and worship, he sent another sun through the sky, which crashed into Man's sun; and all returned again to nebula.

"Yes," he murmured, "it was a good play; I will have it performed again."

Such, in outline, but even more purposeless, more void of meaning, is the world which science presents for our belief. Amid such a world, if anywhere, our ideals henceforward must find a home. That man is the product of causes which had no prevision of the end they were achieving; that his origin, his growth, his hopes and fears, his loves and his beliefs, are but the outcome of accidental collocations of atoms; that no fire, no heroism, no intensity of thought and feeling, can preserve an individual life beyond the grave; that all the labors of the ages, all the devotion, all the inspiration, all the noonday brightness of human genius, are destined to extinction in the vast death of the solar system, and that the whole temple of man's achievement must inevitably be buried beneath the debris of a universe in ruins—all these things, if not quite beyond dispute, are yet so nearly certain that no philosophy which rejects them can hope to stand. Only within the scaffolding of these truths, only on the firm foundation of unyielding despair, can the soul's habitation henceforth be safely built.

How, in such an alien and inhuman world, can so powerless a creature as man preserve his aspirations untarnished? A strange mystery it is that nature, omnipotent but blind, in the revolutions of her secular hurryings through the abysses of space, has brought forth at last a child, subject still to her power, but gifted with sight, with knowledge of good and evil, with the capacity of judging all the works of his unthinking mother. In spite of death, the mark and seal of the parental control, man is yet free, during his brief years, to examine, to criticize, to know, and in imagination to create. To him alone, in the world with which he is acquainted, this freedom belongs; and in this lies his superiority to the resistless forces that control his outward life.

The savage, like ourselves, feels the oppression of his impotence before the powers of nature; but having in himself nothing that he respects more than power, he is willing to prostrate himself before his gods, without inquiring whether they are worthy of his worship. Pathetic and very terrible is the long history of cruelty and torture, of degradation and human sacrifice, endured in the hope of placating the jealous gods: surely, the trembling believer thinks, when what is most precious has been freely given, their lust for blood must be appeased, and more will not be required. The religion of Moloch—as such creeds may be generically called—is in essence the cringing submission of the slave, who dare not, even in his heart, allow the thought that his master deserves no adulation. Since the independence of ideals is not yet acknowledged, power may be freely worshiped and receive an unlimited respect, despite its wanton infliction of pain.

But gradually, as morality grows bolder, the claim of the ideal world begins to be felt; and worship, if it is not to cease, must be given to gods of another kind than those created by the savage. Some, though they feel the demands of the ideal, will still consciously reject them, still urging that naked power is worthy of worship. Such is the attitude inculcated in God's answer to Job out of the whirlwind: the divine power and knowledge are paraded, but of the divine goodness there is no hint. Such also is the attitude of those who, in our own day, base their morality upon the struggle for survival, maintaining that the survivors are necessarily the fittest. But others, not content with an answer so repugnant to the moral sense, will adopt the position which we have become accustomed to regard as specially religious, maintaining that, in some hidden manner, the world of fact is really harmonious with the world of ideals. Thus man created God, all-powerful and all-good, the mystic unity of what is and what should be.

But the world of fact, after all, is not good; and, in submitting our judgment to it, there is an element of slavishness from which our thoughts must be purged. For in all things it is well to exalt the dignity of man, by freeing him as far as possible from the tyranny of nonhuman power. When we have realized that power is largely bad, that man, with his knowledge of good and evil, is but a helpless atom in a world which has no such knowledge, the choice is again presented to us: Shall we worship force, or shall we worship goodness? Shall our God exist and be evil, or shall he be recognized as the creation of our own conscience?

The answer to this question is very momentous and affects profoundly our whole morality. The worship of force, to which Carlyle and Nietzsche and the creed of militarism have accustomed us, is the result of failure to maintain our own ideals against a hostile universe: it is itself a prostrate submission to evil, a sacrifice of our best to Moloch. If strength indeed is to be respected, let us respect rather the strength of those who refuse that false "recognition of facts" which fails to recognize that facts are often bad. Let us admit that, in the world we know, there are many things that would be better otherwise, and that the ideals to which we do and must adhere are not realized in the realm of matter. Let us preserve our respect for truth, for beauty, for the ideal of perfection which life does not permit us to attain, though none of these things meet with the approval of the unconscious universe. If power is bad, as it seems to be, let us reject it from our hearts. In this lies man's true freedom: in determination to worship only the God created by our own love of the good, to respect only the heaven which inspires the insight of our best moments. In action, in desire, we must submit perpetually to the tyranny of outside forces; but in thought, in aspiration, we are free, free from our fellow men, free from the petty planet on which our bodies impotently crawl, free even, while

we live, from the tyranny of death. Let us learn, then, that energy of faith which enables us to live constantly in the vision of the good; and let us descend, in action, into the world of fact, with that vision always before us.

When first the opposition of fact and ideal grows fully visible, a spirit of fiery revolt, of fierce hatred of the gods, seems necessary to the assertion of freedom. To defy with Promethean constancy a hostile universe, to keep its evil always in view, always actively hated, to refuse no pain that the malice of power can invent, appears to be the duty of all who will not bow before the inevitable. But indignation is still a bondage, for it compels our thoughts to be occupied with an evil world; and in the fierceness of desire from which rebellion springs there is a kind of self-assertion which it is necessary for the wise to overcome. Indignation is a submission of our thoughts but not of our desires; the Stoic freedom in which wisdom consists is found in the submission of our desires but not of our thoughts. From the submission of our desires springs the virtue of resignation; from the freedom of our thoughts springs the whole world of art and philosophy, and the vision of beauty by which, at last, we half reconquer the reluctant world. But the vision of beauty is possible only to unfettered contemplation, to thoughts not weighted by the load of eager wishes; and thus freedom comes only to those who no longer ask of life that it shall yield them any of those personal goods that are subject to the mutations of time.

Although the necessity of renunciation is evidence of the existence of evil, yet Christianity, in preaching it, has shown a wisdom exceeding that of the Promethean philosophy of rebellion. It must be admitted that, of the things we desire, some, though they prove impossible, are yet real goods; others, however, as ardently longed for, do not form part of a fully purified ideal. The belief that what must be renounced is bad, though sometimes false, is far less often false than untamed passion supposes; and the creed of religion, by providing a reason for proving that it is never false, has been the means of purifying our hopes by the discovery of many austere truths.

But there is in resignation a further good element: even real goods, when they are unattainable, ought not to be fretfully desired. To every man comes, sooner or later, the great renunciation. For the young, there is nothing unattainable; a good thing desired with the whole force of a passionate will, and yet impossible, is to them not credible. Yet, by death, by illness, by poverty, or by the voice of duty, we must learn, each one of us, that the world was not made for us, and that, however beautiful may be the things we crave, Fate may nevertheless forbid them. It is the part of courage, when misfortune comes, to bear without repining the ruin of our hopes, to turn away our thoughts from vain regrets. This degree of submission to power is not only just and right: it is the very gate of wisdom.

But passive renunciation is not the whole of wisdom; for not by renunciation alone can we build a temple for the worship of our own ideals. Haunting foreshadowings of the temple appear in the realm of imagination, in music, in architecture, in the untroubled kingdom of reason, and in the golden sunset magic of lyrics, where beauty shines and glows, remote from the touch of sorrow, remote from the fear of change, remote from the failures and disenchantments of the world of fact. In the contemplation of these things the vision of heaven will shape itself in our hearts, giving at once a touchstone to judge the world about us and an inspiration by which to fashion to our needs whatever is not incapable of serving as a stone in the sacred temple.

Except for those rare spirits that are born without sin, there is a cavern of darkness to be traversed before that temple can be entered. The gate of the cavern is despair, and its floor is paved with the gravestones of abandoned hopes. There self must die; there the eagerness, the greed of untamed desire, must be slain, for only so can the soul be freed from the empire of Fate. But out of the cavern, the Gate of Renunciation

leads again to the daylight of wisdom, by whose radiance a new insight, a new joy, a new tenderness, shine forth to gladden the pilgrim's heart.

When, without the bitterness of impotent rebellion, we have learned both to resign ourselves to the outward rule of Fate and to recognize that the nonhuman world is unworthy of our worship, it becomes possible at last so to transform and refashion the unconscious universe, so to transmute it in the crucible of imagination, that a new image of shining gold replaces the old idol of clay. In all the multiform facts of the world—in the visual shapes of trees and mountains and clouds, in the events of the life of man, even in the very omnipotence of death—the insight of creative idealism can find the reflection of a beauty which its own thoughts first made. In this way mind asserts its subtle mastery over the thoughtless forces of nature. The more evil the material with which it deals, the more thwarting to untrained desire, the greater is its achievement in inducing the reluctant rock to yield up its hidden treasures, the prouder its victory in compelling the opposing forces to swell the pageant of its triumph. Of all the arts, tragedy is the proudest, the most triumphant; for it builds its shining citadel in the very center of the enemy's country, on the very summit of his highest mountain; from its impregnable watchtowers, his camps and arsenals, his columns and forts, are all revealed; within its walls the free life continues, while the legions of death and pain and despair, and all the servile captains of tyrant Fate, afford the burghers of that dauntless city new spectacles of beauty. Happy those sacred ramparts, thrice happy the dwellers on that all-seeing eminence. Honor to those brave warriors who, through countless ages of warfare, have preserved for us the priceless heritage of liberty and have kept undefiled by sacrilegious invaders the home of the unsubdued.

But the beauty of tragedy does but make visible a quality which, in more or less obvious shapes, is present always and everywhere in life. In the spectacle of death, in the endurance of intolerable pain, and in the irrevocableness of a vanished past, there is a sacredness, an overpowering awe, a feeling of the vastness, the depth, the inexhaustible mystery of existence, in which, as by some strange marriage of pain, the sufferer is bound to the world by bonds of sorrow. In these moments of insight, we lose all eagerness of temporary desire, all struggling and striving for petty ends, all care for the little trivial things that, to a superficial view, make up the common life of day by day; we see, surrounding the narrow raft illumined by the flickering light of human comradeship, the dark ocean on whose rolling waves we toss for a brief hour; from the great night without, a chill blast breaks in upon our refuge; all the loneliness of humanity amid hostile forces is concentrated upon the individual soul, which must struggle alone, with what of courage it can command, against the whole weight of a universe that cares nothing for its hopes and fears. Victory, in this struggle with the powers of darkness, is the true baptism into the glorious company of heroes, the true initiation into the overmastering beauty of human existence. From that awful encounter of the soul with the outer world, renunciation, wisdom, and charity are born; and with their birth a new life begins. To take into the inmost shrine of the soul the irresistible forces whose puppets we seem to be—death and change, the irrevocableness of the past, and the powerlessness of man before the blind hurry of the universe from vanity to vanity—to feel these things and know them is to conquer them.

This is the reason why the past has such magical power. The beauty of its motionless and silent pictures is like the enchanted purity of late autumn, when the leaves, though one breath would make them fall, still glow against the sky in golden glory. The past does not change or strive; . . . it sleeps well; what was eager and grasping, what was petty and transitory, has faded away; the things that were beautiful and eternal shine out of it like stars in the night. Its beauty, to a soul not worthy of it, is unendurable; but to a soul which has conquered Fate it is the key of religion.

The life of man, viewed outwardly, is but a small thing in comparison with the forces of nature. The slave is doomed to worship Time and Fate and Death, because they are greater than anything he finds in himself, and because all his thoughts are of things which they devour. But, great as they are, to think of them greatly, to feel their passionless splendor, is greater still. And such thought makes us free men; we no longer bow before the inevitable in Oriental subjection, but we absorb it and make it a part of ourselves. To abandon the struggle for private happiness, to expel all eagerness of temporary desire, to burn with passion for eternal things—this is emancipation, and this is the free man's worship. And this liberation is effected by contemplation of Fate; for Fate itself is subdued by the mind which leaves nothing to be purged by the purifying fire of time.

United with his fellow men by the strongest of all ties, the tie of a common doom, the free man finds that a new vision is with him always, shedding over every daily task the light of love. The life of man is a long march through the night, surrounded by invisible foes, tortured by weariness and pain, toward a goal that few can hope to reach, and where none may tarry long. One by one, as they march, our comrades vanish from our sight, seized by the silent orders of omnipotent death. Very brief is the time in which we can help them, in which their happiness or misery is decided. Be it ours to shed sunshine on their path, to lighten their sorrows by the balm of sympathy, to give them the pure joy of a never-tiring affection, to strengthen failing courage, to instill faith in hours of despair. Let us not weigh in grudging scales their merits and demerits, but let us think only of their need—of the sorrows, the difficulties, perhaps the blindnesses, that make the misery of their lives; let us remember that they are fellow sufferers in the same darkness, actors in the same tragedy with ourselves. And so, when their day is over, when their good and their evil have become eternal by the immortality of the past, be it ours to feel that, where they suffered, where they failed, no deed of ours was the cause; but wherever a spark of the divine fire kindled in their hearts, we were ready with encouragement, with sympathy, with brave words in which high courage glowed.

Brief and powerless is man's life; on him and all his race the slow, sure doom falls pitiless and dark. Blind to good and evil, reckless of destruction, omnipotent matter rolls on its relentless way; for man, condemned today to lose his dearest, tomorrow himself to pass through the gate of darkness, it remains only to cherish, ere yet the blow fall, the lofty thoughts that ennoble his little day; disdaining the coward terrors of the slave of Fate, to worship at the shrine that his own hands have built; undismayed by the empire of chance, to preserve a mind free from the wanton tyranny that rules his outward life; proudly defiant of the irresistible forces that tolerate, for a moment, his knowledge and his condemnation, to sustain alone, a weary but unyielding Atlas, the world that his own ideals have fashioned despite the trampling march of unconscious power.[15]

MARTIN LUTHER KING, JR. 1929–1968

Martin Luther King, Jr., and Nonviolent Resistance

When Martin Luther King, Jr. (1929–1968), was murdered while preparing to support a strike in Memphis, Tennessee, grief poured out around the world. Although not a technical philosopher, King had lived his life as an active protest to Leibniz's proposition that ours is the best of all possible worlds. King raised his voice against racial hatred, poverty, violence, and the waste of human life for which these conditions were responsible. He outlined the problem of evil as he saw it in a "Letter from Birmingham Jail" (1963):

Lamentably, it is a historical fact that privileged groups seldom give up their privileges voluntarily. Individuals may see the moral light and voluntarily give up their unjust posture; but . . . groups are more immoral than individuals. We know through painful experience that freedom is never voluntarily given by the oppressor; it must be demanded by the oppressed.[16]

King spoke at the massive civil rights rally in Washington, D.C., in 1963, proclaiming that "In spite of the difficulties and frustrations of the moment, I still have a dream. It is a dream deeply rooted in the American dream. I have a dream that one day this nation will rise up and live out the true meaning of its creed: 'We hold these truths to be self-evident: that all men are created equal.' "[17] This famous speech ends with the words: "When we let freedom ring, when we let it ring from every village and every hamlet, from every state and every city, we will be able to speed up that day when all of God's children, black men and white men, Jews and Gentiles, Protestants and Catholics, will be able to join hands and sing in the words of that Negro spiritual, 'Free at last! Free at last! Thank God almighty, we are free at last' " (p. 66). Obviously, King hoped that evil and death do not have the final say. Nor was his hope an academic abstraction. Rather, it undergirded a struggle for survival in a world where too often evil and death do seem to have the last word.

Martin Luther King, Sr., was the pastor of a large and prominent church in Atlanta. His son graduated from seminary at Boston University and served as a pastor himself, a position that made him a leader in the black community. In the 1950s southern blacks held little political power and were effectively deprived of many of their civil rights, often including the right to vote. As the movement to redress these injustices began, King increasingly took a leading role and advocated nonviolent resistance to evil as the best approach. King was a Christian pastor and a political leader, not a philosophical scholar who penned technical treatises such as those by Leibniz or Bertrand Russell. Yet King wrestled with the questions of philosophy: What can I know? What should I do? What may I hope? He did so in the quiet of his study when he prayed or when he prepared his eloquent sermons. He did so while in a jail cell, while marching in protest down southern highways and up northern city streets. He did so, too, as he accepted the 1964 Nobel Prize for peace and as he wrote books explaining *Why We Can't Wait* (1964) and asking *Where Do We Go from Here: Chaos or Community?* (1967). If King was not a professional philosopher, he still professed that words—and deeds—can reveal the truth that helps life make sense.

What Do Death and Evil Mean?

Although Martin Luther King, Jr., can be said to have survived death insofar as his influence will be honored as long as men and women work to eliminate injustice, the vast majority of people do not share this fate. For most of us, the world continues almost as though we had never lived. All of us know we are going to die; few of us have any sensible reason to think we will be remembered for long. We have even less concrete evidence to suggest that personal life somehow does or will continue after we have breathed our last. Life may go on, but for most of us our return to dust appears to give death the final word. Yet human opinions, including those of philosophers, express no unanimity about that conclusion. People believe different things about death because their upbringings vary, their experiences are not identical, and their needs are not the same. We all have reasons—many of them good ones, too—for believing as we do, but agreement among everyone does not follow. Thus, if some philosophers brand as irrational, if not superstitious, views that deny death the final say, it remains a fact that the human thirst for life is unquenched by such pronouncements.

King thought death always smelled of evil. True, sometimes death may be seen as a release from suffering, a liberation from irreversible disease. In such cases it may be welcomed, or, at the culmination of a long, full, and rewarding life, accepted with equanimity. But always, he thought, sorrow was appropriate because something good, life itself, had ended. Grief would be felt even more strongly when men, women, and children were cut down in their prime, their lives wasted by natural causes or by human oppression. In such experiences, King added, the true meaning of evil could best be discerned. His writings often return to this theme.

The term "evil" often functions as a noun, suggesting that evil is an entity. But King argued that **evil** is activity, sometimes *inactivity*, and thus a manifestation of power. Evil powers are those that *waste*. That is, evil happens whenever power is used to ruin or squander life, or whenever power is not used to forestall those results. The kind of evil that most concerned King ignores and violates the personal worth of individuals. Each of us inflicts and receives that sort of pain to some degree. Being a sensitive human being means to be open to being hurt when the actions of others offend us. Yet some individuals, and especially some societies, are far more perverse than others. We measure them by the extent to which their actions waste human existence. As he combated evil, King affirmed his love for life in Christian terms. Through Jesus, preached King, God gives reason to trust that life beyond death is in the future for people of faith. But God also intends this hope to give us courage to take action now for justice, dignity, and freedom.

The Limits of Evil

All philosophies contain undemonstrated and undemonstrable assumptions. King's were religious. He began by affirming that the world and human life are God's creation. God, moreover, is at work in the world, striving with men and women to achieve a humane community. The fatherhood of God, as King frequently emphasized, implies the interdependence—the brotherhood and sisterhood—of humankind. All people, wrote King, "are caught in an inescapable network of mutuality, tied in a single garment of destiny. Whatever affects one directly affects all indirectly. I can never be what I ought to be until you are what you ought to be, and you can never be what you ought to be until I am what I ought to be."[18]

Within this framework of God's love and human interdependence, King attempted to determine the significance of evil. Nothing is more obvious, thought King, than the presence of evil in the universe, its chief manifestation being our brutalizing tendency to hate and to oppress each other. He saw every person's existence as involving a mixture of, and a struggle between, good and evil. We are created in God's image, and human life is good, but it is also stained and shattered by destructive powers. King had no comprehensive theory to explain why evil existed, although he did point to humanity's abuse of freedom as a crucial factor. Instead he focused on the structure of evil, on God's action, and on our human responsibility in responding to both.

"Evil," premised King, "carries the seed of its own destruction" (p. 77). Its forces are powerful and stubborn, never voluntarily relinquishing their hold. But, King argued, "evil cannot permanently organize itself" (p. 73). Evil's nature is to divide, separate, and negate. This description suggests a sense in which evil is self-destructive. It will not destroy itself completely, however; King admitted that new obstacles impede us repeatedly. Yet the consuming force of evil does not exist unchecked. Internally unstable, it is capable of being subdued by the powers of goodness—justice, freedom, and love—which remain vital, however threatened they may be at times. "Looking back," King could say as he surveyed the battle against American racism, "we see the forces of segregation gradually dying on the seashore" (p. 77).

The Authority of Nonviolent Resistance

As for God's action and humanity's responsibility in coping with evil, King held that God is committed to freedom. God permits evil as part of the price to be paid for freedom in the world, but King concurred with

Leibniz in rejecting the view that God wills—directly or indirectly—any specific instance of evil. God's commitment to freedom, however, does have some important ramifications for the way in which God permits evil to exist. For that commitment means not only that people can diverge from the course of action that God wants them to pursue but also that trying to discern and follow God's will entails conscious choices. Furthermore, if divergence from the will of God occurs, God does not always put to immediate use every available means to set things right.

God is not unconcerned about justice, insisted King. God is committed to justice, but within the context of freedom. God's purpose for human life seems to entail our attempt to establish a community of love through our use of freedom, which includes both controlling the potential for evil in human existence and atoning for evil actions that do occur. "Therefore," King contended, "God cannot at the same time impose his will upon his children and also maintain his purpose for man" (p. 79). Yet God will not allow human beings to make creation a total shambles. Evil is kept in check partly by its very nature. Moreover, although God will not do for us what we can do for ourselves, when people turn to God in faith, they can renew courage and strength to attempt what is just and good. "Love," added King, "is the most durable power in the world, . . . the most potent instrument available in mankind's quest for peace and security" (p. 49). Hence the universe is structured to favor love if only men and women will give themselves to that ideal.

Resistance to injustice is indispensable, King emphasized, and the forces of evil must not be allowed to do business as usual. He also raised the strategic issue of identifying the most effective form for resistance to take. King was convinced that hate and violence breed more of the same, even though they sow the seeds of their own destruction. As he pursued the cause of racial justice, he called on his followers to use "a sword that heals."[19] This means, to be involved in effective social action: "collection of the facts to determine whether injustices exist; negotiation; self-purification; and direct action" (p. 78).

King stressed self-purification because the direct action he advocated was nonviolent resistance, a stance he adapted from Jesus' teachings, Thoreau's civil disobedience, and Mahatma Gandhi's opposition to British imperialism in India. Special discipline is required to keep the instinct for violent reactions in check. You should resist evil and even refuse to obey unjust laws, said King, but violence ought to be avoided because it wastes too much. Nonviolent resistance is precisely a sword that heals. The authority of **nonviolent resistance,** King explained, resides in its ability to expose and thwart evil without sacrificing persons. You may experience suffering during such resistance, but this suffering is redemptive. It can strike the human conscience and thus produce a defense of freedom and justice. It can also lead to repentance in those who cause suffering.

Who Is Responsible?

Reviewing the racial strife that wracked Birmingham, Alabama, in the 1960s, King noted that "the ultimate tragedy was not the brutality of the bad people, but the silence of the good people" (p. 50). As a religious man, King knew that some forms of silence show a healthy respect for forces beyond our control, while others can restore our human energies and prepare them for effective use. Prayer and retreats in which people quietly meditate are not to be ignored. But King understood that silence also can indicate a failure of nerve to face issues that do have solutions. Evil must be resisted, urged King, and he counted on concerned men and women to keep trying their best, not only with words but also with actions. Prodding people to travel "the elusive path to freedom" with "the conviction to meet physical force with soul force," King's hope was vindicated by the civil rights movement—but only in part (pp. 32, 30). The clubs, hoses, and dogs unleashed by segregationists did yield to the determination of nonviolent resistance, but it has not been demonstrated that all forms of injustice can be eliminated that way. It seems unlikely, for instance, that nonviolent resistance could have turned back Hitler's oppression. Only military defeat brought Nazism to a halt.

Perhaps, as King claimed, evil is self-destructive because it can never organize itself permanently. Sadly, the historical record makes that premise questionable. Particular evil actions or destructive events may not endure forever, but base forms of evil—hatred, exploitation, prejudice—do not cease. In addition, it does not take a vast organized evil to cancel centuries of worthy effort. Yet even if evil eventually burns itself out, everything good may be reduced to ashes before the flames expire. Although God may exist and act in the world, nothing on earth absolutely ensures the triumph of "soul force." When King sang "We Shall Overcome," he sometimes thought optimistically that the victory he dreamed of was assured and inevitable: the Kingdom of God would indeed break forth within history. In other moments, however, he stressed that "time itself is neutral; it can be used either destructively or constructively" (p. 86). But if time is neutral, then to affirm "We shall overcome someday" may mean that "someday" lies beyond death, if it exists at all.

King's ambivalence, if not inconsistency, about the degree to which moral progress is guaranteed within history stemmed from his equally real convictions that evil is mighty but that God is good and almighty. King emphasized God's opposition to evil. But like King himself, God seems to employ the strategies of nonviolent resistance. That is, there is little evidence that God immediately intervenes to oppose evil when it breaks in to destroy. Evil does not always give way to such subtle pressures. When it does not, one may wonder, in spite of King's apologies for God, whether God could do more and better. Evil and suffering do not simply appear in a vacuum. They have some ultimate source and ground. Human beings are the direct source of a vast amount of human suffering and destruction, but the responsibility for the fundamental structure of the existence into which we are thrown cannot be exclusively human. King stressed God's decision to respect human freedom—even at the cost of temporary defeat—in the hope that freedom would be used creatively and lovingly to achieve a human community. He stressed human responsibility for what happens in the world. As the following selections from *Strength to Love* suggest, however, King left us to wonder about the limits of human responsibility and what those limits might imply about God's responsibility for evil.

THE DEATH OF EVIL UPON THE SEASHORE

AND ISRAEL SAW THE EGYPTIANS DEAD UPON THE SEASHORE (EXODUS 14:30). Is anything more obvious than the presence of evil in the universe? Its nagging, prehensile tentacles project into every level of human existence. We may debate the origin of evil, but only a victim of superficial optimism would debate its reality. Evil is stark, grim, and colossally real.

Affirming the reality of evil in unmistakable terms, the Bible symbolically pictures the conniving work of a serpent which injects discord into the harmonious symphony of life in a garden, prophetically denounces callous injustice and ugly hypocrisy, and dramatically portrays a misguided mob hanging the world's most precious Person on a cross between two thieves. Crystal-clear is the biblical perception of evil. Nor was Jesus unmindful of the reality of evil. Although he never offered a theological explanation of the origin of evil, he never attempted to explain it away. In the parable of the tares, Jesus says that tares are tares, not illusions or errors of the mortal mind. Real weeds disrupt the orderly growth of stately wheat. Whether sown by Satan or by man's misuse of his own freedom, the tares are always poisonous and deadly. Concerning the choking weeds, Jesus says in substance, "I do not attempt to explain their origin, but they are the work of an enemy." He recognized that the force of evil was as real as the force of good.

Within the wide arena of everyday life we see evil in all of its ugly dimensions. We see it expressed in tragic lust and inordinate selfishness. We see it in high places where men are willing to sacrifice truth on the altars of their self-interest. We see it in imperialistic nations crushing other people with the battering rams of social injustice. We see it clothed in the garments of calamitous wars which leave men and nations morally and physically bankrupt.

In a sense, the history of man is the story of the struggle between good and evil. All of the great religions have recognized a tension at the very core of the universe. Hinduism, for instance, calls this tension a conflict between illusion and reality; Zoroastrianism, a conflict between the god of light and the god of darkness; and traditional Judaism and Christianity, a conflict between God and Satan. Each realizes that in the midst of the upward thrust of goodness there is the downward pull of evil.

Christianity clearly affirms that in the long struggle between good and evil, good eventually will emerge as victor. Evil is ultimately doomed by the powerful, inexorable forces of good. Good Friday must give way to the triumphant music of Easter. Degrading tares choke the sprouting necks of growing wheat for a season, but when the harvest is gleaned the evil tares will be separated from the good wheat. Caesar occupied a palace and Christ a cross, but the same Christ so split history into A.D. and B.C. that even the reign of Caesar was subsequently dated by his name. Long ago biblical religion recognized what William Cullen Bryant affirmed, "Truth crushed to earth will rise again," and what Thomas Carlyle wrote, "No lie you can speak or act but it will come, after longer or shorter circulation, like a bill drawn on Nature's Reality, and be presented there for payment—with the answer, No effects."

I. A graphic example of this truth is found in the early history of the Hebrew people. When the children of Israel were held under the gripping yoke of Egyptian slavery, Egypt symbolized evil in the form of humiliating oppression, ungodly exploitation, and crushing domination, and the Israelites symbolized goodness in the form of devotion and dedication to the God of Abraham, Isaac, and Jacob. Egypt struggled to maintain her oppressive yoke, and Israel struggled to gain freedom. Pharaoh stubbornly refused to respond to the cry of Moses, even when plague after plague threatened his domain. This tells us something about evil that we must never forget, namely, that evil is recalcitrant and determined, and never voluntarily relinquishes its hold short of a persistent, almost fanatical resistance. But there is a checkpoint in the universe: evil cannot permanently organize itself. So after a long and trying struggle, the Israelites, through the providence of God, crossed the Red Sea. But like the old guard that never surrenders, the Egyptians, in a desperate attempt to prevent the Israelites from escaping, had their armies go in the Red Sea behind them. As soon as the Egyptians got into the dried up sea the parted waters swept back upon them, and the turbulence and momentum of the tidal waves soon drowned all of them. When the Israelites looked back, all they could see was here and there a poor drowned body beaten upon the seashore. For the Israelites, this was a great moment. It was the end of a frightful period in their history. It was a joyous daybreak that had come to end the long night of their captivity.

The meaning of this story is not found in the drowning of Egyptian soldiers, for no one should rejoice at the death or defeat of a human being. Rather, this story symbolizes the death of evil and of inhuman oppression and unjust exploitation.

The death of the Egyptians upon the seashore is a vivid reminder that something in the very nature of the universe assists goodness in its perennial struggle with evil. The New Testament rightly declares: "No chastening for the present seemeth to be joyous, but grievous: *nevertheless afterward* it yieldeth the peaceable fruit of righteousness." Pharaoh exploits the children of Israel—*nevertheless afterward!* Pilate yields to the crowd which crucifies Christ—*nevertheless afterward!* The early Christians are thrown to the lions and carried to the chopping blocks—*nevertheless afterward!* Something in this universe justifies Shakespeare in saying:

> There's a divinity that shapes our ends,
> Rough-hew them how we will,

and Lowell in saying,

> Though the cause of Evil prosper,
> Yet 'tis Truth alone is strong,

and Tennyson in saying,

> I can but trust that good shall fall,
> At last—far off—at last, to all,
> And every winter change to spring.

II. The truth of this text is revealed in the contemporary struggle between good in the form of freedom and justice, and evil in the form of oppression and colonialism. Of the approximately 3,000,000,000 people in our world, more than 1,900,000,000—a vast majority—live on the continents of Asia and Africa. Less than two decades ago most of the Asian and African peoples were colonial subjects, dominated politically, exploited economically, and segregated and humiliated by foreign powers. For years they protested against these grave injustices. In nearly every territory in Asia and Africa a courageous Moses pleaded passionately for the freedom of his people. For more than twenty years Mahatma Gandhi unrelentingly urged British viceroys, governors general, prime ministers, and kings to let his people go. Like the pharaohs of old, the British leaders turned deaf ears to these agonizing pleas. Even the great Winston Churchill responded to Gandhi's cry for independence by saying, "I have not become the King's First Minister in order to preside over the liquidation of the British Empire." The conflict between two determined forces, the colonial powers and the Asian and African peoples, has been one of the most momentous and critical struggles of the twentieth century.

But in spite of the resistance and recalcitrance of the colonial powers, the victory of the forces of justice and human dignity is gradually being achieved. Twenty-five years ago there were only three independent countries in the whole continent of Africa, but today thirty-two countries are independent. A short fifteen years ago the British Empire politically dominated more than 650,000,000 people in Asia and Africa, but today the number is less than 60,000,000. The Red Sea has opened. The oppressed masses in Asia and Africa have won their freedom from the Egypt of colonialism and now move toward the promised land of economic and cultural stability. These peoples see the evils of colonialism and imperialism dead upon the seashore.

In our own American struggle for freedom and justice, we are seeing the death of evil. In 1619, the Negro was brought to America from the soils of Africa. For more than two hundred years Africa was raped and plundered, her native kingdoms disorganized, and her people and rulers demoralized. In America, the Negro slave was merely a depersonalized cog in a vast plantation machine.

But there were those who had a nagging conscience and knew that so unjust a system represented a strange paradox in a nation founded on the principle that all men are created equal. In 1820, six years before his death, Thomas Jefferson wrote these melancholy words:

But the momentous question [slavery], like a fire-bell in the night, awakened and filled me with terror. I considered it at once as the knell of the Union. . . . I regret that I am now to die in the belief, that the useless sacrifice of themselves by the generation of 1776, to acquire self-government and happiness to their country, is to be thrown away . . . and my only consolation is to be, that I live not to weep over it.

Numerous abolitionists, like Jefferson, were tortured in their hearts by the question of slavery. With keen perception they saw that the immorality of slavery degraded the white master as well as the Negro.

Then came the day when Abraham Lincoln faced squarely this matter of slavery. His torments and vacillations are well known, yet the conclusion of his search is embodied in these words: "In giving freedom to the slave, we assure freedom to the free—honorable alike in what we give and what we preserve." On this moral foundation Lincoln drafted the Emancipation Proclamation, an executive order that brought an end to chattel slavery. The significance of the Emancipation Proclamation was colorfully described by a great American, Frederick Douglass, in these words:

It recognizes and declares the real nature of the contest and places the North on the side of justice and civilization. . . . Unquestionably the first of January, 1863, is to be the most memorable day in American annals. The Fourth of July was great, but the First of January, when we consider it in all its relations and bearings, is incomparably greater. The one had respect to the mere political birth of a nation; the last concerns the national life and character and is to determine whether that life and character shall be radiantly glorious with all high and noble virtues, or infamously blackened forevermore.

The Emancipation Proclamation did not, however, bring full freedom to the Negro,

for although he enjoyed certain political and social opportunities during the Reconstruction, the Negro soon discovered that the pharaohs of the South were determined to keep him in slavery. Certainly the Emancipation Proclamation brought him nearer to the Red Sea, but it did not guarantee his passage through parted waters. Racial segregation, backed by a decision of the United States Supreme Court in 1896 [*Plessy* v. *Ferguson*], was a new form of slavery disguised by certain niceties of complexity. In the great struggle of the last half-century between the forces of justice attempting to end the evil system of segregation and the forces of injustice attempting to maintain it, the pharaohs have employed legal maneuvers, economic reprisals, and even physical violence to hold the Negro in the Egypt of segregation. Despite the patient cry of many a Moses, they refused to let the Negro people go.

Today we are witnessing a massive change. A world-shaking decree by the nine justices of the United States Supreme Court opened the Red Sea and the forces of justice are moving to the other side. The Court decreed an end to the old *Plessy* decision of 1896 and affirmed that separate facilities are inherently unequal and that to segregate a child on the basis of race is to deny the child an equal legal protection. This decision [i.e., *Brown* v. *Board of Education*, 1954] is a great beacon light of hope to millions of disinherited people. Looking back, we see the forces of segregation gradually dying on the seashore. The problem is far from solved and gigantic mountains of opposition lie ahead, but at least we have left Egypt, and with patient yet firm determination we shall reach the promised land. Evil in the form of injustice and exploitation shall not survive forever. A Red Sea passage in history ultimately brings the forces of goodness to victory, and the closing of the same water marks the doom and destruction of the forces of evil.

All of this reminds us that evil carries the seed of its own destruction. In the long run right defeated is stronger than evil triumphant. Historian Charles A. Beard, when asked what major lessons he had learned from history, answered:

> First, whom the gods would destroy they must first make mad with power. Second, the mills of God grind slowly, yet they grind exceeding small. Third, the bee fertilizes the flower it robs. Fourth, when it is dark enough you can see the stars.

These are the words, not of a preacher, but of a hardheaded historian, whose long and painstaking study of history revealed to him that evil has a self-defeating quality. It can go a long way, but then it reaches its limit. There is something in this universe that Greek mythology referred to as the goddess of Nemesis.

III. We must be careful at this point not to engage in a superficial optimism or to conclude that the death of a particular evil means that all evil lies dead upon the seashore. All progress is precarious, and the solution of one problem brings us face to face with another problem. The Kingdom of God as a universal reality is *not yet*. Because sin exists on every level of man's existence, the death of one tyranny is followed by the emergence of another tyranny.

But just as we must avoid a superficial optimism, we must also avoid a crippling pessimism. Even though all progress is precarious, within limits real social progress may be made. Although man's moral pilgrimage may never reach a destination point on earth, his never-ceasing strivings may bring him ever closer to the city of righteousness. And though the Kingdom of God may remain *not yet* as a universal reality in history, in the present it may exist in such isolated forms as in judgment, in personal devotion, and in some group life. "The kingdom of God is in the midst of you."

Above all, we must be reminded anew that God is at work in his universe. He is not outside the world looking on with a sort of cold indifference. Here on all the roads of life, he is striving in our striving. Like an ever-loving Father, he is working through history for the salvation of his children. As we struggle to defeat the forces of evil, the God of the universe struggles with us. Evil dies on the seashore, not merely because of man's endless struggle against it, but because of God's power to defeat it.

But why is God so slow in conquering the forces of evil? Why did God permit Hitler to kill six million Jews? Why did God permit slavery to continue in America for two hundred and forty-four years? Why does God permit blood-thirsty mobs to lynch Negro men and women at will and drown Negro boys and girls at whim? Why does not God break in and smash the evil schemes of wicked men?

I do not pretend to understand all of the ways of God or his particular timetable for grappling with evil. Perhaps if God dealt with evil in the overbearing way that we wish, he would defeat his ultimate purpose. We are responsible human beings, not blind automatons; persons, not puppets. By endowing us with freedom, God relinquished a measure of his own sovereignty and imposed certain limitations upon himself. If his children are free, they must do his will by a voluntary choice. Therefore, God cannot at the same time impose his will upon his children and also maintain his purpose for man. If through sheer omnipotence God were to defeat his purpose, he would express weakness rather than power. Power is the ability to fulfill purpose; action which defeats purpose is weakness.

God's unwillingness to deal with evil with an overbearing immediacy does not mean that he is doing nothing. We weak and finite human beings are not alone in our quest for the triumph of righteousness. There is, as Matthew Arnold wrote, an "enduring power, not ourselves, which makes for righteousness."

We must also remember that God does not forget his children who are the victims of evil forces. He gives us the interior resources to bear the burdens and tribulations of life. When we are in the darkness of some oppressive Egypt, God is a light unto our path. He imbues us with the strength needed to endure the ordeals of

Egypt, and he gives us the courage and power to undertake the journey ahead. When the lamp of hope flickers and the candle of faith runs low, he restoreth our souls, giving us renewed vigor to carry on. He is with us not only in the noontime of fulfillment, but also in the midnight of despair.

In India Mrs. King and I spent a lovely weekend in the State of Karala, the southernmost point of that vast country. While there we visited the beautiful beach on Cape Comorin, which is called "Land's End," because this is actually where the land of India comes to an end. Nothing stretches before you except the broad expanse of rolling waters. This beautiful spot is a point at which meet three great bodies of water, the Indian Ocean, the Arabian Sea, and the Bay of Bengal. Seated on a huge rock that slightly protrudes into the ocean, we were enthralled by the vastness of the ocean and its terrifying immensities. As the waves unfolded in almost rhythmic succession and crashed against the base of the rock on which we were seated, an oceanic music brought sweetness to the ear. To the west we saw the magnificent sun, a great cosmic ball of fire, appear to sink into the very ocean itself. Just as it was almost lost from sight, Mrs. King touched me and said, "Look, Martin, isn't that beautiful!" I looked around and saw the moon, another ball of scintillating beauty. As the sun appeared to be sinking into the ocean, the moon appeared to be rising from the ocean. When the sun finally passed completely beyond sight, darkness engulfed the earth, but in the east the radiant light of the rising moon shone supreme.

To my wife I said, "This is an analogy of what often happens in life." We have experiences when the light of day vanishes, leaving us in some dark and desolate midnight—moments when our highest hopes are turned into shambles of despair or when we are the victims of some tragic injustice and some terrible exploitation. During such moments our spirits are almost overcome by gloom and despair, and we feel that there is no light anywhere. But ever and again, we look toward the east and discover that there

is another light which shines even in the darkness, and "the spear of frustration" is transformed "into a shaft of light."

This would be an unbearable world were God to have only a single light, but we may be consoled that God has two lights: a light to guide us in the brightness of the day when hopes are fulfilled and circumstances are favorable, and a light to guide us in the darkness of the midnight when we are thwarted and the slumbering giants of gloom and hopelessness rise in our souls. The testimony of the Psalmist is that we need never walk in darkness [Psalms 139:7–12].

> Whither shall I go from thy spirit? or whither shall I flee from thy presence? If I ascend up into heaven, thou art there: if I make my bed in hell, behold, thou art there. If I take the wings of the morning, and dwell in the uttermost parts of the sea; even there shall thy hand lead me, and thy right hand shall hold me. If I say, Surely the darkness shall cover me; even the night shall be light about me. Yea, the darkness hideth not from thee; but the night shineth as the day: the darkness and the light are both alike to thee.

This faith will sustain us in our struggle to escape from the bondage of every evil Egypt. This faith will be a lamp unto our weary feet and a light unto our meandering path. Without such faith, man's highest dreams will pass silently to the dust.[20]

PILGRIMAGE TO NONVIOLENCE

In my senior year in theological seminary, I engaged in the exciting reading of various theological theories. Having been raised in a rather strict fundamentalist tradition, I was occasionally shocked when my intellectual journey carried me through new and sometimes complex doctrinal lands, but the pilgrimage was always stimulating, gave me a new appreciation for objective appraisal and critical analysis, and knocked me out of my dogmatic slumber.

Liberalism provided me with an intellectual satisfaction that I had never found in fundamentalism. I became so enamored of the insights of liberalism that I almost fell into the trap of accepting uncritically everything it encompassed. I was absolutely convinced of the natural goodness of man and the natural power of human reason.

I. A basic change in my thinking came when I began to question some of the theories that had been associated with so-called liberal theology. Of course, there are aspects of liberalism that I hope to cherish always: its devotion to the search for truth, its insistence on an open and analytical mind, and its refusal to abandon the best lights of reason. The contribution of liberalism to the philological–historical criticism of biblical literature has been of immeasurable value and should be defended with religious and scientific passion.

But I began to question the liberal doctrine of man. The more I observed the tragedies of history and man's shameful inclination to choose the low road, the more I came to see the depths and strength of sin. My reading of the works of Reinhold Niebuhr made me aware of the complexity of human motives and the reality of sin on every level of man's existence. Moreover, I came to recognize the complexity of man's social involvement and the glaring reality of collective evil. I realized that liberalism had been all too sentimental concerning human nature and that it leaned toward a false idealism.

I also came to see that the superficial optimism of liberalism concerning human nature overlooked the fact that reason is darkened by sin. The more I thought about human nature, the more I saw how our tragic inclination for sin encourages us to rationalize our actions. Liberalism failed to show that reason by itself is little more than an instrument to justify man's defensive ways of thinking. Reason, devoid of the purifying power of faith, can never free itself from distortions and rationalizations.

Although I rejected some aspects of liberalism, I never came to an all-out acceptance of neo-orthodoxy. While I saw neo-orthodoxy as a helpful corrective for a sentimental liberalism, I felt that it did not provide an adequate answer to basic questions. If liberalism was too optimistic concerning human nature, neo-orthodoxy was too pessimistic. Not only on the question of man, but also on other vital issues, the revolt of neo-orthodoxy went too far. In its attempt to preserve the transcendence of God, which had been neglected by an overstress of his immanence in liberalism, neo-orthodoxy went to the extreme of stressing a God who was hidden, unknown, and "wholly other." In its revolt against overemphasis on the power of reason in liberalism, neo-orthodoxy fell into a mood of antirationalism and semi-fundamentalism, stressing a narrow uncritical biblicism. This approach, I felt, was inadequate both for the church and for personal life.

So although liberalism left me unsatisfied on the question of the nature of man, I found no refuge in neo-orthodoxy. I am now convinced that the truth about man is found neither in liberalism nor in neo-orthodoxy. Each represents a partial truth. A large segment of Protestant liberalism defined man only in terms of his essential nature, his capacity for good; neo-orthodoxy tended to define man only in terms of his existential nature, his capacity for evil. An adequate understanding of man is found neither in the thesis of liberalism nor in the antithesis of neo-orthodoxy, but in a synthesis which reconciles the truths of both.

During the intervening years I have gained a new appreciation for the philosophy of existentialism. My first contact with this philosophy came through my reading of Kierkegaard and Nietzsche. Later I turned to a study of Jaspers, Heidegger, and Sartre. These thinkers stimulated my thinking; while questioning each, I nevertheless learned a great deal through a study of them. When I finally engaged in a serious study of the writings of Paul Tillich, I became convinced that existentialism, in spite of the fact that it had become all too fashionable, had grasped certain basic truths about man and his condition that could not be permanently overlooked.

An understanding of the "finite freedom" of man is one of the permanent contributions of existentialism, and its perception of the anxiety and conflict produced in man's personal and social life by the perilous and ambiguous structure of existence is especially meaningful for our time. A common denominator in atheistic or theistic existentialism is that man's existential situation is estranged from his essential nature. In their revolt against Hegel's essentialism, all existentialists contend that the world is fragmented. History is a series of unreconciled conflicts, and man's existence is filled with anxiety and threatened with meaninglessness. While the ultimate Christian answer is not found in any of these existential assertions, there is much here by which the theologian may describe the true state of man's existence.

Although most of my formal study has been in systematic theology and philosophy, I have become more and more interested in social ethics. During my early teens I was deeply concerned by the problem of racial injustice. I considered segregation both rationally inexplicable and morally unjustifiable. I could never accept my having to sit in the back of a bus or in the segregated section of a train. The first time that I was seated behind a curtain in a dining car I felt as though the curtain had been dropped on my self-hood. I also learned that the inseparable twin of racial injustice is economic injustice. I saw how the systems of segregation exploited both the Negro and the poor whites. These early experiences made me deeply conscious of the varieties of injustice in our society.

II. Not until I entered theological seminary, however, did I begin a serious intellectual quest for a method that would eliminate social evil. I was immediately influenced by the social gospel. In the early 1950s I read Walter Rauschenbusch's *Christianity and the Social Crisis,* a book which left an indelible imprint on my thinking. Of course, there were points at which I differed from Rauschenbusch. I felt that he was a victim of the nineteenth-century "cult of inevitable progress," which led him to an unwarranted optimism concerning human nature. Moreover, he came perilously close to identifying the Kingdom of God with a particular social and economic system, a temptation to which the church must never surrender. But in spite of these shortcomings, Rauschenbusch gave to American Protestantism a sense of social responsibility that it should never lose. The gospel at its best deals with the whole man, not only his soul but also his body, not only his spiritual well-being but also his material well-being. A religion that professes a concern for the souls of men and is not equally concerned about the slums that damn them, the economic conditions that strangle them, and the social conditions that cripple them, is a spiritually moribund religion.

After reading Rauschenbusch, I turned to a serious study of the social and ethical theories of the great philosophers. During this period I had almost despaired of the power of love to solve social problems. The turn-the-other-cheek and the love-your-enemies philosophies are valid, I felt, only when individuals are in conflict with other individuals; when racial groups and nations are in conflict, a more realistic approach is necessary.

Then I was introduced to the life and teachings of Mahatma Gandhi. As I read his works I became deeply fascinated by his campaigns of nonviolent resistance. The whole Gandhian concept of *satyagraha* (*satya* is truth which equals love and *graha* is force; *satyagraha* thus means truth-force or love-force) was profoundly significant to me. As I delved deeper into the philosophy of Gandhi, my skepticism concerning the power of love gradually diminished, and I came to see for the first time that the Christian doctrine of love, operating through the Gandhian method of nonviolence, is one of the most potent weapons available to an oppressed people in their struggle for freedom. At that time, however, I acquired only an intellectual understanding and appreciation of the position, and I had no firm determination to organize it in a socially effective situation.

When I went to Montgomery, Alabama, as a pastor in 1954, I had not the slightest idea that I would later become involved in a crisis in which nonviolent resistance would be applicable. After I had lived in the community about a year, the bus boycott began. The Negro people of Montgomery, exhausted by the humiliating experiences that they had constantly faced on the buses, expressed in a massive act of noncooperation their determination to be free. They came to see that it was ultimately more honorable to walk the streets in dignity than to ride the buses in humiliation. At the beginning of the protest, the people called on me to serve as their spokesman. In accepting this responsibility, my mind, consciously or unconsciously, was driven back to the Sermon on the Mount and the Gandhian method of nonviolent resistance. This principle became the guiding light of our movement. Christ furnished the spirit and motivation and Gandhi furnished the method.

The experience in Montgomery did more to clarify my thinking in regard to the question of nonviolence than all of the books that I had read. As the days unfolded, I became more and more convinced of the power of nonviolence. Nonviolence became more than a method to which I gave intellectual assent; it became a commitment to a way of life. Many issues I had not cleared up intellectually concerning nonviolence were now resolved within the sphere of practical action.

My privilege of traveling to India had a great impact on me personally, for it was invigorating to see firsthand the amazing results of a nonviolent struggle to achieve independence. The aftermath of hatred and bitterness that usually follows a violent campaign was found nowhere in India, and a mutual friendship, based on complete equality, existed between the Indian and British people within the Commonwealth.

I would not wish to give the impression that nonviolence will accomplish miracles overnight. Men are not easily moved from their mental ruts or purged of their prejudiced and irrational feelings. When the underprivileged demand freedom, the privileged at first react with bitterness and resistance. Even when the demands are couched in nonviolent terms, the initial response is substantially the same. I am sure that many of our white brothers in Montgomery and throughout the South are still bitter toward the Negro leaders, even though these leaders have sought to follow a way of love and nonviolence. But the nonviolent approach does something to the hearts and souls of those committed to it. It gives them new self-respect. It calls up resources of strength and courage that they did not know they had. Finally, it so stirs the conscience of the opponent that reconciliation becomes a reality.

III. More recently I have come to see the need for the method of nonviolence in international relations. Although I was not yet convinced of its efficacy in conflicts between nations, I felt that while war could never be a positive good, it could serve as a negative good by preventing the spread and growth of an evil force. War, horrible as it is, might be preferable to surrender to a totalitarian system. But I now believe that the potential destructiveness of modern weapons totally rules out the possibility of war ever again achieving a negative good. If we assume that mankind has a right to survive, then we must find an alternative to war and destruction. In our day of space vehicles and guided ballistic missiles, the choice is either nonviolence or nonexistence.

I am no doctrinaire pacifist, but I have tried to embrace a realistic pacifism which finds the pacifist position as the lesser evil in the circumstances. I do not claim to be free from the moral dilemmas that the Christian nonpacifist confronts, but I am convinced that the church cannot be silent while mankind faces the threat of nuclear annihilation. If the church is true to her mission, she must call for an end to the arms race.

Some of my personal sufferings over the last few years have also served to shape my thinking. I always hesitate to mention these experiences for fear of conveying the wrong impression. A person who constantly calls attention to his trials and sufferings is in danger of developing a martyr complex and impressing others that he is consciously seeking sympathy. It is possible for one to be self-centered in his self-sacrifice. So I am always reluctant to refer to my personal sacrifices. But I feel somewhat justified in mentioning them in this essay because of the influence they have had upon my thought.

Due to my involvement in the struggle for the freedom of my people, I have known very few quiet days in the last few years. I have been imprisoned in Alabama and Georgia jails twelve times. My home has been bombed twice. A day seldom passes that my family and I are not the recipients of threats of death. I have been the victim of a near-fatal stabbing. So in a real sense I have been battered by the storms of persecution. I must admit that at times I have felt that I could no longer bear such a heavy burden, and have been tempted to retreat to a more quiet and serene life. But every time such a temptation appeared, something came to strengthen my determination. I have learned now that the Master's burden is light precisely when we take his yoke upon us.

My personal trials have also taught me the value of unmerited suffering. As my sufferings mounted I soon realized that there were two ways in which I could respond to my situation—either to react with bitterness or seek to transform the suffering into a creative force. I decided to follow the latter course. Recognizing the necessity for suffering, I have tried to make of it a virtue. If only to save myself from bitterness, I have attempted to see my personal ordeals as an opportunity to transfigure myself and heal the people involved in the tragic situation which now obtains. I have lived these last few years with the conviction that unearned suffering is redemptive. There are some who still find the Cross a stumbling block, others consider it foolishness, but I am more convinced than ever before that it is the power of God unto social and individual salvation. So like the Apostle Paul I can now humbly, yet proudly, say, "I bear in my body the marks of the Lord Jesus."

The agonizing moments through which

I have passed during the last few years have also drawn me closer to God. More than ever before I am convinced of the reality of a personal God. True, I have always believed in the personality of God. But in the past the idea of a personal God was little more than a metaphysical category that I found theologically and philosophically satisfying. Now it is a living reality that has been validated in the experiences of everyday life. God has been profoundly real to me in recent years. In the midst of lonely days and dreary nights I have heard an inner voice saying, "Lo, I will be with you." When the chains of fear and the manacles of frustration have all but stymied my efforts, I have felt the power of God transforming the fatigue of despair into the buoyancy of hope. I am convinced that the universe is under the control of a loving purpose, and that in the struggle for righteousness man has cosmic companionship. Behind the harsh appearances of the world there is a benign power. To say that this God is personal is not to make him a finite object besides other objects or attribute to him the limitations of human personality; it is to take what is finest and noblest in our consciousness and affirm its perfect existence in him. It is certainly true that human personality is limited, but personality as such involves no necessary limitations. It means simply self-consciousness and self-direction. So in the truest sense of the word, God is a living God. In him there is feeling and will, responsive to the deepest yearnings of the human heart: *this* God both evokes and answers prayer.

The past decade has been a most exciting one. In spite of the tensions and uncertainties of this period something profoundly meaningful is taking place. Old systems of exploitation and oppression are passing away; new systems of justice and equality are being born. In a real sense this is a great time to be alive. Therefore, I am not yet discouraged about the future. Granted that the easygoing optimism of yesterday is impossible. Granted that we face a world crisis which leaves us standing so often amid the surging murmur of life's restless sea. But every crisis has both its dangers and its opportunities. It can spell either salvation or doom. In a dark, confused world the Kingdom of God may yet reign in the hearts of men. (Pp. 165–73.)

Elie Wiesel and the Trial of God

While Martin Luther King, Jr., grew up experiencing segregation and racism in the United States, another boy encountered evil and death in Europe. Dislodged from his home in Sighet, Hungary, Elie Wiesel (b. 1928) lost most of his family in the **Holocaust,** the systematic destruction of six million Jews by the Nazis during World War II. In 1944 Wiesel was imprisoned in the infamous death camp at Auschwitz. He survived and lived in France for a time before finding his way to New York

ELIE WIESEL b. 1928

City. He approached his full literary prowess as King lay dying.

"I never intended to be a philosopher," insists Wiesel, the 1986 recipient of the Nobel Peace Prize. "The only role I sought was that of witness. I believed that, having survived by chance, I was duty-bound to give meaning to my survival, to justify each moment of my life."[21] Thus Wiesel tells stories that remind us of those who lived and died in the Kingdom of Night. "Why do I write?" ponders Wiesel. "Perhaps in order not to go mad. Or, on the contrary, to touch the bottom of madness" (p. 200). Later he gives a different answer to the same question, supplementing the first. "Why do I write? To wrench those victims from oblivion. To help the dead vanquish death" (p. 206). That mission, plus the threat of madness, turns Wiesel to the questions of philosophy, and especially to that most philosophical and ultimate question of all: Why?

What Happened at Auschwitz?

Auschwitz embodied **genocide**. In *Legends of Our Time* (1968), Wiesel observes: "At Auschwitz, not only man died, but also the idea of man. . . . It was its own heart the world incinerated at Auschwitz."[22] The process of destruction exemplified by the Holocaust enlisted the support of diverse human energies and occupations. And for the most part, the people who permitted or carried out the orders were ordinary, decent people much like us. Teachers and writers helped to till the soil in which Hitler's virulent anti-Semitism took root; their students and readers reaped the wasteful harvest. Lawyers helped to draft and enforce the laws that isolated Jews and set them up for the kill. Physicians were among the first to experiment with the gassing of men, women, and children, which would become so much a way of life—and death—at Treblinka, Sobibor, and all the death camps. In the name of science, investigators performed research and tested their racial theories on human beings who had been used as guinea pigs. Business executives found that Nazi concentration camps could provide cost-effective labor: they worked people to death. And artists, such as the filmmaker Leni Riefenstahl, advanced the propaganda that made Hitler's policies persuasive to so many. The list could go on. Genocide requires the complicity of countless talents, persons, and nationalities.

The Holocaust took place in one of the most scientifically advanced, philosophically sophisticated, and technologically competent cultures of all human history. But far from telling us that we inhabit the best of all possible worlds, or that the rational is real and that the actual world is as it ought to be, Auschwitz signifies that virtually everything is permitted—nobody is blessed with a cosmic insurance policy guaranteeing that one's fellow human beings will not commit or condone the mass wasting of human life. Many optimistic assumptions about the innate goodness of human nature, humanity's moral progress, and even love were incinerated at Auschwitz. And yet Wiesel, the survivor, testifies that we must not despair: death deserves no more victories, and evil should never have the last word.

Wrestling with God

Despite injustice and suffering, Martin Luther King, Jr., neither denied God's existence nor thundered out against God in protest. Instead, faith in God was critical to King's conviction that hopes for a triumph over evil and death would be confirmed. Wiesel's experience, infused with Jewish spirituality, produces a tone different from that of the black American Christian. Wiesel finds the Holocaust inexplicable *with* God. He contends that in a certain limited sense the Holocaust may be interpreted without considering God at all. Historical analysis can point to factors such as centuries of anti-Semitism, a world war the Germans had lost, economic collapse in the Weimar Republic, the rise of a fascist state, and advances in technology and bureaucratic management. Such an accounting reveals a logic in the Holocaust that is not without sense. Yet, adds Wiesel, the Holocaust cannot be interpreted *without* God either.

At the very least, the latter claim is true because human beliefs about God figured centrally into the historical pattern that brought the Holocaust about. More than that, however, the Holocaust stands as a major event in the history of the attempt to define hope and faith. "How is one to believe?" asks Wiesel. And he counters that question with another: "How is one not to believe?"[23] As he poses both those questions, Wiesel suggests how the Holocaust produced feelings of forlornness, grief, and rage, but also perhaps of wonder, yearning, and defiance that thrust the question of God upon us and move us to confront God anew. If God cannot be easily accepted after Auschwitz, especially on the terms proposed by Leibniz or King, a refusal to let God go might be one way of testifying that the human heart was not incinerated completely at Auschwitz.

Exploring those possibilities, Wiesel wrestles with God. He has said in his public presentations, for example: "If I told you I believed in God, I would be lying; if I told you I did not believe in God, I would also be lying." How the author can hold these seemingly opposite views simultaneously may be explained by his recent novel *The Testament* (1981). There Wiesel describes the fate of a poet, one of hundreds of Jewish intellectuals in the Soviet Union condemned to death by the dictator Joseph Stalin. Paltiel Kossover writes a letter to his son Grisha, not certain that the boy will ever read it but hoping that a father's words will not be lost. The poet reflects for a time on God. What God "requires is affirmation," says Kossover, "and there I draw the line." And yet he prefaces that comment by writing that "as a source of questioning I would gladly accept Him."[24] This suggests that God provides an approach for asking the right questions, questions that, as long as they are asked, keep men and women human.

Can God and Evil Be Reconciled?

Most people want a perfect God or none at all. In religious quarters, it has not been popular to put God on trial. For centuries human beings have taken themselves to task in order to protect God's innocence, and not without reason. Even at the price of accepting unwarranted guilt, the desire for a neat separation of good and evil is strong. Life is simpler when people put God in the right and God's children in the wrong. Wiesel rejects that neat equation, protesting that too much vindication of God legitimizes evil. Nowhere does he argue for that point more effectively than in his drama *The Trial of God* (1979).

The play is set in the season of Purim, a joyous festival replete with masks and reenactments in celebration of a moment in Jewish history when oppressors were outmaneuvered and Jews were saved. Three traveling Jewish actors have arrived by mistake at the village of Shamgorod. They discover that it is hardly a place for festivity, however, having been ravaged by a murderous pogrom. Only two Jews survived. Berish the innkeeper escaped, but he had to watch while his daughter was unspeakably abused on her wedding night. She now lives, her sanity broken, mercifully out of touch with the world.

In the region of Shamgorod, anti-Jewish hatred festers once again, and a new pogrom may break out. Purim, however, cannot be Purim without a play, and so a *Purimspiel* will be given, but with a difference urged by Berish: this time the play will enact the trial of God. As the characters in Wiesel's drama

begin to organize their play-within-a-play, one problem looms large. The defendant, God, is silent, and on this Purim night no one in Shamgorod wants to speak for him. Unnoticed, however, a stranger has entered the inn, and just when it seems that the defense attorney's role will go unfilled, the newcomer—his name is Sam—volunteers to act the part. Apparently Maria, Berish's Gentile housekeeper, has seen this man before. Have nothing to do with him, she warns, but the show begins.

Berish prosecutes. God, he contends, "could use His might to save the victims, but He doesn't! So—on whose side is He? Could the killer kill without His blessing—without His complicity?"[25] Apologies for God do not sit well with this Jewish patriarch. "If I am given the choice of feeling sorry for Him or for human beings," exclaims Berish, "I choose the latter anytime. He is big enough, strong enough to take care of Himself; man is not" (p. 133). Berish's protest is real; it does not deny God's reality but affirms it by calling God to account.

Sam's style is different. He has an answer for every charge, and he cautions that emotion is no substitute for evidence. In short, he defends God brilliantly, a defense you must read for yourself to appreciate its literary power. Sam's performance dazzles the visiting actors, who have formed the court, and they wonder who he is. Sam will not say, but his identity and the verdict implicit in *The Trial of God* do not remain moot. As the play's final scene unfolds, a mob approaches to pillage the inn at Shamgorod once more. Sensing that the end is near, the Jewish actors choose to die with their Purim masks in place. Sam dons one, too, and as he does so, Maria's premonitions are corroborated. Sam's mask is worthy of his namesake, Samael; both signify Satan. And as a final candle is extinguished and the inn's door flies open as if battered by sudden, deafening sound, Satan's laughter mingles with the murderous roars.

Wiesel as the literary dramatist leaves us in suspense and with no answer, least of all his own as the author. Yet it is clear that Satan and God are joined when evil is concerned.

Could You Have Done Better?

Elie Wiesel witnessed a trial of God in Auschwitz, as he reports in introducing *The Trial of God*, which is set three centuries ago. Wiesel does not mention in that foreword, but has indicated on another occasion, that when the three rabbis who conducted the Auschwitz trial had finished and found God guilty, those pious men noted that it was time for their customary religious observances, and so they bowed their heads and prayed. Apologies for God, warns Wiesel, may be demonic; they may justify God at humanity's expense. But Wiesel's testimony about the rabbis in Auschwitz also warns us to avoid a trap that may lie before us in insisting upon God's guilt. Such insistence could become just another form of scapegoating, one that places a premium on blaming God, leaving the impression that there is really not very much human beings can do.

We do face great odds, admits Wiesel, but there still is much that can be done. Indeed, he argues, we have to act or there will be too little action on humanity's behalf. The world—to too great an extent, no doubt—is in our hands. If God listens and answers, implies Wiesel, it is usually in silence. If the divine is judge or ally, it is less by intervention that metes out justice in total equity and more by letting events fall as they may to reveal the corrupt absurdity, as well as the grandeur, of what human beings do together. The future is more open than it ought to be, Wiesel suggests. We have all that we can do and then some, and if we fail to act well, the waste will only increase. " 'My God, my God, why have you deserted me?' " (Matt. 27:46). Jesus' ancient Jewish question turns out to be contemporary.[26] For Wiesel it evokes still others:

Can we learn not to blame God as a way of covering over our responsibilities? Can we learn to be honest with God and with ourselves as a means to deepen compassion? Wiesel's protests raise these questions; his wrestling with God is the struggle to answer them affirmatively.

Long ago a Jewish family was expelled from Spain. Plagued at every turn, they could find no refuge, except that sleep turned to death for them, one by one. At last only the father was left, and he spoke to God:

> "Master of the Universe, I know what You want—I understand what You are doing. You want despair to overwhelm me. You want me to cease believing in You, to cease praying to You, to cease invoking Your name to glorify and sanctify it. Well, I tell You: No, no—a thousand times no! You shall not succeed! In spite of me and in spite of You, I shall shout the Kaddish [the traditional prayer for the dead], which is a song of faith, for You and against You. This song You shall not still, God of Israel."[27]

As Wiesel recounts that Jewish story, it summarizes well one strand of his case for-and-against God, against-and-for humanity. An ageless dialogue, also restated by Wiesel, reports another. God's creation is at stake. It is far from perfect, and thus . . .

> "Could you have done better?"
> "Yes, I think so."
> "You could have done better? Then what are you waiting for? You don't have a minute to waste, go ahead, start working!"[28]

Those lines are unambiguous, and yet they do contain an ambiguity. Who speaks? Is the conversation between God and humanity, and if so, who speaks which lines? Is the dialogue between two persons, or is it carried on in one mind alone? Or is it all of these at once? If Wiesel leaves the answer up to us, he has little doubt that Auschwitz puts everyone on trial. God, you, we—all of us have something to say about what the verdict of our trial shall be.

Paradigms of Evil

In Leibniz's day, instances of natural catastrophes occupied much of the attention of philosophers and theologians, who wondered about how to account for evil and death. Considering, for example, a great earthquake that devastated Lisbon in 1755, they argued whether such events could be reconciled with the claim that we live in the best of all possible worlds, or whether God could be regarded as omnipotent and totally good. The Lisbon earthquake caused fires and floods; it killed thousands of people. It was also beyond human control. In centuries past, philosophers were well aware that evil and death are produced by human activities that lay waste to life, but their analyses often centered on natural disasters—"acts of God," as they were sometimes called—that human power could not prevent.

Nature's fury demonstrates how fragile our lives can be. But two factors stand out in bold relief in our day. First, human beings now have considerable ability to control some of nature's destructive power. Excellent examples are provided by modern medicine. Smallpox and polio once took a heavy toll. Today those dreaded diseases have been virtually eliminated because human research discovered ways to curtail them. Death still awaits us all, but it need not come as quickly or as painfully as in earlier times. If those results intensify our wonder about the prevalence of what Leibniz called "physical evil," they also tell us that suffering can be reduced, that human life is not completely in the grip of necessities that cannot be broken.

The second point, unfortunately, is less cause for celebration. For if headway has been made against the ill effects of natural catastrophes, the problem of moral evil seems greater than ever. Hence the Holocaust frequently surfaces as the paradigm of evil for the late twentieth century. Violent deaths, caused by the acts of human beings, not by natural disasters, number more than one hundred million in the twentieth century. This is a fundamental fact of our time. We live in an age of refugees, concentration camps, and mass murder, capped by the ultimate dehumanizing threat of nuclear war. Humanity's accumulated record tends to make us doubt that ours is the best of all possible worlds. Yet, even taking into account all its horror, ours is not the worst of all possible worlds either—at least not yet. How to cope with our own power and freedom, how to understand the existence of that power and freedom in the total scheme of things? —Those questions remain. They suggest that the question of whether evil and death will have the last word is still partly open. That openness leaves us to ask "What may I hope?", which is an issue for Elie Wiesel as he contemplates his own writing.

Why do I write? Perhaps in order not to go mad. Or, on the contrary, to touch the bottom of madness.

Like [playwright] Samuel Beckett, the survivor expresses himself "en désespoir de cause," because there is no other way.

Speaking of the solitude of the survivor, the great Yiddish and Hebrew poet and thinker Aaron Zeitlin addresses those who have left him: his father, dead; his brother, dead; his friends, dead: "You have abandoned me," he says to them. "You are together, without me. I am here. Alone. And I make words."

So do I, just like him. I also say words, write words, reluctantly.

There are easier occupations, far more pleasant ones. But for the survivor, writing is not a profession, but an occupation, a duty. Camus calls it "an honor." As he puts it: "I entered literature through worship." Other writers said: "Through anger, through love." Speaking for myself, I would say: "Through silence."

It was by seeking, by probing, silence that I began to discover the perils and power of the word.

I never intended to be a philosopher, or a theologian. The only role I sought was that of witness. I believed that, having survived by chance, I was duty-bound to give meaning to my survival, to justify each moment of my life. I knew the story had to be told. Not to transmit an experience is to betray it; this is what Jewish tradition teaches us. But how to do this? "When Israel is in exile, so is the word," says the Zohar.* The word has deserted the meaning it was intended to convey—impossible to make them coincide. The displacement, the shift, is irrevocable. This was never more true than right after the upheaval. We all knew that we could never, never say what had to be said, that we could never express in words, coherent, intelligible words, our experience of madness on an absolute scale. The walk through flaming night, the silence before and after the selection, the monotonous praying of the condemned, the Kaddish of the dying, the fear and hunger of the sick, the shame and suffering, the haunted eyes, the demented stares. I thought that I would never be able to speak of them. All words seemed inadequate, worn, foolish, lifeless, whereas I wanted them to be searing. Where was I to discover a fresh vocabulary, a primeval language? The language of night was not human; it was primitive, almost animal— hoarse shouting, screams, muffled moaning, savage howling, the sound of beating. . . . A brute striking wildly, a body falling; an officer raises his arm and a whole community walks toward a common grave; a soldier shrugs his shoulders, and a thousand families are torn apart, to be reunited only by death. This is the concentration camp language. It negated all other language and took its place. Rather than link, it became wall. Could it be surmounted? Could the reader be brought to the other side? I knew the answer to be negative, and yet I also knew that "no" had to become "yes." It was the wish, the last will of the dead. One had to break the shell enclosing the dark truth, and give it a name. One had to force man to look.

The fear of forgetting: the main obsession of all those who have passed through the universe of the damned. The enemy counted on people's disbelief and forgetfulness. How could one foil this plot? And if memory grew hollow, empty of substance, what would happen to all we had accumulated along the way?

Remember, said the father to his son, and the son to his friend. Gather the names, the faces, the tears. If, by a miracle, you come out of it alive, try to reveal everything, omitting nothing, forgetting nothing. Such was the oath we had all taken: "If, by some miracle, I emerge alive, I will devote my life to testifying on behalf of those whose shadow will fall on mine forever and ever."

This is why I write certain things rather than others: to remain faithful.

Of course, there are times of doubt for the survivor, times when one would give in to weakness, or long for comfort. I hear a voice within me telling me to stop mourning the past. I too want to sing of love and of its magic. I too want to celebrate the sun, and the dawn that heralds the sun. I would like to shout, and shout loudly: "Listen, listen well! I too am capable of victory, do you hear? I too am open to laughter and joy! I want to stride, head high, my face unguarded, without having to point to the ashes over there on the horizon, without having to tamper with facts to hide their tragic ugliness. For a man born blind, God himself is blind, but look, I see, I am not blind." One feels like shouting this, but the shout changes to a murmur. One must make a choice; one must remain faithful. A big word, I know. Nevertheless I use it, it suits me. Having written the things I have written, I feel I can afford no longer to play with words. If I say that the writer in me wants to remain loyal, it is because it is true. This sentiment moves all survivors; they owe nothing to anyone, but everything to the dead.

*[The "Book of Splendor," principal book of Kabbala, an esoteric commentary on Jewish Scripture.]

I owe them my roots and memory. I am duty-bound to serve as their emissary, transmitting the history of their disappearance, even if it disturbs, even if it brings pain. Not to do so would be to betray them, and thus myself. And since I feel incapable of communicating their cry by shouting, I simply look at them. I see them and I write.

While writing, I question them as I question myself. I believe I said it before, elsewhere: I write to understand as much as to be understood. Will I succeed one day? Wherever one starts from one reaches darkness. God? He remains the God of darkness. Man? Source of darkness. The killers' sneers, their victims' tears, the onlookers' indifference, their complicity and complacency, the divine role in all that: I do not understand. A million children massacred: I shall never understand.

Jewish children: they haunt my writings. I see them again and again. I shall always see them. Hounded, humiliated, bent like the old men who surround them as though to protect them, unable to do so. They are thirsty, the children, and there is no one to give them water. They are hungry, the children, but there is no one to give them a crust of bread. They are afraid, and there is no one to reassure them.

They walk in the middle of the road, like vagabonds. They are on the way to the station, and they will never return. In sealed cars, without air or food, they travel toward another world; they guess where they are going, they know it, and they keep silent. Tense, thoughtful, they listen to the wind, the call of death in the distance.

All these children, these old people, I see them. I never stop seeing them. I belong to them.

But they, to whom do they belong?

People tend to think that a murderer weakens when facing a child. The child reawakens the killer's lost humanity. The killer can no longer kill the child before him, the child inside him.

Not this time. With us, it happened differently. Our Jewish children had no effect upon the killers. Nor upon the world. Nor upon God.

I think of them, I think of their childhood. Their childhood is a small Jewish town, and this town is no more. They frighten me; they reflect an image of myself, one that I pursue and run from at the same time—the image of a Jewish adolescent who knew no fear, except the fear of God, whose faith was whole, comforting, and not marked by anxiety.

No, I do not understand. And if I write, it is to warn the reader that he will not understand either. "You will not understand, you will never understand," were the words heard everywhere during the reign of night. I can only echo them. You, who never lived under a sky of blood, will never know what it was like. Even if you read all the books ever written, even if you listen to all the testimonies ever given, you will remain on this side of the wall, you will view the agony and death of a people from afar, through the screen of a memory that is not your own.

An admission of impotence and guilt? I do not know. All I know is that Treblinka and Auschwitz cannot be told. And yet I have tried. God knows I have tried.

Did I attempt too much or not enough? Out of some fifteen volumes, only three or four penetrate the phantasmagoric realm of the dead. In my other books, through my other books, I try to follow other roads. For it is dangerous to linger among the dead; they hold on to you, and you run the risk of speaking only to them. And so, I forced myself to turn away from them and study other periods, explore other destinies and teach other tales: the Bible and the Talmud, Hasidism and its fervor, the *Shtetl* and its songs, Jerusalem and its echoes; the Russian Jews and their anguish, their awakening, their courage. At times, it seems to me that I am speaking of other things with the sole purpose of keeping the essential—the personal experience—unspoken. At times I wonder: And what if I were wrong? Perhaps I should not have heeded my own advice and stayed in my own world with the dead.

But then, I have not forgotten the dead. They have their rightful place even in the works about Rizhin and Koretz, Jerusalem and Kolvillàg. Even in my biblical and Midrashic tales, I pursue their presence, mute and motionless. The presence of the dead then beckons in such tangible ways that it affects even the most removed characters. Thus, they appear on Mount Moriah, where Abraham is about to sacrifice his son, a holocaust offering to their common God. They appear on Mount Nebo, where Moses enters solitude and death. And again in the Pardés, where a certain Elisha ben Abuya, seething with anger and pain, decided to repudiate his faith. They appear in Hasidic and Talmudic legends in which victims forever need defending against forces that would crush them. Technically, so to speak, they are of course elsewhere, in time and space, but on a deeper, truer plane, the dead are part of every story, of every scene. They die with Isaac, lament with Jeremiah, they sing with the Besht, and, like him, they wait for miracles—but alas, they will not come to pass.

"But what is the connection?" you will ask. Believe there is one. After Auschwitz everything brings us back to Auschwitz. When I speak of Abraham, Isaac, and Jacob, when I evoke Rabbi Yohanan ben Zakkai and Rabbi Akiba, it is the better to understand them in the light of Auschwitz. As for the Maggid of Mezeritch and his disciples, it is to encounter the followers of their followers, that I attempt to reconstruct their spellbound, spellbinding universe. I like to imagine them alive, exuberant, celebrating life and hope. Their happiness is as necessary to me as it was once to themselves. And yet.

How did they manage to keep their faith intact? How did they manage to sing as they went to meet the Angel of Death? I know Hasidim who never vacillated; I respect their strength. I know others who chose rebellion, protest, rage; I respect their courage. For there comes a time when only those who do not believe in God will not cry out to him in wrath and anguish.

Do not judge either. Even the heroes perished as martyrs, even the martyrs died as heroes. Who would dare oppose knives to prayers? The faith of some matters as much as the strength of others. It is not ours to judge; it is only ours to tell the tale.

But where is one to begin? Whom is one to include? One meets a Hasid in all my novels. And a child. And an old man. And a beggar. And a madman. They are all part of my inner landscape. The reason why? Pursued and persecuted by the killers, I offer them shelter. The enemy wanted to create a society purged of their presence, and I have brought some of them back. The world denied them, repudiated them, so let them live at least within the feverish dreams of my characters.

It is for them that I write.

And yet, the survivor may experience remorse. He has tried to bear witness; it was all in vain.

After the liberation, illusions shaped one's hopes. We were convinced that a new world would be built upon the ruins of Europe. A new civilization was to see the light. No more wars, no more hate, no more intolerance, no fanaticism anywhere. And all this because the witnesses would speak. And speak they did, to no avail.

They will continue, for they cannot do otherwise. When man, in his grief, falls silent, Goethe says, then God gives him the strength to sing of his sorrows. From that moment on, he may no longer choose not to sing, whether his song is heard or not. What matters is to struggle against silence with words, or through another form of silence. What matters is to gather a smile here and there, a tear here and there, a word here and there, and thus justify the faith placed in you, a long time ago, by so many victims.

Why I write? To wrench those victims from oblivion. To help the dead vanquish death.[29]

Summary

We began Part III not only with the question "What may I hope?" but also with an epigraph from Elie Wiesel's essay "Why I Write": "It was by seeking, by probing, silence that I began to discover the perils and power of the word" (p. 200). Faced by evil's power,

Wiesel had far more questions than answers. As he reflected on the Holocaust, however, Wiesel added, "I have nothing against questions: they are useful. What is more they alone are. To turn away from them would be to fail in our duty, to lose our only chance to be able one day to lead an authentic life. It is against the answers that I protest, regardless of their basis. Answers: I say there are none."[30] In that recognition and the silence it entails, Wiesel believes that the peril and the power of words reveal themselves. The peril lies in thinking we possess final answers, especially when evil and death are at issue. The power of the word is found in understanding that "answers only intensify the question," an outcome that should keep us probing speech and silence alike.

Wiesel's approach differs dramatically from Leibniz's. While admitting that God's ways elude our complete grasp, Leibniz went on to explain that our world is certainly the best God could create, even if it is not wholly good. In his view, we have the comfort of knowing that there is a reason sufficient to explain and justify every event. Bertrand Russell found Leibniz too optimistic, but as he urged us to become humanists who do everything we can to improve humanity's condition, he also believed that most of the answers are settled where God, evil, and death are concerned. Although Martin Luther King, Jr., knew the risks of the nonviolent resistance he advocated, his confidence about the ultimate outcome of struggle against evil and death is more pronounced than Wiesel's wariness about answers. Wiesel sticks by the questions, leaving us with the struggle to continue searching. God for him is part of this quest, but not in the form of confident conclusions about evil's demise or comforting guarantees about survival beyond death.

Although their approaches differ, all these thinkers recommend facing the problems of evil and death squarely. Each strives to find ways to stop evil and death from robbing life of meaning. "The more I search," Wiesel once wrote, "the more reasons I find for losing hope" (p. 232). And yet even Wiesel does not permit himself to despair completely. Part of being fully human may be to deny—even against strong odds to the contrary—that evil and death have the last word. To keep that hope alive requires keeping questions and questioning alive. That is the theme of the Epilogue, which concludes this book by a reflection on "the adventures of ideas."

GLOSSARY

antecedent will in Leibniz's first **division of will,** the mode of will that exists prior to its own realization in action, which merely "inclines to" or prefers one specific state of affairs. In Leibniz's **theodicy,** the antecedent will represents God's ability to imagine and to realize each and every individual thing that is good.

anthropomorphism the fallacy of describing what is not human in terms proper to the description of human beings; in Leibniz's **theodicy,** this is the fallacy of failing to recognize God's absolute greatness, which sets God apart from and above human beings.

consequent will in Leibniz's first **division of will,** the type of will that consists in the completed act, and in the case of God's act of creating the world represents God's final *decree.* In terms of Leibniz's **theodicy** this means that the particular scheme of things in the world is a reflection of God's consequent will. Furthermore, the consequent will is made up of the concurrence, or interconnection, of many acts of the **antecedent will.** According to Leibniz, evil comes about because the act of the divine consequent will cannot include all possible goods.

despotism Leibniz's term for the theological

fallacy committed by those who fail to admit God's essential and absolute goodness.

division of will Leibniz's analysis of the role of the will in the process of action, extended in Leibniz's **theodicy** to the nature of God's will in the act of creating the world. This analysis is intended to show how God's intention that the world should contain nothing but good things can be consistent with the fact that the world as God actually created it contains some things that are not good (i.e., are **evil**). See also **antecedent, consequent, productive, permissive** (**will**).

evil imperfection, disharmony, cruelty, corruption, or destruction; Leibniz identifies three main types of evil: *metaphysical*, which concerns the order of nature; *physical*, which concerns bodily harm to living beings through accident or illness; and *moral*, which concerns the actions of rational beings. Martin Luther King, Jr., identifies evil with the waste of human life and potential through violence and racial hatred.

genocide the extermination of an entire group or race of persons, as for instance in the **Holocaust**.

Holocaust literally, a sacrifice by fire; a term often used to refer to the systematic mass murder of Jews by the Nazis during World War II.

humanism the belief that no better authority, either religious or mystical, exists for the grounding of human knowledge and the solution of human problems than human intelligence itself.

mysticism the belief that knowledge can be gained through subjective or supernatural insight, intuition, or revelation.

nonviolent resistance the technique of social protest advocated by Gandhi and King, designed to express opposition to the status quo while avoiding the evil waste of life that results from violence.

omnipotence the absolute power to effect change and creation that is possessed by God.

omniscience God's power of absolute knowledge.

permissive in Leibniz's second **division of will**, the type of will that concerns the actions of others, and determines not to interfere with them. In his **theodicy**, Leibniz identifies this will with the **consequent will**, since he believed that God in his goodness could not actively produce evil things by his **antecedent will**. Leibniz believed that God permitted evil because its existence is necessarily linked with significantly good things.

possible worlds the alternative schemes of things that God, in his **omnipotence**, could have created in the place of the scheme of things that actually exist. Leibniz believed that although God has the power to comprehend and realize all possibilities, the world as God created it does not contain all possible goods, since some are contradictory or mutually exclusive. Although God is omnipotent, Leibniz believed that God was logically constrained by the **principle of noncontradiction** in framing the world.

principle of noncontradiction the principle in logic that a proposition and its contradiction cannot both be true simultaneously. The idea that God was constrained by this principle in creating the world is a significant theme in Leibniz's **theodicy**.

principle of sufficient reason the conviction that every event in the world has a cause sufficient to explain its occurrence. That is, there ultimately are no mysteries.

productive in Leibniz's second **division of will**, the type of will that produces action on the part of the agent, prompting the agent to act as he does. Leibniz closely relates this will to the **antecedent will**, the means by which God wills positively that specific goods exist.

providence the absolute benevolence of God, which Leibniz views as being manifest in every detail of the created order of the universe.

theodicy a theory of the relationship between God and human life that seeks to reconcile the apparent existence of **evil** in the world with the doctrine of God's absolute benevolence.

worship veneration, idolization, or ritual celebration of some ideal or deity; Bertrand Russell, as a **humanist,** writes that humanity itself, rather than the traditional God of religion, is the proper object of such an attitude.

STUDY QUESTIONS

1. Can you agree with Leibniz that the world we live in is the best that is possible, even if it is not all good? Cite your reasons for or against.

2. Does it help if every event in the world does have a "sufficient reason," or do you think it possible for there to be events without any logical, rational explanation?

3. What appeals to you most—and least—about Bertrand Russell's outlook? Why?

4. Do you think we have passed the time when religions can be counted on, or be accepted, as providing answers for us?

5. Where evil is concerned, to what extent do you think Martin Luther King's proposal of nonviolent resistance can be effective? Is violent resistance more effective as a response to evil?

6. Do you agree with King that evil carries the seeds of its own destruction and thus will be vanquished in the end?

7. Elie Wiesel faced ultimate evil and destruction in the Holocaust, but can you state what kind of "answer" he provides?

8. How would you define "evil" today? Where would you turn to oppose it or to seek a solution to the problems it poses?

9. Do you hope for life beyond death? Why or why not?

NOTES

[1]Gottfried Wilhelm von Leibniz, *Theodicy,* ed. Diogenes Allen and trans. E. M. Huggard (Indianapolis: Bobbs-Merrill, 1966), p. 10.

[2]Gottfried Wilhelm von Leibniz, *Monadology,* in *Monadology and Other Philosophical Essays,* trans. Paul Schrecker and Anne Martin Schrecker (Indianapolis: Bobbs-Merrill, 1965), pp. 154–55. Reprinted with permission of Macmillan Publishing Company. Copyright © 1965, 1985 by Macmillan Publishing Company.

[3]Leibniz, *Theodicy,* p. 18.

[4]Gottfried Wilhelm von Leibniz, "A Vindication of God's Justice Reconciled with His Other Perfections and All His Actions," in *Monadology and Other Philosophical Essays,* p. 124.

[5]Leibniz, *Theodicy,* p. 41.

[6]Leibniz, "A Vindication of God's Justice," p. 121.

[7]Leibniz, *Theodicy,* p. 36.

[8]Leibniz, "A Vindication of God's Justice," pp. 114–26.

[9]Bertrand Russell, *A Critical Exposition of the Philosophy of Leibniz* (London: George Allen & Unwin, 1958), pp. 1, 202.

[10]Bertrand Russell, "Has Religion Made Useful Contributions to Civilization?" in *Why I Am Not a Christian,* ed. Paul Edwards (New York: Simon & Schuster, 1967), p. 24.

[11]Bertrand Russell, "Why I Am Not a Christian," in *Why I Am Not a Christian,* p. 17.

[12]Bertrand Russell, "A Free Man's Worship," in *Why I Am Not a Christian,* p. 107. Copyright 1957, 1985 by Allen & Unwin Publishers. Reprinted by permission of Simon & Schuster, Inc.

[13]Bertrand Russell, "What I Believe," in *Why I Am Not a Christian*, p. 75.

[14]Bertrand Russell, "Can Religion Cure Our Troubles?" in *Why I Am Not a Christian*, p. 204.

[15]Russell, "A Free Man's Worship," pp. 105–16.

[16]Martin Luther King, Jr., "Letter from Birmingham Jail," in *Why We Can't Wait* (New York: New American Library, 1964), p. 80.

[17]Martin Luther King, Jr., "I Have a Dream," in *Is Anybody Listening to Black America?* ed. C. Eric Lincoln (New York: Seabury Press, 1968), p. 65.

[18]Martin Luther King, Jr., *Strength to Love* (New York: Pocket Books, 1964), pp. 65–66. Copyright © 1963 by Martin Luther King, Jr. Reprinted by permission of Joan Daves.

[19]King, *Why We Can't Wait*, p. 26.

[20]King, *Strength to Love*, pp. 71–81.

[21]Elie Wiesel, "Why I Write," trans. Rosette C. Lamont, in *Confronting the Holocaust: The Impact of Elie Wiesel*, ed. Alvin Rosenfeld and Irving Greenberg (Bloomington: Indiana University Press, 1978),

pp. 200–201. Reprinted by permission of Indiana University Press.

[22]Elie Wiesel, *Legends of Our Time*, trans. Steven Donadio (New York: Avon Books, 1972), p. 230.

[23]Elie Wiesel, *Ani Maamin*, trans. Marion Wiesel (New York: Random House, 1973), p. 25.

[24]Elie Wiesel, *The Testament*, trans. Marion Wiesel (New York: Summit Books, 1981), p. 20.

[25]Elie Wiesel, *The Trial of God*, trans. Marion Wiesel (New York: Random House, 1979), p. 129.

[26]Quoted from the Jerusalem Bible, which designates the Old Testament source of this quotation (Psalms 22:1).

[27]Elie Wiesel, *A Jew Today*, trans. Marion Wiesel (New York: Random House, 1978), p. 136.

[28]Elie Wiesel, *Messengers of God*, trans. Marion Wiesel (New York: Random House, 1976), pp. 35–36.

[29]Wiesel, "Why I Write," pp. 200–206.

[30]Wiesel, *Legends of Our Time*, p. 222.

The Adventures of Ideas

Now you have studied many of the questions of philosophy and met some of the philosophers who have dealt with them. But, you may rightly ask, "What have I learned after all this effort?" Beyond the obvious answer that you have discovered philosophy's considerable variety, you should have come to realize that many, though not all, philosophers are more interested in the questions themselves than in providing final answers. They feel that philosophy's first role is to clarify the questions, because that step is the necessary prelude to rational decision. Thus, we hope you have learned the value of questioning, as well as the different kinds of questions that need to be asked.

Back to the Future

Does our emphasis on questioning and on philosophy's diversity mean that you should be discouraged about coming to a decision on any of philosophy's problems? Certainly not. A diversity in views leaves open to you the adventure of reaching your own conclusions. But perhaps you will admit that it is better to make your decisions on the questions of philosophy in full knowledge of the options others have explored. We have all made a "final decision" only to find that we could not stick with it because we had left so

much out of account. *The Questions of Philosophy* has tried to alert you to the full range of possibilities by providing accounts of the various positions philosophers have worked out to some of life's fundamental issues. Of course, philosophy is not all there is to life. You need to know about questions of economics, health, and politics, which philosophy does not always touch. Nonetheless philosophy can provide you with a basic context or approach that will be helpful in dealing with the adventures life presents. And life does present us with adventure, for human existence is future-oriented. Indeed, it is almost impossible to think about our lives at all without taking the future into account. Our abilities to plan, anticipate, imagine—all these depend on time that lies ahead. Being human keeps the future on our minds.

We think about the future because discovering goodness depends on it. Although we find fulfillment in the past and present, we aim for more. Restlessness looms large in our lives, a symptom of our desire to find something better than we know today. At times, of course, restlessness is not a virtue. We would be better off if our reach did not so often exceed our grasp, and so we need to discover what is and is not possible. The trick is to locate the right balance between too much and too little, and such deliberation produces anxiety. Whether one is young, middle-aged, or elderly, coping with the future is never easy, because life may end at any minute. Thanks to the accumulation of human experience, our futures contain a vast array of opportunities. But much of this array is riddled with awesome, deadly problems. In our age, weapons and hope are inextricably entwined. The collective human future is precarious.

Most of this book's readers are likely to live a considerable portion of their lives in the twenty-first century. Both because of and in spite of human planning, we do not know what that century will bring. Change has always characterized human existence, but its pace has accelerated, shocking us into the recognition that instability is more commonplace than stability. The automobile epitomized change early in the twentieth century, television and jet planes later on. Now the computer transforms the ways we live, and it is only one of the many factors that force us to prepare for the future all over again. But meeting the future is not simply a matter of forming economic forecasts, political stratagems, and organizational flowcharts. It is a philosophical task as well. The future requires us to rethink the fundamentals: What is good? What is just? What is true? We know that philosophers themselves, not to mention students, show frustration over what philosophy has been in its past forms. Perhaps that is as it should be, since changed circumstances require fresh reflection. So the questions of philosophy take us "back to the future." As we head that way, two twentieth-century thinkers—José Ortega y Gasset and Alfred North Whitehead—make effective guides.

José Ortega y Gasset and "What Comes Next?"

In *What Is Philosophy?*, a book published after his death, José Ortega y Gasset (1883–1955)

JOSÉ ORTEGA Y GASSET   1883–1955

observed that "Life is what comes next, what has not yet come to pass. . . . Life is an activity executed in relation to the future."[1] That conviction governed his understanding of what philosophy might accomplish.

Born into an aristocratic family in Madrid, Ortega studied philosophy at Spanish and German universities before receiving a teaching appointment at the University of Madrid in 1910. He taught there until the Spanish Civil War began in 1936, but meanwhile he was also active as a journalist and a politician. An opponent of monarchies and dictatorships, Ortega supported democracy in Spain. He served in the parliament of the Second Spanish Republic and for a time was Madrid's civil governor. When the political tide turned during the Civil War, he had to flee from his country. Not until 1948 was he able to return permanently to Madrid after years of exile in Argentina and several European states.

Much of Ortega's writing was first published in newspaper and magazine articles, and he often reworked this material for his numerous books. The best known of these is *The Revolt of Masses* (1930), which sets forth Ortega's social philosophy. By the time of his death, Ortega was acknowledged to be among the outstanding thinkers in Spanish history and a major contributor to the existential tradition in philosophy.

Collisions with the Future

"Life," asserted Ortega, "is a constant series of collisions with the future" (p. 224). What he called life's "unforeseen character" is present from the beginning and continues until the end (p. 220). Ortega believed, for example, that every person's birth is something like a shipwreck that puts us, without previous consent, "in a world we neither built nor thought about" (p. 220). No one chooses to be born or to exist in the world we enter at birth. But soon enough, contended Ortega, living becomes "a constant process of deciding what we are going to do" (p. 223). That process makes human identity paradoxical, he thought, because one's life "consists not so much in what it is as in what it is going to be: therefore in what it has not yet become" (p. 223).

For Ortega, philosophy is rooted in our collisions with the future. Feeling, thinking, questioning as we do, the undecided, yet-to-be-determined, and therefore unknown elements of existence make philosophy "a thing which is inevitable" (p. 74). But if philosophy is a form of life that arises naturally because we want to know what eludes us, what can philosophy accomplish? Ortega's response to that question produced an instructive adventure.

Philosophy Revitalized

Ortega regarded the recent past as antiphilosophical because science had been thought to render philosophy obsolete. Comte's outlook, for instance, had exerted such power that philosophers had been "humiliated by the imperialism of physics and frightened by the terrorism of the laboratories" (p. 47). The methods of science, it seemed, would provide the answers philosophers had sought in vain. But then science itself had collided with the future, and those developments brought renewed awareness that philosophy had a role to play that no other discipline could fulfill.

According to Ortega, history did not suggest that scientific inquiry produced universal agreement on the absolute superiority of any particular theory. To the contrary, science shows that no scientific theory enables one to observe and do everything. Thus, he argued,

> The sciences are now dominated by a trend which is diametrically opposed to that obtaining toward the end of the nineteenth century. At that time one science or another tried to rule the rest, to extend its own domestic method over them, and the rest humbly tolerated this invasion. Now each science not only accepts its native defects but repels every pretense that another can make laws for it. (P. 59.)

Liberated from the notion that science had superseded it, philosophy might be revitalized. A first step, Ortega asserted, is to recall that philosophy comes into existence in response to the fact that life confronts us with what he called "dramatic questions": "Where does the world come from, whither is it going? What is the definitive power in the cosmos? What is the essential meaning of life?" (p. 66). To answer such questions completely, Ortega explained, requires nothing less than "knowledge of the Universe" (pp. 60–61), and that is how Ortega defined philosophy. But philosophy can be revitalized only if we understand what this definition involves, and that disclosure involves asking whether philosophy is really possible.

Is Philosophy Possible?

Part of Ortega's answer was "I can't be sure." He had several reasons for saying this. No human being, for instance, knows what the Universe is as a whole. Even to speak about the "whole universe" may hide as much as it explains, because "Universe" means "everything there is" (p. 61). Thus, said Ortega, the philosopher "sets sail for the unknown as such" (p. 62). The future of this voyage is profoundly uncertain; no one knows in advance how far it is possible to answer the questions of philosophy. The dilemma is not simply that human intelligence may be too frail to know what is knowable. The origin of philosophy's difficulty lies deeper still:

> . . . there is also the chance that the Universe may be unknowable for a reason which the familiar theories of knowledge ignore—because even though our intelligence may be without limits, the world, the state of being, the universe in itself, in its own texture, may be opaque to thought because in itself it may be irrational. (P. 84.)

Recognizing that we may not be able to satisfy the hunger of philosophy, Ortega nevertheless believed staunchly that we should make the attempt. We can know that we lack knowledge, Ortega thought, and thus we can at least try the philosophical quest. Philosophy is to that extent possible. Joining its adventures, moreover, is one of the qualities that makes us truly human. Therefore, whatever the risks of failure, Ortega thought they are worth taking. See if you concur and are willing to venture into the future as he proposes in the following passage from the essay "The Sportive Origin of the State," as quoted in *What Is Philosophy?*

"Scientific truth is characterized by its exactness and the rigorous quality of its assumptions. But experimental science wins these admirable qualities at the cost of maintaining itself on a plane of secondary problems and leaving the decisive and ultimate questions intact. Out of this renunciation it makes its essential virtue, and for this, if for nothing else, it deserves applause. But experimental science is only a meager portion of the mind and the organism. Where it stops, man does not stop. If the physicist stays the hand with which he delineates things at the point where his methods end, the human being who stands behind every physicist prolongs the line and carries it on to the end, just as our eye, seeing a portion of a broken arch, automatically completes the missing airy curve.

"The mission of physics is to find out from each existent fact just what its beginning was; that is, what was the preceding fact that caused it. But that beginning had in turn an earlier beginning, and thus on back to a first originating principle.

"The physicist renounces the search for this first principle of the Universe; in so doing he does well. But I repeat that the man in whom each physicist is lodged does not give up the search. With his consent or against his will, his soul is drawn toward that first and enigmatic cause. This is natural. To live is certainly to deal with the world, to turn toward it, to act within it, to be occupied with it. Hence, it is literally impossible for man, bound as he is by psychological necessity, to renounce the attempt to possess a complete idea of the world, an integral idea of the Universe. Be it crude or refined, with our consent or without it, that transscientific picture of the world is embodied in every spirit; it comes to govern our existence much more effectively than does scientific truth.

"The past century tried very hard to rein in the human mind and hold it in check within the limits set by exactness. This violence, this turning the back on ultimate problems was called "agnosticism." Such an effort is neither justified nor plausible. That experimental science may be incapable of resolving those fundamental questions in its own way is no reason why it should behave like the fox with the high-hung grapes, should call them "myths" and invite us to abandon them. How can we live deaf to the last, dramatic questions? Where does the world come from, whither is it going? What is the definitive power in the cosmos? What is the essential meaning of life? Confined to a zone of intermediate and secondary themes, we cannot breathe. We need a complete perspective, with foreground and background, not a maimed and partial landscape, not a horizon from which the lure of the great distances has been cut away. Lacking a set of cardinal points, our footsteps would lack direction. To assert that no manner of resolving the ultimate questions has yet been discovered is no valid excuse for a lack of sensitiveness toward them. All the more reason for feeling in the depths of our being their pressure and their hurt! Whose hunger has ever been stilled by knowing that he will not be able to eat? Insoluble though they be, those questions will continue to rise, pathetic, on the clouded vault of the night, blinking at us like the twinkle of a star. As [German poet Heinrich] Heine put it, the stars are the night's thoughts, restless and golden. North and South help to orient us despite their not being accessible cities reached simply by buying a railroad ticket.

"What I mean by this is that we are given no escape from the ultimate questions. Whether we like it or not, they live, in one fashion or another, within us. . . . (Pp. 65–67.)[2]

ALFRED NORTH WHITEHEAD
1861–1947

Alfred North Whitehead and the Adventures of Ideas

Alfred North Whitehead (1861–1947) might have been quoting his contemporary, Ortega y Gasset, when he wrote: "It is the business of the future to be dangerous."[3] If the future were not dangerous, Whitehead thought, there would be little need for philosophy, because much less would urgently need to be figured out. But a dangerous future does beckon, and we will enter it, ready or not. Whitehead urged us to do so with the spirit of adventure that befits "civilized beings . . . who survey the world with some large generality of understanding" (p. 50). That description applies to all the thinkers we have studied, but few went as far as Whitehead in speculative philosophy, which he defined as "the endeavor to frame a coherent, logical, necessary system of general ideas in terms of which every element of our experience can be interpreted."[4] Although Whitehead stressed that such a philosophy would have to be a large-scale working hypothesis, never a finally demonstrated truth, he believed that we would be better equipped to the extent that we approached life with a modernized understanding of things as a whole.

If anyone was qualified to attempt that undertaking, Whitehead was a good candidate. English by birth, he immersed himself in history, mathematics, and science. Bertrand Russell was his pupil at Cambridge, and later they collaborated in *Principia Mathematica* to argue that mathematics could be deduced from the assumptions of formal logic. Whitehead left Cambridge in 1910, teaching next at the University of London and then at the Imperial College of Science and Technology. All the while he was distilling and elaborating his metaphysical vision, although he did not publish most of it until he came to the United States in 1924.

At the age of 63, Whitehead received an invitation to Harvard University. During the next fifteen years he produced a variety of influential books, including: *Science and the Modern World* (1925), *Religion in the Making* (1926), *Process and Reality* (1929), and *Adventures of Ideas* (1933). They form one of the most important philosophical outlooks of our time. To get a feeling of its content, keep in mind that Whitehead counted Plato, Aristotle, Leibniz, and William James among his philosophical heroes.

A Philosophy of Organism

Whitehead called his vision a "Philosophy of Organism" (p. v). Its complexity is immense, but suffice it to say of his basic concept that reality is conceived of as an everlasting creative process. Its fundamental ingredients are "actual entities." They exist through the creative but finite power of a God who makes order by drawing upon the ideal forms that his understanding grasps. Under the persuasive influence of God, these foundational entities develop in communal relationship with each other to form the universe that we experience. All existence is eventful, and no event is isolated. Becoming is ongoing; perishing is perpetual. "There is

no entity, not even God, 'which requires nothing but itself in order to exist.' "[5] But God endures and cares forever. Nothing of value is ever totally lost.

Significantly, Whitehead agreed with many in his assertion that "the modern world has lost God" (p. 72). He also believed that people were still seeking God with a sensitivity—not completely different from Epictetus'—that banks on there being "a wisdom in the nature of things" (p. 138). One of its elements is that the future remains open. There are opportunities for good and evil at every turn. If we are in an iron cage, at least the door has not yet been slammed and the key thrown away. There are ways out, though they are not guaranteed eternally because human existence is not the alpha and omega of reality. Part of life's adventure involves learning and earning our place with respect to the future.

The Aims of Education

Some years before coming to the United States, Whitehead gave an address on "The Aims of Education." Its object, he explained, was "to suggest how to produce the expert without loss of the essential virtues of the amateur."[6] Modern life is specialized. We cannot begin to cope with its possibilities if we lack expertise. As a mathematician, Whitehead was struck especially by the central importance of *quantity*.

> There is no getting out of it. Through and through the world is infected with quantity. To talk sense, is to talk in quantities. It is no use saying that the nation is large—How large? It is no use saying that radium is scarce—How scarce? (P. 7.)

What was true of quantity, and of its implications about the need for training in mathematics, carried over to countless other fields of specialization as well: sociology, psychology, and economics, particularly.

In the modern world, however, one cannot be a specialist in everything. There is too much to know, too much to master. Therefore, the "virtues of the amateur" become more, not less, important. Chief among them, thought Whitehead, are appreciation, curiosity, and versatility. Properly encouraged, they are wellsprings of culture, which Whitehead described as follows:

> Culture is activity of thought, and receptiveness to beauty and humane feeling. Scraps of information have nothing to do with it. A merely well-informed man is the most useless bore on God's earth. (P. 1.)

The aims of education should be as much to stimulate appreciation, arouse curiosity, and nurture versatility as to ensure specialization. In fact, all these activities must supplement each other; in that process culture will lead "as deep as philosophy and as high as art" (p. 1).

To the extent that education is truly successful, Whitehead went on to claim, it results not merely in knowledge-as-power but also in style, "the ultimate morality of mind," as he called it (p. 12). Style may be "the exclusive privilege of the expert," but Whitehead also hoped that a sense of style will mark one's entire life (p. 13). For we need to be expert at living, which is to say that the essential virtues of the amateur—appreciation, curiosity, and versatility—must be linked with "attainment and restraint" (p. 12). Then life displays excellence, efficiency, beauty, and goodness all at once.

The Aim of Philosophy

In 1935 Whitehead enriched his views on education by lecturing on "The Aim of Philosophy." What special function did philosophy have, he asked, in confronting a future "big with every possibility of achievement and of tragedy"?[7] He answered that philosophy should fulfill the aims of education by bringing a sense of style to life. He characterized its contribution as follows:

> Philosophy is an attitude of mind towards doctrines ignorantly entertained. By the phrase "ignorantly entertained" I mean that the full meaning of the doctrine in respect to the infinitude of circumstances to which it is relevant, is not understood. The philosophic attitude is a resolute attempt to enlarge the understanding of the scope of application of every notion which enters our current thought. The philosophic attempt takes every word, and every phrase, in the verbal expression of thought, and asks, What does it mean? It refuses to be satisfied by the conventional presupposition that every sensible person knows the answer. As soon as you rest satisfied with primitive ideas, and with primitive propositions, you have ceased to be a philosopher. (Pp. 233–34.)

In carrying out the philosophic task, however, one must be careful not to fall prey to "the Fallacy of the Perfect Dictionary" (p. 235). Not all the fundamental ideas we need presently exist. The philosopher must not simply clarify what is, but he or she should stretch beyond to find the new expression that sheds light. There must be an adventure of ideas: "The use of philosophy is to maintain an active novelty of fundamental ideas illuminating the social system" (p. 237). Philosophy, then, is "akin to poetry" (p. 237). Not only does philosophy help to place the suggestiveness of the poet into more conventional words that connect those insights with other forms of thought. It also can claim poetic inspiration and imagination when it realizes that the understanding we need must at times outrun "the ordinary usages of words" (p. 68).

Requisites for Social Progress

Whitehead turned more than one poetic phrase during his philosophical career. But if poetry is one of philosophy's siblings, science is another. In *Adventures of Ideas*, he described their relationship in these terms:

> Science and Philosophy mutually criticize each other, and provide imaginative material for each other. A philosophic system should present an elucidation of concrete fact from which the sciences abstract. Also the sciences should find their principles in the concrete facts which a philosophic system presents. The history of thought is the story of the measure of failure and success in this joint enterprise.[8]

Although the story of joint philosophical and scientific effort was full of success—the contributions of Newton, Darwin, and Einstein come to mind—Whitehead believed that recent efforts were insufficient to provide the large-scale visions needed. Prior to the twentieth century, for example, much of science had been dominated by a mechanistic orientation. Philosophy followed suit. One result was the view that individual beings are isolated, not interrelated. Another was a dualistic framework that split mind and matter and divided the universe into two spheres, the organic and the inorganic. There were moral and political ramifications as well. The status of the individual was highlighted, often to good effect. But insofar as that emphasis led us to overlook the fact that existence is fundamentally social and that the world is an interdependent ecological system, the results carried the seeds of disaster. Some of this difficulty concerned the "professionalizing of knowledge."[9] On that score, Whitehead thought, "the specialized functions of the community are performed better and more progressively, but the generalized direction lacks vision" (p. 197).

Whitehead developed these arguments in *Science and the Modern World*. As he ended that book, he found that recent developments in physical and biological theory had a favorable accent because they stressed relations. He also urged that the problem for the future was "not how to produce great men, but how to produce great societies" (p. 205). His point was that isolated individual greatness might destroy the earth, but if societies achieved the excellence for which Whitehead hoped, our collective fate could be fortunate. A major need, he believed, was to encourage a profounder "appreciation of variety of value" (p. 199). If that could be done, we might be converted away from the Gospels of Force and Uniformity and be reborn with faith in a Gospel of Cooperation: "A diversification among human communities is essential for the provision of the incentive and material for the Odyssey of the human spirit. Other nations of different habits are not enemies; they are godsends" (p. 207).

Modern science, Whitehead believed, had not taken us so much into a trap one cannot get out of as into "uncharted seas of adventure" (p. 207). Those seas were less than placid, but Whitehead hoped we would rise to the challenge of the future by refusing to confuse security with civilization. "There is a degree of instability which is inconsistent with civilization," he admitted, but "on the whole, the great ages have been unstable ages" (p. 207). The great ages, he might have added, have been the ages of great ideas. The future, then, may be just as good as the philosophers it spawns. Was Whitehead too optimistic when he hoped the future would add to that company of adventurers in ideas who are "individually powerless, but ultimately the rulers of the world" (p. 208)?

Join the Adventures of Ideas

"Philosophy begins in wonder," said Whitehead, "and, at the end, when philosophic thought has done its best, the wonder remains."[10] He was sure philosophy could give us an urge to explore. Whitehead will be vindicated if philosophy engenders that kind of wonder in you. And for that to happen, you must love the questions of philosophy and take care that they do not fall silent. As you pursue them, Whitehead urges, you must pass the questions on, so that wonder remains to keep the future alive.

Whitehead wrote on many of the questions of philosophy with great effectiveness. We could have introduced him earlier, but we saved him for last because he has such a good sense of the "adventures of ideas," a theme we would like to leave with you at the end. *Adventures of Ideas* was Whitehead's overview of Western civilization. That task belongs to the historian, you might say, but Whitehead saw it as a philosopher's work, too. All human thought and achievement are ours to reflect on, but such reflection will be incomplete unless it puts the questions of philosophy to humanity's accumulated experience. To do so, Whitehead believed, launches us into adventures of ideas.

As Whitehead roamed through Western culture, commenting on its successes and failures, he also developed his own philosophical outlook. He built on what others had done before him, but the needs of the future kept luring him to make a statement of his own that might revise and renew human understanding. Whitehead stressed that it was not enough just to learn from the past. We had to remember that the "classics" were not that when they first appeared. They were, instead, ingenious experiments with new forms and contents—in short, "adventures of ideas."

Advances in human civilization require an adventuresome spirit, and the philosophers we have studied possessed it. We hope you have that feeling about them, and we also hope that you will try, some day if not now, to formulate your own philosophical outlook. To do so constitutes an exciting quest. Having appraised and reappraised the contesting theories of others, your own convictions may now start to take a definite form.

The following passage from *Adventures of Ideas* extends an invitation to join the same adventure. As you study it, consider all the ideas in you just waiting to be thought.

There is no totality which is the harmony of all perfections. Whatever is realized in any one occasion of experience necessarily excludes the unbounded welter of contrary possibilities. There are always "others," which might have been and are not. This finiteness is not the result of evil, or of imperfection. It results from the fact that there are possibilities of harmony which either produce evil in joint realization, or are incapable of such conjunction. This doctrine is a commonplace in the fine arts. It also is— or should be—a commonplace of political philosophy. History can only be understood by seeing it as the theater of diverse groups of idealists respectively urging ideals incompatible for conjoint realization. You cannot form any historical judgment of right or wrong by considering each group separately. The evil lies in the attempted conjunction.

This principle of intrinsic incompatibility has an important bearing upon our conception of the nature of God. The concept of impossibility such that God himself cannot surmount it, has been for centuries quite familiar to theologians. Indeed, apart from it there would be difficulty in conceiving any determinate divine nature. But curiously enough, so far as I know, this notion of incompatibility has never been applied to ideals in the Divine realization. We must conceive the Divine Eros as the active entertainment of all ideals, with the urge to their finite realization, each in its due season. Thus a process must be inherent in God's nature, whereby his infinity is acquiring realization.

It is unnecessary to pursue theology further. But the point stands out that the conceptual entertainment of incompatibilities is possible, and so is their conceptual comparison. Also there is the synthesis of conceptual entertainment with physical realization. The idea conceptually entertained may be identical with the idea exemplified in the physical fact; or it may be different, compatible or incompatible. This synthesis of the ideal with the real is just what happens in each finite occasion.

Thus in every civilization at its culmination we should find a large measure of realization of a certain type of perfection. This type will be complex and will admit of variation of detail, this way or that. The culmination can maintain itself at its height so long as fresh experimentation within the type is possible. But when these minor variations are exhausted, one of two things must happen. Perhaps the society in question lacks imaginative force. Staleness then sets in. Repetition produces a gradual lowering of vivid appreciation. Convention dominates. A learned orthodoxy suppresses adventure.

The last flicker of originality is exhibited by the survival of satire. Satire does not necessarily imply a decadent society, though it flourishes upon the outworn features in the social system. It was characteristic that at the close of the silver age of Roman culture, shortly after the deaths of the younger Pliny and of Tacitus, the satirist Lucian was born. Again, at the close of the silver age of the Renaissance culture, during the eighteenth century, Voltaire and Edward Gibbon perfected satire in their various styles. Satire was natural to the age as it neared the American Revolution, the French Revolution, and the Industrial Revolution. Again a new epoch arose, the first phase of modern industrialism. It flourished with consistent growth for a hundred and fifty years. Its central period has been termed the Victorian Epoch. Within that period, the European races created new methods of industry; they peopled North America; they developed trade with the old civilizations of Asia; they gave new directions to literature and to art; they refashioned their forms of government. The nineteenth century was an epoch of civilized advance—humanitarian, scientific, industrial, literary, political. But at length it wore itself out. The crash of the Great War marked its end, and marked the decisive turn of human life into some new direction as yet

not fully understood. But the close of the epoch has been marked by the rise of satire—Lytton Strachey in England, Sinclair Lewis in the United States of America. Satire is the last flicker of originality in a passing epoch as it faces the onroad of staleness and boredom. Freshness has gone: bitterness remains. The prolongation of outworn forms of life means a slow decadence in which there is repetition without any fruit in the reaping of value. There may be high survival power. For decadence, undisturbed by originality or by external forces, is a slow process. But the values of life are slowly ebbing. There remains the show of civilization, without any of its realities.

There is an alternative to this slow decline. A race may exhaust a form of civilization without having exhausted its own creative springs of originality. In that case, a quick period of transition may set in, which may or may not be accompanied by dislocations involving widespread unhappiness. Such periods are Europe at the close of the Middle Ages, Europe during the comparatively long Reformation Period, Europe at the end of the eighteenth century. Also let us hope that our present epoch is to be viewed as a period of change to a new direction of civilization, involving in its dislocations a minimum of human misery. And yet surely the misery of the Great War was sufficient for any change of epoch.

These quick transitions to new types of civilization are only possible when thought has run ahead of realization. The vigor of the race has then pushed forward into the adventure of imagination, so as to anticipate the physical adventures of exploration. The world dreams of things to come, and then in due season arouses itself to their realization. Indeed all physical adventure which is entered upon of set purpose involves an adventure of thought regarding things as yet unrealized. Before Columbus set sail for America, he had dreamt of the Far East, and of the round world, and of the trackless ocean. Adventure rarely reaches its predetermined end. Columbus never reached China. But he discovered America.

Sometimes adventure is acting within limits. It can then calculate its end, and reach it. Such adventures are the ripples of change within one type of civilization, by which an epoch of given type preserves its freshness. But, given the vigor of adventure, sooner or later the leap of imagination reaches beyond the safe limits of the epoch, and beyond the safe limits of learned rules of taste. It then produces the dislocations and confusions marking the advent of new ideals for civilized effort.

A race preserves its vigor so long as it harbors a real contrast between what has been and what may be; and so long as it is nerved by the vigor to adventure beyond the safeties of the past. Without adventure civilization is in full decay.

It is for this reason that the definition of culture as the knowledge of the best that has been said and done, is so dangerous by reason of its omission. It omits the great fact that in their day the great achievements of the past were the adventures of the past. Only the adventurous can understand the greatness of the past. In its day, the literature of the past was an adventure. Aeschylus, Sophocles, Euripides were adventurers in the world of thought. To read their plays without any sense of new ways of understanding the world and of savoring its emotions is to miss the vividness which constitutes their whole value. But adventures are to the adventurous. Thus a passive knowledge of the past loses the whole value of its message. A living civilization requires learning; but it lies beyond it.[11]

In Philosophy the End May Be the Beginning

Philosophers such as Socrates and Plato felt that philosophy should emphasize clarification of life's questions, not the formulation of answers. Kierkegaard and others we call existentialists agreed. Descartes and theologians such as Luther, on the other hand, thought the quest for certainty important. And Kant thought certainty possible, if only we would rule out some questions as being beyond our bounds and limit the scope of our inquiry accordingly. Naturally, all approaches and all philosophers will not interest you equally. You can choose those whom you feel most insightful, or even reject them all. Either way, you will have by now become a kind of philosopher yourself.

It is sometimes said that philosophy covers every field and is the most wide-ranging of all academic studies. Science, mathematics, and psychology were once a part of philosophy and still are in certain ways. You do not have to accept any one view to be a philosopher. The commitment to search rationally is sufficient, and such a quest is at the heart of the famous statement attributed to Socrates by Plato: "The unexamined life is not worth living."

We hope that this book has encouraged you to make a commitment to the philosophical quest, at least insofar as it fits within your life. Resolve not to let any major question you face go unexamined. We hope that you find added clarity in doing so and thereby make your decisions not only more rational but perhaps also more secure. There is no desire on the part of any philosopher we know to so embroil you in analysis that you become unable to reach a conclusion and act on it. Rather, all hope to instill in you a love of the questions themselves, which may make it no longer necessary for you to demand final answers immediately. Reflection can become a way of life for you without impeding action. One of the greatest Stoic philosophers, Marcus Aurelius, was a Roman emperor. Another, Epictetus, was a slave. No one lifestyle is required of the person who adopts a philosophical outlook. Whatever future you choose, you can take your interest in philosophy with you. It is a life pursuit.

In starting an introductory philosophy course, one student complained: "You make us use muscles we haven't used before." It is fascinating to teach philosophy to beginning students just because it is a new discipline for most. This alone does not prove that it will be ultimately useful to you, but we philosophers maintain that you are more likely to be able to judge about that ten years from now, rather than at the end of your first course. Philosophy is not a matter simply for a semester's study; it is a long-term affair. Once initiated, you may find aspects of philosophical questions coming in your life, and by now you should be able to recognize them as such. If this book and your effort have succeeded, you have gained a new sensitivity to the subtlety involved in questions, terms, and definitions. More than that, we hope your writing style will take on a new clarity. Many students report that philosophy does assist them in this way. They think more clearly and therefore are able to express themselves more clearly, and that is important for almost any work you may do.

Plato's *Republic* asserts that no state will be in good hands until philosophers become kings or kings become philosophers. Plato offered this ideal of the philosopher–king as a symbol for the usefulness of philosophy in all walks of life. He felt that political rulers are all too often unreflective, whereas philosophers are all too often inactive on the public scene. Later, Karl Marx proposed the idea of "praxis," theory put into action, and John Dewey urged a pragmatic approach, one that would encourage people to use philosophy to deal with everyday problems. Unfortunately, there is no single, proven formula on how to do this. For the price of this volume, we cannot give you a precise map on how to use your philosophical learning effectively in civic affairs or in your personal life. Each person must work that out for himself or herself. Nevertheless, we do hope that once you have been inoculated with the philosophical bug, you will never be quite the same again and that you will not rest until

you find a way to make philosophical reflection useful in your own life.

Newcomers to philosophy often expect to find one cohesive enterprise. It can be presented that way, by arguing that philosophy should properly adopt one particular method or point of view; but that approach can work only if all philosophical questions are interpreted from a single perspective. We could have presented philosophy to you in that way; it would have been simpler, easier, and less confusing. But it would have been "cheating," since philosophy is at least as diverse as the many viewpoints we have offered here. There is no collective agreement among philosophers to reduce everything to one view, although as we have seen, parties do arise from time to time arguing that this should be done and offering their programs to set philosophy on a unified footing. Furthermore, life and the world around us are not as unified as some would make them seem. Thus, you can argue that any presentation of philosophy that is too uniform or monolithic will fail, because it is "out of joint" with the real world and its problems. To desire unity and simplicity is to mistake a dream for reality, given the widely diverse views all around us that defy ultimate reconciliation.

Learn to live with plurality and you will be better off—that is one theme of this book. Probably a majority will confine themselves to one context, one career, one religion, one political outlook, and be happy with it. But to do that is surely to avoid facing the almost wild divisions that are all around us. To accept differences of opinion as ultimate, as we recommend, is not to guarantee that you will be successful in dealing with diversity. That will depend more on your political skill than on your philosophy. Your role as a "king" or "queen," your use of your power, is important, but it requires reflective guidance. Reflection does not mean that you cannot work out a unitary view of your own. Such an outcome is probably more desirable than living always in conflict with unreconciled diversity. But surely as it is developed, your view will be more realistic, and less likely to be overturned by events, if you form it in full light of all the variety the world in fact contains.

One can be successful in business or in athletics without much philosophical skill. Some of you are blessed with a practical knack and a persuasive personality, and on certain occasions either of these traits may be more valuable than philosophical reflection. We need different types in our world. And we do not need thousands of new, full-time philosophers; the profession is already crowded. We could, however, use more philosophical sensitivity in a number of fields and areas. Some of us seem condemned to think our way through life. Those who are not so driven may be more successful in terms of popularity or influence, and perhaps even be happier. But if you do find yourself constantly forced to ask "Why?"—that basic philosophical question—don't fight it. Give in; accept your philosophical disposition.

To return to Plato once more, it will perhaps help to note his observation that at times one may think philosophy is worth nothing and then at another time that it is worth everything. Like all love affairs, your flirtation with philosophy should have had its ups and downs as you moved through this book. But we would be disappointed if there were not a few times when you were caught up in your reading or became excited as you tried to put your own thoughts into words. Yet, you would not be normal unless at other times you could not see the sense or the purpose in the whole enterprise. In spite of its hope to be effective, philosophy moves largely on an abstract level, passing from thought to thought without always touching ground. Dealing with that fact provides good training in speculative thinking, in exercising your "new muscles," but it can also be frustrating if you cannot see the forest for the trees. Now,

at the end of your course—or if not now then a decade hence—we hope you can sort things out and come to terms with philosophy. To do so cannot be a bad thing.

Philosophy has been described as a quest, and so it is. Many other affairs in life can be completed and finished. That is a good thing, but some of life's most important enterprises involve a continual searching. In philosophy you need to adjust to a pilgrimage that has no end. Such an adventure can be exciting, if you accept it and do not fight against it. Existential philosophers have been accused of being excessively morbid because they kept talking about death, but they were largely misunderstood. They meant to point out that life involves no automatic spiral upward, no final systematic conclusion. There is just an end at an unpredictable point in time, with the philosophical journey then to be carried on by succeeding generations. More optimistic philosophers believe in intellectual and human progress; you will have to decide for yourself if such an outlook has been vindicated for you.

We hope some of you have been launched on a life-long quest for increased understanding. We would not expect large numbers to do this, but we hope that all who have read this book will benefit to some extent. One nice thing about philosophy is that it introduces you to an "eternal community," not only a group of contemporary men and women but a company stretching far back in time. All the philosophical views ever propounded still have some validity; such is not the case in science or economics. This universal timeliness is exciting in some ways, although disappointing in its lack of conclusiveness and in its inability to settle questions for the contemporary scene. But the problems of humankind are often universal and timeless—are they not? And there is a certain sense of excitement in joining with those who have tried to deal with them. Perhaps most of the time most of us will shun "unanswerable questions" and opt for a practical and immediate way of life. Nonetheless, we hope that your life can always find room for philosophy's questions. With that concluding thought, we wish you well.

NOTES

[1] Ortega y Gasset, José, *What Is Philosophy?*, trans. Mildred Adams (New York: W. W. Norton, 1964), p. 225. Copyright © 1960 by W. W. Norton & Company, Inc. Reprinted by permission of W. W. Norton & Company, Inc.

[2] Ortega's essay, "The Sportive Origin of the State," originally appeared in his book, *Toward a Philosophy of History*, trans. Helene Weyl (New York: W. W. Norton, 1941). Copyright 1941, © 1961 by W. W. Norton & Company, Inc. Copyright renewed 1968 by W. W. Norton & Company, Inc. Reprinted by permission of the publisher.

[3] Alfred North Whitehead, *Modes of Thought* (New York: G. P. Putnam's Sons, 1958), p. 207.

[4] Alfred North Whitehead, *Process and Reality* (New York: Harper Torchbooks, 1960), p. 4.

[5] Alfred North Whitehead, *Religion in the Making* (New York: Meridian Books, 1965), p. 104.

[6] Alfred North Whitehead, *The Aims of Education and Other Essays* (New York: Free Press, 1967), p. 13.

[7] Whitehead, *Modes of Thought*, p. 233.

[8] Alfred North Whitehead, *Adventures of Ideas* (New York: New American Library, 1960), p. 150.

[9] Alfred North Whitehead, *Science and the Modern World* (New York: Free Press, 1967), p. 196.

[10] Whitehead, *Modes of Thought*, p. 232.

[11] Whitehead, *Adventures of Ideas*, pp. 275–79.

Bibliography

CHAPTER ONE

Comte, Auguste. *Cours de philosophie positive.* 6 vols. Paris: 1830–42.

———. *Introduction to Positive Philosophy.* Edited and translated by Paul Descours and Frederick Ferré. Indianapolis: Bobbs-Merrill, 1970.

Plato. *The Dialogues of Plato.* Translated by B. Jowett. 2 vols. New York: Random House, 1920.

———. *Thirteen Epistles of Plato.* Translated by L. A. Post. Oxford: Clarendon, 1925.

Royce, Josiah. *The Hope of the Great Society.* New York: Macmillan, 1916.

———. *The Religious Aspect of Philosophy.* New York: Harper Torchbooks, 1958.

———. *The Spirit of Modern Philosophy.* New York: W. W. Norton, 1967.

CHAPTER TWO

Berkeley, George. *A Treatise Concerning the Principles of Human Knowledge.* In *The English Philosophers from Bacon to Mill,* edited by Edwin A. Burtt. New York: Modern Library, 1939.

———. *Essay, Principles, Dialogues with Selections from Other Writings.* Edited by Mary Whiton Calkins. New York: Charles Scribner's, 1929.

———. *Three Dialogues between Hylas and Philonous.* Edited by Robert M. Adams. Indianapolis: Hackett, 1979.

Hume, David. *A Treatise of Human Nature.* Edited by L. A. Selby-Bigge. Oxford: Clarendon, 1946.

———. *An Enquiry Concerning Human Understanding.* In *The English Philosophers from Bacon to Mill,* edited by Edwin A. Burtt. New York: Modern Library, 1939.

———. *Dialogues Concerning Natural Religion.* Edited by Norman Kemp Smith. Indianapolis: Bobbs-Merrill, 1947.

———. *The History of England.* Indianapolis: Liberty Press, 1983.

Kant, Immanuel. *Critique of Judgment.* Translated by J. H. Bernard. New York: Hafner, 1951.

———. *Critique of Practical Reason.* Translated by Lewis White Beck. Indianapolis: Bobbs-Merrill, 1956.

———. *Critique of Pure Reason.* Translated by Norman Kemp Smith. London: Macmillan, 1963.

———. *Foundations of the Metaphysics of Morals.* Translated by Lewis White Beck. Indianapolis: Bobbs-Merrill, 1959.

———. *Prolegomena to Any Future Metaphysics.* Translated by Lewis White Beck. Indianapolis: Bobbs-Merrill, 1979.

———. *Religion within the Limits of Reason Alone.* Translated by Theodore Greene and Hoyt Hudson. New York: Harper & Row, 1960.

Locke, John. *An Essay Concerning Human Understanding.* In *The English Philosophers from Bacon to Mill,* edited by Edwin A. Burtt. New York: Modern Library, 1939.

———. *Two Treatises of Government.* Edited by Thomas I. Cook. New York: Hafner, 1947.

Rilke, Rainer Maria. *Letters to a Young Poet*. Translated by M. D. Herter Norton. New York: W. W. Norton, 1954.

CHAPTER THREE

Buber, Martin. *Eclipse of God*. Translated by Maurice S. Friedman et al. New York: Harper & Row, 1952.

———. *Good and Evil*. New York: Charles Scribner's, 1952.

———. *I and Thou*. Translated by Ronald G. Smith. New York: Charles Scribner's, 1958.

Descartes, René. *Discourse on Method* and *Meditations on First Philosophy*. Translated by Donald A. Cress. Indianapolis: Hackett, 1980.

Hume, David. *A Treatise of Human Nature*. Edited by L. A. Selby-Bigge. Oxford: Clarendon, 1946.

Freud, Sigmund. *A General Introduction to Psychoanalysis*. Translated by Joan Riviere. New York: Pocket Books, 1975.

———. *An Outline of Psychoanalysis*. Translated by James Strachey. New York: W. W. Norton, 1949.

———. *New Introductory Lectures on Psychoanalysis*. Translated by W.J.H. Sprott. London: Hogarth, 1939.

———. *On Dreams*. Translated by James Strachey. New York: W. W. Norton, 1951.

———. *The Ego and the Id*. Translated by James Strachey. New York: W. W. Norton, 1949.

Smith, Adam. *An Inquiry into the Nature and Causes of the Wealth of Nations*. Edited by R. H. Campbell and A. S. Skinner. 2 vols. Indianapolis: Liberty Press, 1981.

———. *The Theory of Moral Sentiments*. Indianapolis: Liberty Press, 1976.

CHAPTER FOUR

Aristotle. *Metaphysics*. Translated by W. D. Ross. In *The Basic Works of Aristotle,* edited by Richard McKeon. New York: Random House, 1941.

———. *Nicomachean Ethics*. Translated by W. D. Ross. In *The Basic Works of Aristotle,* edited by Richard McKeon. New York: Random House, 1941.

———. *Posterior Analytics*. Translated by G.R.G. Mure. In *The Basic Works of Aristotle,* edited by Richard McKeon. New York: Random House, 1941.

Bacon, Francis. *Novum Organum* ("Aphorisms Concerning the Interpretation of Nature and the Kingdom of Man"). In *The English Philosophers from Bacon to Mill,* edited by Edwin A. Burtt. New York: Modern Library, 1939.

———. *The Advancement of Learning*. Edited by Richard F. Jones. New York: Odyssey, 1937.

———. *The New Organon*. Edited by Fulton H. Anderson. Indianapolis: Bobbs-Merrill, 1960.

Peirce, Charles S. *Charles S. Peirce: Selected Writings*. Edited by Philip P. Wiener. New York: Dover, 1958.

Spinoza, Baruch. *Ethics*. Edited by James Gutmann. New York: Hafner, 1949.

———. *On the Improvement of the Understanding*. Translated by Joseph Katz. New York: Liberal Arts Press, 1958.

Unamuno, Miguel de. *The Tragic Sense of Life in Men and in Peoples*. Translated by J. E. Crawford Flitch. London: Macmillan, 1921.

CHAPTER FIVE

Ayer, A. J. *Language, Truth and Logic,* 2nd edition. New York: Dover, 1946.

James, William. *Pragmatism: A New Name for Some Old Ways of Thinking*. New York: Longmans, Green, 1907.

———. *Some Problems of Philosophy: A Beginning of an Introduction to Philosophy*. New York: Longmans, Green, 1911.

Plato. *Theatetus*. In *The Dialogues of Plato,* translated by B. Jowett. 2 vols. New York: Random House, 1920.

———. *The Republic*. In *The Dialogues of Plato,* translated by B. Jowett. 2 vols. New York: Random House, 1920.

Wittgenstein, Ludwig. "A Lecture on Ethics." In *Ethics: Selections from Classical and Contemporary Writers,* 4th edition, edited by Oliver A. Johnson. New York: Holt, Rinehart & Winston, 1978. The lecture is reprinted from *The Philosophical Review* 74, no. 1 (1965).

———. *On Certainty.* Edited by G.E.M. Anscombe and G. H. von Wright. Translated by Denis Paul and G.E.M. Anscombe. New York: Harper Torchbooks, 1972.

———. *Philosophical Investigations.* Translated by G.E.M. Anscombe. New York: Macmillan, 1960.

———. *Tractatus Logico-Philosophicus.* Translated by D. F. Pears and B. F. McGuinness. New York: Humanities, 1963.

CHAPTER SIX

Calvin, John. *Concerning the Eternal Predestination of God.* Translated by J.K.S. Reid. London: James Clarke, 1961.

———. *Institutes of the Christian Religion.* Translated by Henry Beveridge. 2 vols. London: James Clarke, 1962.

Edwards, Jonathan. *Freedom of the Will.* Edited by Paul Ramsey. New Haven: Yale University Press, 1957.

Erasmus, Desiderius. *On the Freedom of the Will.* Edited and translated by Philip S. Watson and B. Drewery, in *Luther and Erasmus: Free Will and Salvation.* Philadelphia: Westminster Press, 1969.

James, William. *Some Problems of Philosophy: A Beginning of an Introduction to Philosophy.* New York: Longmans, Green, 1911.

———. *The Letters of William James.* Edited by Henry James. 2 vols. New York: Atlantic Monthly Press, 1920.

———. *The Principles of Psychology.* 2 vols. New York: Dover, 1950.

———. "The Dilemma of Determinism." In *The Will to Believe and Other Essays in Popular Philosophy.* New York: Dover, 1956.

Luther, Martin. *On the Bondage of the Will.* Edited and translated by E. Gordon Rupp and A. N. Marlow. In *Luther and Erasmus: Free Will and Salvation.* Philadelphia: Westminster Press, 1969.

Sartre, Jean-Paul. *Being and Nothingness.* Translated by Hazel Barnes. New York: Philosophical Library, 1956.

———. *Nausea.* Translated by Lloyd Alexander. New York: New Directions, 1964.

———. "Existentialism Is a Humanism." Translated by Philip Mairet. In *The Existentialist Tradition: Selected Writings,* edited by Nino Langiulli. Garden City, N.Y.: Doubleday Anchor Books, 1971.

Schopenhauer, Arthur. *Essay on the Freedom of the Will.* Translated by Konstantin Kolenda. Indianapolis: Bobbs-Merrill, 1960.

———. *The World as Will and Idea.* 3 vols. Translated by R. B. Haldane and J. Kemp. London: Routledge & Kegan Paul, 1948.

CHAPTER SEVEN

Aristotle. *Nicomachean Ethics.* Translated by W. D. Ross. In *The Basic Works of Aristotle,* edited by Richard McKeon. New York: Random House, 1941.

Kant, Immanuel. *Foundations of the Metaphysics of Morals.* Translated by Lewis White Beck. Indianapolis: Bobbs-Merrill, 1978.

Mill, John Stuart. *A System of Logic.* New York: Longmans, Green, 1947.

———. *On Liberty.* In *Essential Works of John Stuart Mill,* edited by Max Lerner. New York: Bantam Books, 1965.

———. *Principles of Political Economy.* Edited by Sir W. J. Ashley. New York: A. M. Kelley, 1965.

———. *Utilitarianism.* Edited by George Sher. Indianapolis: Hackett, 1979.

Rawls, John. *A Theory of Justice.* Cambridge, Mass.: Belknap Press of Harvard University Press, 1971.

CHAPTER EIGHT

Augustine, Saint. *Confessions.* Translated by Vernon J. Bourke. New York: Fathers of the Church, 1953.

———. *The City of God.* Translated by Marcus Dods. New York: Modern Library, 1950.

Aurelius, Marcus. *Meditations.* Chicago: Henry Regnery, 1956.

Epictetus. *The Enchiridion.* Translated by Thomas W. Higginson. Indianapolis: Bobbs-Merrill, 1977.

Epicurus. "Letter to Menoeceus." In *Letters, Principle Doctrines, and Vatican Sayings,* translated by Russel M. Greer. Indianapolis: Bobbs-Merrill, 1964.

Kierkegaard, Søren. *Either/Or.* 2 vols. Translated by David F. Swenson and Lillian Swenson. Princeton, NJ: Princeton University Press, 1971.

———. *Philosophical Fragments.* Translated by David Swenson and Howard V. Hong. Princeton, N.J.: Princeton University Press, 1967.

———. *Repetition. An Essay in Experimental Psychology.* Translated by Walter Lowrie. Princeton, N.J.: Princeton University Press, 1946.

Lucretius. *On the Nature of Things.* Translated by W. E. Leonard. New York: E. P. Dutton, 1921.

———. *The Nature of the Universe.* Translated by Ronald Latham. Baltimore: Penguin Books, 1960.

Plato. *The Republic.* In *The Dialogues of Plato,* translated by B. Jowett. 2 vols. New York: Random House, 1920.

CHAPTER NINE

Dewey, John. *A Common Faith.* New Haven: Yale University Press, 1964.

———. "Creative Democracy—The Task before Us." In *Classic American Philosophers,* edited by Max H. Fisch. New York: Appleton-Century-Crofts, 1951.

———. *Democracy and Education: An Introduction to the Philosophy of Education.* New York: Macmillan, 1922.

———. *Experience and Nature.* London: George Allen & Unwin, 1929.

———. *Human Nature and Conduct: An Introduction to Social Psychology.* New York: Random House, 1930.

———. *Individualism Old and New.* New York: Capricorn Books, 1962.

———. *Problems of Men.* New York: Philosophical Library, 1946.

———. *Reconstruction in Philosophy.* Boston: Beacon, 1948.

———. *Schools of Tomorrow.* New York: E. P. Dutton, 1962.

———. "My Pedagogic Creed" (1897). In *The Philosophy of John Dewey,* edited by John J. McDermott. 2 vols. New York: G. P. Putnam's, 1973.

———. *The Quest for Certainty.* New York: G. P. Putnam's, 1960.

Hobbes, Thomas. *Leviathan.* Edited by Herbert W. Schneider. Indianapolis: Bobbs-Merrill, 1958.

———. *The Citizen.* New York: Appleton-Century-Crofts, 1949.

Hospers, John. "What Libertarianism Is." In *Morality in Practice,* edited by James P. Sterba. Belmont, Calif.: Wadsworth, 1984.

Jefferson, Thomas. *Notes on the State of Virginia.* Edited by William Peden. New York: W. W. Norton, 1972.

———. "The Declaration of Independence." In *The Political Writings of Thomas Jefferson,* edited by Edward Dumbauld. Indianapolis: Bobbs-Merrill, 1955.

Locke, John. *An Essay Concerning Human Understanding.* In *The English Philosophers from Bacon to Mill,* edited by Edwin A. Burtt. New York: Modern Library, 1939.

———. *The Second Treatise of Government.* Edited by Thomas P. Peardon. Indianapolis: Bobbs-Merrill, 1952.

———. *Two Treatises of Government.* Edited by Thomas I. Cook. New York: Hafner, 1947.

Paine, Thomas. *Common Sense.* In *Common Sense and Other Political Writings,* edited by Nelson F. Adkins. Indianapolis: Bobbs-Merrill, 1953.

Rand, Ayn. *Anthem.* Caldwell, Idaho: Caxton Printers, 1960.

———. *Atlas Shrugged.* New York: Random House, 1957.

———. *For the New Intellectual: The Philosophy of Ayn Rand.* New York: Random House, 1951.

———. *Philosophy: Who Needs It.* New York: New American Library, 1984.

———. *The Fountainhead.* Indianapolis: Bobbs-Merrill, 1943.

———. *The Virtue of Selfishness.* New York: New American Library, 1964.

———. "Theory and Practice." In Ayn Rand et al., *Capitalism: The Unknown Ideal.* New York: New American Library, 1967.

Rousseau, Jean-Jacques. *Emile or On Education.* Translated by Allan Bloom. New York: Basic Books, 1979.

———. *The Social Contract.* Translated by Maurice Cranston. Baltimore: Penguin Books, 1971.

CHAPTER TEN

Arendt, Hannah. *Eichmann in Jerusalem: A Report on the Banality of Evil.* New York: Penguin Books, 1963.

———. *On Revolution.* New York: Viking Press, 1971.

———. *The Human Condition.* Chicago: University of Chicago Press, 1958.

———. *The Origins of Totalitarianism.* rev. ed. New York: Harcourt Brace Jovanovich, 1973.

Hegel, G.W.F. *Lectures on the Philosophy of History.* Translated by J. Sibree. New York: Wiley, 1944.

Machiavelli, Niccolò. *The Discourses.* Translated by Christian E. Detmold. New York: Modern Library, 1940.

———. *The Prince.* Translated by Luigi Ricci and revised by E. R. P. Vincent. New York: Modern Library 1940.

Malthus, Thomas Robert. *An Essay on the Principle of Population.* Edited by Philip Appleman. New York: W. W. Norton, 1976.

Marx, Karl. *Karl Marx: Selected Writings.* Edited by David McLellan. Oxford: Oxford University Press, 1977.

CHAPTER ELEVEN

Anselm. "Appendix." In *Basic Writings,* translated by Sidney Norton Deane. La Salle, Ill.: Open Court, 1958.

———. *Proslogium.* In *Basic Writings,* translated by Sidney Norton Deane. La Salle, Ill.: Open Court, 1958.

Aquinas, Thomas. *Summa Contra Gentiles.* Translated by Anton C. Pegis. Garden City, N.Y.: Doubleday Image Books, 1955.

———. *Summa Theologica.* In *Basic Writings of Saint Thomas Aquinas,* edited and translated by Anton C. Pegis. 2 vols. New York: Random House, 1945.

Augustine, Saint. *The Enchiridion on Faith, Hope and Love.* Translated by J. F. Shaw. Chicago: Regnery Gateway, 1961.

Hume, David. *Dialogues Concerning Natural Religion.* Indianapolis: Bobbs-Merrill, 1947.

———. *An Enquiry Concerning Human Understanding.* Edited by Eric Steinberg. Indianapolis: Hackett, 1977.

Nietzsche, Friedrich. *Beyond Good and Evil.* Translated by Walter Kaufmann. New York: Vintage Books, 1966.

———. *On the Genealogy of Morals.* Translated by Walter Kaufmann and R. J. Hollingdale. New York: Vintage Books, 1967.

———. *The Gay Science.* Translated by Walter Kaufmann. New York: Vintage Books, 1974.

———. *Twilight of the Idols.* Translated by R. J. Hollingdale. Baltimore: Penguin Books, 1971.

CHAPTER TWELVE

Camus, Albert. *The Myth of Sisyphus and Other Essays.* Translated by Justin O'Brien. New York: Vintage Books, 1955.

———. *The Plague.* Translated by Stuart Gilbert. New York: Random House, 1948.

———. *The Rebel.* Translated by Anthony Bower. New York: Vintage Books, 1956.

———. *The Stranger.* Translated by Stuart Gilbert. New York: Vintage Books, 1958.

Hegel, G.W.F. *Philosophy of Right.* Translated by T. M. Knox. New York: Oxford University Press, 1967.

———. *Reason in History.* Translated by Robert S. Hartman. Indianapolis: Bobbs-Merrill, 1953.

Pascal, Blaise. *Pensées.* Translated by W. F. Trotter. New York: E. P. Dutton, 1958.

Thoreau, Henry David. *Walden.* In *The Portable Thoreau,* edited by Carl Bode. New York: Viking, 1964.

Tillich, Paul. *Systematic Theology.* 3 vols. Chicago: University of Chicago Press, 1951–63.

———. *The Courage to Be.* New Haven: Yale University Press, 1960.

CHAPTER THIRTEEN

King, Martin Luther, Jr. "I Have a Dream." In *Is Anybody Listening to Black America?*, edited by C. Eric Lincoln. New York: Seabury Press, 1968.

———. *Strength to Love*. New York: Pocket Books, 1964.

———. *Where Do We Go from Here: Chaos or Community?* New York: Harper & Row, 1967.

———. "Letter from Birmingham Jail." In *Why We Can't Wait*. New York: New American Library, 1964.

Leibniz, Gottfried Wilhelm von. *Monadology*. In *Monadology and Other Philosophical Essays,* translated by Paul Schrecker and Anne Martin Schrecker. Indianapolis: Bobbs-Merrill, 1965.

———. *Theodicy*. Edited by Diogenes Allen and translated by E. M. Huggard. Indianapolis: Bobbs-Merrill, 1966.

Niebuhr, Reinhold. *The Children of Light and the Children of Darkness*. New York: Charles Scribner's, 1944.

———. *Moral Man and Immoral Society*. New York: Charles Scribner's, 1932.

Russell, Bertrand. *A Critical Exposition of the Philosophy of Leibniz*. London: George Allen & Unwin, 1958.

———. *Marriage and Morals*. New York: Bantam Books, 1929.

———. *Why I Am Not a Christian*. Edited by Paul Edwards. New York: Simon & Schuster, 1967.

Whitehead, Alfred North, and Russell, Bertrand. *Principia Mathematica*. Cambridge: The University Press, 1925.

Wiesel, Elie. *A Jew Today*. Translated by Marion Wiesel. New York: Random House, 1978.

———. *Ani Maamin*. Translated by Marion Wiesel. New York: Random House, 1973.

———. "Why I Write." Translated by Rosette C. Lamont. In *Confronting the Holocaust: The Impact of Elie Wiesel*, edited by Alvin Rosenfeld and Irving Greenberg. Bloomington: Indiana University Press, 1978.

———. *Legends of Our Time*. Translated by Steven Donadio. New York: Avon Books, 1972.

———. *Messengers of God*. Translated by Marion Wiesel. New York: Random House, 1976.

———. *The Testament*. Translated by Marion Wiesel. New York: Summit Books, 1981.

———. *The Trial of God*. Translated by Marion Wiesel. New York: Random House, 1979.

EPILOGUE

Ortega y Gasset, José. *The Revolt of Masses*. Translated by Anthony Kerrigan. Notre Dame, Ind.: University of Notre Dame Press, 1985.

———. "The Sportive Origin of the State." In *Toward a Philosophy of History*. Translated by Helene Weyl. New York: W. W. Norton, 1941.

———. *What Is Philosophy?* Translated by Mildred Adams. New York: W. W. Norton, 1964.

Plato. *The Republic*. In *The Dialogues of Plato*, translated by B. Jowett. 2 vols. New York: Random House, 1920.

Whitehead, Alfred North. *Adventures of Ideas*. New York: New American Library, 1960.

———. *Modes of Thought*. New York: G. P. Putnam's, 1958.

———. *Process and Reality*. New York: Harper Torchbooks, 1960.

———. *Religion in the Making*. New York: Meridian Books, 1965.

———. *Science and the Modern World*. New York: Free Press, 1967.

———. *The Aims of Education and Other Essays*. New York: Free Press, 1967.

Index